Nothing will ever be attempted,
if all possible objections must
first be overcome.
Samuel Johnson

Robertson's
WORDS
for a
MODERN AGE

A Cross Reference of Latin and Greek Combining Elements

Robertson's

WORDS

for a

MODERN AGE

A Cross Reference of Latin and Greek Combining Elements

Compiled and Edited
by

John G. Robertson

Senior Scribe Publications

Eugene, Oregon 1991

Published by:
Senior Scribe Publications
4105 Oak Street
Eugene, OR 97405

Phone numbers: (503) 343 8384 (in U.S.) or 011-49-6122-12273
Fax: 011-49-6122-76659

Library of Congress Catalog Card Number: 91-66803

First printing 1991

10 9 8 7 6 5 4 3 2 1

Manufactured in the United States of America

ISBN 0-9630919-1-3

Dedicated to my wife, who has been my
sine qua non. She has kept me in good health with her
loving concern for my well being and has rarely interfered
with my efforts to strive for my "illusions."

Foreword

I appreciate this book as a necessary part of English education where Latin and Greek are not taught as subjects.

If a thorough knowledge of one's own language is significant for an effective education, knowing the main elements of the vocabulary of that language is important for competence in speaking and reading. As for English, a knowledge of Latin and Greek elements is essential. Although the teaching of Latin and Greek in schools would be the best way to learn the meanings of these languages and their influence on English, they are seldom available in the curricula. The instruction of the key parts of many words which exist in English (such as, prefixes, roots, and suffixes) is the next best way of gaining competence in one's vocabulary development.

For this task, John Robertson's book presents an ingenious and brilliant organization for students of any age who want to acquire an intimate knowledge of many of the special terms that are used not only in academic conversation, but also those which are part of the special fields of medicine, law, the sciences, philosophy, and literature.

Robertson's Words for a Modern Age is organized so that all of the Latin, Greek, and English words and phrases are easy to find in their alphabetical arrangements. A set of fourteen appendices completes the practical utility of the book in several respects, *e.g.* lists of phobias, divinations, oxymora, pleonasms, and Latin phrases used in spoken and written English. This book deserves recognition and utilization by every student who wants to get the most out of his or her formal education.

> Professor, Dr. of Philology, Klaus Günther Sallmann
> Johannes Gutenberg-Universität Mainz

Robertson's Words for a Modern Age is a useful reference of many interesting medical and non-medical words and their origins. The appendices are unique collections of words which are informative and entertaining. This book is a welcome addition to my library where it fills a void between my medical dictionary and my thesaurus.

> Colonel Paul A. Edwards,
> Doctor of Dental Medicine (DMD), Ph.D.
> Chairman of the Department of Oral Pathology
> Wiesbaden Regional Medical Center
> Wiesbaden, Germany

We think with words. If we impoverish the language by not learning Latin and Greek roots and prefixes, we exclude much of the richness which equips us for thinking. This book is dedicated to those who want to develop the skills that will help them understand what they read and to have the tools for greater clarity in thinking.

> John Robertson

Table of Contents

The words in this reference are arranged in **alphabetical order** either from English to Latin and Greek elements or from Latin and Greek elements to English.

English words are in "normal" type while the Latin and Greek entries are in **bold** type.

A a

a-, ab-, abs- (L., from, away, away from) Also see **apo-** for other examples. This is a prefix which is normally used with elements of Latin origin (**abs-** usually joins elements beginning with *c* or *t*).

    Qualifying words: abase, abate, abbreviate, abdicate, abduct, abduction, aberration, abject, ablactation, ablution, abnegate, abnormal, aboral, aborigine, abort, abortion, abrasive, abridge, abrogate, abrupt, abscess, abscise, abscond, absconder, absence, absent, absolve, absorb, abstain, abstemious, abstinence, abstract, abstraction, abstruse, absurd, abterminal, abuse, a priori, aversion, avert

a-, an- (Gk., not, no, without) Also see **in-** and **non-** for additional "no, not" words. A prefix which is normally used with elements of Greek origin, **a-** is used before consonants and **an-** is used before vowels.

    Qualifying words: abiogenesis, abiology, abiophysiology, abiosis, abiotic, abiotrophia, abiotrophy, ablephary, abrachia, abyss, acapnia, acardiohemia, acarpous, acenesthesia, acheilia, acheiropodia, achromatic, acragnosis, acro-agnosis, adactylia, adactylous, adactyly, adipsia, adynamic, agalactia, agamic, agamogenesis, agnath, agnosia, agnostic, agonic, akinesia, alexia, amentia, amnesia, amoral, amorphous, amort, anaerobe, anaerobic, anaerobiosis, anaerobiotic, anaeroplasty, anaesthesia, analgesia, analgia, anarchy, anechoic, anesthesia, anhydrous, anonymous, anorexia, apathy, aphagia, aphasia, aphobic, aphonia, aphyllous, apnea, apteryx, apyretic, asymmetry, asynergia, atheism, atom, atrophy, azoic

ab-, abs- (L., from, away) See **a-, ab-, abs-**.

abdomino-, abdomin-, abdomen- (L., stomach, belly) Also see **coelio-, gastro-,** and **ventri-** for other "stomach" words.

    Qualifying words: abdomen, abdominal, abdominalgia, abdominally, abdominoanterior, abdominocardiac, abdominocentesis, abdominoplasty, abdominoposterior, abdominoscopic, abdominoscopy, abdominothoracic, abdominous, abdominocentesis, intra-abdominal

abdominal wall; soft-body part between the ribs and hip, flank or loin See **laparo-** for examples.

-able, -ably (L., capable of, fit for, able to be done, can be done, inclined to, tending to, given to) A suffix which forms adjectives. Also see **-ible** and SUFFIXES in **Appendix K** for other elements.

    Qualifying words: amicable, believable, curable, durable, eradicable, laudable, lovable, peaceable, perishable, portable, readable

abnormal, excessive See **hyper-** for examples.

abnormal, wrong See **para-** ("by the side of, near") for examples.

abort, aborti- (L., miscarry, pass away, perish by an untimely birth [originally, "to set" or "disappear" (as the sun), from *ab-* (from) and *oriri* (to arise)]) Also see **ectro-** for other "untimely birth" words.

    Qualifying words: abort, abortient, abortifacient, abortigenic, abortion, abortionist, abortive, abortus

above, over, on See **epi-, hyper-, super-, supra-, sur-,** and **ultra-** for examples.

abs- (L., from, away) See **a-, ab-, abs-** for examples.

absence of a body part which is supposed to be normally present See **ectro-** for examples.

abundant growth, excessive growth See **luxur-** for examples.

ac- (L., to, at) See **ad-** for examples.

-ac (Gk. > L., related to, of the nature of, pertaining to) A suffix which forms adjectives. See **-ic** and SUFFIXES in **Appendix K** for other elements.

    Qualifying words: cardiac, demoniac, insomniac, maniac, phobiac

acantho-, acanth-, -acanthid, -acanthous, -acanths (Gk., spiny, thorny) Also see **chaeto-** and **echino-**.

    Qualifying words: acanthaceous, acanthesthesia, acanthite, acanthocarpous, acanthocephala, acanthocephalous, acanthocladous, acanthocyte, acanthoid, acanthology, acanthopod, acanthopterygian, acanthopterygii, acanthosis, acanthous, acanthozooid, acanthus, anacanth, anacanthous, archiacanthocephala, coelacanth, eoacanthocephala, palaeacanthocephala, tragacanth

acaro-, acar-, acari-, acarin- (L., mite [itch]) Also see **amycho-** for other "itch" words.

    Qualifying words: Acarapis, Acari, acarian, acariasis acaricide, acarid, Acaridae, acaridan, acariform, Acarina, acariosis, acarodermatitis, acaroid, acarological, acarologist, acarology, acarophile, acarophilous, acarophily, acarophobia, acarophytism, acarotoxic, acarus, Acarus

accident, providence, chance See **tycho-**.

accidental discovery See **serendipity**.

-aceous (L., having the quality of, of the nature of, characterized by) A suffix which forms adjectives. Also see SUFFIXES in **Appendix K** for additional elements.

This suffix is used with technical combinations, especially biological; "pertaining or belonging to, of the nature of, or characterized by" whatever is meant by the combining root.

Qualifying words: bulbaceous, crustaceous, herbaceous, sebaceous

acerb- (L., bitter, sharp, sour, stinging) Also see **acid, acri-, acut-, oxy-,** and **picro-**.

Qualifying words: acerbate, acerbic, acerbity, acerbophobia, exacerbate, exacerbating, exacerbation

achillo-, achill-, Achilles (Gk. > L., tendon in the heel) Also see **calcaneo-, tendo-,** and **teno-** for other examples.

Qualifying words: Achilles jerk, Achilles tendon, achillobursitis, achillodynia, achillorrhaphy, achillotenotomy, achillotomy

-acid-, -acidi-, acido-, -acidity (L., sour [sharp]) Also see **acerb-, acri-, acut-, oxy-,** and **picro-** for other "sharp or sour" words.

Qualifying words: acid, acidification, acidify, acidimeter, acidity, acidocyte, acidoid, acidophile, acidophilic, acidophily, acidophobe, acidophobic, acidophoby, acidosis, acidotrophic, acidotrophy, acidulate, acidulous, antacid, hydracid, monacid, polyacid, semiacid, subacid

-acious (L., inclined to, tendency to be, abounding in) A suffix which forms adjectives. Also see SUFFIXES in **Appendix K** for additional elements.

Qualifying words: audacious, fallacious, loquacious, mendacious, pugnacious, spacious, tenacious, veracious, vivacious

-acity (L., quality of) A suffix which forms nouns. Also see SUFFIXES in **Appendix K** for additional elements.

Qualifying words: audacity, loquacity, mendacity, pugnacity, tenacity, veracity

acme (Gk., highest point; prime, best time) Also see **acro-** and **alti-** for additional "high" words.

Qualifying words: acme, acmesthesia, acmite

acous-, acou-, acouo-, acouto-, acousti-, -acousia, -acousis, -acoustical, acu- (Gk., hearing, listening, of or for hearing) Also see **audio-** and **ausculto-** for additional "hearing" words. The **acu-** in this element should not be confused with another **acu-** which means "needle" or "sharp."

Qualifying words: acouesthesia, acoumeter, acoumetry, acouophone, acouophonia, acousia, acousma, acousmatagnosis, acousmatamnesia, acoustic, acoustical, acoustically, acoustician, acousticon, acousticophobia, acoustics, acoustigram, acoustogram, acoutometer, acusis, anacousia, anacoustic, bioacoustics, catacoustics, diacoustics, dysacousia, dysacousis, dysacusia, echoacousia, electroacoustics, entacoustic, hyperacousia, hyperacusia, hypoacusis, isacoustic, micracoustic, osteoacusis, paracousis, paracusia, polyacoustic, presbyacousis, presbyacusis

acri- (L., bitter, sour, sharp) Also see **acerb-, acid, acut-,** and **oxy-** for similarities.

Qualifying words: acrid, acridness, acrimonious, acrimoniously, acrimony

acrido-, acrid- (Gk., grasshoper)

Qualifying words: Acridide, acridophage, acridophagous, acridophagy, acridophile, acridophilous, acridophily

acro-, acr- (Gk., high, highest, top, tip, end, outermost; extreme) Also see **acme, alti-,** and **hypso-** for more "high" words.

Qualifying words: acragnosis, acranthous, acroagnosis, acroanesthesia, acroarthritis, acroasphyxia, acroataxia, acrobat, acrocarpous, acrocentric, acrocephalia, acrocephalic, acrocephalosyndactyl, acrocephalous, acrocephaly, acrocinesia, acrocinesis, acrocontracture, acrocyanosis, acrodermatitis, acrodermatoses, acrodermatosis, acrodont, acrodrome, acrodromous, acrodynia, acrodysesthesia, acroesthesia, acrogen, acrogenous, acrognosia, acrognosis, acrohyperhidrosis, acrohypothermia, acrohypothermy, acrolith, acromania, acromegalia, acromegaly, acromion, acromyotonia, acron, acroneurosis, acronym, acronyx, acroparalysis, acroparesthesia, acropathology, acropathy, acropetal, acrophobia, acrophony, acrophyte, acropodium, Acropolis, acropolis, acrostealgia, acrostic, acrotaxia, acrotaxis, acrotropic, acrotropism, acrotrophodynia, Akron (Ohio)

across, through See **dia-, per-,** and **trans-** for examples.

act- See **ag-** for examples.

act, imitate See **mimo-** for examples.

actino-, actin-, actini- (Gk., ray [as of light], radiance, radiating structure) For other "ray" words, see **radio-,** and **roentgeno-**.

Qualifying words: actinal, actinic, actiniform, actinium, actinism, actinobiology, actinocarpic, actinocarpous, actinochemistry, actinocongestion, actinocutitis, actinodermatitis, actinogen, actinogenesis, actinogram, actinograph, actinography, actino hematin, actinoid, actinology, actinometer, actinometric, actinometry, actinomorphic, actinomorphy actinomycosis, actinoneuritis, actinoscopy, actinostome, actinotherapeutics, actinotherapy, actinotoxemia, actinotoxin, actinotrichia, Actinozoa

acu-   (Gk., hearing) See **acous-** for information. Don't confuse this **acu-** with the next **acu-** which means "needle."

acu-   (L., needle) Also see **acut-** and compare with **belono-**. Don't confuse this **acu-** with another **acu-** which means "hearing."

> Qualifying words: acuclosure, acufilopressure, aculeate, aculeolate, aculeus, acuminate, acuologist, acuology, acupression, acupressure, acupuncture, acus, acusection, acusector, acutorsion

acu-   (L., sharp) See **acut-** for information.

acut-, acuti-, acu- (L., sharp, to sharpen, point) Also see **acu-** (needle), and **belono-** for additional "sharp" words. Compare with **acerb-, acid-, acous-, acri-** and **oxy-** for similarities.

> Qualifying words: acuity, acumen, acuminate, acute, acutely, acuteness, acutifoliate, acutilingual, cute

-acy, -cy (L., state, quality, or act). A suffix which forms nouns. Also see SUFFIXES in **Appendix K** for other elements.

> Qualifying words: candidacy, celibacy, infancy, legacy, literacy, primacy, privacy

ad- (L., to, at, direction toward, near). **ad-** appears before vowels and before the consonants *d, h, j, m,* and *v*: addict, address, adept, adequacy, adhere, adhesion, adjective, adjoin, admire, administer, admit, adoption, adverb, adversary, advertise

Before *sc, sp,* and *st,* **ad-** is simplified to **a-**: ascend, ascribe, aspect, aspiration, astringent

Before *c-*, **ad-** is assimilated to **ac-**: accelerate, accept, accident, accord, accumulate, accurate

Before *f,* **ad-** becomes **af-**: affable, affect, affiliate, affinity, affirm, affix, afflict, affluence

Before *g,* **ad-** becomes **ag-**: agglomeration, aggrandize, aggravate, aggregate, aggression, aggressive, aggressor

Before *l,* **ad-** becomes **al-**: allegiance, alleviate, alliteration, allocate, allude

Before *n,* **ad-** becomes **an-**: annex, annihilate, annotate, announce, annul, annulment

Before *p,* **ad-** becomes **ap-**: apparatus, appeal, appearance, append, appendix, appetite, applaud, applause, applicable, appliance, apply, appoint, apprehend, appropriate, approve, approximate

Before *q,* **ad-** becomes **ac-**: acquaint, acquaintance, acquiesce, acquiescence, acquire, acquisition, acquital

Before *r,* **ad-** becomes **ar-**: arrears, arrest, arrive, arrogant

Before *s,* **ad-** becomes **as-**: assault, assemble, associate, assonance, assortment, assuage, assume, assure

adelpho-, -adelphous (Gk., brother) Also see **frater-** for other "brother" words.

> Qualifying words: adelphogamy, adelphoparasite, adelphophagy, adelphotaxis, adelphotaxy, diadelphous, monadelphous, Philadelphia

adeno-, aden- (Gk., gland(s), glandular [from "acorn"])

> Qualifying words: adenalgia, adenasthenia, adenectomy, adenia, adeniform, adenitis, adenocarcinoma, adenodynia, adenofibroma, adenogenesis, adenogenous, adenohypersthenia, adenoid, adenoids, adenoidectomy, adenoiditis, adenology, adenoma, adenomalacia, adenomegaly, adenopathy, adenopharyngitis, adenotomy, adenotonsillectomy, adenovirus

adipo-, adip-, adipos- (L., fat, lard; of or pertaining to fat; fleshy) Also see **eleo-, lipo-, oleo-** (oil), and **steato-**.

> Qualifying words: adipectomy, adipescent, adipic, adipocele, adipocellular, adipocere, adipocyte, adipofibroma, adipogenesis, adipogenic, adipogenous, adipohepatic, adipoid, adipokinesis, adipokinetic, adipoleucocyte, adipolysis, adipolytic, adipoma, adipometer, adiponecrosis, adipopectic, adipopexia, adipophobia, adiposalgia, adipose, adiposis, adipositis, adiposity, adiposuria

adreno-, adren-, -adrenal- (L., glands near the kidneys) Latin **ad-** plus **ren**(es) "kidneys." The name applies to the adrenal glands because of their proximity to the kidneys.

> Qualifying words: adrenal, adrenalectomize, adrenalectomy, adrenaline, adrenalism, adrenalitis, adrenalopathy, adrenalotropic, adrenic, adrenitis, adrenogenous, adrenogram, adrenokinetic, adrenolytic, adrenomegaly, adrenopathy, adrenopause, adrenostatic, adrenotoxin, adrenotrophic, adrenotropic

aego-, aeg-, ego- (Gk., goat) Also see **capri-, hirco-,** and **tragico-** for more "goat" words. Don't confuse the **ego-** in this group with another Latin **ego** which means "I."

> Qualifying words: aegarus, Aegeus, aegicrania, Aegina, Aigina, egicrania, aegis (egis),

aegobronchophony, aegophonic, Aegopodium, aegopodium, egobronchophony, egophonic, egophony

aeluro-, aelur-, ailuro-, ailur-, eluro- (Gk., cat) Also see **feli-, galeo-,** and **gato-** for more "cat" words.

Qualifying words: aelurophile, aelurophobe, aelurophobia, aeluropodous, aeluropsis, ailuromania, ailurophile, ailurophilic, ailurophobia, elurophobia

aero-, aer-, aeri- (Gk., air, mist, wind) For additional "air, wind" words, see **anemo-, pneo-, pneumato-, pneumo-,** and **vent.**

Qualifying words: aerate, aerated, aerating, aeration, aerator, aerial, aerialist, aeriferous, aerification, aerified, aeriform, aerify, aerifying, aero-aquatic, aerobacter, aeroballistics, aerobatics, aerobe, aerobic, aerobics, aerobiology, aerobioscope, aerobiosis, aerobiotic, aerobium, aerodontalgia, aerodontia, aerodontology, aerodrome, aerodromophobia, aerodromphobia, aerodynamic, aerodynamical, aerodynamically, aerodynamics, aerodyne, aeroembolism, aeroemphysema, aerogastria, aerogenesis, aerogenic, aerogenous, aerogram, aerographer, aerographics, aerography, aerohydrotherapy, aerohygrophile, aerohygrophilous, aerohygrophily, aerohygrophobe, aerohygrophobous, aerohygrophoby, aeroionotherapy, aerolite, aerolith, aerolitic, aerologic, aerologist, aerology, aeromancy, aeromantist, aeromechanical, aeromechanics, aeromedical, aeromedicine, aerometeorgraph, aerometer, aerometric, aerometry, aeromorphosis, aeronaut, aeronautic, aeronautical, aeronautically, aeronautics, aeroneurosis, aeronomy, aero-odontalgia, aero-odontodynia, aeropathy, aeropause, aerophagia, aerophagic, aerophagy, aerophil, aerophile, aerophilic, aerophilous, aerophily, aerophobe, aerophobia, aerophobic, aerophore, aerophyte, aeroplane, aeroplankton, aeropulse, aeroscope, aeroscopic, aerosinusitis, aerosol, aerosolization, aerospace, aerosphere, aerostat, aerostatic, aerostatics, aerostation, aerotaxis, aerotherapeutics, aerotherapy, aerothermodynamic, aerothermodynamically, aerothermodynamics, aerothermotherapy, aerothorox, aerotitis, aerotonometer, aerotropic, aerotropism, anaerobe, anaerobic, anaerobiosis, anaerobium, anaerogenic, anaerosis

aesth-, esth-, aesthe-, esthe-, aesthesio-, esthesio-, -aesthesia, -esthesia, -aesthetic, -esthetic, -aesthetical, -esthetical, -aesthetically, -esthetically (Gk., feeling, sensation, perception) Also see **pass-, patho-,** and **sens-** for more "feeling" words.

Qualifying words: acanthesthesia, acenesthesia, acmesthesia, acroanesthesia, acrodyaesthesia, acroesthesia, acroparesthesia, aesthacyte, aesthesis, aesthete, aesthetic, aesthetical, aesthetician, aesthetics, akinesthesia, alganesthesia, algesthesia, allachesthesia, allaesthetic, allesthesia, alloesthesia, amyoesthesis, anaesthesia, anaesthesiologist, anaesthesiology, anaesthetist, anesthecinesia, anesthekinesia, anesthesia, anesthesimeter, anesthesiologist, anesthesiology, anesthetic, anesthetist, anesthetization, anesthetize, anesthetometer, aphemesthesia, aphotesthesia, arthresthesia, bradyesthesia, cacesthesia, cardianesthesia, cardiesthesia, cardioesthesia, caumesthesia, cenesthesia, cenesthesic, cenesthesiopathy, cenesthetic, cheirocinesthesia, cheirokinesthesia, cheirokinesthetic, chromesthesia, coenaesthesia, coenesthesia, cryesthesia, crymoanesthesia, cryptaesthesia, dyesthesia, ergoesthesiograph, esthematology, esthesia, esthesic, esthesiogenesis, esthesiogenic, esthesiography, esthesiology, esthesiometer, esthesiometry, esthesioneurosis, esthesiophysiology, esthesioscopy, esthete, esthetics, gargalesthesia, hyperaesthesia, hypercenesthesia, hyperesthesia, hypesthesia, hyperpallesthesia, hypoesthesia, hypopallesthesia, kinaesthesia, kinesthesia, kinesthetics, macro-esthesia, micraesthetes, monoanesthesia, optesthesia, oxyesthesia, pallanesthesia, pallesthesia, pallyhyperesthesia, paraanesthesia, paraesthesia, parcenesthesia, paresthesia, paracenesthesia, paresthetic, photoparesthesia, photesthesia, postanesthetic, preanesthetic, pseudaesthesia, pseudaesthetic, pseudesthesia, pseudoesthesia, psychroesthesia, psychochromesthesia, radiesthesia, rhinaesthesia, rhinesthesia, somaesthesis, somaesthetic, somatesthesia, somesthesia, somesthetic, synesthesia, synesthesialgia, telaesthesia, thigmesthesia, telesthesia, topesthesia, trichoanesthesia, trichoesthesia, uresiesthesia, uresiesthesiastic, zonesthesia

aether See **ethero-** for examples.

aetio- (Gk., cause, causation) See **etio-** for examples.

af- (L., to, at) See **ad-** for examples.

affirm, vow See **vov-** for examples.

after, behind See **post-** and **postero-** for examples.

ag- (L., to, at) See **ad-** for examples. Don't confuse this element with the next **ag-,** meaning "do."

ag-, ig-, act- (L., do, act, set in motion, drive, lead, conduct, guide) Also see **fac-, -ize,** and **stru-** for other examples which have similar meanings. Don't confuse this **ag-** with the previous **ag-** which means "to, at."

Qualifying words: act, activate, activation, actor, actress, actuate, agenda, agent, agile, agitate, ambiguous, castigate, coact, coagulate, cogitate, congent, exact, exactness, exigency, exiguous, fumigate, fumigation, intransigence, intransigent, litigate, litigation, mitigate, mitigation, navigate, navigation, react, transact, transaction

again, backward See **ana-** (#2), **re-**, **retro-**, and **pali-** for examples.

against See **anti-** and **contra-** for examples.

agito-, agit- (L., excite; characterized by abnormal rapidity or restlessness)

Qualifying words: agitographia, agitolalia, agitophasia, agitate, agitation, agitator

-agogue, -agog, -agogic, -agoguery, -agogy (Gk., lead, leading, bring, take) Also see **duc-** for other "lead, leading" words.

Qualifying words: demagogic, demagogical, demagogism, demagogue, demagoguery, demagogy, galactagogue, hydragogue, hypnagogia, hypnagogic, mystagogia, mystagogic, mystagogue, mystagogy, pedagog, pedagogic, pedagogical, pedagogically, pedagogist, pedagogue, pedagoguery, pedagoguish, pedagogy, psychagogy, synagog, synagogal, synagogue, synagogical, synergagogy (synergogy), xenagogue

agon- (Gk., struggle, a contest, to contend for a prize; *also* to lead, set in motion, drive, conduct, guide, govern; to do, act). Also see **ath-** for other "struggle" words.

Qualifying words: agonist, agonistics, agonizer, agonizing, agonothete, agony, antagonist, deuteragonist, protagonist, tritagonist

agora-, -gor- (Gk., assembly, market place; open space, public speaking; originally, "to unite") Also see **greg-** for other "assemble" words.

Qualifying words: agora, agoranome, agoraphilia, agoraphobia, allegorical, allegory, categorical, category, phantasmagoria

agra-, agri-, agro-, agryp- (Gk. > L., *agrio-, agro-*, pertaining to land or fields) Also see **chthon-, geo-, humus, mundan-,** and **terr-** for more "land, earth" words.

Qualifying words: agrarian, agrestic, agribusiness, agricultural, agriculturalist, agrimotor, agrioecology, agriological, agriologist, agriology, agriothymia, agriotype, agritech, agritechnology, agrizoiatry, agrobiologic, agrobiological, agrobiologist, agrobiology, agrochemical, agroclimatology, agrogeologist, agrogeology, agrological, agrologist, agrology, agromania, agronomical, agronomics, agronomist, agronomy, agrophile, agrophilous, agrophily, agrostographer, agrostography, agrostologic, agrostological, agrostologist, agrostology, agrypnia, agrypnocoma, agrypnodalcoma, agrypnode, agrypnotic

agreeable, pleasing See **grat-** for examples.

agri- (L., land, fields) See **agra-**.

agrio- (Gk., land, fields) See **agra-**.

agro- (Gk., land, fields) See **agra-**.

agryp- (Gk., fields) See **agra-**.

agyio-, agyi- (Gk., street)

Qualifying word: agyiophobia

aigi- (Gk., beach, seashore) See **aigialo-**.

aigialo-, aigial-, aigi- (Gk., beach, seashore) Also see **thino-** for similarities.

Qualifying words: aigialophile, aigialophilous, agialophily, agialosaur, aigialosaurous, aigicole, aigicolous

ailuro- (Gk., cat) See **aeluro-** for examples.

air For examples, see **aero-, anemo-, atmo-, pneo-, pneumato-, pneumo-** and **vent-**.

al- (L., to, at) See **ad-** for examples.

-al (L., of, relating to, characterized by; action, process) Also see **Appendix K** for other SUFFIXES.

Qualifying words: arrival, betrayal, portrayal, refusal, visual, vital

albo-, alb- (L., white) Also see **albumino, cand-,** and **leuco-** .

Qualifying words: alb, albatross, albescent, albicant, albiflorous, albinal, albinic, albinism, albinistic, albino, albinoidism, albinoism, albinotic, albocinereous, albocracy

albumino-, albumi-, albumin-, albumini-, albumo- (L., white) Also examine **albo-, cand-,** and **leuco-**.

Qualifying words: album, albumen, albumimeter, albumin, albuminemia, albuminiferous, albuminiparous, albuminoid, albuminoids, albuminolysis, albuminometer, albuminoreaction, albumoid, albumoscope

alcoholo-, alcohol-, alcoho- (Medieval Latin [1543], *alcohol*, originally "fine powder," then "essence," from Arabic *al-kuhl*, from *al-*, "the," and *kohl, kuhl*, "antimony sulfide [a finely pulverized antimony ore or metallic powder used for painting the eyelids]," which is related to Hebrew *kahal* [Ezekial 23:40]; "He painted the eyelids with antimony."

The original Arabic sense of pulverized antimony powder which was refined by heating to a vapor then condensed to a solid also referred to fluids in 1672. It became a distillate or essence of a liquid; and finally, in 1753, to the spirit of wine and by extension to the spirit of any fermented liquor.

Qualifying words: alcohol, alcoholemia, alcohol-ether, alcoholic, alcoholica, alcoholism, alcoholization, alcoholomania, alcoholometer, alcoholometry, alcoholophilia, alcoholuria, alcoholysis, alcoholytic, alcosol

alectryo-, alectryu-, alecto- (Gk., rooster, cock)

Qualifying words: alectoria, Alectorides, Alectoromorphae, Alectoropodes, Alectrion, alectryomachy, alectryomancy, Alectryon

alert, watchful See **vigi-** for examples.

alexo-, alexi-, alex- (Gk., defend, protect, ward off, keep off) Also see **phylacto-**.

Qualifying words: Alexander, alexin, alexipharmic, alexipyretic, Alexis, alexocyte

alga, algae See **algo-** (L.) and **phyco-** for examples.

algesi-, alge-, alges-, algesio-, algo-, alg-, algio-, -algesia, -algesic, -algetic, -algic, -algia, -algy (Gk., pain, sense of pain) Also see **doloro-** and **odyno-** for other "pain" words.

Qualifying words: aerodontalgia, alganesthesia, algedonia, algedonic, alganesthesia, algesia, algesiac, algesic, algesichronometer, algesimeter, algesimetry, algesiogenic, algesiometer, algesireceptor, algesthesia, algetic, algicide, algid, algiometabolic, algiometer, algiomotor, algiomuscular, algiovascular, algogenesia, algogenesis, algogenic, algolagnia, algometer, algometry, algophilia, algophily, algophobia, analgesia, analgesic, antalgesia, analgetic, analgia, analgic, analgognosia, analgothymia, arthralgia, cardialgia, causalgia, cinesalgia, dermatalgia, gastralgia, hyperalgesia, hypercryalgesia, hyperthermalgesia, hypnalgia, hypoalgesia, kinesalgia, myalgia, nephralgia, neuralgia, nostalgia, nostalgic, nyctalgia, odontalgia, omalgia, onychalgia, ostalgia, otalgia, pantalgia, paralgesia, paralgia, pedalgia, photalgia, pleuralgia, podalgia, psychalgia, pygalgia, rhinalgia, synalgia, synesthesialgia, thermoanalgesia, thermohypalgesia, thermohyperalgesia, trichalgia

algesio- (Gk., pain, sense of pain) See **algesi-** for examples.

-algia (Gk., pain, sense of pain) See **algesi-** for examples.

algio- (Gk., pain, sense of pain) See **algesi-** for examples.

algo- (Gk., pain, sense of pain) See **algesi-** for examples.

algo-, alg- (L., alga, algae) Also see **phyco-** for other "algae" words. Don't confuse this **algo-** with another one which means "pain."

Qualifying words: agologist, agology, algosis

-algy (Gk., pain, sense of pain) See **algesi-** for examples.

ali- (L., other, another) Also see **allo-, alter-, hetero-,** and **vari-** for additional "other" words.

Qualifying words: alias, alibi, alien, alienable, alienate, inalienable, inalienability, inalienably, unalienable

alimento-, aliment- (L., food, nourishment) Also see **bromato-, cibo-, sitio-,** and **troph-** for other "food" words.

Qualifying words: aliment, alimentary, alimentation, alimentology, alimentotherapy

all, every See **omni-** and **pan-** for examples.

allia- (L., garlic, bulb)

Qualifying words: alliaclous, alliaphagia, alliphage, alliaphagy

allelo-, allel- (Gk., one another, of one another; literally, "the other") Closely related to **allo-**, which you should see.

Qualifying words: allele, allelochemics, allelomorph, allelomorphic, allelomorphism, allelopathic, allelopathically, allelopathy, allelotaxis, allelotaxy, diallelon, parallel, parallelism, parallelize, parallelepiped, parallelogram

allo-, all-, allotrio-, allotri- (Gk., different, other, another) Also examine **allelo-, ali-, alter-, hetero-, poikilo-,** and **vari-** additional "other, different" words.

Qualifying words: allachesthesia, allegory, allelotaxis, allenthesis, allergen, allergization, allergy, allesthesia, allesthetic, alloantibody, alloantigen, alloarthroplasty, allobar, allobiosis, allobiosphere, allocarpy, allocentric, allocheiral, allocheiria, allochesthesia, allochiral, allochiria, allochroic, allochroism, allochromacy, allochromasia, allochronic, allochthonous, allocinesia, allodynia, alloeroticism, alloerotism, alloesthesia, alloesthesic, allogamous, allogamy, allogeneic, allogeneous, allogenic, allogotrophia, allograft, allograph, allographic, allography, allokeratoplasty, allokinesia, allokinesis, allokinetic, allolactose, allolalia, allometron, allometry, allomorph, allomorphic, allomorphism, allonomous, allonym, allonymous, allopath, allopathetic, allopathic, allopathically, allopathist, allopathy, allophasia, allophasis, allophidy, allophilous, allophily, allophone, allophylian, alloplasia, allophasis, alloplast, alloplasty, alloploid, allopolyploidy, allopsychic, allopsychosis, allorhythmia, allorhythmic, allosome, allotheism, allotherm, allotoxin, allotransplantation, allotridontia, allotriogeustia, allotriolith, allotriophagy, allotrope, allotropic, allotropism

allotrio- (Gk., different) See **allo-** for examples.

alone, single See **mono-, soli-,** and **uni-** for examples.

alpha (Gk., "beginning," first of anything; first letter of the Greek alphabet; used in physics and chemistry to designate a variety of series or values) Also see **beta-** and the Greek alphabet below.

    Qualifying words: alpha, alpha and omega, alphabet, alphabetical, alphabetize, alphabetology, analphabetical, alphanumeric, alphavirus

    The **Greek alphabet** is used (normally in the lower case) to show terms in chemical elements or to represent physical constants in scientific equations, sometimes with the numerical designations of the Greek alphabet as well as their alphabetical symbols.

    A, α (alpha), 1
    B, β (beta), 2
    Γ, γ (gamma), 3
    Δ, δ (delta), 4
    E, ϵ (epsilon), 5
    Z, ζ (zeta), 6
    H, η (eta), 7
    Θ, θ (theta), 8
    I, ι (iota), 9
    K, κ (kapa), 10
    Λ, λ (lambda), 11
    M, μ (mu), 12
    N, ν (nu), 13
    Ξ, ξ (xi, ksi), 14
    O, o (omicron), 15
    Π, π (pi), 16
    P, ρ (rho), 17
    Σ, σ (sigma), 18
    T, τ (tau), 19
    Y, υ (upsilon), 20
    Φ, ϕ (phi), 21
    X, χ (chi), 22
    Ψ, ψ (psi), 23
    Ω, ω (omega), 24

also-, als- (Gk., forest, woods) See **arbor-, dendro, hylo-, nemo-, sylv-,** and **xylo-** for other "forest, wood" words.

    Qualifying words: alsocole, alsocolous, alsophile, alsophilous, alsophily

alter- (L., different, other, another; to change) Also see **ali-, allo-, hetero-, mut-, poikilo-,** and **vari-** for other "different" words.

    Qualifying words: adulterant (ad + alter), adulterate, adulteration, adulterer, adulter-ine, adulterous, adultery, adultress, alter, alteration, altercation, alter ego, alteregoism, alternate, alternation, alternative, altruism, subaltern, unaltered

alti-, alt-, alto- (L., high, highest, tall, lofty) Also see **acro-** and **hypso-**.

    Qualifying words: altigraph, altimeter, altiplano, altitude, alto, altocumulus, altostratus, exalt, exaltation

always, at all times See **semper** for examples.

amat-, amor-, am- (L., love, loving; fondness for) Also see **aphrodi-, eros, philo-, vener-,** and **venus-** for additional "love" words.

    Qualifying words: amateur, amatory, amicable, amity, amor patriae, amorous, amour, enamored, enamour, inimical, amicable, paramour

amatho-, amath-, amathi- (Gk., sand [dust]) Also see **ammo-, arena, psammo-,** and **silico-** for more "sand" words.

    Qualifying words: amathicole, amathicolous, amathomancy, amathophile, amathophilous, amathophily, amathophobia

ambi-, ambo-, amb- (am-) (L., both, on both sides; around, about) Also see **amphi-, ampho-, circ-, circum-, cyclo-, peri-, rotundi-,** and **sphero-** for more "around" words.

    Qualifying words: ambidexter, ambidexterity, ambidextrous, ambidextrously, ambidextrousness, ambience, ambient, ambiguity, ambiguous, ambiguousness, ambilateral, ambilevosity, ambilevous, ambiopia, ambiquity, ambisexual, ambisinister, ambisinistrous, ambition, ambitious, ambivalence, ambivalency, ambivalent, ambiversion, ambivert, amble, amboceptor, ambomalleal, ambosexual, amputate, amputation, amputator, amputee, circumambient

ambly- (Gk., dull, dullness, dim, dimness, blunt) Also see **narco-** and **torp-** for words with similar meanings.

    Qualifying words: amblyacousia, amblyaphia, amblychromasia, amblychromatic, amblygeustia, amblykusis, amblyopia, amblyopiatrics, amblyoscope, amblypod

ambo- (L., around, about) See **ambi-**.

ambul-, ambulat-, -ambulate, -ambulating, -ambulation, -ambulator, -ambulatory, -ambulant, -ambulic, -ambulism, -ambulist (L., walk, take steps, move around; from "to wander, to go astray") Also see **grad-** and **itiner-**.

    Qualifying words: amble, ambulance, ambulant, ambulate, ambulating, ambulation, ambulator, ambulatory, ambulomancy, funambulism, funambulist, noctambulism, noctambulist, perambulate, perambulation, perambulator, perambulatory, preamble, ramble, somnambulant, somnambulate, somnambulation, somnambulator, somnambulism, somnambulist, somnambulistic, somnambulistically

amnio- (Gk., denotes a thin, transparent, tough membrane lining the fluid-filled cavity which contains the embryo of reptiles, birds, and mammals (*amniotes*); the membrane around a fetus; diminutive of *amnos*, lamb, a bowl in which blood of victims was caught)

Qualifying words: amniocardiac, amniocele, amniocentesis, amniochorial, amniochorion, amniochorionic, amnioclepsis, amnioembryonic, amniogenesis, amniography, amnioma, amnion, amnionitis, amniorrhea, amniorrhexis, amnioscope, amnioscopy, amniotic, amniotome, amniotomy

ammo-, amm- (Gk., sand; used primarily in botany and zoology) Also see **amatho-, arena, psammo-,** and **silico-.**

Qualifying words: Ammobium, ammocalous, ammochaeta, ammochryse, ammochthophile, ammochthophilous, ammochthophily, ammocoete, ammocole, ammocolous, Ammodytidae, ammophile, ammophilous, ammophily, Ammocrypta, Ammophila, ammophilous, ammotherapy

among See **epi-** or **intra-.**

amor- (L., love) See **amat-** for examples.

amphi-, amph- (Gk., around, about, both, on both sides, of both kinds) Also examine **ambi-, ampho-, circ-, circum-, cyclo-, peri-, rotundi-,** and **sphero-.**

Qualifying words: amphiarthrosis, amphiaster, Amphibia, amphibian, amphibiology, amphibiotic, amphibious, amphibiously, amphibiousness, amphicarpogean, amphicentric, amphichroic, amphichromatic, amphicrania, amphicryptophyte, amphicyte, amphidromic, amphigean, amphigory, amphigouri, amphimicrobe, amphiodont, amphipathic, amphipneustic, amphipod, amphipodan, amphipodous, amphiphyte, amphistomatic, amphistomous, amphitheater, amphivorous

ampho- (Gk., both, on both sides, of both kinds) Also see **ambi-, amphi-, circ-, circum-, cyclo-, peri-, rotundi-,** and **sphero-** for additional "around" words.

Qualifying words: amphocyte, amphodiplopia, amphogenic, amphophil, amphophile, amphophilic, amphophilous, amphoteric, amphoterism, amphoterodiplopia, amphoterous, amphotonia, amphotonic, amphotony

amphor- (L., bottle, jar)

Qualifying words: amphora, amphoral, amphore, amphoric, amphoricity, amphoriloquy, amphorophony, amphrous

amycho-, amych- (Gk., scratch, itch) Also see **acaro-** for more "itch" words.

Qualifying words: amychophobia, amyctic

amygdalo-, amygdal- (L., tonsil [almond]) Also see **tonsillo-.**

Qualifying words: amygdal, amygdalin, amygdaline, amygdaloid, amygdalolith, amygdalopathy, amygdalophenin, amygdalothrypsis, amygdalotome

amylo-, amyl- (L., starch)

Qualifying words: amyl, amylaceous, amylase, amylemia, amylin, amyloclastic, amylodextrin, amylodyspepsia, amylogen, amylogenesis, amylogenic, amyloid, amyloidosis, amylolysis, amylolytic, amylopectin, amylophagia, amylopsin, amylose, amylosis, amylosuria, amylum, amyluria

amy- (Gk., "no muscle") See **myo-** for examples.

an- (Gk., not, without) See **a-, an-** (Gk.).

-an (L., pertaining to, like) A suffix which forms nouns. See **-ane** for examples.

an- (L., to, at) See **ad-** for examples.

an- (Gk.) See **ana-** [next] for examples.

ana-, an- (Gk.)

¹ up, upward

Qualifying words: analog, analogous, analogy, anadromous, anagenesis, anaglyph, anaglyptography, anagogy, anakinetic, analeptic, analysis, analyst, analytic, analytical, analyze, anaphase, anaphyte, anastasis, anathema, anatomy

² back, backward, against

Qualifying words: anachronism, anagram, anagrammatical, anamnestic, anamorpha, ananym, anaphrodisiac, anastrophe

³ again, anew

Qualifying words: anabaptism, Anabaptist, anabaptize, anabiosis, anabiotic, anacalypsis, anaclinal, anadipsia, anadipsic, anagenesis, anahaemin, anamnesis, anamorphosis, anaplasty, anastomosis

-ance, -ancy (L., quality or state of; being; condition; act or fact of _____ ing) A suffix which forms nouns. Also examine **-ence, -ency** and SUFFIXES in **Appendix K** for additional elements.

Qualifying words: annoyance, avoidance, connivance, contrivance, hesitancy, importance, nonchalance, obeisance, vigilance

anchyl- (Gk., stiff, not movable) See **ankylo-** for examples.

ancient See **archae-** (arche-), **palaeo-** (paleo-), and **proto-** ("first") for examples.

ancon- (Gk. > L., elbow) Also see **ulno-** for other "elbow" [forearm] words.

> Qualifying words: anconad, anconagra, anconal, aconal, anconeal, anconitis, anconoid

-ancy (L., quality, state of) See **-ance.**

-ander (Gk., man) See **andro-** for examples.

andr- (Gk., man) See **andro-** for examples.

andro-, andr-, -ander, -andria, -andrian, -andric, -andrism, -androus, -andry (Gk., man, male) Also see **anthropo-, homo-** (L.), and **vir-.**

> Qualifying words: adynamandrous, adynamandry, adynamogynous, adynamogyny, anandria, anandrous, andranatomy, andriatrics, andriatry, andric, androcentric, androconium, androcracy, androcyte, androgalactozemia, androgen, androgenesis, androgenetic, androgenic, androgenous, androgophobia, androgynous, androgyny, android, andrology, andromania, andromorphous, andropathy, androphagous, androphile, androphilia, androphilic, androphilous, androphobia, androsome, androsphinx, androspore, apandrous, apandry, gymandromorph, gynandrous, heterandrous, misandry, monandrous, monandry, pachysandra, philander, polyandry, pseudandrous, pseudandry

-androus (Gk., man) See **andro-.**

-andry (Gk., man) See **andro-** for examples.

-ane, -an (L., pertaining to, like, belonging to, having the character of) A suffix which forms nouns. Also see SUFFIXES in **Appendix K.**

> Qualifying words: human, humane, mundane, urban, urbane, veteran

anemo-, anem- (Gk., air, wind, breath) Also see **aero-, pneo-, pneumato-, pneumo-,** and **vent-** for additional "air" words.

> Qualifying words: anemochore, anemograph, anemographic, anemography, anemological, anemology, anemometer, anemometric, anemometrical, anemometry, anemopathy, anemophilia, anemophile, anemophilous, anemophily, anemophobia, anemophobic, anemophoby, anemophyte, anemoplankton, anemotactic, anemotaxis, anemotropism, anemotrophic

angelo-, angel- (Gk., messenger, divine messenger)

> Qualifying words: angel, Angela, angelic, Angelica, angelical, angelically, Angelina, angelicize, angelize, angelolatry, evangelist

angio-, angi-, angei- (Gk. [receptacle] > L., vessel, often a blood vessel; "covered by a seed or vessel")

> Qualifying words: anangioid, anangioplasia, angialgia, angialgistic, angiasthenia, angiectomy, angiectopia, angiitis (angitis), angina, anginal, anginiform, anginoid, anginophobia, angioarchitecture, angioataxia, angiocardiogram, angiocardiography, angiocardiokinetic, angiocardiopathy, angiocarditis, angiocarpic, angiocarpous, angiocinematography, angioderm, angiodermatitis, angiodiascopy, angiodynia, angiodynography, angiodystrophy, angiofibrosis, angiogenesis, angiogenic, angiogram, angiograph, angiography, angioid, angiokeratoma, angiokinesis, angiokinetic, angioleucitis, angiolith, angiology, angiolymphitis, angiolysis, angioma, angiomegaly, angiometer, angiomyoma, angionecrosis, angioneuralgia, angioneurectomy, angioneuropathy, angioneurotomy, angionoma, angioparalysis, angiopathology, angiopathy, angioplasty, angiopneumography, angiopoiesis, angiopoietic, angioscope, angioscopy, angiosperm, angiotitis, angiotome, angiotomy, angiotoxis, angiotrophic, angitis

angle, angu- (L., corner, a bend) Also see **gon-** (Gk.) for more "corner" words.

> Qualifying words: angle, angular, angulate, angulated, angulation, nonangle, quadrangle, rectangle, septangle, septangular, triangle

angu- (L., corner) See **angle** for examples.

angui- (L., serpent, snake) Also see **herpeto-** (reptile), **ophio-, reptil-** (creeping), and **sauro-** (lizard) for other "serpent" words.

> Qualifying words: anguiform, anguilliform, anguine, anguineous, anguiped

anhydro- (Gk., without water) See **hydro-** for "water" words.

anima-, anim- (L., animal life; breath; soul; mind) Also see **fauna, spir-, therio-** and **zoo-** for more related words. Compare with **bio-** and **vita-.** *Anima* is "a living being" from a Latin form meaning, "of air, having a spirit, living," which in turn comes from another form meaning, "breath of air, air, soul, life."

> Qualifying words: animal, animalcule, animalism, animalization, animalize, animate, animated, animater, animation, animatism, animator, animism, animistic, animosity, animus, equanimity, unanimity, unanimous

animal(s) See **anima-, fauna, therio-,** and **zoo-** for examples.

animal adjectives See **-ine** for examples.

ANIMAL CATEGORIES See **Appendix A.**

animal groups See ANIMAL CATEGORIES in **Appendix A** and GROUP NAMES in **Appendix M** for examples of the specialized animal-group names.

animal life See **anima-** for examples.

aniso-, anis- (Gk., unequal, unsymmetrical) A combination of **an-** (Gk.), "negative" or "no," plus **iso-**, which means "equal."

> **Qualifying words:** anisocarpous, anisochromatic, anisochromia, anisocytosis, anisodactylous, anisodactyly, anisodont, anisogamy, anisognathous, anisomastia, anisomorphic, anisophylly, anisopia, anisopogonous, anisopterous, anisorhythmia, anisotonic, anisotropic, anisotropy

ankle See **tarso-** for examples.

anklebone See **astragalo-** and **talo-** for examples.

ankylo-, ankyl-, anky-, anchylo-, anchyl-, ancylo- (Gk., stiff, not movable; adhesion [originally, "bent, hooked, crooked, curved"])

> **Qualifying words:** anchyloblepharon, anchylosis, ancylotic, ankyloblepharon, ankylocheilia, ankylodactyly, ankyloglossia, ankylomele, ankylophobia, ankylopoietic, ankyloses, ankylosis, ankylotic, ankylotomy, ankylurethria, ankyrism, ankyroid

ann-, annu- (L., year) Also see **-enni-** for other "year" words.

> **Qualifying words:** annalist, annals, anniversary, Anno Domini (A.D.), anno mundi, annual, annually, annuitant, annuity, biannual, interannual, per annum, semiannual, semiannually, superannuate, superannuated, triannual

anopheli-, anophel- (Gk. > L., mosquito) Also see **culci-** for other "mosquito" words.

> **Qualifying words:** Anopheles, anophelicide, anophelifuge, Anophelinae, anopheline, Anophelini, anopheliphobia, anophelism

another See **ali-, allelo-, allo-, alter-, hetero-,** and **vari-** for examples.

anseri-, anser- (L., geese [as well as swans and ducks]) Also see **cyg-** for other "geese" words.

> **Qualifying words:** anserated, anseriform, Anseriformes, Anserinae, anserine, anserous

ant (insect) See **formic-** and **myrmeco-** for examples.

ante-, anti-, ant- (L., before, in front of, prior to) Also see **antero-** and **pre-** for more "before" words. Compare this element with **anti-**, meaning "against." **Anti-** with the meaning of "before" is found in very few words, such as: *antipasto* (from Italian) and *anticipate* with its various forms.

> **Qualifying words:** anteaural, antebellum, antecede, antecedence, antecedent, anteceding, antechamber, antebrachial, antebrachium, ante cibum, antedate, antedated, antedating, antediluvian, antedorsal, antefebrile, anteflect, anteflex, anteflexion, antegrade, antemeridian, ante meridian, antemeridiem, ante meridiem, antemortem, ante mortem, antenatal, antenuptial, antepartum, antepyretic, anterior, anteroom, anticipant, anticipate, anticipated, anticipating, anticipation, anticipatory, antipasto(It.), antique, antorbital, antrorse

antero- (L., before, in front of) Also see **ante-** and **pre-** for additional "before" words.

> **Qualifying words:** anterior, anterodorsal, anteroexternal, anteroinferior, anterograde, anterointernal, anterolateral, anteromedial, anteromedian, anteroposterior, anterosuperior, anteroventral

antho-, anth-, -anthic, -anthous, -anthus (Gk., flower; that which buds, sprouts). Also see **flori-** for more "flower" words.

> **Qualifying words:** anantherous, ananthous, anthecology, anther, antheridium, anthesis, anthesmotaxis, anthobian, anthocarp, anthocarpous, anthochlore, anthocyanin, anthodium, anthoecology, anthogenesis, antholite, anthologist, anthology, anthomania, anthophagous, anthophile, anthophilous, anthophily, anthophobia, anthophore, anthophyte, anthotaxia, anthotaxis, anthotaxy, anthotropic, anthotropism, Anthoxanthum, Anthozoa, anthozoan, anthozoic, anthozoon, Chrysanthemum, clinanthium, dysanthic, dysanthous, exanthema, hydranth, isanthous, monoanthous, perianth, polyanthous, polyanthus, Zoanthus

anthraco-, anthrac-, anthra- (Gk., coal, charcoal, carbuncle; carbon-dioxide) Also see **carbo-** for other "coal" words.

> **Qualifying words:** anthracene, anthracobionic, anthracoid, anthracometer, anthraconecrosis, anthracosilicosis, anthracosis, anthracotherapy, anthracotic, anthrageny

anthropo-, anthrop-, -anthrope, -anthropic, -anthropical, -anthropically, -anthropism, -anthropist, -anthropoid, -anthropus, -anthropy (Gk., man [including male and female members of the human race]; human being, mankind, people) Also see **andro-, homo-**(L.), and **vir-** for more "man" words.

> **Qualifying words:** anthropic, anthropobiology, anthropocentric, anthropocentrism, anthropodermic, anthropogenesis, anthropo-

genic, anthropogeny, anthropogeography, anthropoglot, anthropography, anthropoid, anthropokinetics, anthropolatry, anthropologist, anthropology, anthropometer, anthropometric, anthropometry, anthropomorphic, anthropomorphically, anthropomorphism, anthropomorphous, anthroponomy, anthropopathic, anthropopathically, anthropopathism, anthropopathy, anthropophage, anthropophagi, anthropophagic, anthropophagist, anthropophagous, anthropophagy, anthropophilic, anthropophilous, anthropophily, anthropophobia, anthropopithecus, anthropopsychism, anthroposophy, anthroposphere, Anthropozoic, anthropozoonosis, anthropozoophilic, anthroptomy, apanthropy, cynanthropy, dendranthropologic, dendranthropological, dendranthropology, Eoanthropus, lycanthrope, lycanthropy, misanthrope, misanthropic, misanthropism, misanthropy, philanthropic, philanthropical, philanthropist, philanthropy, Pithecanthropus, Sinanthropus, synanthropic, synanthropy, therianthropic, therianthropy, zoanthropy, zooanthroponosis

anti- (L., before) See **ante-** for an explanation and special examples. Don't confuse this **anti-** with the next one which means "against, opposed to."

anti-, ant- (Gk., against, opposed to, preventive) Also see **contra-**.

    Qualifying words: antacid, antagonize, antarctic, antiaircraft, antibacterial, antiballistic, antibiogram, antibiont, antibiosis, antibiotic, antibody, antiantibody, antiantidote, antiantitoxin, antibromic, anticlimactic, anticlimax, anticoagulant, anticontagious, anticorrosive, anticyclone, antidisestablishmentarianism, antidotal, antidote, antidromic, antidromy, antifebrile, antifertility, antifoliate, antifungal, antigalactic, antihidrotic, antihypnotic, antilithic, antilogy, antimacassar, antimalarial, antinomic, antipathetic, antipathy, antipepsin, antipodes, antiposia, antipyretic, anti-Semitic, anti-Semitism, antiseptic, antitoxic, antitoxin, antivivisection, antivivisectionist, antonym, antonymous

anus See **procto-** and **recto-** for examples.

antro-, antr- (Gk., cave, cavern; in medicine, "of or pertaining to a [bodily] cavity or sinus;" a term in anatomical nomenclature, especially to designate a cavity or chamber within a bone) Also see **speleo-** for more "cave" words.

    Qualifying words: antrobuccal, antrocele, antroduodenectomy, antrodynia, antronalgia, antronasal, antroneurolysis, antroscope, antroscopy, antritis, antrostomy, antrotome, antrotomy, antrotympanic, antrotympanitis, antrum

ants See **formic-** and **myrmeco-** for examples.

aorto-, aort-, aortico- (Gk., lower extremity of the windpipe; by extension, extremity of the heart, the great artery) Also see **broncho-** and **tracheo-**.

    Qualifying words: aorta, aortae, aortal, aortalgia, aortectomy, aortic, aorticopulmonary, aortitis, aortocoronary, aortogram, aortography, aortolith, aortopathy, aortorrhaphy, aortosclerosis, aortotomy

ap- (to, at) See **ad-** for examples.

apart, aside, without See **se-** for examples.

ape, monkey See **pitheco-** and **simia-**.

appetite (hunger) See **limo-** and **orexi-**.

aphrodi-, -aphrodisia, -aphrodisiac, -aphroditic (Gk., Greek goddess of love; originally from αφροσ ["foam"] because Aphrodite was thought to have been born from the foam of the sea) Also see **amat-, eroto-, philo-,** and **vener-**.

    Qualifying words: anaphrodisia, aphrodisia, aphrodisiac, aphrodisian, Aphrodite, hermaphrodite, hypaphrodisia

api- (L., bee) Also see **melli-** (honey).

    Qualifying words: Acarapis, apian, apiarian, apiarist, apiary, apiaries, apicultural, apiculture, apiculturist, apimania, apiologist, apiology, apiophobia, apiotherapy, apiphobia, apitoxin, apivorous

apo-, ap-, aph- (Gk., from, away from, asunder, separate) Also see **a-, ab-, abs-** (L.).

    Qualifying words: aphorism, apobiotic, apocalypse, apocarp, apocarpous, apocentric, apocynum, apocyte, apoderma, apogamy, apogee, apogeotropic, apogeotropism, apology, apophyllous, apoplexy, aporrhysa, apostasy, apostrophe, apothanasia, apothecary, apotome

appear, show See **phantasm** and **oriri-** for examples.

appearance, form See **morpho-** for examples.

apt- (ept-) (L., fit, fitted, suited)

    Qualifying words: adapt, adaptation, adept, apt, aptitude, aptness, inept, ineptitude

aqua-, aquatic-, aqui-, aqu-, -aquatically, -aqueous (L., water) Also see **hydro-** for more "water" words. Compare this element with **humid-, hyeto-, hygro-, mari-, ombro-, pluvial, udo-,** and **uro-**.

    Qualifying words: aqua(s.), Aqua Caliente, aquacade, aquacultural, aquaculture, aquae(pl.), aquafarm, aqualung, aquamarine, aquanaut, aquaphobia, aquaplane, aquaplaned, aquapolis, aquapontic, aquapontics, aquapuncture, aqua pura, aquarelle, aquarian, aquarist, aquarium, Aquarius, aquarius, aquatel, aquatic, aquaticole, aquaticolous, aquatics, aquatint, aquavit, aqueduct, aqueous, aqueously, aqueousness, aquiculture, aquifer, aquiferous, aquiparous, aquosity, pseudoaquatic, subaquatic, subaqueous, terraqueous, transaquatic,

aquatic animal See **lutra-** (otter) for examples.

ar- (L., to, at) See **ad-** for examples.

-ar (L., pertaining to, of the nature of) Also see **-ary** and SUFFIXES in **Appendix K** for other examples.

> **Qualifying words:** circular, insular, lunar, popular, regular, similar, solar, stellar

arachno-, arachn- (Gk., spider; when used in medicine, this Greek element refers to a membrane, veins, or any web-like structure) Also see **histo-** for "web" examples and **arano-** for other "spider" words.

> **Qualifying words:** arachnactis, arachnean, arachnephobia, arachnid, Arachnida, arachnidism, arachnidium, arachnidologist, arachnidology, arachniform, arachnitis, arachnivorous, arachnodactylia, arachnodactyly, arachnogastria, arachnoid, arachnoidal, arachnoidea, arachnoideae, arachnoidism, arachnoiditis, arachnologist, arachnology, arachnolysin, arachnophagous, arachnophobia, arachnopia, arachnorhinitis, subarachnoid

arano-, aran- (L., spider) Also see **arachno-** for other "spider" words.

> **Qualifying words:** aranea, Araneae, Araneidae, araneola, araneophage, araneophagic, araneophagy, araneus

arbor- (L., tree) Also see **also-, dendro-, hylo-, ligni-, nemo-, sylvan,** and **xylo-** for other "tree, forest" words.

> **Qualifying words:** arbor(s.), arboraceous, arboreal, arborean, arboreous, arbores(pl.), arborescence, arborescent, arboresque, arboretum, arborical, arboricide, arboricole, arboricolous, arboriculture, arboriform, arborisation, arborist, arborization, arborize, arboroid, arborophilia, arborous, arborvirus, arbor vitae (arborvitae)

arch-, archi-, archo- (Gk. > L., chief, principal, leader, first [in position or rank]) Don't confuse this **arch-** with the next one, which means "to govern." Also see **capit-, prim-,** and **prin-**.

> **Qualifying words:** archagenesis, archangel, archangelic, archbishop, archduke, archiater, archicarp, archicerebrum, archigony, archipelago, architect, architectonic, architectural, architecturally, architecture

-arch, -archic, -archical, -archism, -archy Gk., govern, rule, ruler, chief [first in position]) Don't confuse this **-arch** with the previous **arch-,** which means "chief,

principal." Also see **crat-, -cracy,** and **regi-** for additional "govern, rule" words.

> **Qualifying words:** anarchism, anarchy, antarchy, archmonarchy, aristarchy, aristomonarchy, autarchy, biarchy, chiliarchy, cryptarchy, crystarchy, decarchy, dekarchy, diarchy, dodecarchy, duarchy, dyarchy, ecclesiarch, ecclesiarchy, endarchy, ethnarch, ethnarchy, exarchy, gynandrarchy, gynarchy, hagiarchy, hecatonarchy, heptarchy, heroarchy, hierarchy, hyperanarchy, Hyptarchy, iatrarchy, matriarch, matriarchal, matriarchate, matriarchic, matriarchical, matriarchy, monarch, monarchial, monarchic, monarchical, monarchism, monarchy, myriarchy, neurarchy, octarchy, oligarch, oligarchic, oligarchical, oligarchy, panarchy, pantarchy, patriarch, patriarchical, patriarchy, pentarchy, phylarch, phylarchy, polemarchy, polyarchy, septarchy, squirearchy, synarchy, tetrarchy, tetradarchy, thearchy, toparchy, triarchy

archaeo-, archeo-, archae-, arche-, archa- (Gk., original [first in time], ancient, primitive, from the beginning) Also see **palaeo-** and **proto-**.

> **Qualifying words:** archaeological, archaeology, Archaeopteryx, archaeorius, archaeornis, Archaeozoic, archaic, archaically, archaism, archaist, archebiosis, archecentric, archeology, Archeopteryx (Archaeopteryx), archezoic, archive, archives, archivist, archtype

-archy (Gk., govern, rule) See **-arch**.

arcto-, arct- (Gk., of the bear, bear [the animal]; or the north, northern) Also see **ursus** for additional "bear" words.

> **Qualifying words:** antarctic, antarctical, arctic, arctoid, arctomachy, arctophile, arctophilist, Arthur, cynarctomachy, nearctic

ard- (L., fire, burn) See **ars-** for examples.

arena (*harena*) (L., sand, sandy place, seashore; place of combat [literally, "place strewn with sand"]; the floors of the amphitheaters of ancient Rome had to be covered with absorbent sand because so much blood was spilled in the gladiatorial contests held there and therefore resulted in the name given to the structure) Also see **amatho-, ammo-, psammo-,** and **silico-** for more "sand" words.

> **Qualifying words:** arena, arenaceous, arenaria, arenation, arenicole, arenicolous, arenoid

argent-, argenti-, argento- (L., silver) Also see **argyro-** for more examples.

> **Qualifying words:** argent, argentation, argentic, argentiferous, Argentina, argentine,

argentite, argentophil, argentophile, argentum, argenti

argillo-, argill- (Gk. > L., clay) See **chledo-, limi-,** and **pelo-.**

    Qualifying words: argillaceous, argillicole, argillicolous, argillophile, argillophilous, argillophily

argyro-, argyr- (Gk., silver) Also see **argent-.**

    Qualifying words: argyanthous, argyremia, argyron, argyrophil, argyrophile, argyria

-arian (L., a person who, a thing which) A suffix which forms nouns. Also see SUFFIXES in **Appendix K** for other examples of word endings.

    Qualifying words: grammarian, libertarian, librarian, millenarian, nonagenarian, seminarian

aristo-, arist- (Gk., best)

    Qualifying words: aristarchy, aristocracy, aristocrat, aristocratic, aristocratical, aristocratically, aristocratism, aristogeneses(pl.), aristogenesis(s.), aristogenetic, aristogenics, aristopherenia

-arium (s.), **-aria** (pl.), **-ariums** (pl.) (Gk. > L., a place for; abounding in or connected with something; "a place containing or related to" that which is specified by the root) Also see **-ary, -orium,** and **-ory.**

    Qualifying words: alvearium, aquarium, aquaria, caldarium, calidarium, cinerarium, frigidarium, herbarium, hippolarium (hipposolarium), insectarium, leprosarium, ossuarium, panarium (bread), planetarium, pollenarium, ranarium, sanitarium, solarium, septarium, sudarium, tepidaria, termitarium, terrarium, vaporarium, vivaria, vivarium

arm- (L., weapon) Don't confuse this element with the English "arm," meaning "upper limb." Also see **strato-** ("army").

    Qualifying words: arm, armada, armadillo, armament, armamentarium, armature, armigerous, arminger, armipotent, armistice, armor, armory, armour, army, disarmament

arm See **brachio-** for information.

armpit For related words, see **axillo-, hirco-** (goat), and **maschal-.**

army See **arm-** or **strato-** for examples.

around See **ambi-, amphi-, circ-, circum-, cyclo-,** and **peri-** for examples.

arrangement See **nomo-, taxi-,** and **cosmo-.**

arrow See **sagitto-** and **toxo-** for examples.

ars-, ard- (L., fire) Also see **caust-, crema-, flagr-, flam-, ign-, incend-, pyro-,** and **volcan-** for other "fire" words.

    Qualifying words: ardent, ardor, arson, arsonist

art, skill, craft See **art-** and **techno-.**

art-, arti- (L., skill, handicraft, trade, occupation, art) Also see **techno-** for other "skill" words.

    Qualifying words: art, artful, artifact, artifice, artificial, artist, artiste, artistic, artistry, artless, *art nouveau,* arty

arterio-, arteri-, arter- (Gk. > L., artery, blood vessel, *or* vein) Also see **angio-, arteriolo-** ("small artery"), **phlebo-, vaso-,** and **veno-** for more "vessel" or "vein" words.

    Qualifying words: arteria, arterial, arterialization, arteriectomy, arterioatomy, arteriogram, arteriography, arteriolith, arteriolitis, arteriology, arterionecrosis, arteriomalacia, arteriometer, arteriopathy, arteriophlebotomy, arterioplasty, arteriostenosis, arteriotome, arteriotomy, arteriovenous, arteritis, artery

arteriolo-, arteriol- (Gk. > L., windpipe, artery; *arteriole,* "small artery") Also see **arterio-** for other "windpipe" examples.

    Qualifying words: arteriola(s.), arteriolae(pl.), arteriolar, arteriolonecrosis, arteriolonephrosclerosis, arteriolovenous

arthro-, arthr- (Gk., joint, pertaining to the joints)

    Qualifying words: arthralgia, arthrectomy, arthresthesia, arthrifuge, arthritis, arthroclasia, arthrodynia, arthroendoscopy, arthrography, arthrokinetic, arthrology, arthrometry, arthropathology, arthropathy, arthroplasty, arthropod, Arthropoda, arthroscope, arthrosis, arthrotomy, arthrotropic, synarthrosis

-ary (L., a person who, a place where, a thing which, *or* pertaining to) Also see **-arium, -ar, -orium, -ory,** and SUFFIXES in **Appendix K** for other word endings.

    Qualifying words: apiary, apothecary, arbitrary, aviary, commissary, dictionary, estuary, formicary, fragmentary, functionary, granary, library, mercenary, military, mortuary, notary, ossuary, penitentiary, piscary, sanctuary, sedentary, seminary, stationary, subsidiary, termitary, vespiary, vocabulary

as- (to, at) See **ad-** for examples.

ascari-, ascarid- (Gk., worm; maw-worm; intestinal worm) For more "worm" words, see **helmintho-, scoleco-,** and **vermo-.**

    Qualifying words: ascariasis, ascaridal, ascaricide, ascarid, ascaridosis, ascariosis

ashes See **ciner-, spodo-,** and **tephro-.**

aside, apart See **se-** for examples.

ask, seek See **peti-, quir-,** and **rog-** for examples.

aspido-, aspid- (Gk., shield)
> Qualifying words: aspidate, aspidium, aspidomancy, aspis

assemble, gather together For examples, see **agora-** and **greg-**.

aster- (Gk., star) Also examine **astra-, astro-, sidero-,** and **stell-** for other "star" words.
> Qualifying words: aster, asteriated, asterisk, asterism, asteroid, diaster, disaster, disastrous, disastrously

astheno- (Gk., without strength) See **stheno-**.

astra- (L., star) Also see **aster-, astro-, sidero-,** and **stell-** for other "star" examples.
> Qualifying words: astral, astrally, astraphobia

astragalo-, astragal- (Gk., anklebone, talus, ball of ankle joint; dice, die [the Greeks made these from ankle bones]) Also see **talo-** for other "ankle" words.
> Qualifying words: astragalectomy, astragalocalcanean, astragalomancy, astragaloscaphoic, astragaloscaphoid, astragalotibial, astragalus

astrapo-, astrap- (Gk., lightning; the Greek verb *strapto* means "to hurl") Also see **bronto-, cerauno-,** as well as **tonitro-**.
> Qualifying words: astrapomancy, astrapomania, astrapophobia, astrapotheria

astro-, astr- (Gk., star) Also see **astra-, aster-, sidero-,** and **stell-** for more "star" words.
> Qualifying words: astrobiology, astrocompass, astrocyte, astrocytic, astrodome, astrodynamics, astrogation, astrogator, astrogeology, astrogeny, astrognosy, astrogony, astrogeology, astrographic, astrography, astroid, astrokinetic, astrolabe, astrolater, astrolatry, astrologer, astrologic, astrological, astrologically, astrology, astromancer, astromancy, astromantic, astrometer, astrometry, astronaut, astronautical, astronautics, astronavigation, astronavigator, astronomer, astronomic, astronomical, astronomy, astrophile, astrophilic, astrophobia, astrophotograph, astrophotography, astrophysical, astrophysicist, astrophysics, astropodia, astrosphere, radioastronomy

at all times, always See **semper** for examples.

at, toward See **ad-** for examples.

ataxo-, ataxia- (Gk., disorder, without order) See **taxi-** for examples.

-ate (L.) [1] A suffix which forms nouns, office of, holder(s) of the office of: electorate, magistrate, senate

[2] A suffix which forms verbs: alleviate, amalgamate, annihilate, compensate, prevaricate

atelo- (Gk., imperfect, incomplete) See **teleo-** for "end, completion" words.

ath-, athl- (Gk., struggle, a contest [in war or sports], to contend for a prize) Also see **agon-** (Gk.) for other "struggle, contest" words.
> Qualifying words: athlete, athletic, athletically, athleticism, athletics, biathlon, decathlon, heptathlon, hexathlon, pentathlon, triathlon

-ation (Gk. > L., action, process, state, or condition) Also see SUFFIXES in **Appendix K** for more examples.
> Qualifying words: brachiation, civilization, perspiration, vaporization

atmo-, atm- (Gk., vapor, steam; air, gas; respiration) Also examine **aero-, anemo-, atmo-, -pnea, pneumato-, pneumo-,** and **vent-** for other "air, wind" words.
> Qualifying words: atmiatrics, atmobios, atmocausis, atmograph, atmology, atmolysis, atmometer, atmophyte, atmosphere

atmospheric pressure See **baro-** for examples.

atrio-, atri- (L., entrance hall or chamber; upper heart chamber)
> Qualifying words: atriomegaly, atriotomy, atrioventricular, atrium

attaching to, fixing [of a specified *body* part] See **-pexy** for examples.

attain, hold, clasp See **prehend-** for examples.

attack (a violent attack) See **-lepsy**.

atto- (Danish, eighteen; 10^{-18}, 0. 000 000 000 000 000 001) [U.S.: quintillionth; U.K.: trillionth], or one-millionth of a millionth of a millionth. Also see METRIC GROUPS in **Appendix F**.
> Qualifying words: attogram, attotesla

attraction to See **philo-** for examples.

auc- (Gk., increase, growth). See **auxano-**.

audio-, aud-, audi-, audit- (L., hearing, listening, perception of sounds) Also see **acous-** and **ausculto-**.
> Qualifying words: audibility, audible, audibleness, audibly, audiclave, audience, audient, audile, audio, audioanalgesia, audiofrequency, audiogenic, audiogram, audiological, audiologist, audiology, audiometer, audiometrist, audiometry, audiophile, audiophiliac, audiovisual, audiphone, audit, audition, auditive, auditognosis, auditor, auditories, auditorily, auditorium, auditory, clairaudience, clairaudient

aug- (Gk., increase, grow) See **auxano-** for examples.

auri-, auriculo-, auricul-, auro-, aur- (L., ear) Also see **oto-** for more "ear" words. Don't confuse this element with the next **auri-**, which means "gold."

Qualifying words: aural, auricle, auricula(s.), auriculae(pl.), auricular, auriculate, auriculid, auriculocranial, auriculotemporal, auriculoventricular, auriform, aurilave, auripuncture, auris, auriscope, aurist, auroscope, aurometer, dextraurality, levoaurality, sinistraurality

auri-, auro-, aur- (L., gold, yellow) Also see **chryso-, ochro-,** and **xantho-** for more "yellow" words. Don't confuse this **auri-** with the previous one which means "ear."

Qualifying words: aureate, aureole, auriargentiferous, auric, aurid, aurific, auriferous, aurify, aurimine, aurivorous, aurochromoderma, aurigraphy, aurous, aurotherapy, oriole

auriculo- (L., ear) See **auri-** (ear).

aurora (L., dawn) Also see **eo-** and **ostro-**.

Qualifying words: Aurora, aurora, auroral, Aurora Australis, Aurora Borealis, auroraphobia

auspic-, auspec- (L., from *auspex* [genitive form, *auspicis*] *avi-*, stem of *avis*, "bird" plus *-spex*, "observer," from *specere*, "to look, observe")

A Roman priest, or *auspex*, was appointed to foretell or divine the future outcome of an important event by observing the flights of birds, listening to their songs, observing the food they ate, and by examing their entrails (intestines, etc.). Favorable omens came to be known as *auspicious*. Later, the Roman *auspex* was replaced with the *augur* as the interpreter-observer of bird signs, his name being derived from the Latin *avis*, "bird," and *garrire*, "to talk or tell." His interpretation, or *augurism* became the English word augury, an omen, and the Latin *inaugurare*, "to install an official after consulting the birds," became our word "inaugurate."

Also see **avi-** and **ornitho-**.

Qualifying words: auspex, auspicate, auspices, auspicious, auspiciously, auspiciousness, inauspicious, inauspiciously, inauspiciousness

ausculto-, auscult- (L., listen, hear) Also see **acous-** and **audio-**.

Qualifying words: auscultate, auscultation, auscultatory, auscultoplectrum

austro-, austr-, austral-, auster- (L., south, south wind, southern) Also see **boreal**, "north." This element also means "dry" (*austeros*) in Greek.

Qualifying words: Aurora Australis, Auster, austere, austral, australic, Australia, Australian, australopithecines, australopithecus, Austro-Asiatic, Austrocolumbia, austromancer, austromancy, Austronesia, Austronesian, Austrophil, austrophil, circumaustral, *terra australis*

auto-, aut- (Gk., self) Also see **sui-, ego** (I), **idio-,** and **ipse** for related words.

Qualifying words: autarchy, autecology, autoantibody, autoantitoxin, autobiographer, autobiographical, autobiography, autocarp, autocatalysis, autocephalous, autochthonous, autocinesis, autocracy, autoclasia, autoclasis, autocrat, autocratic, autocratical, autocratically, autodermic, autodiagnosis, autodidactic, autoecology, autogamous, autogamy, autogenesis, autogenetic, autogenous, autognosis, autograph, autographic, autohemotherapy, autohypnosis, autohypnotic, autoimmunity, autointoxication, autokinesia, autokinesis, autokinetic, autolatry, autologous, autology, autolysis, autolytic, automatic, automatically, automation, automnesia, automobile, automotive, automysophobia, autonarcosis, autonomic, autonomous, autonomy, autonym, autonymous, autonymy, autopathography, autophagia, autophagous, autophagy, autophile, autophilia, autophilic, autophilous, autophobia, autophony, autophyllogeny, autophyte, autoplasty, autopotamic, autopsy, autopsychosis, autopsychotherapy, autosmia, autosomatognosis, autosomatognostic, autosuggestion, autotherapy, autotomy, autotopagnosia, autotoxin, autotoxemia, autotoxicosis, autotropism, autoxenous, dermatoautoplasty

auxano-, auxi-, auxo-, auso-, aug-, auc-, auct- (Gk., increase, growth) Also see **cresc-** for more "increase, grow" words.

Qualifying words: auction, auctioneer, augment, augmentation, augur, augurate, augury august, August, author, auxanogram, auxanography, auxanology, auxanometer, auxesis, auxiliary, auxiliometer, auxilytic, auxocardia, auxodrome, auxoflore, auxology, inaugurate, inauguration

auxo- (Gk., increase, growth) See **auxano-** for examples.

avi-, av- (L., bird) See **auspic-** and **ornitho-** for other "bird" words.

Qualifying words: avarist, Aves, avian, aviaries, aviary, aviate, aviation, aviator, aviatrix, avicide, aviculture, aviculturist, avifauna, avifaunal, avigation, avinosis, avionics

awareness, perception Examine **aesth-, pass-, path-,** and **sens-** for related words.

away, away from See **a-, ab-, abs-** (L.); **apo-**; **ex-, ec-, e-** (Gk.), and **se-** (L.) for examples.

axillo-, axill- (L., armpit) Also see **hirco-** (goat) and **maschalo-** for other "armpit" words.

> **Qualifying words:** axial, axil, axilla(s.), axillae(pl.), axillar, axillary, axillary artery, axillary fossa, axillary gland, axillary nerve, axillary vein

B b

babbling (speech) See **lalo-** for examples.

bacci- (L., berry)

> **Qualifying words:** bacciferous, bacciform, baccivorous

bacilli-, bacill-, bacillo- (L., rod, staff; a rod-shaped bacterium) Also see **bacterio-** and **cocc-** for more examples.

> **Qualifying words:** actinobacillosis, actinobacillus, bacillemia, bacillicide, bacilliculture, bacilligenic, bacilli(pl.), bacillosis, bacilluria, bacillus(s.), bacillotherapy, diplobacillus, lactobacillus

back, on the back See **dorso-** for examples.

backward, again See **ana-, an-**; **re-**; **retro-**; and **pali-** for examples.

bacteria See **bacterio-, bacilli-,** and **cocc-** for examples.

bacterio-, bacter-, bacteri-, -bacteria, -bacterial, -bacterially, -bacterium (Gk., rod-shaped micro-organism; used in biomedical terminology) Also see **bacilli-** and **cocc-** for more examples.

> **Qualifying words:** bacteremia, bacteria, bacterial, bacteria(pl.), bactericidal, bactericide, bacteriocinogens, bacterioclasis, bacteriogenic, bacteriogenous, bacterioid, bacteriological, bacteriologist, bacteriology, bacteriolysin, bacteriolysis, bacteriolytic, bacteriophage, bacteriophagia, bacteriophagology, bacteriopexy, bacteriosis, bacteriostasis, bacteriostat, bacteriostatic, bacteriotoxic, bacteriotropic, bacterium(s.), bacteriuria, bacteroid, bacteriocidal, mycobacterium

back, backward See **ana-** (#2); **pali-, re-** (red-), and **retro-** for examples.

bad See **caco-, dys-, mal-,** and **mis-** for examples.

bad odor, stink See **bromo-** and **osmo-** for examples.

bag, sac See **bursa-, cysto-,** and **scroto-** for examples.

ball, round See **glob, glom,** and **sphero-** for examples.

ballo-, ball-, bolo-, bol-, -bola, -bole, -bolic, -bolism, -bolite, -boly (Gk., throw, send, put) Also see **jet-** and **miss-** for more "throw" words.

> **Qualifying words:** amphibole, anabolism, ballista, ballistic, ballistics, ballistocardiogram, ballistocardiograph, bolograph, bolometer, boloscope, boule, catabolic, catabolism, diabolic, ecbolic, embolism, epibolic, hyperbola, hyperbole, hyperbolic, hyperbolically, hyperbolism, hyperbolize, hyperbolizes, hyperbolizing, metabolism, parable, parabola, parabolic, symbol, symbolic, symbolism

balneo-, balne- (L., bath, wash) Also see **lav-, luto-,** and **purg-** for more "wash, clean" words.

> **Qualifying words:** balneary, balneography, balneology, balneologist, balneotherapeutics, balneotherapy

bank, mound, hill See **ochtho-** for examples.

bapti- (Gk., dip, immersion, dipping in water) Also see **merg-** for more "dip, immerse" words.

> **Qualifying words:** Anabaptism, Anabaptist, antipaedobaptism, antipedobaptism, baptisaphily, baptism, baptist, Baptist, baptistery, baptistry, baptize, catabaptist, hemerobaptism, holobaptism, halobaptist, parabaptism, parabaptist, paedobaptism, paedobaptist, pedobaptism, pedobaptist

barba-, barb- (L., beard, beardlike) For related words, see **pogo-** for more "beard" examples and see **pilo-** [hair], **hirsute** [hair], and **tricho-** [hair]. Don't confuse this element with **barbar-,** meaning "foreign."

> **Qualifying words:** barb, Barbarossa, barber, barbette, barbical, barbituric, barbule, Lombard

barbar- (Gk. > L., foreign, strange, outlandish) Also see **xeno-** (pronounced "zeno") for more "foreign" examples. From Greek *barbaros*, "non-Greek, foreign, barbarous," from an Indo-European imitative base *barb-*, "to stammer, stutter; unintelligible." Don't confuse this element with the previous **barba-** which means "beard."

> **Qualifying words:** Barbara, barbaralalia, barbarian, barbarianism, barbaric, barbarically, barbarism, barbarity, barbarization, barbarize, barbarized, barbarizing, barbarous, barbarously, Barbary

baro-, bar-, bary- (Gk., weight, heavy; atmospheric pressure) Also see **grav-.**

> **Qualifying words:** abaragnosia, abarognosis, baragnosia, baragnosis, baranesthesia, baresthesia, baroagnosis, barognosis, barograph, barokinesis, barokinetic, barology, barometer, barophile, barophilia, barophilic, barophily, barophilic, baraphobia, baroscope, baroscopic, baroscopical, barostat, barotactic, barotaxis, barotropic, barotropism, barycenter, barycentric, baryesthesia, baryglossia, barylalia, barymorphic, barymorphosis, baryphonia, baryseisma, baryseismic, barythymia, barytone (baritone), centrobaric

bary- (Gk., heavy, weight) See **baro-** for examples.

bat(s) See **vespertillio** for examples.

bath See **balneo-, lav-, luto-,** and **purg-** for examples.

bathe, clean, bath, wash See **balneo-, lav-, luto-,** and **purg-** for examples.

batho- (Gk., depth) See **bathy-** for examples.

bathy-, batho- (Gk., deep, depth). Also see **bentho-** for more "deep" words.

> **Qualifying words:** bathesthesia, batholite, bathometer, bathomorphic, bathophobia, bathos, bathyaesthesia, bathybius, bathycardia, bathycentesis, bathycolpian, bathyesthesia, bathyhyperesthesia, bathyhypesthesia, bathyhypoesthesia, bathylimnetic, bathylittoral, bathymeter, bathymetry, bathypelagic, bathyphile, bathyphilous, bathyphily, bathyplankton, bathypnea, bathyscaph, bathysphere, bathyanesthesia

batracho-, batrach- (Gk., frog) Also see **rani-** for more "frog" words.

> **Qualifying words:** Batrachia, batrachian, batrachite, batrachivorous, batrachoherpetomachia, batrachoherpetomachy, batrachophobia, batrachophagous, batrachophagy, batrachoplasty, batrachotoxin

battle line See **phalango-** for examples.

battle, war See **belli-, -machy,** and **milit-**.

beach, seashore See **aigialo-** for examples.

bear (animal) See **arcto-** and **ursus**.

bear (verb), carry, take See **fer-, later-, phoro-,** and **port-** for examples.

bearing, producing young See **nasc-** and **para-** for examples.

beard, beard-like See **barba-** and **pogo-** for examples.

beast, wild animal See **therio-** for examples.

beat, whip See **flagello-** for examples.

beautiful See **bell-, calli,** and **kali-**.

becoming See **-esce** and **-escent** for examples.

bed; slant, slope See **clino-** for examples.

bee See **api-** for examples.

beer See **zymo-** for examples.

before, in front of See **ante-, antero-, anti-** (rarely with this meaning), **pre-,** and **pro-** for examples.

beg, ask See **peti-, rog-,** and **quir-** for examples.

beginner, novice See **tyro-** for examples.

beginning, first See **alpha** for examples.

beginning to be See **-esce** and **-escent** for examples.

behind, after See **post-, postero-,** and **retro-** for examples.

being, existing See **onto-** for examples.

believe, belief See **cred-, dox-,** and **fid-** for examples.

bell-, bel- (L., pretty, beautiful) Also see **calli-** for additional "beautiful" words.

> **Qualifying words:** belladonna, bellafigura, belle, belle epoque, *belles-lettres*, Belleville, Bellevue, belvedere, embellish, embellished, embellishes, embellishing, embellishment

belli- (L., war, fight). Also see **-machy, milit-,** and **pugn-** for more "war" words.

> **Qualifying words:** antebellum, bellatrix, bellicose, bellicosely, bellicoseness, bellicosity, belligerence, belligerency, belligerent, belligerently, bellona, rebel, rebellion, rebellious, rebelliously, rebelliousness

belly (stomach) For examples, see **abdomino-, coelio-, gastro-,** and **ventri-**.

beloved, pleasing See **grat-** for examples.

belonging to See **-ane** for examples.

below, under Examine **hypo-, infra-, sub-,** and **subter-** for examples.

belono-, belon- (Gk., needle) Also see **acu-** for other "needle, sharp" words.

> **Qualifying words:** belonephobia, belonoskiascopy, belonoid

bend, corner See **angle** and **gon-** for examples.

bend, turn See **flect-, gyro-, -plex, stroph-, tors-, trop-, verg-, vers-,** and **volv-** for information and examples.

bene-, ben- (L., good, well) Also see **bon-** and **eu-** for more "good" words. Compare with **caco-, dys-,** and **mal-** for words with opposite meanings.

> **Qualifying words:** benediction, benedictory, benefaction, benefactor, benefactress, beneficence, beneficent, beneficently, beneficial, beneficially, beneficiary, benefit, benevolence, benevolent, benign, benignant, benignity, benignly, benison

beneath See **hypo-, infra-, sub-,** and **subter-** for examples.

bentho-, benth- (Gk., sea bottom, depth) Related to **bathy-,** which you should see for similarities.

> **Qualifying words:** abyssobenthic, archibental, archibenthic, archibenthos, benthic, benthogenic, benthon, benthonic, benthos, benthophilia, benthophyte, benthopleustophyte, benthopotamous, endobenthic, endobenthos, epibenthic, epibenthos, haptobenthos, holobenthic, holobenthos, hyperbenthic, hyperbenthos, macrobenthos, microbenthos, mesobenthos, nektobenthic, nectobenthos, phytobenthos, rhizobenthic, rhizobenthos

berry See **bacci-** for examples.

beside, close by See **juxta-** for examples.

beside; past; beyond See **para-** for examples.

besides See **epi-** for examples.

best See **aristo-** for examples.

beta- (Gk., ß, second letter of the Greek alphabet) Also see **alpha** for the Greek alphabet.

> **Qualifying words:** alphabet, alphabetical, alphabetology, analphabetic, betatron

better See **meliorat-** for examples.

between See **inter-** for examples.

beyond See **extra-, extro-, para-,** and **per-** for examples.

bi- (Gk., life) See **bio-** for examples. Don't confuse this **bi-** with the next **bi-** which means "two."

bi- [before *s, c,* or a *vowel*], **bin-, bino-, bis-** (L., two, twice, double, twofold) Also see **deutero-, di-, duo-** for other examples and see NUMBERS in **Appendix G** for a list of other numerical elements. Don't confuse this *bi-* with another *bi-* which means "life."

> **Qualifying words:** biangular, biannual, biaruricular, biaxial, bicameral, bicentenary, bicentennial, bicentric, bicentricity, bicephalous, biceps, bicorporal, bicuspid, bicycle, bicyclic, bicycling, biennia, biennial, biennium, bifocal, bifocals, bifoliate, bigamist, bigamous, bigamously, bigamy, bihourly, bilabial, bilateral, bilateralism, bilaterally, bilinear, bilingual, bilingualism, billion, bimanual, bimanually, bimetallic, bimillennium, bimonthly, binary, binaural, binauricular, binocle, binocular, binomial, binomially, binophthalmoscope, binoscope, biparous, bipartite, biped, bipedal, biplane, bipod, bipolar, bipolarity, biquarterly, biracial, biradial, biscuit, bisect, bisected, bisection, bisectional, bisector, bisexual, bisexualism, bisexuality, bisexually, bitheism, bivalence, bivalent, bivalve, biweeklies, biweekly, biyearly, combination, combine, combinatory

bib-, bibi- (L., drink) Also see **dipso-, poto-,** and **-posia** for more "drink" words.

> **Qualifying words:** beverage, bib, bibaceous, bibation, bibitory, bibulous, imbibe, imbibed, imbiber, imbibing, imbibitional, imbibition

bibli-, bibl- (Gk., book) Also see **libr-** for more "book" words.

> **Qualifying words:** Bible, Biblical, Biblicist, biblioclasm, biblioclast, bibliofilm, bibliogenesis, bibliognost, bibliogony, bibliograph, bibliographer, bibliographical, bibliographically, bibliography, biblioklept, bibliokleptomania, bibliokleptomaniac, bibliolater,

bibliolatrous, bibliolatry, bibliologist, bibliology, bibliomancy, bibliomania, bibliomaniac, bibliomanical, bibliopegist, bibliopegy, bibliophage, bibliophagous, bibliophagy, bibliophil, bibliophile, bibliophilism, bibliophilist, bibliophilistic, bibliophily, bibliophobe, bibliophobia, bibliopole, bibliopolic, bibliopolism, bibliopolist, bibliopoly, bibliotaph, bibliotaphic, bibliotaphy, bibliotheca, bibliothecal, bibliotherapeutic, bibliotherapist, bibliotherapy, bibliotist, bibliolatry, bliophagy, photobibliography

big See **grand-, magni-, macro-, major-, maxi-,** and **mega-** for examples.

bile, gall See **cholo-** for examples.

billionth of a unit See **nano-** for examples.

bin- (L., two) See **bi-** (L.) for examples.

bind oneself, pledge See **spond-** for examples.

bio-, bi-, -bia, -bial, -bian, -bion, -biont, -bius, -biosis, -bium, -biotic, -biotical, -biotic (Gk., life) Also see **vita-** for more "life" words. Don't confuse this element with another **bi-** which means "two." This element is etymologically related to **anim-, psycho-, spir-** and **zoo-**. For *antonyms,* see **death.**

> **Qualifying words:** abiogenesis, abiogenic, abiogenous, abiological, abiology, abiophysiology, abiosis, abiotic, abiotrophy, aerobicamphibious, anabiosis, anabiotic, antibiosis, antibiotic(s), autobiosphere, bathybius, bioacoustics, bioaeration, bioastronautics, biocenosis, biochronology, biocidal, biocide, bioclast, bioclastic, bioclimatology, biocompatibility, biocomputer, biocybernetics, biocycle, biodegradable, biodegradation, biodegrade, biodemography, biodynamic, biodynamical, biodynamics, bioecological, bioecologist, bioecology, bioelectric, bioelectricity, bioenergetics, bioethical, bioethics, biofeedback, biogenesis, biogenetic, biogenic, biogenous, biogeny, biogeographic, biogeochemistry, biogeographic, biogeography, biograph, biographical, biography, biohazard, bioherm, biohermal, biohydraulic, biokinetics, biologist, biology, bioluminescence, bioluminescent, biolysis, biolytic, biomagnetism, biomass, biome, biomedical, biometeorology, biometer, biometrics, biometry, bion, bionecrosis, bionics, bionomics, bionomy, biopesticide, biophage, biophagism, biophagous, biophagy, biophilia, biophile, biophily, biophotogenesis, biophysics, biophysiologist, biophysiology, biophyte, biopsy, biorhythm, bioscience, bioscope, bioseisma, biospeleology, biosphere, biospheric, biostatics, biosynthesis, biosynthetic, biosystematics, biota, biotaxis, biotherapy, biotic, biotomy, biotoxicology, biotoxin, cenobite, coenobite, cryptobiosis, cryptobiotic, ectosymbiont, ectosymbiosis, endosymbiont, endosymbiosis, endosymbiotic, exobiologist, exobiology, exobiotic, geobiologist, geobiology,

macrobe, microbial, macrobiotic, macrobiotics, microbe, microbiotic, necrobiosis, necrobiosis, neurobiology, paleobiologist, paleobiology, sociobiologist, sociobiology, symbion, symbiont, symbiosis, symbiote, symbiotic, symbiotical, symbiotism

bird See **auspic-, avi-,** and **ornitho-** for examples.

birth, born See **genus, nasc-, oriri-, -para,** and **toco-** for examples.

bis- (L.,twice, double, twofold) See **bi-** for examples.

bite, sting See **pung-** for examples.

bitter See **acerb-, acid-, oxy-,** and **picro-** for examples.

black See **melano-, niger-,** and **nigri-.**

bladder See **cysto-** for examples.

blasto-, blast-, -blast, -blastic (Gk., germ, bud; shoot, formative cell or layer; of or pertaining to an embryonic or germinal stage of development)

> **Qualifying words:** blast, blastema, blastocyte, blastoderm, blastodermic, blastogenesis, blastogenic, blastogeny, blastolysis, blastolytic, blastoma, blastomatoid, blastomatosis, blastophyllum, ectoblast, hematoblast, hemoblastic, heteroblastic, holoblastic, mesoblast, neuroblast

blaze See "fire" and locate any of the elements you desire from that list.

blepharo-, blephar- (Gk., eyelid; of or pertaining to the eyelid[s] or eyelash[es]) Also see **cilio-** for other "eyelid" words.

> **Qualifying words:** ablepharia, ablepharon, ablepharous, ablephary, ablepsis, ablepsy, ableptical, acyanoblepsia, blepharal, blepharectomy, blepharedema, blepharitis, blepharopachynsis, blepharoplastic, blepharoplasty, blepharoplegia, blepharorrhaphy, blepharospasm, blepharosphincterectomy, blepharostat, blepharotomy, macroblepharia, symblepharon

blind See **typhlo-** for examples.

blind gut See **ceco-** for examples.

blindness, darkness See **scoto-** and **skoto-** for examples.

blood See **-emia, hemo-,** and **sangui-** for examples.

blood (clot) See **thrombo-** for examples.

blood vein See **angio-, arterio-, capillaro-, phlebo-, vaso-,** and **veno-** for related words.

blow, a puff of wind See **flat-** for examples.

blue See **cyano-** for examples.

boat-shaped See **scapho-** for examples.

bodily cavity See **bursa-** for examples.

bodily injury, wound See **traumato-.**

bodily part See **organo-** for examples.

body See **corp-** and **soma-** for examples.

boil See **ferv-** for examples.

bol- (Gk., throw) See **ballo-** for examples.

-bole (Gk., throw) See **ballo-** for examples.

balo- (Gk., thorw, thrown) See **ballo-** for examples.

bon- (L., good) Also see **bene-** and **eu-** for other examples of "good" words. Compare this element with those in **caco-, dys-,** and **mal-** for words with opposite meanings.

> **Qualifying words:** *bon vivant, bon voyage, bona fide,* bonanza, bonbon, bonhomie, Boniface, bonification, bonny, bonus, bonuses, boon, bounty, debonair, *magnum bonum*

bone(s) See **ilio-, os-, osteo-, sacro-²,** and **skeleto-** for examples.

bone between two joints of a finger or toe See **phalango-** for examples.

book See **biblio-** and **libr-** for examples.

boreal (Gk. > L., north, northern) Also see **austro-** (south).

> **Qualifying words:** antiboreal, Aurora Borealis, boreal, borealization, Boreas, circumboreal, Hyperborean, hyperboreus

border See **fin-** for examples.

born, birth See **genus, nasc-, oriri-, para-,** and **toco-** for examples.

bos- (L., cow) See **bov-** for examples.

botano-, botan- (Gk. > L., plants, plant life [originally, "herb, grass, pasture"]) Also see **phyto-** for more "plant" words.

> **Qualifying words:** botanic, botanical, botanically, botanist, botanology, botanomancy, botanophily, botany, botinize, ethnobotanic, ethonobotanist, ethnobotany

both, on both sides For examples, see **ambi-, amphi-, ampho-, circ-, circum-, cyclo-,** and **peri-.**

botryo-, botry- (Gk., cluster of grapes, clusterlike, grapes)

> **Qualifying words:** botryogen, botryoid, botryomycosis, botryose, botryotherapy, botrytimycosis

bottle, jar See **amphor-** for examples.

bottom See **bentho-** for examples.

bou-, bu- (Gk., cow, ox) Also see **bovo-** and **vacc-** for more "cow" words.

> **Qualifying words:** boulemia, bouphonia, boustrophedon, bucolic, bucranium, bugle, bulimarexia, bulimia, bulimiac, bulimic, bulimorexia

boundary, end   Examine **fin-, teleo-, term-,** and **ultim-** for related words.

bovo-, bov-, bos- L., cow)   Also see **bou-** and **vacc-** for other "cow" words.

> Qualifying words: Bos, Bosphorus (or Bosporus), bovate, bovia, boviculture, bovid, boviform, bovine, bovovaccination

boy, child   See **puer-** and **pedo-** (Gk.) .

brachio-, brachi- (Gk., arm [especially the upperarm from the shoulder to the elbow]).

> Qualifying words: abrachia, abrachiocephalia, abrachiocephalus, abrachiocephaly, abrachius, brachia, brachial, brachialgia, brachiate, brachium, brachiathon, brachiocephalic, brachiofaciolingual, brachiogram, brachipod, brachiopod, brachioradialis, brachiosaurus, brachiotomy, brachium(s.), brachia(pl.), macrobrachia

brachy-, -brachy, -brach (Gk., short, small [also expressed as "slow"]) For similarities, see **brady-** (slow) and **brevi-** (short).

> Qualifying words: amphibrach, brachycardia, brachycephalic, brachycephalous, brachycephaly, brachydactyl, brachydactylia, brachydactylic, brachydactylous, brachydactyly, brachydont, brachydontia, brachyglossal, brachygnathous, brachygraphic, brachygraphy, brachylogy, brachymorphic, brachypodous, brachypterous, brachyrhinia, brachytherapy, brachymorphic, brachyural, brachyuran, brachyurous

brady- (Gk., slow, delayed, tardy)   Also see **brachy-** for possible "slow" examples. Compare with **tacho-**, "fast."

> Qualifying words: bradyacusia, bradycardia, bradycinesia, bradycrotic, bradyesthesia, bradyglossa, bradyglossia, bradykinesia, bradykinesis, bradykinetic, bradykinin, bradylalia, bradylexia, bradylogia, bradypepsia, bradypeptic, bradyphagia, bradyphasia, bradyphemia, bradyphrasia, bradypnea, bradypod, bradypodiadae, bradypsychia, bradypus, bradyseism, bradyseismic, bradytachycardia, bradyteleocinesia, bradyteleokinesis, bradytelic, bradytrophia, bradytrophic

brain   See **cerebello-, cerebro-, encephalo-,** and **phren-** for examples.

bread   See **pan-** for examples.

break   See **clast-, frag-, -orrhexis,** and **rupt-**.

breast   Examine **mammo-, masto-, mazo-,** and **pectoro-** for examples.

breath of life   See **anima-** and **spir-**.

breathing, breath   See **anemo-, hal-, pneo-, pneumato-,** and **pneumo-** for examples.

brevi-, brev- (brie-, bri-) (L., short) Also see **brachy-** for more "short" words.

> Qualifying words: abbreviate, abbreviated, abbreviation, abbreviator, abridge, abridged, abridger, abridgment, breve, brevet, breviary, brevicaudate, brevifoliate, brevilingual, breviloquent, breviped, brevity, brief, briefly, unabridged

bring, carry   See **-fer, later-, port-,** and **phoro-**.

bring forth, produce   See **nasc-** and **-parous**.

bring, lead   See **agogue-** and **duc-** for examples.   Compare with **port-** (carry).

bristle, spine   See **acantho-** and **chaeto-**.

bristling, shaking   See **hor-** for examples.

broad, flat surface; ankle   See **tarso-** for examples.

broad leaf   See **forbi-** for examples.

broad, upper bone of the pelvis   See **ilio-** for examples.

broad, wide   See **eury-** and **platy-**.

broken, break   See **clast-, frag-,** and **rupt-**.

bromato-, bromat-, broma- (Gk., food)   Also see **alimento-, cibo-, sitio-,** and **tropho-**.

> Qualifying words: bromatherapy, bromatology, bromatotherapy, bromatotoxin, bromatoxism

bromo-, brom- (Gk., stench, stink, bad odor; unpleasant bodily odor)   Also see **odori-, olfacto-, osmo-,** and **osphresio-** for other examples.

> Qualifying words: antibromic, bromhidrosis, bromide, bromidic, bromidrosiphobia, bromidrosis, bromine, bromohyperhidrosis, bromomania, bromomenorrhea, bromopnea, podobromhidrosis, podobromidrosis

broncho-, bronch-, bronchi-, bronchio- (Gk., windpipe [trachaea])   See **aorto-** and **tracheo-** for other "windpipe" examples.

> Qualifying words: bronchi(pl), bronchia, bronchial, bronchialgenic, bronchiloguy, bronchiospasm, bronchiolitis, bronchoclysis, bronchitis, bronchography, broncholith, bronchomotor, bronchoplasty, bronchopneumonia, bronchopulmonary, bronchoscope, bronchoscopy, bronchospasm, bronchospirometry, bronchostomy, bronchotomy, bronchotracheal, bronchus(s), tracheobronchial

bronto-, bront- (Gk., thunder) Also examine **cerauno-** and **tonitro-** for additional "thunder" words.

> Qualifying words: brontograph, brontology, brontometer, brontophobia, brontosaur, Brontosaurus, brontotherium

brother   See **adelpho-** and **frater-**.

bruxo-, brux- (Gk., gnashing the teeth) Also see **tribo-** and **-tripsy** for other "grind" words.

> Qualifying words: bruxating, bruxism, bruxomania (also brychomania), bruxophobia

bryo- (Gk., moss; blossom)

> **Qualifying words:** bryochore, bryocole, bryocolous, bryophile, bryophilous, bryophily, bryological, bryology, Bryophyta, bryophyte, bryophytic, Bryozoa, bryozoan

bu- (from "cow") See **bov-** for examples.

bucco-, bucc- (L., cheek)

> **Qualifying words:** bathybuccal, bucca, buccal, buccoclusion, buccocervical, buccoclination, buccofacial, buccogingival, buccoglossopharyngitis, buccolabial, buccolingual, buccolingually, bucconasal, bucconasopharyngeal, buccoplacement, buccoversion, buccula, gingivobuccoaxial, umbobuccal

bud, germ See **blasto-** for examples.

bufo- (L., toad) Also see **batracho-, phryno-,** and **rani-** (frog) for other "toad" words.

> **Qualifying words:** Bufo, *Bufo marinus*, Bufonidae, bufotenin, bufotenine, bufotherapy, bufotoxin

bug See **entomo-** and **insecti-** for examples.

build See **ag-, fac-, -ize** and **stru-** for examples.

bulima (morbid hunger) See **bou-** (cow).

bull See **bou-** and **tauro-** for examples.

burial See **tapho-** for examples.

burn, fire See **ars-, caust-, crema-, ethero-, flagr-, flam-, ign-, incend- pyro-,** and **volcan-** for examples.

bursa-, bruso-, burs- (L., bag, sac, saclike, purse; in anatomy and medicine, a bodily cavity, especially one located between joints or at points of friction between moving structures and filled with a viscid fluid and situated at the various places in the tissues at which friction would otherwise develop)

> **Qualifying words:** bourse, bursa, bursae, bursal, bursalogy, bursar, bursary, burse, bursectomy, bursiform, bursitis, bursolith, bursopathy, bursotomy, bursula, disburse, imburse, purse, reimbursable, reimburse, reimbursement

burso- (L., bag) See **bursa-** for examples.

bursting, a breaking forth See **-orrhexis.**

bush, thicket See **lochmo-** for examples.

butter See **butyro-** for examples.

butterflies, moths See **lepidopter-** for examples.

buttocks, rump See **pygo-** for examples.

butyro-, butyr- (Gk. > L., butter; from *bou(s),* "ox, cow" plus *tyro(s),* "cheese")

> **Qualifying words:** butter, butyric, butyromel, butyrometer, butyroscope

by means of, through See **per-** for examples.

C c

caco-, cac-, kako-, kak- (Gk., bad, harsh, wrong, poor) Also see **dys-, mal-,** and **mis-** for other "bad" examples. Compare with **bene-, calli-, eu-** and **ortho-** for opposite meanings.

> **Qualifying words:** cacesthesia, cacesthesia, cacexia, cacidrosis, cacodemon, cacodemonia, cacodemonomania, cacodontia, cacodoxy, cacodoxian, cacodoxical, cacoepy, cacoethes, *cacoethes loquendi, cacoethes scribendi,* cacoethic, cacogalactin, cacogastric, cacogenesis, cacogenic, cacogeusia, cacoglossia, cacography, cacolalia, cacology, cacomorphosis, caconym, cacopathy, cacophemism (*antonym* of euphemism), cacophonia, cacophonic, cacophonical, cacophonous, cacophony, cacoplasia, cacoplastic, cacorhythmic, cacorrhinia, cacosmia, cacothanasia, cacothenics, cacothrophy, kakergasia, kakergasic, kakesthesia, kakistocracy, kakosmia, kakotrophy

cad-, cas-, cid- (L., fall) Also see **-ptosia.**

> **Qualifying words:** accident, accidental, cadaver, cadaverous, cadence, cadent, cadenza, caducous, cascade, casual, casualty, coincide, coincidental, decadence, decadent, decay, deciduous, incidence, incident, incidental, occasion, occidental, recidivism

caino- (Gk., new, recent, fresh) See **ceno-** for examples.

cal- (L., heat) See **calori-** for examples.

calcaneo-, calcane- (L., heel bone [back of the *tarsus*]) Also see **achilles.**

> **Qualifying words:** calcaneal, calcanean, calcaneum, calcaneitis, calcaneoapophysitis, calcaneodynia, calcaneotibial, calcaneum, calcaneus, calcanodynia

calci-, calc-, calcio-, calco-, calx (L., lime, calcium; heel, bone of the tarsus; to tread [derived from *calx, calcis,* limestone, lime, pebble; from Gk. words *khalix* and *psephos* meaning "small stone, pebble"])

> **Qualifying words:** calcareous, calcaroid, calcemia, calces, calcic, calcicole, calcicosis, calciferous, calcific, calcification, calcify, calgerous, calcinosis, calciotropism, calciphilia, calciprivia, calcium, calcoglobule, calculable, calculate, calculation, calculator, calculi, calculus, calk, calx, calxes, calyces, calycine, calycle, causeway, chalk, chalkboard, chalkline, chalkstone, inculcate, recalcitrant

cale- (L., heat) See **calori-** for examples.

call, speak See **voc-** for examples.

calli-, cali-, callo-, calo-, kalli-, kali-, kaleido- (Gk., beautiful) Also see **bell-** for other examples of "beautiful" words. Compare this element with **caco-** for antonyms.

> **Qualifying words:** calibraphist, caligraphy, calisthenic, calisthenical, calisthenically, calisthenics, calligraph, calligrapher, calligraphic, calligraphical, calligrapist, calligraphy, Calliope, calliopsis, calliphony, Calliphora, callipygian, Callipygian Venus, callipygous, callomania, callomaniac, Calonyction, Calophyllum, calotype, kaleidophone, kaleidoscope, kaleidoscopic, kaleidoscopically

calm, peaceful See **pac-, plac-,** and **quies-** for examples.

calo- (L., heat) See **calori-** for examples.

calor- (L., heat) See **calori-** for examples.

calor-, calori-, calo-, cal-, cale- (L., heat; related to **cau(s)t**) Also examine **ferv-** and **thermo-** for other "heat" words.

> **Qualifying words:** caldarium, caldron, calefacient, calefaction, calefactory, calescent, caliduct, California, calorescence, calorescent, calorgenic, caloric, caloricity, calorie, calorifacient, calorific, calorigenesis, calorification, calorifics, calorigenetic, calorigenic, calorimeter, calorimetric, calorimetry, caloripuncture, calorismetry, caloriscope, caloritropic, calorose, calory, cauldron, decalescent, nonchalance, nonchalantly, nonchalantness, nonchalent, scald

calypo-, calyp- (Gk., L., covered, cover, hide, hidden, conceal, concealed) For additional "secret" words, examine **adelo-, clandestine, crypto-, krypto-, leth-, myster-,** and **occult-.** Also see **stego-** for other "cover" words.

> **Qualifying words:** anacalypsis, apocalypse, Calypso, calyptoblastic, calyptobranchiate, calyptomerous, calyptra, Eucalyptus, spermiocalyptrotheca

calx (L., lime, heel) See **calci-** for examples.

camp (L., flat space, plain, field)

> **Qualifying words:** camp, campaign, camper, campestral, campo, campus, decamp, encamp, encampment

cancer See **cancero-** for examples.

cancero-, cancer-, canceri-, cancri-, cancro- (L., crab; malignant tumor [according to Galen, the swollen veins surrounding a malignant tumor resemble the legs of a crab]) Also see **carcino-, -oma,** and **onco-** for other "tumor" words.

> **Qualifying words:** cancer, canceremia, cancericidal, cancerigenic, cancerism, cancerite, cancerocidal, canceroderm, cancerogenic, cancerophobia, cancerous, cancerphobia, cancriform, cancrivorous, cancrocirrhosis, cancroid

cancri-, cancro- (L., tumor) See **cancero-.**

cand-, cend- (L., glow; white) Also see **albo-**, **albumino-**, and **leuco-**.

    Qualifying words: candelabra(pl.), candelabrum(s.), candent, candescent, candid, candidate, candle, candor, chandelier, incandescent, incendiary, incense

cani-, can- [*canis*] (L., dog) Also see **cyno-**.

    Qualifying words: canary, canicola, Canicula, canicular, canicule, canine, caniniform, Canis, *canis lupus*, Canis Major, Canis Minor, *dentes canini*

cantho-, canth- (Gk. > L., corner of the eye)

    Qualifying words: canthectomy, canthi, canthitis, cantholysis, canthoplasty, canthorrhaphy, canthotomy, canthus

cap-, cip-, capt-, cept-, -ceive, -ceipt, -ceit (L., catch, seize, take hold of, take, hold) Also see **prehend-** and **ten-** for other "seize, hold" words.

    Qualifying words: accept, acceptance, anticipate, anticipatory, capability, capable, capableness, capably, capacious, capacitor, capacity, capsule, caption, captious, captivate, captivation, captive, captivity, captor, capture, capturer, conceit, conceited, conceive, concept, conception, deceit, deceitful, deceitfully, deceitfulness, deceive, deceived, deceiver, deception, deceptive, emancipate, encapsulate, except, exceptional, forceps, imperceptible, incapable, incapacitate, incapacitation, inception incipiency, incipient, inconceivable, intercept, intercepted, interceptor, interception, interceptor, misconception, municipality, occupation, occupy, participant, participate, participating, participation, participle, perceive, percept, perceptible, perception, perceptive, preconceive, principal, principle, receipt, receive, receptacle, reception, receptionist, receptive, receptor, recipe, recipient, recuperate, susceptibility, susceptible, unacceptable, unprincipled

capillaro-, capillar-, capillario-, capilli- (L., of, pertaining to, or resembling hair; minute [hairlike] blood vessels that connect the *arterioles* and the *venules*) Also see other "hair-type" words, such as: **chaeto-** (spine, bristle), **crino-, hirsute, tricho-, pilo-,** and **pogo-** (beard).

    Qualifying words: capillarectasia, capillariomotor, capillaritis, capillarity, capillaroscopy, capillary, capilliculture, capillifolious, capilliform

capit-, capt-, ceps-, chapt-, chef, cip-, -cup- (L., head, leader, chief, *or* first) Also see **cephalo-, cranio-, prim-,** and **prin-** for other examples with similar meanings.

    Qualifying words: achieve, achievement, achiever, biceps, cape, capital, capitalism, capitalize, capitate, capitation, capitol, capit-ulate, capitulation, capitulatory, captain, captaincy, caption, cattle, chapter, chattel, chef, chief, chieftain, decapitate, decapitated, decapitating, decapitation, decapitor, handkerchief, kerchief, mischief, per capita, precipice, precipitable, precipitance, precipitant, precipitantly, precipitate, precipitation, precipitous, precipitously, precipitousness, quadriceps, recap, recapitulate, recapitulated, recapitulater, recapitulating, recapitulation, recapitulative, recapitulatory, receive, received, triceps

capno-, capn- (Gk., smoke; vapor; sooty [extended meaning is *carbon dioxide*]) Also see **fumi-** and **typho-** [stupor, clouding of the mind] for additional "smoke" words.

    Qualifying words: acapnia, acapnial, acapnic, acapnotic, capnogram, capnograph, capnography, capnohepatography, capnomancy, capnometry, capnophilic, hypercapnia, misocapnic, misocapnist

capri-, capr- (L., goat, resembling a goat) Also examine **aego-** (*ego-*), **hirco-** and **tragico-** for other "goat" words.

    Qualifying words: capella, caper, capric, caprice, capricious, capricorn, Capricorn, caprifoliaceous, caprigenous, capriloquism, caprine, capriola, capriole, capripede, chevron (Fr.), Chevrolet (Fr.)

capsule, case See **theco-** for examples.

carbo-, carb- (L., coal, charcoal) Also check **anthraco-** for other "coal" words.

    Qualifying words: carbide, carbohydrate, carbolic, carbon, carbonaceous, carbonado, carbonated, carboniferous, Carboniferous, carbonize, carboraceous, carborundum, carbuncle, carbuncular, carburet, carburetor, escarbuncle

carbon dioxide See **anthraco-** and **carbo-**.

carcino-, carcin- (Gk., cancer ["crab"]) Also see **cancero-, -oma,** and **onco-** for other "cancer" words.

    Qualifying words: adenocarcinoma, carcinectomy, carcinemia, carcinogen, carcinogenesis, carcinogenic, carcinoid, carcinology, carcinolysin, carcinolysis, carcinolytic, carcinoma, carcinomatoid, carcinomatophobia, carcinomatosis, carcinomorphic, carcinophilia, carcinophilic, carcinophobia, carcinosis, carcinostatic, carcinous

card, map See **carto-** for examples.

cardio-, cardi-, card- (Gk., heart, pertaining to the heart). Also see **cor-** for other "heart" words.

    Qualifying words: acardia, acardiac, a-cardiotrophia, acardius, bradycardia, bradycardiac, cardiagra, cardialgia, cardianesthesia, cardiant, cardiataxia, cardiatoxico, cardiectomized, cardiectomy, cardioaccelerator, cardioactive, cardioanesthesia, cardioangiology, cardiocentesis, cardiocinetic, cardiodynamics, cardiodynia, cardiogram, cardiograph, cardiographic, cardiography, cardiohepatic, cardioid, cardiokinetic, cardiolipin, cardiologist, cardiology, cardiometer, cardiometry, cardiomotility, cardiomyoliposis, cardionecrosis, cardiopathia, cardiopath, cardiopathy, cardiophobia, cardiophone, cardiophony, cardioplasty, cardioplegia, cardioplegic, cardiopneumatic, cardiopneumograph, cardiopulmonary, cardiopuncture, cardiotachometer, cardiotachometry, cardiotherapy, cardiotomy, cardiotoxic, cardiovalvulitis, cardiovascular, carditis, dexiocardia, diplocardiac, electrocardiogram, endocardium, epicardium, megalocardia, myocardia, pericardium, tachycardia

care, to till (the ground) See **cult-**.

carno-, carn-, carne-, carni- (L., flesh, meat) Also see **creo-** and **sarco-**.

> **Qualifying words:** carnage, carnal, carnality, carnalize, carnation, carneous, carnification, carnigen, carnine, carnival, carnivora, carnivore, carnivorous, carnivorously, carnivorousness, carnophobia, carnosity, chili con carne, incarnate, incarnation, reincarnate, reincarnation

carpo-, carp-, -carp, -carpic, -carpium, -carpous, -carpus (Gk., fruit; to cut, to pluck) Also see **pomo-** for "apple" words. Don't confuse this **carpo-** with another one in medicine, which means "wrist."

> **Qualifying words:** acarpous, acrocarpous, allocarpy, amphicarpic, apocarpous, carpel, carpet, carpogenic, carpogenous, carpolite, carpolith, carpology, carpophagous, carpophagy, carpophile, carpophily, carpophore, chrysocarpous, cremocarp, endocarp, epicarp, excerpt, excerption, mericarp, mesocarp, monocarpic, monocarpous, pericarp, scarce, schizocarp, syncarp, xylocarp

carpo-, carp-, -carpals, -carpus (Gk., wrist [literally, "that which turns"]) Don't confuse this element with another **carpo-** (Gk.) which means "fruit."

> **Qualifying words:** carpal, carpale, carpectomy, carpitis, carpocarpal, carpopedal, carpoptosis, carpus, metacarpal, metacarpectomy, metacarpus, midcarpal, radiocarpal, radiocarpus

carry, bring See **phoro-, port-** and compare with **agogue-, duc-,** and **ger-**.

cartilage See **chondro-** for examples.

carto- (Gk., L., map, card [playing]; piece of papyrus, paper)

> **Qualifying words:** cartel, carton, cartoon, cartridge, cartogram, cartography, cartomancy

carve, engrave See **glypto-** for examples.

case- (L., cheese) Also see **tyro-** for other "cheese" words.

> **Qualifying words:** caseasation, casease, caseate, caseic, casein, caseinate, caseogenous, caseose, caseous, caseum

case, capsule See **theco-** for examples.

cas See **miss-** for examples.

cat See **aeluro-, feli-, galeo-,** and **gato-**.

cata-, cat-, cath-, kata- (Gk., down, downward; against; entirely, in accordance with, completely, back)

> **Qualifying words:** acataphasia, catabaptist, catabolic, catabolism, catachronobiology, cataclastic, cataclysm, cataclysmal, catacomb, catadromous, catagenesis, catalepsy, cataleptic, catalog, catalogia, catalogue, catalysis, catalyst, catalytic, catamnesis, cataphasia, cataphora, cataphyll, cataplasm, catapult, cataract, catarrh, catastrophe, catathermometer, catatonia, catatonic, catatropia, catechism, cathedral, cathode, catholic, catoptrics, catropia, kataphylaxis, katatropic, katatropism

catch, seize See **cap-** for examples.

caterpillar See **eruci-** for examples.

catheter (Gk, a tubular, flexible, surgical instrument for withdrawing fluids from [or introducing fluids into] a cavity of the body, especially one for introduction into the bladder through the urethra for the withdrawal of urine) From **cata-**.

> **Qualifying words:** catheter, catheterization, catheterize, catheterostat, catheometer

catoptro-, catoptr- (Gk., mirror; from *kat-(a)* "against, back" plus *op-(tos)* "seen" plus the noun-forming suffix *-tron*) Also see **eisoptro-** for other "mirror" words.

> **Qualifying words:** catoptric, catoptrical, catoptrics, captoptromantic, catoptromancy, catoptrophobia, catoptroscope

caudo-, caud- (L., tail, toward the tail; downward) Also see **peni-** and **uro-** for other "tail" words.

> **Qualifying words:** acaudal, acaudate, brevicaudate, cauda, caudal, caudalis, caudate, caudation, caudiform, caudocephaled, cephalocaudal, coward, cowardly, longicaudate

cauli-, caul-, col- (Gk. > L., stem, stalk)

> **Qualifying words:** acaulescent, caulescent, caulicarpous, caulicle, cauline, cauliculus, cauliflory, cauliflower, cauliform, cauligenous, cole, coleslaw, caulocarpous, folicaulicole, folicaulicolous, kohlrabi

cause, causation See **etio-** and **fac-**.

cause to go See **miss-** for examples.

caust-, caus-, caut-, cau- (Gk., fire, burn; from *kauter*, "branding iron") See ars-, crema-, flagr-, flam-, ign-, incend-, pyro-, and volcan-.

> Qualifying words: caumesthesia, causalgia, caustic, caustically, causticity, causticize, cauter, cauterant, cauteries, cauterization, cauterize, cauterized, cauterizing, cautery, cryocautery, diacaustic, electrocauterization, electrocautery, encaustic, eremacausis, galvanocautery, hippocaust, holocaust, holocaustal, holocaustic, hypocaust, ink, photocautherization, photocautery, thermocautery

caut- (L., fire, burn) See caust- for examples.

cauter- (L., fire, burn) See caust- for examples.

cave, cavern See antro- and speleo- for examples.

ceco-, cec-, caeco-, caec- (L., blind, blind gut [first part of the large intestine, forming a dilated pouch into which open the *ileum*, the *colon*, and the *appendix vermiformis*]; any blind pouch) Also see typhlo-.

> Qualifying words: caecal, caecotomy, cecalcecitis, cecocentral, cecocolic, cecocolon, cecocolostomy, cecofixation, cecoileostomy, cecopexy, cecorrhaphy, cecostomy, cecotomy, cecum

-cede, -ceed, -cess, -cease (L., go, go away, yield, give up, withdraw)

> Qualifying words: abscess, accede, access, accessory, ancestor, antecede, antecedence, antecedent, cease, cede, cessation, cession, concede, concession, decease, epicede, exceed, excess, excessive, incessant, intercede, intercession, necessary, precede, precedent, precession, predecessor, procedure, proceed, process, procession, recede, recess, recession, retrocede, secession, secessionist, secede, succeed, success, unprecedented

ceiv- (L., catch, seize) See cap- for examples.

cele- (Gk., abdomen, belly) See coeli- for examples.

celeo- (Gk., abdomen, belly) See coeli- for examples.

celio- (Gk., abdomen; belly, stomach) For examples, see coeli-.

celest- [*caelestis*] (L., heaven, sky) Also see urano- for more "heaven" words and ethero- for words with similar meanings.

> Qualifying words: ceiling, celesta, celestial, celestiality, celestially, celestial equator, celestial latitude, celestial sphere, Selina (Céline, French from Latin *caelum, caelestis*)

celer- (L., fast, speed, swift, rapid) Also see tacho- and veloci- for additional "fast" words. Compare this with brady- for words with opposite meanings.

> Qualifying words: accelerant, accelerate, acceleration, accelerator, accelerometer, celerity, decelerate, deceleration

celi-, celio-, celo- (Gk., abdominal relationship; hollow) See coelio- for examples.

cell, hollow See cyto- for examples.

cemetery See tapho- for examples.

cend- (L., glow; white) See cand- for examples.

-cene (Gk., new, denotes certain "recent" eons when naming geological periods) Also see ceno-, "new."

> Qualifying words: Eocene, miocene, Oligocene, Paleocene, Pleistocene, Pliocene

ceno-,[1] cen-, ceoen-, coeno-, coino-, kaino-, koino- (Gk., common, shared) Also see coeno- and commu- for more "common" words. Don't confuse this ceno- with others which mean "new" or "empty."

> Qualifying words: acenesthesia, biocenosis, cenadelphus, cenesthesia, cenesthesic, cenesthetic, cenesthopathy, cenobite, cenobian, cenobium, cenocyte, cenosite, cenotype, cenotrope, coenesthesia, coenobite, coenocyte, koinonia, koinotropic, koinotropy

ceno-,[2] cen-, caeno-, caen-, caino-, cain-, kaino-, kain- (Gk., new, recent, fresh) Also see -cene, neo-, and novo- for more "new" words. Don't confuse this ceno- with those which mean "common" and "empty."

> Qualifying words: caenogenesis, caenophithecus, caenozoic, cainophobia, cainozoic, cenogenesis, cenopsychic, cenotaph, cenotype, Cenozoic, cenozoology, Eocene kainophobia, miocene, recent

ceno-,[3] caeno-, keno- (Gk., empty) Don't confuse this ceno- with others which mean "common" or "new."

> Qualifying words: cenophobia, cenotaph, cenotaphic, cenotoxin, kenophobia, kenotoxin

-centesis (Gk., perforation, puncture, or tapping, as with an aspirator or needle)

> Qualifying words: abdominalcentesis, amniocentesis, cardiocentesis, celioparacentesis, colocentesis, enterocentesis, paracentesis, pneumonocentesis, thoracocentesis

centi-, cent- (L., hundred; 10^{-2} [0.01] or one-hundredth) Also see hecto- for other "hundred" words. See NUMBERS in Appendix G and METRIC GROUPS in Appendix F for additional numerical elements. In the metric system, **centi-** denotes 1/100th of a unit or, in other words, fractions of a unit.

    Qualifying words: bicentenary, bicentennial, cent, centenarian, centenary, centennial, centennium, centesimal, centesimate, centigrade, centigram, centiliter, centimeter, centimilli, centipede, centuple, centurion, century, percent (*per centum*, %), percentage, quadricentennial, quincentenary, quincentennial, sesquicentennial, sexcentenary, tercentenary, tercentennial

centro-, centr-, centri-, kentro- (Gk., center) This element originally meant "sharp point, goad, spur."

    Qualifying words: acentric, androcentric, anthropocentric, biocentric, center, centering, centipedal, central, centralize, centre, centric, centrical, centricity, centrifugal, centrifuge, centripetal, centrist, centrobaric, centrocecal, centrodorsal, centrokinesia, centrokinetic, centro-osteosclerosis, centrosphere, cerebrocentric, concentrate, concentrated, concentration, concentrator, concentric, eccentric, eccentricity, egocentric, egocentricity, epicenter, geocentric, heliocentric, kentrokinesia, paracentric

cephalo-, cephal-, -cephalous; sometimes they are also: **kephal-** or **kephalo-** (Gk., head) Also see **capit-** and **cranio-**.

    Qualifying words: acephalous, acrocephalic, anencephalic, autocephalous, bicephalous, brachycephalic, brachycephalism, brachycephalous, brachycephaly, cephalad, cephalalgia, cephalate, cephalic, cephalitis, cephalocaudal, cephalodynia, cephalodynic, cephaloid, cephalomancy, cephalometer, cephalometric, cephalometrical, cephalometry, cephalopathy, cephaloplegia, cephalopod, cephalothorax, cephalotomy, cephalotripsy, cephalous, cynocephalous, encephalalgia, encephalitis, encephaloma, encephalon, hydrocephaloid, hydrocephalus, isocephalic, isocephalism, isocephalous, isocephaly, kephalin, kephalogram, macrocephalic, macrocephalia, macrocephalism, macrocephalous, macrocephaly, megacephalic, mesocephalic, metencephalon, microcephalism, microcephalous, microcephaly, orthocephalic, rhinencephalon, stenocephaly

ceps- (L., head) See **capit-** for examples.

cer- (Gk., wax) See **cero-** for examples.

cerato-, cerat-, kerato-, kerat-, ker-, kera-, kerat- (Gk., horn, horny; cornea) Also see **corn-** for other "horn" words.

    Qualifying words: angiokeratoma, cerotid, ceratoid, keratalgia, keratic, keratin, keratinophile, keratinophilic, keratinophily, keratinophile, keratinophilic, keratinophily, ke-

ratitis, keratoderma, keratodermis, keratodermo, keratogenesis, keratogenous, keratohemia, keratoid, keratolysis, keratolytic, keratoma, keratome, keratomalacia, keratometer, keratometry, keratopathy, keratoplasty, keratosis, keratotomy, megaceros, rhinoceros, tetracerous, triceratops

cerauno-, kerauno- (Gk., thunderbolt, thunder, lightning [literally, "smasher, crusher"]) Also see **bronto-** and **tonitro-**.

    Qualifying words: ceraunograph, ceraunography, ceraunophilia, ceraunophobia, ceraunoscopia, keraunograph, keraunography, keraunoneurosis, keraunophilia, keraunophobia, keraunoscopia

cerebello-, cerebell- (L., brain) Also examine **cerebro-, encephalo-,** and **phreno-**.

    Qualifying words: cerebellar, cerebellifugal, cerebellitis, cerebellum

cerebro-, cerebr-, cereb-, cerebri- (L., brain [that part of the brain which is concerned with the coordination of body movements]) Also see **cerebello-, encephalo-,** and **phreno-**. Compare with **capit-, cephalo-,** and **cranio-** (meaning "head").

    Qualifying words: acerebral, cerebral, cerebralgia, cerebrasthenia, cerebriform, cerebritis, cerebrocardiac, cerebroncentric, cerebroid, cerebrology, cerebroma, cerebromalacia, cerebrometer, cerebro-ocular, cerebropathia, cerebropathy, cerebropsychosis, cerebroscope, cerebrosis, cerebrospinal, cerebrotomy, cerebrum

cero-, cer-, kero-, keri- (Gk., wax, waxy) Also see **cerum-** for other "wax" words.

    Qualifying words: acerotous, adipocere, ceraceous, cerago, ceral, cerate, cerated, ceratonosus, cere, cereous, cere perdue, ceriferous, cerograph, cerographic, cerographical, cerographist, cerography, ceroid, cerolipoid, cerolite, cerolysin, ceroma, ceromancy, ceromel, cerophage, ceraphagous, cerophagy, ceroplastic, ceroplastics, ceroplasty, ceromen, cerumen, ceruminal, ceruminolytic, ceruminosis, ceruminous, keritherapy, kerotherapy, kerosene, sincere, sincerely, sincerest, sincerity, Tricerion

cerum-, cerumini- (Gk., [from *keros*, beeswax, wax] formed of wax) Also see **cero-** for more "wax" words.

    Qualifying words: cerumen, ceruminal, ceruminolysis, ceruminolytic, ceruminoma, ceruminosis, ceruminous

cervi-, cerv- (L., deer) Don't confuse this element with the next one which means "neck."

    Qualifying words: cervanthropy, cervicaprine, cervicide, cervicorn

cervico-, cervici-, cervic-, cervi- (L., neck, head-joint, throat) Also see **esophago-, gutturo-, laryngo-, pharyngo-, thoraco-** and **trachelo-** for other "neck" words.

> Qualifying words: cervical, cervicalgia, cervicalis, cervicectomy, cervicicardiac, cervicies, cervicispinal, cervicitis, cervicoauricular, cervicoaural, cervicoaxillary, cervicobrachial, cervicobrachialgia, cervicodorsal, cervicodynia, cervicofacial, cervicohumeral, cervicolingual, cervicomuscular, cervico-occipital, cervicoplasty, cervicovaginal, cervicovaginitis, cervicovesical, cervicoscapular, cervicothoracic, cervicotomy, cervicouterine, cervimeter, cerviplex, cervix, linguocervical

ceto-, cet-, -cete, -ceti (Gk., whales [dolphins, porpoises])

> Qualifying words: archaeocetes, Archaeoceti, Cetacea, cetacean(s), cetologists, cetology, Mysticeti, mysticeti, Odontocetes, Odontoceti, Protocetidae, spermaceti

chaeto-, chaet-, chaeti-, cheto-, chet- (Gk., spine, bristle ["long, flowing hair"]) See **acantho-, capillaro-, crino-,** and **hirsute** for other "hair" words.

> Qualifying words: achaetous, chaeta, chaetic, chaetiferous, Chaetodon, chaetodont, chaetognath, chaetophorous, Chaetopod, chaetotaxy, Coleochaete, Oligochaeta, spirochete

chalico-, chalic- (Gk., gravel, pebbles, rubble)

> Qualifying words: chalicophile, chalicophilous, chalicophily, chalicophyte

chamber, entrance hall See **atrio-**.

chance, fortune See **tycho-** for examples.

change, changeable See **alter-** and **mut-**.

chapt- (L., head) See **capit-** for examples.

character, manners See **ethi-** and **mor-**.

charcoal, coal See **anthraco-** and **carbo-**.

cheek See **bucco-** for examples.

cheese See **case-** and **tyro-** for examples.

cheilo-, cheil-, chilo-, chil- (Gk., lip, lips; edge or brim)

> Qualifying words: acheiles, acheilia, achilia, Achilles, achillobursitis, achillodynia, achillogram, cheilalgia, cheilectomy, cheilectropion, cheilion, cheilitis, cheiloangioscopy, cheilocarcinoma, cheilognathoschisis, cheilophagia, cheiloplasty, cheilorrhaphy, cheilosis, cheilostomatoplasty, cheilotomy, chilalgia, chilitis, chilophagia, chiloplasty, chilotomy, macrocheilia, xerocheilia

cheiro-, cheir-, chiro-, chir- (Gk., hand) Also see **manu-**. Compare with **dactylo-** (finger) and **digit** (finger).

> Qualifying words: acheiria, acheiropodia, acheirus, achiral, achiria, allocheiral, allo-

cheiral, allochiria, brachycheirous, cheiragra, cheiralgia, cheirarthritis, cheirobrachialgia, cheirocinesthesia, cheirocosmetic, cheirognomist, cheirognomy, cheirognostic, cheirograph, cheirography, cheirokinesthesia, cheirokinesthetic, cheirology, cheiromancy, cheiromegaly, cheironomy, cheiroplast, cheiroplasty, cheiropodalgia, cheirospasm, cheirotomy, chiragra, chiral, chirality, chirally, chirocosmetic, chirognomist, chirognomy, Chirognostic, chirograph, chirography, chirokinesthesia, chirology, chiromancy, chironomy, chiroplast, chiroplasty, chiropodalgia, chiropodist, chiropody, chiropractic, chiropractor, chiropraxis, chiroptera, chiropteran, chiropterophile, chiropterophilous, chiropterophily, chiroscope, chirospasm, chirothesia, chirotony, chirurgenic, chirurgery, chirurgic, dyscheiria, dyschiria, dyschirography, encheiresis, enchiridion, macrocheiria, Megachiroptera, megachiropteran, Microchiroptera, microchiropteran, syncheiria

chela-, cheli- Gk., claw, pincer) Also examine **onycho-** and **unguo-** for "nail" words.

> Qualifying words: chela, chelate, chelation, cheliferous, cheliform, cheliped, nonchelated

chelono-, chelon- (Gk., tortoise)

> Qualifying words: chelone, chelonite, chelonography, chelonologist, chelonology

chemo-, chem-, chemico-, chemi- (Arabic > Gk. > L.; from Arabic: (the) art of combining base metals [to make gold]; from Greek, *chemia,* "Egypt," supposedly where the art of changing metals into gold existed. The art of combining base elements which form matter, or a reference to their scientific studies.

> Qualifying words: alchemy, chemexfoliation, chemiatric, chemical, chemically, chemicobiological, chemicobiology, chemist, chemobiotic, chemoluminescence, chemistry, chemoautotroph, chemoautotrophic, chemobiotic, chemocautery, chemocautry, chemokinesis, chemokinetic, chemoluminescence, chemoluminescent, chemolysis, chemomorphosis, chemoprophylaxis, chemoreception, chemoreceptor, chemoreflex, chemosensory, chemostat, chemotactic, chemotaxis, chemotherapy, chemotropism, chemurgy

chest See **pectoro-, pleuro-** (chest membrane), **stetho-,** and **thoraco-** for examples.

chest membrane See **pleuro-** for examples.

chief See **arch-, capit-, prim-,** and **prin-**.

child See **pedo-** (Gk.), **proli-** (offspring), **puer-,** and **juveni-** for examples. Don't confuse the Greek **ped-**, "child," with the Latin **ped-**, which means "foot."

childbirth See **nasc-, para,** and **toco-**.

chilo-, chil- (Gk., lip, lips) See **cheilo-**.

chimno-, chimn-, chimono-, chimon-, chim-, chimo- (Gk., winter)

> Qualifying words: chimnochlorous, chimonophile, chimonophilous, chimonophily, chimopelagic, chimous

chin See **genio-** and **mento-** for examples.

chiono-, chion- (Gk., snow, like snow) Also see **nivi-** for other "snow" words.

> Qualifying words: chionablepsia, chionophile, chionophilous, chionophily, chionophobe, chionophobia, chionophobous, chionophoby, chionophyte

chir- (Gk., hand) See **cheiro-** for examples.

chiro- (Gk., hand) See **cheiro-** for examples.

chledo-, chled- (Gk., debris, mud, dirt) Also see **argillo-, limi-**, and **pelo-**.

> Qualifying words: chledophile, chledophilous, chledophily, chledophyte

chloro-, chlor- (Gk., green, yellow-green) Also see **verdant** and **virid-**.

> Qualifying words: chloremia, chlorine, Chloris (Greek goddess), chlorite, chlorocyte, chloroform, chloroleukemia, chlorophyl, chlorophyll, chloropia, chloroplast, chloropsia, chlorosis

cholecysto-, cyholecyst- (L., gall bladder) Also see **cholo-** for similarities.

> Qualifying words: cholecyst, cholecystagogic, cholecystagogue, cholecystalgia, cholecystatony, cholecystectony, cholecystenteric, cholecystenteroanastomosis, cholecystenterorrhaphy, cholecystenterostomy, cholecystgastrostomy, cholecysticcholecystis, cholecystitis, cholecystocholangiogram, cholecystocolotomy, cholecystogastric, cholecystogastrostomy, cholecystogram, cholecystography, cholecystoileostomy, cholecystointestinal

cholo-, chol-, chole- (Gk., bile, gall) Also see **cholecysto-** for similarities.

> Qualifying words: cholagogic, cholagogue, cholaligneic, cholangiogram, cholangiography, cholangiohepatis, cholangiohepatoma, cholangiole, cholangiotomy, cholangitis, cholanopoiesis, cholate, cholechromopoiesis, cholecyanin, choler, cholera, choleraic, choleric, cholesterine, cholesterol, cholic, cholithic, cholohemothorax, chololith, cholopoiesis, choloscopy, cholothorax, choluric, melancholy

chondro-, chondr-, chrondrio-, chondri-, -chondriac, -chondrias, -chondromatous, -chondroma, -chondromas, -chondromata (Gk., cartilage, gristle, or a relationship to cartilage)

> Qualifying words: chondralgia, chondralloplasia, chondrectomy, chondric, chondrification, chondritis, chondrocranium, chon-

drocyte, chondrodermatitis, chondrodynia, chondrodystrophy, chondrogenesis, chondrography, chondroid, chondroitic, chondrology, chondrolysis, chondroma, chondronecrosis, chondro-osseous, chondropathology, chondropathy, chondroplastic, chondroplasty, chondroskeleton, chondrosternoplasty, chondrotome, chondrotomy, chondrotrophic, enchondroma, hypochondria, hypochondriac, hypochondriacal, hypochondriasis, hypochondrium, osteochondritis, perichondrium, synchondrosis

-chore, -choric, -chorous, -chory (Gk., to spread, disperse; to withdraw, advance, go)

> Qualifying words: anemochore, anemochorous, anemochory, anthropochore, anthropochoric, anthropochorous, anthropochory, autochore, autochorous, autochory, bryochore, bryochoric, clitochore, clitochorous, clitochory, cryochore, cryochory, dendrochore, dendrochoric, dendrochory, entomochore, entomochoric, entomochory, eurychore, eurychoric, eurychorous, hydrochoric, hydrochory, stenochoric, stenochorous, xerochore, xerochoric, xerochorous, xerochory, zoochore, zoochorous, zoochory

choreo-, chore-, chorei-, choro-, -choreatic, -chorea, -choreal, -choreic (Gk., dance; in medicine, it is used to denote "a nervous disorder of organic or from an infectious origin") Also see **orches-**.

> Qualifying words: chorea, choreal, choreic, choreiform, choreographer, choreograph, choreographic, choreography, choreomania, choreophrasia, choromania, chorus, labiochorea, pseudochorea, orchichorea

chromato-, chromat-, chromo-, chrom-, -chrome, -chromasia, -chromia, -chromy, -chromatism, -chromatic, -chromatically, -chromasias, -chromy (Gk., color) Also see COLORS for additional elements.

> Qualifying words: achromachia, achromacyte, achromasia, achromatic, achromatism, achromatocyte, achromatognosia, achromatophil, achromatophilia, achromatopsia, achromaturia, achromia, achromoderma, achromodermia, achromophil, achromophilic, achromotrichia, basichromatic, biochrome, chromagogue, chromasphere, chromatic, chromatism, chromatogenesis, chromatogram, chromatography, chromatology, chromatometer, chromaturia, chromoblast, chromocyte, chromodynamics, chromogenesis, chromolithography, chromolysis, chromometer, chromophil, chromophilic, chromoplasm, chromopsia, chromosome, chromosphere, chromotype, dichromatopsia, ferrochrome, heterochromatic, hyperchromatism, polychromatic, monochromatic, panchromatic,

polychromatist, lithochromatic, oxychromatic, panchromatic, polychromic, polychromy, psychochromesthesia, trichromaopsia, xanthochromous

chrono-, chron- (Gk., time) Also see **horo-** and **tempo-** for other "time" words.

Qualifying words: allochronic, anachronism, anachronistic, anachronous, chronaxia, chronaxie, chronaximeter, chronaximetric, chronaximetry, chronaxy, chronokymograph, chronic, chronicity, chronicle, chronobiology, chronocinematography, chronocline, chronognosis, chronogram, chronograph, chronokinetics, chronological, chronology, chronometer, chronometry, chronomyometer, chronon, chronopher, chronophobia, chronophotograph, chronoscope, chronotherapy, chronotropism, chrony, diachronic, geochronology, isochronous, metachronism, parachronism, synchromesh, synchronic, synchronicity, synchronize, synchronology, synchronous, tautochrone, thermochronology

chryso-, chrys- (Gk., gold, golden, golden yellow) See **auri-, ochro-,** and **xantho-** for other "yellow" words and see COLORS for additional related elements.

Qualifying words: chrysalis, chrysaniline, chrysalis, chrysanthemum, chryselephantine, chrysocarpous, chrysoderm, chrysoderma, chrysography, chrysoleptic, chrysology, chrysophyll, chrysotherapy

chthon- (Gk., earth, of the earth, soil) Also see **agra-, geo-, humus, mundan-,** and **terr-.**

Qualifying words: allochthonous, allochthony, antichthon, autochthon, autochthonal, autochthonic, autochthonism, autochthonous, autochthony, chthon, chthonal, chthonian, chthonic, chthonism, chthonography, chthonophagia, chthonophagy, chthonous, nosochthonography

church See **ecclesi-** for examples.

cibo-, -cibal (L., food, meal) For other "food" words, see **alimento-, bromato-, sitio-,** and **tropho-.**

Qualifying words: antecibal, cibarian cibarious, cibophobia, postcibal

cicatri-, cicatr- (L., scar)

Qualifying words: cicatrectomy, cicatrical, cicatrices(pl.), cicatricotomy, cicatrix(s.), cicatrization

ciconi-, cicon- (L., stork)

Qualifying words: Ciconia, ciconmia, Ciconiidae, ciconiiform, ciconiiformes, ciconine, ciconiine

-cide (L., cut) Don't confuse this element with another **-cide** which means "to kill." See **-cise** for examples.

-cide, -cides, -cidal (L., kill, killer; murder, to cause death) Also see **letha-, mort-,** **neci-, necro-,** and **thanato-.** Don't confuse this element with the previous **-cide** which means "to cut," although **-cide,** "death," is related to **-cise, -cide,** "to cut down."

Qualifying words: aborticide, acaricide, algicide, algiocide, amebicidal, amebicide, amicicide, apicide, apricide, arachnidcide, avicide, bactericide, biocide, biopesticide, bovicide, canicide, cervicide, ceticide, cimicide, culicicide, ecocide, ethnocide, febrificide, felicide, femicide, feticide, filicide, floricide, formicide, fratercide, fratricidal, fratricide, fungicide, gallicide, gallinicide, genocide, genocidal, germicide, giganticide, gynaecide, gynecide, herbicide, herpecide, herpicide, hiricide, hirudicidal, hirudicide, homicidal, homicide, homicidomania, homocidal, hospiticide, hosticide, infanticidal, infanticide, insecticide, larvicide, logocide, lupicide, macropicide, macropocide, mariticidal, mariticide, maritocide, matricidal, matricide, microbicide, miticide, mundicide, omnicide, ovicide, oxyuricide, parenticide, parricidal, parricide, parricidism, patricidal, patricide, pesticide, petracide, phyocide, pisicide, prolicide, pulicide, regicidal, regicide, rodenticide, senicide, serpenticide, sororicidal, sororicide, spermatocide, spermicidal, spermicide, suicidal, suicide, taeniacide, talpicide, tauricide, teniacide, tyrannicide, ursicide, uxoricidal, uxoricide, vaccicide, vaticide, verbicide, vermicide, vespacide, viricide, vulpicide

cilio-, cili-, cil- (L., the eyelid or its outer edge; hairs growing on the edges of the eyelids, eyelashes) Also see **blepharo-** for other "eyelid" words.

Qualifying words: ciliariscope, ciliarotomy, ciliary, ciliastatic, Ciliata, ciliate, ciliation, ciliectomy, ciliocytophoria, ciliogenesis, ciliograde, Ciliophora, ciliophoran, cilioretinal, ciliotomy, ciliotoxicity, cilium(s.), cilia(pl.), cillo, cillosis, Euciliatia, kinocilium, multiciliate, palpicil, Protociliata, stereocilia, superciliary, supercilious, superciliously, superciliousness

cine-, cinem-, cinema-, cinemat-, cinemato-, -cinesia, -cinesis, -cinetic, -cinesias, -cineses, -cinetical, -cinetically (Gk., move, movement, set in motion) Also see **kine-, mob-** and **mot-** for additional "move" words. Don't confuse the elements in **cine-** with **ciner-,** "ashes."

Qualifying words: adiadochocinesia, adiadochocinesis, allocinesia, allocinesis, allocinetic, anesthecinesia, cine, cineangiocardiography, cinedance, cinema, *cinema verite*, cinema-goer, cinematics, cinematography, cinemicrography, cineplastics, cineplasty, cineradiography, cinerama, cineroentgenography, cinesalgia, oxycinesis

ciner-, cine- (L., ashes) Also see **conio-** (dust) and **spodo-** for additional examples. Don't confuse this **ciner-** with **cine-,** which means "to move."

> **Qualifying words:** cinefaction, cinenary, Cineraria, cinerarium, cinerator, cinereous, cinerescent, cinerous, incinerate, incineration, incinerator

circ- (L., circle [a ring; wheel]) For additional "circle" words, see **-cycle, cyclo-, orb-, peri-, rotundi-,** and **sphero-.**

> **Qualifying words:** circa, circle, circled, circlet, circling, circuit, circuitous, circuitously, circuitry, circular, circularity, circularization, circularize, circularizer, circulate, circulated, circulating, circulation, circulator, circulatory, circus, encircle

circle, round See **circ-, circum-, cyclo-, orb-,** and **rotundi-** for examples.

circular motion See **gyro-** for examples.

circum- (L., around, about, surrounding, on all sides; literally, "in a circle.") Also examine **ambi-, amphi-, circ-, cyclo-, peri-, rotundi-,** and **sphero-** for other "round" or "circle" words.

> **Qualifying words:** circumambience, circumambiency, circumambient, circumambulate, circumambulation, circumambulator, circumambulatory, circumcise, circumcision, circumference, circumflex, circumflexion, circumfluence, circumfluent, circumfusion, circumgyrate, circumgyration, circumlocution, circumlocutional, circumlocutionist, circumnavigable, circumnavigate, circumnavigation, circumnavigator, circumplanetary, circumpolar, circumscribe, circumscriber, circumscript, circumscription, circumsolar, circumspect, circumspection, circumspectly, circumstance, circumstantial, circumstantiality, circumstantially, circumstantiate, circumstantiation, circumstellar, circumterrestrial, circumvent, circumvention, circumventive, circumvolution, circumvolve, circumvolving

-cise, -cis, -cide (L., cut) Also see **-ectomy, sec-, -tom,** and **tomo-.** From this combining form, we also get the element **-cide,** "kill," but don't confuse the two elements because they have different meanings.

> **Qualifying words:** chisel, circumcised, circumcision, concise, concisely, conciseness, concision, decide, decision, decisive, excide, excise, excision, incise, incision, incisive, incisor, precise, precisely, preciseness, precisian, precisianist, precision precisionist, scissors

cit- See **civi-** for examples. Don't confuse this element with the next **cit-,** which means "to talk").

cit-, citat- (L., talk, speak, say; "to put into quick motion, excite, provoke, call urgently; summon") Also see **clam-, dic-, locu-, loqu-, mythico-, ora-, -phasia, -phemia,** and **voc-** for other "talk, speak" words.

> **Qualifying words:** citable, citation, cite, citing, excitable, excitation, excite, excited, excitement, exciting, excitingly, incite, incitement, inciting, recital, recitation, recite, resuscitate, resuscitation, resuscitator, solicit, solicitation, solicitor, solicitous, solicitude, suscitate

citat- (L., talk) See **cit-** for examples.

citizen See **civi-** for examples.

city See **civi-, polis-,** and **urban** for examples.

civi-, civ-, cit- (L., city, citizen) See **polis-** and **urban** for other "city" examples.

> **Qualifying words:** citadel, citizen, city, civic, civically, civics, civil, civilian, civilities, civility, civilization, civilize, civilized, civily, incivil, incivility, uncivil, uncivilized

claim (L., talk) See **clam-** for examples.

clam- (cla-), clamat-, claim- (L., talk, call out, speak, say, shout) Also see **cit-, dic-, locu-, loqu-, logo, mythico-, ora-, -phasia, -phemia,** and **voc-** for additional "talk" words.

> **Qualifying words:** acclaim, acclamation, acclamatory, acclimation, claim, claimant clamor, clamorous, declaim, declaimed, declamation, declamatory, disclaim, disclaimer, exclaim, exclamation, nomenclator, nomenclature, proclaim, proclaimed proclamation, reclaim, reclamation, unclaimed

clandestine (L., secret, hidden) Also examine **calyp-, crypto-, krypto-, leth-, myster-,** and **occult-** for other "secret" words.

> **Qualifying words:** clandestine, clandestinely, clandestineness

clair- (L., through French, clear; perceiving through extrasensory perception)

> **Qualifying words:** clairaudience, clairsentience, clairvoyant

clasp, seize, reach See **prehend-** for examples.

class, kind See **genus** for examples.

clast-, -clastic, -clast, -clase, -classia, -clasis, -classis, -clasmic, -clasm, -clysm (Gk., break, break in pieces; broken, broken in pieces, crush) Also see **frag-** and **rupt-** for other "break" words.

> **Qualifying words:** aclastic, anaclastic, anemoclastics, anticlastic, atmoclastics, autoclastics, biblioclasm, biblioclast, bioclasm, bioclastics, calamitous, calamity, cataclasm, cataclasmic, cataclast, cataclysm, clastic,

clastothrix, cranioclast, cryptoclastic, dendroclastic, epiclastic, glycoclastic, haloclastics, hydroclastics, iconoclasm, iconoclast, iconoclastic, limnoclastics, mythoclastic, oligoclase, oligoclastic, orthoclase, orthoclastic, osteoclasis, panclasm, panclastic, periclase, plagioclase, potamoclastics, proteoclastic, pyroclasm, pyroclastic, thromboclastic

claud- (L., close, shut) See **clud-** for examples.

claus- (L., close, shut) See **clud-** for examples.

claustro- (L., close, shut) See **clud-** for examples.

clavi-, clav- (L., key; a collarbone) Also see **cleido-** for other "key" and "collarbone" words.

> **Qualifying words:** autoclave, clavelization, claviature, clavichord, clavicle, clavicorn, clavicotomy, clavicula, clavicular, clavicularium, claviculectomy, clavier, clavieristic, claviform, claviger, claviol, clavipectoral, clavier, clavis, clef, conclave, enclave, infraclavicular, scapulaclavicular, sternoclavicular, subclavian, subclavicular, supraclavicular

claw, nail See **chela-, onycho-,** and **unguo-** for examples.

clay See **argillo-** for examples. Also examine **chledo-, limi-,** and **pelo-** for words with similar meanings.

-cle (L., small, insignificant) Also see **-cule** and **lepto-** for other "small" words.

> **Qualifying words:** cubicle, cuticle, denticle, muscle, particle

clean, trim See **put-** for examples.

clean, wash See **balneo-, lav-, luto-,** and **purg-** for examples.

cleft, split See **schisto-** and **schizo-** for examples.

cleido-, cleid-, clido-, clid- (Gk., key; a means or thing which locks a door; a key, bar, or hook; a combining form which denotes the **clavicle** or collarbone) Also see **clavi-** for other "key" and "collarbone" words.

> **Qualifying words:** cleidal, cleidarthritis, cleidocostal, cleidocranial, cleidohumeral, cleidohyoid, cleidomancy, cleidomastoid, cleidorrhexis, cleidoscapular, cleidosternal, cleidotomy, cleidotripsy, clidomancy

cleisto-, cleist-, clisto-, clist- (Gk., closed)

> **Qualifying words:** cleistocarp, cleistocarpous, cleistogamic, cleistogamous, cleistogamous, cleistogamy, cleistothecium, thermocleistogamic, thermocleistogamy

clepto-, clept- (Gk., steal, theft) See **klepto-** for examples.

climb, mount See **scan-** and **scend-** for examples.

clino-, clin- (Gk., bed; slope, slant) Also see **loxo-** for other "slant" words.

> **Qualifying words:** acclivity, client, clientel, climacteric, climacterium, climactic, climate, climax, clinic, clinical, clinician, clinograph, clinomania, clinometer, clinotherapy, declension, declination, decline, declivity, enclitic, inclination, incline, isoclinic, microcline, monoclinal, pericline, proclivity, recline, synclinal

-clois (L., close, shut) See **clud-** for examples.

close (close, shut) See **clud-** for examples.

closed See **cleisto-** for examples.

close, shut See **clud-** for examples.

close by See **juxta-** for examples.

clot (blood) See **thrombo-** for examples.

clothe, clothing See **habili-** for examples.

cloud See **nephelo-** for examples.

-clois (L., close, shut) See **clud-** for examples.

-close (L., close, shut) See **clud-** for examples.

close to, near See **juxta-** and **proximo-** for examples.

clot (blood) See **thrombo-** for examples.

claud- (L., close, shut) See **clud-**.

clud-, claud-, claus-, clos-, -clude, -clois, -cluding, -cluded, -clus, -clusion, -clusive (L., close, shut)

> **Qualifying words:** clause, claustral, claustrophilia, claustrophobia, claustrophobic, clavicle, cloister, close, closet, closure, conclude, concluded, concluding, conclusion, conclusive, conclusively, conclusiveness, disclose, disclosure, enclose, enclosure, excludable, exclude, excluded, excluding, exclusion, exclusionary, exclusionist, exclusive, exclusiveness, foreclose, foreclosure, inclose, inclosure, includable, include, included, including, inclusion inclusive, inclusively, inclusiveness, malocclusion, occlude, occluded, occluding, occlusion, occlusive, preclude, precluded, preclusion, preclusive, recluse, reclusion, reclusive, seclude, secluded, secluding, seclusion, seclusive

-clus (L., close, shut) See **clud-** for examples.

cluster of grapes See **botryo-** for examples.

-clysm (Gk., break) See **-clast** for examples.

co- (L., together, with) See **com-** for examples.

coal, charcoal See **anthraco-** for examples.

cocc- (Gk., bacteria; literally, a "berry") Also see **bacilli-** and **bacterio-** for additional "bacteria" examples.

> **Qualifying words:** coccal, cocci, coccidiosis, cocciferous, coccobacillus, coccoid, coccolite, coccosphere, cocculus, coccus, cryptococcosis, diplococci, meningococcus, micrococci, pneumococcal, pneumococcus, pneumococci, streptococci, staphylococci, staphylococcus, streptococcal

coccygo-, coccyg-, coccyge-, coccyo-, coccy- (Gk., from κοκκυ[χ] κοκκυ[γοσ], "cuckoo"; the end of the vertebral column in man and in some apes; the rudiment of a tail. This bone was probably identified with this nomenclature because of its supposed resemblance to a *cuckoo's beak*)

> **Qualifying words:** coccyalgia, coccycephalus, coccydynia, coccygalgia, coccygeal, coccygectomy, coccygodynia, coccygotomy, coccyodynia, coccyx

cochle-, cochl-, cochleo-, cochlio- (Gk, spiral shell, snail with a spiral shell; pertaining to the *cochlea*, the spiral tube in the inner ear)

> **Qualifying words:** cochlea, cochlear, cochleitis, cochleoid, cochleotopic, cochleovestibular, cochlitis,

cock, rooster See **alectryo-** for examples.

coelio-, coelo-, coel-, -coele, coeli-, celeo-, cele-, celi-, celio- (Gk., abdomen [hollow, cavity of the body]) In addition, examine **abdomino-, gastro-,** and **ventri-** for other "stomach" words.

> **Qualifying words:** celiac, celialgia, celiectomy, celiocentesis, celiodynia, celioenterotomy, celiogastrotomy, celiohysterectomy, celioma, celiomyalgia, celiomyomectomy, celiomyomotomy, celiomyositis, celiopathy, celiorrhaphy, celioscope, celioscopy, celiotomy, celitis, celozoic, coelenterata, coelia, coeliac, coelodont, encelialgia, enceliitis, encelitis, entocoel

coeno-, coen-, coino-, coin-, koino-, koin- (Gk., common) Also examine **ceno-** and **commu-** for other "common" words.

> **Qualifying words:** coenaesthesis, coenangium, coenanthium, coenesthesia, coengenesis, coenobium, coenoblast, coenocyte, coenoecium, coenogamy, coenosarc, coenosite, coenosteum, coenotrope, coenozygote, coenurus, koinonia, koinotropy, phytocoenology, zoocoenosis

cog- (L., together) See **com-** for examples.

cogni-, cogn-, cognosc- (L., know, learn) Also see **gno-, epistemo-, intellect-, mne-, not-,** and **sci-** for other "know" words.

> **Qualifying words:** cognition, cognitional, cognitive, cognizable, cognizance, cognizant, cognoscente, cognoscenti, connoisseur, incognita, incognito, incognizance, incognizant, metacognition, metacognitive, precognition, recognition, recognizability, recognizable, recognizance, recognize, recognized, recognizing, recognizance, reconnoiter

coil, spiral See **helico-** for examples.

coino- (Gk., common) See **coeno-** for examples.

col- (Gk. > L., stem, stalk) See **cauli-**.

col- (L., together) See **com-** for examples.

cold See **crymo-, cryo-, crystallo-,** and **frigo-** for examples.

-cole, -coles, -colid, -coline, -colous (L., to inhabit, to live in, on, or among; used in botanical and biological terminology to denote a plant or organism; having or characterized by a habitat as specified by the combining root)

> **Qualifying words:** agaricole, agaricolous, aigicole, aigicolous, algicole, algicoline, algicolous, alsocole, alsocolous, amathicole, amathicolous, ammocole, ammocolous, amnicole, amnicolous, aphidicole, aphidicolous, aquaticole, aquaticolous, arboricole, arboricolous, arenicole, arenicolous, argillicole, argillicolous, bryocole, bryocolous, cadavericole, cadavericolous, calcicole, calcosaxicole, cavernicolous, calcosaxicolous, crenicole, crenicolous, crinicole, crinicolous, dendrocole, dendrocolous, epicole, epicolous, fimbricole, fimbricolous, fimicole, fimicolous, folicaulicole, folicaulicolous, folicole, folicolous, franchicole, franchicolous, fructicole, fructicolous, fungicole, fungicolous, gallicole, gallicolous, geocole, geocolous, graminicole, graminicolous, halicole, halicolous, herbicole, herbicolous, hylacole, hylacolous, lapidicolous, lichenicole, lichenicolous, lignicole, lignicoline, lignicolous, limicole, limicolous, limnicole, limnicolous, lucicole, lucicolous, luticole, luticolous, luticole, luticolous, myrmecocole, myrmecocolous, nervicole, nervicolous, nidicole, nidicolous, nivicole, nivicolous, omnicole, omnicolous, petricole, petricolous, petrocole, petrocolous, phreaticole, phreaticolous, piscicole, piscicolous, planticole, planticolous, potamicole, potamicolous, radicicole, radicicolous, ripicole, ripicolous, rupicole, rupicolous, sanguicole, sanguicolous, sanguicoline, saxicole, saxicoline, saxicolous, sepicolous, silicole, silicolous, silvicole, silvicolous, sylvicole, sylvicolous, telmicole, telmicolous, termiticole, termiticolous, thinicole, thinicolous, tiphicole, tiphicolous, tubicole, tubicolous, umbraticole, umbraticolous, urbicole, urbicolous

collarbone See **clavi-** and **cleido-**.

collectives (the terminology of groups) See GROUP NAMES in **Appendix M** for examples.

colo-, col- (Gk., colon or large intestine [that part which extends from the secum to the rectum])

> **Qualifying words:** colocecostomy, colocentesis, colocutaneous, colodyspepsia, coloenteritis, coloysis, colometrometer, colon, colonalgia, colonic, colonitis, colonopathy, colonorrhagia, colonorrhea, colonoscope, colonoscopy, enterocolitis

colon See **colo-** for examples.

color See **chromato-** for examples.

COLORS

> black: see **melano-** and **niger-** for examples.
>
> blue: see **cyano-** for examples.
>
> green: see **chloro-**, **verdant-**, and **virid-** for examples.
>
> red: see **erythro-**, **rub-**, **rhodo-**, and **roseo-** [pink] for examples.
>
> silver: See **argent-** and **argyro-** for examples.
>
> yellow (gold): see **auri-**, **chryso-**, **ocher,** and **xantho-**.
>
> white: see **albo-**, **albumino-**, and **leuko-** for examples.

colpo-, colp-, kolpo-, kolp- (Gk., womb, fold; vagina) See **episio-**, **hyptero-**, **vagino-**, **vulvo-**, and **utero-** for related "female-reproductive-organ" words.

> **Qualifying words:** colpalgia, colpectasia, colpectomy, colpedema, colpeurysia, colpitis, colpocele, colpoceliotomy, colpocleisis, colpocystic, colpocystitis, colpocystoplasty, colpocystotomy, colpodynia, colpohyperplasia, colpohysterectomy, colpohysteropexy, colpohysterorrhaphy, colpomicroscope, colpomicroscopy, colpomycosis, colpomyomectomy, colpoperineoplasty, colpoperineorrhaphy, colpopexy, colpoplasty, colpopoiesis, colpopolypus, colporectopexy, colporrhagia, colporrhaphy, colporrhea, colposcope, colposcopy, colpospasm, colpostat, colpostenosis, colpostenotomy, colpotherm, colpotomy, colpoureterocystotomy, colpoureterotomy, colpoxerosis, kolpalgia, kolpectasia, kolpectomy, kolpedema, kolpeurysia, kolpitis, kolpocele, kolpoceliotomy, kolpocleisis, kolpocystic, kolpocystitis, kolpocystoplasty, kolpocystotomy, kolpodynia, kolpohyperplasia, etc. (The letter "k" may be used for any of the above words which begin with "c".)

com- (co-, cog-, col-, con-, cor-) (L., together, with) These elements are assimilated to **col-** before *l*; **cor-** before *r* ; **con-** before *c, d, g, j, n, q, s, t, v*; and **co-** before *h, w,* and all *vowels.* Also see **syn-**.

> **Qualifying words:** coagulate, coeducation, coequate, coerce, coeternal, coexist, cogitate, cohabitation, coherence, cohesion, collate, collateral, colleague, collect, colloquial, combat, combatant, combination, combine, combustible, combustion, commemorate, commit, compact, companion, companionable, company, comparison, compassion, compatible, compile, complete, component, comport, compose, conceal, conceive, concentrate, concert, conduct, conductor, constancy, constant, constellation, contract, contraction, correct, correlate, correspond, corrigible

coma[1] (Gk., a deep, sound sleep, lethargy, trance without sleep) Don't confuse this **coma** with the next one which means "hair of the head, foliage." Also examine **dorm-**, **hypno-**, **narco-**, **somni-**, and **sopor-** for other "sleep" words.

> **Qualifying words:** coma, comatose [many medical comas exist]: agrypnodal coma (vigil coma), alcoholic coma, apoplectic coma, deanimate coma, deep coma, diabetic coma, epileptic coma, hepatic coma, coma hepaticum, hypoglycemic coma, hypopituitary coma, hypothermic coma, irreversible coma, trance coma, vigil coma (agrypnodal coma), etc.

coma[2] (Gk. hair of the head, tuft of hairs, hair, foliage) Don't confuse this **coma** with the previous **coma** which means "deep sleep." Also see **hirsute, tricho-,** and **pilo-** for other "hair" words.

> **Qualifying words:** coma, comet

command, order See **manda-** for examples.

come See **vent-** for examples.

common See **ceno-, coeno-,** and **commu-**.

common people See **demo-, pleb-, popu-, publi-,** and **vulg-** for examples.

commotion, confusion See **turb-** for examples.

commu- (L., common, multitude and common people) Also see **coeno-, demo-, ethno-, ochlo-, pleb-, popu-, pub-,** and **vulg-** for additional "common" examples.

> **Qualifying words:** communal, communalism, communalist, communalization, commune, communicable, communicate, communication, communicative, communicator, communion, communique, communism, communist, communistic, community, excommunicate, incommunicable, incommunicado, uncommunicative

compact, thick See **dense** and **pykno-** for examples.

complete, whole See **holo-** for examples.

compress, draw tight See **string-** for examples.

con- (L., together, with) See **com-** for examples.

concealed, unseen See **adelo-** for examples.

concealed, secret Examine **adelo-, calyp-, clandestine, crypto- myster-,** and **occult** for examples.

concho-, conch-, conchi- (L., shell, sea shells)

> **Qualifying words:** concha, conchiferous, conchiform, conchoid, conchologist, conchology

condition, process See **-osis** for examples.

conduct See **ag-** (do, act) for examples.

confidence, trust See **cred-, dox-,** and **fid-** for examples.

confusion, disorder See **turb-** for examples.

conio-, coni-, -coniosis, -conite, konio-, koni-, kono-, kon- (Gk., dust) Also see **ciner-** (ashes) and **tephro-** for other "dust" or "ashes" examples.

> **Qualifying words:** anthraconite, anthraphobia, coniasis, conidia, conidial, conidiophore, conidium, coniofibrosis, coniology, coniolymphstasis, coniophage, coniophile, coniophilous, coniophily, coniophora, coniosis, coniotheca, coniothyrium, coniotoxicosis, dermatoconiosis, konimeter, konimetric, konimetry, koniology, koniometer, koniscope, konometer, otoconium, pneumoconiosis, pneumokoniosis, pneumonoconiosis, pneumonokoniosis

One of the longest words in the English language is **pneumonoultramicroscopicsilicovolcanoconiosis**, which can be divided into the following segments: **pneu/mono/ultra/micro/scopic/silico/ volcano/coni/osis**; and means "miner's lung disease," or "a disease of the lungs caused by the inhalation of very fine silicate or quartz dust and occurring especially in the lungs of miners."

conquer, overcome See **vinc-** for examples.

consciousness, threshold See **limen** for examples.

consider, reckon See **put-** for examples.

consume, eat See **phago-** and **vor-** for examples.

container, receptacle See **theco-** for examples.

contend for a prize See **agon-** for examples.

contest, struggle See **ath-, agon-,** and **-machy** for examples.

contra-, contro-, counter, contre- (L., against, opposed to, opposite, contrary) Also see **anti-** for other "against" examples.

> **Qualifying words:** contraband, contrabandist, contrabass, contrabassist, contrabassoon, contraception, contraceptive, contradict, contradictable, contradiction, contradictory, contradistinction, contradistinctive, contradistinctively, contradistinguish, contraindicate, contraindicated, contraindication, contraindicative, contralto, contraposition, contrariety, contrariness, contrarious, contrariwise, contrary, contrast, contrastable, contrastive, contravene, contravened, contravening, contravention, contrecoup, contredanse, contretemps, control, controversial, contraversialist, contraversially, controversy, controvert, controvertible, controvertibly, counterblow, counteract, counterattack, counterbalance, counterbalanced, counterbalancing, countercharge, countercharged, counterclaim, counterclockwise, counterculture, counterespionage, counterfeit, counterfeiter, counterforce, counterinsurgency, counterin-
> telligence, counteriritant, countermand, countermarch, countermeasure, countermove, countermoving, counteroffensive, counteroffer, counterplot, counterplotted, counterplotting, counterproductive, counterproposal, counterpunch, counterreformation, counterrevolution, counterrevolutionary, counterrevolutionist, counterspy, counterweigh, counterweight, encounter, incontrovertible

contracted, narrow See **steno-** for examples.

contre- (L., against, opposed to) See **contra-**.

contro- (L., against, opposed to) See **contra-** for examples.

copro-, copr-, kopro-, kopr- (Gk., feces, dung, excrement; filth, dirt) For other "dung" words, see **feco-, fimbri-,** and **scato-**.

> **Qualifying words:** autocoprophage, autocoprophagous, autocoprophagy, copracrasia, copremesis, coproantibody, coprobiont, coprobiontic, coprocolous, coproculture, coprogen, coprolabia, coprolagnia, coprolalia, coprolalomania, coprolite, coprolith, coprologic, coprological, coprology, coprophagia, coprophagous, coprophagy, coprophil, coprophile, coprophilia, coprophilous, coprophily, coprophobia, coprophasia, coprophyte, coprophytic, coprostasis, coprostasophobia, coprozoa, coprozoic, coprozoite, hippocoprosterol, ornithocoprophile, ornithocoprophilous, ornithocoprophily

cor- (L., together, with) See **com-** for examples. Don't confuse this **cor-** element with the next **cor-** which means "heart."

cor-, cord-, cour- (L., heart) Also see **cardio-** for other "heart" examples. Don't confuse this **cor-** element with the previous **cor-** which means "together."

> **Qualifying words:** accord, accordance, according, accordingly, concord, concordance, condordant, cordate, cordial, cordiality, cordially, cordialness, cordiform, core, courage, discord, discordance, discordant, discordantly, discourage, discouragement, discouraging, discouragingly, encourage, encouragement, encouraging, encouragingly, obcordate, record, recordable, recorder, recording

cord- (L., heart) See **cor-** for examples.

cord, string See **lin-** and **mito-** for examples.

corn- (L., horn, horny) Also see **cerato-** for other "horn" examples.

> **Qualifying words:** bicorn, Capricorn, capricorn, corn, cornea, corneous, corniculum, cornification, corniform, cornu, cornucopia, cornule, cornulite, cornute, longicorn, tricorn, unicorn

cornea See **cerato-, kerato-** for examples.

corner See **angle** and **gon-** (Gk.) for examples.

corner of the eye See **cantho-** for examples.

corp-, corpor-, corpus- (L., body) Also see **soma-** for other "body" examples.

Qualifying words: corporal, corporality, corporally, corporate, corporation, corporative, corporeal, corporis, corps, corpse, corpulence, corpulency, corpulent, corpus, corpuscle, corpuscula, *corpus delicti, habeas corpus,* incorporate, incorporated, incorporation, incorporeal

correct, right See **ortho-** and **recti-**.

cosmo-, cosm- (Gk., world, universe [to order, arrange, adorn; well-ordered, regular]) Also see **nomo-** and **taxi-** for additional "order, arrange" examples. Compare this element with **agra-, agri-, agro-, geo-, humus, mundan-,** and **terr-**.

Qualifying words: cosmecology, cosmetic, cosmetology, cosmic, cosmism, cosmogenesis, cosmogonic, cosmogonist, cosmogony, cosmographer, cosmographic, cosmographical, cosmography, cosmological, cosmologist, cosmology, cosmonaut, cosmonautic, cosmonautics, cosmopolis, cosmopolitan, cosmorama, cosmos, cosmotheism, cosmotheist, cosmozoism, macrocosm, macrocosmic, microcosm, microcosmic, microcosmically, nucleocosmochronology, pancosmic, pancosmism

costo-, cost-, costi- (L., rib, side)

Qualifying words: accost, chondrocostal, costa(s.), costae(pl.), costal, costalgia, costalis, costatectomy, costectomy, costicartilage, costicervical, costiferous, costiform, costispinal, costocentral, costochondral, costoclavicular, costogenic, costopneumopexy, costotome, costotomy, costovertebral, intercostal, subcostal, supracostal

count, reckon See **put-** for examples.

counter (L., against, opposed to) See **contra-**.

counterfeit, false See **fals-** and **pseudo-**.

cour- (L., heart) See **cor-** for examples.

course, running See **cur(r)-** and **dromo-**.

cover See **calyp-** and **stego-** for examples.

cow See **bou-, bov-,** and **vacc-** for examples.

crab, cancer See **carcino-** for examples.

coxa-, coxo-, cox- (L., hip [anatomy], hipbone, hip joint)

Qualifying words: coxa, coxal, coxalgia, coxankylometer, coxarthritis, coxarthropathy, coxarthrosis, coxitis, coxodynia, coxofemoral, coxotuberculosis, coxotomy

-cracy (Gk., govern, rule) See **-crat**.

craft, art, skill See **art-** and **techno-**.

cranio-, crani-, cran- (Gk., head, skull) Also see **capit-** and **cephalo-**.

Qualifying words: amphicrania, cranial, craniectomy, cranioaural, craniocerebral, craniograph, craniography, craniological, craniologist, craniology, craniomalacia, craniometer, craniometric, craniometry, craniopathy, cranio-

plasty, craniotomy, cranitis, cranium, hemicrania, pericranium

-crat, -cracy, -cratic, -cratism, -cratically, -cracies (Gk., govern, rule; strength, power) Also see **arch-** and **regi-**.

Qualifying words: acreocracy, albocracy, androcracy, androcratic, angelocracy, aristocracy, aristocrat, aristocratic, aristodemocracy, arithmocracy, autocracy, autocrat, autocratic, bureaucracy, bureaucrat, bureaucratic, chirocracy, chromatocracy, chrysoaristocracy, chrysocracy, cosmocracy, democracy, democrat, democratic, demonocracy, diabolocracy, doulocracy, dulocracy, ergatocracy, esquirearchy, ethnocracy, gerontocracy, gerontocrat, gynocracy, gynaeocracy, gynecocracy, gynecratic, gynocracy, hagiocracy, hagiocrat, hetaerocracy, hierocracy, hierocratic, hierocratical, isocracy, kakistocracy, kleptocracy, lairdocracy, logocracy, merocracy, mesocracy, metrocracy, millionocracy, mobocracy, mobocratic, monocracy, monocrat, neocracy, neocrat, nomocracy, ochlocracy, ochlocrat, ochlocracy, oligocracy, oligocratic, pantisocracy, physiocracy, physiocrat, plantocracy, plutocracy, plutocrat, pornocracy, slaveocracy, slavocracy, sociocrat, sosiocracy, stratocracy, stratocrat, technocracy, technocrat, thalassocracy, theatrocracy, theocracy, theocrat, theodemocracy, timocracy, timocrat, tritheocracy

crauno- (Gk., well, spring) See **creno-**.

crea-, creato-, creatin- (Gk., flesh, meat) See **creo-** for examples.

creatin- (Gk., flesh, meat) See **creo-**.

creating, making See **fac-, ger-** [carry; produce], **-parous,** and **-poeia** for examples.

cred-, credit-, creed- (L., believe, belief, faith, confidence, trust) Also see **dox-** and **fid-** for other "believe" examples.

Qualifying words: accredit, accreditation, accredited, credence, credential, credibility, credible, credibleness, credit, creditable, creditor, credo, credulity, credulous, credulously, credulousness, creed, discredit, discreditable, discreditably, incredible, incredibleness, incredibly, incredulity, incredulous, incredulously, miscreant, recreant

creed- (L., believe) See **cred-** for examples.

crema- (L., burn [fire]) Also see **caust-, flagr-, flam-, ign-, incend-, pyro-,** and **volcan-** for other "fire" words.

Qualifying words: cremate, cremation, cremationist, cremator, crematorium, crematory

creno-, cren-, crauno-, crouno- (Gk., well head, spring, fountain, mineral spring) Also see **namato-** and **pego-** for additional "spring, fountain" words.

Qualifying words: craunology, craunotherapy, crenic, crenicole, crenicolous, crenogenic meromixis, crenology, crenophile, crenophilous, crenophily, crenotherapy, crenothrix, crounotherapy, Hippocrene, Hippocrenian, limnocrene

creo-, cre-, creato-, crea-, creatin-, kreo-
(Gk., flesh, meat) Also examine **carn-** and **sarco-** for additional "meat" examples.

Qualifying words: acreophagist, acreophagous, acreophagy, creatinase, creatinemia, creatinuria, creatotoxin, creatoxin, creophage, creodont, creophagism, creophagist, creophagous, creophagy, creosote, creotoxin, creotoxism, kreotoxicon, kreotoxin, kreotoxism

cresc-, -cret, -crease, -cru (L., increase, grow)
Also see **auxano-** for other "grow" words.

Qualifying words: accrue, concreate, create, creation, creative, creator, decrease, increase, increment, procreate, procreation, recreate, recreation

crest, ridge See **lopho-** for examples.

crim-, crimino- (L., judicial decision, verdict, object of reproach, offense) Also see **jud-** and **jus-** for other "judicial" words.

Qualifying words: crime, criminal, criminality, criminate, criminology, discriminate, discrimination, incriminate, incrimination, indiscriminate, recriminate, recrimination

crino-, crin-, crini- (L., hair) Also examine **capillaro-, chaeto-, coma², hirsute, pilo-, pogo-** (beard), and **tricho-**.

Qualifying words: crinal, crinatous, crinet, criniculture, criniparous, crinite, crinoline

cross See **cruci-** for examples.

crowded, thick For examples, examine **densi-, pachy-,** and **pykno-**.

cruci-, crux (L., cross)

Qualifying words: across, crucial, crucially, cruciate, crucible, cruciferous, crucified, crucifier, crucifix, crucifixion, cruciform, crucify, cruciverbalist, cruciverbalophile, cruise, cruiser, crusade, crusader, crux, cruzeiro, excruciate, excruciating, excruciation

crush See **tribo-** and **-tripsy** for examples.

crymo-, crym-, krymo-, krym- (Gk., cold, frost, chill) Also see **cryo-, crystallo-, frigo-,** and **psychro-**.

Qualifying words: crymnion, crymoanesthesia, crymodynia, crymohemic, crymophile, crymophillia, crymophillic, crymophilous, crymophily, crymophylactic, crymophyte, crymotherapeutics, crymotherapy, krymotherapy

cryo-, cry-, kryo-, kry- (Gk., cold, freezing) Also examine **crymo-, crystallo-, frigo-,** and **psychro-** for other "cold" examples.

Qualifying words: cryalgesia, cryalgia, cryanesthesia, cryesthesia, cryobiologist, cryobi-

ology, cryobiosis, cryobirth, cryocardioplegia, cryocauterist, cryocautery, cryochemist, cryochemistry, cryochore, cryoconite, cryoelectronics, cryoextraction, cryoextractor, cryofibrinogen, cryogen, cryogenic, cryogenics, cryogeny, cryoglobulin, cryohemia, cryohemic, cryolite, cryology, cryolysis, cryometer, cryometry, cryonicist(s), cryonics, cryopathy, cryopedologic, cryoplankton, cryophilia, cryophil, cryophile, cryophilic, cryophillia, cryophillic, cryophilous, cryophily, cryophobia, cryophorus, cryophylactic, cryophytes, cryoplankton, cryoprecipitate, cryoprecipitation, cryopreservation, cryoprobe, cryoprotectant, cryroprotection, cryoprotective, cryopumping, cryoscope, cryoscopic, cryoscopy, cryospasm, cryostat, cryosurgery, cryosurgeon, cryotherapy, cryotolerant, cryotron, cryotronics, cryotropic, cryotropism, cryoturbation, hypercryalgesia, hypercryesthesia, hypocryalgesia, hypocryesthesia, kryoscop, urinocryoscopy

crypto-, crypt-, krypto-, krypt- (Gk., secret, hidden, concealed) For other "secret" words, see **calyp-, clandestine, krypto-, leth-, myster-,** and **occult**.

Qualifying words: anticryptic, apocryphal, crypt, crypta, cryptaesthesia, cryptamnesia, cryptanalysis, cryptanalyst, cryptectomy, cryptesthesia, cryptesthetic, cryptic, cryptically, cryptitis, cryptobiosis, cryptocarp, cryptocephalus, cryptoclimate, crypto-communist, cryptofauna, cryptogam, cryptogamian, cryptogamic, cryptogamist, cryptogamous, cryptogamy, cryptogenetic, cryptogenic, cryptogram, cryptogramic, cryptogrammatic, cryptograph, cryptographer, cryptographic, cryptographical, cryptographically, cryptographics, cryptography, cryptoleukemia, cryptolith, cryptologist, cryptology, cryptometer, cryptomitosis, cryptomnesia, cryptomnesic, cryptoneurous, cryptonym, crypton, cryptophyte, cryptoplasmic, cryptopodia, cryptopoite, cryptopsychic, cryptopsychism, cryptorchid, cryptotoxic, cryptxanthin, cryptozoa, cryptozoic, cryptozoite, cryptozoology, data encryption, decrypt, decryption, encrypt, encryption, excrypt, excryption, hemicryptophyte, holocryptic, krypt, kryptography, kryptomnesia, kryptomnesic, krypton

crystallo-, crystall- (Gk., crystal, ice, freeze, congeal, frost; icelike, transparent) Also see **crymo-, cryo-, frigo-,** and **psychro-**.

Qualifying words: crystal, crystalline, crystallogram, crystallographer, crystallography, crystalloic, crystallomancy, crystallophobia, crystalluria

culci-, culici-, culc- L., gnat, mosquito) Also see **anopheli-** for other "mosquito" words.

Qualifying words: Culex, culicicide, Culicidae, culicidal, culicide, culicifuge, Culicinae, culicine, Culicoides, culicosis

-cule, -cula, -culo, -culus, -culum (L., small, tiny) A suffix which forms nouns or adjectives. Also see **-cle, micro-,** and **mini-** for other "small" words.

> Qualifying words: animalcule, auriculocranial, auriculotemporal, auriculoventricular, auriculid, minuscule, molecule, ossicula(pl), particular

cult-, -culture (L., to care for, to till [the ground], to cherish; to dwell, to inhabit)

> Qualifying words: agricultural, agriculture, agriculturist, apiculture, apiculturist, aquaculture, aquiculture, arboriculture, arboriculturist, aviculture, aviculturist, aviculture, aviculturist, bicultural, citriculture, citriculturist, colonial, colonist, colonize, colony, cult, cultic, cultigen, cultism, cultist, cultivable, cultivar, cultivatable, cultivate, cultivated, cultivating, cultivation, cultivator, cultural, culture, cultured, culturist, feticulture, floriculture, floriculturist, hirudiniculture, hirudiniculturist, horticultural, horticulture, horticulturist, mariculture, monocultural, monoculture, pisciculture, pisciculturist, polyculture, polyculturist, pomiculture, puericulture, silviculture, sericulture, sericulturist, stirpiculture, stirpicultural, terriculture, viniculture

cumulo-, cumul- (L., a heap, heap up)

> Qualifying words: accumulate, cumulate, cumulative, cumul, cumuliform, cumulose, cumulous, cumulus

cur(r)-, curs-, -course (L., run, go) Also see **dromo-** for additional "run" examples.

> Qualifying words: concourse, concur, concurrent, corral, corridor, courier, course, currency, current, curricula, curricular, curriculum, cursive, cursor, cursory, discourse, discursive, excursion, incur, incursion, intercourse, occur, occurrence, precursor, precursory, recourse, recur, recurrence, recurrent

cura-, cur- (L., heal, cure [care for, give attention to, to take care of]) Also see **iatro-, medi-, sana-,** and **therap-**.

> Qualifying words: accurate, curable, curative, curate, curator, cure, cured, cureless, curing, curious, inaccurate, incurability, incurable, incurableness, incurably, insecure, insurance, manicure, manicurist, pedicure, pedicurist, procurator, procure, secure, security, sinecure, sure, surety

cure, heal See **cura-, -iatry, medi-, sana-,** and **therap-** for examples.

current, new See **ceno-, neo-,** and **nove-**.

curvature, curved See **scolio-** for examples.

curve, turn See **flect-, gyro-, -plex, stroph-, tors-, trop-, verg-, vers-,** and **volv-** for examples.

custom, habit See **ethi-** and **mor-** for examples.

cut (incision) See **-cise, -ectomy, sec-, -tom,** and **tomo-** for examples.

cuti-, cutan-, cutis (L., skin) For other "skin" words, see **derma-**.

> Qualifying words: cutaneous, cuticle, cuticolor, cuticula, cuticularization, cuticulin, cutin, cutinization, cutireaction, cutis, *cutis vera,* cutisector, endocuticle, enterocutaneous, epicuticle, epicutis, exocuticle, gastrocutaneous, intracutaneous, neurocutaneous, pleurocutaneous, percutaneous, procuticle, subcutaneous, subcuticular, subcutis, transcutaneous

-cy (singular); **-cies** (plural) (L., a state, condition, office of, or act of) A suffix which forms nouns. Also see **-acy** and SUFFIXES in **Appendix K** for other examples of word endings.

> Qualifying words: advocacy, bankruptcy, captaincy, celebacy, democracy, fallacy, residency

cyano-, cyan-, kyano-, kyan- (Gk., blue, dark blue) Also see COLORS for other elements dealing with colors.

> Qualifying words: acrocyanosis, acyanoblepsia, acyanopsia, acyanotic, cyanate, Cyanea, cyanic, cyanid, cyanide, cyanidetoxicity, cyanin, cyanite, Cyanocita, cyanoderma, cyanogen, cyanogenic, cyanogenesis, cyanometer, cyanometry, cyanopathy, cyanophil, cyanophile, cyanophilous, cyanophyll, cyanopsia, cyanosis

cyber- (Gk., steersman, pilot, helmsman; to steer, guide, govern) *Cybernetics,* introduced in 1948 by an American mathematician, Norbert Wiener (1894-1964), refers to the science which studies and compares systems of communication and control, such as those in the brain and those in electronic or mechanical devices.

> Qualifying words: cybernate, cybernated, cybernating, cybernation, cybernetic, cybernetical, cybernetics, cybernetician, cyberneticist, cyberphobe, cyberphobia, cyberphobic, cyborg (cyb[ernetic] + org[anism]), cyberthon, cyberspace

cyclo-, cycl-, -cycle, -cyclic, -cyclical, -cycles (Gk., around, round, circle, circular) See **ambi-, amphi-, circum-, peri-, rotundi-,** and **sphero-** for other "round, around" examples.

> Qualifying words: acyclic, bicycle, cycle, cyclic, cycloid, cyclometer, cyclone, cyclopean, cyclops, cyclorama, cycloramic, cyclotherapy, cyclotomy, cyclotron, encyclical, encyclopedia, epicycle, kilocycle, megacycle, monocyclic, motorcycle, pericycle, recycle, tricycle, unicycle

cyg- (L., swan) Also see **anseri-** for additional "swan" words.

> Qualifying words: cygneous, cygnet, Cygnus, cygnus, dendrocygna

cymo-, cym-, cymo- (Gk., wave; sprout) Also see **kymo-** for other "wave" examples and see **fluct-, liqu-, rheo-, rheum-, undu-,** and **vacilla-** for related words.

    Qualifying words: cymograph, cymometer, cymophobia, cymophone, cymoscope, cymotrichy

cyno-, cyn-, kyno-, kyn- (Gk., dog) Also see **cani-** for other "dog" examples.

    Qualifying words: apocynum, cynanthropy, cynegetics, cynias, cyniatric, cyniatrics, cynic, cynobex, cynocephalic, cynocephalous, cynodont, cynoglossum, cynoid, cynologist, cynology, cynophobia, cynosure, kynophobia, kynurin, misocyny, philocynic, philocynical, philocynism, philocyny

cypri- (L., a prostitute; of or pertaining to Cypress, the reputed birthplace and center of the cult that worshipped Aphrodite [goddess of love in Greek mythology, corresponding to the Roman goddess Venus]; a lewd or licentious woman whose conduct was inspired by Aphrodite) Also see **fornicate** and **porno-** for related words.

    Qualifying words: cyprian (Cyprian), cyprianophobia, cypridology, cypridopathy, cypripareunia, cypriphobia

cysto-, cyst-, cysti-, cystido- (Gk., sac or bladder which contains fluid [or *gas*, as in *pneumatocyst*]; most frequently used in reference to the urinary bladder) Also see **bursa-** for other "sac" examples.

    Qualifying words: cholecystogram, cholecystitis, cystocarcinoma, cystochromoscopy, cystodynia, cystogram, cystography, cystoid, cystolith, cystolithectomy, cystolithic, cystolithotomy, cystoma, cystometer, cystometrogram, cystometrography, cystometry, cystomorphous, cystoneuralgia, cystophorous, cystoplasty, cystoplegia, cystorrhea, cystoscope, cystoscopy, cystospasm, cystotome, cystotomy, enterocyst, hydrocyst, pneumatocyst, urocystitis,

cyto-, cyt-, -cyte (Gk., cell, hollow)

    Qualifying words: chlorocyte, cytobiology, cytobiotaxis, cytochrome, cytocidal, cytocide, cytocinesis, cytodiagnosis, cytogenesis, cytogenetics, cytogenic, cytogenous, cytogeny, cytoid, cytokinesis, cytologic, cytologist, cytology, cytolysin, cytolysis, cytolytic, cytomachia, cytometer, cytometry, cytomorphology, cytomorphosis, cyton, cytonecrosis, cytopathic, cytopathogenesis, cytopathogenetic, cytopathogenic, cytopathology, cytophagocytosis, cytophagous, cytophagy, cytophil, cytophillic, cytophotometer, cytophotometric, cytophotometry, cytophysics, cytophysiology, cytoplasm, cytoscopy, cytose, cytosome, cytostasis, cytostatic, cytostome, cytotactic, cytotaxis, cytotherapy, cytotoxic, cytotoxicity, cytotoxin, cytotropic, cytotropism, cytozoic, erythrocyte, hematocyte, leucocyte, lymphocyte, melanocyte, pericyte, phygocytic

D d

dacryo-, dacry- (Gk., tear(s), tear drop) Also see **lacri-** for other "tear" words.

   Qualifying words: adacrya, dacryadenalgia, dacryadenitis dacryagogatresia, dacryagogic, dacryagogue, dacryoadenalgia, dacryoadenectomy, dacryoadenitis, dacryocyst, dacryocystalgia, dacryocystectomy, dacryocystitis, dacryocystorhinostomy, dacryocystotomy, dacryogenic, dacryohemorrhea, dacryolith, dacryoma, dacryops, dacryorrhea, dacryostenosis, oligodacrya

dactylo-, dactyl-, dactylio-, -dactyl, -dactyla, -dactylia, -dactylic, -dactylism, -dactyloid, -dactylous, -dactyly (Gk., finger, toe) Also see **digit-**.

   Qualifying words: acrocephalosyndactylia, adactylia, dactyl, dactylate, dactyledema, dactylic, dactylioglyph, dactylioglyphic, dactylioglyphy, dactylioglyphist, dactyliograph, dactyliographer, dactyliographic, dactyliography, dactyliologic, dactyliology, dactyliomancy, dactylion, dactyliotheca, dactylithic, dactylitis, dactylocampsodynia, dactylodynia, dactylograde, dactylogram, dactylograph, dactylographer, dactylography, dactyloid, dactylology, dactylolysis, dactylomegaly, dactylonomy dactylophasia, dactyloscopist, dactyloscopy, dactylose, dactylospasm, dactylotheca, dactylozooid, dactylus, didactyl, ectrodactylia, ectrodactylism, ectrodactyly, heterodactylous, hexadactylism, macrodactylia, monodactylic, monodactylous, monodactyly, pentadactylate, pentadactyl, pentadactylic, pentadactylism, pentadactylous, perissodactylate, perissodactylic, perissodactylism, perissodactylous, polydactylism, polydactyly, pterodactyl, sclerodactylia, syndactyl, syndactylism, syndactyly, zygodactyl

daemono- (Gk., an intermediary spirit between gods and men which could be good or evil) "...a *daemon* and a *demon* are not one and the same thing. And it is *daemon*, in its Platonic sense of a being intermediary between gods and men—not *demon* with its Judaeo-Christian import of an unclean, evil, or malignant spirit that we must keep in mind." J.L. Lowes in *Webster's New International Dictionary, Second Edition*, ©1950. For examples, see **demono-**.

-daemonic (Gk., demon, evil deity) Examine **demono-** for samples.

-daimonic (Gk., demon, evil deity) Examine **demono-** for samples.

dance, dancing See **choreo-** and **orches-**.

darkness, night See **nocti-, nycti-, scoto-,** and **skoto-** for examples.

dasy- (Gk., thick with hair or leaves, shaggy, woolly; density) Also see **hirsute, pilo-,** and **tricho-** for other "hair" words.

   Qualifying words: dasymeter, dasyphyllous, Dasypus, dasypygal, dasyure, dasyurine, dasyuroid, *ursine dasyure*

daughter, son See **fili-** for examples.

dawn See **aurora, eo-,** and **ostro-**.

day See **dies** (DEE uhs) and **hemero-**.

DAYS OF THE WEEK See **Appendix B** for a list.

de- (L.) Many words are formed with this prefix; many more than those which are listed next.

[1] from, away from, off

   Qualifying words: debar, decapitate, decease, deceased, decide, decipher, decrease, deface, deflect, deflection, deflector, deform, deformed, deformity, delegate, delete, deletion, delight, delightful, delineate, delude, demise, depreciate, derivation, derive, derogatory, desciduous, describe, description, desirable, desire, detour, deviate, devious

[2] down

   Qualifying words: decadence, decadent, decal, decalcomania, decelerate, decline, decompose, deduce, deduct, deductible, deflate, deflation, degradation, degrade, degrading, degree, degression, deject, dejected, depends, depose, deposit, depreciation, depress, descend, descendant, descent, detest, detestable, devolution, devolve

[3] wholly, entirely, utterly, completely

   Qualifying words: declaim, declamation, declamatory, declaration, declare, decry, dedicate, dedication, deflatrate, denigrate, denominate, denomination, deny, depict, deport, deportation, desiccate, detonate, detonator, devastate, devour

[4] reverse the action of; undo; the negation or reversal of the notion expressed in the primary word

   Qualifying words: deactivate, debilitate, debilitation, debug, declassify, decode, decompress, decongestant, decontrol, decrypt, deemphasize, defloration, defoliant, defrost, defuse, dehumanize, dehumidify, dehydrate, dehydration, dehypnotize, deice, demerit, demilitarize, demobilize, denationalize, denaturalize, deodorant, deodorize, deplane, deplume, depopulate, derail, desalination, desalt, desensitize, detach, detoxification, detoxify, detrain

dead   See **-cide, lethal, mort-, neci-, necro-,** and **thanato-** for examples.

deadly   See **neci-** for examples.

dear, grateful   See **grat-** for examples.

death   See **-cide, lethal, mort-, neci-, necro-,** and **thanato-** for examples.

debris, mud   See **chledo-** for examples.

deca-, dec-, deka-, dek- (Gk., ten)   Also see **decem-** for more "ten" examples. In the metric system, **deca-** is used to show whole units. See NUMBERS in **Appendix G** and METRIC GROUPS in **Appendix F** for other numerical elements and words.

> **Qualifying words:** decachord, decade, decagon, decagonal, decagram, decagramme (British), decahedra, decahedral, decahedron, decahedrous, decaliter, decalitre (British), Decalog, Decalogue, Decameron, decameter, decametre (British), decangular, decanormal, decapeptide, decapod, Decapoda, decapodal, decapodan, decapodous, decarch, decarchy, decastyle, decasyllabic, decasyllable, decathlon

decaying, rotten   Examine **sapro-** and **sepsi-** for examples.

decem-, decim-, deci- (L., ten)   Also see **deca-** for additional "ten" words. In the metric system, **deci-** is used to show 1/10 of a unit. See NUMBERS in **Appendix G** and METRIC GROUPS in **Appendix F** for other numerical elements and words.

> **Qualifying words:** December, decemvir, decemviral, decemvirate, decennaries, decennary, decenniad, decennial, decennially, decennium, decibel, decigramme (British), deciliter, decilitre (British), decillion, decimal, decimalism, decimalist, decimalization, decimalize, decimally, decimate, decimation, decimeter, decimetre (British), decimvir, duodecennial, duodecimal, duodecimo, undecennary, undecennial, quindecennial

deception, untrue   See **fals-** and **pseudo-** for examples.

deci- (L., ten)   See **decem-** for this element and NUMBERS for other numerical examples.

Decibels   See **Appendix C** for a list of decibel levels and the examples which show the causes of the various decibel scales.

decide, judge   See **jud-** for examples.

decrease in, not enough   Examine **-penia** for examples.

deep, depth   Examine **-bathy** and **bentho-** for examples.

defect of a body part   See **ectro-** for examples.

defend, protect   Examine **alexo-, -fend-,** and **phylacto-** for examples.

dei-, div- (L., God, god [deity, divine nature])   Also see **theo-** for additional "God, god" words.

> **Qualifying words:** adieu (Fr.), deicidal, deicide, deific, deification, deified, deiform, deify, deifying, deism, deist, deistic, deistical, deistically, deity, diviner, divination, divine, divinely, divining, divinity

deity (L., God and god)   See **dei-** for examples.

deka- (L., ten)   See **deca-** for examples.

delayed, slow   See **brachy-** and **brady-** for examples.

delicate, fine, thin   See **lepto-** and **nemato-** for examples.

demi- (L., half)   Also see **hemi-** and **semi-** for other examples.

> **Qualifying words:** demigod, demigoddess, demilune, demimonde, demirelief, demirep, demisemiquaver, demitasse, demivolt

demo-, dem-, -demic, -deme, -demically (Gk., people, from *district, country, land, and the people who inhabit those territories*)   Also see **ethno-, ochlo-** (mob), **pleb-, popu-, publi-,** and **vulg-** for other "people" examples.

> **Qualifying words:** demagogue, democracy, democrat, democratic, democratically, democratization, democratize, democratized, democratizing, demogoric, demographer, demographic, demographically, demographics, demography, demomania, demophil, demophile, demophilia, demophobia, demotic, endemic, epidemic, epidemical, epidemiologist, epidemiology, pandemic, polydemic, zoanthrodemic

demon, devil   See **demon-, diabolo-, Lucifer,** and **Satan** for examples.

demono- demon-, -demonic, -demon, -demonical, -demoniac, -demoniacally, daemono-, -daemonic, -daemonical, -daemon, -daemoniac, -daemonia, -daemoniacally, -daimon, -daimonic (Gk., devil, demon [evil spirit])   Also see **diabolo-, Lucifer,** and **Satan** for other "devil-type" examples.

> **Qualifying words:** ademonist, cacodemon, cacodemonia, cacodemoniac, cacodemonic, daemon, Daemonelux, daemonic, daemonurgy, daemony, demon, demoniac, demonian, demonianism, demoniac, demonian, demonianism, demonic, demonize, demonocracy, demonolatry, demonologic, demonological, demonologist, demonology, demonomancy, demonomania, demonopathy, demonophobia, demonurgy, eudemonia, eudemon, pandemonism, pandemonium, polydaemonism, polydaemonistic, polydemonism, polydemonistic

D

dendro-, dendr-, dendri-, -dendria, -dendrite, -dendritic, -dendra, -dendron (Gk., tree, tree-like structure) Also see **also-, arbor-, hylo-, ligni-, nemo-,** and **sylv-** for words with related meanings.

> **Qualifying words:** acrodendrophile, acrodendrophilous, acrodendrophily, adendritic, dendranthropologic, dendranthropological, dendranthropology, dendraxon, dendric, dendriceptor, dendriform, dendrite, dendritic, dendrochronologist, dendrochronology, dendroclimatologist, dendrocole, dendrocolous, dendrodate, dendrogram, dendrograph, dendrography, dendroid, dendrolatrous, dendrolatry, dendrolite, dendrologic, dendrological, dendrologist, dendrology, dendrometer, dendron, dendrophagous, dendrophagus, dendrophagy, dendrophilia, dendrophilous, dendrophily, dendrophobia, epidendrous, epidendric, lepidodendron, neurodendrite, neurodendron, oligodendria, philodendron, rhododendron, telodendria, telodendron, zoodendria, zoodendron

dense, thick See **densi-, pachy-,** and **pykno-.**

densi-, dens- (L., thick, thickly set, crowded) Also see **pachy-** and **pykno-** for additional "thick" words.

> **Qualifying words:** condensable, condensation, condense, dense, densely, denseness, densimeter, density

dento-, dent-, denta-, dentino-, denti-, dentin- (L., tooth, teeth) Also see **odonto-** for other "tooth" examples.

> **Qualifying words:** dandelion (Fr.), dental, dentalgia, dentaphone, dentate, denticle, denticulate, denticulated, dentification, dentiform, dentifrice, dentigerous, dentilabial, dentilingual, dentimeter, dentinalgia, dentine, dentinitis, dentinogenesis, dentinogenic, dentinoid, dentiparous, dentist, dentistry, dentition, dentofacial, dentographydentoid, dentoid, dentoiden, dentolingual, dentomechanical, dentonomy, dentosurgical, dentotropic, denture, Edentata, edentate, edentulous, indent, indentation, indention, indenture, interdental, mastodon, orthodontist, peridontal, soricident, trident

depth, deep See **bathy-** and **bentho-.**

deprive of See **ex-** (L.) for examples.

dermo-, derm-, derma-, dermato-, dermat-, -derma, -dermatic, -dermatous, -dermis, -dermal, -dermic, -dermoid, -dermatoid (Gk., skin) Also see **cuti-** for more "skin" words.

> **Qualifying words:** adermia, adermogenesis, anthropodermic, blastoderm, cynoderma, derma, dermabrasion, dermagen, dermagraph, dermagraphy, dermahemia, dermal, dermalgia, dermametropathism, dermanaplasty, dermaskeleton, dermatalgia, dermata-

neuria, dermatergosis, dermatic, dermatitis, dermatocele, dermatodysplasia, dermatoglyphics, dermatograph, dermatogrphia, dermatographic, dermatographism, dermatography, dermatoheteroplasty, dermatologist, dermatology, dermatolysis, dermatome, dermatomycosis, dermatomyositis, dermatopathia, dermatopathic, dermatopathology, dermatopathy, dermatophyte, dermatoplasty, dermatosclerosis, dermatosis, dermatotherapy, dermatotropic, dermatotrophy, dermatozoon, dermatozoonosis, dermatrophia, dermatrophy, dermiatrics, dermic, dermis, dermitis, dermochrome, dermoglyphics, dermograph, dermagraphia, dermographic, dermographism, dermography, dermohemia, dermoid, dermoidectomy, dermolipoma, dermolysis, dermometer, dermometry, dermomycosis, dermonecrotic, dermoneurosis, dermonosology, dermopathic, dermopathy, dermophobe, dermophyte, dermoplasty, dermoptera, dermoreaction, dermoskeleton, dermotactile, dermotoxin, dermotropic, dermovaccine, dermovirous, dermographia, diadermic, ectoderm, ectodermosis, endoderm, epidermis, leucoderma, mesoderm, mesodermal, pachyderm, pachydermia, scleroderma, somatoderm, taxidermic, taxidermist, taxidermy, transdermal, transdermic, xeroderma, xerodermia, xerodermic

descent, origin See **genus** for examples.

desert See **eremo-** for examples.

detrio-, detri-, detriti- (L., fragmented organic material, worn away)

> **Qualifying words:** detriophage, detriophagous, detriophagy, detritivore, detritivorous, detritivory, detrital, detritus

destroy, strike See **flic-** for examples.

deutero-, deuter-, deut- (Gk., two; second [in a series]) Also see **bi-, di-** and **duo-** for other "two" examples.

> **Qualifying words:** deuteranopia, deuterate, deuteric, deuterize, deuterogamy, deuteromorphic, Deuteronomy, deuteropathic, deuteropathy, deuterotoxin, deutoplasm

device, instrument See **-tron** for examples. A suffix which forms nouns.

devil See **demono-, diabolo-, Lucifer,** and **Satan** for examples.

devour, eat See **phago-** and **vor-** for examples.

dew See **droso-** for examples.

dexter-, dextra-, dextro- (L., right, right hand, to the right; therefore, "skillful, fortunate") Also see **ortho-** and **recti-** for additional "right" examples; and examine **sinistro-** ("left") for words with opposite meanings.

> **Qualifying words:** ambidexterity, ambidextrous, dexter, dexterity, dexterous, dextrad, destral, dextrality, dextraural, dextra-

urality, dextren, dextrocardia, dextrocardiogram, dextrocerebral, dextroclination, dextrocularity, dextroduction, dextrogastria, dextrogyral, dextrogyration, dextromanual, dextropedal, dextrophobia, dextroposition, dextrorotation, dextrorotatory, dextrosinistral, dextrotorsion, dextrotropic, dextrous, dextroversion, dextroverted, sinistrodexterity, sinistrodextral, sinistrodextrous

dextro- (L., right, to the right) See **dexter-**.

di, dies (L., day) See **dies** for examples.

di- (Gk., through) See **dia-** for examples.

di- (L., apart) See **dis-** for examples.

di-, dicho- (Gk., two, twice, divided, double) Also see **bi-** (L.), **deutero-**, and **duo-** for other examples of "two" words. See NUMBERS in **Appendix G** for additional numerical elements.

> **Qualifying words:** diadelphous, diarchy, dibrachia, dicephalous, dicephaly, dicheilia, dicheria, dichogamous, dichogamy, dichogeny, dichotic, dichotomy, dichroism, dichromatic, dichromatism, dichromic, dichromophil, dichromophilism, dicyclic, didactylism, didactylous, digametic, digamous, digamy, digastric, digenetic, diglossia, diglot, diglyph, digram, digraph, dihedral, dihysteria, dilemma, dimeter, dimorphic, dimorphism, dimorphobiotic, dimorphous, dioxide, diphonia, diphthong, diphyllous, diploma, diploid, dipodia, dipolar, Diptera, dipteral, Dipterocarpus, dipterous, dipteryx, dipus, disyllable, ditheism, dittograph, diurnal, divide, dizygotic

dia-, di- (Gk., through, thoroughly, across, entirely, utterly) Also see **per-** and **trans-**.

> **Qualifying words:** adiathermance, adiathermancy, diabetes, diabetic, diabolic, diachronous, diacoustic, diacoustics, diacritic, diacritical, diadem, diadochokinesia, diadochokinesis, diadochokinetic, diagnosis, diagnostic, diagnosticate, diagnostication, diagonal, diagram, diagrammatic, diagraph, diaheliotropism, diakinesis, dialect, dialectic, dialectologist, dialectology, dialog, dialogic, dialogist, dialogue, dialysis, diamagnetic, diamagnetism, diameter, diaphanous, diaphragmatic, diarrhea, diarrhoea, diarthrosis, diathermancy, diathermanous, diathermic, diathermy, diatribe

diabolo-, diabol-, devil (Gk., devil, demon [literally, "to throw across;" then, "to attack, to slander"]) Also see **demono-, Lucifer,** and **Satan** for other "devil" examples.

> **Qualifying words:** adiabolist, devil, deviltry, diabolepsy, diabolical, diabolism, diabolist, diabolize, diabology, diabolology, diabolonian, monodiabolism, monodiabolistic, polydiabolism, polydiabolistic

diaphragm See **phren-** for examples.

dic-, dict- (L., talk, speak, say, tell, declare) Also see **cit-, clam-, fa-, legi-, locu-, logo-, mythico-, ora-, -phasia, -phemia,** and **voc-** for other examples of "talk" words

> **Qualifying words:** abdicate, abdication, addict, addicted, addiction, adjudicate, benediction, contradict, contradiction, contradictory, dedicate, dictate, dictation, dictator, dictatorial, diction, dictionary, dictograph, dictim, dictum, edict, ediction, indicate, indication, indict, interdict, interdiction, jurisdiction, malediction, maledictory, obiter dictum, predicate, predict, prediction, valediction, valedictorian, valedictory, verdict, vindicate, vindication, vindictive

dicho- (Gk., two) See **di-** for examples.

dict- (L., talk, speak) See **dic-** for examples.

diem (L., day) See **dies** (DEE uhs).

dies (DEE uhs), **di** (L., day) Don't confuse this element with "death" or "two." also see **hemero-** for other "day" words.

> **Qualifying words:** adjournment (Fr.), antemeridian [also *antemeridiem*], *carpe diem*, circadian, dial, diary, *dies non*, dismal, diuria, diurnal, diurnation, diurnule, journal (Fr.), meridian, meridional, per diem, postmeridian (P.M.) [also *postmeridiem*], quotidian, semidiurnal, *sine die*, sojourn (Fr.)

dif- (L., apart, asunder) See **dis-** for examples.

different See **allo-, alter-, hetero-,** and **vari-** .

difficult See **dys-** for examples.

dig, dug; fossil See **orycto-** for examples.

digest, digestion See **pepto-** for examples.

digit (L., finger, toe) Also see **dactylo-**.

> **Qualifying words:** digit, digital, digitaliform, digitalis, digitate, digitation, *digiti*(pl.), digitiform, digitigrade, *digiti pedis*, digitorium, *digitus*(s.), *digitus medius*, *digitus minimus*, interdigit, interdigitation, prestidigitate (Fr.), prestidigitation, prestidigitator

dim, dull See **ambly-** and **narco-** for examples.

dino-, din- (Gk., fearful, frightful; terrible, powerful) Also see PHOBIA WORDS in **Appendix I** for examples of other "fear" words.

> **Qualifying words:** Dinocera, Dinornis, dinosaur, Dinosaura, dinothere, Dinotherium

dip, immerse See **bapti-** and **merg-**.

diplo-, dipl- (Gk., double [two-fold]) Also see **di-** for additional examples of "two" and see **-plex** and **-ploid** for other examples of "fold."

> **Qualifying words:** anadiplosis, diplobacillus, diplobacteria, diplobacterium, diploblastic, diplocardia, diplocardiac, diplococcus, di-

plogaster, diplogenesis, diplogram, diploic, diiploid, diploma, diplomyelia, diploneural, diplophonia, diplopia, diplopiaphobia, diplopodia, diploscope, diplosomia

dipping in water See **bapti-** for examples.

dipso-, -dipsia, -dipsy, -dipsias (Gk., thirst [toward "drink"]) Also see **bib-, poto-,** and **-posia** for other examples of "drink."

> **Qualifying words:** adipsa, adipsia, adipsous, adipsy, anadipsia, dipisa, dipsesis, dipsetic, dipsia, dipsogen, dipsogenic, dipsomania, dipsomaniac, dipsomanophobia, dipsopathy, dipsophobia, dipsorexia, dipsosis, dipsotherapy, dysdipsia, dipsotherapy, paradipsia, pollakidipsia, polydipsia

direction, toward See **ad-** for examples.

dirt (sand) For examples, see **amatho-, arena,** and **psammo-** for examples.

dirty, unclean See **myso-** and **rhypo-.**

discharge, flow See **rheum-** for examples.

dis-, di-, dif- (L., apart, asunder) This prefix is used with a great number of words. The meaning of **dis-** varies with different words as shown by the numbered explanations below.

> [1] *separation* (apart, asunder)
>
> [2] *removal* (away, from)
>
> [3] *negation,* deprivation, undoing, reversal (utterly, completely)

> **Qualifying words:** disable, disadvantaged, disagree, disagreeable, disappear, disappoint, disapprove, disarm, disarmament, disassociate, disaster, disastrous, disciple, discipline, disclaim, disconnect, discontent, discord, discourse, disequilibrium, dishonest, disinfect, disinfectant, dissatisfy, dissect, dissemble, disseminate, dissent, dissertation, disservice, dissident, dissimilar, dissimulate, dissipate, dissociate, dissoluble, dissolute, dissolve, dissonance, dissuade, distribute

> **dif-,** assimilated form of **dis-** before *f*: differ, difference, differentiate, difficile, difficult, diffident, difform, difformity, diffuse, diffusion

> **di-,** form of **dis-** before *b, d, g, l, m, n, r, v*: digest digestion, digress, digression, dilate, diligent, dilute, dilution, diluvial, diluvium, diminish, direct, diversion, divorce

discovery by accident See **serendipity.**

disease, disease of See **noso-, -osis, -otic,** and **patho-** for examples.

disorder See **ataxia-** and **ataxo-** in the **taxi-** group for examples.

disorderly, agitated See **turb-** for examples.

disperse, spread See **-chore** for examples.

dissolving, dissolution See **-lysis** and **solv-.**

distance (at a distance) See **tele-.**

diurn (L, day) See **dies** (DEE uhs).

div- (L., god) See **dei-** for examples.

divine, God, god See **dei-** and **theo-.**

diversity, different See **vari-, ali-, allo-, alter-,** and **hetero-** for examples.

divination, prophecy See **Mancy** Words in **Appendix E** for examples. Divination is the act of trying to foretell the future or the unknown by some occult [*secret* or *esoteric*] means. Divination is related to *mania,* ("madness, frenzy").

divine messenger See **angelo-** for examples.

do See **ag-** and **fac-** for examples.

doc-, doct- (L., teach, instruct)

> **Qualifying words:** docile, docility, doctor, doctoral, doctorate, doctorial, doctrinal, doctrinate, doctrine, document, documentary, indoctrinate, indoctrination, indoctrinator

dodeca-, dodec- (Gk., twelve) Also see **duodecim-** and NUMBERS in **Appendix G** for other "twelve" words.

> **Qualifying words:** dodecadactylitis, dodecadactylon, dodecagon, dodecahedral, dodecahedron, dodecaphonic, dodecaphony, dodecarchy, dodecasyllabic, dodecasyllable, dodecatheon, duodecahedral

dog-, dogma- (Gk., believe) See **dox-** for examples. Don't confuse this **dog-** with the next one which refers to a *quadriped fauna.*

dog (animal) See **cani-** and **cyno-** for examples Don't confuse this *dog* with the previous **dog-** which refers to "belief."

dogma- See **dox-** for examples.

doloro-, dolor-, dolori- (L., feel pain, sorrow, grief; mourning) Also see **algesi-** and **odyno-** for other examples of "pain" words.

> **Qualifying words:** condole, condolence, dole, doleful, dolor(s.), dolores(pl.), dolorific dolorifuge, dolorimeter, dolorimetry, dolorogenic, dolorogenous, dolorology, dolorous, indolence, indolent

dolphins See **ceto-** for examples.

dom- (*domus*) (L., house, home ["master, lord" of the house]) Also see **eco-, habit-, nosto-,** and **oiko-.**

> **Qualifying words:** domain, domestic, domesticable, domestically, domesticate, domestication, domesticity, domify, domicile, domiciliary, dominant, domineer, dominion, indomitable, major domo, polydomous, predominance, predominate, zoodomatia

dont- (tooth, teeth) See **odonto-.**

door, gate, entrance See **Janus** and **port-**.

dorm-, dormi- (L., sleep, sleeping) Also examine **coma[1]**, **hypno-**, **narco-**, **somni-**, and **sopor-** for other examples of "sleep."

> Qualifying words: dormancy, dormant, dormifacient, dormition, dormitive, dormitory, dormouse

dorso-, dors-, dorsi-, -dorsal (L., back, on the back, pertaining to the back, near the back)

> Qualifying words: antedorsal, centrodorsal, dorsa, dorsad, dorsal, dorsalgia, dorsalis, dorsiduct, dorsiferous, dorsiflexion, dorsigerous, dorsispinal, dorsoanterior, dorsocephalad, dorsodynia, dorsointercostal, dorsolateral, dorsolumbar, dorsomedian, dorsonasal, dorsoposterior, dorsoscapular, dorsoventral, dorsum, endorse, endorsee, endorsement, endorser, iliodorsal, lumbodorsal, middorsal

dot, mark, pinpoint See **pung-** for examples.

double See **diplo-** for examples.

down   See **cata-** (*direction*) or **ptilo-** (*soft feathers*) for examples.

downward, toward the tail See **caudo-** and **uro-** for examples.

dox-, dog-, dogma- (Gk., believe, belief; opinion; praise; confidence) Also see **cred-**, **fid-**, and **laud-** for additional examples of "believe" or "praise" words.

> Qualifying words: dogma, dogmatic, dogmatism, doxastic, doxographer, doxological, doxology, heterodox, heterodoxy, orthodox, orthodoxy, paradox, paradoxical, paradoxically, pseudodox, unorthodox, unorthodoxy

drag, draw together See **tra-** for examples.

draw, describe See **glyph-**, **gram-**, **grapho-**, and **scrib-** for examples.

draw, lead See **duc-** for examples.

draw tight, compress See **string-**, **strict-**.

draw together See **tra-** for examples.

dream See **hallucina-** and **oneiro-**.

drifting passively See **plankton** for examples.

drinking   See **bib-**, **dipso-** (thirst), **poto-**, and **-posia** for examples.

dripping See **stalac-** for examples.

drive See **ag-** for examples.

drive, push See **pel-** for examples.

drive away, flee See **fug-** for examples.

-drome (Gk., running, course) See **dromo-**.

dromo-, drom-, -drome, -dromic, -dromical, -dromous (Gk., running, course) Also see **cur(r)-**.

> Qualifying words: acrodrome, adromia, aerodrome, aerodromic, anadromous, anadromy, antidromic, catadromous, diadro-

mous, dromedary, dromic, dromograph, dromomania, dromond, dromophobia, dromotropic, dromotropism, heterodromous, hippodrome, hippodromic, homodromous, katadromous, lampadedromy, loxodromic, monodromia, monodromic, orthodromic, oceanodromous, palindrome, potanadromous, prodromal, prodrome, syndrome

drooping, sagging See **-ptosia** for examples.

dropping See **stalac-** for examples.

droso-, dros- (Gk., dew)

> Qualifying words: drosograph, drosometer, Drosophila, drosophila, drosophile, drosophilous, drosophily, drosphilous, drosopterin

drug, medicine See **pharmaco-** for examples.

drum See **tympano-** for examples.

dry See **sicca-** and **xero-** for examples.

duc-, -duce, -duct, -ductor, -duction, -ductive, -ducer, -ducement, -ducation (L., lead, leading, bring, take, draw) Also see **-agogue** for other examples of "leading."

> Qualifying words: abduce, abducent, abduct, abduction, abductor, adduce, aqueduct, archducal, conduce, conducive, conduct, conductance, conduction, conductive, conductivity, conductor, conduit, deduce, deduct, deduction, ducal, ducat, duchen, duchess, duct, ductile, duke, educate, education, educe, educt, eductive, induce, induct, inductance, inducted, inductee, inductible, inducting, induction, inductive, inductivity, inductor, introduce, introduction, introductory, produce, producer, producible, product, production, productive, productivity, reduce, reductant, reduction, reproduce, reproduction, reproductive, seduce, seduction, seductive, subdue, traduce, transducer, transduction, viaduct

ducks (*anserine*) See **anseri-** for examples.

dug, dig, fossil See **orycto-** for examples.

-duct (lead, *the verb form*) See **duc-** for examples.

dulci-, dulc- (L., sweet, pleasant, charming) Also see **gluco-**, **glyco-**, and **sacchar-** for other "sweet" words.

> Qualifying words: dulcet, dulciana, dulcifluous, dulcify, dulcigenic, dulciloquy, dulciloquent, dulcimer, Dulcinea, dulcitude

dull, dullness See **ambly-**, **narco-**, and **torp-** for examples.

dull, foolish See **moro-** for examples.

dulo-, dul- (Gk., slave)

> Qualifying words: dulocracy, dulocratic, dulosis, dulotic, hierodule

dung, excrement See **copro-**, **feco-**, **fimbri-**, and **scato-** for examples.

duo-, du- (L., two) Also see **bi-**, **deutero-**, and **di-** for other "two" words. See NUMBERS in **Appendix G** for additional numerical elements.

Qualifying words: conduplicate, double, doubloon, doubt, dual, dualism, dualist, dualistic, duality, dualize, dualpurpose, duarchy, dubious, duet, deuce, dulogue, duo, duodecennial, duodecimal, duomachy, duopoly, duotone, duple, duplex, duplexity, duplicate, duplication, duplicative, duplicator, duplicities, duplicitous, duplicity, dyarchy, dyotheism, indubitable, reduplicate

duodecim-, duodec- (L., twelve) Also see **dodeca-** for other "twelve" words and NUMBERS in **Appendix G** for additional numerical elements.

Qualifying words: duodecimal, duodecimo

duodeno-, duoden- (L., first part of the small intestine) Also see **entero-** for other examples of "intestine" words.

Qualifying words: duodenal, duodenectomy, duodenitis, duodenogram, duodenohepatic, duodenoscopy, duodenotomy, duodenum, gastroduodenostomy,

duro-, dur-, dura- (L., hard [as wood], lasting) Also see **rigi-** and **sclero-** for other examples of "hard" words.

Qualifying words: dour, *dura mater*, durability, durable, durably, durance, duraplasty, durate, duration, durematoma, duress, during, duroarachnitis, durometer, durosarcoma, endurable, endurance, endure, enduring, indurate, indurated, induration, obduracy, obdurary, obdurate

dust See **ciner-** (ashes), **conio-**, and **tephro-**.

dust (sand) For examples, see **amatho-, arena**, and **psammo-**.

dwarf (very small; "billionth of a unit") See **nano-** for examples.

dwell, have See **habit-** and **ten-** for examples.

dyna-, dyn-, dynamo-, -dyne, -dynamia, or **-dynamic** (Gk., power, strength, force, mightiness) For additional words meaning "power," see **firm-, fort-, poten-, stheno-,** and **valid-**.

Qualifying words: adynamia, adynamic, aerodynamics, aerodyne, dynamic, dynamical, dynamically, dynamics, dynamism, dynamist, dynamite, dynamiter, dynamo, dynamogenesis, dynamogenic, dynamograph, dynamometer, dynamometry, dynamoscope, dynastic, dynasty, dynatherm, dynatron, dyne, electrodynamics, hydrodynamics, hypodynamia, neurodynamia, neutrodyne, photodynamic, thermodynamics, toxicodynamics

-dyne (pain) See **odyno-** for examples.

-dynia (pain) See **odyno-** for examples.

dys- (Gk., bad, harsh, wrong; ill; hard to, difficult at; slow of) Also see **caco-, mal-,** and **mis-** for additional examples of "bad" words. For words with opposite meanings, see **eu-**.

Qualifying words: dysacousia, dysacousis, dysacusia, dysanagnosia, dysantigraphia, dysaudia, dyscephaly, dyschiria, dyschromia, dyschronism, dyscinesia, dysdipsia, dysentery, dysenteric, dysequilibrium, dysesthesia, dysesthetic, dysfunction, dysfunctional, dysgalactia, dysgenic, dysgenics, dysgenopathy, dysgeusia, dysglandular, dysgnosia, dysgraphia, dyskinesia, dyskinetic, dyslexia, dyslexic, dyslogia, dyslogistic, dysmnesia, dysmnesic, dysmorphia, dysmorphism, dysmorphology, dysmorphobia, dysmorphosis, dysodontiasis, dysorexia, dysosmia, dysostosic, dyspathy, dyspepsia, dyspeptic, dysphagia, dysphagic, dysphagy, dysphasia, dysphasic, dysphemia, dysphemism, dysphonia, dysphoria, dysphoric, dyspnea, dyspneic, dyspnoea, dysrhythmia, dyssomnia, dyssomic, dyssymmetry, dystaxia, dysteleology, dystemper, dystonia, dystopia, dystopian, dystrophia, dystrophic, dystrophy, dysuria, dysuric, dysvitaminosis

E e

e- (L., out of, from) See **ex-** for examples.

ear See **auri-** and **oto-** for examples.

ear, inner See **cochle-** for examples.

eardrum membrane Examine **myringo-** and **tympano-** for samples.

earnest, ardent See **ferv-** for examples.

earth See **agra-, chthon-, geo-, humus, limi-, mundan-, pelo-,** and **terr-** for examples.

earthquake See **seismo-** for examples.

east See **eo-** and **ostro-** for examples.

eat away, gnaw See **rod-** for examples.

eat, consume See **phago-** and **vor-.**

ec- (Gk., out of, away from) See **ex-** (Gk.).

ecclesi-, ecclesiastico- (Gk., called out; church)

    Qualifying words: ecclesia, ecclesial, ecclesiarch, ecclesiast, Ecclesiastes, ecclesiastic, ecclesiastical, ecclesiastically, ecclesiasticism, ecclesiasticize, ecclesiography, ecclesiolatry, ecclesiologically, ecclesiologist, ecclesiology

echidno-, echidn- (Gk., viper)

    Qualifying words: echidnase, echidnin, Echidnophaga, echidnotoxin, echidnovaccine

echino-, echin- (Gk., spiny, prickly) Also see **acantho-** and **chaeto-.**

    Qualifying words: echinate, echinidium, echinite, echinochrome, echinocyte, echinoderm, Echinodermata, Echinoderms, Echinodorus, echinoid, echinosis, echinus

echo-, ech- (Gk., sound, noise) For additional "sound" words, see **phono-, son-,** and **ton-.**

    Qualifying words: anecho, anechoic, catechism, catechist, catechize, catechumen, echeosis, echo, echoacousia, echoacusis, echocardiogram, echocardiograph, echocardiography, echoencephalography, echogenic, echogram, echograph, echographer, echographia, echography, echoism, echokinesia, echokinesis, echolalia, echolocation, echomimia, echomotism, echopathy, echophonia, echophony, echophotony, echophrasia, echopraxia, echoscope

eco- (*oeco-*) (Gk., house, household affairs [environment, habitat]) Also examine **dom-, habit-, nosto-,** and **oiko-.**

    Qualifying words: antecology, anthoecology, autecology, bioecologist, bioecology, ecobiotic, ecobiology, ecocidal, ecocide, ecogeographic, ecogeographical, ecography, ecogeography, ecoid, ecological, ecologist, ecology, ecomania, econometrics, economic, economics, economist, economy, ecoparasite, ecophobia, ecophysiology, ecopoiesis, ecosite, ecospecies, ecosphere, ecospheric, ecostatism, ecosystem(s), ecotage [environmental sabotage], ecotaxis, ecotone, ecotoxicology, ecotoxicologist, ecotype, ecotypic, ecumenic, ecumenical, genecology, macroecology, microecology, myrmecology, paleoecology, synecology

ecto-, ect- (Gk., out, outside of, out of, external, beyond) Also see **ex-** (Gk.) and **exo-** for other "out, outside" words.

    Qualifying words: ectobiology, ectoblast, ectocardia, ectocytic, ectoderm, ectodermal, ectodermatosis, ectodermic, ectodermoidal, ectoenzyme, ectogenic, ectogenous, ectoglobular, ectogony, ectohormone, ectomorph, ectomorphic, ectomorphy, ectoophage, ectoophagous, ectoophagy, ectoparasite, ectophage, ectophagous, ectophagy, ectophyte, ectophytic, ectoplasm, ectoplasmatic, ectoplastic, ectosarc, ectoscopy, ectoskeleton, ectosphere, ectosuggestion, ectosymbiont, ectotherm, ectothermal, ectothermic, ectotoxemia, ectotoxin, ectotrophic, ectotropism, ectozoa, ectozoon

-ectomy, -ectome, -ectomize (Gk., cut, surgical removal of) Also see **-cise, sec-, -tom,** and **tomo-.**

    Qualifying words: adrenalectomy, apicoectomy, appendectomy, arthrectomy, bursectomy, cardiectomy, celiectomy, celiomyomectomy, costectomy, craniectomy, cryptectomy, cystectomy, gastrectomy, glossectomy, hysterectomy, laryngectomy, lumpectomy mammectomy, mastectomy, mastoidectomy, neurectomy, oophorectomy, ostectomy, osteoectomy, ovariectomy, pneumectomy, pneumonectomy, thoracectomy, thyroidectomy, tonsillectomy, uvulectomy

ectro- (Gk., abortion, untimely birth; primarily used to mean "congenital absence" or "defect" of a part which is normally present) Also see **abort-.**

    Qualifying words: ectrocardia, ectrocheiry, ectrochiry, ectrodactylia, ectrodactylism, ectrodactyly, ectrogenic, ectrogeny, ectromelia, ectromelic, ectromelus, ectrometacarpia, ectrometatarsia, ectrophalangia, ectropody, ectrosis, ectrosyndactylia, ectrosyndactly, ectrotic

-ee (L., a person who; a thing which) Also see **-eer, -ist,** and SUFFIXES in **Appendix K** for other elements.

    Qualifying words: appointee, devotee, divorcee, draftee, employee, nominee, payee, refugee, transferee, trainee, vendee

-eer (L., a person who) Also see **-ee, -ist,** and SUFFIXES in **Appendix K** for more examples.

    Qualifying words: auctioneer, profiteer

egg See **oo-, oophoro-, ova-, ovi-,** and **ovum.**

ego (L., I) Don't confuse this **ego** with another one which means "goat." Also see **auto-** (self) and **sui-** (self) for words which are similar in meaning.

    Qualifying words: alterego, alteregoism, ego, egoaltruistic, egocentric, egocentricity, egodystonic, egoism, egoist, egomania, egomaniac, egophonic, egophony, egotheism, egotism, egotist, egotistic, egotistical, egotropic, superego

ego- (Gk., goat) See **aego-** for information. Don't confuse this **ego-** with the previous one which means "I."

eido-, eid-; ido-, id- (Gk., image, figure, form, shape) Also see **form-, icono-, idol, morpho-,** and **-oid** for other "form" words.

    Qualifying words: eiconometer, eidetic, eidogen, eidograph, eidoptometry, eidonometer, eidoid, idyl, idyll, kaleidophone, kaleidoscope

eight See **octo-** for information.

eisoptro- (Gk., mirror) Also see **catoptro-** for other "mirror" words.

    Qualifying words: eisoptrophobia, eisoptrophobic

elbow See **ancon-** and **ulno-** for examples.

electro-, electr-, electri- (L., electric, electricity [amber, resembling amber], generated from amber which when rubbed vigorously [as by friction], produced the effect of static electricity, as described by Dr. William Gilbert [1540-1603] in a treatise on the magnet in 1600) The word "electricity" was first used by the English physician Sir Thomas Browne (1605-1682) in 1646. The word "electrode" was coined by the English physicist and chemist Michael Faraday (1791-1867). The words "electrolysis" and "electrolyte" were introduced by Faraday at the suggestion of the Reverend William Whewell. *Cf.* **cyber-** for electronics.

    Qualifying words: dielectric, electric, electrical, electricity, electrify, electroacupuncture, electroanalgesia, electroanalysis, electroanesthesia, electroappendectomy, electrobasograph, electrobiology, electrobioscopy, electrocardiogram, electrocardiograph, electrocardiography, electrocardiophonograph, electrocardioscopy, electrocatalysis, electrocautery, electrochemistry, electrochromatography, electrocision, electrocoagulation, electrocochleography, electrocute, electrocution, electrode, electrodeposit, electrodermal, electrodermatome, electrodiagnosis, electrodiagnostics, electrodynamic(s), electroencephalogram, electroencephalograph, electroencephalography, electroexcision, electrogastroenterostomy, electrogastrogram, electrogastrograph, electrogastrography, electrogenesis, electrogoniometer, electrogram, electrograph, electrography, electrogustometry, electrohemostasis, electrohysterogram, electrohysterography, electroimmunodiffusion, electrojet, electrokinetic, electrolepsy, electrolithotrity, electroluminescence, electrolysis, electrolyte, electrolytic, electrolyze, electromagnet, electromagnetic, electromanometer, electrometer, electrometrogram, electromigratory, electromotion, electromotive, electromyogram, electromyograph, electromyography, electron, electronarcosis, electronegative, electroneurography, electroneurolysis, electroneuromyography, electronic, electro-olfactogram, electro-osmosis, electroparacentesis, electropathology, electrophile, electrophilic, electrophorus, electrophotometer, electrophysiologic, electrophysiology, electroplax, electroplexy, electropositive, electroradiometer, electroretinography, electrosalivogram, electroscission, electroscope, electrosection, electrosome, electrostatic, electrostethograph, electrosurgery, electrotaxis, electrothanasia, electrotherapeutics, electrotherapeutist, electrotherapist, electrotherapy, electrotherm, electrotome, electrotomy, electrotonic, electrotropism, electroureterography, electrovagogram, electrovalence, electrovalent, electroversion, electrovert, electrum

eleo-, elaeo-, elaio- (Gk., oil, olive oil) Also see **adipo-, lipo-, oleo-,** and **steato-** for other "oil" or "fat" words.

    Qualifying words: elaeoplast, elaiopathy, eleometer, eleotherapy, eleothorax

eleuthero-, eleuther- (Gk., free) Also examine **liber-** for other "free" words.

    Qualifying words: eleutherarch, Eleutherian, eleutherism, eleutherodactyl, Eleutherodactylous, eleutheromania, eleutheropetalous, eleutherophilia, eleutherophobia, eleutherophyllous, meleutherosepalous

eleven See **hendeca-** as well as NUMBERS in **Appendix G** for information.

eluro- (Gk., cat) See **aeluro-** for examples.

embolo-, embol-, emboli- (Gk. > L., that which is thrust into something; wedge, stopper; interpolation, obstruction; from "throw in" or "throw into")

    Qualifying words: emboliform, embolism, emboli, embololalia, embolomycotic, embolophrasia

emesi-, emeti-, emeto-, emet-, -emea, -emetic, -emesis (Gk., vomit)

    Qualifying words: antiemesia, antiemetics, autemesia, dysemesia, emesia, emesis, emetatrophia, emetic, emeticology, emetomania, emetomorphine, emetophobia, emetotherapy, hematemesis, hyperemesis, matutemia, tyremesis

-emia, -aemia (Gk., blood, usually a diseased condition of the blood) Also see **hemo-** and **sangui-** for additional "blood" words.

Qualifying words: anoxemia, chloremia, erytheremia, hydemia, hyperaemia, hyperemia, hyperlipoproteinemia, leukemia, melanaemia, melanemia, pachyaemia, pachyemia, sapraemia, sapremia, septicemia, uraemia, uremia, xanthemia

empori- (Gk. > L. traveler, trader, merchant; a trading place, market; pertaining to trade or traveling) Also see **itiner-**.

Qualifying words: emporia(pl.), emporiatric, emporiatrics, emporiatrician, emporium(s.)

empty See **vacu-** for information.

en-, em- (Gk., in; within) Also see **endo-, ento-, en-, in-, intra-,** and **intro-**.

Qualifying words: encephalitis, embolism, embryo, empathy, emphasis, emphysema, emporium, encircle, encyclical, encyclopedia, enemy, energy, engrave, enthusiasm, enzootic, enzyme

-ence, -ency (L., state, quality, or condition of) A suffix which forms nouns. Also see **-ance** for other examples with similar meanings and SUFFIXES in **Appendix K** for other word endings.

Qualifying words: acquiescence, confidence, fluency, influence, insolence, iridescence, transience

encephalo-, encephal- (Gk., brain) Also see **cerebello-, cerebro-,** and **phreno-** for additional examples of "brain" words. Compare with **noo-** and **psycho-**.

Qualifying words: electroencephalogram, encephalalgia, encephalitis, encephalatrophy, encephalogram, encephalography, encephaloid, encephalology, encephalomalacia, encephalomyelitis, encephalomyocarditis, encephalon, encephalopathy

end, last Examine **fin-, omega, teleo-, term,** and **ultim-** for information.

end, outermost See **acro-** for examples.

ending, last of anything See **omega**.

endo-, end- (Gk., within, inside, into, in, on, inner) Also see **en-, em-; ento-; eso-; in-; intra-;** and **intro-**.

Qualifying words: endaortic, endo-abdominal, endobiotic, endocardial, endocarditis, endocranial, endocystic, endocyst, endocyte, endoderm, endodermal, endodontia, endodontitist, endodontitis, endodontics, en-

doepidermal, endogamy, endogastric, endogastrectomy, endogastritis, endogenous, endoparasite, endophasia, endophyte, endophytic, endopodite, endorhinitis, endoscope, endoscopic, endoscopy, endoskeletal, endoskeleton, endosoma, endosome, endosymbiont, endosymbiosis, endothermal, endothermia, endothermic, endothermy, endoscope, endotoxemia, endotoxic, endotoxin, endotoxoid, endovaccination, endovasculitis, endovenous

engrave, carve See **glypto-** for information.

ennea-, enne- (Gk., nine) Also see **nona-** and **novem-** for other "nine" words, as well as NUMBERS in **Appendix G** for additional numerical elements.

Qualifying words: enneacotahedron, ennead, enneagon, enneagynous, enneahedron, enneander, enneapennate, ennearchy, enneatic

-enni, -ennial, -ennium (L., year or years) Also see **ann-** for other examples.

Qualifying words: bicentennial, biennial, biennium, centennial, centennium, decennial, decennary, decennium, duodecennial, millenial, millennial, millennium, novennial, octennial, perennial, quadrennial, quadrennium, quadricentennial, quincentennial, quindecennial, quinquenniad, quinquennial, quinquennium, semicentennial, septennary, septennate, septennial, septennium, sesquicentennial, sexennial, sexennium, tercentennial, tricennial, tricentennial, triennial, triennium, undecennial, vicennial

-ennial (L., year) See **enni-** for examples.

-ennium (L., year) See **enni-** for examples.

eno- (Gk., wine) See **oeno-** for information.

enough See **satis-** for information.

entero-, enter- (Gk., intestines, gut) Also see **duodeno-**.

Qualifying words: dysentery, enteralgia, enterectomy, enteric, enteritis, enteroantigen, enterobacteriotherapy, enterocinesia, enterocinetic, enterocutaneous, enterodynia, enterogastric, enterogastritis, enterogenous, enterogram, enterograph, enterography, enterohepatitis, enterokinesia, enterokinetic, enterology, enterolysis, enteromycosis, enteroneuritis, enteronitis, enteropathy, enteroplasty, enteroptosis, enterorrhagia, enterorrhea, enterotomy, enterotoxemia, enterotoxin, enterotropic, enterozoic, enterozoon, gastroenteritis

entire, whol See **holo-** for information.

ento-, ent- (Gk., within, inside, inner) Also see **en-, endo-, eso-, in-, intra-,** and **intro-**.

Qualifying words: entoblast, entocranial, entocyte, entoderm, entodermal, entodermic, entogastric, entophyte, entoplasm, entoplastic, entoptic, entoptoscopy, entorganism, entosarc, entozoa, entozoon

entomo- (Gk., insect, bug; literally, "cut up, cut in pieces;" an insect because it appears to be segmented) Also see **insecti-** for other "bug" words.

Qualifying words: dientomophilous, dientomophily, entomogenous, entomological, entomologist, entomology, entomophagous, entomophilous, entomophily, entomophobia, entomophyte, entomological, entomophagous, entomophilous, entomophily, entomotomy

entrance, door See **Janus** and **port-**.
entrance hall, chamber See **atrio-**.
entrance, opening See **ora-** for examples.
environment, house See **eco-** for information.

eo-, eoso- (Gk., dawn [east], daybreak; early) Also see **aurora** and **ostro-** for additional examples of "dawn" or "east" words.

Qualifying words: eoan, Eoanthropus, Eocene, Eocine, Eogaea, Eogene, Eohippus, eohippus, eolith, eolithic, Eos, eos, eophobia, eophyte, eosophobia, Eozoic, eozoon

-eous (L., composed of, of the nature of) A suffix which forms adjectives. Also see SUFFIXES in **Appendix K**.

Qualifying words: aqueous, gaseous, vitreous

epi-, ep- (Gk., above, over, on, upon; besides; in addition to; toward; among Also see **hyper-, super-, supra-, sur-,** and **ultra-** for additional examples of "above, over" words.

Qualifying words: ephemeral, ephemerid, ephemeris, ephemeron, Ephemeroptera, epibenthos, epibenthic, epibiont, epibiosis, epibiotic, epiblast, epicalyx, epicanthus, epicardium, epicarp, epicenter, epicentral, epicotyl, epicranial, epicranium, epicritic, epicutis, epicycle, epicycloid, epidemic, epidemical, epidermatoplasty, epidemiography, epidemiologist, epidemiology, epidendric, epidermal, epidermis, epidermitis, epidermodysplasia, epidermoid, epidermolysis, epidermomycosis, epifauna, epifilter, epifocal, epigastralgia, epigastric, epigastrium, epigeal, epigean, epigenesis, epigenetic, epigenous, epigeotropic, epigeotropism, epiglottis, epigram, epigrammatic, epigraph, epigrapher, epigraphic, epigraphist, epigraphy, epilepsy, epileptic, epileptoid, epilithic, epilithophyte, epilithophytic, epilog, epilogue, epiphyll, epiphyte, epiphytology, epiphytotic, episode, episodic, epistemology, epitaph, epithet, epithetic, epithetical, epitome, epitomize, epixylous, epizoic, epizoicide, epizoology, epizoon, epizoonosis, epizootic, epizootiology, eponym, eponymic, eponyous, eponymy, epornithic, epornithology

episio-, episi- (Gk., denotes the *vulva* or region of the pubes) Also see **colpo-, hystero-,** **vagino-, vulvo-,** and **utero-** for related "female-reproductive-organ" words.

Qualifying words: episioclisia, episioelytrorrhaphy, episiohematoma, episioitis, episioperineoplasty, episioperineorrhaphy, episioplasty, episiorrhagia, episiorrhaphy, episiotenosis, episiotomy

epistemo-, epistem- (Gk., knowledge, understand, believe) Also examine **cogni-, gno-, intellect-, mne-, not-,** and **sci-** for additional examples of "knowledge."

Qualifying words: epistemic, epistemolater, epistemolatry, epistemology, epistemophilia

ept- (L., fit, suited) See **apt-** for examples.

equ-, equi- (L., same, equal, similar, even) Also see **homo-** (Gk.), **iso-, -oid, pari-, peer-, simal-,** and **tauto-** for additional examples of "same, similar" words. Don't confuse this **equ-** with the one which means "horse."

Qualifying words: adequacy, adequate, coequal, coequate, equable, Ecuador, equal, equalitarian, equality, equalize, equalizer, equanimity, equate, equation, equator, equatorial, equiangular, equidistant, equilateral, equilibrium, equinimity, equinoctial, equinox, equipotential, equipotentiality, equitable, equity, equivalence, equivalent, equivocal, equivocate, equivocation, equivocator, equivogue, inequality, inequity, iniquity

equ-, eque-, equi- (L., horse) Also see **hippo-** for additional "horse" words. Don't confuse this **equ-** with the previous one meaning "same, equal."

Qualifying words: equerry, eques, equestrian, equestrianism, equestrienne, Equidae, equid, equine, Equisetophyta, equitation, equiod, Equus

equal See **equ-, homo-** (Gk.), **homeo-, iso-, -oid, pari-, peer-, simal-,** and **tauto-**.

eremo-, erem-, eremi- (Gk., lonely, solitary; hermit; desert) Also compare with **soli-** (one) for similarities.

Qualifying words: eremiophobia, eremitic, eremite, eremitic, eremitical, eremitish, eremitism, eremobionic, eremobryoid, eremologist, eremology, eremophile, eremophilous, eremophily, eremophobe, eremophobia, eremophyte, eremophytic

ereuth- (Gk., red) See **erythro-** for words.

ergasio- (Gk., work) See **ergo-** for examples.

ergo-, erg-, ergasio-, ergasi-, ergas-, ergat- (Gk., work) Also see **labor-, oper-, pono-,** and **urg-** for other "work" words.

Qualifying words: allergies, allergy, energetic, energy, erg, ergasia, ergasiaphyte, ergasiapophyte, ergasiatrics, ergasiatry, ergasidermatosis, ergasiology, ergasiomania, ergasiomaniac, ergasiophobia, ergasiophobic, ergasthenia, ergastic, ergatandromorph, ergatandromorphic, ergatandrous, ergate, ergatogynomorph, ergatogynomorphic, ergatogynomorphous, ergatogyne, ergatogynous, ergatoid, ergatomorphic, ergocardiogram, ergocardiography, ergocheiron, ergodermatosis, ergodic, ergodynamograph, ergodynamorph, ergoesthesiograph, ergogenic, ergogram, ergograph, ergographic, ergology, ergomania, ergomaniac, ergometer, ergonometrics, ergonomic, ergonomically, ergonomics, ergonomist, ergonomy, ergophile, ergophillia, ergophobia, ergostat, ergotherapy, ergotocracy, ergotropy, George, kilerg, stigmergy, synergetic, synergism, synergistic, synergagogy, synergogy, telergy

eros (love) See **eroto-** for information.

eroto-, erot-, ero-, eros (Gk., love [more of a sexual love]) Also see **amat-, aphrodi-, philo-,** and **vener-** for additional examples of "love" words.

   Qualifying words: autoerotism, erogenous, Eros, erotic, erotica, eroticism, eroticize, eroticomania, erotism, erotize, erotogenesis, erotogenic, erotographomania, erotology, erotomania, erotomaniac, erotopath, erotopathy, erotophobia, erotosexual

err-, errat- (L., wander, stray, rove) Also see **migr-, nomad-,** and **vaga-** for additional examples of "wander" words.

   Qualifying words: aberrant, aberration, arrant, err, errant, errantic, erratum, erroneous, error, inerrant, unerring

eruci-, eruc- (L., caterpillar)

   Qualifying words: erucivore, erucivorous, erucivory, eruciform, eruciphile, eruciphilous, eruciphily

erythro-, erythr- (Gk., red) Also see **rube-, rhodo-,** and **roseo-.**

   Qualifying words: erythralgia, erythrin, erythrism, erythrocyte, erythroderma, erythrodermatitis, erythremia, erythrogenic, erythron, erythropathy, erythrophages, erythrophilous, erythrophobia, erythrophyll, erythropia, zooerythrin

-esce, -escent, -escence (L., beginning to be, becoming) A suffix which forms nouns and adjectives. See the SUFFIXES in the **Appendix K** section for other word endings.

   Qualifying words: adolescence, adolescent, calescent, coalescent, convalescence, convalescent, crescent, effervescence, effervescent, efflorescence, florescence, florescent, fluorescence, fluorescent, frondescence, fructescence, incandescence, juvenescence, juvenescent, nascence, nascent, incandescent, luminescence, luminescent, obsolescence, obsolescent, pearlescence, pearlescent, pubescence, pubescent, rejuvenescence, rejuvenescent, revirescence, revirescent, senescence, senescent

eso- (Gk., inward, within) Also see **en-, endo-, ento-, intra-,** and **intro-.**

   Qualifying words: esocataphoria, esodeviation, esoethmoiditis, esogastritis, esophagostenosis, esophagotome, esophoria, esotoxin, esotropia, esotropic

esophago-, esophag- (Gk., gullet, throat [passage from the mouth to the stomach]) Also see **cervico-, gutturo-, laryngo-, thoraco-, trachelo-,** and **pharyngo-** for additional "throat" words.

   Qualifying words: esophagalia, esophageal, esophagectomy, esophagism, esophagitis, esophagocardiomyotomy, esophagocele, esophagocologastrostomy, esophagocoloplasty, esophagoduodenostomy, esophagodynia, esophagogastric, esophagogastroplasty, esophagogastroscopy, esophagogastrostomy, esophagogram, esophagography, esophagology, esophagomalacia, esophagometer, esophagostoma, esophagostomy, esophagotrachea, esophagus, presbyesophagus

esth-, aesth- (Gk., feeling, sensation, perception) See **aesth-** for examples.

-et (French) (small) Also examine **-cle, -cule, -lepto-, micro-, mini-, nano-, oligo-, pauci-, pico-,** and **-ule** for other "small, little" words.

   Qualifying words: booklet, eaglet, floweret, giblet, leaflet, owlet, piglet, ringlet, starlet

ethero-, ether-, aethero-, aether- (Gk. > L., burn, shine, to kindle; light up; the heavens) Also see additional "burn" and "fire" words such as, **ars-, caust-; crema-; flagr-; flam-; ign-; incend-; pyro-;** and **volcan-.** See **celest-** and **urano-** for other "heaven" words.

   Qualifying words: ether, etherated, etherized, ethereal, etherial, ethereality, etheriality, etherealization, etherialization, etherealize, ethereally, etherially, etherealness, etherean, etherian, ethereous, etherious, etheric, etherical, etherification, etheriform, etherify, etherism, etherization, etherize, etheromania, etheromaniac, etherous, ethyl

ethi-, eth-, etho- (Gk., custom, habit, character, manners) Also see **mor-** (*mora-*) for additional examples of "custom" or "manner" words.

   Qualifying words: cacoethes, ethic, ethical, ethicize, ethics, ethnic, ethnocentricity, ethogram, ethograph, ethnography, ethology, ethos, polyethism

ethno-, ethn- (Gk., people, race, nation) Also see **demo-, genus, pleb-, popu-, publi-,** and **vulg-** for other examples of elements which refer to "people."

Qualifying words: ethnarchy, ethnic, ethnicity, ethnobiology, ethnobotanic, ethnobotanical, ethnobotanist, ethnobotany, ethnocentric, ethnocentricity, ethnocentrism, ethnodicy, ethnogenic, ethnogenist, ethnogeny, ethnographer, ethnographic, ethnographical, ethnography, ethnohistorian, ethnohistory, ethnolinguistic, ethnologic, ethnological, ethnologist, ethnology, ethnomusicologist, ethnomusicology, ethnopsychology, ethnozoology, polyethnic

etho- (Gk., custom, habit) See **ethi-** for examples.

etio-, aetio- (Brit.) [aetio-, atio-] (Gk., cause, causation, originating, that which causes or originates something)

Qualifying words: aetiological, etiogenic, etiolated, etiolation, etiologic, etiological, etiologist, etiology (aetiology), etiopathic, etiopathology, etiopathy, etiotropic

-ette (French, small) Also see "small" for other elements which mean "small, little," etc.; and see SUFFIXES in **Appendix K** for other word endings.

Qualifying words: cigarette, dinette, kitchenette, novelette

etym- (Gk., truth, true meaning, real [the root meaning, true meaning or literal meaning of a word]) Also see **veri-** for additional examples of "truth" words.

Qualifying words: etyma, etymography, etymological, etymologist, etymologize, etymology, etymon

eu- (Gk., good, well, happy, pleasing) Also see **bene-** and **bon-** for other examples of "good" words. Compare this element with those found in **caco-, dys-,** and **mal-** for words with opposite meanings.

Qualifying words: eubiotics, eucalyptus, eucentric, eucharist, euchromatopsy, eudaemonia, eudaemoniac, eudaemonism, eudemon, eudemonia, eudemoniac, eudemonism, eudipsia, eudora, euesthesia, Eugene, Eugenia, eugenics, eugnosia, eugnostic, eugonic, euhaline, euhydrophile, euhydrophilous, euhydrophily, eukinesis, eukinesia, eukinetic, eulogy, eumetria, eumorphics, eumorphism, eunomy, euosmia, eupepsia, eupepsy, eupeptic, euphagia, euphemise, euphemism, euphemistic, euphile, euphilous, euphonic, euphony, euphoretic, euphoria, euphoric, euphoristic, euphoropsis, eupnea, eupneic, eupnoea, eupotamic, eupraxia, eupyrexia, eurhythmia, eurhythmics, eustatic, eusthenia,

eusthenuria, eutelegenesis, euthanasia, euthenic, euthenics, eutherapeutic, euthermic, euthymia, euthyroid, euthyroidism, eutocia, eutrophia, eutrophic, euthrophication, eutrophy

eury- (Gk., wide, broad) Also see **platy-** and **tarso-** for other "flat" words. For antonyms, see **steno-**.

Qualifying words: aneurysm, aneurysmectomy, aneurysmograph, aneurysmoplasty, aneurysmotomy, eurybaric, eurybath, eurybathic, eurybenthic, eurybenthous, eurybiontic, eurycephalic, eurychoric, eurychorous, Eurydice, eurygnathic, eurygnathism, euryhaline, euryhydric, euryhygric, eurylumic, euryopia, euryphage, euryphagous, euryphagy, euryphotic, eurypterid, eurysome, eurytherm, eurythermal, eurythermic, eurythermophilic, eurythmics, eurytopic, eurytrophic, eurytropic, euryxenous

evening, west See **hesperian** and **vesper.**

ever, always See **semper** for examples.

every, all See **omni-** and **pan-** for examples.

evil, bad See **mal-** for information.

ex- (e-, ef-) (L., [1] out of, from; or [2] upward; or [3] completely, entirely; or [4] to remove from, deprive of; or [5] without; or [6] former) Also see **ecto-, exo-,** and **ex-** (Gk.) for additional examples of "out, outside" words.

[1] out of, from

Qualifying words: exit, expel, educe, excise, egress, emit, evict, excerpt, exonerate, exorbitant, expand, expatriate, expect, expectorate, expedient, expedite, expel, expire, educate, efface, effluent

[2] upward

Qualifying words: exalt, effervesce, excel, extol

[3] completely, entirely

Qualifying words: execute, exterminate

[4] to remove from, deprive of

Qualifying words: expropriate, effete

[5] without

Qualifying word: exanimate

[6] former

Qualifying words: ex-president, ex-convict

ex-, ec-, e- (Gk., out of, away from) **ex-** goes before vowels, **ec-** goes before consonants. This is a prefix which is supposed to be used with words or roots of *Greek origin*. Also see **ecto-, ex-** (L.), and **exo-** for words with similar meanings.

> **Qualifying words:** eccentric, eccentricity, ecclesia, ecclesiastic, ecclesiastical, eclectic, eclipse, ecliptic, ecsomatice, ecstasy, ecstatic, ectoderm, ectogenous, ectopia, exarch, exegate, exegesis, exodont, exodontist, exodus, exosmosis, exostosis

exa- [from *hexa-*, "six"] (Gk., one-quintillion [U.S.], 10^{18} [1 000 000 000 000 000 000]) Also see the METRIC GROUPS in **Appendix F** for other units of the metric system.

> **Qualifying word:** exameter

examine See **scope-** and **spec-** for examples.

excess, have in excess; abundant growth See **luxur-** for examples.

excessive, abnormal See **hyper-** for examples.

excite See **agito-** for information.

excrement, dung See **copro-, feco-, fembri-,** and **scato-** for examples.

existence, being See **onto-** for information.

exo-, ex- (Gk., outer, outside) Also see **ecto-, ex-** (L.), **ex-** (Gk.), and **extra-** for other "outer, outside" examples.

> **Qualifying words:** exobiology, exobiotic, exocardia, exocardiac, exocardial, exocarp, exocentric, exocuticle, exocytosis, exoderm, exodermis, exogamous, exogamy, exogastric, exogastritis, exogenous, exonym, exopathic, exopathy, exophytic, exoplasm, exopodite, exoskeletal, exoskeleton, exosphere, exothermal, exothermic, exotoxin, exotoxins, exotropia, exotropic

external See **ecto-, ex-** (Gk.), **exo-,** and **extra-** (L.) for information.

extra-, extro- (L, beyond, outside, on the outside, outward, external) Also see **ecto-, ex-** (L.), **ex-** (Gk.), and **exo-** (Gk.) for other "outside" words.

> **Qualifying words:** extracellular, extracerebral, extracontinental, extracorporeal, extracurricular, extrafamilial, extragalactic, extragovernmental, extrajudicial, extramarital, extramundane, extramural, extraneous, extraordinary, extraplanetary, extraprofessional, extrasensory, extrasocial, extrasolar, extraterritorial, extravagant, extraversion, extrofloral, extrospection, extroversion, extrovert, extroverted

extreme, outermost end or top See **acro-** for examples.

extro- (L., beyond, outside) See **extra-** for examples.

eye, corner of See **cantho-** for examples.

eye(s) See **ocul-, op-, opthalmo-, pupillo-,** and **retino-** for references to the "eye."

eyelid See **blepharo-, cili-,** and **tarso-** (eyelid edge) for examples and information.

F f

fa-, fam-, fan-, fat-, -fess (L., talk, speak, say, spoken about) Also see cit-, clam-, dic-, lalo-, legi-, locu-, logo-, loqu-, mythico-, ora-, -phasia, -phemia, and voc- for additional examples of "talk" words.

Qualifying words: affable, affableness, affably, confess, confession, confessor, defamation, defamatory, defame, fable, fabulous, fame, famous, fascinate, fate, fateful, fib, ineffable, infamous, infamy, infancy, infant, infanticide, infantile, infantilism, infantry, nefarious, preface, prefatory, profess, professed, profession, professional, professionalism, professor

fac-, fact-, feas-, -feat, -fect, -feit, -facient, -faction, fic-, -fy, facil- (L., make, do, build, cause, produce; forming, shaping) Also see ag-, -ize, -poeia, and stru- for additional "making" words and plasmo- for other "forming, molding" words.

Qualifying words: absorbifacient, affair, affect, affected, affection, artifact, artifice, artificial, artificially, benefaction, benefactor, beneficent, beneficial, beneficiary, benefit, calorifacient, certificate, certify, chafe, chauffeur, clarify, coefficient, confit, confection, confetti, configuration, counterfeit, counterfeiter, defacto, defeat, defect, defective, deficient, deficit, deify, diffect, difficacious, difficult, difficulty, dignify, discomfit, disfigure, diversify, edification, edifice, edify, effect, effectual, efficacious, efficacy, efficient, effigy, *ex post facto*, exemplify, facient, facile, facileness, facilitate, facilitation, facility, facsimile (a new term, *fax* [facsimile], is often used in office lingo or computerese), fact, faction, factious, factitious, factor, factory, factotum, factual, faculty, falsify, fashion, feasance, feasibility, feasible, feasibly, feat, feature, febrifacient, feckless, fetish, fiction, fictitious, figment, figure, forfeit, fortify, fructify, glorify, gratify, horrific, horrify, identify, imperfect, imperfection, indemnify, infect, infection, inflect, intensify, *ipso facto*, justify, liquefy, magnificence, magnificent, magnificently, magnifico, magnify, malefactor, malefic, maleficence, maleficent, malfeasance, manufacture, misfeasance, modify, mollify, mortify, munificence, munificent, nonfeasance, notify, nullify, office, official, officiate, officious, olfactory, orifice, pacific, pacifist, pacify, perfect, perfecto, personify, petrify, pluperfect, pontiff, pontificate, prefect, proficient, proficiency, proficiently, profit, prolific, putrefy, qualify, ramify, rarefy, ratify, rectify, refectory, sacrifice, sanctify, satisfaction, satisfy, *savoir-faire*, scientific, significant, signify, simplify, solidify, somnifacient, specific, spe-

cify, stratify, stupefy, suffice, sufficient, superficial, surface, surfeit, terrific, terrify, testify, transfigure, typify, unify, verify, vilify, vivify

face, surface See -hedral for examples.

-facient (L., make, do, build) See fac- for examples.

facil-, facult- (L., make easy) See fac- for examples.

fact- (L., made, do, build) See fac- for examples.

-faction (L., made, do, build) See fac- for examples.

faith, trust See cred-, dox-, and fid-.

fall See cad- and -ptosia for information.

fall, slip See laps- for examples.

falling down of a body organ See -ptosia for information.

fals-, fall- (L., false, deception, untrue) Also see pseudo- for additional examples of "false" words.

Qualifying words: default, fallacious, fallacy, false, falsetto, falsification, falsify, falter, fault, faulty, infallible

fam-, fan- (L., talk, speak, say) See fa- for examples.

FAMILY GROUPS

> parr- (Gk. > L.) close relative, parent
> See parr- for examples.
> pater-, patr- (L.) father
> See pater- for examples.
> mater-, matri- (L.) mother
> See mater- for examples.
> matro-, matr- (Gk., mother)
> See matro- for examples.
> metro-, metr- (Gk.) mother (in medicine, "uterus, womb") See metro- for examples. Don't confuse this metro- with another Greek metro- which means "measure."
> uxor- (L.) wife See uxor- for examples.
> fili- (L.) son (*filius*), daughter (*filia*)
> See fili- for examples
> frater- (L., brother
> See frater- for examples.
> soro-, sorori- (L.) sister
> See soro- for examples.

fan- (L., talk, speak, say) See fa-.

far away, far off See tele- for examples.

farm animals See the ANIMAL GROUPS section in Appendix A for information.

fast, swift   For examples, see **agito-, celer-, tacho-,** and **veloci-**.

fat- (L., talk, speak, say) See **fa-** for examples.

fat See **adipo-, lipo-, oleo-,** and **steato-**.

fate, fortune See **tycho-** for examples.

father See **pater-** for examples.

fatigue, work hard See **pono-** for examples.

fauna (L., animal) Also see **anima-, therio-,** and **zoo-** for other "animal" words.

> **Qualifying words:** avifauna, epifauna, Fauna, fauna, faunal, faunation, faunist, faunistically, faunistics, faunizone, faunology, faunula, Faunus, infauna, infaunal, macrofauna, meiofauna, microfauna

fear See **-phobia** for information.

fearful, frightful See **dino-** for examples.

feas- (L., made, do, build) See **fac-**.

feat- (L., made, do, build) See **fac-**.

feather, wing See **plum-, ptero-, pterygo-,** and **ptilo-** for examples.

febri- (L., fever) Also see **pyeto-** and **pyro-** (fire) for additional "fever" examples.

> **Qualifying words:** afebric, afebrile, antefebrile, antifebrile, febricant, febricide, febricity, febricula, febriculose, febriculosity, febrifacient, febriferous, febrific, febrificide, febrificulous, febrifugal, febrifuge, febrile, febriphobia, febris, februs

feco-, fec-, faeco-, faec-, feci- (L., excrement, dung; from *faeces,* plural of *faex,* "dregs, sediment") Also see **copro-, fimbri-,** and **scato-** for other "dung" words.

> **Qualifying words:** caryofecia, defecalgesiophobia, defecate, defecation, faecal, faeces, fecal, fecalith, fecaloid, fecaloma, fecaluria, fecanalgia, feces, fecogenous, feculence, feculent

-fect (L., make, do, build) See **fac-** for examples.

feeble minded See **moro-** for information.

feeling, sensation See **aesthe-, pass-, patho-,** and **sens-** for examples.

feet See **ped-**(L.) and **pod-** for examples. Also compare with **dactylo-** (finger).

-feit (L., make, do, build) See **fac-** for examples.

feli- (L., cat) Also see **aeluro-, galeo-,** and **gato-** for additional "cat" words.

> **Qualifying words:** felicide, felid, Felidae, feline, felinity, felinophile, felinophobia, philofelist

fem-, femi- (L., woman) Also see **gyno-** and **-trix** for additional examples.

> **Qualifying words:** effeminate, female, femicide, feminality, femineity, feminine,

feminism, femininity, feminist, feminity, feminize, *femme fatale*

female, woman See **fem-, gyno-,** and **-trix** for examples.

female-genital organ(s) See **colpo-, episio-, hystero-, utero-, vagino-,** and **vulvo-**.

femur See **femoro-** for examples.

femto- (Danish, represents fractions of fifteen digits, 10^{-15} [0.000 000 000 000 001]) Also see METRIC GROUPS in **Appendix F** for other metric measurements. Used in naming units of measurement to indicate one-quadrillionth (10^{-15}) of the unit designated by the root with which it is combined or one-thousandth of a millionth of a millionth.

> **Qualifying words:** femtoampere, femtogram, femtojoule, femtoliter, femtometer, femtomole, femtosecond, femtovolt

femoro-, femur (L., thigh) Also see **mero-** (# 2) for additional information.

> **Qualifying words:** femora(pl.), femoral, femorocaudal, femorocele, femoroiliac, femorotibial, femur(s.), femorotibial

-fend- (L., ward off, strike, keep off, defend, guard, protect; from *fendere* [found only in compounds]) Also see **alexo-** and **phylacto-**.

> **Qualifying words:** defend, defendant, defense, defensible, defensive, fence, fencer, fencing, fend, fender, offend, offense, offensive

-fer-, -ferous (L., bear, carry; produce) Also see **ger-, later-, phoro,** and **port-** for additional examples of "carry" words.

> **Qualifying words:** afferent, aquifer, auriferous, circumference, confer, conferee, conference, conferred, conferring, conifer, coniferous, crucifer, cruciferous, defer, deference, deferential, deferment, deferred, deferring, differ, difference, different, differential, differentiate, differentiated, differentiating, differentiation, differently, efferent, ferriferous, ferry, fertile, fertility, fetiferous, fructiferous, herbiferous, infer, inference, inferential, inferred, inferring, interfere, interference, Jennifer, lactiferous, Lucifer, odoriferous, offer, offered, offering, prefer, preferable, proffer, refer, referee, reference, referenda(pl.), referendum(s.), referent, referral, referred, referring, sanguiferous, somniferous, suffer, sufferable, sufferance, suffered, sufferer, suffering, suffers, transfer, transferable, transferal, transferee, transference, transferor, transferred, transferring, vociferate, vociferous

ferment, fermentation See **zymo-** for examples.

-ferous (L., bear, carry) See -fer for examples.

ferro-, ferr-, ferri- (L., iron) Also see sidero- for examples of other "iron" words.

> Qualifying words: ferreous, ferric, ferriferous, ferroalloy, ferrochromium, ferroconcrete, ferrocyanide, ferromagnetic, ferromanganese, ferrometer, ferrotherapy, ferrotype, ferrous, ferruginous, ferrule

ferv- (L., to boil; hot; deeply earnest; ardent) Also see calor- and thermo- for additional examples of "hot, heat" words.

> Qualifying words: effervesce, effervescence, effervescent, ferment, fermentation, fervency, fervent, fervently, fervescence, fervescent, fervid, fervidly, fervor, fervour

-fess (L., talk, speak) See fa-, fat- for examples.

fet- (an unborn offspring) See feto- for examples.

feti- (an unborn offspring) See feto- for examples.

feto-, fet-, feti- (L., an unborn offspring) Also examine nasc-, para, and toco- for other "birth" references.

> Qualifying words: effete, fetal, fetalism, fetalization, fetation, feticulture, feticidal, feticide, fetiferous, fetography, fetologist, fetology, fetometry, fetoscope, fetoscopy, fetus

fever See febri-, pyreto-, and pyro- for examples.

few See oligo- and pauci- for examples.

fiber See fibro- for examples.

fibro-, fibr- (L., fiber [an elongated, threadlike structure]) Also see lin- and mito- for other examples of "fiber" words.

> Qualifying words: angiofibrosis, fibremia, fibrenemia, fibriform, fibril, fibrilation, fibrin, fibrinogen, fibrinogenesis, fibrinoid, fibrinolysis, fibroid, fibroadipose, fibromyalgia, fibromyositis, fibrosis, fibrous, fibrositis

fic- (L., make, do, build) See fac- for examples.

fid-, fidel- (L., believe, belief, trust, faith) Also see cred- and dox- for additional examples of "believe" or "trust" words.

> Qualifying words: affidavit, bona fide, confidant, confidante, confide, confidence, confident, confidentially, defiance, diffidence, diffident, diffidently, fealty, fidelity, fiducial, fiduciary, infidel, infidelity, mala fide, perfidious, perfidy, semper fidelis

field See agra-, agrio-, and camp for examples.

fight, war See belli-, -machy, milit-, and pugn- for examples.

figure For examples, see eido-, form-, icono-, idol-, morpho-, and -oid.

fili- (L., son, daughter; offspring) Also see FAMILY GROUPS for additional words.

> Qualifying words: affiliate, affiliation, filial, filiality, filiate, filiation, filicidal, filicide, filiety

fill See ple-, and pleio- for examples.

filth, unclean Examine copro-, feco-, myso-, rhypo-, and scato- for examples.

fimbri-, fimbr-, fimi-, fim- (L., dung, excrement) Also see copro-, feco-, and scato- for other "dung" words.

> Qualifying words: fimbricole, fimbricolous, fimbriphilous, fimbrivore, fimbrivorous, fimbrivory, fimetarius, fimicole, fimicolous, fimiphilous, fimiphily, fimivore, fimivorous, fimivory

fimi- (L., dung) See fimbri- for examples.

fin- (finis) (L., end, last, limit, boundary, border) Also see omega, teleo-, term-, and ultim- for additional examples of "end" words.

> Qualifying words: ad infinitum, affinity, confine, define, definite, definitely, definition, definitive, final, finale, finalism, finalize, finalization, finalist, finality, finally, finance, financial, fine, finesse, finish, finite, finitely, finiteness, finitude, indefinite, infinite, infinitesimal, infinitive, infinitely, infinitude, infinity, refine, refinery, refinement, unfinished, paraffin

final See fin-, teleo-, term-, and ultim- for examples.

fine, delicate See lepto- and nemato- for examples.

finger, toe See dactylo- and digit for words.

finger nail See onycho- for examples.

fire, burn See ars-, caust-, crema-, flagr-, flam-, ign-, incend-, pyro-, and volcan- for other "fire" words .

firm- (L., strong, firm) Also see dyna-, fort-, poten-, stheno-, and valid- for other examples of "strong" words.

> Qualifying words: affirm, affirmable, affirmation, affirmative, affirmatively, confirm, confirmable, confirmation, confirmative, confirmed, firm, firmament, infirm, infirmary, infirmities, infirmity, reaffirm, reaffirmation, reaffirmed, reaffirming, reaffirms

firm, solid See firm- and stereo- for examples.

first See alpha, archae-, paleo-, prim-, prin-, and proto- for examples.

fish See ichthyo- and pisci- for examples.

fit, suited See apt- for examples.

five See **penta-** and **quinqu-** for examples and NUMBERS in the **Appendix G** section for other numerical elements.

fixed, standing See **stato-** for examples.

fixing (of a specified part to something) For examples, see **-pexy**.

flag See **vexill-** for examples.

flagello-, flagell- (L., to whip, whip)

> **Qualifying words:** biflagellate, choanoflagellate, dinoflagellate, flagella, flagellant, flagellar, flagellate, flagellation, flagelliform, flagellum, microflagellate, nanophytoflagellate, phytoflagellate, silicoflagellate, zooflagellate

flagr- (L., fire; burn, blaze) Also see **ars-, caust-, crema-, flam-, ign-, incend-, pyro-,** and **volcan-** for other "fire" words.

> **Qualifying words:** conflagrate, conflagration, conflagrative, deflagrate, deflagration, flagrancy, flagrant, flagrantly, *in flagrante delicto,* inflagrante

flake, scale See **lepidoptera-** for examples.

flam- (L., fire, burn, blaze) Also see **ars-, caust-, crema-, flag-, ign-, incend-, pyro-,** and **volcan-.**

> **Qualifying words:** flamboyant, flame, flamiferous, flamingo, flamivomous, flammable, inflame, inflammable, inflammation, inflammatory

flank or loin See **laparo-** for examples.

flat- (L., blow, a puff of wind; accumulation of gas in the stomach or bowels)

> **Qualifying words:** afflatus, conflate, conflation, deflate, deflation, flatulency, flatulent, flatus, inflate, inflation, inflationary, inflationism, perflation, reflate, sufflate

flat, broad Examine **eury-** and **platy-** for other "flat" words.

flat space See **camp** for examples.

flat surface, broad; ankle See **tarso-** for examples.

flea (bug) See **pulic-** for examples.

flect-, flex- (L., bend, curve, turn) Also see **gyro-, -plex, stroph-, tors-, trop-, verg-, vers-,** and **volv-** for other examples of "bend, turn" words.

> **Qualifying words:** anteflexion, biflex, circumflex, deflect, deflection, flection, flex, flexibility, flexible, flexuous, flexure, genuflection, inflect, inflection, inflexible, reflect, reflection, reflective, reflex, retroflex, retroflexion

flee, run away See **fug-** for examples.

flesh, meat See **carno-, creo-,** and **sarco-** for examples.

flesh (skin) See **dermo-** and **cuti-** for examples.

fleshy (fat) See **adipo-, lipo-, steato-,** and **oleo-** (oil) for examples.

flex- (L., bend) See **flect-** for examples.

flic-, flig- (L., strike, destroy, dashed down, damaged)

> **Qualifying words:** afflict, afflicted, affliction, conflict, confliction, inflict, infliction, profligacy, profligate

fling See **ballo-, jac-,** and **jet-** for examples.

float, flow, sail See **neusto-** and **pleusto-** for examples.

flori-, flor-, flora-, -florous (L., flower; *flora, plants* of a general region or period) Also see **antho-** for other examples of "flower" words.

> **Qualifying words:** defloration, effloresce, Flora, flora, florabunda, floral, Florence, florescence, floriculture, florid, Florida, floriferous, florin, florish, florist, floristics, florology, florula, inflora, inflorescence, macrofloria, microflora, multiflorous, uniflorous

flow, float, sail See **neusto-** and **pleusto-.**

flow, wave See **fluct-, liqu-, rheo-, -rrhea, rheum-, undu-,** and **vacilla-** for other "flow" words.

flower See **antho-** and **flori-** for examples.

flu- (L., flow) See **fluct-** for examples.

fluct-, flucti-, flux-, flu- (L., flow, wave) Also see **cymo-, -fus-, liqu-, rheo-, rheum-, -rrhea, undu-,** and **vacilla-** for additional examples of "flow" words.

> **Qualifying words:** affluence, affluent, afflux, circumfluent, confluence, confluent, conflux, effluence, effluent, effluvium, efflux, fluctuate, fluctuation, flue, fluency, fluent, fluently, fluid, fluidity, fluidic, fluidics, fluidity, fluidize, fluidness, flume, flush, fluvial, fluvioglacial, fluviology, flux, fluxion, influence, influent, influenza, influx, millifluent, mellifluous, reflux, superfluity, superfluous

fluvio-, fluvi- (L., river) Also see **potamo-.**

> **Qualifying words:** fluvial, fluviatic, fluviatile, fluvioglacial, fluviologist, fluviology, fluviomarine, fluvioration, fluvioterrestrial

flux- (L., flow) See **fluct-** for examples.

fold See **diplo-, -plex,** and **-ploid.**

folii- (l., leaf, sheet) See **folio-** for examples.

folio-, foli-, folii- (L., leaf) Also see **forbi-** (broad leaf) and **phyllo-** for additional examples of "leaf" words.

> **Qualifying words:** bifoliate, bifoliation, defoliate, defoliation, foil, exfoliate, foliaceous, foliage, foliar, foliate, foliated, foliating, foliation, foliature, folic, folicaulicole, folicau-

licolous, foliicole, foliicolous, folicole, folicolous, foliiferous, folligerous, folio, foliolate, foliole, foliose, folium, folivore, folivorous, folivory, graminifolious, latifoliate, multifoliate, perfoliate, portfolio, trifolium

follow See **sequ-** for examples.

fondness for For examples, see **amat-, eros, philo-,** and **-mania.**

fondness for (excessive), madness for something See **-mania** for examples.

food, nourishment See **alimento-, bromato-, cibo-, sitio-,** and **tropho-** for examples.

foolish See **moro-** for examples.

foot See **ped-** (L.) and **podo-** for examples.

footprint, track See **ichno-** for examples.

for See **pro-** for examples.

forbi-, forb- (Gk., fodder, food; any herb other than grass, a broadleaf herb; a weed) Also examine **folio-** and **phyllo-** for other "leaf" words.

> **Qualifying words:** forbicole, forbicolous, forbiphilous, forbiphily, forbivore, forbivorous, forbivory

forc- (L., power, strength) See **fort-** for examples.

force, power See **dyna-, firm-, fort-, poten-,** and **valid-** for examples.

foreign, strange Examine **barbar-, Gallo-,** and **xeno-** for examples.

forest, woods (trees) See **also-, arbor-, hylo-, nemo-, sylvan-, xylo-,** and **dendro-** for examples.

forget, forgetfullness See **leth-** for examples.

foretell, predict See **-mancy** for information.

forgetful, forgetfullness See **leth-** for examples.

form-, -form, forma-, format- (L., shape, form, figure, appearance) Also see **eido-, ideo-, morpho-,** and **plasmo-** for additional "shape" words. Also compare these elements with **icono-** and **idol.**

> **Qualifying words:** biform, conform, conformation, conformer, conformist, conformity, cordiform, deform, deformed, deformity, dentiform, formal, formalism, formalist, formality, formalization, formalize, format, formation, formative, formless, formula, formulate, inform, informal, informant, information, informative, informed, informer, nonconformist, oviform, perform, performance, performed, reform, reformation, transform, transformation, transformational, uniform

formed, shaped See **form-, morpho-,** and **plasmo-** for examples.

former See **ex-** (L.) for examples.

formic-, form-, -formic (L., ant) For additional "ant" words, see **myrmeco-** (Gk.).

> **Qualifying words:** chloroform, formaldehyde, formic, Formica, formicarian, formicarium, formicary, formicate, formication, formicative, Formicidae, formicide, formicine, formicivore formicivorous, formiphagia, formiphagy, formiphobia, formivore, formivorous, iodoform

forming, shaping See **ag-, fac-, -ize, -poeia,** and **stru-** for examples.

fornicate (L., whoredom [from "arch, vault; brothel"]) Also see **cypri-** and **porno-** for similar examples. Brothels were called *fornices,* i.e. "arches," because prostitutes used to gather "under the arches" of certain buildings of ancient Rome.

> **Qualifying words:** fornicate, fornication, fornicator, fornicatress

fort-, forc- (L., power, strength, strong) Also see **dyna-, firm-, poten-, stheno-,** and **valid** for other "power" words.

> **Qualifying words:** comfort, comfortable, comfortless, comfortlessly, discomfort, effort, enforce, enforceable, enforcement, force, *force majeure,* forcible, forcibly, fort, forte, fortification, fortifier, fortify, fortifying, fortissimo, fortitude, fortress, reinforce

fountain, mineral spring See **creno-** and **pego-.**

fortune, chance See **tycho-** for examples.

fossil, mineral; dig, dug Examine **orycto-** for examples.

four See **quadri-** and **tetra-** for examples.

forward See **pro-** for examples.

fox See **vulpi-** for examples.

fract- (L. break) See **frag-** for examples.

frag-, frang-, fract-, fring- (L., break) Also see **clast-, -orrhexis,** and **rupt-** for other "break" words.

> **Qualifying words:** diffract, diffraction, fracas, fractal, fractile, fraction, fractional, fractionize, fractious, fracture, fragible, fragile, fragility, fragment, fragmental, fragmentary, fragmentate, fragmentation, fragmentize, frail, frailty, frangible, frangile, infraction, infrangible, infringe, infringement, refactory, refract, refraction, refractor, refractory, saxifrage, suffrage

frang- (L., break) See **frag-** for examples.

frater-, frat- (L., brother) Also see **adelpho-** and FAMILY GROUPS for other elements.

> **Qualifying words:** confraternity, fraternal, fraternity, fraternize, fratricide

free See **eleuthero-** and **liber-** for examples.

freezing, cold Examine **frigo-, crymo-, cryo-, crystallo-,** and **psychro-** for examples.

frequent, frequently See **pollaki-** and **pykno-**.

friction, rub See **bruxo-, tribo-,** and **-tripsy** for examples.

frigo-, frig- (L., cold, frost) Also see **cryo-, crymo-, crystallo-,** and **psychro-**.

> **Qualifying words:** frigid, frigidity, frigidly, frigidness, frigolabile, frigophile, frigophilic, frigophily, frigorific, frigorimeter, frigorism, frigostabile, frigostable, frigotherapy, refrigerator

fring- (L., break) See **frag-** for examples.

frog See **batracho-** and **rani-** for examples.

from, away See **a-, ab-, abs-; apo-;** and **de-** for examples.

front of (in front of) See **ante-, pre-,** and **pro-** for examples.

frost, freezing Examine **frig-, crymo-, cryo-, crystallo-,** and **psychro-** for examples.

fruit See **carpo-** and **pomo-** for examples.

fug-, -fuge, -fugit (L., drive away, flee, run away)

> **Qualifying words:** centrifugal, febrifuge, fugacious, fugitive, fugue, refuge, refugee, solifugal, subterfuge, vermifuge

full, fill Examine **ple-, pleio-,** and **opulen-** for examples.

fumi-, fum- (L., smoke, vapor) See **capno-** and **typho-** for additional "smoke" words.

> **Qualifying words:** fumarium, fumarole, fumatorium, fumatory, fume, fumiferous, fumigate, fumigation, fumitory, fumous, fumy, perfume

fun- (L., pour, melt) See **fus-** for examples.

funeral See **tapho-** for examples.

fungi-, fung- (L., mold, mushroom) Also see **myco-** for other "mold" words.

[1]Any of a group of plants including mushrooms, molds, mildews, etc.

[2]In medicine, a spongy, morbid growth.

> **Qualifying words:** fungal, fungi(pl.), fungicide, fungicole, fungicolous, fungiform, fungistasis, fungistat, fungistatic, fungitoxic, fungitoxicity, fungivorous, fungoid, fungosity, fungous, fungus(s.)

fus-, fun-, fut- (-**found**-, through French) (L., pour, melt, blend)

> **Qualifying words:** affusion, circumfuse, circumfusion, confound (through French), confuse, confusion, diffuse, diffusion, effuse, effusion, effusive, foundry, funnel, fuse, fusible, fusion, futile, infuse, infusion, interfuse, interfusion, profound (through French), profuse, profusion, refund, refuse, suffuse, suffusion, transfuse, transfusion

fut- (L., pour, melt) See **fus-** for examples.

future (prediction of) See **-mancy** for examples.

-fy (L., make, do, build, cause, produce) See **fac-** for examples and see SUFFIXES in **Appendix K** for other word endings.

G g

galacto-, galact-, -galaxy (Gk., milk) Also see **lacto-** for additional "milk" words.

> **Qualifying words:** agalactia, agalactosis, agalactous, agalorrhea, androgalactozemia, antigalactic, dysgalactia, extragalactic, galactagogue, galactase, galactia, galactic, galactin, galactodendron, galactoid, galactometer, galactophage, galactophagous, galactophorous, galactopoietic, galactorrhea, galactorrhoea, galactose, galactostasis, galactrophic, galaxy, ischiogalactic, metagalactic, metagalaxy

-galaxy (Gk., milk) See **galacto-**.

galeo-, gale- (Gk., cat [*marten, weasel*]) Also see **aeluro-, feli-,** and **gato-**.

> **Qualifying words:** galeanthropy, galeophilia, galeophobia

gall, bile See **cholo-** for examples.

gall bladder See **cholecysto-** for examples.

Gallo-, Gall- (L., of or pertaining to Gaul, a region which is now modern-day France and Northern Italy [from the Germanic root meaning "foreigner, stranger" which includes English *Wales, Welsh, Wallachian, and Walloon*])

> **Qualifying words:** Gallic, Gallomania, Gallophile, Gallophilia, Gallophobe, Gallophobia, Gallo-Romance

gamo-, gam-, -gamy, -gamous (Gk., marriage, union)

> **Qualifying words:** adelphogamy, agamete, agamic, agamobium, agamocytogeny, agamogenesis, agamogenetic, allogamous, allogamy, autogamous, autogamy, bigamist, bigamy, cleistogamy, deuterogamy, dichogamous, dichogamy, digamist, digamous, digamy, endogamy, epigamic, exogamy, gamic, gamogenesis, gamomania, gamophobia, heterogamous, hologamy, homogamy, hypergamy, hypogamy, microgamy, misogamist, misogamous, misogamy, monogamist, monogamous, monogamy, pantagamy, pentagamist, pentagamy, polygamy, quadrigamist, quadrigamy, syngamy, tetragamy, trigamy

garlic See **allia-** for examples.

gas in the stomach or bowels See **flat-**.

gas, vapor See **atmo-** for examples.

gastro-, gastr-, gastero-, gaster-, gastri-, -gastria- (Gk., stomach, belly) Also see **abdomen-, coelio-,** and **ventri-** for additional "stomach" words.

> **Qualifying words:** agastria, arachnogastria, digastric, endogastric, endogastritis, en-

gastrius, epigastric, epigastrium, gastral, gastralgia, gastralgic, gastralium, gastrectomy, gastric, gastrilegous, gastriloquist, gastrin, gastritis, gastroblast, gastrocardiac, gastrocentral, gastrochaena, gastrocolic, gastrocutaneous, gastrodermal, gastrodermis, gastroduodenal, gastroduodenitis, gastroenteric, gastroenteritis, gastroenterocolostomy, gastroenterologist, gastroenterology, gastrogenic, gastrohepatic, gastrointestinal, gastrolith, gastrologer, gastrological, gastrologist, gastrology, gastrolysis, gastromancy, gastronomic, gastronomist, gastronomy, gastrophilus, gastropod, gastroptosis, gastropulmonary, gastrorrhagia, gastrotherapy, gastrotomy, gastrotoxin, melanogaster, microgastria, neogastropod, photogastroscope, polygastria, transgastric

gate, door, entrance See **port-** for examples.

gather together See **agora-** and **greg-** for more information and examples.

gato- (Spanish, from Latin *cattus*, cat) Also see **aeluro-, galeo-,** and **feli-** for other "cat" examples.

> **Qualifying words:** gatomania, gatophilia, gatophobia

geese See **anseri-** and **cyg-** for information and examples.

gelo-, geloto- (Gk., laughter, laughing)

> **Qualifying words:** gelastic, gelogenic, gelomancy, geloplegia, geloscopy, gelotherapy, gelotolepsy, gelotometer

genesis- (L., birth, origin) See **genus** for examples.

genio-, geni- (Gk., chin) Also see **mento-** for other "chin" words.

> **Qualifying words:** genial, geniocheiloplasty, genioglossal, genioglossus, geniohyoid, genion, genioplasty

genital organs (female) See **colpo-, utero-, vagino-,** and **vulvo-** for examples.

genu- (L., knee) Also examine **gony-** for other "knee" words.

> **Qualifying words:** genuclast, genicula(pl.), genicular, geniculate, geniculum(s.), genu, genucubital, genuflect, genuflection, genuflexion, genupectoral

genus, genesis-, -genesis, -genetic, -genous (L., birth, descent, origin, creation, inception, beginning, race, sort, kind, class) Also see **gono-, nasc-, para,** and **toco** for additional "birth" words.

> **Qualifying words:** autogenous, benign, biogenesis, congenial, cosmogony, degenerate, degeneration, endogenous, exogenous, engender, erogenous, eugenic(s.), gender, genealogical, genealogist, genealogy, general, generate, generated, generating, generation,

generative, generator, generic, generous, genesiology, genesis, genetal, genetical, genetically, genetics, genetrix, genial, genitive, genius, genocidal, genocide, genomic imprints, genre, hematogenous, heterogeneous, homogeneous, homogenize, indigenous, malign, malignancy, malignant, miscegenation, pathogenesis, philoprogenitive, photogenic, phylogenesis, phylogenetic, phylogenetically, phylogenic, phylogeny, primogeniture, progeny, regenerate, regeneration, telegenic, ultimogeniture

geo-, ge- (Gk., earth, world) Also see **agra-, chthon-, cosmo-, humus, mundan-, pelo-** (mud), and **terr-** for additional "earth" words.

   Qualifying words: ageotropic, ageotropism, amphigean, apogee, archaeogeology, archeogeological, archeogeology, biogeocoenology, biogeography, biogeosphere, diageotropic, diageotropism, endogean, epigean, geoaesthesia, geobenthos, geobiology, geobiontic, geobionts, geobios, geobotany, geocarpic, geocarpy, geocentric, geochronological, geochronologist, geochronology, geochronometry, geocole, geocolous, geocryptophyte, geode, geodestic, geodesy, geodetic, geodiatropic, geodiatropism, geognostic, geognosy, geogony, geographic, geography, geohydrology, geohydrology, geoid, geoisotherm, geology, geomagnetic, geomagnetism, geomancy, geomantic, geomantist, geomedicine, geometric, Geometridae, geometry, geomorph, geomorphologist, geomorphology, geonastic, geonasty, geonyctitropic, geonyctitropism, geophagia, geophagism, geophagist, geophagous, geophagy, geophilous, geophone, geophysical, geophysics, geophyte, geopolitics, geoponic, geoponics, geophyte, geotropic, geotropism, George, geoseism, geosphere, geostrophic, geotaxis, geotectnology, geotectonics, geothermal, geotropic, geotropism, hydrogeology, hypogean, hypogeous, isogeotherm, perigee, phytogeography, thermogeographic, thermogeography

gero-, ger-, geronto-, geront- (Gk., old age, old man, old people) Also see **presbyo-** and **sen-** for more "old age" words. Don't confuse this **ger-** with the next **ger-** which means "carry" or "produce."

   Qualifying words: acrogeria, agerasia, gerascophobia, gerasophobia, geratology, geriatics, geriatrician, geriatrics, geriatry, geriopsychosis, gerodermia, gerodontics, gerodontology, geromorphism, gerontal, gerontic, gerontio, gerontocracy, gerontology, gerontophilia, gerontophobia, gerontopia, gerontotherapeutics, gerontotherapy, progeria, psychogeriatrics, quadragenarian

ger-, ges- (L., carry, produce) Also see **fer-, phoro-, -poeia** [produce], and **port-** for other examples. Don't confuse this **ger-**

with the previous Greek **ger-** which means "old age."

   Qualifying words: belligerent, congest, congested, congestion, congestive, digest, digestible, digestion, egest, exaggerate, exaggerated, exaggerating, exaggeration, gestation, gesticulate, gesture, indigestion, ingest, ingestion, progestion, suggest, suggestion

germ, bud See **blasto-** for examples.

geronto- (Gk., old age, old people) See **ger-** (Gk.) for examples.

ges- (L. carry, produce) See **ger-** (L.).

geus-, geuma-, -geusia, -geusic, -geustia, (Gk., taste) Also see **gust-**.

   Qualifying words: ageusia, ageusic, ageustia, allotriogeusia, ambageusia, amblygeusia, cacogeusia, dysgeusia, geumaphobia, glycogeusia, hemiageusia, hypergeusia, hypogeusia, oxygeusia, parageusia, picrogeusia, pseudogeusesthesia, pseudogeusia

ghost; shade, shadow See **scio-** for examples.

giant See **giga-** and **giganto-** for examples.

giga- (Gk., "giant," billion [10^9] [1 000 000 000]) Also see **giganto-, grand, macro-, magni-, major, maxi-, mega-, megalo-** and METRIC GROUPS in **Appendix F** for additional units.

   Qualifying words: gigabit, gigabyte, gigacycle, gigaelectrovolt, gigajoules, gigahertz, gigameters, (British: *gigametres*), gigapascal, gigavolt, gigawatt, gigohm

giganto-, gigant- (Gk., giant; giantlike; very large) Also see **giga-, grand, macro-, magni-, major, maxi-, mega-,** as well as **megalo-** for other "big, large" words.

   Qualifying words: gigantoblast, gigantocyte, gigantosoma, gigantism

gingivo-, gingiv- (L., the gums of the mouth)

   Qualifying words: gingiva, gingivae, gingival, gingivalgia, gingivectomy, gingivitis, gingivobuccoaxial, gingivoglossitis, gingivolabial, gingivolinguoaxial, gingivoplasty, gingivostomatitis

girl, young girl See **partheno-** and **virgo-**.

gladi- (L., sword) Also see **xipho-** for other "sword" words.

   Qualifying words: gladiate, gladiator, gladiatorial, gladioli(pl.), gladiolus(s.) [*also*: gladiola], gladius, Orca gladiator

gland (male reproductive) Examine **orchio-** and **testi-** for sample words.

glands near the kidneys Examine **adeno-** for sample words.

glandular See **adeno-** for examples.

glass, glassy See **hyalo-** and **vitreo-**.

glob-, glom- (L., ball, round) For other "round" words, see **sphero-**.

> **Qualifying words:** agglomerate, agglomeration, conglomerate, conglomeration, globe, globoid, globular, globule, glomeration, hemoglobin

glom- (L., ball, round) See **glob-** for examples.

glosso-, gloss-, glotto-, glot-, -glott (Gk., tongue, language) Also see **linguo-** for additional "tongue" words.

> **Qualifying words:** aglossal, aglossia, aglosstomia, anklyoglossia, anthropoglot baryglossia, bradyglossia, cacoglossia, cynoglossum, diglot, epiglottis, gloss, glossa, glossarist, glossal, glossalgia, glossary, glossectomy, glossematics, glossitis, glossocinesthetic, glossocoma, glossdynamometer, glossograph, glossographer, glossography, glossokinaesthetic, glossolalia, glossology, glossomantia, glossopathy, glossophagine, glossophobia, glossoplegia, glossoplegic, glossopyrosis, glossoscopy, glossospasm, glossotomy, glottal, glottis, glottochronological, glottochronology, glottological, glottology, hypoglossal, hypoglossally, isogloss, monoglot, monoglottic, pachyglossal, pachyglossia, polyglot, tachyglossus, xenoglossay

glotto-, glot- (Gk., tongue, language) Examine **glosso-** for examples.

glow; white See **cand-** for examples.

gluco-, gluc- (Gk., sweet, sweetness) Also see **dulci-, glyco-** and **racchar-** for other "sweet" words.

> **Qualifying words:** glucogenesis, glucogenic, glucohemia, glucokinetic, glucolysis, glucolytic, glucose

glyco-, glyc- (Gk., sweet, sugar) Also examine **gluco-** and **racchar-**.

> **Qualifying words:** aglycositosis, glycemia, glycerine, glycine, glycobiology, glycobrosis, glycoclastic, glycogen, glycogenesis, glycogenolysis, glycogeusia, glycohemia, glycolimia, glycolipid, glycolysis, glycolytic, glycopathia, Glycophagus, glycophagus, glycophilia, glycoproteins, glycorrhea, glycosites, glycositosis, glycostatic, glycotaxis, glycotropic, hyperglycemia, hypoglycemia, hypoglycositosis, proteoglycans

-glyph (Gk., carve, engrave) See **glypto-**.

glypto-, glypt-, -glypha, -glyph, -glyphic, -glyphous (Gk., carve, carving; engrave) Also see **grapho-, -gram**, and **scrib-** for related "writing" words.

> **Qualifying words:** anaglyph, bioglyph, bioglyphic, dactylioglyph, diglyphic, glyph, glyphic, glyphograph, glyphography, glyphology, glyptic, glyptogenesis, glyptograph, glyptography, hieroglyph, hieroglyphic(s), petroglyph, petroglyphic(s), triglyph

gnashing of teeth See **bruxo-** for examples.

gnat, mosquito See **anopheli-** and **culci-**.

gnatho-, gnath-, -gnatha, -gnathan, -gnath, -gnathi-, -gnathic, -gnathous (Gk., jaw) Also see **mandibulo-** and **maxillo-** for other "jaw" words.

> **Qualifying words:** Cynognathas, eurygnathism, gnathalgia, gnathic, gnathion, gnathism, gnathitis, gnathocephalus, gnathodynamia, gnathodynamics, gnathodynamometer, gnathodynia, gnathography, gnathology, gnathoplasty, gnathopod, gnathoschisis, gnathosoma, gnathostatics, gnathostomatous, gnathotheca, hemignathous, holognathous, macrognathia, menognathous, orthognathic, orthognathism, orthognathist, orthognathous, prognathism, prognathous

gnaw, eat away See **rod-** for examples.

gno-, gnos-, gnoto-, -gnostic, -gnosia, -gnomic, -gnomonic, -gnomical, -gnomically, -gnomy, -gnosia, -gnostic, -gnosis (Gk., know, learn) Also examine **cogni-, epistemo-, intellect-, mne-, not-**, and **sci-** for other "know" words.

> **Qualifying words:** abaragnosia, acognosia, acognosy, agnogenetic, agnogenic, agnosia, agnosic, agnostic, agnosticism, atopognosia, atopognosis, baragnosia, baragnosis, chirognomic, chirognomy, craniognomic, diagnose, diagnosed, diagnosis, diagnostic, diagnostician, diagnostics, dysanagnosia, dysgnosia, geognosis, gnosis, gnotobiotic, gnotobiology, gnotobiota, gnotobiote, gnotobiotics, gnotophoresis, ignoramus, ignorance, ignorant, ignore, logagnosia, pathognomic, pathognomy, physiognomy, pragmatagnosia, prognosis, prognostic, prognosticate, prognosticated, prognosticating, prognostication, prognosticator, pyrognomic, toxignomic

go See **-cede** and **itiner-** for examples.

goat See **aego-, capri-, hirco**, and **tragico-** for examples.

god, deity See **dei-** and **theo-** for examples.

goddess of love See **aphrodi-** for examples.

-gogy (Gk., lead, leading) See **-agogue**.

gold, yellow See **auri-, chryso-, ocher**, and **xantho-** for examples. Don't confuse this **auri-** with another **auri-** which means "ear."

golden (color) See **chryso-** for examples.

gon-, gonio-, -gon, -gonal, -gonally, -gony (Gk., corner, bend, angle) Also see **angle** for other examples. Don't confuse this **gon-** with the next **gono-**, which means "seed, kind, race," etc.

> **Qualifying words:** agonic, decagon, diagon, diagonal, dodecagon, enneagon, gonio-

meter, goniometry, hendecagonal, heptagon, hexagon, isogonic, nonagon, octagon, orthogonal, pentagon, polygon, tetragon, trigon, trigonometry

gono-, gon-, goni-, -gonic, -gony (Gk., seed, kind, race, sexual, reproductive, procreation, generation) Also see **spermo-** and **sporo-** for other examples. Don't confuse this **gono-** with the next one ("knee"), or the previous one ("corner").

Qualifying words: andromerogony, bibliogony, cosmogony, gamogony, gonad, gonadal, gonadectomize, gonadectomy, gonadocentric, gonadogenesis, gonadokinetic, gonadoma, gonadopathy, gonadopause, gonadotherapy, gonadotropic, gonadotropism, gonaduct, ganophage, geogony, gonad, gonidium, gonococcus, gonocyte, gonophore, gonorrhea, gonotoxemia, theogony

gony-, gon- (Gk., knee) Don't confuse this **gon-** with the previous one which means "seed." Also see **genu-**.

Qualifying words: gonalgia, gonarthron, gonarthritis, gonarthrotomy, gonitis, gonocampsis, gonycampus, gonybatia, gonyoncus

good, well See **bene-, bon-,** and **eu-**.

govern, rule See **-arch, -crat,** and **regi-** for examples.

gra- (L., beloved, pleasing) See **grat-**.

grac- (L., beloved, pleasing) See **grat-** for examples.

grad-, -grade, -gred, -gree, -gress (L., walk, step, take steps, move around) Also see **ambul-** and **itiner-** for other "walk, step" words.

Qualifying words: aggradation, aggression, aggressive, aggressor, biodegradable, centigrade, congress, congressional, degrade, degradation, degree, digitigrade, digress, digression, egress, gradate, gradation, gradational, grade, grades, gradient, gradual, gradualism, gradually, graduate, graduated, graduation, ingredient, ingress, pinnigrade, plantigrade, progress, progression, progressive, pronograde, regress, regression, regressive, retrogradation, retrograde, retrogress, retrogression, saltigrade, tardigrade, transgress, transgressed, transgression, transgressor, vermigrade

gram-, -gram, -grammatic, -grammactically, -gramme, -grammatical, -grammic (Gk., write, that which is written, a letter, a written record) Also see **grapho-, glypto-** (carve), and **scrib-**.

Qualifying words: anagram cablegram, chronogram, cryptogram, decagram, diagram, diagrammed, epigram, grammar, grammarian, grammatical, grammatologist, gramma-

tology, gramophone, ideogram, logogram, microgram, monogram, monogrammatic, myriagram, program, programmable, programmed, programmer, programming, telegram

grand (L., large, great) For other examples, see **giga-, giganto-, macro-, magni-, major, maxi-, mega-,** and **megalo-**.

Qualifying words: aggrandize, grand, grandeur, grandiflora, grandiloquence, grandiloquent, grandiose, grandiosity

grapes, cluster of See **botryo-** for examples.

grapho-, graph-, -graphy, -grapher, -graphia (Gk., write, record, draw, describe) Also see **glypto-, -gram,** and **scrib-** for other "write" words.

Qualifying words: agraphia, agraphesthesia, agraphic, allograph, autobiographer, autobiographic, autobiographical, autobiography, autograph, autographer, autographic, autographically, autography, bibliographic, bibliographical, bibliography, biograph, biographer, biographic, biographical, biography, cacographer, cacographic, cacographical, cacography, cacography, calligraphy, calligrapher, calligraphic, calligraphical, calligraphist, calligraphy, cartograph, cartography, cerography, chalcographic, chalcography, cheirograph, cheirography, chirograph, chirographic, chirographical, chirography, choreographer, choreography, chrysographer, chrysography, cinematograph, cinematography, cosmography, cryptograph, cryptographer, cryptography, crystallography, crystallography, dactylograph, dactylography, demographer, demographics, demography, digraph, digraphy, dittography, epigraph, epigraphy, ethnography, flexography, geography, geographical, graft, graph, graphemic, graphemics, graphic, graphite, graphologist, graphology, graphomania, graphonomy, graphopathological, graphopathologist, graphopathology, graphophobia, graphomancy, haplography, holograph, holographic, holography, homograph, hydrography, ichthyography, ideograph, ideographic, ideographical, ideography, isographic, isographical, isography, lexicograph, lexicographer, lexicography, lipography, lithograph, lithography, logograph, logographer, logographic, logography, metallography, mimeograph, mimeography, monograph, monographic, monographology, oceanography, ondograph, ondography, orthographer, orthographic, orthographical, orthography, paleography, pantograph, paragraph, paragraphism, paragraphist, petrography, phonograph, phonographer, phonographic, phonographist, phonography, photograph, photographer, photography, photomicrograph, physiography, pictograph, pictographic, pictography, polygraph, pornographer, pornographic, pornography, pseudagraphia, pterylography, pyrograph, pyrography, radiographer, radiographic, radiography, scenography, scolography, scotography, seismograph, seismographer, seismography, sematography, semeiography, skiagraph, skiagraphy, stelography, stenographer, stenographic, stenographical, stenography, tachygrapher, tachygraphic, tachygraphical, tachygraphy, telautograph, telautography, telegraph, telegrapher, telegraphic, telegraphy, telephotography, tomographic, topography, trigraph, typography, xerograph, xerography, xeroradiography, zoogeographer, zoogeographic, zoogeography, zoography

grasp, hold See **ten-** for examples.

grasshopper See **acrido-** for examples.

grass See **herb-** for examples.

grat-, gra-, grac- (L., beloved, pleasing, dear, agreeable; grateful, thankful, pleased)

> **Qualifying words:** agree, congratulate, congratulation, disagree, disgrace, disgraceful, grace, graceful, graceless, gracious, grateful, gratification, gratify, gratis, gratitude, gratuitous, gratuity, gratulate, ingrate, ingratiate

grav-, griev- (L., heavy, weighty) Also see **baro-** and **gravid-** (pregnant).

> **Qualifying words:** aggravate, aggravated, aggravation, grave, gravid, gravimeter, gravimetric, gravimetry, gravisphere, gravitate, gravitating, gravitation, gravitational, gravitometer, gravity, grief, grievous

grave, tomb See **tapho-** for examples.

gravel See **chalico-** for examples.

gravid- (L., pregnant, pregnancy [from **grav-,** *heavy*]). Also see **para-**[1] (giving birth to)

> **Qualifying words:** decigravida, gravid, gravida, gravidic, gravidism, graviditas, gravidity, gravidocardiac, gravidopuerperal, multigravida, nonigravida, octigravida, primigravida, secondigravida, tertigravida, quartigravida, quintigravida, septigravida, sextigravida

grease; tallow, suet See **sebo-** for examples.

great, large For examples, see **giga-, giganto-, grand, macro-, magni-, major, maxi-, mega-,** and **megalo-.**

-gred (L., walk) See **grad-** for examples.

-gree (L., walk, step) See **grad-.**

Greek alphabet See **alpha** for the complete list.

green See **chloro-, verdant,** and **viri- for** examples.

green crop See **herb** for examples.

greg-, -gregate, -gregation (L., assemble, gather, gather together) Also see **agora-** for "assemble" or "market-place" words.

> **Qualifying words:** aggregate, aggregation, congregate, congregating, congregation, Congregationalist, congregator, desegregate, de-

segregation, desegregationist, egregious, gregarious, segregate, segregation, segregationist

-gress (L., walk) See **grad-** for examples.

grief, sorrow See **doloro-** for examples.

griev- (L., heavy, weighty) See **grav-.**

grind, friction See **tribo-** and **-tripsy.**

ground, soil See **agra-, chthon-, geo-, humus, mundan-,** and **terr-** for examples.

groups, collectives Examine GROUP NAMES in the **Appendix M** section for examples.

grow, increase See **auxano-** and **cresc-.**

growth (excessive, abundant) See **luxur-.**

grow, inhabit See **-cole** for examples.

growth (morbid growth) See **-oma.**

guard, protect, preserve For examples of these meanings, examine **alexo-, -fend-,** and **phlacto-.**

guide See **ag-** for examples.

gums of the mouth See **gingivo-.**

gust-, gusti- (L., taste, tasting) For other examples, see **geus-.**

> **Qualifying words:** degust, degustation, disgust, disgusted, disgusting, gust, gustation, gustatious, gustatism, gustative, gustatory, gustful, gustin, gusto, gustometer, gustometry, ragout

gutturo-, guttur- (L., throat) Also examine **cervico-, esophago-, laryngo-, thoraco-, trachelo-,** and **pharyngo-.**

> **Qualifying words:** guttur, guttural, gutturalism, gutturalize, gutturonasal, gutturophony, gutturotetany

gymno-, gymn- (Gk., naked, uncovered) Also see **nudo-** for other "naked" words.

> **Qualifying words:** gymnasium, gymnastic, gymnobacteria, gymnocarpic, gymnocarpous, gymnocyte, gymnogenous, gymnopedia, gymnophobia, gymnopterous, gymnoscopic, gymnosophist, gymnosophy, gymnosperm, gymnospore

gynaeco- (Gk., woman) See **gyno-** .

gyno-, gyn-, gynaeco-, gyneco-, gyne-, -gynia, -gynic, gynec-, -gynist, -gynous, -gyny (Gk., woman, female) Also see **fem-,** and **-trix** for additional "woman" words.

> **Qualifying words:** agynary, androgynous, gynaeceum, gynaecolatry, gynaecopathic, gynaecopathy, gynaeocracy, gynandromorph, gynandromorphic, gynandromorphism, gynandromorphous, gynandrous, gynandry, gynarchies, gynarchy, gynecium, gynecocracy, gynecogenic, gynecography, gynecoiatry, gynecoid, gynecolater, gynecolatry, gynecological, gynecologist, gynecology, gynecomania, gynecomastia, gynecopathic, gynecopathy, gynecophobia, gyneocology, gyneocracy, gyneolatry, gynephobia, gyneplasty, gyniatrics,

gyniatry, gynocracy, gynolater, gynolatry, gynopathy, gynopathic, gynophobia, gynoplastics, gynoplasty, hypogynous, hypogyny, misogynic, misogynist, misogynous, misogyny, monogynous, monogyny, oligogynous, oligogyny, philogynist, philogynous, philogyny, polygynous, polygyny, pseudogynous, pseudogyny, pseudopolygyny

gyro-, gyr- (Gk., turning, spinning, whirling, bend, circular motion; originally, "circle, curved, ring") Also see **flect-, -plex, stroph-, tors, trop-, verg-, vers-,** and **volv-** for additional "turning" words.

Qualifying words: dextrogyrate, dextrogyrating, gyre, dextrogyration, gyral, gyrate, gyration, Gyrinidae, gyrocompass, gyromancy, gyroplane, gyroscope, gyrospasm, gyrostabilizer, sinistrogyrate, sinistrogyrating, sinistrogyration

H h

habili-, habil- (L., clothe, clothing; make fit; from *habere*, to "have")

    Qualifying words: habiliment, habilitate, habilitation, habit, rehabilitate, rehabilitation

habit, custom See **ethi-** and **mor-** for examples. Don't confuse this *habit* with the next one which means "dwell."

habit-, hab-, -hibit (L., dwell; have, hold [from *habere*, to "have"]) Also see **dom-, eco-, nosto-,** and **oiko-** for other examples of "home" or "house" words.

    Qualifying words: cohabit, cohabitation, exhibit, exhibition, *habeas corpus*, habiliments, habit, habitable, habitant, habitat, habitation, habitual, habituate, habitude, Homo habilis, inhabit, inhabitant, inhibit, inhibition, prohibit, prohibition, prohibitive, rehab, rehabilitate

habitat, place of residence See **eco-** and **habit-** for examples.

haemo-, haem- (Gk., blood) See **hemo-** for examples.

hagio-, hagi- (Gk., sacred, holy) Also examine **hiero-, sacro-,** and **sanct-.**

    Qualifying words: hagiarchy, hagiocracy, hagiographa, hagiograph, hagiographer, hagiographic, hagiography, hagiolatry, hagiolith, hagiologist, hagiology, hagioscope

hair See **capillaro-** (hair-like), **chaeto-** (spine, bristle), **coma², crino-, hirsute, pilo-, tricho-,** and **pogo-** (beard) for examples.

hal-, hali-, -haled, -haling, -halant, -halent, -halation (L., breathe, breath) Also examine **pneo-, -pneumato,** and **-pneum** for additional "breath" words. Don't confuse this **hal-** with another one which means "salt."

    Qualifying words: exhalation, exhale, halitosis, halitus, inhalation, inhale

half See **demi-, hemi-,** and **semi-** for examples.

hallucina-, hallucinat- (Gk. > L., to wander in mind, dream) Also see **oneiro-** for other "dream" words.

    Qualifying words: hallucinate, hallucinated, hallucinates, hallucinating, hallucination, hallucinational, hallucinative, hallucinatory, hallucinogen, hallucinogenic, hallucinosis

halo-, hal-, hali- (Gk., salt) Also see **sal-** for other "salt" words. Don't confuse this

halo-, hal- with the previous **hal-** (L.) which means "breathe, breath."

    Qualifying words: euhaline, euryhaline, halicole, halicolous, halide, haliplankton, halite, halobacterium, halobiont, halobiontic, halobios, halobiotic, halocline, halodermia, haloduric, halogen, haloid, halolimnetic, halolimnic, halomancy, halometer, halometry, halomorphic, halophil, halophile, halophilic, halophilous, halophily, halophobe, halophobic, halophyte, halophytic, haloplankton, halosere, holeuryhaline, mesohaline, oligohalabous, oligohaline, polyhaline, polyhalophile, polyhalophilic, polyhalophily, polystenohaline, stenohaline

hand See **chiro-** and **manu-** for examples.

handicraft, skill See **art-** and **techno-** for examples.

handle, touch See **hapto-, tang-,** and **thigmo-** for examples.

hang, weigh See **pend-** for examples.

haplo-, hapl- (Gk., simple, simply; single, once) Also examine **mono-, soli-,** and **uni-** for similar meanings.

    Qualifying words: haplobiont, haplodermatitis, haplodiploid, haplodiploidy, haplodont, haplography, haploid, haplology, haplometrosis, haplometrotic, haplomitosis, haplopathic, haplopathy, haplopetalous, haplophase, haplophyte, haplopia, haplosis, haplozygous, haptic

hapto-, hapt-, -hapte (Gk., touch, seizure) Also see **tang-** and **thigmo-** for additional "touch" words.

    Qualifying words: aphaptotropic, aphaptotropism, aphaptophobia, aphephobia, haptalgesia, haptephobia, hapteron, haptic, haptics, haptobenthos, haptometer, haptophil, haptophile, haptophobia, haptophore, haptotaxis, haptotropism

harbor See **port-** for examples.

hard See **duro-, rigi-,** and **sclero-** for examples.

hare, rabbit See **lepor-** for examples.

harlot, prostitute See **fornicate** and **porno-** for examples.

harmful See **nox-** and **neci-** for examples.

harsh, bad See **caco-** and **dys-** for examples.

hate, hater See **miso-** for examples.

have, hold See **habit-** and **ten-** for examples.

head See **capit-, cephalo-,** and **cranio-** for examples.

heal, cure See **cura-, -iatry, medi-, sana-,** and **therap-** for examples.

healthy, wholesome See **hygieio-** for examples.

heap up, a heap See **cumulo-** for examples.

hearing, listening Examine **acous-**, **audio-**, and **ausculto-** for examples.

heart See **cardio-** and **cor-** for examples.

heart chamber See **atrio-** for examples.

heat See **calor-**, **ferv-**, and **thermo-**.

heaven, sky See **celest-**, **ethero-**, and **urano** for examples.

heavy See **baro-** and **grav-** for examples.

hecto-, hect-, hecato-, hecaton-, hekto-, hekt- (Gk., a hundred) Also see **centi-** for other "hundred" words. In addition, see NUMBERS in the **Appendix G** section and METRIC GROUPS in **Appendix F** for other numerical elements. In the decimal system, **hecto-** is used to show whole units; a hundred, 10^2 (100).

Qualifying words: hecatophyllous, hectare, hectogram, hectograph, hectoliter, hectometer, hektare, hektometer

hedono-, hedon-, -hedonia, -hedonic (Gk., pleasure)

Qualifying words: anhedonia, hedonic, hedonical, hedonics, hedonism, hedonist, hedonistic, hedonomania, hedonometer, hedonophobia, hyperhedonia, hyphedonia

-hedral (adj.), **-hedron** (n.) (Gk., face, faces; surface, surfaces)

Qualifying words: cathedral, dodecahedron, enneacotahedron, hexahedral, hexahedron, holohedral, holohedron, icosahedral, icosahedron, polyhedral, polyhedron, tetartohedral, tetartohedron, tetrahedral, tetrahedrally, tetrahedrite, tetrahedron

heel (tendon or bone) See **achilles, calcaneo-,** and **calci-** for examples.

hekto- (Gk., a hundred) See **hecto-**.

helo-, hel- (Gk., marsh) Also examine **limno-, telmato-,** and **tipho-** for other "marsh" words.

Qualifying words: helobious, helodric, helohylophile, helohylophilous, helohylophily, helophile, helophilous, helophily, helophyte, heloplankton

helico-, helic-, helici-, heli- (Gk., spiral, coil; twisted, bent) Also examine **flect-, gyro-, helico-, -plex, stroph-, tors-, trop-, verg-, vers-,** and **volv-** for related "turn" words.

Qualifying words: helical, helicograph, helicogyrate, helicogyre, heliciform, helicoid, helicopter, helix

helio-, heli- (Gk., sun) Also see **sol-**.

Qualifying words: anheliophile, anheliophilous, anheliophily, aphelion, apheliotropic, apheliotropism, diaheliotropic, diaheliotro-

pism, heliocentric, heliograph, heliography, heliogravure, heliolatrist, heliolatry, heliolith, heliolithic, heliology, heliometer, heliometry, heliophil, heliophile, heliophilic, heliophilous, heliophily, heliophobia, heliophobic, heliophyll, heliophyllous, heliophyte, Helios [god of the sun], heliosciophyte, helioseismology, heliosis, heliostat, heliotaxis, heliothermic, heliotherapy, heliotrope, heliotropism, helioxerophile, helioxerophilous, helioxerophily, perihelion

helmintho-, helminth-, helminthi-, -helminth (Gk., worm) Also see **ascari-, scoleco-,** and **vermo-** for additional "worm" words

Qualifying words: antihelmintic, helminth, helminthic, helminthicide, helminthoid, helminthologist, helminthology, helminthophobia, helminthophobic, helminthous, platyhelminthes

hem- (Gk., blood) Examine **hemo-**.

hema-, haema- (Gk., blood) See **hemo-**.

hemat-, haemat- (Gk., blood) See **hemo-** for examples.

hemato-, haemato- (Gk., blood) See **hemo-** for examples.

hemi- (Gk., half) Also see **demi-** and **semi-**.

Qualifying words: hemialgia, hemicrania, hemicycle, hemidemisemiquaver, hemiepiphyte, hemigamy, hemignathous, hemiparasite, hemisphere, hemitropous

hemero-, hemer- (Gk., day) Also see **dies** for other "day" words.

Qualifying words: Ephemera, ephemera, ephemeral, ephemerality, ephemerally, ephemeralness, ephemeran, Ephemerid, ephemerid, Ephemerida, Ephemeridae, ephemerides, ephemeris, ephemerist, ephemeromorph, ephemeron, ephemerous, hemeralope, hemeralopia, hemeralopic, hemeranthous, hemeranthy, hemeraphonia, Hemerobaptism, Hemerobaptist, Hemerobius, Hemerocallis, Hemerocampa, hemerocology, hemerologium, hemerology, hemerophile, hemerophilous, hemerophily, hemerophyte

hemo-, haemo-, hem-, haem-, hema-, haema-, hemato-, haemato-, hemat-, haemat-, -hemia, -haemia, -hemic, -haemic (Gk., blood) Also see **-emia** and **sangui-**.

Qualifying words: anhematosis, anhemolytic, haemachrome, haemacyte, haemaphobia, haemapoietic, haematidrosis, haematobic, haematobium, haematochrome, haematocytozoon, haematogenous, haematolysis, haematophagous, haematophyte, haematothermal, haematothermic, haematozoon, haemophage, haemophagous, haemophagy, haemoplastic, haemopoiesis, haemopoietic, haemotoxin, haemotropic, hemadynamometry, hemaphobia, hemarthrosis, hematidrosis, hematocyst, hematologist, hematology, hematolysis, hematoma, hematomancy, hematophagous, hematophagy, hematophobia, hematopoiesis, hematopoietic, hematozoon, hemoglobin, hemoid, hemophile, hemophilia, hemophilic, hemophobia, hemorrhage, hemorrhoidal, hemorrhoids, hemostat, pseudohemophilia

hendeca-, hendec- (Gk., eleven) Also examine NUMBERS in the **Appendix G** section for other numerical units.

    Qualifying words: hendecagon, hendecagonal, hendecahedral, hendecahedron, hendecandrous, hendecasemic, hendecasyllable, hendecasyllabic

hepatico- (Gk., liver) See **hepato-** for examples.

hepato-, hepat-, hepatico- (Gk., liver)

    Qualifying words: hepatalgia, hepatatrophia, hepatectomy, hepatic, hepaticoduodenostomy, hepaticoenterostomy, hepaticogastrostomy, hepaticolithotomy, hepaticolithotripsy, hepaticopulmonary, hepaticostomy, hepaticotomy, hepatism, hepatitis, hepatocyte, hepatodynia, hepatofugal, hepatogastric, hepatogenic, hepatogenous, hepatogram, hepatography, hepatohemia, hepatoid, hepatolith, hepatologist, hepatology, hepatolysis, hepatolytic, hepatoma, hepatomalactia, hepatomegaly, hepatomelanosis, hepatometry, hepatopath, hepatopathy, hepatoxcopy, hepatoportal, hepatotherapy, hepatotomy, hepatotoxicity, hepatotoxin, hepatotropic, parahepatitis

hepta-, hept- (Gk., seven) Also see **septem-** and NUMBERS in **Appendix G** for other numerical elements.

    Qualifying words: heptachord, heptachromic, heptadactylism, heptad, heptagon, heptagynous, heptahedron, heptahydrate, heptaldehyde, heptameter, heptandrous, heptangular, heptarchy, heptatonic

-her-, -hes- (L., stick to)

    Qualifying words: adhere, adherence, adherent, adhesion, adhesive, cohere, coherence, coherency, coherent, cohesion, cohesive, hesitant, hesitate, incoherence, incoherent, inhere, inherent

herb- (L., green crop, grass)

    Qualifying words: herbaceous, herbage, herbal, herbarium, herbary, herbicide, herbiferous, Herbivore, herbivore, herbivorous, herborist, herborize

hermit See **eremo-** for examples.

herpes (Gk., reptile, to creep, crawl, creeping animal; a skin disease) Herpes may refer to either the "disease" or to "reptiles." The diseases are either "herpes simplex" or "herpes zoster." See **herpeto-** for examples based on this element.

herpeto-, herpet-, herp- (Gk., creeping thing, reptile; snake) Also see **angui-, ophio-** (snake), **reptil-,** and **sauro-** (lizard).

    Qualifying words: batrochoherpetomachia, batrochoherpetomachy, herpes, herpesian, herpetic, herpetiform, herpetism, herpetofauna, herpetogeny, herpetography, herpetoid, herpetologic, herpetological, herpetologist, herpetology, herpetophobia, herpetotomy, herpism, herpobenthic, herpobenthos, herpon

hes- (L., stick to) See **her-** for examples.

hesperian (Gk. > L., west, evening) Also see **vesper** for additional examples.

    Qualifying words: hesper, Hesperides, hesperian

hetero-, heter- (Gk., different, other, another, unlike) Also examine **ali-, allo-, alter-, poikilo-,** and **vari-.**

    Qualifying words: heteracanthous, heteractinal, heterandrous, heteraxial, heterocarpous, heterochromatic, heterochromatism, heterochronism, heterocycle, heterocyclic, heterodactylous, heterodermic, heterodont, heterodox, heterogamous, heterogeneous, heterointoxication, heterogenous, heterography, heterogynous, heterometric, heteromorphic, heteromorphism, heteronomous, heteronym, heteronymous, heteronymy, heterophage, heterophagous, heterophagy, heterophyllous, heterophyte, heteroplasm, heterosexual, heterosexuality, heterosporous, heterotaxis, heterotherapy, heterothermal, heterothermy, heterotroph, heterotrophic, heteroxenous, heteroxeny

hex-, hexa- (Gk., six) Also see **sex-** (the number) for other examples. See NUMBERS in **Appendix G** for additional numerical elements.

    Qualifying words: hexacanth, hexactinal, hexactine, hexacyclic, hexad, hexadactylia, hexadactylism, hexadactyly, hexadecimal, hexagon, hexahedral, hexahedron, hexameter, hexapod, hexode, hexaphyllous, hexaploid, hexaploidy, hexapod, Hexapoda, hexapody, hexarchy, hexasyllable, hexathlon, hexavaccine, hexavalent, hexode

-hibit- (L., dwell) See **habit-** for examples.

hidden, secret For examples of these words, examine **adelo-, calypto-, clandestine, crypto-, myster-,** and **occult.**

hide, cover See **adelo-, calypto-, clandestine, crypto-, myster-,** and **occult** .

hidero-, hider-, hidro-, hidr-, -hidrosis, -hidrotic (Gk., sweat, sweat gland) Also see **sudor-** for other "sweat" words.

    Qualifying words: acrohyperhidrosis, anhidrosis, anhidrotic, antihidrotic, cacidrosis, chromhidrosis, cyanephidrosis, dyshidrosis, ephidrosis, hemathidrosis, hidradenitis, hidroadenitis, hidrocystoma, hidropathy, hidroplankton, hidropoiesis, hidropoietic, hidrorrhea, hidroschesis, hidrosis, hidrotherapy, hidrotic, hyperephidrosis, hyperhidrosis, hypohidrosis, maschalephidrosis, olighidria, osmidrosis, phosphorhidrosis, podobromhidrosis, podohidrosis, polyhidria, polyhidrosis, synhidrosis, urhidrosis (uridrosis, urinidrosis)

hidro- (Gk., sweat) See **hidero-** for examples.

hiero-, hier- (Gk., sacred, holy) For additional "sacred" words, see **hagio-, sacro-,** and **sanct-**.

    Qualifying words: hierarchy, hieratic, hierocracy, hierodule, hieroglyph, hieroglyphics, hierophant, hierogram, hierolatry, hierology, hieromania, hierophobia, hierotherapy, hierurgy

high, highest Also examine **acme, acro-, alti-, hypso-,** and **sum-** for examples.

highest See **acme, acro-, hyper-, sum-,** and **super-** for examples.

hill, mountain See **mont-, ochtho-,** and **oro-** for words with *similar* meanings.

hinder, inhibit See **koly-** for examples.

hip See **coxa-** for examples.

hip bone See **ilio-** for examples.

hippo-, hipp- (Gk., horse) Also see **equ-**.

    Qualifying words: Eohippus, ephippium, hipparch, hippiatric, hippiatry, hippic, hippocampus, hippocaust, hippocene, hippocentaur, hippocoprosterol, hippocrepiform, hippodrome, hipodromist, hippogastronomy, Hippoglossus, hippogriff, hippogriffin, hippogryph, hippoid, hippolarium (hippo-solarium), hippology, Hippolyte, Hippolytidae, Hippolytus, hippomachy, hippomania, hippomaniac, hippometry, hipponosological, hipponosology, hippopathology, hippophagi, hippophagism, hippophagous, hippophagy, hippophile, hippophobia, hippopotamous, hippopotamus, hippopotomy, Hipposelinum, hippotherapy, hippuric, Hippuris, Mesohippus, Miohippus, Orohippus, Philip, Pliohippus, Protohippus

Hippocrates of Cos (late 5th century B.C. [about 460 - 377 B.C.]) See **Appendix D** for information.

Hippocratic oath See **Hippocrates of Cos** in **Appendix D** for the full text of the oath and other Hippocrates' quotations.

hirco-, hirc- (L., goat) Also see **aego-, capri-,** and **tragico-** for additional examples.

    Qualifying words: hirci(pl.), hircine, hircism, hircismus, hircinous, hircocervus, hircosity, hircus(s.)

hirsute (L., hair, shaggy, bristly) Also see **coma², crino-, dasy-, pilo-, tricho-, barba-** (beard), and **pogo-** (beard) for other related "hair" words.

    Qualifying words: hirsute, hirsuteness, hirsutism

hirudin-, hirudi-, hirud- (L., leech, leeches)

    Qualifying words: hirudicidal, hirudicide, hirudin, Hirudinaria, Hirudinea, hirudiniasis, hirudiniculture, hirudiniculturist, hirudinization, hirudinize, Hirudo

histo-, hist- (Gk., tissue [web]) Also examine **arachno-** (spider) for additional "tissue" words.

    Qualifying words: histioid, histio-irritative, histoblast, histoclastic, histocompatibility, histodiagnosis, histogenesis, histogenous, histography, histohematogenous, histohydria, histoid, histoincompatibility, histokinesis, histologist, histology, histolysis, histoma, histomorphology, histoneurology, histonomy, histopathology, histotherapy, histotomy, histotoxic, histotroph, histotropic, histozoic, neurohistology

hodo-, hod- (Gk., way, a going, a traveling) Also see **odo-** and **via-** for other "way" words.

    Qualifying words: hodograph, hodology, hodometer, hodometry, hodoneuromere, hodophobia

hog, pig See **porc-** for examples.

hold, grasp See **cap-, prehend-,** and **ten-**.

hold, have See **habit-** for examples.

hollow, cell See **cyto-** for examples.

holo-, hol- (Gk., whole, entire, complete)

    Qualifying words: holandry, holoantigen, holism, holistic, holobenthic, holocarpic, holocaust, holocryptic, holodont, holognathous, hologram, holograph, holographic, holography, hologynic, holohedral, holomorphic, holomorphosis, holoparasite, holophote, holophrasis, holophrastic, holophyte, holophytic, holopneustic, holosaprophyte, holotrichous, holozoic

holy, sacred See **hagio-, hiero-, sacro-,** and **sanct-** for examples.

home, house Examine **dome, eco-, oiko-,** and **habit-**.

homeo-, homoeo-, homio-, (homoio-, British spelling) (Gk., same, like, resembling, sharing in common, similar, equal) Also see **equ-, homo-** (Gk.), **ido-, -oid, pari-, simal-,** and **tauto-**.

    Qualifying words: homeokinesis, homeomorphism, homeopathy, homeoplasia, homeostasis, homeostat, homeostatic, homeotherapy, homeotherm, homeothermy, homeotoxic, homeotoxin, homeozoic, homoioplastic, homoiosmotic, homoiostasis, homoiothermal, homoiothermic, homoiothermous

homo-, hom- (Gk., same, equal, like, similar) Also see **equ-, homeo-, iso-, -oid, pari-, simal-,** and **tauto-** for other "same" words. Don't confuse this Greek **homo-** element with the following Latin **homo-**.

   Qualifying words: homobium, homocarpous, homocentric, homochromous, homodermic, homodermous, homodont, homodromous, homodynamic, homogamous, homogamy, homogenesis, homogenize, homogenized, homogenous, homoglandular, homograph, homolateral, homology, homomorphic, homonym, homonymic, homophone, homophonic, homoplast, homopterous, homosexual, homosomal, homotaxis, homothermal

homo-, hom-, hum- (L., human beings, mankind, man) Also see **andro-, anthropo-,** and **vir-** for additional "man" examples. This Latin **homo-** is related to *humus*, "earth" or "born," and so it is said to mean "earthly being" or "born of the earth" and also refers to all of humanity. Don't confuse this Latin **homo-** with the Greek **homo-** which means "same" or "equal."

   Qualifying words: homage, homicidal, homicide, hominid, hominivorus, hominoid, Homo erectus, Homo habilis, Homo sapiens, homunculus, human, humane, humanitarian, humanity, humanoid, inhumanity

homoio- (like, similar) See **homeo-** (Gk.).

honey   See **melli-** for examples.

hor-, horr- (L., bristling, roughness, rudeness, shaking, trembling)

   Qualifying words: abhor, abhorrence, abhorrent, horrendous, horrent, horrescent, horribility, horrible, horrid, horrific, horrification, horrify, horripilate, horripilation, horror

horn   See **cerato-** (*kerato-*) and **corn-**.

horo- (Gk., hour, period of time, season, time) Also see **chrono-** and **tempo-** for other "time words.

   Qualifying words: horography, horologe, horologic, horologiography, horologist, horology, horometer, horometry, horoscope

horse   See **equ-** and **hippo-** for examples.

horti- (L., a garden, of a garden, a gardener)

   Qualifying words: horticulture, horticultural, horticulturist

hot   See **calor-, ferv-,** and **thermo-**.

house, home   Examine **dom-, eco-, habit-,** and **oiko-** for examples.

hull-shaped   See **scapho-** for examples.

hum- (L, earth)   See **humus** for examples.

hum- (L., human being)   Examine **homo-** for examples.

humanity   See **anthropo-** and **homo-** (L.).

humero-, humer- (L., shoulder, upper arm) Also see **omo-** (L.) for other "shoulder" words.

   Qualifying words: humeral, humeri, humeroradial, humeroscapular, humeroulner, humerus

humid- (L., moist, wet) Also examine **hygro-** for examples and compare with **aqua-** and **hydro-**.

   Qualifying words: humid, humidification, humidifier, humidify, humidistat, humidity, humidor

humus, hum- (L., earth, ground, soil) Also see **agra-, chthon-, geo-, mundan-,** and **terr-** for other "earth" words.

   Qualifying words: exhume, exhumation, human, humble, humic, humiliate, humiliating, humiliation, humility, humus, inhume, inhumation, posthumous

hundred   See **hecto-** and **centi-** for examples.

hunger, appetite   See **bou-** (*bulima*), **limo-,** and **orexi-** for examples.

hurl   See **ballo-, jac-, jet-,** and **miss-**.

hyalo-, hyal- (Gk., glass, glassy; transparent) Also see **vitreo-** for other "glass" words.

   Qualifying words: hylin, hyaline, hyalinization, hyalite, hyalodermis, hyalogrphy, hyaloid, hyalophagia, hyalophagy, hyalopterous, hyalosome, hyalosporous

hydro-, hydra-, hydr-, hyd- (Gk., water) For other "water" words, see **aqua-** and see **humid, hygro-, hyeto-, omoro-, pluvial, udo-,** and **uro-** for similarities.

   Qualifying words: anhydrase, anhydrous, anhydration, anhydrobiosis, aphydrotactic, aphydrotaxis, dehydrate, dehydration, euhydrophile, euhydrophilous, euhydrophily, hydragogue, hydrant, hydranth, hydrate, hydraulic, hydraulically, hydraulics, hydremia, hydrobiology, hydrobios, hydrocarpic, hydrocephalus, hydrocephaly, hydrochimous, hydrochoric, hydrochory, hydrochthophyte, hydrocleistogamic, hydrocleistogamy, hydrocole, hydrocolous, hydrocryptophyte, hydrocycle, hydrodynamic, hydrodynamics, hydroelectricity, hydrofoil, hydrogen, hydrogeology, hydrogeophyte, hydrographer, hydrographic, hydrography, hydrohemicryptophyte, hydroid, hydrokinetic, hydrokinetically, hydrolatry, hydrologist, hydrology, hydrolysis, hydromancer, hydromancy, hydromechanics, hydromegathermic, hydromel, hydrometallurgy, hydrometeor, hydrometer, hydrometric, hydrometrical, hydrometry, hydromorph, hydromorphic, hydronastic, hydronasty, hydro-naut, hydronymy, hydropathology, hydropa-thy, hydrophile, hydrophilic, hydrophilous, hydrophobe, hydrophobia, hydrophobicity, hydrophone, hydrophyte, hydroplane, hydro-planing, hydropneumothorax, hydroponicist, hydroponics, hydroponist, hydropower, hy-droscope, hydroseisma, hydrosol, hydro-space, hydrosphere, hydrostatics, hydrotac-tic, hydrotaxis, hydrotherapeutics, hydrother-apy, hydrothermal, hydrotribophile, hydrotri-bophilous, hydrotribophily, hydrotropic, hy-drotropism, hydrozoan, hydrus, magnetohy-drodynamics, pneumohydrothorax

hyeto-, hyet- (Gk., rain, rain fall) Also see **ombro-, pluv-, udo-, urino-,** and **uro-** for other "rain" words.

    Qualifying words: hyetography, hyeto-graphic, hyetographical, hyetography, hyeto-logical, hyetologist, hyetology

hygieio-, hygiei-, hygio-, hygi- (Gk., healthy, healthful, wholesome, sound [in body]) Also see **cura-, iatro-, medi-,** and **sana-** for related "healing" words.

    Qualifying words: Hygeia, Hygea, hygeio-latry, Hygia, hygieiology, hygiene, hygienic, hygienics, hygienist, hygieology, hygiology

hygio- See **hygieio-** for examples.

hygro-, hygr- (Gk., moist, wet) See **humid** and compare with **aqua-** and **hydro-** for related "wet, water" words.

    Qualifying words: aerohygrophile, aero-hygrophilous, aerohygrophily, aerohygro-phobe, aerohygrophobous, aerohygrophoby, hygroblepharic, hygrocole, hygrocolous, hy-grograph, hygrophanous, hygrography, hy-grokinesis, hygrokinetic, hygromania, hygro-maniac, hygrometer, hygrometric, hygrome-try, hygro-orthokinesis, hygro-orthokinetic, hygropetric, hygrophilly, hygrophilous, hygro-phobia, hygrophobic, hygrophyte, hygro-scope, hygroscopic, hygroscopically, hygro-scopicity, hygroscopy, hygrotactic, hygrotax-is, hygrothermal, hygrothermograph, hygro-thermography, hygrothermometer hygrotro-pic, hygrotropism,

hyl- (wood, forest) See **hylo-** for examples.

hyle- (wood, forest) See **hylo-** for examples.

hylo-, hyle-, hyl- (Gk., wood, forest, sub-stance, matter) Also see **also-, arbor-, dendro-, ligni-, nemo-, sylv-,** and **xylo-** for additional "forest, woods" words.

    Qualifying words: helohylophile, helohy-lophilous, helohylophily, hylacole, hylaco-lous, hyle, hylephobia, hylergography, hylic, hylodophile, hylodophilous, hylodophily, hy-lodophyte, hylodophytic, hylogenesis, hylo-geny, hylologist, hylology, hyloma, hylo-pathism, hylopathist, hylophage, hylopha-gous, hylophagy, hylophile, hylophilous, hy-

lophily, hylophobia, hylophyte, hylotheism, hylotheist, hylotomous, hylotropy, hylozoic, hylozoism, hylozoist

hymeno-, hymen- (Gk., membrane, skin; vir-ginal membrane; *hymen* originally denot-ed any membrane. In its present specific meaning, it was first used by Vesalius in 1550)

    Qualifying words: hymen, Hymen (god of marriage in Greek mythology, a refrain of the song sung at the marriages of the ancient Greeks), hymenal, hymeneal (wedding or bridal song), hymenectomy, hymenia, hymen-itis, hymenography, hymenology, Hymen-optera, hymenopteran, hymenopterism, hy-menopterous, hymenorrhaphy, hymenotome, hymenotomy

hyo- (Gk., denoting υ-shaped [upsilon-sha-ped]; hyoid bone, literally, "mere or sim-ple *y*," *ypsilon*)

    Qualifying words: hyoepiglottic, hyoglos-sal, hyoglossus, hyoid, hyolaryngeal, hyo-mandibular, hyomental, hyosternal, hyothy-roid, thyrohyoid

hyper- (Gk., above, over; excessive; abnormal excess [in medicine]; abnormally great or powerful sensation [in physical or patho-logical terms]; highest [in chemical com-pounds]) For additional "over, above" words, see **epi-, super-,** and **ultra-** and compare with **hypo-** and **sub-** for words with opposite meanings.

    Qualifying words: hyperacidity, hyperac-tive, hyperactivity, hyperacusia, hyperacusis, hyperadiposis, hyperadiposity, hyperaesthe-sia, hyperaesthetic, hyperalgesia, hyperalge-sic, hyperalgetic, hyperalgia, hyperaliminta-tion, hyperanakinesis, hyperanakinesia, hy-perbaric, hyperbarism, hyperbenthic, hyper-benthos, hyperbola, hyperbole, hyperbolic, hyperbolically, hyperbolize, hyperbolized, hy-perbolizing, hyperborean, hyperbrachyceph-aly, hypercapnia, hypercapnic, hypercardia, hypercenesthesia, hyperchromatic, hyper-cinesia, hypercinesis, hypercorrection, hyper-critical, hypercryalgesia, hypercryesthesia, hypercytosis, hyperdacryosis, hyperdactylia, hyperdactylism, hyperdactyly, hyperdipsia, hyperdipsic, hyperdontia, hyperdynamia, hy-perdynamic, hyperemia, hyperemesis, hyper-ergasia, hyperereyesthesia, hyperesthesia, hy-peresthetic, hypergamy, hypergeusia, hyper-geusesthesia, hyperglycemia, hyperglycemic, hypergnosis, hyperhidrosis, hyperhypnosis, hyperirritability, hyperkeratosis, hyperkera-totic, hyperkinesia, hyperkinesis, hyperkinet-ic, hyperlogia, hypermarket, hypermastia, hy-permetropia, hypermnesia, hypermyesthesia, hyperorexia, hyperosmia, hyperparasite, hy-perpathia, hyperpepsia, hyperphagia, hyperphonia, hyperphrenia, hyperpnea, hyperpneic, hyperpyretic, hyperpyrexia, hypersaline, hypersensitive, hypersensitivity, hypersensitization, hypersomnia, hypersomnia, hypersonic, hypertension, hyperthermal, hyperthermalgesia, hyperthermia, hyperthermoaesthesia, hyperthermoesthesia, hyperthyroidism, hypertonic, hypertrichosis, hypertrophic, hypertrophy, hyperventilate, hyperventilation

hyphen (Gk. > L., together, in one, as a single word; from **hypo-** [under]; a short line (-) joining parts of a word)

    Qualifying words: hypheme, hyphen, hyphenate, hyphenated, hyphenic, hyphenism, hyphenize, hyphenization

hypno-, hypn- (Gk., sleep) Also see **coma**[1], **dorm-, narco-, somni-,** and **sopor-** for additional "sleep" words.

    Qualifying words: ahypnia, anhypnia, ahypnosis, anhypnosis, archehypnotic, autohypnosis, autohypnotic, euhypnia, hyperhypnosis, hypnagogic, hypnagogue, hypnalgia, hypnanalysis, hypnapagogic, hypnesthesia, hypnic, hypnoanalytic, hypnocatharsis, hypnocinematograph, hypnocyst, hypnodontics, hypnogenesis, hypnogenic, hypnogenous, hypnogogic, hypnoid, hypnoidal, hypnolepsy, hypnologist, hypnology, hypnonarcoanalysis, hypnonarcosis, hypnopathy, hypnopedia, hypnophobia, hypnopompic, Hypnos, hypnosis, hypnotherapy, hypnotic, hypnotise, hypnotist, hypnotize, hypnotizer, hypnotoid, hypnotoxin, hypnudism, Hypnus, parahypnosis

hypo-, hyp- (Gk., under, below, beneath; less than; too little) Also see **infra-, sub-,** and **subter-** for other "under, below" words.

    Qualifying words: acrohypothermy, hypalgesic, hyphen, hypnagogue, hypoacidity, hypoacusis, hypoalgesia, hypobaric, hypobaropathy, hypobiosis, hypobiotic, hypocapnia, hypocarpogean, hypocarpogenous, hypocaust, hypocenter, hypochondria, hypochondriac, hypochromemia, hypochromic, hypocrisy, hypocrite, hypodactylia, hypodactylism, hypodactyly, hypoderma, hypodermal, hypodermatic, hypodermic, hypodermis, hypodipsia, hypodontia, hypodynamia, hypodynamic, hypoemia, hypoertgia, hypoergy, hypoesthesia, hypogaeic, hypogalactia, hypogalactous, hypogastric, hypogastrium, hypogean, hypogeous, hypogeusia, hypoglossitis, hypoglottis, hypognathous, hypohidrosis, hypohidrotic, hypohydremia, hypohypnotic, hypokinemia, hypokinesia, hypokinesis, hypokinetic, hypoleucocytosis, hypoleukemia, hypoliposis, hypolithic, hypologia, hypomania, hypomastia, hypomazia, hypomnesia, hypomnesis, hypomotility, hypomyotonia, hyponeuria, hypophonia, hypophrasia, hypophyllous, hypopnea, hypoopteran, hyposarca, hyposensitiveness, hyposomia, hyposomniac, hypostasis, hypotaxia, hypotxis, hypotension, hypo-

tenuse, hypothermal, hypothermesthesia, hypothermic, hypothermia, hypothesia, hypothetical, hypotoxicity, hypotrichosis, hypotrophy, hypoventilation, hypovitaminosis, hypoxemia, hypoxia

hypso-, hyps-, hypsi- (Gk., high, highest, height; on high) Also see **acro-** and **alti-**.

    Qualifying words: hypsicephalic, hypsithermal, hypsodont, hypsographic, hypsographical, hypsography, hypsokinesis, hypsometer, hypsometric, hypsometrist, hypsometry, hypsophobia, hypsophyll, hypsotherapy

hystero-, hyster-, hysteri- (Gk., the womb or uterus; hysteria) Hysteric disturbances, which most frequently occur in women were ascribed erroneously by ancient Greeks to the influence of the womb and were, for this reason, called *hysteria*, "disease of the womb."

    See **colpo-, episio-, vagino-, vulvo-,** and **utero-** for other for related words.

    Qualifying words: hysteralgia, hysterectomy, hysteresis, hysteria, hysteric(s), hysterical, hystericism, hysterics, hysteriform, hysterocatalepsy, hysterodynia, hysteroepilepsy, hysterogenic, hysterogram, hysterography, hysteroid, hysterolith, hysterology, hysterolysis, hysterometer, hysteromyoma, hysteromyomectomy, hysteropathy, hysteroplasty, hysteropsychosis, hysterorrhexis, hysteroscope, hysteroscopy, hysterothermometry

I i

I   See **ego** (L.) for examples. Also see **auto-** (self) and **sui-** (self) for similarities.

-ia   (Gk. > L., a suffix which forms nouns):
     ¹ names of countries, such as *Germania*
     ² names of diseases, such as *pneumonia*
     ³ names of chemical alkaloids, such as *morphia*
     ⁴ names of flowers from the names of the discoverer or the person who introduced the flower, such as *begonia*
     ⁵ names of classes and orders in botany and zoology, such as *Amphibia*
     See **-ia** in the SUFFIXES section in **Appendix K** for more *examples* of the above and for other word endings.

-ial   (L., a suffix which forms English adjectives from Latin adjectives ending with **-is** or **-ius** with meanings which include "pertaining to or relating to, or characterized by") Also see the SUFFIXES section in **Appendix K**).
     Qualifying words: clestial, financial, industrial, managerial, ministerial, racial

-iasis   (Gk. > L.)
     ¹ a process
          Qualifying word: odontiasis
     ² a morbid condition
          Qualifying word: elephantiasis

iatro-, iatr-, -iatry, -iatria, -iatric, -iatrics, -iatry, -iatrist (Gk., physician, heal, cure, treat; medical) Also see **cura-, medi-, sana-,** and **therap-** for additional "healing" words and **hygieio-** for "healthful" words.
     Qualifying words: emporiatric, emporiatrics, emporiatrician, geriatricism, geriatrics, gyniatrics, hippiatric, hippiatry, iatrarchy, iatric, iatrochemical, iatrochemist, iatrochemistry, iatrogenesis, iatrogenic, iatrology, iatromechanical, iatrophilia, iatrophysical, iatrophysicist, iatrophysics, iatrotechnical, iatrotechnique, odontoiatria, pediatrician, pediatrics, physiatrics, podiatrist, podiatry, psychiatric, psychiatry, zoiatria, zoiatrist

     Iatrogenesis refers to any illness, injury, or fatality that is the direct result of medical intervention (doctor induced), ranging from inappropriate treatment to harmful drug interaction, misinterpretation of a lab test, or a fatal reaction to an injection of penicillin or other medication. Adverse side effects and dangerous interactions between drugs are probably the most common types of *iatrogenic* illnesses.

-ibility   (L., a suffix which means *able to* [be]; a variation of **-ability**) Also examine SUFFIXES in **Appendix K** for more word endings.
     Qualifying word: defensibility, flexibility, sensibility,

-ible   (L., can be done, worthy of being, able to be, tending to, capacity for) For other examples, see **-able** and the SUFFIXES section in **Appendix K**.
     Qualifying words: contemptible, contractible, credible, discernible, edible, flexible, invisible, irresistible, legible, reducible, visible

-ic   (Gk., pertaining to; of the nature of; in chemistry, it denotes a higher valence of the element than is expressed by **-ous**) Also see **-ac, -tic,** and SUFFIXES in the **Appendix K** section for additional examples.
     Qualifying words: avionic, electronic, epidemic, logic, logomachic, music, nitric, rhetoric, slavonic

-ice   (L., quality of, state of) A suffix which forms nouns. See **-ice** in **Appendix K** for other examples.
     Qualifying words: accomplice, avarice

ice, crystal   See **crystallo-** for examples and compare with **crymo-, cryo-, frig-,** and **psychro-** for similarities.

ichno-, ichn-   (Gk., track, trace, footprint) Also examine **pedi-** and **podo-** for other "foot" words.
     Qualifying words: ichnite, ichnocoenosis, ichnofauna, ichnoflora, ichnofossil, ichnogram, ichnographic, ichnographical, ichnographically, ichnography, ichnolite, ichnolithology, ichnological, ichnology, ichnomancy, neoichnology, palaeoichnology

ichthyo-, ichthy-, ichth-   (Gk., fish) Also see **pisci-** for additional "fish" words.
     Qualifying words: ichthic, ichthin, ichthism, ichthus, ichthyodont, ichthyofauna, ichthyographic, ichthyography, ichthyoid, ichthyolatrous, ichthyolatry, ichthyolite, ichthyologic, ichthyological, ichthyologically, ichthyologist, ichthyology, ichthyomancy, ichthyomantist, ichthyomorphic, ichthyomor-

phous, ichthyomorphs, ichthyoneuston, ichthyoneustont, ichthyophagia, ichthyophagi, ichthyophagist, ichthyophagous, ichthyophagus, ichthyophagy, ichthyophobia, ichthyoplankton, ichthyopterygia, ichthyornis, ichthyosarcotoxin, ichthyosaur, ichthyosauria, ichthysaurian, ichthyosaurous, ichthyosaurus, ichthyosis, ichthyotoxicology, ichthyotoxin, ichthys, ichthysimus, ichthyosarcotoxism, palaeichthyology, paleichthyology, paleoichthyology

The Greek word for fish was also an acronym for *Iesous CHristos, THeon Yios, Soter* (Jesus Christ, God's Son, Saviour) and it is said to be the secret symbol used by early Christians to communicate with each other. They did this by drawing a fish-like sign or symbol: ⟨⤬ This symbol is found on many seals, rings, urns, and tombstones from the early Christian period; and for some, it was a mystical charm.

-ician (Gk., specialist in, practitioner of) Also see the SUFFIXES section in **Appendix K** for other word endings.

> **Qualifying words:** electrician, technician

icono-, icon- (Gk., image, likeness; sacred image) Also see **eido-** and **idol** for other "image" words.

> **Qualifying words:** icon, iconic, iconically, iconicity, iconism, iconoclasm, iconoclast, iconoclastic, iconographer, iconographic, iconography, iconolater, iconolatry, iconological, iconologist, iconology, iconomachy, iconomania, iconomatography, iconometer, iconophil, iconophobia, iconophobe, iconophobic, iconometry, iconoscope, iconostasis, iconotrophy, iconotype

icosa-, icos-, icosi-, eicosa- (Gk., twenty) Also see the NUMBERS section in **Appendix G** for other numerical elements

> **Qualifying words:** icosacolic, icosandrous, icosahedron, icosanoid, icosasemic, icosidodecahedron

-ics (Gk., a suffix which forms nouns and is usually used to form names of arts and sciences) Also see the SUFFIXES section in **Appendix K** for other word endings.

> **Qualifying words:** dynamics, electronics, gymastics, mathematics, optics, physics, polymics

-id (L., state, condition; having, being, pertaining to) Also see the SUFFIXES section in **Appendix K** for other word endings.

> **Qualifying words:** avid, florid, frigid

-ida (L., a suffix used to form names of zoological groups, classes, and orders) Also see **-idae** and SUFFIXES in **Appendix K** for other word endings with the same or similar meanings.

> **Qualifying word:** Arachnida

-idae (Gk. > L., a suffix used to form the names of families in zoology) For additional words of this type, see **-ida.**

> **Qualifying words:** Basilosauridae, Protocetidae, Mesonychidae, Agorophiidae, Balaenopteridae, Balaenidae, Eschrichtiidae, Platanistidae, Monodontidae, Delphinidae

idea See **ideo-** for examples.

ideo- (Gk., idea, form)

> **Qualifying words:** ideational, ideoglandular, ideogram, ideograph, ideographic, ideography, ideoligial, ideologist, ideologue, ideology, ideometer, ideomotor, ideophrenia

idi- (Gk., peculiar, personal) See **idio-.**

idio-, idi- (Gk., peculiar, one's own, personal, private; of or pertaining to one's self; distinct, separate, alone) For other related "self" words, see **auto-, ipse,** and **sui-.**

> **Qualifying words:** idiobiology, idioblast, idiochromatic, idiocrasy, idiocy, idiodynamic, idiodynamics, idiogamous, idiogamy, idiogenesis, idioglossia, idioglottic, idiogram, idiograph, idiographic, idiohypnotism, idiolalia, idiolect, idiom, idiomatic, idiomatric, idiomorphic, idiomorphism, idiomorphous, idiomuscular, idiopathic, idiopathy, idioplasm, idiosyncrasy, idiosyncratic, idiot, idiotic, idiotropic, idiot savant

-idium (Gk., a suffix meaning smaller or lesser) Also see the SUFFIXES section in **Appendix K** for other word endings.

ido-, id- (Gk., image, figure) See **eido-** for examples.

idol (L., image, likeness, specter, apparition) Also see **eido-** and **icono-** for other "image" words and compare with **form-** and **morpho-.**

> **Qualifying words:** idolater, idolatress, idolatrous, idolatry, idolism, idolize, idolomania

ig- (L., do, act; not, without) See **in-**[1] or **ag-** (do, act) for examples. Don't confuse this **ig-** with the next one which means "fire" or "burn".

ign-, igni-, ignis- (L., fire, burn) Also see **ars-, caust-, crema-, flagr-, incend-, pyro-,** and **volcan-** for additional "fire, burn" words.

> **Qualifying words:** gelignite, igneous, ignescent, igniextirpation, ignigenous, ignioper-

ation, ignipedites, ignipotent, ignipuncture, ignis, ignisation, ignite, ignition, ignitron, ignivomous, *ignus fatuus*

ignorant See **rudi-** for examples.

il- (L., not, without) See **in-**[1] for examples.

-ile (L., ability to, capable of, suitable for, pertaining to) Also see SUFFIXES in **Appendix K** for additional elements and examples.

> **Qualifying words:** agile, docile, domicile, facile, fertile, fragile, infantile, juvenile, mobile, puerile, senile, tactile, virile, volatile

ileo-, ile- (Gk > L., [from L. *ile, ileum,* or *ilium* (s.), *ilia* (pl.), groin, flank, lower part of the body, gut, bowels, abdomen, loins; from Gk. *eileos,* verbal of *eilein,* to roll or twist up tightly; used earlier interchangeably with *ilium,* but later referred to the entire intestine], last division of the small intestine) A combining form which denotes the *ileum* or the lower section of the small intestine. Also see **ilio-** for related words.

> **Qualifying words:** gastroileostomy, ileitis, ileocecal, ileocecostomy, ileocecum, ileocolic, ileocolitis, ileocolonic, ileocolotomy, ileocutaneous, ileopathy, ileotomy, ileum, ileus

ilio-, ili- (Gk. > L., [from L. *ile, ileum,* or *ilium* (s.), *ilia* (pl.), groin, flank, lower part of the body, gut, bowels, abdomen, loins, from Gk. *eileos,* verbal of *eilein* to roil or twist up tightly; early used interchangeably with *ileum,* but later used with os, bone (*os ilium*) to denote the bone of the soft parts], hip bone) A combining form denoting the illium or one of the broad upper bones of the pelvis. Also examine **ileo-** for other "groin, gut" words and **os-, osteo-, sacro-,** and **skeleto-** for other "bone" words.

> **Qualifying words:** iliococcygeal, iliocolotomy, iliocostal, iliodorsal, iliofemoral, iliofemoroplasty, iliohypogastric, iliolumbar, iliometer, iliopelvic, iliosacral, iliotibial

-ility (L., ability, ability to) See the SUFFIXES section in **Appendix K** for additional examples.

> **Qualifying words:** capability, fragility, sensibility

illusion, show See **phantasm** for examples.

im- (L., not, without) See **in-**[1] for examples.

image, likeness For examples, examine **eido-, icono-, idol, morph-,** and **-oid**.

immerse, plunge See **bapti-** and **merg-** for examples.

immersion, dip See **bapti-** and **merg-** for examples.

imitate, act See **mimo-** for examples.

imperfect See **atelo-** for examples.

impulse, push See **osmo-** (#2) for examples.

in, within See **en-** for examples.

in-[1] (ig-, il-, im-, ir-) (L., not, without) Also see **a-, an-** (Gk.) and **non-** for other "not" words. This **in-** becomes **i-** before *gn,* **il-** before *l,* **im-** before *b* and *m,* and **ir-** before *r.* Don't confuse this **in-** with the following **in-,** which means "in, within," etc.

> **Qualifying words:** ignorance, illegal, illiterate, imbalance, immaculate, immature, immovable, improbable, inaccurate, inactive, incorrect, irrational, irregular

in-[2] (il-, ir-, im-) (L., in, into, within, inside, on, toward) Also examine **endo-, ento, intra-,** and **intro-** for additional "in" words. The **in-** changes or is assimilated to **il-** before *l,* as with illuminate, to **im-** before *b,* as with imbibe; before **m,** as with immediate; before *p,* as with implant; and to **ir-** before *r,* as with irrigate. Note the differences between this **in-** and the previous one.

> **Qualifying words:** illuminate, imbibe, immigrate, import, inaugurate, incalescent, incandescent, inflammable, inject, inscribe, irradiate

incarcerat-, incarcera- (L., from *in-* + *carcer;* prison, jail; an enclosed place)

> **Qualifying words:** cancel, carcer, incarcerate, incarcerated, incarcerating, incarceration, incarcerator

incend-, incens- (L., fire; to burn, to set fire to, to kindle [from *in-* and *candere,* to shine, be white; to glow with heat]) Also see **ars-, caust-, crema-, flagr-, flam-, ign-, pyro-,** and **volcan-** for additional "fire" words.

> **Qualifying words:** censer, frankincense, incendiaries, incendiarism, incendiary, incense, incensed, incensing

incens- (L., fire, burn) See **incend-** for examples.

incision, cut See **-cise, -ectomy, sec-, -tom,** and **tomo-** for examples.

inclination See **clino-** for examples.

incline, slant See **clino-** for examples.

incline, tend toward See **flect-, gyro-, tors-, trop-, -plex, stroph-, vers-,** and **volv-**.

incomplete See **atelo-** for examples.

increase, grow See **auxano-** and **cresc-**.

individual, being See **onto-** for examples.

-ine (L.) Also see SUFFIXES in **Appendix K** for other word endings.

> ¹ of, pertaining to; of the nature of, like
>
> > **Qualifying words:** acarine, accipitrine, adulterine, aedine, alaudine, alcidine, alectoridine, anatine, anguine, anopheline, anserine, antelopine, aquiline, asinine, aspine, avine, bisontine, bombycine, bovine, bubaline, buteonine, caballine, cameline, canine, caprine, capreoline, cathartine, ceratorhine, cervine, cervuline, charadine, ciconine, colubrine, columbine, corvine, cricetine, crocodiline, crotaline, cuculine, culicine, cygnine, cyprine, dacelonine, delphine, didelphine, didine, elaphine, elephantine, equine, ermine, falconine, feline, formicine, fringilline, fulciline, fuliguline, galline, garruline, gazelline, giraffine, glirine, herpestine, hippocampine, hippopotamine, hippotigrine, hircine, hirundine, homarine, hominine, hyenine, hylobatine, hystricine, ibidine, icterine, lacertine, lapine, larine, lemurine, leonine, leopardine, leporine, limacine, lumbricine, lupine, lutrine, lyncine, macropine, macropodine, manatine, megapterine, meleagrine, meline, mephitine, milvine, mimine, moschine, murine, muscapine, musine, musteline, myrmicine, nestorine, noctilionine, octopine, odontophorine, oryctolagine, osine, ostracine, ovibovine, ovine, pantherine, pardine, passerine, pavonine, perdicine, percesocine, phasianine, phocaenine, phocine, picine, piscine, porcine, poscine, procyonine, psittacine, pteropine, pulicine, ralline, rangiferine, ranine, rhinocerine, rucervine, rupicaprine, sabelline, salamandrine, salamandrine, saline, sciurine, sealine, serpentine, soricine, strigine, struthine, sturnine, suilline, suine, talpine, tapirine, taurine, tetraonine, tineine, tigrine, tolypeutine, tringine, trochiline, trochilidine, turdine, ursine, vaccine, vespine, viperine, vituline, viverrine, volucrine, vulpine, vulturine, zebrine
>
> ² forms abstract nouns
>
> > **Qualifying words:** discipline, doctrine, medicine
>
> ³ forms feminine common nouns
>
> > **Qualifying word:** heroine
>
> ⁴ also forms chemical words
>
> > **Qualifying words:** bromine, chlorine, cocaine, cystine, gasoline, quinine, saline

infero- (under, below) See **infra-** for examples.

inflammation See **-itis** for examples.

infra-, infero-, infer- (L., under, below, beneath) Also see **hypo-, sub-,** and **subter-** for other "under, below" words.

> **Qualifying words:** inferior, inferiority, inferobranchiate, inferolateral, inferomedian, inferoposterior, infracardiac, infraclavicular, infraclusion, infracostal, infraglotic, infraclusion, *infra dignitatem*, infraglottic, infrahuman, infralabial, inframandibular, inframaxillary, inframundane, infranasal, infrapsychic, infrared, infrasonic, infrasound, infrastructure, infratracheal, infraversion

inhabit, reside See **-cole** for examples.

inhibit, hinder See **koly-** for examples.

injurious, harmful See **nox-** for examples.

inner ear See **cochle-** for examples.

inquiry, request See **rog-** for examples.

insecti-, insecto- (L., a bug; literally, "cut into," from *insectum*, with a notched or divided body) Also see **entomo-** for additional "insect" words.

> **Qualifying words:** insectaries, insectarium, insectary, insecticidal, insecticide, insectifuge, insectiphobia, Insectivora, insectivore, insectivorous, insectology, insectologist

inside, within See **endo-, intra-,** and **intro-**.

instrument, device See **-tron** for examples. A suffix which forms nouns.

insula-, insulino-, insulin-, insulo-, insul-, isle (L., island) For other "island" words, see **neso-**.

> **Qualifying words:** isolate, isolation, isolationist, insular, insularity, insulation, insulator, insulin, insulinase, insulinemia, insulinlipodystrophy, insulinogenesis, peninsular, insulism, insulopathic, peninsula

intellect-, intellig- (L., know, learn) Also see **cogni-, epistemo-, gno-, mne-, not-,** and **sci-** for other "know" words.

> **Qualifying words:** intellect, intellectual, intellectualism, intellectualization, intelligence, intelligent, intelligentsia, intelligible, unintelligible

intellig- (L. know) See **intellect-**.

inter- (L., between [also: among, mutually, together]) Compare with **intra-** and **intro-**.

> **Qualifying words:** interact, interactive, intercede, intercellular, intercept, intercommunication, intercontinental, intercostal, interdental, interdict, interdigital, interdigitation, interdigitory, interface, interfere, intergalactic, interim, interior, interject, interjection, interkinesis, interlock, interlocution, interlude, interlunar, intermarry, intermodal, internal, international, interrogate, interrupt, intersect, interurban, intervene, interview

intestines See **duodeno-, entero-,** and **ileo-**.

into See **endo-, ento-, intra-,** and **intro-**.

intra- (L., within, inside, on the inside) Also see **en-, endo-, eso-, into-, in-,** and **intro-** for other "within, inside" words.

>Qualifying words: intra-abdominal, intra-aural, intracardiac, intracellular, intracoastal, intracorporeal, intracranial, intracutaneous, intradermal, intradermic, intrados, intrafebrile, intragalactic, intragastric, intrahepatic, intramural, intramuscular, intramyocardial, intranational, intraocular, intrapsychic, intrapyretic, intrastate, intravenous, *intra vitam*

intro- (L., within, inside, into, inward) Also examine **en-, endo-, ento-, eso-, in-,** and **intra-** and note the differences between **intro-** and **intra-**.

>Qualifying words: introduce, introduction, introductory, introflection, introflexion, introgastric, introjection, intromission, introrse, introspect, introspection, introversion, introvert

investigation, search See **scrut-** for examples.

invisible, concealed Examine **adelo-, calyp-, clandestine, crypto-, myster-,** as well as **occult-** for related words.

-ior (L., pertaining to) Also see the SUFFIXES section in **Appendix K** for additional word endings.

>Qualifying words: anterior, excelsior, inferior, posterior, superior

ipse, ipsi-, ipso (L., self) Also see **auto-** and **sui-** for similar examples.

>Qualifying words: ipsative, *ipse dixit*, ipsefact, ipsilateral, ipsilaterally, *ipsissima verba*, ipsiversive, ipso facto, *ipso jure*

ir- (L., not, without) See **in-**[1] for examples.

irido-, irid-, iri-, iris- (Gk., iris [relating to the eye]; the rainbow; colored portion of the eye [originally, "something bent *or* curved"]) Also see **pupillo-** for relationships to the "eye."

>Qualifying words: iridalgia, iridectomy, iridemia, irides, iridescence, iridiagnosis, iridic, iridescent, iridium, iridization, iridochoroiditis, iridocyte, iridodiagnosis, iridokinesia, iridokinesis, iridokinetic, iridology, iridolysis, iridomalacia, iridomotor, iridesis, iridopathy, iridopupillary, iridotomy, iris, Iris, irisopsia, iritic, iritis, iritomy

iris- See **irido-** for examples.

iron See **ferro-** and **sider-** for examples.

irregular, contrary See **para-** for examples.

irregular, varied See **poikilo-** for examples.

-ise (L., do, make, cause) Examine **-ize** and SUFFIXES in **Appendix K** for examples.

island See **insula-** and **neso-** for examples.

-ism (Gk., belief in, practice of, condition of) Also see **-ist** for similar examples and SUFFIXES in **Appendix K** for additional word endings.

>Qualifying words: agnosticism, alcoholism, altruism, antagonism, asceticism, atheism, colloquialism, communism, deism, dogmatism, euphemism, fatalism, geocentrism, hypnotism, malapropism, misologism, myrmecophilism, narcissism, neologism, plagiarism, prohibitionism, robotism, sexism, somnambulism, spoonerism, vandalism

iso-, is- (Gk., same, equal, similar, alike) Also see **equ-, homo-** (Gk.), **homeo-, -oid, pari-, simal-,** and **tauto-** for additional "same" words and examine **aniso-** (Gk.) for similar meanings.

>Qualifying words: anisogamy, geoisotherm, isacoustic, isandrous, isobaric, isobar, isobathytherm, isochromatic, isochron, isochronal, isochronism, isochronous, isocracy, isodactylous, isodactyly, isodemic, isodont, isodynamic, isogamy, isogenetic, isogeotherm, isogeothermal, isogeothermic, isogloss, isognathous, isogonal, isogonic, isohaline, isolateral, isolume, isomerous, isomeric, isometric isomorph, isomorphic, isomorphism, isomorphous, isonymous, isonomy, isonym, isopach, isopachous, isopathy, isophagous, isophot, isophyllous, isopluvial, isoptera, isopterous, isopters, isosceles, isoseismal, isotach, isotachy, isotherm, isothermal, isothermic, isotonic, isotope, isotoxic, isotoxin, isozoic

-ist (Gk. and L., one who believes in; one who is engaged in) Also see **-ee, -eer, -ism** and SUFFIXES in **Appendix K**.

>Qualifying words: antagonist, apologist, archeologist, bigamist, biologist, cardiologist, chemist, chiropodist, communist, dentist, dermatologist, dramatist, entomologist, evangelist, gastrologist, geologist, gerontologist, graphologist, gynecologist, herpetologist, ichthyologist, internist, microbiologist, monarchist, naturalist, neurologist, oculist, ophthalmologist, optometrist, ornithologist, orthodontist, orthopedist, pathologist, phonologist, phrenologist, podiatrist, psychiatrist, psychologist, scatologist, seismologist, socialist, spelologist, symbolist, terrorist, toxicologist

it- (L., travel) See **itiner-** for examples.

itch See **acaro-** and **amycho-** for examples.

-ite (Gk., one connected with, inhabitant of [also used to indicate chemicals, minerals, etc.]) Also see the SUFFIXES section in **Appendix K** for other word endings.

>Qualifying words: graphite, Israelite

itiner-, it-, -it (L., go, walk, way; travel, journey) Also see **ambul-, empori-,** and **grad-** for words with similar meanings.

Qualifying words: adit, ambition, circuit, circuitous, circuitously, circuitousness, coition, coitus, exit, inevitable, initial, initiate, introit, itinerancy, itinerant, itinerary, itinerate, janitor, limit, obituary, sedition, seditionary, seditioinist, seditious, seditiously, transient, transiently, transientness, transit, transition, transitional, transitory, transitive

-itious (L., tending to, characterized by) Also see SUFFIXES in **Appendix K** for other word endings.

Qualifying word: adventitious, ambitious, expeditious, fictitious

-itis (Gk., inflammation, burning sensation; by extension, disease associated with inflammation) This suffix has come to mean "inflammation of" but originally it meant "pertaining to" or "of the." The Greek word **nosos** ("disease") was either expressed or understood, although it might not be included with the basic element. For example, *bursitis nosos* would mean "disease of the bursa."

Qualifying words: acroarthritis, acrodermatitis, acromastitis, actilnoneuritis, adenitis, adipositis, adrenalitis, allergyrhinitis, angiitis, angioleukitis, angiopancreatitis, angiotitis, appendicitis, arachnitis, arachnoiditis, arachnorhinitis, arteritis, arthritis, blepharitis, bronchiolitis, bronchitis, bursitis, capsulitis, carditis, celiomositis, celitis, cellulitis, cerebellitis, cerebritis, cervicitis, cheilitis, cheirarthritis, cholecystitis, chondritis, colitis, chorditis, conjunctivitis, coxitis, cystitis, dermatitis, dermatomyositis, diverticulitis, duodenitis, encephalitis, endocarditis, endometritis, enteritis, enterocolitis, epididymitis, fibrositis, gastritis, gingivitis, hepatitis, hyalitis, ileitis, iritis, keratitis, laminitis, laryngitis, lymphadenitis, lymphangitis, mastitis, mastoiditis, meningomyelitis, metritis, meningitis, myelitis, myocarditis, myositis, nephritis, neuritis, omphalitis, onychitis, oophoritis, oophorosalpingitis, ophthalmitis, osteitis, osteochondritis, otitis, ovaritis, pancreatitis, panophthalmitis, panotitis, pansinusitis, parotitis, perialienitis, periappendicitis, pericarditis, perimastitis, periodontitis, periostitis, peritendinitis, peritonitis, perixenitis, pharyngitis, phlebitis, phrenitis, pleuritis, pneumonitis, poikilodermatonyositis, poliomyelitis, retinitis, rhinitis, sinusitis, sphenoiditis, splenitis, spondylitis, stomatitis, tendinitis, tendonitis, tenonitis, thrombophlebitis, tephromyelitis, tonsilitis, toxicodermatitis, tracheitis, tympanitis, ulitis, uloglossitis, utheritis, uteritis, vaginitis, vulvitis, valvulitis

-ive (L., tending to; of the quality of) Also see SUFFIXES in **Appendix K** for additional examples.

Qualifying words: cursive, festive, pensive, pervasive, regressive, sedative

-ize (**-ise**) (L., do; make; cause) Also see **ag-, fac-, stru-,** and SUFFIXES in **Appendix K** for additional meanings.

Qualifying words: amortize, ostracize, satirize, sterilize, subsidize, temporize

J j

jac- (L., throw) See **jet-** for examples.

jail, prison See **incarcerat-** for examples.

Janus (L., door, entrance) Janus was god of gates and doors, represented with two faces. Also see **port-** for other "door" words.

> **Qualifying words:** janiceps, janitor, janitrix, January, Janus

jar, bottle See **amphor-** for examples.

jaw See **gnatho-, mandibulo-,** and **maxillo-** for examples.

jet-, -ject, -jecting, -jected, -jection, -jector, -jectory; jac- (L., throw, send, fling, hurl, cast; gush; spurt) Also see **ballo-** and **miss-** for additional meanings.

> **Qualifying words:** abject, abjectly, abjectness, adjacent, adjective, conjectural, conjecture, deject, dejected, dejection, ejaculate, ejaculation, eject, ejection, inject, injection, interject, interjection, jactation, jactitation, jaculatory, jet, jetsam, jettison, jetty, jut, object, objection, objectionable, objective, project, projectile, projection, projectionist, projective, projector, reject, rejecter, rejection, subjacent, subject, subjective, subjectivity, traject, trajectory

-ject (L., throw) See **jet-** for examples.

jest, play See **lud-** for examples.

join, unite See **junct-** for examples.

joining in a seam See **-rhaph** for examples.

joint(s) between bones See **arthro-** for examples.

journey, travel See **itiner-** for examples.

jud-, judic- (L., decide, judge) Also examine **crim-** and **jus-** for other examples.

> **Qualifying words:** adjudge, adjudicate, judge, judicatory, judicial, judiciary, judicious, judgmatic, judgment, judicable, judicature, judicial, judiciary, judicious, prejudge, prejudice, prejudicial,

junct, join, jug- (L., join, unite)

> **Qualifying words:** adjoin, adjunct, conjoin, conjoint, conjugal, conjugate, conjugation, conjunct, conjunction, conjunctive, conjuncture, disjoin, disjoint, disjointed, disjunct, disjuncture, enjoin, heterojunction, injunction, joinder, joint, junction, juncture, junta, rejoin, rejoiner, subjoin, subjugate, subjugation, subjunctive

jus-, just-, jur- (L., right, justice, law) Also see **crim-** and **jud-** for additional examples.

> **Qualifying words:** abjure, adjure, conjuration, conjure, conjurer, conjuring, conjuror, injury, juridical, jurisconsult, jurisdiction, jurisprudence, jurist, juror, jury, just, justice, justification, justify, objurgation, perjure, perjuror, perjury

justice, law See **crim-, jud-,** and **jus-** for examples.

juveni- (L., young, youthful)

> **Qualifying words:** junior, juvenal, juvenescence, juvenescent, juvenile, juvenilia, juvenility, rejuvenate, rejuvenation, rejuvenator, rejuvenescence, rejuvenescent

juxta-, juxt- (L., beside; close by, close to, near) Also see **para-** (by the side of, *or* near) and **proximo-** for additional "near" words.

> **Qualifying words:** juxta-articular, juxtapose, juxtaposition, juxtaspinal

K k

kaino-, kain- (Gk., new, recent, fresh) See **ceno-²** for examples.

kako-, kak- (Gk., bad, harsh, wrong) Examine **caco-** for examples.

kak- (Gk., bad) See **caco-** for examples.

kalei- (Gk. beautiful) See **calli-** for examples.

kali- (Gk., beautiful) See **calli-** for examples.

kata- (Gk., down, downward) See **cata-** for examples.

keno- (Gk., empty) See **ceno-³** for examples.

kerato- (Gk., horn) See **cerato-** for examples.

kerato-, kerat- (Gk., horn) See **cerato-** for examples.

keep, protect Check with **alexo-**, **-fend-**, and **phylacto-** for examples.

keno- (Gk., empty) See **ceno-** (empty) for examples.

kentro- (Gk., center) See **centro-** for examples.

kephal- (Gk., head) See **cephalo-** for examples.

kerauno- (Gk., thunderbolt) See **cerauno-** for examples.

kero- (Gk., wax) See **cero-** for examples.

kettledrum, eardrum See **tympano-** for examples.

key See **clavi-** and **cleido-** for examples.

kidney See **nephro-, pyelo-,** and **reno-** for examples.

kill, murder See **-cide, mort-,** and **nox-** for examples.

kilo- (Gk., one thousand) In the metric system,

> **kilo-** denotes a whole unit, 10³ (1 000). Also see **giga-** and **milli-** for similar examples; as well as the NUMBERS section in **Appendix G** and the METRIC GROUPS in **Appendix F** for additional numerical and metrical elements.

> **Qualifying words:** kiloampere, kilobaud, kilobit, kilobytes, kilocalorie, kilocurie, kilocycle, kilodyne, kilogram, kilogrammeter, kilohertz, kilohm, kiloliter, kilomegacycle, kilometer, kilo-ohm, kiloparsec, kilopascal, kilorad, kiloroentgen, kilosecond, kiloton, kilounit, kilovolt, kilowatt, kilurane

kind, class See **genus** for examples.

kine-, kin-, kino-, kinesio-, kinesi-, kineto-, kinet-, -kinesia, -kinesis, -kinetic, -kinesias, -kineses, -kinetical, -kinetically (Gk., move, set in motion) Also examine **cine-, mob-,** and **mot-** for other "motion" words.

> **Qualifying words:** akinesia, akinesic, adiadochokinesia, adiadochokinesis, akinaesia, akinaesis, akinaesthesia, akinaesthetic, akinesia, akinesis, akinesthesia, akinesthetic, akinete, akinetic, allokinesis, allokinetic, anaesthekinesia, anesthekinesia, angiokinesis, angiokinetic, archeokinetic, autokinetic, bradykinesia, chronokinetics, dactylakinesia, dyskinesia, electrokinetics, hydrokinesia, hydrokinetics, hyperkinesia, hyperkinesis, kinaesthetic, kineaesthesia, kineaesthetic, kinematics, kinematograph, kinemia, kinemic, kineplastics, kineplasty, kinesalgia, kinescope, kinesia, kinesialgia, kinesiatrics, kinesics, kinesi-esthesiometer, kinesimeter, kinesiology, kinesiometer, kinesioineurosis, kinesiotherapy, kinesiphony, kinesitherapy, kinestasis, kinesthesia, kinesthesiometer, kinesthetic, kinetia, kinetic, kineticist, kinetics, kinetocardiography, kinetogenic, kinetographic, kinetosis, kinetotherapy, kinocilia, kinology, kinomometer, kinopsis, kinotoxin, klinokinesis, orthokinesis, pharmacokinetics, podactylakinesia, psychokinesis, telokinesia, toxicokinetics

kinesi- (Gk., movement) See **kine-** for examples.

kino- (Gk., move) See **kine-** for examples.

kiss See **oscula-** for examples.

klepto-, klept-, clepto-, clept- (Gk., theft, thief, steal) Also see **plagiar-** for additional "stealing" words.

> **Qualifying words:** cleptobiosis, cleptomania, cleptoparasite, cleptoparasitism, kleptobiosis, kleptocracy, kleptohemodeipnonism, kleptolagnia, kleptomania, kleptomaniac, kleptoparasitism, kleptoparasite, kleptophobia, biblioklept, bibliokleptomania

knee See **genu** and **gony-** for examples.

know, learn For examples, check the elements **cogni-, epistemo-, gno-, intellect-, mne-, not-,** and **sci-**.

knowledge For examples, check the elements **cogni-, gno- epistemo-, intellect-, mne-, not-, sap-, sci-,** and **sopho-**.

koino- (Gk., common, shared) See **ceno-¹** for examples.

kolpo- (Gk., womb) See **colpo-** for examples.

koly- (Gk., hinder, inhibiting, to cut short, stop) Also written as **coly-**.

> **Qualifying words:** kolypeptic, kolyphrenia, kolyseptic, kolytic

kon- (dust) See **conio-** for examples.

konio- (dust) See **conio-** for examples.

kopro- (Gk., feces, dung) See **copro-**.

kreo- (Gk., flesh, meat) See **creo-**.

krymo-, krym- (Gk., cold, frost) See **crymo-** for examples.

kryo-, kry- (Gk., cold, freezing) See **cryo-, cry-** for examples.

krypto-, krypt- (Gk., secret; hidden, concealed) See **crypto-** for examples.

kyano- (Gk., blue) See **cyano-** for examples.

kymo-, kym- (Gk., wave, sprout; swollen) Also see **cymo-** and **undul-** for other "wave" words.

> **Qualifying words:** kymatology, kymocyclograph, kymogram, kymograph, kymography, kymoscope, kymotrichous, roentgenkymography

kyno- (Gk., dog) See **cyno-** for examples

kyto- (Gk., hollow) See **cyto-** for examples.

L 1

labio-, labi- (L., lips) Also see **cheilo-**.

    Qualifying words: bilabial, chasmalabia, labia, labiate, labial, labiodental, labioglossal, labiograph, labiolingual, labiology, labiomancy, labionasal, labioplasty, synlabia

labor-, laborat- (L., work) Also see **ergo-, oper-, pono-,** and **urg-**.

    Qualifying words: belabor, belabored, belaboring, belabors, collaborate, collaborated, collaborating, collaboration, collaborationist, collaborator, elaborate, elaborated, elaborately, elaborating, elaboration, elaborator, labor, laboratory, labored, laborer, laboring, laborious, laboriously, laboriousness, laborite, labors

lacri-, lacrimo-, lacrim-, lachrym-, lacrymo-, lacrym-, lacrymi-, lachry- (L., tears, tear) Also see **dacryo-**.

    Qualifying words: lacrima, lacrimal, lacrimalin, lacrimation, lacrimator, lacrimatory, lacrimonasal, lacrimotome, lacrimotomy, lacrymal, lacrymonasal, lachrymose, lacrymiform, nasolacrimal

lacrymo- (L., tear) See **lacri-** for examples.

lacto-, lact-, lacti- (L., milk) For additional "milk" words, see **galacto-**.

    Qualifying words: ablactation, Lactarius, lactase, lactate, lactation, lacteal, lactesce, lactescence, lactescent, lactic, lactide, lactiferous, lactifuge, lactigenous, lactiphagous, lactivorous, lactochrome, lactogen, lactogenesis, lactogenic, lactometer, lactory, lactose, lactotherapy, lactotoxin, lactovegetarian, nomolactia

laevo- (L., left) See **levo-** for examples.

-lagnia, -lagny (Gk. > L., lust, lustful, lecherous; a sexual predilection specified by the combining root)

    Qualifying words: algolagnia, algolagny, coprolagnia, coprolagny, ecdemolagnia, iconolagnia, iconolagny, kleptolagnia, necrolagnia, necrolagny, pyrolagnia, pyrolagny, urolagnia, zoolagnia

lake, marsh See **limno-** for examples.

lalo-, lalio-, lal-, -lalia, -lalic (Gk., speech, babbling, chattering) Also see **cit-, clam-, dic-, fa-, legi-, locu-, logo-, loqu-, mythico-, ora-, -phasia, -phemia,** and **voc-** for other "speak, talk" words.

    Qualifying words: allolalia, anililagnia, bradylalia, coprolalia, cunnilalia, echolalia, endytolagnia, glossolalia, idiolalia, laliatry, laliophobia, lallation, lalochezia, lalognosis, lalomania, lalomaniac, laloneurosis, lalopathy, lalophilic, lalophilly, lalophobia, laloplegia, lalorhea, lalorrhea, matutolagnia, neolagnia, osphresiolagnia, tachylalia, tantalolagnia, titallagnia, vernalagnia

land See **agra-, agri-, agro-, geo-,** and **terr-** for examples.

language, tongue See **glosso-** and **linguo-**.

laparo-, lapar- (Gk., the soft part of the body between the ribs and the hip, flank, loin; denotes (1) the flank or loin, (2) the abdominal wall)

    Qualifying words: laparacolpotomy, laparectomy, laparocele, laparocholecystotomy, laparocolectomy, laparocolotomy, laparocolpotomy, laparocystectomy, laparocystidotomy, laparocystotomy, laparocystovariohysterotomy, laparoenterostomy, laparoenterotomy, laparogastroscopy, laparogastrotomy, laparohepatotomy, laparohysterectomy, laparohystero-oophorectomy, laparohysterosalpingo-oophorectomy, laparohysterotomy, laparoileotomy, laparomonodidymus, laparomyitis, laparomyomectomy, laparomyomotomy, laparomyositis, laparonephrectomy, laparorrhagia, laparorrhaphy, laparoscope, laparoscopy, laparosplenotomy, laparotome, laparotomy, laparouterotomy, laparovaginal

lapid-, lapis- (L., stone, rock) Also see **litho-, petro-,** and **saxi-** for other "rock" words.

    Qualifying words: dilapidated, dilapidation, lapidarion, lapidary, lapidate, lapidation, lapideous, lapidicolous, lapidify, lapilliform, lapis, lapis lazuli

laps- (L., to slip, to fall)

    Qualifying words: collapse, collapsible, collapsing, elapse, infralapsarian, lapsable, lapse, lapsed, *lapsus linguae*, prolapse, relapse, supralapsarian

large, great Examine **giga-, giganto-, grand, macro-, magni-, major, maxi-, mega-,** and **megalo-** for examples.

laryngo-, laryng- (Gk., throat, upper part of the windpipe; the vocal-chord area of the throat) Also see **cervico-, esophago-, gutturo-, pharyngo-, thoraco-,** as well as **trachelo-** for additional "throat" examples.

    Qualifying words: laryngalgia, laryngeal, laryngectomy, laryngitis, laryngologist, laryngology, laryngometry, laryngopathy, laryngophanton, laryngophony, laryngoplasty, laryngoplegia, laryngorhinology, laryngoscope, laryngoscopy, laryngostomy, laryngotomy, laryngotracheal, larynx

last, end See **fin-, omega, teleo-, term-,** and **ultim-** for examples.

lasting, hard See **duro-** for examples.

later, subsequent See **post-** and **postero-**.

later-, lateral-, -late, -lat, -lation, -lative (L., bear; carry) Also see **-fer, phoro-,** and **port-** for other "carry" words. Don't confuse this **later-** with **latero-,** "side."

Qualifying words: adulation, Atlantic, Atlas, belated, collate, collatron, collation, correlate, dilatory, elate, elation, legislate, legislation, legislator, oblation, prelate, relate, relation, relative, speculate, speculation, superlative, superlatively, translatable, translate, translation, translator

latero-, later-, lateri-, -lateral, -laterally (L., side, sideways; flank) Don't confuse this **latero-** with the previous **later-,** which means "bear, carry."

Qualifying words: bilateral, bilateralism, bilaterally, collateral, collaterally, collaterality, contralateral, equilateral, laterad, lateral, laterality, lateralization, lateriflexion, laterigrade, latero-abdominal, laterodeviation, laterodorsal, lateroduction, lateroflexion, laterognathism, laterograde, lateroposition, lateropulsion, laterotorsion, laterotrusion, lateroversion, latitude, latitudinarian, multilateral, quadrilateral, trilateral, unilateral, unilateralism, unilateralist, unilaterally

-latry, -olatry, -later, -olater, -latress, -olatress, -latria, -latrous, -olatrous (Gk., worship; excessively, fanatically devoted to someone or something; "service paid to the gods") Also examine **cred-, dox-, fid-,** and **laud-** for words which have related meanings.

Qualifying words: angelolatry, anthropolatry, arborolatry, archaeolater, archaeolatrous, archaeolatry, astrolater, astrolatry, autolatry, babyolatry, bardolater, bardolatry, bibliolater, bibliolatrous, bibliolatry, cosmolatry, cynolatry, duratolatry, demonolatry, dendrolatry, diabolatry, diabololatry, ecclesiolatry, gastrolatry, geniolatry, gyneolatry, gynolatry, hagiolatry, heliolatry, herolatry, hierolatry, hydrolatry, hygeiolatry, ichthyolatry, iconolatry, idiolatry, idolater, idolatress, idolatrize, idolatrized, idolatrizing, idolatrous, idolatrously, idolatry, juvenolatry, latria, litholatry, logolatrous, logolatry, lunolatry, Mariolatry, martyrolatry, mobolatry, monolatry, neolatry, onolatry, ophiolatry, palaeolatry, paleolatry, parthenolatry, patriolatry, patrolatry, physiolatry, phytolatry, plutolatry, popolatry, pseudolatry, pyrolatry, selenolatry, solarolatry, staurolatry, taurolatry, thaumatolatry, theolatry, theriolatry, topolatry, uranolatry, urbanolatry, verbolatry, zoolater, zoolatrous, zoolatry

laud- (L., praise) Also see **dox-** for other words with similar meainigs.

Qualifying words: laudability, laudable, laudation, laudatory

laughter See **gelo-** for examples.

lav- (L., wash, bathe) Also see **balneo-, luto-,** and **purg-.**

Qualifying words: latrine, launder, laundry, lava, lavabo, lavage, lavation, lavatory, lave, lavement, laver, lavish, lotion

law, order See **crim-, jud-, jus-,** and **nomo-.**

lax- (L., loose; slack). Also examine **-lysis** and **solv-** for related words.

Qualifying words: laxate, laxation, laxative, laxity, relax, relaxant, relaxation

layer, horizontal See **strati-** for examples.

lead (the *verb*) See **-agogue** and **duc-.**

lead (the *metal*) See **plumbo-** and **molybd-.**

leader, chief See **capit-** for examples.

leading See **-agogue** and **duc-** for examples.

leaf, leaves See **folio-, forbi-** (broad leaf), and **phyllo-** for examples.

learn, know Examine **cogni-, epistemo-, gno-, intellect-, mne-** [remember], **not-,** and **sci-** for examples.

leaves, leaf See **folio-, forbi-** (broad leaf), and **phyllo-** for examples.

lecherous, lustful See **-lagnia** for examples.

lect- (L., read, readable) See **legi-.**

leech, leeches See **hirudin** for examples.

left, left side See **levo-** and **sinistro-** for examples.

leg See **skel-** for examples.

legi-, leg-, ligi-, lig-, lect-, lex-, -lexia, -lexis, -lexic, -lectic (L., read, readable [to choose words; gather, collect; to pick out, choose; to read, recite]) Closely related to **lexico-,** which you should see. Also see **cit-, clam-, dic-, intellect-, locu-, logo-, mythico-, ora-, -phasia, -phemia,** and **voc-** .

Qualifying words: alexia, bradylexia, colleague, collect, collection, collective, college, dialect, diligence, diligent, dyslexia, dyslexic, eclectic, elect, election, elective, electorate, elegant, eligible, elite, idiolect, illegible, intellect, intelligence, intelligent, intelligentsia, intelligible, lectern, lection, lecture, legacy, legal, legation, legend, legible, legion, legislation, legitimate, legume, lesson, lexical, lexicographer, lexicography, lexicon, ligneous, neglect, negligee, negligence, negligent, predilection, recollect, religion, sacrilege, select, selection, selective, sortilege

leio-, lei-, li-, lio- (Gk., smooth)

Qualifying words: leiasthenia, leiodermia, leiodystonia, leiomyoblastoma, leiomyofibroma, leiomyoma, leiomyosarcoma, leiotrichous, leiotrichous, leiotrichy, leomyoma

lepido-, -lepis (flake, scale) For "moth" or "butterfly" words, see **lepidopter-**.

> **Qualifying words:** lepidodentroid, lepidolite, lepidophyllous, lepidophyte, lepidotrichium

lepidopter- (Gk., moths, butterflies; a combination of **lepido-**, "flake" or "scale" and **ptero**, "wing") Also see **ptero-** and **pterygo-** for related "wing" words. See **lepido-** for "scale, flake" words.

> **Qualifying words:** Lepidoptera, lepidopterid, lepidopterist, lepidopterology, lepidopteron, lepidopterophilous, lepidopterophily, lepidopterous, Macrolepidoptera, Microlepidoptera

lepor- (L., rabbit, hare)

> **Qualifying words:** leporid, Leporidae, leporine, lepus

-lepsy, -lepsia, -lepsis, -leptic (Gk., a violent attack, a seizing)

> **Qualifying words:** analeptic, analepsy, androlepsy, catalepsy, epilepsy, epileptic, narcolepsy, nympholepsy, organoleptic, organolepsy, prolepsis, syllepsis

lepto-, lept- (Gk., thin, small, fine, delicate) Also see **micro-, mini-, nano-, nemato-,** and **pico-** for other examples.

> **Qualifying words:** leptocephalous, leptocephaly, leptochromatic, leptodactyl, leptodactylous, leptodactyly, leptodermatous, leptodermic, leptodontous, leptology, leptophonia, leptophonic, leptophyll, leptopodal, leptorrhine, leptosomatic, leptosome, neuraleptanesthesia, neuroleptanesthetic

less; smaller See **mio-** for examples.

less than See **hypo-** for examples.

let go See **miss-** for examples.

leth- (L., lie hidden, secretely; forgetfulness, forget, inactive through forgetfulness; also sleepy, drowsy, dull, sluggish) Also see **crypto-** and **krypto-** for additional "hidden, secret" words; and see **narco-** and **sopor-** for other "sleep" words. From *Lethe*: 1. A river of Hades, whose water when drunk caused forgetfulness of the past. 2. Forgetfulness, oblivion.

> **Qualifying words:** lethargic, lethargical, lethargize, lethargy, Lethe, Lethean, lethologica, lethonomia

letha- (L., deadly, mortal) Also examine **-cide, mort-, neci-, necro-,** and **thanato-** for additional "death" words.

> **Qualifying words:** lethal, lethality, Lethe, semilethal

letter See **liter-** for examples.

leuco-, leuc-, leuko-, leuk-, -leukemia (Gk., white) Also see **albo-, albumino-,** and **cand-** for additional "white" words.

> **Qualifying words:** aleukemia, aleukemic, aleukia, aleukocyte, leucocytometer, leucine, leucite, leucocarpous, leucocyan, leucocyte, leucocythemia, leucocytosis, leucoderma, leucodermia, leucoma, leucoplast, leucopoiesis, leucopterin, leucotactic, leucotomy, leukemia, leukemogen, leukemogenesis, leukemogenic, leukemoid, leukocyte, leukocytology, leukocytophagy, leukocytotherapy, leukocytotoxin, leukoderma, leukodermia, leukodermic, leukodont, leukodontia, leukogram, leukokinesis, leukokinetic, leukokinetics, leukonecrosis, leukonychia, leukopathia, leukopathy, leukophyll, leukoplast, leukoscope, leukotactic, leukotaxis, leukotherapy, leukotome, leukotomy, leukotoxic, leukotoxicity, leukotoxin, pseudoleukemia

lev- (L., light in weight, lightness; raise, lift)

> **Qualifying words:** alleviate, alleviation, elevate, elevator, lever, levee, levitate, levitation, levity, levy

-leukemia (Gk. > L., in medicine, a disease with an excessive number of white blood cells) See **leuco-** for examples.

levo- (laevo-, British) (L., left, to the left, toward, or on the left side) Also examine **sinistro-** for other "left" words.

> **Qualifying words:** laevorotary, levoangiocardiography, levoaural, levoaurality, levocardia, levocardiogram, levoclination, levocular, levocycloversion, levoduction, levoglucose, levogram, levogyrate, levogyration, levomanual, levophobia, levorotation, levorotatory, levotorsion, levotropic, levotropous, levoversion

lex- (L., read, readable; words) See **legi-**.

lexico-, lexi-, lex- (Gk., a word; a saying, a phrase; speaking) Also see **legi-, logo-,** and **verb** for other "word" examples.

> **Qualifying words:** alexia, alexio, lexeme, lexemic, lexica, lexical, lexicalize, lexicographer, lexicographian, lexicographical, lexicography, lexicological, lexicologist, lexicology, lexicon, lexiconist, lexiconize, lexicostatistic, lexigram, lexigraphic, lexigraphy, lexiphanes, lexiphanic, lexiphanicism, lexiphonic, lexis

libel- (book) See **libr-** for examples

liber- (L., free) Also see **eleuthero-** for other "free" words.

> **Qualifying words:** liberal, liberality, liberalize, liberate, liberation, liberator, libertarian, liberticide, libertine, liberty

libr-, libel (*liber*) (L., book) Also see **bibli-** for additional "book" words.

> **Qualifying words:** ex-libris, libel, libelous, librarian, library

lieno-, lien- (Gk. > L., spleen) Also examine **spleno-** for other "spleen" words.

> **Qualifying words:** lienography, lienointestinal, lienomalacia, lienopancreatic, lienopathy, lienorenal, lienotoxin

life See **bio-** and **vita-** for examples.

lift, raise See **lev-** for examples.

-lig- (L., read) See **legi-** for examples.

light, shine See **ethero-, luco-, lumen-, lun-, lustr-, phospho-, photo-,** and **scintill-**.

lightness, lift See **lev-** for examples.

lightning See **astrapo-** for examples.

ligni-, lign- (L., wood) Also see **also-, arbor-, dendro-, hylo-, nemo-, sylv-,** and **xylo-**.

> **Qualifying words:** ligneous, lignescent, lignicole, lignicolous, lignification, ligniferous, ligniform, lignify, lignin, ligniperdous, lignite, lignitic, lignivore, lignivorous, lignivory, lignocellulose, lignophile, lignophilic, lignophily, pyroligneous

like, same See **equ-, homo-** (Gk.), **iso-, -oid, pari-, simal-,** and **tauto-** for examples.

limestone, lime See **calci-** for examples.

limen, lim- (L., threshold [of consciousness]; boundary, limit) Also see **fin-, teleo-, term-,** and **ultim-**.

> **Qualifying words:** eliminate, elimination, illimitable, liminal, liminometer, liminoscope, limit, limitation, limited, preliminary, sublimate, sublimation, sublime, subliminal, superliminal, unlimited

limi-, lim- (L., mud) See **argillo-, chledo-,** and **pelo-** for other "mud" words.

> **Qualifying words:** limicole, limicoline, limicolous, limivorous, limous, pollute, pollution

limit, boundary See **fin-, teleo-, term-,** and **ultim-** for examples.

limno-, limn- (Gk., lake, marshy lake, pool, marsh) Also see **helo-, telmato-,** and **tipho-** for other "lake, marsh" words.

> **Qualifying words:** bathylimnetic, epilimnion, hypolimnetic, hypolimnion, limanth, limnion, limitrophic, limnanthes, limnemia, limnemic, limnemia, limnetic, limnimetere, limnimetric, limnobiology, limnobiont, limnobiontic, limnobios, Limnobium, limnocrene, limnocryptophyte, limnograph, limnological, limnologist, limnology, limnometer, limnomia, limnonekton, limnophil, limnophile, limnophilous, limnophobia, limnophyte, limnoplankton, metalimnetic, metalimnion

limo-, lim- (Gk., hunger, appetite) Also see **bou-** (*bulima*) and **orexi-** for similarities.

> **Qualifying words:** bulimia, bulimiac, bulimic, limophobia, limophoitas, limophthsis, limosis, limotherapy

lin-, line- (L., line, thread, string, cord) Also see **fibro-, flax-,** and **mito-** for additional thread-type words.

> **Qualifying words:** align, alignment, alineate, collimate, collinear, delineate, delineation, line, lineage, lineal, linear, lineate, linen, lining, linseed, lint, lingerie, matrilineal, patrilineal, rectilinear

linguo-, lingu-, lingua-, -linguist, -linguistic, -linguistical, -linguistically (L., tongue, language) Also see **glosso-** for other "tongue" words.

> **Qualifying words:** bilingual, cunnilinguist, cunnilingus, faciolingual, language, *lapsus linguae, lingua franca,* lingual, linguate, linguist, linguistics, linguodental, linguoversion, metalinguistics, monolingual, multilingual, psycholinguistic, sociolinguistic, sublingual, trilingual

lip, lips See **cheilo-** and **labio-** for examples.

lipo-, lip-, -lipid, -lipoid, -lipoma, -lipomatous (Gk., fat, fatty) Also see **adipo-, eleo-, oleo-** [oil], and **steato-** for other "fat" words.

> **Qualifying words:** alipogenic, alipoidic, alipotropic, apolipoprotein, hyperlipidaemia, hyperlipidemia, hyperlipoproteinemia, glycolipide, lipacidemia, lipaciduria, liparous, lipase, lipasuria, lipectomy, lipemia, lipid(e), lipidosis, lipoarthritis, lipoblast, lipoblastoma, lipocardiac, lipocere, lipochondroma, lipochrome, lipoclasis, lipoclastic, lipocyte, lipodieresis, lipodologist, lipodology, lipodystrophy, lipoferous, lipofibroma, lipogenesis, lipogenetic, lipogenic, lipogenous, lipogranuloma, lipoid, lipoidal, lipoidema, lipoidous, lipoiduria, lipolipoidosis, lipolysis, lipolytic, lipoma, lipomyoma, lipophage, lipophagia, lipophagic, lipophagy, lipophilia, lipophil, lipophilic, lipoprotein, liposis, liposome, lipostomy, lipotropic, lipotropism, lipuria, osteolipoma, angiolipoma, fibrolipoma, phospholipase, phospholipid, phospholipidemia

-lipoma (Gk. > L., in medicine, it denotes a tumor made up of fatty tissue) See **lipo-**.

liqu- (L., flow, fluid, wave) Also see **cymo-, fluct-, rheo-, kymo-, -rrhea, undu-,** and **vacilla-** for other "flow, wave" words or examples.

> **Qualifying words:** deliquesce, liquifacient, lliquefy, liqueur, liquid, liquidate, liquidity, liquor

listen, hear See **acous-, audio-,** and **ausculto-**.

liter- (L., letter)

> **Qualifying words:** alliterate, alliteration, belles-lettres, illiteracy, illiterate, literacy, literal, literally, literary, literate, *literati,* literature, obliterate, obliteration, transliterate, transliteration

literary thief See **plagiar-** for examples.

litho-, lith-, -lith, -lithic, -lite, -liths, -lites (Gk., stone, rock) See **lapid-, petro-,** and **saxi-** for additional "rock" words.

Qualifying words: angiolith, biolith, cerolite, chrysolite, coprolite, coprolith, coprolithic, endolith, endolithic, endolithophyte, endolithophytic, eolith, Eolithic, exolithophyte, exolithophytic, glyptolith, granulite, grapholite, hypolithic, lithic, lithiication, lithify, lithium, lithofacies, lithogenesis, lithograph, lithoid, lithoidolatry, lithodomus, litholatry, lithological, lithology, lithomancy, lithometer, lithometry, lithophage, lithophagic, lithophagy, lithophagous, lithophile, lithophilous, lithophily, lithophyll, lithophyte, lithophytic, lithoseisma, lithosol, lithosphere, lithostratigraphy, lithostratigraphic, lithotomous, lithotomy, lithotriper, lithotripsy, lithotype, lithoxyle, megalith, monolith, monolithic, nephrolith, oolite, phytolith, rhabdolith, rhinolith, zoolith, zoolithic

little, small See **-cle, -cule, -et** (Fr.), **lepto-, micro-, mini-, nano-, oligo-, pauci-, pico-,** and **-ule.**

little nerve See **radiculo-** for examples.

live, life See **bio-, -cole** (inhabit), **vita-,** and **viva-** for examples.

liver See **hepato-** for examples.

lizard See **sauro-** for examples.

loc- (L., talk, speak) See **locu-** for examples.

local, localized See **loco-** and **topo-** for examples.

lochmo-, lochm- (Gk., thicket, bush)

Qualifying words: lochmocole, lochmocolous, lochmodophile, lochmodophilous, lochmodophily, lochmodophyte, lochmophile, lochmophilous, lochmophily, lochmophyte, lochmophytic

loci- See **loco-** for examples.

loco- (*locus*) (L., place, from place to place; where something is placed) Also see **pon-, sist-, the-,** and **topo-** for additional "place" words.

Qualifying words: allocate, allocation, collocation, dislocate, dislocation, local, locale, locality, localize, locate, location, locomotion, locomotive, loculus, locus, relocate, relocation

locu-, loc- (L., talk, speak, say, word, speech) Also examine the following roots: **cit-, clam-, dic-, fa-, lalo-, legi-, logo-, loqu-, mythico-, ora-, -phasia, -phemia,** and **voc-** for additional "speaking" words.

Qualifying words: allocution, circumlocution, elocution, elocutionist, interlocutor, locution, locutionist, prolocutor

locus (L., place) See **loco-** for examples.

logo-, log-, -logia, -logical, -logism, -logician, -logian, -logist, -logy, -logue (Gk., talk, speech, speak; word) Also check out the following elements: **cit-, clam-, dic-, fa-, lalo-, legi-, locu-, loqu-, mythico-, ora-, -phasia, -phemia,** and **voc-** for additional "talk, speak" words.

Qualifying words: alogia, analogue, analogy, apologize, apologue, apology, battology, battologe, battologizing, biology, catalog, catalogue, decalog, decalogue, dialogue, duologue, dyslogy, eclogue, eulogy, epilogue, eulogize, eulogy, genealogic, genealogy, homologous, hyperlogia, hypologia, illogical, logagnosia, logagraphia, logamnesia, loganamnosis, logaphasia, logarithm, logastellus, logasthenia, logic, logical, logician, logistic, logo, logocide, logoclonia, logocracy, logodaedalus, logodiarrhea, logogogue, logogram, logograph, logographer, logography, logokophosis, logolatrous, logolatry, logolept, logologist, logology, logomachia, logomachy, logomancy, logomania, logomisia, logomonomania, logoneurosis, logonomy, logopaedia, logopaedics, logopathy, logopedia, logopedics, logophasia, logophilia, logophile, logophobia, logophasia, logoplegia, logorrhea, logos, logospasm, macrologist, macrology, monologue, multiloquous, neologism, neologist, paralogism, paralogy, pauciloquous, pharmacologic, pharamacology, philoloogist, philology, prologue, syllogism, tautologism, tautology, tetralogy, travelogue, trilogy

-logy (Gk., a speaking of; science of, study of) See **logo-** and **-ology** for examples.

lonely, solitary See **eremo-** and **soli-** for examples.

look at, see Examine **-orama, -scope, spec-,** and **vid-** for examples.

loose, slack See **lax-, -lysis,** and **solv-.**

loosen, untie See **lax-, -lysis,** and **solv-** .

lop, trim See **put-** for examples.

lopho-, loph- (Gk., ridge; crest) lophobranch, lophodont, lophophore, lophotrichous

love, loving Examine **amat-, aphrodi-, eroto, philo-,** and **venus** for examples.

loving one's self, self-love See **narciss-.**

loqu-, -loquence, -loquent, -loquently (L., talk, speak, say) Also see **cit-, clam-, dic-, lalo-, legi-, locu-, logo-, mythico-, ora-, -phasia, -phemia, phras-,** and **voc-** for other "talk, speak" words.

Qualifying words: amphoriloquy, breviloquence, breviloquent, colloquial, colloquialism, colloquium, colloquy, eloquence, eloquent, grammalogue, grandiloquence, grandiloquent, loquacious, loquaciousness, loquacity, magnilo- quence, magniloquent, obloquy, pauciloquy, paucilloquence, paucilloquency, soliloquy, soliquize, somniloquist, ventriloquism, ventriloquist

lower, below See **hypo-, infra-, sub-,** and **subter-** for examples.

lower extremity of the windpipe See **aorta-**.

loxo-, lox- (Gk., slanting, oblique) Also see **clino-** for other "slant" words.

   Qualifying words: loxia, loxodromic, loxolophodont, loxophthalmus, loxotomy

luco-, luc-, luci-, lux, -lucence, -lucent (L., light, shine) For other "light" words, see **lumen-, lun-, lustr-, phospho-, photo-,** and **scintill-**.

   Qualifying words: elucidate, elucidation, lucent, lucicole, lucicolous, lucid, lucidly, lucidness, lucidity, Lucifer, luciferase, luciferous, lucifugal, lucifugous, lucimeter, Lucina, lucipetal, luciphile, luciphilous, luciphily, lucite, lucotherapy, lux, noctiluca, omnilocence, omnilocent, pelluced, pellucidness, pelucidity, radiolucent, relucent, translucence, translucent

Lucifer (L., devil, demon, Satan; Lucifer literally means "light-bringer" or "bringing light") Also examine **demono-, diabolo-, phospho-,** and **Satan** for other other "devil" examples and see **luc-** for "light" words.

   Qualifying words: Lucifer, Luciferphobia

lucr- (L., wealth, wealthy, rich; gain, profit, money) Also see **opulen-** and **pluto-**.

   Qualifying words: lucrative, lucre

lud- (*ludere*), **ludicro-, lus-** (L., play, make sport of, jest; sportive)

   Qualifying words: allude, allusion, allusive, collusion, delude, deluder, delusion, delusive, delusory, elude, eluded, eluding, elusion, elusive, elusory, illusion, illusionary, illusionist, illusive, illusory, interlude, ludicropathetic, ludicroserious, ludicrosity, ludicrous, ludicrously, ludification, postlude, prelude

   In Roman antiquity, *ludi publici* (LYOO digh PUB li sigh) were public games and spectacles, including athletic competitions, horse and chariot races, exhibitions of the arena and theater. *Ludi Cercenses* (sur SEN seez) were games of the Circus; *ludi scenici* (SEN i sigh) of the theater. Some were named for particular festivals: *ludi Apollinares* (uh pol" i NAY reez), in honor of Apollo, chiefly theatrical; *ludi Romani* (roh MAY nigh),

in honor of Jupiter, in September; *ludi Megalenses* (meg" uh LEN seez), in honor of the *Magna Mater*, April 4 to April 10.

luer- (L., wash) See **lu-** for examples.

lum- (L., light) See **lumen-** for examples.

lumbo-, lumb- (L., loin [the lower part of the back on either side of the backbone between the hipbones and the ribs])

   Qualifying words: lumbago, lumbar, lumboabdominal, lumbocostal, lumbodorsal, lumbodynia, thoracolumbar, supralumbar

lumen-, lumin-, lum- (L., light, shine; source) Also see **luco-, luno-, lustr-, phospho-, photo-,** and **scintill-** for additional "light" words.

   Qualifying words: bioluminescence, bioluminescent, electroluminescence, illuminate, illuminance, illumination, illuminati, lumen, luminal, luminance, luminary, luminescence, luminescent, luminiferous, luminoscope, luminosity, luminous, lumisome, noctiluca, noctilucine, photoluminescence, photoluminescent, radioluminescence, sonoluminescence, sonoluminescent, thermoluminescence, triboluminescence, triboluminescent

luna-, luni-, lun-, lunu- (L., moon, light, shine) Also see **seleno-** for other "moon" words. Related to **luco-, lumen-, lustr-, phospho-, photo-,** and **scintill-**.

   Qualifying words: apolune, demilune, interlunar, interlunation, loony, luna, lunabase, lunacy, lunambulism, lunar, lunarian, lunarite, lunate, lunatic, lunation, lunatism, lune, lunette, lunisolar, lunitidal, perilune, plenilunary, semilunar, sublunar, sublunary

lung(s) See **pulmo-** and **pneumo-** for examples.

lup- (L., wolf) See **lupus** for exasmples.

lupus, lup- (L., wolf [pertaining to or connected with a "wolf"]; in medicine, a tuberculous disease of the skin because ulcerations resemble a wolf's bite) Also see **lyco-** for other "wolf" words.

   Qualifying words: Canis lupus, lobo (Sp.), lupanar, Lupercalia, lupia, lupiform, lupine, Lupinus, lupoid, lupus

lust, lecherous See **-lagnia** for examples.

lustr-, lust- (L., light up, shine) Also examine **luco-, lumen-, luno-, phospho-, photo-,** and **scintill-** for other "light" words.

   Qualifying words: illustrate, illustration, illustrious, luster, lustral, lustrate, lustrical, lustrous, lustrum

luto-, lut-, luv-, lu- (L., wash, clean) Latin *luere*, "to wash upon or against" is related to *lavare*. Also see **balneo-, lav-,** and **purg-** for other "wash, clean" words.

Qualifying words: abluent, ablution, ablutomania, alluvia, alluvial, alluvium, antediluvian, colluvial, deluge, deluged, dilute, diluter, dilution, dilutor, diluvial, diluvialism, diluvian, diluvianism, elutriate, eluvia, eluvial, eluviation, eluvium, pediluvium, postdiluvial, postdiluvium, solution

lutra-, lutr- (L., otter; aquatic animal)

Qualifying words: Lutra, lutrine

lut- (wash, clean) See **luto-** for examples.

luv- (wash, clean) See **luto-** for examples.

lux (L., light, shine) See **luco-** for examples.

luxur- (L., excess, have to excess; grow profusely) Don't confuse this **luxur-** element with **lux,** "light," because there is no connection between the two elements.

Qualifying words: luxuriant, luxuriate, luxurious, luxury

lyco-, lyc-, lycos- (Gk., wolf) Also see **lupus** for other examples.

Qualifying words: lycanthrope, lycanthropy, lycomania, lycopodium, lycopus, lycorexia, lycosid

lyso-, lyo-, ly-, -lysin, -lys-, -lysis, -lytic, -lyt-, -lyz- (Gk., loosing, dissolving, dissolution) Also see **lax-** and **solv-** for other "loose" words.

Qualifying words: analyst, analytic, analyze, angiolysis, autolysis, autolytic, biolysis, biolytic, carcinolysin, carcinolysis, carcinolytic, catalysis, catalyst, catalytic, catalyze, chromolysis, cytolysis, dialyphyllous, dialysis, dialytic, dialyze, electrolysis, electrolyte, glycolysis, haematolysis, haemolysis, haemolytic, hematolysis, hemolysis, hepatolytic, heterolysis, histolysis, hydrolysis, hydrolytic, hydrolyze, lipolysis, litholyte, lyencephalous, lyophilic, lyophobia, lyophobic, lyosorption, lyotropic, lysimeter, lysin, lysine, lysis, lysism, lysobacteria, lysocline, lysoform, lysogenesis, lysogenic, lysogenization, lysogenize, lysogeny, lysol, lysosome, lysostaphin, lysozyme, lytic, macroanalysis, nephrolysis, nephrolytic, neurolysis, orchilytic, palsy, paralysis, paralytic, paralyze, peptolysis, peptolytic, photolysis, psychoanalysis, psychoanalyst, psychoanalyze, psychoanalysis, pyrolysis, thermolysis, thrombolysis, thrombolytics

-lytic (Gk., adjective form of **-lysis**) See **lyso-** for examples.

M m

machine See **mechano-** for examples.

-machy, -machia, -machist, -machic, -machical (Gk., battle, war, contest, fight) Also see **belli-**, **milit-**, and **pugn-**.

> **Qualifying words:** alectoromachy, alectryomachy, andromachy, angelmachy, batrachoherpetomachia, centauromachia, cynarctomachy, cytomachia, duomachy, gamomachia, gamomachy, gigantomachia, hippomachia, hippomachy, gigantomachy, hieromachia, hieromachy, iconomachy, logomachia, logomachy, machozoid, naumachia, naumachy, pyromachy, psychomachia, psychomachy, sciamachy, tauromachia, tauromachian, tauromachy, theomachist, theomachy, telemachy, Titanomachy, trimachia, trimachy

macro-, macr- (Gk., large, great; long [in extent or duration]; enlarged, or enlongated) For additional "large" words, see **giga-**, **giganto-**, **grand-**, **magni-**, **major**, **maxi-**, **mega-**, and **megalo-**.

> **Qualifying words:** macroaesthesia, macrobiosis, macrobiote, macrobiotic, macrobiotics, macroblepharia, macrobrachia, macrocardia, macrocardius, macrocarpous, macrocephalus, macrocheilia, macrocheiria, macrochiria, macrococcus, macroclimate, macrocosm, macrocyte, macrodactylia, macrodactylism, macrodactylous, macrodactyly, macrodont, macrodontia, macrodontism, macroesthesia, macrofauna, macroflora macrofloral, macroglossia, macrognathia, macrognathic, macrograph, macrography, macrogyne, macrology, macromania, macromolecule, macron, macronychia, macroparasite, macropathology, macrophage, macrophagic, macrophagocyte, macrophagous, macrophyllous, macrophyte, macrophytic, macroplankton, macropodia, macropsia, macropterous, macropygia, macrorhinia, macroscopic, macroscopy, macroseism, macrosomatous, macrosomia, macrospheric, macrosymbiont, macrosymbiote, macrothermophyte, macrotia, macrotaxonomy, macrotrichia

made, formed See **form -** and **plasmo-**.

madness, excessive fondness for something See **-mania** for examples.

magni-, magn- (L., large, big, great) Also see **giga-**, **giganto-**, **grand**, **macro-**, **magni-**, **major**, **maxi-**, **mega-**, and **megalo-** for other "large" words.

> **Qualifying words:** magnanimous, magnate, *magna cum laude*, magnification, magnificence, magnificent, magnify, magniloquence, magniloquent, magniscope, magnitude, magnum, *magnum opus*

maiden, a girl See **partheno-** and **virgo-** for examples.

major (L., larger, greater) Also see **grand-**, **macro-**, **magni-**, **maxi-**, and **mega-** for other examples.

> **Qualifying words:** majestic, majestical, majesty, major, major domo, majority, majuscular, majuscule

make See **fac-** and **-poeia** for examples.

make fit See **habili-** for examples.

make visible, see See **phenero-** and **phant-** for examples.

mal-, male- (L., bad, badly, harsh, wrong; ill; evil; abnormal, defective) For other "bad" words, see **caco-**, **dys-**, and **mis-**. This combining form has nothing to do with the word *male*, meaning "man" or "masculine."

> **Qualifying words:** malabsorption, maladjustment, maladminister, maladroit, malady, malaise, malalignment, malapropism, malapropos, malaria, malarial, malariology, malarious, malassimilation, malcontent, maldigestion, malediction, maledictory, malefaction, malefactor, malefic, maleficence, maleficent, malevolence, malevolent, malfeasance, malformation, malformed, malfunction, malice, malicious, maliferous, malign, malignance, malignancy, malignant, malignity, malinger, malingerer, malingering, malinterdigitation, malnourished, malnutrition, malocclusion, malodorous, malodorously, malpractice, malrotation, maltreat, maltreatment, malversation (chiefly British)

malaco-, malac-, malako-, -malacia (Gk., soft, softness)

> **Qualifying words:** arteriomalacia, cardiomalacia, chondromalacia, craniomalacia, encephlalomalacia, gastromalacia, hepatomalacia, malacia, malacic, malacology, malacoma, malacoplakia, malacosarcosis, malacostean, malacotic, malacotomy, malacozoology, malakoplakia, nephromalacia, osteomalacia, pneumomalacia, scleromalacia

male, man See **andro-**, **anthropo-** (humans in general), **homo-** (L.) (humans in general), and **vir-** for examples.

male reproductive gland See **orchio-** and **testi-** for examples.

male sex organ See **peni-** for examples.

mammill-, mammilli-(Gk. >L., breast, nipple) Also see **mammo-**, **masto-**, **mazo-**, and **pectoro-** for other "breast" words.

> **Qualifying words:** mammilla, mammillate, mammillary, mammillated, mammillation, mammilliform, mammillitis, mammilloid, mammilliplasty

mammo-, mamm-, mammi- (L., breast) Also examine **mammill-, masto-, mazo-,** and **pectoro-** for other "breast" words.

    Qualifying words: mama, mamma, mammal, mammalgia, Mammalia, mammalogy, mammaplasty, mammary, mammectomy, mammiferous, mammiform, mammiplasia, mammitis, mammodynia, mammogen, mammogenesis, mammogram, mammography, mammoplasia, mammoplasty, mammose, mammotomy, mammotroph, mammotrophic, mammotropic

man, male See **andro-, anthropo-** (humans in general), **homo-** (L.) (humans in general), and **vir-** for examples.

-mancy, -mancer, -mantic, -mantical, (Gk., divination, prophecy; to interpret signs so "practical" decisions can be made [related to *mania*]) Divination is considered the willful exploration of the future or the discovery of hidden things by various practices. Most common divinations are *astrology, dowsing, dreams, cards, numerology, crystal-gazing, omens, palmistry, etc.* See **Appendix E** for an extensive list of **Mancy Words**.

manda-, mandat- (L., to command, order; literally "to give into one's hand")

    Qualifying words: commandeer, command, commandant, commander, countermand, demand, mandate, mandatory, recommend, remand

mandibulo-, mandibul-, mandibuli- (L., jaw, lower jaw) Also examine **gnatho-** and **maxillo-** (upper jaw).

    Qualifying words: mandible, mandibular, mandibulary, mandibulate, mandibuliform, mandibulohyoid, mandibidomaxillary, mandibulopharyngeal,

-mania, -maniac, -maniacal, -manic, -manically, -maniacally (Gk., 1. A specific *mental disorder* or obsessive preoccupation with something; madness, frenzy; obsession, or abnormal desire for or with something or someone. 2. *Excessive enthusiasm* or *fondness* for something.) Opposite of **phobia**; however, it is related to **-mancy**.

    Qualifying words: ablutomania, acromania, acronymania, agoramania, agromania, agyiomania, ailuromania, alcoholomania, amaxomania, amenomania, Americamania, andromania, androphonomania, Anglomania, anthomania, aphrodisiomania, apimania, arithmomania, automania, autophonomania, ballistomania, bibliokleptomania, biblioklep-

tomaniac, bibliomania, bibliomaniac, bibliomaniacal, bruxomania, cacodemonomania, callomania, camphorormania, catabythismomania, catapedamania, chaeromania, cheromania, Chinamania, chionomania, choreomania, choromania, chrematomania, cleptomania, clinomania, cocainomania, coprolalomania, coprolamania, cratomania, cremnomania, cresomania, cyclomania, cynomania, dacnomania, decalcomania, decalcomaniac, decalomania, demomania, demonomaniac, dipsomania, dipsomaniac, doramania, doromaniac, drapetomania, dromomania, dysmorphomania, ecdemiomania, ecdemomania, ecomania, edecomania, egomania, egomaniac, eleutheromania, eleuthromania, emetomania, empleomania, enomania, enosimania, entheomania, entomomania, eremiomania, ergasiomania, ergomania, ergomaniac, eroticomania, erotodromomania, erotographomania, erotomania, erotomaniac, erythromania, esthesiomania, etheromania, florimania, Francomania, Gallomania, gamomania, gamomaniac, gamonomania, gephyromania, Gallomania, gamomania, gamomaniac, gamonomania, gephyromania, Germanomania, gigmania, graphomania, graphomaniac, Grecomania, gymnomania, gynecomania, habromania, hamartomania, hedonomania, heliomania, Hellenomania, hieromania, hippomania, hodomania, homicidomania, hydrodipsomania, hydromania, hylomania, hypermania, hypnomania, hypomania, hypomaniac, hypolepsiomania, hysteromania, ichthyomania, iconomania, idolomania, Italomania, kainomania, kathisomania, kinesomania, klazomania, kleptomania, kleptomaniac, klopemania, lalomania, letheomania, lethomania, logomania, logomaniac, logomonomania, lycomania, lypemania, lypermania, macromania, mania, maniac, maniacal, maniaphobia, manic, megalomania, megalomaniac, melomania, melomaniac, mentulomania, mesmeromania, metromania, micromania, monomania, morphiomania, monomania, monomaniac, musicomania, musomania, mythomania, narcomania, narcomaniac, necromania, necromaniac, narcomaniac, nautomania, necromania, noctimania, noctomania, nosomania, nostomania, nudomania, nymphomania, nymphomaniac, ochlomania, oestromania, oestromaniac, oikomania, oinomania, oligomania, oniomania, oniomaniac, onomatomania, onychotillomania, ophidiomania, opiomania, opsomania, orchidomania, oreximania, ornithomania, paramania, parousiamania, pathomania, phagomania, phaneromania, pharmacomania, philopatridomania, phonomania, photomania, phrenomania, phronemomania, phthisiomania, planomania, plutomania, politicomania, poriomania, pornographomania, potichomania, potomania, pseudomania, pyromania, pyromaniac, Russomania, satyromania, schizomania, scribblemania, scribomania, siderodromomania, sideromania, sitiomania, sitomania, sitomaniac, sophomania, squandermania, submania, supermania, symmetromania, Teutonomania, thalassomania, thanatomania, theatromania, theomania, theomaniac, timbromania, tomomania, toxicomania, trichokryptomania, trichomania, trichorrhexomania, trichotillomania, tristimania, tromomania, Turkomania, typomania, uteromania, verbomania, xenomania, zoomania, zoomaniac

manifest, visible See **phanero-** and **phant-** for examples.

mankind, human See **anthropo-** and **homo-** (L.) for examples.

manners, custom See **ethi-** and **mor-**.

-mantic (divination) See **-mancy**.

manu-, man-, mani- (L., hand) For other "hand" words, see **chiro-**.

> **Qualifying words:** amanuensis, bimanous, bimanual, emancipate, emancipation, manacle, manage, manageable, management, manager, manicure, manifest, manifestation, manifesto, maniloquism, manipulate, manipulation, manoeuvre, manual, manufactory, manufacture, manumission, manumotor, manure, manuscript, quadrumanous

many, much See **multi-** and **poly-**.

map See **carto-** for examples.

mare, mari- (L., sea) Also see **pelago-** and **thalasso-** for other "sea" words.

> **Qualifying words:** mare, *mare liberum,* mariculture, marigraph, marina, marinade, marine, mariner, marinotherapy, maritime, mariposia, submarine, submariner, supramarine, transmarine, ultramarine

margarito- (L., pearls)

> **Qualifying words:** margarid, margarite, margaritiferous, margaritomancy

mari- (L., sea) See **mare** for examples.

mark, reproach See **stigma** for examples.

mark, sign See **semeio-** and **sig-** for examples.

market place See **agora-** for examples.

marriage, union See **gamo-** for examples.

marriageable girl See **partheno-** and **virgo-**.

marsh, marshy See **helo-, limno-, telmato-,** and **tipho-** for examples.

marsupium (Gk., pouch) Also see **thyla-**.

> **Qualifying words:** marsupial, marsupialia, marsupium

marvel, monster See **terato-** for examples.

marvelous, wonderful See **prodigy** for examples.

maschal- (Gk., armpit) Also see **axillo-** for other "armpit" words.

> **Qualifying words:** maschaladenitis, maschalephidrosis, maschaliatry, maschalomadesis, maschaloncus, maschalyperidrosis, tragomaschalia

mass, tumor See **carcino-, -oma,** and **onco-**.

masto-, mast-, -mastia, -masty (Gk., breast) For other "breast" words, see **mammill-, mammo-, mazo-,** and **pectoro-**.

> **Qualifying words:** acromastitis, amastia, bimastism, macromastia, mastalgia, mastatrophy, mastectomy, mastitis, mastocarcinoma, mastodon, mastodontic, mastodynia, mastogram, mastography, mastoid, mastoidal, mastoidalgia, mastoidectomy, mastoiditis, mastoidotomy, mastology, mastopathis, mastopathy, mastopexy, mastoplasia, mastoplastia, mastoplasty, mastotomy, pleomastia

mastoido-, mastoid- (Gk., *masto-[e] id[es]*, "breast-shaped" [from *mast[os]*, breast plus the adjective-forming suffix *-oid*, like], used in the specialized sense as "of or pertaining to the [breast-shaped] mastoid process of the temporal bone") Also see **mammo-, mammil-, masto-, mazo-,** and **pectoro-** for other "breast" words; and **temporo-** for "side of head" words.

> **Qualifying words:** mastoid, mastoidalgia, mastoidectomy, mastoiditis, mastoidotomy

mater-, matri-, matr- (L., mother) Also see FAMILY GROUPS, **matro-,** and **metro-**.

> **Qualifying words:** alma mater, material, maternal, maternity, matriarch, matriarchy, matricentric, matricide, matriculate, matrilineage, matrilineal, matrilinear, matrilocal, matrilocality, matrimony, matrix, matron, matronly, matronymic

matter See **chemo-** and **hylo-** for examples.

matr- (L., mother) See **mater-** for examples.

matri- (L., mother) See **mater-** for examples.

matro-, matr- (Gk., mother) Also see **mater-** and **metro-** for other "mother" words.

> **Qualifying words:** matron, matronal, matronage, matronize, matronly, matronymic, matroclinous

maxi- (L., large, great, greatest) Also examine **giganto-, grand, macro-, magni-, major-,** and **mega-** for other "large" words.

> **Qualifying words:** maxim, maxima, maximal, maximize, maximum

maxillo-, maxill- (L., jaw, upper jawbone) Also see **gnatho-** and **mandibulo-** (lower jaw) for other "jaw" words.

> **Qualifying words:** maxilla(s.), maxillae(pl.), maxillary, maxilliform, maxillofacial, maxillomandibular, maxillopharyngeal

mazo-, -mazia (Gk., breast) See **mammo-, mammill-, masto-,** and **pectoro-** for other "breast" words.

> **Qualifying words:** Amazon, gynecomazia, mazodynia, mazoplasia, tetramazia

meadow, field, open woodland See **orgado-** for examples.

meal See **cibo-** for examples.

measure See **mens-** and **meter-** for examples.

meat, flesh For examples, see **carno-**, **creo-** (**kreo-**), and **sarco-**.

meato-, meat-, mea- [*meatus*] (L., opening or passageway in the body, bodily opening or canal; to pass, passage)

> **Qualifying words:** impermeable, irremeable, meatal, meatomastoidectomy, meatome, meatometer, meatoplasty, meatorrhapy, meatoscope, meatoscopy, meatotome, meatotomy, meatus, permeability, permeable, permeance, permeant, permeate, permeation

mechano-, mechan- (Gk., machine, contrivance; of or pertaining to a machine or to the workings of a machine)

> **Qualifying words:** mechanics, mechanocardiography, mechanocyte, mechanogymnastics, mechanotherapy, mechanothermy

medi-, med- (L., heal, cure) Also see **cura-**, **iatro-**, **sana-**, and **therap-** for additional "heal" words. Don't confuse this **medi-** element with the one in **medio-** which means "middle." Also see **hygieio-** for "healthy" words.

> **Qualifying words:** medical, medicament, medicant, medicate, medication, medicinal, medicine, remediable, remedial, remedy

medicine, drug(s) See **pharmaco-**.

medio-, medi- (L., middle) Also see **meso-** for other examples. Don't confuse this **medi-** with the previous one which means "cure, heal."

> **Qualifying words:** immediacy, immediate, immediately, intermediary, intermediate, intermezzo, media, medial, median, mediant, mediate, mediator, medieval, medifrontal, mediocre, mediocrity, mediolateral, Mediterrranean, medium, meridian

mega-, meg- (Gk., large, great, powerful; when measuring, it means a *million* [10^6]) See **giga-, giganto-, grand-, macro-, magni-, major, maxi-, megalo-,** and the METRIC GROUPS section in **Appendix F** for additional units and examples.

> **Qualifying words:** acromegaly, megabit, megabyte, megacephalic, megacephalous, megacurie, megacycle, megadactyl, megadactylia, megadactylism, megadactyly, megadont, megadontism, megadyne, megaelectron, megaelectrovolt, megaelectronvolt-curie, megaesophagus, megagauss, megagnathia, megagram, megahertz, megajoule, megalgia, megalith, megalopolis, megaparsec, mega-

phyllous, megapod, megarad, megascope, megascopic, megasecond, megaseism, megathere, megatherium, megatherm, megathermophyte, megaton, megavitamis, megavolt, megawatt, megohm, megohmmeter, omega

megalo-, megal-, -megalia, -megaly (Gk., large) Also see **giga-, giganto-, grand-, macro-, magni-, major, maxi-,** and **mega-** for additional "large" words.

> **Qualifying words:** megalaesthetes, megalocardia, megalocheira, megalochiria, megalodactylia, megalodactylism, megalodactyly, megalodont, megalodontia, megalogastria, megaloglossia, megalohepatia, megalomania, megalomaniac, megalopia, megalopodia, megalopolis, megalosyndactyly, megalosyndactylia

meio- (Gk., smaller, less) See **mio-**.

mel- (L., honey) See **melli-** for examples.

melano-, melan-, mela-, melen- (Gk., black) Also see **niger-** for other "black" words and examine COLORS for related words.

> **Qualifying words:** hepatomelanosis, melancholia, melancholiac, melancholic, melancholy, melanemia, Melanesia, melangeophile, melangeophilous, melangeophily, melaniferous, melanin, melanism, melanocarcinoma, melanocyte, melanoderm, melanoderma, melanodermatitis, melanodermic, melanogaster, melanogenesis, melanoglossia, melanoid, melanoleukoderma, melanoma, melanonychia, melanopathy, melanosis, melanotrichous, pneumonomelanosis

meliorat- (L., better) Compare with **pejor-** (worse) for words with opposite meanings.

> **Qualifying words:** ameliorate, meliorable, meliorate, meliorated, melioration, meliorating, meliorism, meliorist, melioristic, meliority

melli-, meli-, melit-, melito-, mellit-, mellito-melo-, -mel, -melic, -melitic (Gk. > L., honey) Also see **api-** (bee) for related examples.

> **Qualifying words:** caramel, hydromel, meliphage, meliphagous, meliphagy, melis, melittology, melittophile, melittophilous, melittophily, melliferous, mellifluence, mellifluent, mellifluous, melliphagous, mellisugous, mellivorous, mellivory, Melissa, molasses, oenomel, oxymel, philomel

melt, pour See **fus-** for examples.

membrane of the chest See **pleuro-**.

membrane around a fetus See **amnio-**.

membrane lining See **amnio-** for examples.

membrane, skin See **hymeno-** for examples.

membrane of the ear, tympanic See **myringo-** and **tympano-** for examples.

membranes of the brain and the spinal cord See **meningo-** for examples.

memor-, memen- (L., memory, remember) Also see **mne-**.

> Qualifying words: commemorate, commemoration, commemorative, immemorial, memento, memento mori, memoir, memorabilia, memorable, memoranda, memorandum, memorial, memorialize, memorize, memory, remember, remembrance

meningo-, mening-, meninge-, meningeo-, meningi- (Gk., membranes enveloping the brain and spinal cord)

> Qualifying words: menina, meninges, meningitic, meningitis, meningoencephalitis, meningomyelitis, pseudomeningitis

meno-, men-, meni-, -mena (Gk., [lunar] month; moon denotes the *menses*)

> Qualifying words: amenia, catamenia, dysmenorrhea, menhidrosis, menolipsis, menology, menometrorrhagia, menopause, menorrhagia, menorrhalgia, menorrhea, mensal, menstasia, menostasis, menostaxis, menses, menstrual, menstruate, menstruation, mensual, myelomenia, premenstrual, postmenstrual

mens- (L., measure) Also see **meter-**.

> Qualifying words: commensurable, commensurate, dimension, immense, immensurable, mensurable, mensural, mensurate, mensuration

menses (Gk., "monthly period") See **meno-**.

menstrual See **meno-** (month) for examples.

mental, mind See **noo-**, **phren-**, and **psycho-**.

mento-, ment-, menti- (L., chin)

> Qualifying words: mentigerous, mentoanterior, mentolabial, mentoplasty, mentoposterior, mentotransverse

merg-, mers- (L., dip, immerse, plunge) Also examine **bapti-**.

> Qualifying words: emerge, emergency, emergent, emersion, immerge, immerse, immersion, merge, merger, submerge, submersion

mero-, mer-, meri- (Gk., [1] part, partial; segment)

> Qualifying words: merergastic, merispore, meroacrania, meroblastic, merocrine, merogenesis, merogenic, merogony, merology, meromelia, meromicrosomia, meromorphosis, meromyosin, meronecrobiosis, meronecrosis, merosmia, meropia, meroplankton, merorachisis, merosmia, merostotic, merotomy, merozoite, merozygote

> (Gk., [2] thigh [anatomy] Also see **femuro-** for other "thigh" words.

> Qualifying words: meralgia, merocoxalgia, merophilous, merosthenic

mers- (L., dip, immerse) See **merg-**.

meso-, mes-, mesio- (Gk., middle) Also see **medio-** for additional "middle" words.

> Qualifying words: mesiolingual, mesioversion, mesoappendix, mesobenthos, mesocardia, mesocarp, mesocephalic, mesocosm, mesoderm, mesodont, mesogastric, mesognathous, mesohaline, mesohippus, mesohydrophyte, mesohydrophytic, mesolit, mesolithic, mesology, mesomorph, mesomorphic, mesopause, mesophil, mesophyll, mesophyllous, mesophyte, mesophytic, mesoplankton, mesoplastic, Mesopotamia, mesopsammon, mesorhinal, mesorrhine, Mesosauria, mesosaprobe, mesosaprobic, mesosphere, mesotherm, mesotic, mesotrophic, mesotropic, Mesozoa, Mesozoic, mesozooid

messenger See **angelo-** for examples.

meta-, met-, meth- (Gk., [1] after, behind) Also see **post-** for other "after, behind" words.

> Qualifying words: metacognition, metacognitive, metagastric, metakinesis, metalimnetic, metalimnion, metaphysical, metaphysics, metaphyte, metaplasis, metapterygium, metaptile, metathroax, metazoan, metazoon, metencephalon, metoesthetism, metoxenous

> (Gk., [2] changed in form, altered)

> Qualifying words: metabolic, metabolism, metachromy, metachrosis, metagnathous, metamorphic, metamorphism, metamorphosis, metaplasia

> (Gk., [3] higher [used to designate a higher degree of a branch of science])

> Qualifying word: metabisulfate, metachemistry, metaphosphate

metall-, metall- (Gk., mineral, metal)

> Qualifying words: metallesthesia, mettallophobia, metallophil, metallophilia, metallophilic, metalloscopy, metallotherapy

meter-, metro-, metr-, -metrical, -metrically, -metron, -metric, -metrist, -meters, -metry, -metre (Gk., measure) Also see **mens-** and NUMBERS in **Appendix G** and the METRIC GROUPS in **Appendix F** for additional "measure" words. Don't confuse this element with another **metro-** which means "mother" or "uterus" [in the medical world].

> Qualifying words: absorptiometer, accelerometer, acetimeter, acidimetry, algometer, altimeter, anemometer, asymmetrical, asymmetry, atmometer, audiometer, autometry, barometer, bathometer, biometrics, biometry, calorimeter, centimeter, cephalometer, chromoptometer, chronometer, clinometer, craniometer, cryometer, cryometry, cyclometer, cyclometry, decimeter, densimeter, diameter, diametrically, dioptometer, dissymmetrical,

dosimeter, drunkometer, dynamometer, econometrics, ergometer, ergometry, erythrocytometry, eudiometer, extensometer, fluorometer, fluviometer, fluxmeter, galactometer, galvanometer, galvanometry, geometry, goniometer, goniometry, gravimeter, gyrometer, halometry, heliometer, heliometry, horometer, hydrometer, hygrometer, hypsometer, hypsometry, isometrics, isometry, kinesimeter, konimeter, konimetry, kryometer, lactometer, megameter, meter, metrical, metrics, metrograph, metrography, metrologist, metrology, metromania, metronome, micrometer, odometer, ohmmeter, oleometer, ombrometer, ondometer, oometer, osmometer, osteometry, pachymeter, parameter, pedometer, perimeter, phonometer, photometer, planometer, plastometer, plastometry, pluviometer, pneumatometer, psychometrics, psychometry, pulmometer, pulsimeter, pyrheliometer, pyrometer, pyrometry, radiometer, radiometry, rheometry, saccharimeter, salimeter, salinometer, scintillometer, seismometer, sensitometer, sonometer, spectrometer, speedometer, sphygmomanometer, spirometer, stereometry, stethometer, symmetric, symmetrical, symmetrophobia, symmetry, tachometer, tachymeter, tachymetry, taximeter, telemeter, telemetry, terameter, tetrameter, thalassometer, thermometer, trigonometry, turbidimetry, udometer, velocimeter, viameter, viatometer, vinometer, viscometer, voltmeter, volumetry, zymometer, zoometry

metro-, metr- (Gk., mother) Also see **mater-** and **matro-** and FAMILY GROUPS for additional examples. Don't confuse "mother" examples with those in "measure" (**meter-**, et al.) and another **metro-** used in medicine which means "uterine" or "womb."

  Qualifying words: haplometrosis, haplometrotic, metrocracy, metrocyte, metronymic, metronymy, metropolis, metropolitan, pleometrosis, pleometrotic

metro-, metra-, metr- (Gk., uterus, womb) Also see **hystero-** for related information. Don't confuse this **metro-** with another **metro-** which means "mother;" and be careful of **meter-**, "measure."

  Qualifying words: endometrorrhagia, endometriosis, endometritis, endometrium, metritis, metrocele, metrodynamometer, metrodynia, metroendometritis, metrogenous, metrography, metromalacia, metronania, metroparalysis, metropathia, metropathy, metroperitoneal, metroperitonitis, metrophlebitis, metroplasty, metrorrhagia, metrorrhea, metrorrhexis, metroscope, metrostasis, metrotomy, metrotoxin

-metry (Gk., measure) See **meter-**.

mice, mouse See **muso-** for examples.

micro-, micr- (Gk., small, tiny; one millionth part of [something]; 10^{-6} [0.000 001]) Also see **lepto-, mini-, nano-, pico-,** and the METRIC GROUPS section in **Appendix F** for other related elements.

  Qualifying words: micracoustic, micraesthetes, microanalysis, microbe, microbiology, microbiophagy, microbiophobia, microbiota, microbivorous, microcosm, microcurie, microdont, microdot, microearthquake, microecology, microfarad, microfaunal, microfilm, microflora, microfloral, microgyne, microhabitat, microhenry, microhm, micrometer, micromicrocurie, micromicrofarad, Micronesia, Micronesian, microorganism, microparasite, microphages, microphagic, microphil, microphone, microphyllous, microphyte, microphytology, microplankton, micropodous, micropterism, micropterous, microseism, microscopic, microsomia, microsurgery, microsurgical, microtaxonomy, microtherm, microtomy, microtrichia, microwatt, microzoon, photomicrograph

middle See **medio-** and **meso-** for examples.

mighty, powerful Examine **dyna-, firm-, fort-, poten-, stheno-,** and **valid-** for examples.

migr-, migrat- (L., wander, moving) Also see **err-, nomad-,** and **vaga-**.

  Qualifying words: commigration, emigrant, emigrate, emigration, emigre (Fr.), immigrant, immigrate, immigration, migrant, migrate, migration, migratory, transmigrate, transmigration

milit- (L., soldier, fight) For additional "war" words, see **belli-, -machy,** and **pugn-**.

  Qualifying words: demilitarize, militancy, militant, militarist, militate, militia, military

milk See **galacto-** and **lacto-** for examples.

mili- (L., thousand) See **milli-** for examples.

milli-, mille-, mill-, mili- (L., thousand; 10^{-3} [0.001] or one-thousandth) Also examine **giga-** and **kilo-** for other examples and see the NUMBERS section in **Appendix G** and the METRIC GROUPS section in **Appendix F** for other numerical elements. Note: in the metric system, **milli-** denotes 1/1,000 of a unit.

  Qualifying words: mile, millefiori, millenary, millennial, millennium, Millennium, millepede, millesimal, milliampere, milliard, millibar, millicurie, millienarian, millienarianism, millifarad, milligram, milliliter, millilitre, millimeter, millimetre, milliohm, million, millionaire, millipede, millirad, milliroentgen, millisecond, millivolt, milliwatt

mill- (L., thousand) See **milli-** for examples.

million See **mega-** for examples.

mimo-, mim-, -mimesis, -mimia, -mimetic, -mime, -mimic, -mimical, -mimically (Gk., imitate, act, simulation)

> Qualifying words: mime, mimeograph, mimesis, mimetic, mimic, mimicry, mimographer, mimosis, mimotype, necromimesis, neuromimesis, pantomime, pathomimesis

mind, mental See **noo-, phreno-,** and **psycho-**.
mineral spring, fountain See **creno-** and **pego-**.
mingle, mix See **misce-** for examples.

mini-, minor-, minut-, minu- (L., small, little) Also see **-cle, -cule, -icle, -le, lepto-, -let, -ling, micro-, mio-, nano-, oligo-, pauci-, pico-,** and **-ule** .

> Qualifying words: comminute, diminish, diminuendo, diminution, diminutive, minify, minima, minimal, minimize, minimum, miniscule, minister, minometer, minor, minority, minuend, milnuet, minus, minuscule, minute, minutia, minutiae

mio-, meio- (Gk., smaller, less) Also examine **-cle, -cule, -icle, -le, lepto-, -let, -ling, micro-, mini-, nano-, oligo-, pauci-, pico-,** and **-ule** for other "small" words.

> Qualifying words: meiofauna, meioflora, meiophyly, meiosis, meiospore, meiotherm, meiosis, miobyte, miocardia, Miocene, miocrystalline, miohippus, miophone, mioplasma, mioplasmia, miopus, miosis, miotic

miracle, wonder See **thaumato-** for examples.
mirror See **catoptro-** and **eisoptro-**.
mis- (Anglo-Saxon, bad, harsh, wrong) This **mis-** is not related to the **miso-, mis-** in "hate." Also see **caco-, dys-,** and **mal-** for additional "bad" words.

> Qualifying words: misadventure, misbehave, misconstrue, misdeed, misdemeanor, misfortune, mistrust

miscarry, untimely birth For examples, see **abort-** and **ectro-**.
misce-, misc- (L., mix, mingle)

> Qualifying words: antimiscegenation, immiscible, meddle, medley, miscegenation, miscellanea, miscellaneous, miscellaneously, miscellany, mixture, promiscuity, promiscuous, promiscuously

miso-, mis- (Gk., hate, hater, hatred) Don't confuse this element with another **mis-** which means "bad, harsh, wrong."

> Qualifying words: misandria, misandrist, misandry, misanthrope, misanthropy, misarchist, misarchy, misocainia, misocapnist, misocapny, misocynist, misocyny, misogamy, misogamist, misogrammatist, misogrammar, misogynist, misogyny, misologia, misologist, misology, misomania, misomaniac, misomater, misoneism, misoneist, misopater, misopa-

trist, misopedist, misopedia, misopedist, misopogonist, misoscopist, misosophist, misosophy, misotheism, misotheist, misoxene, misoxenist

miss-, -miss, -mis-, -mit, -mitt- (L., send, let go, cause to go; throw, hurl, cast) Also see **ballo-** and **jet-**.

> Qualifying words: admission, admit, admittance, Christmas, commissar, commissary, commission, commit, commitment, committee, compromise, demise, demit, dismiss, dismissal, emissary, emission, emit, immission, immit, intermission, intermit, intermittent, intromission, intromit, manumission, Mass, message, missal, missile, mission, missionary, missive, noncommital, omission, omit, permission, permit, premise, pretermission, pretermit, promise, remiss, remission, remit, remittance, submission, submissive, submit, surmise, transmission, transmit

mist, air See **aero-** for examples.
-mit, -mitt (L., send, throw) See **miss-**.
mite(s) See **acaro-** for examples.
mito-, mit- (Gk., thread) Also see **fibro-** and **lin-** for similarities.

> Qualifying words: karyomitotic, mitochondria, mitochondrion, mitogen, mitogenesia, mitogenesis, mitogenetic, mitokinesis, mitome, mitoplasm, mitoschisis, mitoses, mitosis, mitosome, mitotic

mix, mingle See **misce-** and **mixo-**.
mixo-, mix-, -mixia (Gk., a mixing, mingling, intercourse)

> Qualifying words: mixobarbaric, mixoploid, mixoscopia, mixoscopy, manmixia

mne-, mnem-, mnemon-, mnes-, -mnesia, -mnesiac, -mnesic, -mnestic (Gk., memory, to remember) Also see **memor-** for other "remember" words and compare with **cogni-, epistemo-, not-,** and **sci-** for words with related meanings.

> Qualifying words: amnemonic, amnesia, amnesiac, amnesic, amnestic, amnesty, anamnestic, antimnemonic, automnesia, cryptomnesia, mnemic, mnemonic, mnemonics, mnemonists, mnemotaxis, panmnesia, paramnesia

mob, people See **ochlo-** for examples.
mobi- (L., move) See **mobil-** for examples.
mobil-, mobi- (L., move, moving, to set in motion) Also see **cine-, kine-,** and **mot-**.

> Qualifying words: automobile, immobile, immobility, immobilization, mob (*mobile vulgus*), mobile, mobility, mobilization, mobilize, mobocracy

moist, wet See **hygro-** and **humid-**.
mold, mushroom See **fungi-** and **myco-**.

molded, shaped   See **plasmo-** for examples.

molybd- (Gk., lead [the metal]) Also see **plumbo-** for other "lead" [metal] words.

> Qualifying words: molybdenum, molybdenos, molybdic, molybdous

mond- (L., earth, world) See **mundan-**.

money, profit   See **lucr-** for examples.

monkey, ape   See **pitheco-** and **simia-**.

mono-, mon- (Gk., one, alone, single) Also see **haplo-, soli-,** and **uni-** for other "one" words and see the NUMBERS section in **Appendix G** for related elements.

> Qualifying words: monadelphous, monandrous, monanthous, monarch, monarchy, monaster, monastery, monastic, monatheism, monaural, monk, monoandry, monoanesthesia, monoblepsia, monobrachia, monocardia, monocardian, monocarp, monocarpic, monocarpous, monocellular, monocentric, monocephalous, monochromatic, monochronic, monociliated, monocle, monocracy, monocular, monocyclic, monodactylia, monodactylism, monodactylous, monodactyly, monodiplopia, monogamy, monogastric, monogenesis, monogenous, monogeny, monogomy, monogram, monograph, monogyny, monolingual, monolith, monolithic, monologue, monomania, monomial, monomaniac, monomorphic, mononym, monoma, monopathy, monophagia, monophagism, monophasia, monoplegia, monopodal, monopodia, monopoly, monopus, monorhinal, monorhinic, monotheism, monothermal, monothermia, monotony, monotrophic, monotropic, monoxenous, monoxylic

monster   See **terato-** for examples.

mont-, mount- (L., mountain, hill) Also see **ochtho-** and **oro-** (mountain).

> Qualifying words: amount, catamount, insurmountable, montage, mount, mountebank, paramount, piedmont, promontory, rodomontade, surmount, tantamount

month   See **meno-** for examples.

-mony (L., action, result of an action or condition) A suffix which forms nouns. Also see the SUFFIXES section in **Appendix K** for other word endings.

> Qualifying words: acrimony, patrimony, sanctimony, testimony

moon   See **luna-** and **seleno-** for examples.

mor-, mora- (L., custom, habit, manner) Also see **ethi-** for other "custom" words. Don't confuse this element with those in **mort-,** "death."

> Qualifying words: amoral, demoralize, immoral, immorality, moral, morale, morality, moralize, mores, morose

more   See **pluri-** for examples.

mori- (L., death) See **mort-** for an example.

moro-, mor-, -moria (Gk., a feeble minded person; foolish; dull)

> Qualifying words: monomoria, moran, moronic, moronism, morosoph, oxymoron, phantasmatomoria, sophomore, sophomoric

morpho-, morph-, -morphous, -morphically, -morphia, -morphosis, -morphously, -morphy, -morphic, -morphism (Gk., shape, form, figure, appearance) Also see **eido-, icono-, idol,** and **-oid** for additional "form" words.

> Qualifying words: adelomorphous, allomorph, amorphous, anthropomorphic, atmometamorphism, chemomorphosis, ectomorph, endomorph, endomorphic, exomorphic, geomorph, geomorphology, hydrometamorphism, isomorphic, isomorphous, mesomorph, metamorphosis, morpheme, Morpheus, morphine, morphobiometry, morphocytology, morphography, morphogenesis, morphogeny, morphology, morphometrical, morphometry, morphon, morphonomic, morphonomy, morphoplasy, morphosis, pantomorphic, perimorphous, polymorphic, polymorphism, promorphologist, promorphology, pseudomorph, pseudomorphic, pyrometamorphism, tetramorph, tetramorphism, zoomorphosis

mort-, mor-, mori- (L., death, dead) Also see **-cide, letha-, neci-, necro-,** and **thanato-** for additional "death" words.

> Qualifying words: abmortal, admortal, amort, amortality, amortize, ante mortem, benemortasia, biomort, biomortia, immortal, immortality, moribund, mortal, mortality, mortgage, mortician, mortification, mortify, mortuary, neomort, neomortia, post-mortem, postmortem

mosquito   See **anopheli-** and **culci-**.

moss   See **bryo-** for examples.

most, more, full   See **pleio-, plen-,** and **pluri-**.

mot-, moto-, -motile, -motility, -motorial, -motoric, -motive, -motored (L., move) Also see **cinem-, kine-,** and **mob-**.

> Qualifying words: commotion, demote, demotion, emotion, emotional, locomotion, locomotive, moment, momentaneous, momentary, momentous, momentum, motile, motility, motion, motivate, motivation, motive, motometer, motor, promote, promoter, promotion, remote, remove

moths, butterflies   See **lepidopter-**.

mother   See **mater-** and **metro-** for examples.

mouse, mice   See **muso-** for examples.

mound, hill, bank   See **ochtho-** for examples.

mouth   See **ora-, oscula-,** and **stomato-**.

mount- (mountain, hill) See **mont-**.

mount (verb), climb   See **scan-** and **scend-**.

mountain See **mont-** and **oro-** for examples.

move, movement See **ambul-, cinem-, kine-, mobi-,** and **mot-** for examples.

move in a certain direction, stretch See **tend-, tendo-, teno-,** and **ton-** for examples.

moving around, wandering See **err-, migr-, nomad-,** and **vaga-** for examples.

much, many See **multi-** and **poly-**.

mud, earth See **argillo-, chledo-, limi-** and **pelo-** for examples.

multi-, mult- (L., many, much) Also see **poly-** for other "many" words.

> **Qualifying words:** multicellular, multicolored, multifarious, multifold, multiform, multigraph, multilateral, Multilith, multiparous, multiple, multiplex, multiplication, multiplicity, multiply, multitude, multitudinous

multitude, people See **commu-, demo-, ethno-, ochlo-, pleb-, popu-, publi-,** and **vulg-**.

mundan-, mond- (L., earth, world) Additional "earth, world" words will be found if you examine **agra-, agri-, agro-, chthon-, cosmo-, geo-, humus,** and **terr-**.

> **Qualifying words:** demimonde, extramundane, monde, mound, mundane, mundanely, mundaneness, mundanity, transmundane, ultramondane, ultramundane

murder See **-cide** and **mort-** for examples

muri- (L., mouse) Also see **muso-** for other "mouse" words.

> **Qualifying words:** murid, Muridae, muricidal, muriform, murine

muscle See **myo-** for examples.

Muses, goddesses of the various fine arts. There were nine beautiful daughters of *Zeus* and *Mnemosyne* (ne MOS i nee), a Titaness, from which we have words meaning "memory," and "mnemonic." The Muses were goddesses of poetic inspiration and poets of ancient times, and even of early-modern times, would always start important poems by calling on the Muses for inspiration.

In ancient times, poetry, drama, and other forms of recitation were done from memory with the accompaniment of melodious sounds which came to be known as "music."

Temples built in honor of the Muses were devoted to study and learning and these temples became known as "museums."

The nine Muses were in charge of different branches of the fine arts. *Calliope* (kuh LIGH uh pee) was head of the Muses. She was the Muse of heroic poetry and eloquence.

Clio (KLEE oh), was the muse of history. *Erato* (ER uh toh) and *Urania* (yoo RAY nee uh) are two Muses with the feminine names of Eros and Uranus. *Erato* is the Muse of love poetry and *Urania* is the Muse of astronomy.

Euterpe (yoo TUR pee) is the Muse of ordinary music and *Polyhymnia* (PAHL ee HIM nee uh) is the Muse of religious music.

Thalia (tha LIGH uh) is the Muse of comedy and *Melpomene* (mel POM i nee) is the Muse of tragedy.

The ninth Muse is *Terpsichore* (terp SIK oh ree), goddess of the dance. Even today, dancing is sometimes jokingly spoken of as the "terpsichorean art."

mushroom, mold See **fungus** and **myco-** for examples.

musico-, music- (Gk., music [*mousiko(s)*], pertaining to the Muses, especially the Muses of lyric poetry and song." From *Muse* plus *-icos*, meaning "the art of combining sounds in sequence so as to produce aesthetic pleasure in the listener."

> **Qualifying words:** musicogenic, musicologist, musicology, musicomania, musicotherapy

muso-, mus- (Gk., mouse, mice) Also spelled **myo-** (Gk., muscle) when used in medical terms. Also see **muri-** for other "mouse" words.

> **Qualifying words:** musomania, musophile, musophilia, musophobia

mut- (L., change, changeable) Other examples can be seen in **alter-**.

> **Qualifying words:** commute, immutable, molt, mutable, mutant, mutate, mutation, mutual, permutation, permute, remuda, transmutation, transmute

myceto- (fungus, fungi) See **myco-**.

myco-, myc-, myceto-, mycet-, -mycetous, -mycetic, -mycetous, -mycosis, -mycin (Gk., fungus, fungi) Also see **fungi-** for additional "fungi" examples and examine **phyco-** for "algae" words.

> **Qualifying words:** actinomyces, actinomycetes, actinomycosis, blastomycosis, chromoblastomycosis, dermatomycosis, mycelial, mycelium, mycetocyte, mycetogenic, mycetoid, mycetology, mycetoma, mycetophage,

mycetophagous, mycetophagy, mycobiont, mycobiota, mycoderm, mycogen, mycoid, mycological, mycologist, mycology, mycophagous, mycorhiza, mycorrhiza, mycosis, mycotic, mycotoxincosis, mycotoxic, mycotoxin, mycotrophic, mycotrophy, myocosis, neomycin, phaeohyphomycosis, pharyngomycosis, phycomyces, rhinomycosis, Saccharomyces, schizomycete

myelo-, myel- (Gk., bone marrow; the spinal cord and medulla oblongata; the myelin sheath of nerve fibers)

> **Qualifying words:** amyelencephalia, amyelia, amyeloneuria, amyelotrophy, myelinoclasis, myelitis, myeloblast, myelocytes, myelodysplasia, myelography, myeloid, myeloma, muyelomalacia, myelopathy, myelotoxic, myesthesia, neuromyelitis, osteomyelitis, poliomyelitis

myo-, my-, myos- (Gk., muscle ["mouse"]) Also see **myelo-** for additional examples. From Greek *mu*(s), *my*(os), meaning "mouse," as in *myomancy*.

> **Qualifying words:** amyocardia, amyoesthesis, amyoplasia, amyostasia, amyosthenia, amyosthenic, amyotaxia, amyotaxy, amyotonia, amyotrophia, amyotrophic, amyotrophy, amyous, cardiomyopathy, encephalomyocarditis, myasthenai, myoathrophy, myoatrophy, myobradia, myocardial, myocarditis, myocardium, myochrome, myodynamic, myofibril, myofibroma, myofibrosis, myofibrositis, myogenic, myogenesis, myogram, myograph, myography, myoid, myolipoma, myology, myoma, myomancy, myopathy, myospasm, myotaxy, myotherapy, myotonia

myria-, myrio-, myri- (Gk., ten thousand; very numerous, countless) Also see the NUMBERS section in **Appendix G.**

> **Qualifying words:** myriacanthous, myriad, myriagram, myrialiter, myriameter, myriapod, myriarch, myrioama, myriophyllous, myriopod, myriosporous, myriotheist

myringo-, myring- (Gk. > L., membrane, tympanic [drum] membrane) Also see **tympano-** for other "drum" or "eardrum" words.

> **Qualifying words:** myringa, myringitis, myringectomy, myringodectomy, myringodermatitis, myringomycosis, myringoplasty, myringorupture, myringotome, myringotomy

myrio- (Gk., countless) See **myria-.**

myrmeco-, myrmec-, myrme-, myrmic-, myrmi- (Gk., ant *or* ants) For additional "ant" words, see **formic-.**

> **Qualifying words:** adelomyrmex, *Cyphomyrmex, Dorymyrmex, Erebomyrma antiqua, Gesomyrmex, Iridomyrmex, Myrmecia,* myrmecide, *Myrmecinae,* myrmecobiosis, myrme-

cochore, myrmecochorous, myrmecochory, myrmecoclepty, *Myrmecocystus,* myrmecodomatia, myrmecodomus, myrmecological, myrmecologist, myrmecology, *Myrmecophaga,* myrmecophagia, *Myrmecophagia tridactyla, Myrmecophagidae,* myrmecophagous, myrmecophagy, myrmecophil, myrmecophile, myrmecophilous, myrmecophily, myrmecophobia, myrmecophobic, myrmecophyte, myrmecophytism, myrmecosymbiotic, myrmecosymbiosis, myrmecotrophic, myrmecotrophy, myrmecoxenous, myrmecoxeny, *Myrmeleontidae, Myrmica,* myrmicine, *Oligomyrmex, Pogonomyrmex, Prionomyrmex longiceps, Pristomyrmex, Pseudomyrma, Thaumatomyrmex, Trachymyrmex*

myso-, mys- (Gk., uncleanness of body or mind; filth; anything disgusting) Also see **rhypo-** for other "filth" words and compare with **sapro-** and **sepsi-** for similar meanings.

> **Qualifying words:** mysophilia, mysophobia, mysophobiac, mysophobic, automysophobia

myster-, myst- (Gk. > L., secret, occult [probable literal meaning is "one whose eyes are closed"]) Also examine the elements: **calyp-, clandestine, crypto-, krypto-, leth-,** and **occult** for additional "hidden, secret" words.

> **Qualifying words:** mystagogic, mystagogue, mystagogy, mysterious, mystery, mystic, mystification, mystify

mythico-, mytho-, myth-, -mythical, -mythical, -mythically, -mythic (Gk., talk, speech, word, story) Examine **cit-, clam-, dic-, fa-, lalo-, legi-, locu-, logo-, loqu-, ora-, -phasia, -phemia,** and **voc-** for additional "talk, speech, story" words.

> **Qualifying words:** antimythic, myth, mythical, mythographer, mythological, mythologist, mythologize, mythology, mythomania, mythopeic, mythophobia, mythopoeic, mythopoetic, polymythic

N n

nail, claw See **chela-, onycho-**, and **unguo-**.

naked, uncovered See **gymno-** and **nudo-**.

nemato-, namat- (Gk., spring (water), fountain) Also see **creno-** and **pego-** for other "spring, water" words.

    Qualifying words: namatophile, namatophilous, namatophily, namatophyte

name See **nom-, onomato-**, and **-onym** for examples.

nano-, nan-, nanno-, -nania (Gk., dwarf, dwarfish; pygmy; very small or tiny [one billionth of a unit] 10^{-9} [0.000 000 000 001]) Also see **micro-, mini-, mio-**, and **pico-** and the METRIC GROUPS section in **Appendix F** for additional units.

    Qualifying words: metronania, nanander, nanocranous, nanism, nannandrous, nannofossil, nannoplankton, nanocephalia, nanocephalous, nanocephaly, nanocircuit, nanocurie, nanoequivalent, nanofabrication, nanofossil, nanogram, nanoid, nanoliter, nanometer, nanomole, nanon, nanophanerophyte, nanophyll, nanophyllous, nanoplankton, nanosecond, nanosomia, nanosomus, nanosurgery (nannosurgery), nanotechnology, nanotribologist, nanotribology, Nanotyrannnus, nanounit, nanous, nanovolt, nanowatt, nanozooid

narciss-, narcis- (Gk. > L., morbid self love) Also see **ego-** (L.) for related words.

    Qualifying words: narcism, narcissine, narcissism, narcissist, narcissistic, Narcissus

narco-, narc-, -narcotic, -narcosis, -narcoticism (Gk., numbness, dullness; sleep, stupor) Also see **ambly-, coma**[1]**, dorm-, hypno-, leth-, somni-, sopor-**, and **torp-** for other "sleep" words.

    Qualifying words: autonarcosis, narcoanalysis, narcoanesthesia, narcohypnia, narcohypnosis, narcolepsy, narcoma, narcomania, narcomaniac, narcose, narcosis, narcostimulant, narcosynthesis, narcotherapy, narcotic, narcotism, narcotize

narrow, contracted See **steno-** for examples.

nasc-, nat- (L., born) Also see **genus, para-**, and **toco-** for other "birth" words.

    Qualifying words: antenatal, agnate, innate, inpregnate, intranatal, nascent, natal, natatorium, nation, native, nativity, natural, naturalism, nature, naturopathy, neonatal, neonate, neonatus, perinatal, perinatally, perinatologist, perinatalogy, postnatal, pregnant, prenatal, renaissance, renascent

naso-, nas- (L., nose) For other "nose" words, see **rhino-** and **rhyncho-**.

    Qualifying words: nasal, nasalis, nasality, nasalization, nasalize, nasally, nasitis, nasoantritis, nasobronchial, nasofrontal, nasograph, nasolabial, nasological, nasologist, nasology, nasopalatine, nasophryngitis, nasophranx, nasoscope, nasoseptal, nasoseptitis, nasosinusitis, nasospinale, nasus, nasute, nasutus, postnasal

nata- (L., to swim, swimming) Also examine **necto-** and **neusto-** for other "swimming" examples.

    Qualifying words: natant, natation, natatoria(pl.), natatorial, natatorium(s.)

nat- (born) See **nasc-** for examples.

nation, race See **ethno-** for examples.

nature See **nasc-** and **physico-** for examples.

naus-, nau- (Gk., sailor; ship) Also see **naut-** and **nav-** for other "sailor, ship" examples.

    Qualifying words: ad nauseam, naumachia, naupathia, nausea, nauseant, nauseate, nauseated, nauseous

naut-, -naut, -nautical, -nautics (Gk., ship; sailor; navigation) Also see **naus-** and **nav-** for related words.

    Qualifying words: aeronaut, aeronautics, aquanaut, astronaut, cosmonaut, nautical, nautiloids, nautilus

nav- (L., sailor; ship) Also see **naus-** and **naut-** for other "sailor" words.

    Qualifying words: circumnavigate, circumnavigation, naval, navicular, navigable, navigate, navigation, navigator, navy

navel, bellybutton See **omphalo-** and **umbili-** for examples.

ne- (Gk., new) See **neo-** for examples. The **ne-** element in this section is not the same as the Latin **ne-** which means "negative."

ne- (L., no, not) See **neg-** for examples. Don't confuse this element with the previous **ne-** (*neo-*) which means "new."

near, close For examples, see **juxta-, para-**, and **proximo-**.

near the back See **dorso-** for examples.

neci-, nici- (L., death, kill, deadly, murderous, destructive) Related to **nox-** and **necro-**. Also see **-cide, letha-, mort-, necro-**, and **thanato-** for additional "death" words.

    Qualifying words: internecine, pernicious, perniciously

neck, throat See the following for examples: **cervico-, esophago-, gutturo-, laryngo-, pharyngo-, trachelo-**, and **thoraco-**.

necro-, necr-, necron-, -necrosis, nekro- (Gk., dead, death, dead body, dead tissue, corpse) Also see **-cide, letha-, mort-,** and **thanato-** for other "death" words. Compare with **neci-** and **nox-**.

Qualifying words: adiponecrosis, angionecrosis, meronecrosis, necremia, necretomy, necrobia, necrobiosis, necrobiotic, necrocytosis, necrocoenosis, necrocytotoxin, necrodermatitis, necroectomy, necrogenic, necrogenous, necrographer, necrohormone, necrolatry, necrologic, necrological, necrologically, necrologist, necrologue, necrology, necromancer, necromancy, necromania, necromantic, necrometer, necromimesis, necronectomy, necroparasite, necrophagia, necrophage, necrophagous, necrophagy, necrophile, necrophilia, necrophiliac, necrophilism, necrophilous, necrophily, necrophobe, necrophobia, necrophobic, necrophoresis, necrophoric, necrophorus, necrophytophage, necrophytophagous, necrophytophagy, necropneumonia, necropolis, necropsies, necropsy, necropyoculture, necrosadism, necroscopy, necrose, necroses, necrosin, necrosis, necrotic, necrotize, necrotizing, necrotomy, necrotoxin, necrotrophic, synnecrosis, postnecrosis, postnecrotic, rhinonecrosis, steaonecrosis

necto-, nect-, nekto-, nek- (Gk., swimming) Also see **nata-, neusto-** and **pleusto-**.

Qualifying words: epinekton, epinektonic, holonekton, meronekon, nectism, nectobenthid, nectobenthos, nectocalyx, necton, Nectonema, nectophore, nectopod, nectosome, nectozooid, Nectria, nectridia, Necturus, nekton, nektonic

needle See **acu-** and **belono-** for examples.

neg- (L. [*negare*], no, not, deny, nullify)

Qualifying words: abnegate, abnegation, denegation, negation, negationist, negative, negatively, negativeness, negativism, negativist, negativity, negator, negatory, neglect, negligent, negotiate (from: *neg otium est*, "there is no leisure"), neuter, never, renegade, renege

negr- (L., black) See **niger-** for examples.

-neir (Gk., dream) See **oneiro-** for examples.

neither See **neutr-** for examples.

nekro- (Gk.) See **necro-** for examples.

nekto- (Gk., swimming) See **necto-** for examples.

nemato-, nemat-, nemati- (Gk., thread, that which is spun; pertaining to a thread-like structure) Also see **lepto-** for additional "thread" words.

Qualifying words: nema, nemaline, nemathelminth, nemathelminthiasis, nematicide, nematocide, nematocyst, nematoid, nematologist, nematology, Nematomorpha, Nematospermia

nemo-, nem- (Gk., wooded pasture, glade; grove; woods, forest) Also see **also-, arbor, dendro-, hylo-, ligni-,** and **sylv-**.

Qualifying words: Nemophilia, nemophilist, nemophilous, nemophily, nemoral

neo-, ne- (Gk., new, recent, current) Also see **-cene, ceno-,** and **novo-**.

Qualifying words: misoneism, neobiogenesis, neocarpy, neoclassic, neoclassicism, neolalia, neolith, Neolithic, neologism, neologist, neologize, neomorph, neomorphosis, neomort, neomortia, neomycin, neon, neonate, neonatal, neonatology, neontology, neoorthodoxy, neophilia, neophilism, neophily, neophobia, neophyte, neoplasm, neoplastic, neoptile, neoteric, neoterism, neozoic

nephelo-, nephel-, nepho- (Gk., cloud)

Qualifying words: nephanalysis, nepheligenous, nephelogist, nephelognosy, nephelogram, nephelograph, nephelometer, nephelometric, nephelometry, nephelopsychosis, nepheloscope, nephelosphere, nephology, nephelopia, nephophobia

nephro-, nephr-, -nephric (Gk., kidney) Also see **pyelo-** and **reno-**.

Qualifying words: epinephroma, hepatonephric, mesonephroma, nephralgia, nephralgic, nephrectomy, nephric, nephritic, nephritis, nephrocardiac, nephrogenic, nephrogenous, nephrogram, nephrography, nephroid, nephrolith, nephrolithiasis, nephrolithotomy, nephrologist, nephrology, nephrolysis, nephrolytic, nephromalacia, nephromegaly, nephropathic, nephropathy, nephropexy, nephrophagiasis, nephroplasty, nephropoietic, nephroscope, nephrosis, nephrosonography, nephrotome, nephrotomy, nephrotoxic, nephrotoxicity, nephrotoxin, oligonephria, paranephritis, paranephroma, pronephric

nervo-, nerv-, nervi- (L., nerve fiber or sinew) Also examine **achillo-, neuro-, polio-, radiculo-, tend-, tendo-, teno-,** and **ton-**.

Qualifying words: enervate, nerve, nervi(pl.), nervimotility, nervimotor, nervine, nervocidine, nervomuscular, nervosism, nervous, nervousness, nervus(s.)

neso-, nes-, -nesia (Gk., island) For other examples of "island" words, see **insula-**.

Qualifying words: Austronesian, Indonesia, Melanesia, Micronesia, nesomania, nesomaniac, Peloponnesia, Polynesia, Polynesian

net, netlike See **reticulo-** for examples.

neuro-, neur-, neuri-, -neuroma, -neurotic, -neurosis, -neuron, -neural, -neuria (Gk., nerve, tendon, sinew, cord) For other "nerve, tendon" words, see **achillo-, nervo-, tend-, tendo-, teno-,** and **ton-**.

Qualifying words: neuradynamia, neural, neuralgia, neuralgic, neurarchy, neurasthenia, neuratrophia, neuratrophy, neuraxis, neurectomy, neurergic, neuriatria, neuriatry, neuritic, neurimotility, neuritis, neuroarthropathy, neurobiotaxis, neurocardiac, neurodermatitis, neurodynamic, neurodynia, neurogastric, neurogram, neurography, neurology, neurolysis, neurolytic, neuromalacia, neuromyelitis, neuronitis, neuronophage, neuronophagia, neuronophagy, neuroplasty, neuropsychosis, neuro-otology, neurosis, neurosomatic, neurotherapeutics, neurotherapy, spinoneural, stereoneural, trineural

neusto-, neust-, -neuston, -neustonic (Gk., swim, float) Also see **nata-, necto-** and **pleusto-** for other "swim, float" words.

Qualifying words: anemoneuston, bacterioneuston, epineuston, epineustonic, hyponeuston, hyponeustonic, ichthyoneuston, ichthyoneustont, neuston, neustonic, neustonology, neustonphage, neustophagous, neustophagy, zooneuston, zooneustonic

neutr-, neut- (L., neither)

Qualifying words: neuter, neutered, neuterized, neutral, neutralism, neutralist, neutrality, neutralization, neutralize, neutrino, neutroclusion, neutron, neutropenia, neutrophil, neutrophile, neutrophilic, neutrosphere

new, recent See **ceno-, neo-,** and **nov-**.

next, near See **proximo-** for examples.

niger-, nigri-, negr- (L., black) Also examine **melano-** and COLORS for other examples. The word *Negro* comes from Latin *neger* through French *nègre* and Spanish and Portuguese *negro*.

Qualifying words: denigrate, denigration, Negress, Negritic, Negrito, Negro, Negroid, Negrophile, Negrophila, Negrophobia, Negrophobe, nigrescence

nigri- (L., black) See **niger-** for examples.

night See **nocti-, nycti-,** and **scoto-**.

nine Examine **ennea-, nona-, novem-,** and the NUMBERS section in **Appendix G**.

-nit- (L., know) See **not-** for examples.

nivi-, niv-, nivos- (L., snow) Also see **chiono-**.

Qualifying words: nival, nivation, niveoglacial, nivicole, nivicolous, nivose, nivosity

nivos- (L., snow) See **nivi-** for examples.

no, not See **a-, an-** (Gk.); **ne-** (L.), and **non-**.

noc- (L., harmful) See **nox-** for examples.

nocti-, noct-, nox (L., night) Also see **nycti-** and **scoto-** for additional "night" words. Don't confuse the **nox** in this element with another **nox** (**noc-**) which means "harmful, injurious."

Qualifying words: equinox, equinoctial, noctambulation, noctambulism, noctambulist, noctiluca, noctilucent, noctilucine, noctimania, noctinavigation, noctiphobia, nocto-

phobic, noctuary, noctuid, Noctuidae, noctule, nocturn, nocturna, nocturnal, nocturne, Nox, pernoctation

noise See **echo-, phono-, son-,** and **ton-**.

nom-, nomen-, nomin-, -nomia, -nomic (L., name) Also see **-onomato-** and **-onym** for additional "name" words. Don't confuse this element with the Greek **nomo-** which means "law."

Qualifying words: agnomen, anomaly, anomia, antonomasia, binomial, binomialism, cognomen, cognomination, comiconomenclaturist, denominate, denominated, denomination, denominator, dysnomia, ignominious, ignominy, innominate, misnomer, multinomial, nomancy, nomenclature, nomenclator, nominal, nominate, nomination, nominee, paranomia, polynomial, praenomen, surnomial, taxonomic, toponomy, trinomen, trinomial, trinomialism

nomad- (L., wander, moving around) Also see **err-, migr-,** and **vaga-**.

Qualifying words: nomad, nomadic, nomadical

nomen- (L., name) See **nom-** for examples.

nomo-, nom-, -nomy, -nome, -nomic, -nomous, -nomical, -nomically (Gk., law, order, arrangement, systematized knowledge of [something]; usage) Compare with **taxi-** and **cosmo-** for similarities.

Qualifying words: agronomy, anomalopia, anomie, anomocarpous, anomophyllous, anomaloscope, antinomy, astronomy, autonomic, autonomous, autonomy, binomial, Deuteronomy, economic, economy, ergonomics, ergonomy, eunomy, gastronomy, genomic, imprints, heteronomous, hydronomy, hetronomy, isonomy, metonomy, metronome, multinomial, nomism, nomogenesis, nomograph, nomography, nomology, nomothetic, nomotopic, nomography, physiognomist, plutonomic, plutonomics, plutonomist, plutonomy, taxonomy, technonomy, trinomial

-nomy (Gk., law) See **nomo-** for examples.

non- (L., not) Also see **a-, in-,** and **neg-** for other "no, not" words.

Qualifying words: nonconformist, nondescript, nonego, nonentity, nonsense, non sequiter, nonviable [plus hundreds of others which can be found in dictionaries]

nona-, noni-, non- (L., nine) Also see **ennea-** and **novem** for additional "nine" words. See NUMBERS in **Appendix G** for other numerical elements.

Qualifying words: nonagenarian, nonagon, nonan, nonapeptide, nonigravida, nonillion, noniparce, nonose, November, novena

none See **nul-** for examples.

noo- (Gk., mind, thought)   Also see **phreno-** and **psycho-** for other "mind" words.

Qualifying words: nookleptia, nookleptic, noological, noology, noopsyche, nooscopic, noosphere, noothymopsychic

north   See **boreal** for examples.

nosc- (L., know)   See **not-** for examples.

nose   See **naso-, rhino-,** and **rhyncho-** for examples.

noso-, nos-, -nosia, -nosis (Gk., disease, sickness)   Also see **-osis, -otic,** and **patho-** for other "disease" words.

Qualifying words: anosognosia, anosognosic, dermatonosology, dermonosology nosetiology, nosocomial, nosogenesis, nosogenic, nosogeny, nosogeography, nosographer, nosographic, nosography, nosointoxication, nosologic, nosological, nosologist, nosology, nosomania, nosometry, nosomycosis, nosonomy, nosoparasite, nosophilia, nosophobia, nosophyte, nosopoietic, nosotaxy, nosotherapy, nosotoxic, nosotoxicity, nosotoxicosis, nosotoxin, nosotrophic, nosotrophy, notable, notice, notified, notion, notoriety, notorious, zoonosia, zoonosis, zoonotic

nosto-, nost- (Gk., return home)   Also examine **dom-, eco-,** and **oiko-.**

Qualifying words: nostalgia, nostology, nosomania

not   See **a-, an-** (Gk.); **in-; negate;** and **non-.**

not any   See **nul-** for examples.

not-, no-, nosc-, -nit- (L., know)   Also see **cogni-, epistemo-, intellect-, mne-, not-,** and **sci-** for additional "know" words.

Qualifying words: connoisseur, ennoble, noble, notary, notation, note, notice, notify, notification, notion, notoriety, notorious, reconnaissance, reconnoiter

not enough, decrease in   See **-penia.**

not movable   See **ankylo-** for examples.

not moving, standing   See **stato-** for examples.

not one   See **nul-** for examples.

nourishment, food   See **aliment-, bromato-, cibo-, sitio-,** and **tropho-** for examples.

novo-, nov-, novi- (L., new, recent)   Also see **ceno-** and **neo-** for examples.

Qualifying words: innovation, nova, novel, novelty, novepithel, novice, novilunar, novitiate, novobiocin, novoscope, renovate, renovation

novem-, nona- (L., nine)   Also see **ennea-** and **nona-** for additional "nine" words. See the NUMBERS section in **Appendix G** for other numerical elements.

Qualifying words: nonagenarian, nonagon, November, novena, novennial

nox-, noxi-, noc-, nui-, nic-, nec- (L., harmful, injurious; kill)   Also see **-cide** and **neci-.** Don't confuse this **nox-** with the following Latin **nox,** which means "night."

Qualifying words: innocent, innocuous, innoxious, nocent, nocuous, noxious, obnoxious, obnoxiously, obnoxiousness

nox (L., night)   See **nocti-** for examples. Don't confuse this **nox** with the previous **nox-** which means "harmful."

nudo-, nudi- (L., naked, uncovered)   Also see **gymno-** for additonal "naked" words.

Qualifying words: denude, nude, nudiflorous, nudiped, nudism, nudist, nudity

nui- (L., harmful)   See **nox-** for examples.

nul-, null-, nulli- (L., not one, not any, none)

Qualifying words: annul, annulment, null, nullification, nullify, nulliparous, nullisomatic, nullity

numb, stupor   See **ambly-, narco-,** and **torp-.**

number   See **numer-** for examples.

numbers   See NUMBERS in **Appendix G** for and extensive list.

numbness   See **narco-** and **torp-** for examples.

numer- (L., number)

Qualifying words: enumerate, innumerable, numeral, numerate, numeration, numerator, numerical, numerosity, numerous, supernumerary

numerous, very many   See **myria-.**

nutrition   See **alimenti-** and **tropho-.**

nycti-, nyct-, nycto-, nyc- (Gk., night)   Also see **nocti-** and **scoto-.**

Qualifying words: acronycal, geonyctitropic, geonyctitropism, nyctalgia, nyctolope, nyctalopia, nyctanthous, nyctaphonia, nycterine, nycterohemeral, nyctohemeral, nyctigamous, nyctigamy, nyctipelagic, nyctitropic, nyctitropism, nyctophilia, nyctophobia, nyctophonia, nycturia, Nyx (Greek goddess of night)

-nym (Gk., name)   See **-onym** for examples.

nympho-, nymph- (Gk., young bride; woman of marriageable age; from *nymph,* one of a class of inferior female deities presented as inhabiting the sea, springs, wells, woods, etc.; a young, not fully developed insect; a pupa, chrysalis; sometimes in medical anatomy, the inner lips of the vulva)

Qualifying words: nymph, nympha, nymphae, Nymphaea, nymphal, nymphean, nymphitis, nympholepsy, nympholept, nymphomania, nymphitis, nymphomaniac, nymphotomy, paranymph

O o

oath, **Hippocratic** See **Hippocratic Oath** in **Appendix D** (p. 185).

ob- (L.) before *c*, ob- becomes *oc-*;
  before *f*, ob- becomes *of-*;
  before *g*, ob- becomes *og-*;
  before *p*, ob- becomes *op-*;
  before *m*, ob- becomes *o-*

¹ toward, to, before

  Qualifying words: oblige, obsequious, obstetrics, obverse, obvert

² against

  Qualifying words: obdurate, objection, obloquy, obnoxious, obsesse, obstacle, obstruct, oppose, opposition, oppress, oppression, oppressive

³ across, over, upon (in the way)

  Qualifying words: obfuscate, object, obscure

⁴ down

  Qualifying word: occasion

⁵ completely, totally

  Qualifying words: obsolete, observe, obsess, occupy

oblique, slant See **loxo-** for examples.

occult- (L., secret, hidden, concealed) For additional "secret" words, examine **calyp-, clandestine, crypto-, krypto-, leth-,** and **myster-**.

  Qualifying words: occult, occultist, occultation, occultism

ochero-, ochr- (Gk., yellow; pale, wan, or sallow) Also see **auri-, chryso-,** and **xantho-** for additional "yellow" words.

  Qualifying words: ocher, ochroid, ochrometer, xantochroi

ochlo-, ochl- (Gk., mob [people]) Also see **demo-, ethno-, popu-, publi-,** and **vulg-** for other "people" words.

  Qualifying words: ochlocracy, ochlocratic, ochlomania, ochlophilia, ochlophobia, ochlotheocracy

ochtho-, ochth- (Gk., any elevation, bank, hill, mound) Also see **mont-** and **oro-** for other "hill or mountain" words.

  Qualifying words: ochthophile, ochthophilous, ochthophily, ochthophyte

octa-, octo-, oct-, octi-, octon- (Gk. > L., eight, eighth) For additional numerical elements, see the NUMBERS section in **Appendix G.**

  Qualifying words: octachord, octad, octagon, octagonal, octagynous, octahedral, octahedron, octamerous, octameter, octandrous, octangular, octant, octarchy, octave, octavo, octennial, octet, octette, octillion, octiparous, October, octodecimo, octodont, octogenarian, octogynous, octolateral, octonocular, octopetalous, octopod, octopus, octuple, octuplet, octuplicate

ocul-, oculo- (L., eye[s]; sight) Also see **op-** and **opthalmo-**.

  Qualifying words: binocular, inoculate, inoculation, inoculator, monocular, monocle, ocular, oculate, oculist, oculometer, oculomotor, oculopathy

od- (way, a going) See **odo-** for examples.

ode, -odal, -odeon, -ody (Gk. > L., song, poem) Don't confuse this **ode** with the next **odo-** which means "road, way."

  Qualifying words: melodeon, melodious, melodic, melody, nickelodeon, ode, parody, prosody, rhapsody

odo-, od-, -ode, -odic, -odically (Gk., road, way) Also see **hodo-** and **via-** for additional examples. Don't confuse this **odo-** element with **ode** (Gk. > L.), which means "song" or "poem" as in *melody*. Primary meanings are "way, path."

  Qualifying words: anode, anodize, cathode, diode, electrode, episode, exodus, method, odograph, odometer, period, periodic, periodical, synod

odonto-, odont-, -odont, -odonic, -odontic, -odontia, -odontoid (Gk., tooth, teeth) Also see **dent-**.

  Qualifying words: aerodontalgia, aerodontia, aerodontics, aerodontology, anodont, anodontia, cacodontia, creodont, dontopedalogy, exodontia, heterodont, homodont, hypodontia, isodontic, labyinthodont, mastodon, megadontic, microdontic, odontalgia, odontectomy, odontiasis, odontitis, odontoclast, odontograph, odontography, odontoiatria, odontoid, odontologist, odontology, odontopathy, odontophobia, odontophore, odontopteryx, orthodontia, orthodontics, orthodontist, pathodontia, pedodontics, periodontia, polyodontia, radiodontis, saprodontia

odor, smell See **bromo-** and **osmo-**.

odori-, odoro- (L., smell [noun form]) Also see **bromo-, olfacto-, osmo-,** and **osphresio-** for other "smell" words.

  Qualifying words: inodorous, malodor, malodorous, odor, odorant, odoriferous, odorimetry, odoriphore, odorivector, odorimeter, odorography, odorous

odyno-, odyn-, -odynia, odynic,-odyne, -odyn
(Gk., pain) Also see **algesi-** and **doloro-**
for other "pain" words. Limited to medical terms. Original meaning is literally
"that which eats or consumes."

    Qualifying words: achillodynia, acrody-
nia, agiodynia, angiodynography, anodyne,
anodynia, arthrodynia, arthrodynic, calca-
neodynia, cardiodynia, cephalodynia, cervico-
dynia, crymodynia, dactylodynia, encephalo-
dynia, esophagodynia, gastrodynia, glosso-
dynia, hysterodynia, neurodynia, odontodyn-
ia, odynacusis, odynolysis, odynometer, ody-
nophagia, odynophilia, odynophobia, odyn-
phagia, ophthalmodynia, osteodynia, oto-
dynia, photodynia, pododynia, rhinodynia,
tenodynia, thoracodynia, trachelodynia, thoracodynia

oeno-, oen-, eno- (Gk., wine) Also see **vini-**
for other "wine" words. This element is
also spelled **eno-**, as in *enology*.

    Qualifying words: enology, enomania, oe-
nanthic, oenologist, oenology, oenomancy,
oenomania, oenomel, oenometer, oenophilia,
oenophilist, oenophily, oenophobia, oenopho-
bist

of the nature of See **-ac** and the SUFFIXES section in **Appendix K** for other examples
of word endings.

offspring See **proli-** for examples.

of one another See **allelo-** for examples.

-oid, -oidal, -oidism (Gk., like, resembling,
similar to) Also see **eido-, equ-, form-,
homo-** (Gk.), **iso-, morpho-, pari-,
simal-,** and **tauto-**.

    Qualifying words: acanthoid, alkaloid,
android, anthropoid, anthropoidal, arach-
noid, asteroid, butyroid, carpoids, cycloid,
cystoids, ellipsoid, factoid, fatoids, geoid, gy-
necoidism, haloid, helioid, hexaploid, hypno-
toid, ichthyoid, lipoid, megazooid, Mongoloid,
Negroid, nephrotyphoid, pleurotyphoid, odontoid, oozooid, ovoid, planetoid, Polaroid, pteridoid, speroid, sporozooid, tabloid, tetraploid,
trapezoid, triploid, xyloid

oiko- (oec-, ecu-) (Gk., house, home) Also see
dom-, eco-, habit-, and **nosto-** for additional "house" words.

    Qualifying words: coenoecium, ecumenic,
ecumenical, ecumenism, ecumenist, oiko-
fugic, oikomania, oikophobia

oil, fat See **adipo-, lipo-, oleo-,** and **steato-**.

-olatry, -olater, -olatress (Gk., worship) Examine **-latry** for examples.

old, old age See **gero-, presbyo-,** and **sen-**.

old, primitive Examine **archaeo-, palaeo-,** and
proto- for examples.

oleo-, ole-, -oleic, ol- (L.) ([olive] oil, fat)
Also see **adipo-, eleo-, lipo-,** and **steato-**
for additional "fat" words.

    Qualifying words: lanolin, linoleic, lino-
leum, oleaginous, oleic, oleiferous, oleoar-
throsis, oleochrysotherapy, oleogranuloma,
oleograph, oleoinfusion, oleomargarine, oleometer, oleotherapy, oleovitamin, petrol, pe-
troleum

olfacto-, olfact- (L., to smell; pertaining to the
sense of smell) Also see **odori-** (smell),
osmo- (odor, smell), **osphresio-** (smell),
and examine **bromo-** for additional examples.

    Qualifying words: olfact, olfactic, olfac-
tion, olfactism, olfactology, olfactometer, ol-
factometry, olfactophobia, olfactory

oligo-, olig- (Gk., few, small; abnormally few
or small) Also see **pauci-** for additional
examples.

    Qualifying words: oligacanthous, oligan-
drous, oligarch, oligarchical, oligarchy, olig-
carpous, oligochronometer, oligemia, olig-
emic, oligocardia, oligocarpus, oligocythemia,
oligodacrya, oligodactylia, oligodactylism, oli-
godactyly, oligodipsia, oligodontia, oligody-
namic, oligogalactia, oligogenesis, olighidria,
olighydria, oligohidrosis, oligohydruria, oligo-
morphic, oligonatality, oligonucleotides, oligo-
pela, oligopelic, oligopepsia, oligophagous,
oligophagy, oligophrenia, oligophrenic, oligo-
plastic, oligopnea, oligopoly, oligopsony, oligo-
rophic, oligosaprobe, oligosaprobic, oligosyl-
labic, oligotherm, oligothermic, oligotrichia,
oligotrichosis, oligotrophic, oligotrophy, oligo-
xenous, oligoxeny

-ologist (Gk., one who speaks about, writes
about, or studies) All **-ology** words can
be made into **-ologist** forms. For example: adenologist, allergologist, etc.

-ology (Gk., study of, science of) From "talk,
speak;" "one who speaks" (in a manner);
"one who deals with a specific topic."

    Qualifying words: acarology, adenology,
allergology, amphibiology, anaesthesiology,
anemology, anesthesiology, angiology, antho-
logy, anthropology, anthropobiology, arach-
nology, archaeology, arthrology, astrology,
audiology, bacteriology, batology, biology,
brachylogy, bryology, caliology, campanology,
cardiology, carcinology, carpology, cerebrolo-
gy, cetology, choledology, chondrology, cho-
rology, chronology, climatology, conchology,
cosmetology, cosmology, craniology, criminology, crustaceology, cryptology, cytology, dactylology, dendrology, dermatology, dipterolo-
gy, ecology, electrophysiology, embryology,
emetology, endocrinology, enology, enterology, entomology, epidemiology, epistemology,
ethnology, ethology, etiology, etymology, exo-

biology, futurology, gastroenterology, gastrology, genealogy, geology, gerontology, glottochronology, glyptology, gynaecology, gynecology, haematology, hagiology, helminthology, hematology, hemipterology, hepatology, herniology, herpetology, heterology, hippology, histology, histopathology, horology, hydrology, hypnology, iatrology, ichthyology, ichthyopaleontology, immunology, laryngology, lepidopterology, leprology, lexicology, limnology, lithology, malacology, mammalogy, mastology, menology, merology, meteorology, metrology, microbiology, mineralogy, morphology, muscology, musicology, mycology, myology, myrmecology, nematology, neonatology, nephrology, neurology, neuropathology, neurology, nomology, nosology, odontology, oenology, oncology, oneirology, ontology, oology, ophthalmology, ophiology, ornithology, orology, osteology, otolaryngology, otology, otorhinolaryngology, paleo-ornithology, paleontology, paleozoology, palynology, parasitology, pathology, pedology, penology, petrology, pharmacology, philology, phonology, phrenology, physiology, phytology, pneumatology, polemology, pomology, posology, potamology, proctology, promorphology, protozoology, psephology, psychology, pteridology, phytology, radiobiology, radiology, reflexology, rheology, rheumatology, rhinology, scatology, seismology, selenology, semiology, sinology, sitology, sociology, somatology, speleology, stomatology, syndesmology, tautology, technology, tegestology, teleology, tenology, teratology, theology, topology, toxicology, traumatology, tribology, trichology, typhlology, ufology, uranology, urology, venereology, vexillology, virology, zoology, zoopaleontology, zymology

-oma, -ome, -omatoid (Gk., tumor, morbid growth; to swell, bulge) For other "cancer" words, see **cancero-, carcino-,** and **onco-.**

Qualifying words: adenoma, angiokeratoma, angioma, carcinoma, fibroma, glaucoma, glioma, lipoma, lymphoma, mycetoma, myeloma, neuroma, osteosarcoma, sarcoma, scotoma, syphiloma, trachoma

ombro- (Gk., rain) Also see **hyeto-, pluv-, udo-, urino,** and **uro-** for other "rain" words.

Qualifying words: ombratropic, ombratropism, ombrocleistogamic, ombrocleistogamy, ombrograph, ombrologist, ombrology, ombrometer, ombrophile, ombrophilous, ombrophily, ombrophobe, ombrophobia, ombrophobic, ombrophoby, ombrophyte, ombrotiphic, ombrotrophic, ombrotrophy

omega (Gk., [Ω, ω] the ending, the last of anything; the 24th and last letter of the Greek alphabet). Also see **fin-, mega-, teleo-, term-,** and **ultim-** for additional "end" words; and see the Greek alphabet under **alpha** (beginning).

Qualifying words: alpha and omega, omega, omega melancholicum

omni-, omn- (L., all, every) Also see **pan-** for other "all" words.

Qualifying words: omniactive, omnibearing, omnibenevolent, omnibus, omnicide, omnicole, omnicolous, omnicorporeal, omnicredulity, omnicredulous, omnidirectional, omnidistance, omnierudite, omnifarious, omniferous, omnigenous, omnigraph, omnigraphy, omni-ignorant, omnilingual, omniloquent, omnilucent, omnimeter, omnipotence, omnipotent, omnipresence, omnipresent, *omni quadrante hora*, omnirange, omniscience, omniscient, omnist, omniumgatherum, omnivision, omnivoracious, omnivoracity, Omnivore, omnivore, omnivorous

omo-, om- (L., shoulder) Also see **humero-** for other "shoulder" words. Don't confuse this element with another **omo-** (Gk.), meaning "raw."

Qualifying words: omalgia, omarthritis, omitis, omodynia, omoplate

omphalo-, omphal- (Gk., navel, umbilicus) Also see **umbili-** for other "navel" words.

Qualifying words: cirsomphalous, exomphalos, omphalectomy, omphalelcosis, omphalic, omphalitis, omphaloangiopagus, omphalocele, omphalochorion, omphalodidymus, omphalogenesis, omphaloma, omphalomesaraic, omphalomesenteric, omphaloncus, omphalopagus, omphalophlebitis, omphalorrhagia, omphalorrhea, omphalorrhexis, omphalos, omphalosite, omphalospinous, omphalotaxis, omphalotomy, omphalus, variomphalus

omo- (Gk., raw, unripe) Don't confuse this element with another **omo-** (L.), meaning "shoulder."

Qualifying words: omomania, omophagia, omophagic, omophagous, omophilia, omophobia

on See **epi-, hyper-, super-,** and **ultra-.**

once, simply See **haplo-** for examples.

onco-, oncho-, -oncus (Gk., "mass, bulk;" denotes relationship to a tumor, swelling, or mass) For additional "cancer" words, see **cancero-, carcino-,** and **-oma.**

Qualifying words: oncocyte, oncocytoma, oncocytosis, oncogeneic, oncogenesis, oncogenetic, oncogenic, oncogenous, oncography, oncoides, oncologist, oncology, oncolysis, oncolytic, oncoma, oncometer, oncometric, oncometry, oncosis, oncotherpy, oncothlipsis, oncotic, oncotomy, oncotropic, oncovirus

one See **mono-, soli-,** and **uni-** for examples.

one and a half See **sesqui-** for examples.
one fourth See **tetarto-** for examples.
oneiro-, oneir-, oniro-, onir-, -neir- (Gk., dream) Also see **hallucina-** and **somni-** for "sleep"[or dream] words.

> **Qualifying words:** euneirophrenia, malneirophrenia, oneiric, oneirism, oneiroanalysis, oneirocritic, oneirocritical, oneirocriticon, oneirodelirium, oneirodynia, oneirogenic, oneiroid, oneirologist, oneirology, oneiromancy, oneiromantic, oneironosus, oneirophrenia, oneiroscopist, oneiroscopy, oniric, onirogenic, oniroid

one's own, personal See **idio-** for examples.
onio- (Gk., sell, for sale) Also see **-poly** for other "sell" words.

> **Qualifying word:** oniomania, oniomaniac

oniro- (Gk., dream) See **oneiro-** for examples.
only, single Examine **haplo-, mono-, soli-,** and **uni-** for examples.
onomato-, onoma- (Gk., name) For additional "name" words, see **nom-** and **-onym.**

> **Qualifying words:** antonomasia, onomancy, onomasiology, onomastic, onomasticon, onomatist, onomatology, onomatomania, onomatophobia, onomatopoeia, onomatopoeic, onomatopoetic

on the back, near the back See **dorso-.**
onto- (Gk., a being, individual; being, existence)

> **Qualifying words:** ontocycle, ontogenesis, ontogenetic, ontogeny, ontologism, ontology, paleontography, paleontology

onycho-, onych-, ony-, -onychial, -onychium (Gk., claw, nail; finger nails, toe nails) For other "claw" words, see **chela-** and **unguo-.**

> **Qualifying words:** anonychia, anonychosis, Baryonyx Walkeri, eponychia, leukonychia, onychalgia, onychatrophia, onychectomy, onychia, onychitis, onychoclasis, onychocryptosis, onychodystrophy, onychogenic, onychogram, onychograph, onychography, onychoid, onychology, onycholysis, onychoma, onychomalacia, onychomycosis, onypathic, onychopathology, onychopathy, onychophagia, onychophagy, onychoptosis, onychorrhexis, onychorrhiza, onychoschizia, onychosis, onychotomy, onypathic, onyx, onyxis, onyxitis, paronychia, schizonychia, scleronychia

-onym, -onymy, -onymic, onymically, -onymous, -onymously, -nym (Gk., name) Also see **nom-** and **onomato-** for additional "name" words.

> **Qualifying words:** acronym, allonym, anonym, anonymity, anonymous, antonym, antonymous, anthroponymy, aptronym, autonym, bacronym, caconym, caconymic, capitonym, charactonym, consonym, contronym, cryptonym, cryptonymous, cryptonymic, cryptonymous, domunym, eponym, eponymic, eponymous, eponymy, euonym, euonymous, euonymy, exonym, heteronym, homonym, hydronymy, hyponym, malonym, matronymic, metonym, metonymical, metonymous, metonymously, metonymy, metronym, metronymic, mononym, numeronym, paronymous, patronymic, poikilonymy, polynym, polyonymous, polyonymy, pseudonym, retronym, synonym, synonymous, tautonym, teknonymic, toponym, toponymic, toponymist, toponymous, toponymy, typonym

oo- (Gk., egg or eggs) Also see **oophoro-, ova-, ovi-, ovo-,** and **ovum** for additional "egg" words.

> **Qualifying words:** ectoophage, ectoophagous, ectoophagy, endoophage, endophagy, ooblast, oocenter, oocephalus, oocinesia, oocinesis, oocinete, oocyan, oocyanin, oocyesis, oocyst, oocytase, oocyte, oogamous, oogamy, oogenesis, oogenetic, oogenic, oogenous, oograph, ooid, ooidal, ookinesis, ookinete, oolite, oolith, oological, oologic, oologist, oology, oometer, oomycetous, oomycosia, oophagia, oophagous, oophagy, oophorectomy, oophoritis, oophoroma, oophyte, ooplasm, oorhodein, ooscopy, oosome, oosperm, oosphere, ootheca, ootherapy, ooxanthine, oozoid, oozooia

oophoro-, oophor- (Gk., ovary, egg [literally, "egg-carrier"]) Also see **oo-, ova-, ovi-, ovo-,** and **ovum** for other "egg" words.

> **Qualifying words:** oophoralgia, oophorectomize, oophorectomy, oophorites, oophoritis, oophorocystectomy, oophorocystosis, oophoroepilepsy, oophorogenous, oophorohysterectomy, oophoroma, oophoromalacia, oophoropathy, oophoropexy, oophoroplasty, oophorostomy, oophorotomy, oophorrhagia

op-, opt-, -opia, -ops, -opsia, -opsis, -opsy, -optic, -opic, -opy (Gk., eye[s]; sight; vision) Also see **ocul-** and **opthalmo-** for other "eye" words. Also examine words with similar meanings in **-orama, -scope, spec-** and **vid-.** Also see **pupillo-.**

> **Qualifying words:** achromatopsia, aglaucopsia, aglaukopsia, ambiopia, amblopia, amblyopia, anisopia, autopsy, biopsy, cyanopia, deuteranopia, diplopia, diopter, erythropsia, hypermetropia, hyperopia, isomatropia, myopia, myopic, necropsy, nyctalopia, opesthesia, optical, optician, optics, optometer, optometrist, optometry, presbyopia, protanopia, stereopsis, stereopticon, synopsis, synoptic, tetartanopia, thanatopsis, tritanopia

open space See **agora-** for examples.
open woodland, meadow Examine **orgado-** for examples.
opening, entrance See **ora-** for examples.

opening, passageway in the body See **meato-**.

oper-, opus (L., work) Also see **ergo-, labor-, pono-,** and **urg-**.

> Qualifying words: cooperate, cooperatively, cooperativeness, inoperable, inoperative, magnum opus, opera, operability, operable, operate, operation, operational, operator, operetta, operose, opus

ophidio- (Gk., serpent, snake) See **ophio-** for examples.

ophio-, ophi-, -ophid, ophidio-, -ophidia, -ophis (Gk., snake, serpent) Also examine **angui-, herpeto-** (reptile, serpent), **reptil-,** and **sauro-** (lizard).

> Qualifying words: Hydrophis, ophic, ophicalcite, Ophicephalidae, Ophichthyidae, ophidia, ophidian, ophidiophobia, ophidiophobe, ophidious, ophiocephaloid, ophiography, ophiolater, ophiolatrous, ophiolatry, ophiolite, ophiolitic, ophiological, ophiologist, ophiology, ophiomancy, ophiomorphic, ophiomorphous, ophiophage, ophiophagous, ophiophagy, ophiophilism, ophiophilist, ophiophobe, ophiophobia, ophiosaurus, ophiotoxemia, ophiotoxicology, ophiotoxin, ophis, ophisaurus, ophite, ophitic, scolecophidian, thanatophidia, toxicophidia

-opia (Gk., eye; sight; vision) See **op-**.

opinion, belief See **dox-** for examples.

opposed to See **anti-** and **contra-** for examples.

ophthalmo-, ophthalm-, -ophthalmia, -ophthalmic, -ophthalmos (Gk., eye; sight) Also see **ocul-, op-,** and **pupillo-**.

> Qualifying words: exophthalmic, heterophthalmia, lagophthalmic, microphthalmic, ophthalmagra, ophthalmalgia, ophthalmia, ophthalmiatrics, ophthalmitis, ophthalmodynia, ophthalmograph, ophthalmography, ophthalmologist, ophthalmology, ophthalmometer, ophthalmometry, ophthalmopathy, ophthalmoplasty, ophthalmoplegia, ophthalmoscope, ophthalmoscopy, ophthalmostasis, ophthalmostat, ophthalmothermometer, periophthalmia

-ops, -opsia (Gk., eye) See **op-** for examples.

opt- (eye[s]) See **op-** for examples.

opulen (L., wealth, wealthy, rich [power, might; abundance, plenty]) Also examine **lucr-** and **pluto-**.

> Qualifying words: copious, copy, cornucopia, opulence, opulent

opus (L., work) See **oper-** for examples.

-or (L., state of, result of) A suffix which forms nouns. British usage is -our. Also see SUFFIXES in **Appendix K** for other word endings.

> Qualifying words: conservator, error, furor, incisor, innovator, mediator, speculator

ora-, orat- (L., talk, speak, say; mouth, face; opening, entrance) For additional "talk" words, see **cit-, clam-, dic-, lalo-, legi-, locu-, logo-, loqu-, -phasia, -phemia, phras-,** and **voc-**. From Latin, *oris*, "mouth, face; opening, entrance." Also see **os-** for similarities.

> Qualifying words: aboral, adorable, adoration, adore, exorable, inexorable, inexorably, oracle, oracular, oral, orate, oration, orator, oratorium, oratory, oratrix, orifice, peroration

-orama, -oramic, -rama (Gk., view; sight; see, that which is seen) Also see **scop-, spec-,** and **vid-** for additional "see, view" words.

> Qualifying words: cinerama, cosmorama, cyclorama, diorama, myriorama, panorama, sonorama

orb-, orbito- (L., circle, ring, round surface, disk; rut or track made in the ground by a wheel) Also see other "round" words in **ambi-, amphi-, circum-, cyclo-, peri-, rotundi-,** and **sphere**.

> Qualifying words: orb, orbiculate, orbiculated, orbicular, orbit, orbital

orches- (Gk., dance, pertaining to dancing) Also examine **choreo-** for other "dance" words.

> Qualifying words: orchesography, orchestic, orchestics, orchestra, orchestral, orchestrate, orchestration, orchestromania

orchido-, orchid- (Gk. > L., testes; orchid, from testicle. So called because of the resemblance of the roots to testicles) Also see **orchio-** and **testi-** for other "testicle" words.

> Qualifying words: cryptorchidism, orchid (flower), orchidalgia, orchidectomy, orchidic, orchiditis, orchidocelioplasty, orchidocelioplasty, orchidology (flower), orchidoptosis, orchidorraphy

orchio-, orchi- (Gk., testicle or testes) Also see **orchido-** and **testi-** for other related words.

> Qualifying words: orchalgia, orchectomy, orchialgia, orchiatrophy, orchic, orchidalgia, orchidatrophia, orchidatrophy, orchidectomy, orchidic, orchidion, orchiditis, orchidometer, orchidoncus, orchidopathy, orchidopexy, orchidoplasty, orchidorrhaphy, orchidotherapy, orchidotomy, orchiectomy, orchilytic, orchiocatabasis, orchiocele, orchiodynia, orchiomyeloma, orchioncus, orchioneuralgia, orchiopathy, orchiopexy, orchioplasty, orchiorrhaphy, orchiotherapy, orchiotomy, orchis, orchitic, orchitis, orchitolytic, orchotomy

ord-, -ordin-, -ordinate, -ordinating, -ordinated (L., order, row, regular series, class, rank) Also see **cosmo-, nomo-,** and **taxi-** for additional "order" words.

Qualifying words: coordinate, coordination, disorder, extraordinary, foreordain, inordinate, insubordinate, ordain, order, ordinal, ordinance, ordinary, ordinate, ordination, ordinance, preordain, subordinate, subordination

order See **cosmo-, crim-, jud-, jus-, nomo-, ord-,** and **taxi-** for examples.

order (verb) See **manda-** for examples.

ordin- (L., order, row, et al.) See **ord-.**

orexi-, orex-, -orexia, -orexic, -oretic, -orectic, -rexia (Gk., appetite [hunger]) Also see **bou-** (*bulima,* "cow") and **limo-.**

Qualifying words: anorectic, anorexia (*nervosa*), anorexiant, anorexic, anorexigenic, bulimarexia, cynorexia, dysorexia, lycorexia, orexia, orexic, orexis, orexifugic, orexigenic, oreximania, orexis, pseudoanorexia, parorexia, xenorexia

orgado-, orgad- (Gk., open woodland, meadow, field) Also see **agra-** and **agrio-.**

Qualifying words: orgadocole, orgadocolous, orgadophile, orgadophilous, orgadophily, orgadophyte

organo-, organ- (Gk., an organized structure; pertaining to a specific bodily part with a specific function or set of functions; instrument, tool)

Qualifying words: organic, organism, organization, organize, organofaction, organogel, organogen, organogenesis, organology, organoma, organomegaly, organonomy, organopathy, organopexia, organopexy, organophilic, organophilism, organoscopy, organotaxis, organotherapy, organotrophic, organotropism, organotropy, organum

-oria (L., a place used for something) For examples, see **-orium.**

origin See **genus-** and **oriri-** for examples.

original (first in time) See **archaeo-, palaeo-,** and **proto-** for examples.

originating, causing See **etio-** for examples.

-orium, -oria (L., a place or a thing used for something) Also see **-arium, -ary,** and SUFFIXES in **Appendix K** for other word endings.

Qualifying words: auditorium, conservatorium, crematorium, ejaculatorium, emporium, incubatorium, lavatorium, lubritorium, natatorium, oratorium, sanatorium, sanitarium, scriptorium(s.), scriptoria(pl.), sensorium, sudoria, sudorium, vaporium, vivisectorium

ornitho-, ornith-, -ornithic, -ornithes, -ornithoid (Gk., bird) Also see **auspic-** and **avi-** for other "bird" words.

Qualifying words: dinornithic, ichthyornis, ornis, Ornithgalum, ornithic, ornithin, ornithine, ornithivorous ornithocephalous, ornithocoprophile, ornithocoprophilous, ornithocoprophily, ornithogenic, ornithoid, ornithological, ornithologist, ornithology, ornithomancy, ornithomania, ornithophilous, ornithophily, ornithophobia, Ornithopoda, ornithopter, ornithorhynchus, ornithoscopy, ornithosis, ornithotomist, ornithotomy, palaeornithology, panornithic, pholornithic, stereornithic

oriri-, orir-, ori-, or- (L., to rise, be born; the rising sun, east; to rise, become visible, appear)

Qualifying words: abort, abortifacient, abortion, abortive, orient, oriental, orientate, orientation, Oritntal, Orientalism, Orientalist, Orientalize, origin, original, originality, originate, origination

oro- (Gk., mountain) Also examine **mont-** and **ochtho-** for related "hill" words. Don't confuse this element with other unrelated words, such as **oro-** ("oral, mouth") or **or-** ("gold").

Qualifying words: oread, orobathymetric, orocratic, orogen, orogenesis, orogenetic, orogenic, orogeny, orographic, orographical, orography, Orohippus, orohydrography, orohylile, orological, orologist, orology, orometer, orometric, orophile, orophilous, orophily, orophytes, orophytic

-orrhea (flow, flowing) See **-rrhea.**

-orrhaphy (suture, stitching) See **-rhaph.**

-orrhexis, -rhexis, -rrhexis (Gk., rupture of an organ or vessel; a breaking forth, bursting)

Qualifying words: angiorrhexis, arteriorrhexis, cardiorrhexis, cystorrhexis, enterorrhexis, hepatorrhexis, hysterorrhexis, phleborrhexis

ortho-, orth- (Gk., right, straight, correct, true; designed to correct) Also see **dexter-** and **recti-** for additional "right" words.

Qualifying words: anorthography, orthocarpus, orthocephalic, orthocephalous, orthochromatic, orthoclastic, orthodontia, orthodox, orthodoxy, orthodromic, orthoepy, orthogenesis, orthognathic, orthognathism, orthognathous, orthognathy, orthogonal, orthograde, orthographer, orthography, orthoheliotropic, orthoheliotropism, orthokinesis, orthokinetics, orthopedic, orthopedics, orthopedist, orthopedy, orthophototropic, orthophototropism, orthophony, orthoplera, orthopnea, orthopneic, orthopnoea, orthopraxy, orthopraxis, Orthoptera, orthopteran, orthopterous, orthoptic, orthoscopic, orthothanasia, orthotherapy, orthosis, orthotist, orthotropic, orthotropism

-ory (from Latin, **-orium**) (L., place where) Also see **-ary (-arium)** and the SUFFIXES section in **Appendix K**.

> Qualifying words: conservatory, crematory, directory, dormitory, factory, laboratory, lavatory, observatory, oratory, purgatory

orycto-, oryct- (Gk., fossil, mineral; dug, dig; literally "thing dug")

> Qualifying words: oryctological, oryctologist, oryctology

Oryza (Gk., L., rice)

> Qualifying words: Oryza, Oryza sativa, Oryzaglaberrima, oryzivore, oryzivorous, Oryzomys, Oryzopsis

os-, oss-, ost- (L., bone) Also see **osseo-** and **osteo-**. Don't confuse this **os-** with the **os-** which means "mouth."

> Qualifying words: interosseous, osseous, ossicle, ossiculectomy, ossiculum, ossiferous, ossific, ossification, ossify, ossiphone, ossuary, ostalgia, ostarthritis, ostitis

os-, or- (L., mouth) Compare this combining form with **ora-, orat-** (L.) and don't confuse this element with the **os-** meaning "bone." For other "mouth" words, see **ora-, oscula-,** and **stomato-**.

> Qualifying words: aborad, aboral, oracle, oral, orifice, oscular, osculate, ostiary

oscillo-, oscill- (L., swing, vibrate; from **oscillum,** a diminutive form of *oso(ris)* "mouth, face," meaning "small face" and, by extension, "small mask of the god Bacchus" which was hung in Roman vineyards to honor the god of wine while scaring off grape-eating birds as it vibrated in the breeze)

> Qualifying words: oscillate, oscillation, oscillator, oscillatory, oscillogram, oscillograph, oscillometer, oscillopsia, oscilloscope

oscula- (L., kiss; little mouth; lip [diminutive of **os-,** "mouth"]) For related examples, see **ora-** and **stomato-**.

> Qualifying words: osculate, osculation

-ose (-iose), -osic, -osity, -osely [1] (L., full of, having much, or many) A suffix which forms adjectives. Also examine **-ous** and the SUFFIXES section in **Appendix K**.

> Qualifying words: bellicose, bulbose, cerebrose, comatose, grandiose, granulose, jocose, lachrymose, morose, verbose, vesculose

[2] (Gk., sweet wine) A suffix which forms nouns meaning a carbohydrate, especially sugar, such as cellulose, fructose, glycose, lactose, sorbose; a primary product of hydrolysis, such as apiose, caseose, proteose

-osis, -sis (Gk. > L., actor, process, condition, or state of; expresses a state or condition; in *medicine,* an abnormal condition or process of some disease) Also see **noso-, -otic,** and **patho-** for other "disease" words and see SUFFIXES in **Appendix K** for other word endings.

> Qualifying words: acidosis (med.), dermatosis (med.), halitosis (med.), heterosis, hypnosis, metamorphosis, neurosis (med.), osmosis, phychosis, psychosis (med.), symbiosis, thrombosis (med.), tuberculosis (med.)

[1]**osmo-, osmia-, osmi-, -osmia, -osmatic** (Gk., odor; smell, smelling) Also see **bromo-, odori-, olfacto-,** and **osphresio-** for other "smell" words. Don't confuse this **osmo-** with the next one which means "impulse, thrust."

> Qualifying words: anosmatic, anosmia, anosmic, aosmics, autosmia, dysosmia, hyperosmia, hyposmia, merosmia, osmatic, osmazone, osmesis, osmesthesia, osmics, omidrosis, osmium, osmodysphoria, osmolagnia, osmolarity, osmology, osmometer, osmonosology, osmophilic, osmophobia, osmoscope, parosmia, pseudosmia

[2]**osmo-, osmia-, osmi-, -osmia, -osmatic** (Gk., impulse, thrust, push, impel) Don't confuse this **osmo-** with the previous one which means "odor, smell."

> Qualifying words: endosmosis, exosmosis, hyperosmosis, hyperosmotic, hypo-osmosis, hypo-osmotic, osmology, osmometer, osmometry, osmosis, osmosology, osmostat, osmotaxis, osmotherapy, osmotic, osmotropic, osmotropism, poikilosmosis, poikilosmotic,

osphresio-, osphresi- (Gk., to smell; pertaining to odor or to the sense of smell) Also see **bromo-, odori-, olfacto-** and **osmo-**.

> Qualifying words: osphresiolagnia, osphresiology, osphresiometer, osphresiometry, osphresiophobia, osphresis, osphretic

oss- (L., bone) See **os-** for examples.

osseo-, osse-, ossi- (L., bone, bony) Also see **os-, osteo-,** and **skeleto-** for other "bone" words.

> Qualifying words: ossein, osseoaponeurotic, osseocartilaginous, osseofibrous, osseoligamentous, osseosonometer, osseosonome-

try, osseous, ossiculectomy, ossiculoplasty, ossiculotomy, ossiculum, ossiferous, ossifluence, ossiform

osteo-, oste-, ost- (Gk., bone) Also see **os-** (L.), "bone;" **osseo-**, and **skeleto-**.

    Qualifying words: ostalgia, ostarthritis, ostealgia, ostectomy, osteitis, osteoacusis, osteoanesthesia, osteoarthropathy, osteodynia, osteodysplasty, osteodystrophy, osteogen, osteography, osteoid, osteologia, osteologist, osteology, osteolysis, osteolytic, osteoma, osteomalacia, osteomalacic, osteomantic, osteomancy, osteometry, osteomiosis, osteomyelitis, osteonecrosis, osteoneuralgia, osteopath, osteopathia, osteopathy, osteopathology, osteophage, osteophagia, osteophone, osteophony, osteoplasty, osteopoikilosis, osteotomy, osteotrophy

ostreo-, ostrei- (Gk., oyster)

    Qualifying words: ostraceous, ostracosis, ostreiculture, ostreophagous, ostreophagy, ostreotoxism

ostro- (L., east) Also see **auroa** and **eo-** for other "east" or "dawn" words.

    Qualifying words: Ostrogoth

osyter See **ostreo-** for examples.

other, another, different See **ali-, allelo-, allo-, alter-, hetero-,** and **vari-** for examples.

-otic (Gk., a suffix which means state or condition of; diseased condition of) Also see **noso-, -osis, -patho-** for additional "disease" words and SUFFIXES in **Appendix K** for other word endings.

    Qualifying words: hypnotic, psychotic

ot- (Gk., ear) See **oto-** for examples.

oto-, ot-, -otic (Gk., ear) Also see **auri-**.

    Qualifying words: dichotic, ectotitis, endotic, endotitis, entotic, epiotic, macrotia, otalgia, otalgic, otary, otiatrics, otiatry, otic, otitis, otocariasis, otocyst, otodynia, otogenic, otogenous, otogenous, otography, otolaryngology, otolith, otologist, otology, otomycosis, otoneuralgia, otoneurology, otopathy, otophone, otoplasty, otorhinolaryngologist, otorhinology, otorrhagia, otorrhea, otoscope, otoscopy, otosis, ototoxic, ototoxicity, panotitis, parotic, parotid, periotic, polyotia, prootic

otter See **lutra-** for examples.

-ous (**-ious, -eous**) (L., possessing the qualities of, full of, pertaining to) Also see **-ose** and the SUFFIXES section in **Appendix K.**

    Qualifying words: acidulous, ambiguous, barbarous, bibulous, bigamous, carnivorous, conspicuous, credulous, famous, gregarious, herbaceous, incredulous, innocuous, inodorous, mellifluous, odorous, oviparous, pluvious, poisonous, polygamous, populous, solicitous, tempestuous, various

out, outside, outer See **ecto-, ex-** (Gk.), and **exo-** for examples.

out of, from, away from See **ec-** and **ex-** (L.) and **ex-** (Gk.) for examples.

outer, outside See **exo-** (Gk.) for examples.

outermost See **acro-** for examples.

outside, beyond See **extro-** (L.) for examples.

ova- (L., egg) Also see **oo-, oophoro-, ovi-, ovo-,** and **ovum.**

    Qualifying words: ova, oval, ovate, ovaphagous, ovariotomy, ovaritis, ovary

ovari-, ovario-, ova-, -ovaria, -ovarial (L., egg) For other "egg" words, see **oo-, oopharo-, ova-, ovo-,** and **ovum.**

    Qualifying words: anovaria, hyperovaria, hypovaria, ovaphagous, ovarialgia, ovarian, ovariectomy, ovariopathy, ovariotherapy, ovariotomy, ovaritis, ovarotherapy, ovary, ovate

ovary (L., egg) Examine **ovari-, oo-, ovo-,** and **oopharo-** for examples.

over, through See **per-** and **trans-.**

over, upon, above See **epi-, hyper-, super-, supra-, sur-,** and **ultra-** for examples.

overcome, conquer See **vinc-** for examples.

ovi- (L., egg) Also see **oo-, oophoro-, ova-, ovo-,** and **ovum-** for additional "egg" words. Don't confuse this **ovi-** with the next **ovi-** which means "sheep."

    Qualifying words: ovicide, oviduct, oviferous, oviform, ovigenesis, ovigenic, ovipara, oviparism, oviparity, oviparous, oviposit, oviposition, ovipositor, ovium, semioviparous

ovi- (L., sheep) Don't confuse this element with the above **ovi-** which means "egg."

    Qualifying words: Ovibos, Ovibovine, ovibovine, Ovidae, ovigorm, ovination, ovine, ovinia, Ovis

ovo- (L., egg) Also see **oo-, oophoro-, ova-, ovi-,** and **ovum.**

    Qualifying words: ovogenesis, ovoid, ovolysin, ovolytic, ovotherapy, ovovivipara, ovoviviparism, ovoviviparity, ovoviviparous

ovum-, ovu- (L., egg) For additional "egg" words, see **oo-, oophoro-, ova-, ovi-,** and **ovo-.**

    Qualifying words: ovulate, ovule, ovulm

ox- (Gk., cow) See **bou-** for examples.

oxy-, -oxia, -oxic (Gk., sharp, pointed, keen, acidic, pungent) Also see **acid-, acerb-, acri-, acut-,** and **picro-** for meanings which are the same or similar in nature.

    Qualifying words: amphioxious, anoxemia, anoxia, asthenoxia, hyperoxia, hypoxia, oxalis, oxide, oxyacid, oxyacusis, oxyalgia, oxybenzene, oxyblepsia, oxycalcium, oxycephalia, oxycephalous, oxychromatic, oxychromatin, oxycinesis, oxydactyl, oxydactylic, oxmel, oxydation, oxyesthesia, oxygen oxygenize, oxygnathous, oxyhemoglobin, oxyhexaster, oxyhydrogen, oxymora(pl.), oxymoron(s.), oxyntic, oxyopia, oxyopter, oxyosmia, oxyperitoneum, oxyphil(e), oxyphilous, oxyphobe, oxyphonia, oxyphyte, oxyrhine, oxytone, oxyuricide, oxyurid, paroxyosm

oxymora, pronounced ahk" si MOR uh, is plural; **oxymoron**, pronounced ahk" si MOR ahn, is singular, ["pointedly foolish," from Greek, *oxy-*, "point, sharp" and *moron*, "foolish, dull"]. See **Appendix H** for an extensive list of **Oxymora**.

oyster See **ostreo-** for examples.

P p

pac-, peac-, peas- (L., peace, calm)   Also see **plac-** for additional "peace" words.

　　Qualifying words: appease, appeasement, appeaser, pacifiable, pacific, Pacific, pacification, pacified, pacifier, pacifist, pacifism, pacifist, pacify, pacifying, pax, peace, peaceable, peaceful, peacefully, peacefulness

pachy-, pacho-, pach- (Gk., thick, dense) Also see **densi-** and **pykno-** for other "thick" words.

　　Qualifying words: isopach, isopachous, myopachynsis, pachemia, pachometer, pachycephalia, pachycephalic, pachycephalosaurian, pachycephaly, pachyderm, pachyderma, pachydermal, pachydermatoid, pachydermatous, pachydermai, pachydermic, pachydermoid, pachydermous, pachyglossal, pachyglossia, pachygnathous, pachymeaningitis, pachymeter, pachynema, pachypod, pachypteron, pachysandra, pachyrhinic, pachysomia, Riftia pachyptila (the tube worm, a dominant deep-sea vent animal)

paed- (Gk., child) Examine **pedo-** (Gk.).

paid- (Gk., child) Examine **pedo-** (Gk.).

pain See **algesi-, doloro-,** and **odyno-**.

pair (L., equal) See **pari-** for examples.

pairs, yoke See **zygo-** for examples.

palaeo-, palae-, paleo-, pale- (Gk., original, ancient, primitive, old) Also see **archaeo-** and **proto-**.

　　Qualifying words: palaeethnology, palaeobiologist, paleobotony, paleography, paleolith, paleolithic, paleology, paleontology, paleopsychology, paleozoic, paleozoology

paleo- See **palaeo-** for examples.

pali-, palin-, palin- (Gk., recurrence, repetitious; back, backward, again) Also see **re-** and **retro-** for other "back, again" words.

　　Qualifying words: palicinesia, paligraphia, palikinesia, palilalia, palilexia, palilogia, palilogy, palinal, palindrome, palindromia, palindromic, palinesthesia, palingenesis, palingenetic, palingraphia, palinmnesia, palinopsia, palinphrasia, palirrhea

pall- (Gk., shake, vibration) Also see **seismo-** for additional "shake" words.

　　Qualifying words: hyperpallesthesia, hypopallesthesia, pallanesthesia, pallesthesia, pallesthetic, pallyhyperesthesia, pallhypesthesia

palyn- (Gk., pollen, spores) The Greek *palynein* means "to sprinkle."

　　Qualifying words: palynologic, palynological, palynologically, palynologist, palynology

pan- [*panis*] (L., bread)   Don't confuse this **pan-** with the next **pan-** which means "all" or "every."

　　Qualifying words: accompany, companion, companionable, companionship, panarium, panivorous, pannier, pantry

pan-, panto-, pant- (Gk., all, every)   Also see **omni-** for other "all, every" words. Don't confuse this **pan-** with the previous one which means "bread."

　　Qualifying words: Pan, panacea, pan-American, panangiitis, panarthritis, panasthenia, panatrophy, panautonomic, pancarditis, panchromatic, panchromia, pancreas, pancreatectomy, pancreatic, pancreatolith, pancreatolysis, pancreatopathy, pancreatotomy, pancyclopedic, pandemic, pandemicity, pandemonium, Pandora, panegyric, panencephalitis, panendoscope, panepizootic, panesthesia, panesthetic, Pangaea, pangenesis, pangitis, panglossia, panhydrometer, panhyperemia, panic, panimmunity, panleukopenia, panophobia, panoply, panoptic, panorama, panosteitis, panotitis, panphobia, pan-Satanism, pansinusitis, pansophist, pansophy, pantachromatic, pantagamy, pantalgia, pantamorphia, pantamorphic, Panthalassa, pantheisis, pantheism, pantheon, pantherapist, pantogamy, pantograph, pantology, pantomine, pantomorphia, pantomorphic, pantophagous, pantophagy, pantophobia, pantophobic, pantoscopic, pantotropic, pantropic, panzootic

-pand-, -pans-, -pass- (*pandere*) (L., stretch, spread)

　　Qualifying words: apace, compass, encompass, expand, expanse, expansionism, impasse, overpass, pace, pacemaker, pass, passable, passacalgia, passage, passbook, passé, passenger, passport, past, pastime, spandrel, spawn, surpass, trespass

-pans- (L., stretch, spread) Examine **-pand-** for examples.

panto- (Gk., all, every)   See **pan-**.

par (L., same, equal) Examine **pari-** for examples.

para-¹, par-, -para, -parity, -parous, -parously, -partum (L., to bring forth, to bear; producing viable offspring; giving birth to; brood) Also see **genus, nasc-,** and **toco-** for similarities.   Don't confuse this element with the next **para-** which means "near, by the side of," or another **para-** which means "to protect." Also see **gravid-** (pregnant).

　　Qualifying words: ambiparous, andropara, androparous, bipara, biparous, decipara, dentiparous, deuteripara, dorsiparous, duipara, floriparous, larviparous, laviparity, multipara, multiparous, nonipara, nullipara, nulliparous, octipara, ovipara, oviparous, ovovivipara, ovoviviparity, ovoviviparous, parent, paroventron, parous, parturient, parturifacient, parturition, pluriparous, postpartum, postparturitional, preparturient, preparturition, primipara, primiparous, pupiparous, quadripara, quartipara, quintipara, secundipara, secundiparity, secundiparous, semioparous, septipara, sextipara, sudoriparous, tertipara, tripara, unipara, uniparous, vivipara, viviparity, viviparous

para-², par- (Gk., by the side of, near; past, beyond; contrary, wrong; abnormal, irregular) Also see **juxta-** and **proximo-** for other "near" examples. Don't confuse this **para-** with the following one which means "to protect" or with the previous one meaning "to bring forth, to bear."

> **Qualifying words:** para-analgesia, para-anesthesia, parabiont, parabiosis, parablast, paracardiac, paracenesthesia, paracinesia, paracousis, paracusia, paracusis, paradigm, paradipsia, paradox, paradoxical, parady, paradysentery, parageusia, parageusic, paraglossia, paragon, paragraph, paragraphia, parahelion, parahepatic, parahepatitis, parahypnosis, parakinesis, parakinetic, paralexia, paralgesia, paralgia, parallel, paralytic, paramania, paramedical, paramnesia, paramorphic, paranephritis, paranoia, paranoid, paranomia, paranormal, paranosis, paraphernalia, parappendicitis, paraphasia, paraphobia, paraphonia, paraphrase, paraplegia, paraplegic, parapsychology, parasite, parasitic, parasiticidal, parasitism, parasitogenic, parasitoid, parasitologist, parasitology, parasitosis, parasitotropic, parasomnia, parasthenia, paratrophy, parazoon, paregoric, parentheses(pl.), parenthesis, paresthesia(s.), parenthetic, parkinesis, parodontal, paroxysm

para-³, par- (Gk., that which protects) Also see the previous **para-²** which means "by the side of, near," etc., and the **para-¹** which means "to produce," etc.

> **Qualifying words:** parachute, parapet, parasol

paralysis See **-plegia** and **polio-** for examples.

pari-, par- (Gk., same, equal, equality, equal value) Also examine **equ-, homeo-, homo-** (Gk.), **iso-, -oid, peer-, simal-,** and **tauto-.**

> **Qualifying words:** comparable, compare, disparage, disparity, impair, pair, par, parisyllabic, parity, parlay, peerless, umpire

-parous (L., to bring forth, to bear; birth) See **para-** (L.) for examples.

parr- (L., close relative, parent) Also examine FAMILY GROUPS for additional elements.

> **Qualifying words:** parricidal, parricide

part, partial See **mero-¹** for examples.

part of the body See **organo-** for examples.

partheno-, partho- (Gk., virgin, maiden, young girl) Also examine **virgin** for other "maiden" or "young girl" words.

> **Qualifying words:** parthenocarpy, parthenogenesis, parthenology, parthenon, Parthenon, parthenophobia, parthogenesis

partho- (Gk., virgin, maiden, young girl) See **partheno-** for examples.

-partum (L., birth) See **para-¹** for examples.

-pass- (L., stretch, spread) See **-pand-** for examples. Don't confuse this **-pass-** with the next **pass-** (suffering).

pass-, pati- (L., suffering, feeling; enduring) Also see **aesth-, patho-,** and **sens-** for other "feeling" words.

> **Qualifying words:** compassion, compassionate, compatible, compatibility, dispassion, dispassionate, impassion, impassionate, impassioned, impassible, impassive, impatience, impatient, incompatible, passion, passionate, passive, passivity, patience, patient

pass away, miscarry See **abort** for examples.

passageway, opening Examine **meato-** as well as **poro-** for examples.

passively drifting or wandering See **plankton.**

past, beyond See **para-** for examples.

pater-, patr- (L., father) Also examine FAMILY GROUPS for additional elements.

> **Qualifying words:** allopatric, Cleopatra, expatriate, expatriation, paternal, paternity, patriarch, patricentric, Patricia, patrician, patricide, patrilineage, patrilineal, patrilocal, patrilocality, patrimony, patriot, patriotic, patristic, patron, patronage, patroness, patronize, patronymic, philopatric, philopatry, repatriate

path, way, road See **odo-** and **via-.**

patho-, -path-, -pathia, -pathic, -pathology, -pathetic, -pathize, -pathy (Gk., feeling, sensation, perception, suffering, [in medicine, it usually means "one who suffers from a disease of, or one who treats a disease"]) Also see **aesth-, pass-, sens-,** and **noso-** (disease) for additional related examples.

> **Qualifying words:** allopath, allopathetic, allopathy, antipathetic, antipathy, apathetic, apathy, arthropathology, cardiomyopathy, cardiopathy, cryopathy, dyspathic, dyspathy, empathetic, empathy, homeopathy, isopathy, metropathy, osteopath, osteopathy, pathergasia, pathetic, pathoformic, pathogen, pathogenesis, pathologic, pathological, pathologist, pathology, pathophilia, pathophobia, pathos, psychopath, psychopathic, psychopathy, sociopathy, sympathetic, sympathize, sympathy, telepathic, telepathy

-pathy (Gk., feeling *or* a disease) See **patho-** for examples.

pati- (L., feeling, suffering) Examine **pass-** for examples.

patr- (L., father) See **pater-** for examples.

patria (L., fatherland) Examine **pater-** for examples.

pauci- (L., few, little) Also examine **oligo-** for other "few" words.

> Qualifying words: pauciflorous, paucifoliate, paucioquence, paucioquent, paucity, paucioquy, pauciradiate, pauper

peac- (L., peace) See **pac-** for examples.

peace, quiet See **pac-, plac-,** and **quies-** for examples.

pearls See **margarito-** for examples.

peas- (L., peace) See **pac-** for examples.

pebble See **calci-** for examples.

pebbles, gravel See **chalico-** for examples.

pectoro-, pector- (L., breast, chest) Also see **mammill-, mammo-** (breast), **mazo-** (breast), **masto-** (breast), **sterno-** (chest), **stetho-** (chest), **thoraco-** (chest) for related words.

> Qualifying words: angina pectoris, pectoral, pectoralgia, pectoralis, pectoriloquy, pectorophony

peculiar, personal See **idio-** for examples.

ped-, pedi-, -pedal, -ped, -pede, -pedia (L., foot) For additional "foot" words, see **podo-** and **-pus.** Remember that the Latin **ped-** means "foot," while the Greek **ped-** means "child."

> Qualifying words: biped, bipedal, bipedaling, bipedalism, centipede, expedience, expediency, expedient, expedite, expedition, expeditious, impede, impeded, impeder, impediment, impedimenta, impeding, pedal, pedaled, pedate, peddle, pedestal, pedestrian, pedialgia, pedicab, pedicle, pedicure, pedicurist, pediform, pedigree, pediluvium, pedionalgia, pediphalanx, peditis, pedodynamometer, pedograph, pedometer, pedopathy, pedorthic, pedorthics, pedorthist, quadruped, remiped, unimpeded, velocipede

pedo-, paedo-, ped-, paed-, paido-, paid- (Gk., child) Also see **puer-** and **proli-** for additional "child" words. Remember that the Greek **ped-** means "child" while the Latin **ped-** means "foot."

> Qualifying words: encyclopedia, orthopedic(s), orthopedica, orthopedist, paedobaptist, paedogenesis, paedomorphic, paedomorphosis, paedophage, paedophagous, paedophagy, paideutics, paidological, paidologist, paidology, pedagog, pedagogic, pedagogical, pedagogics, ped-agogue, pedagogy, pediadontia, pediadontist, pediadontology, pediatric(s), pediatrician, pediatrics, pediatry, pedobaptism, pedodontics, pedodontist, pedodontistry, pedologist, pedology, pedomorphism, pedopathy, pedophilia, pedophile, pedophilic, pedophobia, pedophobic, pedoplania

peer, pair (L., same, equal, similar) For other "same, equal" words, see **equ-, homo-** (Gk.), **iso-, -oid, pari-, simal-,** and **tauto-.**

> Qualifying words: peer, peerage, peerless

pego-, -pegic (Gk., spring, fountain, mineral spring) Also see **creno-** and **namato-** for other "spring, fountain" words.

> Qualifying words: pegologist, pegology, pegomancy, pegotherapist, pegotherapy, thermopegic

pejor- (L., worse) Also examine **meliorat-** (better) for opposite meanings.

> Qualifying words: pejoration, pejorative, pejoratively

-pel, -peal, -pell (L., drive, push, beat) Also examine **puls-** [another form of **-pel**] for other "drive" words.

> Qualifying words: appeal, appellant, appellate, appellation, appellative, compel, compelled, compelling, compellingly, dispel, expel, impel, peal, propel, propellant, propeller, propelling, rappel, repeal, repel, repellant, repelled, repellency, repellent

pelago-, pelag- (Gk. > L., sea, pertaining to the sea) Also examine **mare** and **thalasso-** for other "sea" words.

> Qualifying words: abyssopelagic, allopelagic, autopelagic, bathypelagic, chimopelagic, epipelagic, eupelagic, halopelagic, holopelagic, meropelagic, mesopelagic, neritopelagic, nyctipelagic, oligopela, oligopelic, pelagial, pelagian, pelagic, pelagophile, pelagophilous, pelagophily, pelagophyte, pelagophytic, tychopelagic

pelo-, pel- (Gk., mud, earth) Also see **angillo-** [clay], **chledo-** [mud, clay], **geo-** [earth], **limi-** [mud], and **terr-** [earth] words with similar meanings.

> Qualifying words: pelochthophile, pelochthophilous, pelochthophily, pelochthophyte, pelogenous, pelohemia, peloid, pelology, pelopathy, pelophilous, pelopathy, pelophile, pelophyte, pelophytic, pelosammic, pelotherapy

pelvic bone See **ilio-** for examples.

pend-, pens, -pense, -pending, -pended (L., hang, weigh)

> Qualifying words: append, appendage, appendant, appendectomy, appendicitis, appendix, compendious, compendium, compensate, compensation, depend, dependency, dependent, dispensary, dispensation, dispense, expend, expendable, expenditure, expense, expensive, im-

pend, impending, imponderable, independency, independent, indispensible, pendant, pendent, pending, pendulum, pendulus, pendulous, pension, pensive, penthouse, perpendicular, ponder, ponderable, ponderance, ponderate, ponderation, ponderous, preponderance, preponderant, preponderate, propensity, recompense, supension, suspend, suspended, suspenders, suspense, suspenseful, suspension, suspensory

peni-, peno-, peo- (Gk. > L., tale; male organ of copulation, the penis) Also see **caudo-** and **uro-** for other "tail" words.

　　Qualifying words: pencil, penectomy, penial, penicillin, penile, penis, penischisis, penitis, penoscrotal, penotherapy, peotillomania, peotomy

-penia-, -penic, pen-, penia- (Gk., abnormal reduction, decrease in, not enough, deficiency; originally, Greek for "poverty, need") Don't confuse this element with **peni-,** "male organ."

　　Qualifying words: calcipenia, calcipenic, erythrocytopenia, leukocytopenia, leukopenia, lymphopenia, lymphopenic, monopenia, penalgia, peniaphobia, thrombopenia, thrombopenic

pens- (L., hang) See **pend-** for examples.

penta-, pent-, pente-, pento- (Gk., five) Also see **quinqu-** for other examples. Examine the NUMBERS section in **Appendix G** for other numerical elements.

　　Qualifying words: pentacle, pentact, pentactinal, pentacular, pentacyclic, pentad, pentadactyl, pentadelphous, pentagamist, pentagamy, pentaglot, pentagon, Pentagon, pentagonal, pentagynous, pentahedral, pentahedron, pentalogy, pentameter, pentandrous, pentangular, pentapetalous, pentapterous, pentarchy, pentasyllable, Pentateuch, pentathlete, pentathlon, pentatonic, Pentecost, pentode, pentomic

peo- (Gk. > L., male organ) Examine **peni-.**

people Examine **demo-, ethno-, ochlo-, pleb-, popu-, publi-,** and **vulg-** for examples.

-pepsia (Gk., digestion) Examine **pepto-.**

pepto-, pept-, -peptic, pepsi-, -pepsia, -pepsy (Gk., digestion, promoting digestion, able to digest; cook)

　　Qualifying words: apepsia, apepsinia, bradypepsia, dyspepsia, dyspeptic, eupepsia, eupeptic, hyperpepsinia, hypopepsinia, pepsin, pepsinate, pepsinia, pepsiniferous, pepsinogen, pepsinogenous, peptase, peptic, peptide, peptinotoxin, peptolysis, peptolytic, peptone, peptonize, peptotoxin, eupepsia, eupeptic

per- (L., through, across, over; beyond, by means of) Also see **dia-** and **trans-.**

　　Qualifying words: impervious, perambulate, perambulated, perambulating, perambula-

tion, perambulator, per annum, per capita, perceive, per cent, perception, perceptive, percolate, percolating, percolation, percolator, percussion, percutaneous, per diem, perennial, perennially, perfect, perfection, perfectionist, perfectly, perfidious, perfidy, perforate, perforated, perforating, perforation, perforator, perfume, perfumer, perfumery, perfunctory, perfuse, perfusion, permanence, permanency, permanent, permanently, permeability, permeable, permeance, permeate, permeation, permeator, permission, permissive, permissiveness, permit, permutation, permute, perpendicular, perpendicularity, perpetrate, perpetual, perpetually, perpetuate, perpetuation, perpetuator, perpetuity, perplex, perplexity, perquisite, persecute, persecution, persecutor, perseverance, persevere, persist, persistence, persistent, persistently, perspective, perspectively, perspicacious, perspicaciously, perspicacity, perspicuity, perspicuous, perspiration, perspire, perspired, perspiring, persuade, persuaded, persuader, persuading, persuasible, persuasion, persuasive, persuasively, persuasiveness, pertain, pertinacity, pertinent, perturb, perusal, peruse, perused, perusing, pervade, pervaded, pervading, pervasion, pervasive, pervasively, pervasiveness, pervious, semipermeable

perceive See **spec-** and **vid-** for examples.

perception Examine **aesth-, pass-, patho-,** and **sens-** for related words.

perfection, completion See **teleo-** for related words.

perforation, puncture See **-centesis.**

peri- (Gk., around, about, near, enclosing) Also see **ambi-, amphi-, circ-, circum-, cyclo-,** and **sphero-** for other "around" words.

　　Qualifying words: perianth, periarthritis, pericardial, pericarditis, pericardium, pericarp, perichrome, pericranium, pericycle, periderm, periodontia, perifoliary, perigee, periglossitis, periglottic, periglottis, perihelia, perihelion, perihepatic, perimeter, perimetric, perinatal, period, periodic, periodical, periodontal, periosteum, peripatetic, peripheral, peripherally, periphery, periphrasis, periphrastic, perisarc, periscope, periscopic, peristome, peritoneum, peritonitis, peritrichous

person, especially a child, who is endowed with extraordinary qualities Examine **prodigy** for examples.

person who (thing which) For examples of these meanings, go to suffixes **-ee, -eer,** and **-ist.** Also see **Appendix K** for other word endings.

personal, private See **idio-** for examples.

pertaining to the back Examine **dorso-.**

pertaining to, of the nature of Suffixes with these meanings: **-ac, -ane, -ar,** and **-ary.**

peta- [from **penta-**] (Gk., one quadrillion [U.S.] 10^{15} [1 000 000 000 000 000]) For other units, also see METRIC GROUPS in **Appendix F**.

    Qualifying words: petagram, petameter

peter- (Gk., stone, rock) Examine **petro-** for examples.

peti-, pet-, -pit- [*petere*] (L., seek, ask, request; strive after) Also examine **quir-** and **rog-** for other examples.

    Qualifying words: appetite, appetizer, compete, competent, competition, competitor impetuous, impetus, perpetual, petition, petulant, propitious, repeat, repetition

petr- (Gk., stone, rock) See **petro-**.

petro-, petr-, peter- (Gk., stone, rock) Also see **lapid-, litho-,** and **saxi-** for otherr "stone, rock" examples.

    Qualifying words: Peter, petracide, petricole, petricolous, petrifaction, petrified, petrify, petrobiont, petrobiontic, petrochthophile, petrochthophilous, petrochthophily, petrochthophyte, petrocole, petrocolous, petrodophile, petrodophilous, petrodophily, petrodophyte, petroglyph, petroglyphic, petroglyphics, petrographer, petrographic, petrographical, petrographically, petrography, petrol, petroleum, petrologic, petrological, petrologist, petrology, petrophile, petrophilous, petrophily, petrophyte, petrophytic, petrous, saltpeter

-pexia (Gk., fixing to) See **-pexy**.

-pexy, -pexia, -pexes, -pexic, -pexis (Gk., fixing [of a specified part]; attaching to, a fastening; used in medical nomenclature to denote "a surgical fixation" of that which is specified by the combining root)

    Qualifying words: calcipexis, cecopexy, cholecystopexy, colopexy, colpohysteropexy, colpopexy, cordopexy, cryptorchidopexy, cystopexy, enteropexy, gastropexy, hepatopexy, hysteropexy, mastopexy, mesenteriopexy, mesopexy, nephropexy, nephrosplenopexy, omentopexy, oophoropexy, orchidopexy, orchiopexy, organopexy, pexia, pexic, pexin, pexis, pneumopexy, pneumonopexy, retinopexy, scapulopexy, scrotopexy, sigmoidpexy, syndesmopexy, toxicopexis, tympanolabyrinthopexy, vaginapexy, viropexis

phago-, phag-, phag, phage, -phagi, -phagic, -phagically, -phagia, -phagism, -phagist, -phagism, -phagic, -phagous, -phag (Gk., eat, consume) Also see **vor-**.

    Qualifying words: acridophage, acridophagous, acridophagy, adephagia, adephagous, aerophagia, aerophagy, allotriophagia, allotriophagy, androphagous, anthophagous, anthophagy, anthropophagi(pl.), anthropophagus(s.), aphagia, aphagosis, araneophage, araneophagic, araneophagy, autocoprophage, autocoprophagous, autocoprophagy, autophage, autophagous, autophagy, bacteriophage, bacteriophagous, bacteriophagy, batrachophagous, bibliophagic, bibliophagy, biophagery, biophagism, biophagous, biophagy, bradyphagia, bradyphagy, carcinophagous, cardophagus, carpophagous, cerophagia, cerophagous, cerophagy, cheilophagia, chthonophagia, coprophagous, coprophagy, creophagic, creophagism, creophagous, creophagy, dendrophagous, dendrophagy, dysphagia, dysphagy, Echidnophaga, endoophage, endoophagous, endoophagy, endophage, endophagous, endophagy, Entomophaga, entomophagous, entomophagy, esophagus, euryphagous, exophagus, fuciphagous, galactophage, galactophagia, galactophagous, galliphage, galliphagous, galliphagy, geophagist, geophagous, geophagy, haematophagous, hematophagous, hematophagy, hippophagism, hippophagist, hippophagous, hippophagy, histophagous, homophagia, hyalophagia, hyalophagy, hylophagous, hyperphagia, ichthyophagous, ichthyophagy, larviphagic, larviphagy, lipophage, lipophagic, lithophaga, lithophagous, lithophagy, mallophaga, meliphagous, meliphagy, monophagism, monophagous, monophagy, mycophagous, myrmecophagous, necrophagous, necrophagy, oligophagous, oligophagy, omophagia, omophagic, omophagous, omophagy, onychophagia, onychophagist, onychophagy, oophagous, oophagy, ophiophagous, ophiphagous, ostreophagous, ostrephagous, panthophagis, pantophagous, pantophagy, phagelysis, phagocyte, phagologist, phagology, phagolysis, phagomania, phagophobia, phagotherapy, phagozoite, phyllophagous, phyllophagy, phytophagous, pleophagous, pneumophagia, poltophagy, polyphagia, polyphagous, polyphagy, psomophagia, psomophagy, rhizophagous, rhizophagy, saprophagous, saprophagy, sarcophago, sarcophagous, sarcophagus, sarcophagy, saurophagous, scatophagous, scatophagy, sialoaerophagia, sialoaerophagy, stenophagous, stenophagy, tachyphagia, thermophagy, trichophagy, xylophaga, xylophage, xylophagist, xylophagous, xylophagy, zoophagous, zoophagy

phalango-, phalang- (Gk., bone between two joints of a finger or toe; line of battle, [*phalanx*], heavy infantry in close order [Greek antiquity])

    Qualifying words: phalangeal, phalangectomy, phalanges, phalangitis, phalangophalangeal, phalangosis, phalanx

phanero-, phaner-, -phane, -phanic, -phanous, -phany (Gk., to show; visible, manifest, open) Also examine **phant-** for other "show; visible" words.

    Qualifying words: allophane, cellophane, diaphanous, epiphany, Epiphany, lithophany, phanatron, phanerite, phaneritic, phanerocarpae, phanerocryst, phanerogenic, phanereglossia, phaneromania, phaneromaniac, phanerophyte, phaneroscopy, phanerosis, phanerozoic, phanerozoite, phanerozonia, phanotron

phant-, phanta-, -phant (Gk., illusion, show, appear, make visible, display, visible, show [through], shine [through]) Also examine **phanero-** for other "visible" words.

Qualifying words: emphasis, fantasy, hierophant, phantasmagoria, phantasmal, phantasmic, phantasy, phantom, phenomena, phenomenon, sycophant, theophanty, tomophant

pharmaco-, pharmac-, -pharmic (Gk., drug, medicine; poison)

Qualifying words: alexipharmic, antipharmic, pharmaceutic, pharmaceutical, pharmacist, pharmacochemistry, pharmacodynamic, pharmacogenetics, pharmacognosist, pharmacognostics, pharmacognosy, pharmacography, pharmacokinetics, pharmacologist, pharmacology, pharmacomania, pharmacophobia, pharmacopoeia, pharmacopsychosis, pharmacotherapeutics, pharmacy, polypharmic, polypharmacy

pharyngo-, pharyng- (Gk., pharynx [the alimentary canal between the palate and the esophagus]; part of the neck or throat) Also examine **cervico-, esophago-, gutturo-, laryngo-, thoraco-,** and **trachelo-.**

Qualifying words: adenopharyngitis, pharyngology, pharyngoscope

-phasia, -phasic, -phasis, -phasy (Gk., talk, speak, say) Also examine **cit-, clam-, dic-, fa-, locu-, logo-, loqu-, mythico-, ora-, -phemia, -phras-,** and **voc-** for other "talk, speak" words.

Qualifying words: acataphasia, aphasia, aphasiac, aphasic, apophasis, bradyphasia, dysphasia, euphasia, hyperphasia, monophasic, paraphasia, polyphasic, tachyphasia, tonaphasia

-phemia, -phemic, -phemism, -pheme (Gk., speak, speech) Also examine the items under **-phasia** [shown above] for related "speak" words.

Qualifying words: aphemesthesia, aphemia, aphemic, ataxiophemia, blame, blaspheme, blasphemous, blasphemy, bradyphemia, cacophemism, cacophemistic, dysphemis, euphemis, euphemism, euphemist, euphemistic, euphemistical, euphemistically, euphemize, euphemizer, Polyphemus, prophecy, prophesy, prophet, prophetess, prophetic

philo-, -phil-, -phile, -phila, -philia, -philic, -philous, -phily, -philiac, -philist, -philism, -philite (Gk., love, loving, friendly to, fondness for, attraction to, strong tendency toward, affinity for) Note: under some circumstances, **-philia** means "unwholesome

sexual attraction" to something or someone, as in *paedophilia* (*pedophilia*). Also examine **amat-, aphrodi-, eroto-,** and **vener-** for additional "love, fondness, *and* attraction to" words.

Qualifying words: acidophil, acidophilous, aelurophile, aelurophilist, aerohygrophile, aerohygrophilous, aerohygrophily, aerohygrophobia, aerohygrophobe, aerohygrophobous, aerohygrophoby, aerophilia, ailurophile, ailurophily, aithalophile, aithalophilous, aithalophily, algophilia, anemophilous, anemophily, anglophile, aphilophrenia, arctophilist, audiophile, autophilia, autophilous, autophily, basophile, basophilous, basophily, bathophile, bathophiloous, bathophily, bibliophile, bibliophilism, bibliophily, biophile, biophilous, biophily, brandophily, cacophily, capnophilic, capnophily, cartophily, cibophile, cibophily, cinephile, cryophilia, cryophilic, cynophilist, cynophilous, demophil, demophile, dendrophilous, dipsophile, dipsophily, dubiophilia, electrophile, electrophilic, entomophilous, euhydrophile, euhydrophilous, euhydrophily, gastrophile, gerontophilia, gymnophile, gynephile, gynephily, gymnophily, halophilous, halophily, heliophile, heliophily, hematophilia, hemophilia, hydrophil, hydrophilia, hydrophilic, hydrophilous, hygrophilous, hygrophily, iatrophilia, iatrophile, iatrophily, iconophilist, laborphily, lyophilic, malacophilous, mazophilous, meadophily, merophilous, mymecophilous, mymecophily, necrophilia, necrophilic, necrophilous, necrophily, nemophilist, nemophilous, neophiliac, neophily, neutrophils, nucleophile, nyctophilia, ochlophile, ochlophilia, oenophilist, ornithocoprophile, ornithocoprophilous, ornithocoprophily, ornithophilous, oxyphil, oxyphile, oxyphilous, paedophilia, paleophilist, paniphile, paniphilous, paniphily, pedophile, pedophily, Philadelphia, philagrypnia, philander, philanderer, philanthropic, philanthropical, philanthropist, philanthropy, philatelist, philately, philharmonia, philharmonic, philodendron, philogynist, philologist, philology, philornithic, philosopher, philosophic, philosophical, philosophize, philosophy, philotheist, philotherm, philoxeny, philter, photophile, photophilia, photophilous, photophily, potamophilous, psychrophile, psychrophilic, psychrophily, pygophilous, pyrophilia, saprophilous, saprophily, scopophilia, stegophilist, termitophile(s), termitophilic, termitophilous, termitophily, thalassophilous, thalassophily, thermophil, thermophile, thermophilous, thermophily, tropophilic, tropophilous, tropophily, xenophile, xenophilist, xenophily, xerophil, xerophilous, xerophily, zoophilia, zoophile, zoophilous, zoophily

phlebo-, phleb- (Gk., blood vein) Also see **angio-, arterio-, vaso-,** and **veno-.**

Qualifying words: arteriophlebotomy, phlebalgia, phlebectomy, phlebectopy, phlebitic, phlebitis, phlebocarcinoma, phlebodynamics, phlebogram, phlebograph, phlebography, phleboid, phlebolite, phlebolith, phlebology, phlebo-plasty, phleborrhagia, phlebosclerosis, phlebo-stasis, phlebotomy, phlebotropism

-phobia, -phobias, -phobe, -phobiac, -phobist, -phobic, -phobism, -phobous; phobo-, phob- (Gk., fear, extreme fear of, morbid fear of, *excessive* fear of, *irrational* fear or terror of something or someone; however, sometimes this Greek element means a strong *dislike* or *hatred* for something) Noun endings are formed with **-phobia** and **-phobe**; while adjectives end with **-phobic**. Also see **timi-** for other "fear" words. See **Appendix I** for an extensive list of over five hundred phobias which are given from English to the "phobic" name or vice versa.

phono-, phon-, -phone, -phonia, -phonic, -phonetic, -phonous, -phonically, -phonetically, -phonious, -phony (Gk., sound; voice) Also examine **echo-, son-,** and **ton-** for other "sound" words.

Qualifying words: amphorophony, antiphony, aphonia, aphonic, cacophonic, cacophonous, cacophony, cardiophone, diaphony, diplophonia, dysphonia, earphone, electrophone, euphonious, euphonous, euphony, gramaphone, homophone, hydrophone, hypophonia, idiophone, kinetophone, magnetophone, megaphone, microphone, optophone, orthophonic, oxyphonia, phoneme, phonetic, phonetician, phonetics, phoniatrics, phonic, phonics, phonocardiography, phonogram, phonograph, phonographic, phonography, phonolite, phonological, phonologist, phonology, phonometer, phonomyography, phonomyogram, phonophore, phonoreceptor, phonoscope, polyphonic, radiophone, radiotelephone, saxophone, sousaphone, sphygmophone, stethophone, symphonic, symphony, tautophony, telephone, telephonic, tracheophonesis, tracheophony, trachyphonia, videophone, xylophone

phoro-, phor-, -phora, -phorous, -phoresis, -phore, -phori, -phoria, (Gk. > L., bearer, to bear, carrying) Also examine **fer-, ger-, later-,** and **port-** for other "carrying, bearing" words.

Qualifying words: anthophore, Christopher, chromatophore, cryophorous, dysphoria, esophoria, euphoria, exophoria, hypophoria, metaphore, nectarophore, oophoro, oophorous, phorologist, phorology, phorometer, phorozoon, phosphoric, phosphorous, phyllophosphoric, phyllophorous, pneumatophore, semaphore, siphonophore, spodophorous, thermophore

phospho-, phosph-, phosphoro-, phosphor- (Gk., light, shine; morning star; a nonmetalic chemical element which ignites when exposed to air) Also examine **luco-, Lucifer,** **lumen-, luna-, lustr-, photo-,** and **scintill-** for additional "light" words.

Qualifying words: phosis, phosphate, phosphated, phosphatic, phosphatization, phosphatize, phosphene, phosphite, phospholipase, phospholipid, phospholipidemis, Phosphor, phosphorated, phosphorescence, phosphorescent, phosphorhidrosis, phosphoric, phosphorize, phosphorolysis, phosphoroscope, phosphorous, phosphorus

photo-, phot-, -photic, -phote (Gk., light) Also examine **luc-, lumen-, luna-, lustr-, phospho-,** and **scintill-** for other "light" words.

Qualifying words: aphotic, aphototactic, aphototaxis, aphototropic, aphototropism, diaphototactic, diaphototaxis, diaphototropic, diaphototropism, dysphotic, euphotic, euryphotic, phot, euphototropic, euphototropism, photalgia, photaugiaphobia, photic, photism, photinos, photoallergy, photoautotrophic, photoautotrophy, photobiology, photobiotic, photocautherization, photocautery, photocell, photochemical, photochemistry, photochromatic, photocleistogamic, photocleistogamy, photocomposition, photocopy, photocutaneous, photocytes, photodegradable, photodermatitis, photodermatosis, photodynia, photoesthesia, photoesthetic, photodynamics, photoelectric, photoelectron, photoemissive, photoengraving, photogenic, photography, photohyponastic, photohyponasty, photokinesis, photolethal, photology, photoluminescence, photoluminescent, photolysis, photolytic, photometer, photometric, photometry, photomicrograph, photomorphosis, photopathy, photoperception, photophilia, photophilic, photophilous, photophobia, photophobic, photophobotactic, photophobotaxis, photophone, photophore, photopsia, photopsy, photoptometer, photoptometry, photorespiration, photoretinitis, photoretinopathy, photoreversal, photoscopy, photosensitive, photosensitization, photosphere, photostat, photostatic, photosynthesis, photosynthetic, phototactic, phototaxis, phototherapy, photothermal, photothermy, phototoxic, phototoxicity, phototoxis, phototropic, phototropism, stenophotic, sthenophotic

phras-, phra-, -phrasia, -phrase, -phrastic (Gk., talk, speak, say) Also see **cit-, clam-, dic-, fat-, -fess, lalo-, locu-, logo-,** and **loqu-** for additional "talk" words.

Qualifying words: angiophrasis, angophrasis, bradyphrasia, dysphrasia, holophrasis, holophrastic, metaphrase, paraphrase, periphrasis, phrase, phraseograph, phraseogram, phraseologist, phraseology

phreato-, phreat-, phreati- (Gk., well, reservoir, ground water)

Qualifying words: phreatic, phreaticole, phreaticolous, phreatobiology, phreatophyte, phreatophytic

phreno-, phren-, -phrenia, -phrenic, phrenically (Gk., mind, brain, or the diaphragm) Also see **cerebello-, cerebro-, encephalo-, noo-,** and **psycho-**.

Qualifying words: oligophrenia, oligophrenic, phrenalgia, phrenectomy, phrenetic, phrenic, phreniclasia, phrenism, phrenocardia, phrenodynia, phrenogastric, phrenoglottic, phrenograph, phrenolegia, phrenologist, phrenology, phrenopathy, phrenoplegia, phrenosplenic, phrenotropic, prysbyophrenia, schizophrenic

phryno-, phryn- (Gk., toad) Also see **bufo-** for examples.

Qualifying words: phrynin, phrynoderma, phrynodermia, phrynolysin, phrynolysine, Phrynosoma

phyco-, phyc- (Gk., alga, algae) Also examine **algo-** for other "algae" words and **fungi-** and **myco-** for "fungi" words.

Qualifying words: phycobiont, phycocoenoloby, phycology, phycophage, phycophagic, phycophagous, phycophagy, phycophile, phycophilic, phycophily

phylacto-, phylact-, phylax- (Gk., guard, preserve) Also examine **alexo-** and **-fend-** for other "guard, defend" words.

Qualifying words: anaphylaxis, crymophylactic, phylacagogic, phylactery, phylactic, phylactocarp, phylactotransfusion, phylaxin, phylaxiology, phylaxis, prophylactic

phyllo-, phyll-, -phyll, -phyllous (Gk., leaf, leaves) Also see **folio-** and **forbi-** (broad leaf) for other "leaf" words.

Qualifying words: aphyllous, aphylly, aphytic, chlorophyll, diphyllous, eleutherophyllous, heterophyllous, hydrophyllium, Phyllis, phyllobiology, phyllogenetic, phylloid, phyllomancy, phyllomania, phyllomorphosis, phyllophagous, phyllophorous, phyllorhiza, phyllosphere, phyllotaxis, phyllotaxy, Phylloxera, phyllozooid, phylogeny, sporophyll, xanthophyll

phylo-, phyl- (Gk., tribe)

Qualifying words: allophylian, monophyletic, phyla(pl.), phylarch, phyle, phyletic, phyletically, phylogenetic, phylogenetical, phylogenetically, phylogenic, phylogeny, phylon, phylum(s.), polyphylesis

physico-, physio-, physi- (Gk., nature, natural [make grow, produce]) Also see **phyto-** (plant) for related elements.

Qualifying words: apophysis, diaphysis, geophysics, hypophysis, metaphysics, monophysitic, paraphysis, physiatrician, physiatrics, physiatrist, physiatry, physic, physical, physically, physician, physicotherapeutics, physicotherapy, physicist, physics, physiocracy, physiocrat, physiocratic, physiogeny, physiognomical, physiognomist, physiognomonic, physio-gnomy, physiognosis, physiographer, physiographic, physiographical, physiography, physiological, physiologist, physiologize, physiologue, physiology, physiolysis, physiometry, physioneurosis, physiopathic, physiopathology, physiopyrexia, physiotherapeutics, physiotherpeutist, physiotherapist, physiotherapy, physique, symphysis

phyto-, phyt-, -phyte, -phyto- (Gk., a plant [growing in a specified way or place; produce]) Also see **botano-** and **physico-**.

Qualifying words: aerophyte, Anthophyta, atmophyte, aulophyte, autophyte, autophytic, biophyte, biophytic, bryophyta, cataphyll, Chlorophyta, chlorophyte, Chrysophyta, chrysophyte, cryptophyte, cryptophytic, dermophyte, dermotophyte, dissophyte, ectophyte, endophyte, endophytic, epiphyte, epiphytology, epiphytotic, exophytic, gametophyte, geophyte, halophytes, haptophyte, helophyte, helophytic, hemihydrophytes, holophyte, holophytic, hydrophyte, hygrophytes, hypsophyll, lithophyte, mesopleustophyte, microphyte, neophyte, oophyte, phytobiology, phytobiotic, phytochemistry, phytochrome, phytocidal, phytocide, phytocoenology, phytoconenosis, phytodemic, phytoderma, phytogenesis, phytogenous, phytogeographer, phytogeography, phytographer, phytographic, phytographist, phytography, phytoid, phytolith, phytology, phytome, phytomorphic, phytoparasite, phytopathogen, phytopathology, phytopathy, phytopathology, phytophage, phytophagous, phytophagy, phytophilous, phytopharmacology, phytoplankton, phytopleuston, phytosis, phytosociologist, phytosociology, phytotomy, phytotoxin, phytotrophic, phytotype, protophyta, protophytes, pteridophyte, phytotomy, pteridophyta, pteridophytes, Pyrrophyta, Rhodophyta, saprophyte, sciophytes, spermatophyta, spermatophytes, sporophyll, sporophyte, thallophytes, tracheophyte, tropophytes, xerophytes, xerophytic, zoophyte

pici-, pic- (L., woodpecker)

Qualifying words: Picidae, Picinae, piciform, Piciformes, picine, picoid, picologist, picology

pico- (L., woodpecker) See **pici-** for examples.

pico- (Italian, very small; one-trillionth part of something; 10^{-12} [0.000 000 000 001]) Also see METRIC GROUPS in **Appendix F** for additional elements.

Qualifying words: picoammeter, picoampere, picocurie, picofarad, picogram, picolife, picoliter, picometer, picomole, Picornaviridae, piconavirus, picopicogram, picoplankton, picoplanktonic, picosecond, picounit, picowatt

picro-, picr- (Gk., bitter, sharp, pungent) Also see **acerb-, acid-,** and **oxy-**.

Qualifying words: picric, picrocarmine, picrogeusia, picrotoxin, picrotoxinism

pierce, sting See **pung-** for examples.

pig, pork See **porc-** for examples.

pilo- (L., hair) Also see **coma²**, **crino-**, **dasy-**, **hirsute**, **tricho-**, **barba-** (beard), and **pogo-** (beard) for related words.

> **Qualifying words:** capillary, caterpillar, depilate, depilatory, epilation, horripilation, pilapanthia, pilar, pile, pileous, piliation, piliform, piloerection, piloid, pilojection, pilology, pilomotor, pilose, pilosis, pilosism, pilosity

pinpoint, sharp point See **pung-** for examples.

pipe, tube See **syringo-** for examples.

pisci-, pisc- (Gk., fish) Also see **ichthyo-** for other "fish" words.

> **Qualifying words:** piscan, piscary, piscation, piscatology, piscator, piscatorial, piscatory, Pisces, pisces(pl.), piscide, piscicolous, piscicultural, pisciculture, pisciculturist, piscifauna, pisciform, pisciformis, piscina, piscine, piscinity, piscis(s.), Piscis Austrinus, piscivorous, piscivory

-pit- (L., seek, ask, request) See **peti-**.

pitheco-, pithec-, -pithecan, -pithecoid (Gk., ape, monkey) Also see **simia-**.

> **Qualifying words:** Australopithecus, Archeopithecus, cercopithecini, Cercopithecus, Gigantopithecus, Archeopithecus, Leontopithecus, Nyctipithecus, Ouranopithecus macedoniensis, pithecanthrope, pithecanthropic, pithecanthropine, pithecanthropoid, Pithecanthropus, Pitheca, pithecoid, pithecological, pithecology

plac-, placi-, -plais (L., peace, calm; to please, satisfy) Also see **pac-** for other examples.

> **Qualifying words:** complacence, complacent, complaisant, implacable, placate, placebo, placid, placidity, placoid, plea, plead, pleasance, pleasurable, pleasure

place or thing used for something See **-arium**, **-ary**, and **-orium** for examples.

place, to put See **loco-, pon-, sist-** and **the-**.

place, a position See **loco-, pon-** and **topo-**.

place where See **-ory** for examples.

plagiar- (L., a literary thief; "plunderer, oppressor, kidnapper" [one who "abducts the child or slave of another"]; to take and use the thoughts, writings, etc. of someone else and represent or claim them as one's own) Also see **klepto-** for related words.

> **Qualifying words:** plagiarism, plagiarist, plagiaristic, plagiarization, plagiarize, plagiarizer

plain, field See **camp** for examples.

plankton (collective name for plant and animal organisms floating on or in the seas [coined by the German physiologist Viktor Hensen, 1835-1924]) See **plano-**.

plano-, plankton (Gk., passively drifting, wandering, or roaming) Another meaning for **plano-** is "level, flat," from Latin. Also see **neusto-** and **pleusto-**.

> **Qualifying words:** aerial plankton, aeroplankton, baterioplankton, cryoplankton, elaioplankton, epiplankton, epiplanktontic, femtoplankton, haliplankton, hidroplankton, helioplankton, holoplankton, holoplanktonic, ichthyoplankton, macroplankton, macrozooplankton, megaplankton, megaloplankton, meroplankton, meroplankters, meroplanktonic, metazooplnktonic, microzooplankton, morphoplankton, nanoplankton, nanoplanktonic, neidioplankton, neritoplankton, phytoplankters, phytoplankton, phytoplanktonic, picoplankton, picoplanktonic, planet, planetarium, planetary, planetesimal, planetoid, plankton, planktonic, planktophile, planktophilous, planktophily, plantophyte, planktotroph, planktotrophic, plantotrophy, potamoplankton, protozooplankton, pseudoplankton, rheoplankton, saproplankton, tychoplankton, virioplankton, zooplankters, zooplanktonic

plant (vegetation) See **botano-** and **phyto-** for examples.

plasmo-, plasm-, plast- plasma-, plasmat-, -plasmato-, -plasia, -plasis, -plasm, -plasmatic, -plasmic, -plast, -plastic, -plasy, -plasty (Gk., something made, molded, or formed)

> **Qualifying words:** abdominoplasty, anaplasia, aplasia, aplastic, arterioplasty, arthrodysplasia, arthroplasty, bioplast, blepharoplasty, cheiloplasty, chondroplasia, chondrodysplasia, cineplasty, cytoplasm, cytoplasmic, dermatoplastic, dermatoplasty, dysplasia, dysplasty, ectoplasm, ectoplasmic, exoplasm, gastroplastic surgery, heteroplasia, heteroplasy, homoplasia, hyperplasia, hypoplasia, hypoplastic, labioplasty, mammilliplasty, mammoplasty, metaplasm, myelodysplasia, neoplasm, osteoplasty, osteochondrodysplasia, otoplasty, phleboplasty, photoplasm, plasma, plasmatic, plasmatorrhexis, plasmic, plasmodium, plasmolysis, plasmolytic, plasmolyze, plasmosome, plasson, plaster, plastic, plastically, plasticism, plasticity, plasticization, plasticize, plasticider, plastic, plastodynamia, plastolysis, plastometer, protoplasm, protoplast, rhinoplastic, rhinoplasty, tenoplasty, theleplasty, thelyplasty, thoracoplasty, tonoplast, uvulopalatopharyngoplasty

-plasty- See **plasm-** for examples.

platy-, plat-, platt- (Gk., broad, wide, flat, level) Also see **eury-** and **tarso-**.

> **Qualifying words:** plat, Plataleidae, plataleine, platband, plate, plateasm, plateau, plateiasm, platelet, platen, platform, platformer, platformist, platitude, platitudinarian, platitudinarianism, platitudinism, platitudinist, platitudinization, platitudinize, platitudinizer, Plattdeut-

sch, platten, platter, platydactyl, platyhelminth, Platyhelminthes, platypod, platypus, platyrrhine, platysma, platytrope

play See **lud-** for examples.

-ple (L., bend) See **-plex** for examples.

ple-, pleini-, plen-, plet- (L., fill, full) See **ple-, pleio-,** and **opulen-.**

Qualifying words: accomplish, accomplishment, complement, complemental, complementary, complete, completely, completeness, completion, compliment, comply, deplete, depletion, expletive, implement, implementation, plenary, plenipotentiary, plenitude, plenteous, plentiful, plenty, plenum, plethora, replenish, replenishment, replete, supplement, supplemental, supplementary, supplementation, supply

plead, pray See **ora, orat-** for examples.

pleasing See **bene-, bon-, eu-, grat-,** and **plac-** for examples.

pleasure See **hedono-** for examples.

pleb- (L., common people, common multitude [as opposed to the PATRICIANS of Roman times]) Also see **commu-, demo-, ethno-, popu-, publi-,** and **vulg-.**

Qualifying words: plebe, plebeian, plebeianism, plebes, plebian, plebianize, plebicolist, plebifaction, plebiscite, plebs

pledge, promise See **spond-** for examples.

-plegia, -plegic, -plegy (Gk., paralysis [stroke, blow, strike]) Also see **polio-.**

Qualifying words: blepharophegia, cardioplegia, cardioplegic, cephaloplegia, cephaloplegic, cryocardioplegia, gastroplegia, gastroplegic, glossoplegia, glossoplegic, hemiplegia, hemiplegic, laloplegia, laloplegic, paraplegia, paraplegic, paraplegiform, plegia, polyplegia, polyplegic, quadraplegia, quadraplegic, thermoplegia

pleio-, plei-, pleo-, pleon-, pleio- (Gk., more, most, full) Also examine **ple-, plen-,** and **pluri-** for other "more, full" words. You should also see the **Appendix J** section for a list of **PLEONASMS** (redundancies).

Qualifying words: pleiocyclic, pleiomerous, pleiomorphous, pleiopetalous, pleiophyllous, pleiotaxis, pleiotaxy, pleiotropic, pleiotropy, pleiotropy, pleioxenous, Pleistocene, pleochroic, pleochromatic, pleogamy, pleomastia, pleometrosis, pleometrotic, pleomorphic, pleomorphism, pleonasm, pleonastic, pleonotia, pleophagous, pleophagy, pleopod, Pliocene

plenty Examine **opulen-, ple-,** and **pleio-** for appropropriate words.

pleo- (Gk., more, most, full) See **pleio-.**

pleuro-, pleur- (Gk., side, rib; a thin membrane with two layers which line the chest cavity; one lining the outside of the lungs and the other the inside of the chest cavity; fluid between the two layers provides lubrication and so allows smooth, uniform expansion and contraction of the lungs during breathing)

Qualifying words: pleura, pleuralgia, pleuralgic, pleurectomy, pleuric, pleurisy, pleuritic, pleurobronchitis, pleurocarpous, pleurocentesis, pleuroclysis, pleurocutaneous, pleurodont, pleurodynia, pleurogenic, pleurography, pleurohepatitis, pleuropericardial, pleuropneumonia, pleurosoma, pleurosomus, pleurotomy

pleusto-, pleust- (Gk., to sail, to float; flow) Also see **necto-** and **neusto-.**

Qualifying words: acropleustophyte, acropleustophytic, benthopleustophyte, benthopleustophytic, epipleuston, epipleustonic, phytopleuston, pleustohelophyte, pleuston, pleustonic, pleustont, pleustophyte

-plex, -plexity, -plexus,-ple, -pli, -plic, -plicat, -plicit, -plicate, -plication, -ply, plici- (L., bend, curve, turn, fold, twine, twist, interweave, weave) See **flect-, gyro-, stroph-, tors-, trop-, verg-, vers-,** and **volv-** for additional "bend" examples and see **-ploid.**

Qualifying words: accomplice, applicability, applicable, application, apply, complaint, complex, complexity, compliance, compliancy, compliant, complicate, complicated, complication, complicity, comply, decemplex, deploy, diplex, duplex, duplicate, duplication, duplicity, explicable, explicate, explicit, exploit, exploitation, implex, implicate, implication, implicit, imply, inexplicable, multiple, multiplex, multiplicand, multiplication, multiplicative, multiplicity, multiplier, multiply, octuplex, perplex, perplexity, plexus, pliable, pliancy, pliant, plicate, plication, pliciform, plier, ply, proplex, quadruple, quadruplicate, quadruplex, replica, replicate, replication, replied, replies, reply, sextuple, simple, simplicity, supple, simplex, supplication, triple, triplicate

-pli (bend, fold) See **-plex** for examples.

-plic (bend, fold) See **-plex** for examples.

-plicat (bend, fold) See **-plex** for examples.

plici- (bend, fold) See **-plex** for examples.

-plicit (bend, fold) See **-plex** for examples.

-ploid, -ploidy (Gk., a fold) Also see **-plex.**

Qualifying words: alloploidy, amphidiploidy, aneuploidy, autoploid, autoploidy, diploidy, haplodiploid, haplodiploidy, haploid, hexaploid, ploidy, polyploid, polyploidy, tetraploid, triploid, triploidy

plum-, plumi-, -plume (L., feather) Also see **ptero-, pterygo-** [wing], and **ptilo-** [feather] for other examples.

Qualifying words: corniplume, deplume, *nom de plume*, pennoplume, pluma, plumage, plumalar, plumate, plume, plumelet, plumicorn, plumigerous, plumiped, plumose, plumula, plumulate, plumule, plumy, pulviplume, semiplume

plumbo-, plumb-, plumbi- (L., lead, Pb, [the metal]) Also see **molybd-**.

    Qualifying words: aplomb, plumb, plumbago, plumbeous, plumber, plumbiferous, plumbing, plumbism, plumbite, plumbous, plumbum, plummet, plumbocalcite, plumbosolvency, plumbotherapy, plummet, plunge

plunge, dip See **merg-** for examples.

pluri-, plur-, plu- (L., more, many) Also see **ple-, pleio-,** and **opulen-**.

    Qualifying words: plural, pluralism, pluralist, plurality, pluralization, pluralize, plurally, pluriflorous, plurifoliate, plurilocular, pluripara, pluriparous, pluriresistent, plurisegmental, plurivorous, plus, pluses, surplus.

pluto-, plut- (Gk., wealth, wealthy, rich) Also see **lucr-** and **opulen-**.

    Qualifying words: Plutarch, plutarchy, Pluto, plutocracy, plutocrat, plutocratic, plutogogue, plutolatry, plutologist, plutology, plutomania, plutomaniac, plutonian, plutonic, plutonium, plutonomy

pluv-, pluvio-, pluvi- (L., rain) For other "rain" related words, see **hyeto-, ombro-, udo-, urino-,** and **uro-**.

    Qualifying words: isopluvial, pluvial, pluvialphobous, pluviofluvial, pluviograph, pluviographic, pluviographical, pluviography, pluviometer, pluviometric, pluviometrical, pluviometrically, pluviometry, pluviophile, pluviophilous, pluviophily, pluviophobe, pluviophoby, pluvioscope, Pluviose, pluviosity, pluvious

-ply (L., bend) See **-plex** for examples.

pneo-, -pnea, -pneic, -pnoea, -pnoeic, -pneo (Gk., air, wind; breathing) Also examine **aero-, anemo-, hal-, pneumato-, pneumo-, spir-,** and **vent-**.

    Qualifying words: anapnea, apnea, apneic, apneumis, bradypnea, dyspnea, dyspeic, eupnea, hyperpnea, hypnoapnea, orthopnea, pneogaster, pneograph, pneodynamics, pneograph, pneometer, pneometry, pneoscope, polypnea, sleepapnea, tachypnea

-pnea, -pneo (Gk., air, vapor, breath) Examine **pneo-** for examples.

pneumato-, pneumat-, -pneumonia, -pneumonic (Gk., air, wind, breath; presence of air; spirit) Also see **aero-, anemo-, hal-, pneo-, pneumo-, spir-,** and **vent-**.

    Qualifying words: apneumatic, pneumatic, pneumatics, pneumatinuria, pneumatism, pneumatists, pneumatization, pneumatized, pneumatocardia, pneumatocele, pneumatocyst, pneumatogram, pneumatograph, pneumatohe-

mia, pneumatology, pneumatometer, pneumatophore, pneumatorrhachis, pneumatoscope, pneumatosis, pneumatotherapy, pneumatothorax, pneumaturia

pneumo-, pneum-, pneumono-, pneumon- (Gk., lung [breath]) Also see **pulmo-** for other "lung" examples. Compare with **aero-, anemo-, -pnea, pneumato-, spir-,** and **vent-** for similar meanings.

    Qualifying words: apneuses, apneustic, bronchopneumonia, gastropneumonia, gastropneumonic, hepatopneumonia, hepatopneumonic, peripneumonia, pleuropneumonia, pneuma, pneumarthrosis, pneumectomy, pneumoangiography, pneumoarthrography, pneumarthrosis, pneumocardial, pneumocephalus, pneumochirurgia, pneumocolex, pneumoconiosis, pneumoderma, pneumodynamics, pneumography, pneumohemia, pneumohemothorax, pneumohydrothorax, pneumohypoderma, pneumology, pneumolysis, pneumomalacia, pneumometer, pneumonectomy, pneumonia, pneumonic, pneumonitis, pneumonocentesis, pneumonomelanosis, pneumonopexy, pneumonopathy, pneumonotomy, pneumonorrhagia, pneumonoultramicroscopicsilicovolcanoconiosis, pneumopexy, pneumophagia, pneumostome, pneumotachometer, pneumotaxis, pneumotaxic, pneumotherapy, pneumothoractic, pneumotomy, pneusis, postpneumonia, synpneumonia, synpneumonic

podo-, pod-, -poda, -pod, -pode, -podium, -podia, -podial -podous, -pody (Gk., foot, feet) Also see **ped-** (L.) and **-pus** for other "foot" words.

    Qualifying words: amphipod, antipodes, apod, apodal, apodia, apodous, apody, arthropod, cephalopod, chiropodist, chiropodous, chiropody, copepod, dactylopodite, decapod, endopodite, exopodite, gastropod, heteropod, lycopod, megapod, monopode, myriapod, ornithopod, pleopod, podagra, podagric, podagrous, podal, podalgia, podobromhidrosis, podalic, podiatrist, podiatry, podia, podium, podocarpous, podoconiosis, pododerm, pododynia, podogram, podograph, podology, podophyllin, podotheca, polypod, propodium, pseudopod, pteropod, sympodium, tripod

-poeia, -peia, -poiesis, -poesis, -poeic, -poetic, -poietic, -poetical, -poietical, -poetically, -poietically (Gk., making, producing, creating, creative, forming, for- mation; in medical terminology, the "creation" or "production" of that which is named by the combining root.) Also examine **fac-, form-, morpho-,** and **-plasia**.

    Qualifying words: angiopoietic, autopoiesis, biopoiesis, cosmopoietic, ecopoiesis, galactopoietic, haemapoietic, hematopoiesis, hemopoietin, hormopoiesis, leucopoiesis, monocytopoeisis, myelopoiesis, mythopoieic, nephropoietic, onomatopoieia, onomatopoeic, onomatopoeic, onomatopoetic, pharmacopoeia, poem, poet, poetic, poetomachia, poetry

poem, song See **ode** for examples.

pogo-, pogono-, -pogon (Gk., beard) Also see **barba-** (beard), **hirsute** (hair), and **tricho-** (hair).

    Qualifying words: pogomaniac, pogomys, pogonatum, pogonia, pogoniasis, pogoniate, pogonion, pogonite, pogonofora, pogonological, pogonologist, pogonology, pogonomania, pogonomyrmex, pogonophile, pogonophobia, pogonotomy, pogonotrophy

poikilo-, poikil- [on some occasions, **poecilo-, poecil-**] (Gk., varied, irregular, mottled) For additional "varied, different" words, see **ali-, alter-, hetero-,** and **vari-**.

    Qualifying words: osteopoikilosis, Poecilide, poikilergasia, poikiloblast, poikilocyte, poikilocytosis, poikilodentosis, poikiloderma, poikilohaline, poikilonymy, poikilotherm, poikilothermal, poikilothermic, poikilothermy

poison See **toxico-, veno-,** and **viru-** for examples.

point, pointed See **acut-** and **oxy-** for examples.

polio- (Gk., gray; pertaining to the gray matter of the nervous system, brain, and the spinal cord)

    Qualifying words: poliocidal, polioclastic, poliodystrophia, poliodystrophy, polioencephalitis, polioencephalomalacia, polioencephalomyelitis, polioencephalotropic, poliomyelencephalitis, poliomyelitis, poliosis, poliothrix, poliovirus

polis-, polit-, poli- (Gk., city, method of government) Also see **civi-** and **urban**.

    Qualifying words: acropolis, Annapolis, apolitical, aquapolis, Constantinople, cosmopolis, cosmopolitan, cosmopolitanism, cosmopolite, decapolis, geopolitical, geopolitics, heliopolis, Indianapolis, isopolity, megalopolis, metropolis, metropolitan, Minneapolis, Napolean, *Neapolis* (Naples), Neapolitan, necropolis, police, policed, policeman, policize, policy, political, politician, politic(s), polity, propolis, tetrapolis, Thermopolis, Tripoli

pollaki- (Gk., frequent, frequently) Also see **pykno-** for other "frequent" examples.

    Qualifying words: pollakidipsia, pollakiuria

pollen (L., fertilizing male elements of flowers; "fine flour; milldust; spores; powder")

    Qualifying words: pollen, pollinate, pollination, pollinic, polliniferous, pollinium, pollinosis

poly- (Gk., many, much; too many, too much, excessive) Also examine **multi-** for other "many" words. Don't confuse this **poly-** with another **-poly** which means "to sell."

    Qualifying words: polyacoustics, polyadenitis, polyalgesia, polyandry, polyanthus, polyarthric, polyarthritis, polycheiria, polychiria, polychord, polychromatic, polydactyl, polydactyly, polydaemonism, polydemic, polydipsia, polydontia, polyesthesia, polyesthetic, polygalactia, polygamous, polygamy, polyglot, polygon, polygraph, polygyny, polyhedron, polyhidrosis, polymorph, polymorphism, polymorphous, polymyalgia, Polynesia, polynomial, polyodontia, polyonymous, polyonymy, polyopia, polyorexia, polypetalous, polyphage, polyphagia, polyphagous, polyphonic, polyphony, polyphrasia, polyphyllous, polyphyodont, polyplastic, polyplegic, polypnea, polypod, polypodia, polyrhizal, polyrhizous, polysarcous, polysensory, polysomic, polysomitic, polysyllable, polytechnic, polytheism, polythermic, polytrichia, polytrichous, polytropic, polyuria

-poly, -pole, -polism, -polist, -polistic, -polistically (Gk., sale, selling; one who sells; pertaining to selling) Don't confuse this element with another **poly-** which means "many." Also see **onio-** for other "selling" words.

    Qualifying words: bibliopole, bibliopolism, bibliopolist, bibliopoly, duopole, duopoly, monopole, monopoly, multipoly, oligopole, oligopolies, oligopoly, xylopolist, xylopoly

pomo-, pom-, pomi- (L., fruit) For other "fruit" words, see **carpo-** [don't confuse this **carpo-** (fruit) with another **carpo-** meaning "wrist"].

    Qualifying words: pomaceous, pomiculture, pomiferous, pomiform, pomological, pomologist, pomology, Pomona [city in California]

pon-, posit-, pos-, -poning, -poned, -ponency, -ponent, -ponement, -pound (L., place, put) Also see **loco-, sist-, the-,** and **topo-** for other "place" words.

    Qualifying words: appose, apposite, apposition, compone, component, compose, composite, composition, compost, composure, compound, counterpose, decomposition, depone, depose, deposit, deposition, depository, depot, dispose, disposition, exponent, expose, exposition, expound, impose, imposition, impostor, imposture, indispose, interpose, interposition, juxtapose, juxtaposition, opponent, oppose, opposite, pose, posit, position, postpone, posture, prepose, preposition, propone, proponent, proposal, propose, proposition, propound, purpose, repose, repository, superimpose, superpose, suppose, supposition, transpose, transposition

pond- (L., hang, weight) See **pend-**.

pond, pool, marsh See **helo-, limno-, telmato-,** and **tipho-** for examples.

pono-, pon-, -ponic, -ponics (Gk., toil, labor, work hard, fatigue; exertion; also, in some words, "pain") See **ergo-, labor-, oper-,** and **urg-** for other "work" words.

Qualifying words: aponia, aponic, aquaponics, geoponic, geoponics, hydroponic, hydroponics, hydroponist, ponesiatrics, ponograph, ponopalmosis, ponophobia

pool, lake See **limno-** and **tipho-**.
poor, wrong See **caco-, dys-, mal-,** and **mis-**.

popu- (L., people) Also see **commu-, demo-, ethno-, ochlo-, pleb-, publi-,** and **vulg-**.

Qualifying words: depopulate, depopulated, depopulation, populace, popular, popularity, popularize, populate, population, populous

population, people See **popu-** for examples.
por- (L., before) See **pro-** for examples.
porc-, pork- (L., pig, hog)

Qualifying words: porcine, porcupine, porpoise, pork, porker, porky

porno-, porn- (Gk., harlot, prostitute [originally, "bought, purchased, exported, sold;" prostitutes in ancient Greece having largely been victims of the slave trade]) Also see **cypri-** and **fornicate** for related words.

Qualifying words: philopornist, pornerastic, porn, porno, pornocracy, pornogenitore, pornographer, pornographic, pornographist, pornography, pornolagnia

porpoises See **ceto-** and **porc-** for examples.
poro-, por-, pori- (Gk. > L., passageway; pertaining to a *pore*, a small orifice)

Qualifying words: poradenitis, poriferous, porocephalosis, poroid, poroplastic, porosis, porosity, porotomy, porous

-pos (Gk., drink) See **poto-** for examples.
port- (L., door, gate, entrance, harbor) Don't confuse this **port-** with the following one which means "to carry." Also see **Janus**.

Qualifying words: airport, hall porter, opportune, opportunity, passport, porch, port, portal, porter (doorman), porthole, portico, portside, Portugal, seaport

port-, portat- (L., carry, bring, bear) Also see **-fer-, ger-, later-,** and **phoro-** for other "carry" words. Don't confuse this **port-** with the previous one which means "door," etc.

Qualifying words: comport, deport, deportation, deportment, deportee, disport, disportation, export, exportation, exporter, import, important, importation, importer, portable, portage, porter, portfolio, portmanteau, purport, report, reporter, sport, sportsman, support, supporter, teleport, teleportation, transport, transportation

-posia (Gk. > L., drinking; a word termination [suffix] denoting a relationship to drinking or the intake of fluids) For other "drinking" words, see **bib-, dipso-,** and **poto-**.

Qualifying words: antiposia, antiposic, pariposia, symposiac, symposiarch, symposiast, symposia(pl.), symposium(s.), thalassoposia, uriposia

posit- (L., place, put) See **pon-** for examples.
position, place Examine **loco-** and **topo-** for samples.
-posium (Gk., drinking) Examine **-posia** for samples.
poss- (L., power, strength) Examine **poten-** for samples.
post- (L., after, behind, later, subsequent) Also examine **postero-** for other "after" words.

Qualifying words: a posteriori, anteroposterior, postabortal, post-bellum, postcibal, postclassical, postconnubial, postdate, postdiluvian, postdoctoral, posterior, posterity, postexilic, postfebrile, postfix, postglacial, postgraduate, posthumous, posthypnotic, postlude, postmeridian, postmeridiem, postmillenarian, postmillenial, post mortem, post-mortem, postmortem, postnasal, postnatal, postnatus, postnati, postnecrosis, postnecrotic, postnuptial, post-obit, postorbital, postpartum, postpone, postscript, posttest, postwar, preposterous

postero- (L., after, behind, following) Also see **post-** for other "after" words.

Qualifying words: posteroanterior, posteroexternal, posterointernal, posterolateral, posteromedial, posteromedian, posterosuperior

potamo-, potam- (Gk., river) Also see **fluvio-**.

Qualifying words: autopotamic, autopotamous, benthopotamous, eupotamic, hippopotamus, Mesopotamia, Micropotamogale, potamian, potamic, potamicole, potamicolous, potamodromous, Potamogale, Potamogeton, potamographer, potamographic, potamography, potamological, potamologist, potamology, potamometer, potamophile, potamophilous, potamophily, potamophyte, potamophobia, potamoplankton, potamous

pot- (L., power, strength) See **poten-** for examples.
poten-, pot-, poss-, -potent, -potence, -potency, -potential (L., power, strength, ability) Also see **dyna-, firm-, fort-, stheno-,** and **valid-** for other "power" words.

Qualifying words: ignipotent, impossibility, impotence, impotency, impotent, magnipotence, omnipotence, omnipotent, plenipotentiary, posse (*posse comitatus*), possess, possession, possible, possibly, potency, potent, potentate, potential, potentiality, potentiometer, potestate, prepotent, viripotent, viripotency

poto-, pot-, pos- [see **-posia**] (L., drink) Also examine **bib-, dipso-,** and **-posia.**

> Qualifying words: *aqua potabile*, Hydropotes, poison, potable, potation, potification, potion, potomania, potomaniac, potometer, potometry, Potua [goddess of drinking], potus

pouch Examine **marsupium-** and **thyla-** for examples.

-pound (place, put) See **pon-** for examples.

pour, melt See **fus-** for examples.

poverty, not enough See **-penia** for examples.

power For examples, see **dyna-, firm-, fort-, poten-, stheno-,** and **valid-.**

powerful Examine **dyna-, firm-, fort-, poten-, stheno-,** and **valid-** for examples.

praise See **dox-** and **laud-** for examples.

pray See **ora-** for examples.

pre- (*prae-*) (L., before [both in time and place]) Also see **ante-, antero-, por-,** and **pro-** for other "before" words.

> Qualifying words: preamble, preamplifier, prearrange, precancel, precancerous, precaution, precede, precedence, precedent, precession, precipice, precipitant, precipitate, precipitation, precipitous, précis, precise, preclude, preclusion, precocious, precocity, precognition, preconceived, preconception, precondition, preconscious, precook, precursor, predate, predecessor, predestinate, predestination, predetermine, predicable, predicament, predicate, predict, predictable, prediction, predigest, predilection, predispose, preempt, preexist, preexistence, prefab, prefabricate, preface, prefer, preferable, preference, prefix, preflight, pregnancy, pregnant, prehistoric, prehistorical, prejudge, prejudice, prejudicial, prelate, preliminary, prelude, premarital, premature, premedical, premeditate, premeditation, premonition, prenatal, prenuptial, preoperative, preordain, preparation, prepare, preposition, prepositional, prepossess, prepossession, preposterous, prerequisite, prerogative, presage, prescient, prescribe, prescription, present, presentation, preservation, preserve, preside, presidencey, president, presume, presumption, pretence, pretend, pretense, prevail, prevalence, prevalent, prevaricate, prevarication, prevent, preventable, previous, prevision, prevue

pregnant, pregnancy See **gravid-** for examples.

prehend-, prehens- (L., to clasp, seize, reach, attain, hold) Also examine **cap-** and **ten-** for other "clasp, seize" words.

> Qualifying words: apprehend, apprehending, apprehensible, apprehension, comprehend, comprehensible, comprehension, comprehensive, incomprehensibility, incomprehensible, prehensible, prehensile, prehensioin, reprehend, reprehensible, reprehensibleness, reprehension, reprehensive

presbyo-, presby- (Gk., old, relationship to old age) Also examine **gero-** and **sen-.**

> Qualifying words: presbyacousia, presbyacusia, presbyatrics, presbycardia, presbycousis, presbycusis, presbyesophagus, presbyope, presbyophrenia, presbyope, presbyopia, presbyopic, presbyter, Presbyterian, presbytery

preserve, guard Examine **alexo-, -fend-,** and **phylacto-** for examples.

press-, presso-, pressi-, -prim-, -prin- (L., press, to bear down on or against)

> Qualifying words: compress, compressibility, compression, compressor, decompress, depress, depressant, depressed, depression, depressor, express, expression, expressionism, expressway, fingerprint, footprint, impress, impression, impressionism, impressive, imprimatur, imprint, irrepressible, misprint, oppress, oppression, press, pressing, pressure, pressurize, print, printout, repress, repression, reprimand, suppress, suppression, voiceprint

pressure, tension See **tono-** for examples.

pretty See **bell-** and **calli-** for examples.

prickly, spiny For examples, see **acantho-, chaeto-,** and **echino-.**

prim-, primi-, primo- (L., first, chief, foremost) Also examine **archae-, prin-,** and **proto-** for other "first, chief" words.

> Qualifying words: prima ballerina, prima donna, prima facie, primacy, primal, primarily, primary, primate, prime, primer, primeval, primigenial, primigravida, primiparous, primitive, primogeniture, primordial, prior, priority, Priscilla

-prim- See **press-** for examples.

primitive, first See **archae, palaeo-, prim-, prin-,** and **proto-** for examples.

prin- L., first, chief) Also see **archae-, prim-,** and **proto-** for other "first, chief words.

> Qualifying words: prince, princess, principal, principality, principle, principled

-prin- See **press-** for examples.

prior to, before See **ante-, antero-,** and **pre-.**

prison, jail See **incarcerat-** for examples.

pro-, por- (Gk. > L.)

[1] before

> Qualifying words: portend, portent, procerebrum, prodigy, prodrome, profound, progenitor, progeny, progeria, progeria, prognosis, prognostic, prognosticate, prognostication, program, prologue, promise, promitosis, prophyllum

[2] forward

> Qualifying words: procedure, proceed, process, proclivity, procrastinate, procreate, prognathous, progress, progression, project,

promote, promoter, propel, propensity, prospect, protractor, reciprocal

3 for, in favor of

Qualifying words: pro bono publico, pro-American, procure, proforma, prohydrotropism, proponent, proslavery

4 in front of

Qualifying words: proboscis, profane, profanity, prologue

5 in place of, on behalf of

Qualifying words: proconsul, pronoun

process, condition See **-osis** for examples.

procto-, proct- (Gk., anus, rectum) Also see **recto-** for other "anus" words.

Qualifying words: proctagra, proctalgia, proctitis, proctoclysis, proctocolitis, proctocolonoscopy, proctocolpoplasty, proctodynia, protologic, proctologist, proctology, proctoparalysis, protophobia, protoplasty, protoplegia, proctoscopy, proctostasis, proctotomy

prodigy (L., sign, omen, portent; a wonder, a person [especially a child] endowed with extraordinary qualities])

Qualifying words: prodigious, prodigiously, prodigiousness, prodigy

produce, bear See **fac-, fer-,** and **para-.**

producing, making See **-poeia** for examples.

proli-, prol- (L., offspring, child) Also see **pedo-** (Gk.) and **puer-** for other "child" examples.

Qualifying words: eoproligerous, opsiproligerous, opsiproligery, prolegeron, prolicide, proliferate, proliferation, proliferous, prolific, proligerous

producing young See **para** for examples.

promise, pledge See **spond-** for examples.

prophecy, prophesy, divination See **-mancy** for examples.

prostitute, harlot Examine **cypri-, fornicate,** and **porno-** for examples.

protect, defend, save For examples, see **alexo-, -fend-,** and **phylacto-.**

protects from See **para-** for examples.

proto-, prot- (Gk., first, original) Also examine **archae-, palaeo-, prim-,** and **prin-.**

Qualifying words: Protoabia, protobiont, protobios, protocol, protoderm, protoepiphyte, protogynous, protogyny, protolithic, protomartyr, proton, protopathic, protophyte, protoplasm, protoplasmic, protoptile, prototrophic, prototype, protoxylem, protozoa, protozoacide, protozoan, protozoiasis, protozoic, protozoology, protozoon, protozoophage, protozootherapy

provident, accident See **tycho-** for examples.

proximo-, proxim- (L., nearest, next) Also see **juxta-** and **para-** for other "near" words.

Qualifying words: approximal, approximate, approximately, approximation, proximal, proximate, proximity, proximoataxia, proximoceptor

prune, trim (verbs) See **put-** for examples.

psammo-, psamm-, psamme- (Gk., sand) Also see **amatho-, ammo-, arena,** and **silico-** for other "sand" words.

Qualifying words: endopsammon, epipsammic, epipsammon, mesopsammon, psammism, psammolittoral, psammite, psammofauna, psammoma, psammomatous, psammon psammophilic, psammophily, Psammophis, psammophilous, psammophore, psammophyte, psamosere, psammotherapy, psammous, suprapsammon, uropsammus

pseudo-, pseud- (Gk., false, deception, lying, untrue, counterfeit) Also see **fals-.**

Qualifying words: faux pas (French, foh PAH), pseudacousis, pseudacusis, pseudagraphia, pseudalbuminuria, pseudandrous, pseudandry, pseudannual, pseudarthrosis, pseudencephalus, pseudepigraphy, pseudesthesia, pseudoacousma, pseudoaesthetic, pseudoagraphia, pseudoanemia, pseudoangina, pseudoantagonist, pseudoanodontia, pseudoanthropology, pseudoappendicitis, pseudoaquatic, pseudoarthrosis, pseudobenthos, pseudocarp, pseudochromethesia, pseudochromia, pseudochronism, pseudochronology, pseudoderm, pseudodextrocardia, pseudodipsia, pseudodont, pseudodox, pseudodoxy, pseudodysentery, pseudoemphysema, pseudoepidemic, pseudoesthesia, pseudofoliaceous, pseudogaster, pseudogestation, pseudogeusesthesia, pseudogeusia, pseudogeustia, pseudoglottic, pseudoglottis, pseudograph, pseudographia, pseudography, pseudogynous, pseudogyny, pseudohelminth, pseudohemophilia, pseudohermaphrodite, pseudohypertrichosis, pseudohypertrophic, pseudohypertrophy, pseudointellectual, pseudoism, pseudoisochromatic, pseudolalia, pseudolatry, pseudoleukemia, pseudologia, pseudologist, pseudologue, pseudology, pseudomancia, pseudomancy, pseudomania, pseudomaniac, pseudomantic, pseudomantist, pseudomelanosis, pseudomelia, pseudomnesia, pseudomorph, pseudomorphic, pseudomorphism, pseudomorphose, pseudomorphosis, pseudomyopia, pseudomyrmecine, pseudomyrmex, pseudonarcotic, pseudoneuritis, pseudonym, pseudonymity, pseudonymous, pseudonymously, pseudoparasite, pseudophotesthesia, pseudoplatelets, pseudopneumonia, pseudopod, pseudopodia, pseudopodium, pseudopterygium, pseudoscience, pseudotrophic, pseudovolcanic, pseudovolcano

psycho-, psych-, -psyche, -psychic, -psychical, -psychically (Gk., the mind or the mental processes) Etymologically, this element includes such meanings as, "breath, life, soul, spirit, mind," and "consciousness." Also examine **noo-** and **phreno-** for other "mind" words.

> **Qualifying words:** anthropopsychism, psychagogy, psychalgia, psychataxia, psychauditory, psychedelic, psyche, psychiatrics, psychiatrist, psychiatry, psychic, psychinosis, psychoacoustics, psychoactivator, psychoallergy, psychoanalysis, psychoanalyst, psychoataxia, psychoauditory, psychobiology, psychochrome, psychochromesthesia, psychochronometry, psychodiagnosis, psychodrama, psychodynamics, psychodysleptic, psychogalvanic, psychogalvanometer, psychogenesis, psychogenic, psychogeriatrician, psychogeriatrics, psychogeusic, psychognosis, psychogogic, psychogram, psychography, psychokinesia, psychokinesis, psycholepsy, psycholinguistics, psychologist, psychology, psychomaticist, psychometrician, psychometrics, psychometry, psychomotor, psychoneurosis, psychonomics, psychonomy, psychonosis, psychonosology, psychonoxious, psychopathia, psychopathic, psychopathist, psychopathology, psychopath, psychopathy, psychopharmacology, psychophobia, psychophylaxis, psychophysics, psychophysiologist, psychophysiology, psychoplegia, psychoprophylactic, psychoprophylaxis, psychosensory, psychosis, psychosomatic, psychosurgery, psychosynthesis, psychotechnics, psychotherapeutics, psychotherapist, psychotherapy, psychotic, psychotropic

psychro- (Gk., cold) Also examine **crymo-**, **cryo-**, **crystallo-**, and **frigo-** for additional "cold" words.

> **Qualifying words:** psychralgia, psychric, psychroalgia, psychrocleistogamic, psychroesthesia, psychrolusia, psychrometer, psychrometry, psychrophil, psychrophile, psychrophilic, psychrophobia, psychrophobic, psychrophore, psychrophyte, psychrotherapy

pterido-, pterid- (Gk., fern [from *pter(on)*, "feather, wing"])

> **Qualifying words:** pteridology, pteridomania, Pteridophyta, pteridophyte

ptero-, pter-, -ptera, -pteron, -pteryx, -ptery, -pterous (Gk., feather, wing, winglike) Also see **plum-**, **pterygo-**, and **ptilo-**.

> **Qualifying words:** apterex, apteria, apterous, Archaeopteryx, archipterygium, brachypterous, chiropterygium, coleoptera, Dermaptera, dermoptera, diptera, dipteral, dipterous, embiopteran, eurypterid, helicopter, Hemiptera, heteroptera, hexapterous, homopteran, homopterous, hyalopterous, hymenopteran, hymenopterous, isopterous, Lepidoptera, lepidoptera, lepidopteral, lepidopteran, lepidopterous, macropterous, megachiroptera, microchiroptera, micropterism, micropterous, Orthoptera, orthopteran, peripteral, Plecoptera, pseudopterygi-

um, pteridoid, pteridological, pteridology, pteridophyta, pteridophyte, pteridophytic, pteris, pterodactyl, pterographic, pterography, pteroid, pteronophobia, pteropod, Pteropoda, pteropodial, pterosaur, pterotheca, pterygoid, siphonaptera, subapterous, teleoptile, trichoptera

pterygo-, pteryg- (Gk., wing) Also see **plum-**, **ptero-**, and **ptilo-** for other "wing" words.

> **Qualifying words:** apterygial, apterygotosis, cheiropterygium, pterygium, pterygoid, ptergomandibular, pterygomaxillary, pterygosteum, pteryla, pterylography, pterylology, pterylsis

-pteryx (Gk., feather, wing) See **ptero-** for examples.

ptilo-, ptil-, ptilono- (Gk., feather [soft], down) For other "feather" or "wing" words, see **plum-**, **ptero-**, and **pterygo-**.

> **Qualifying words:** mesoptile, protoptile, ptilopaedic, ptilosis

ptoma- (Gk., fall, a falling down of an organ; drooping, sagging) See **-ptosia** for examples.

-ptosia, -ptosis, ptoma-, -ptot- (Gk., fall, a falling down of an organ; drooping, sagging) Also see **cad-** for other "fall" words.

> **Qualifying words:** cardioptosis, carpoptosis, laryngoptosis, mastoptosis, panoptosis, ptomaine, ptomainemia, ptomainotoxism, ptomatopsia, ptomatopsy, ptosis, ptotic, symptom, symptomatic, symptomatology

publi-, pub- (L., people, concerning people, population) Also examine **commu-**, **demo-**, **ethno-**, **popu-**, and **vulg-** for other "people" or "common" words.

> **Qualifying words:** public, publication, publicity, publish, publisher, republic, republican, Republican

public place See **agora-** for examples.

puer- (L., child, boy) Also see **pedo-** (Gk.), and **proli-** for other "child" words.

> **Qualifying words:** puericulture, puericulturist, puerile, puerilely, puerilism, puerility, puerpera, puerperal, puerperalism, puerperant, puerperium

puff of wind, blow See **flat-** for examples.

pugn-, pug- (L., fight) For other "fight" words, see **belli-**, **-machy,** and **milit-**.

> **Qualifying words:** impugn, oppugn, pugil, pugilant, pugilism, pugilist, pugilistic, pugnacious, pugnacity, repugnable, repugnance, repugnancy, repugnant, repugnate

pulic-, puli- (L., flea)

> **Qualifying words:** pulicatic, Pulex, pulicene, pulicicide, pulicid, Pulicidae, pulicidal, pulicide, pulicologist, pulicology, pulicosis, puligenous

pull, tear, pluck See **tillo-** for examples.

pulmo-, pulmoni-, pulmono-, pulmon-, -pulmonary, -pulmonic (L., lung) Also see **pneumo-** for other "lung" words.

> **Qualifying words:** apulmonic, intrapulmonic, gastropulmonic, pulmoaortic, pulmocardiac, pulmocutaneous, pulmogastric, pulmogram, pulmograph, pulmolith, pulmometer, pulmometry, pulmonal, pulmonary, pulmonectomy, pulmonic, pulmonitis, pulmonohepatic, pulmonologist, pulmonology, pulmotor

puls-, pulsi-, pulso-, -puls, -pulse, -pulsion, -pulsive (L., push, beat, strike, knock, drive; another form of **pel-**) Also see **pel-**.

> **Qualifying words:** compulsion, compulsive, compulsively, compulsory, expulsion, expulsive, impulse, impulsive, propulsion, pulsar, pulsate, pulsation, pulsator, pulse, pulsejet, pulsimeter, push, pusher, pushup, pushy, repulse, repulsed, repulsing, repulsion, repulsive, repulsiveness

pulse See **sphygmo-** for examples.

puncture, perforation See **-centesis**.

pung-, punc-, point (L., pierce, sting, bite; dot, mark, sharp point, pinpoint)

> **Qualifying words:** appoint, appointment, compunction, disappoint, disappointment, expugn, expunction, expunge, impugn, interpunction, punctilious, punctual, punctuate, punctuation, puncture, pungency, pungent

pupillo-, pupill- (L., [diminutive of *pupa*, a young girl, doll (puppets)] the pupil of the eye; the larva of insects) Also see **irido-** for related "eye" words as well as **entomo-**, "insect," for some of the *bug* words. The term *pupil* came into existence because when one looked closely into another person's eyes, he could see the reflections of little images (dolls or puppets) of himself.

> **Qualifying words:** interpupillary, pupa, pupal, pupate, pupil, pupilloconstriction, pupillograph, pupillography, pupillometer, pupillometry, pupillomotor, pupilloplegia, pupilloscope, pupilloscopy, pupillostatometer, Pupipara, pupiparous, pupivorous

purg- (L., clean, cleanse, purify) Also examine **balneo-, lav-,** and **luto-** for other "clean, words.

> **Qualifying words:** compurgation, expurgate, expurgation, impure, pure, purgation, purgative, purgatorial, purgatory, purge, purification, purify, puritanic, purity, unpurged, spurge

-pus (Gk., foot) Also see **ped-** (L.) and **podo-** (Gk.) for other "foot" words.

> **Qualifying words:** dipus, octopus, platypus, Pteopus, Xenopus

push, thrust See **osmo-** (#2) and **trud-** for examples.

push, drive See **pel-** for examples.

put See **pon-** for examples.

put, place, stand See **loco-, pon-, sist-,** and **the-** for examples.

-pute, -puter (L., count, reckon) See **put-** for examples.

put-, puta-, -pute, -puter, -puting, -putation, -putative (L., trim, prune, lop, clean; think over, consider, reckon, count)

> **Qualifying words:** amputate, amputation, computable, computation, compute computer, computist, count, depute, deputize, deputy, disputation, dispute, disreputable, disrepute, imputation, impute, indisputable, putative, reputation, repute, reputed

putrid, rotten See **sapro-** and **sepsi-** for examples.

pyelo-, pyel- (Gk., pelvis of the kidney; from *tub, vat*) Also see **nephro-** and **reno-** for other "kidney" words.

> **Qualifying words:** pyelic, pyelitis, pyelocystitis, pyelogram, pyelography, pyelometer, pyelometry, pyelopathy, pyelophlebitis, pyeloplasty, pyeloscopy, pyelostomy, pyelotomy, pyeloureteroplasty, pyelovenous, ureteropyelitis, ureteropyelography, ureteropyelonephritis, ureteropyelonephrostomy, ureteropyeloplasty, ureteropyelostomy

-pygy (Gk., rump, buttocks) See **pygo-** for examples.

pygo-, pyg-, -pyga, -pygia (Gk., rump, buttocks; the posterior part of the body, especially in insects)

> **Qualifying words:** callipygia, callipygian, callipygous, callipygy, dasypygal, Eurypyga, macropygia, Macropygia, ovopygian, planopygian, pleopygian, pygal, pygalgia, pygia, pygidia, pygidial, pygidium, pygist, pygoamorphus, pygophilous, pygotripsis, spheropygian, steatopygia, steatopygian, steatopygic, steatopygous, steatopygy, uropygial, uropygium

pykno- (Gk., thick, compact, dense; frequent) Also see **dens-** and **pachy-** for other "thick" words.

> **Qualifying words:** pyknic, pyknocyte, pyknocytoma, pyknocytosis, pyknolepsy, pyknometer, pyknometry, pyknomorphic, pyknomorphous, pyknophrasia, pyknophrasis, pyknosis

pyreto-, -pyrexia, -pyrexias (Gk., fever, burning heat) Also see **febri-** and **pyro-** for other "fever" words.

> **Qualifying words:** alexipyretic, antipyresis, antipyretic, apyrexia, eupyrexia, hyperpyrexia, pyretherapy, pyretic, pyreticosis, pyretogen, pyretogenesis, pyretogenetic, pyretogenic,

pyretogenous, pyretography, pyretology, pyretolysis, pyretotherapy, pyretotyphosis, pyrexia, pyrexial, pyrexiogenic, pyrexy

-pyrexia (Gk., fever) See **pyreto-**.

pyro-, pyr- (Gk., fire, burn; and sometimes "fever") Also see **ard-, caust-, crema-, febri-** (fever), **flagr-, flam-, ign-, incend-, pyreto-** (fever), and **volcan-** for additional words with "fire, heat" related meanings.

Qualifying words: antipyrotic, apyretic (*athermic*), apyrexia, apyrexial, empyrean, eupyrexia, pyracantha, pyroclastic, pyrheliometer, pyrolater, pyrolatry, pyre, pyretic, pyrexia, pyrite, pyrocantha, pyroclastic, pyrogenesis, pyrogenetic, pyrogenics, pyrogenous, pyrognomic, pyrograph, pyrographic, pyrography, pyrogravure, pyrolagnia, pyrolater, pyrolatry, pyroligneous, pyrology, pyrolysis, pyrolytic, pyromachy, pyromancer, pyromancy, pyromania, pyromaniacal, pyromanic, pyromantist, pyrometer, pyrometric, pyronyxis, pyrophile, pyrophilia, pyrophilous, pyrophobia, pyropbobic, pyrophoric, pyrophotography, pyroptothymia, pyropuncture, pyrophyte, pyroscope, pyroseisma, pyrosis, pyrosphere, pyrospheric, pyrotechnic, pyrotechnical, pyrotechnics, pyrotechnist, pyrotechny, pyrotherapy, pyrotic, pyrotoxin, pyroxylin, pyroxylophile, pyroxylophilous, pyroxylophily, pyrurgy

Q q

quadri-, quad-, quadru-, quatr- (L., four) Also see **tetra-** for other "four" words. See NUMBERS in **Appendix G** for other numerical elements.

Qualifying words: quadragenarian, quadrangle, quadrangular, quadrant, quadraphonic, quadraphony, quadraplegic, quadrat, quadrate, quadratic, quadratics, quadrennia, quadrennial, quadrennium, quadricentennial, quadriceps quadricycle, quadrifoliate, quadrilateral quadrilingual, quadrille, quadrillion, quadrinomial, quadriphonic(s), quadriplegia, quadriplegic, quadrireme, quadrisect, quadrisyllable, quadrivium, quadrumane, quadrumanous, quadrumvirate, quadruped, quadrupeda, quadruple, quadruplets, quadruplex, quadruplicate, quadruplicity

quart- (L., fourth) See **quadri-** for examples.

quartz- See **silico-** for examples.

quer- (L., ask; seek) See **quir-** for examples.

quest- (L., ask; seek) See **quir-** for examples.

quies-, -quiet-, -quit- (L., rest, quiet) Also see **pac-** and **plac-**.

Qualifying words: acquiesce, acquit, disquietude, quiescent, quiet, quietus, quit, quite, requiem, *requiescat in pace* (R.I.P.), requite, requited, tranquil, unrequited

quiet, calm See **pac-, plac-,** and **quies-** for examples.

quin- (L., five) See **quinqu-** for examples.

quinqu-, quinque-, quin- (L., five) Also see **penta-** and **quint-** for other examples of "five" and NUMBERS in **Appendix G** for other numerical elements.

Qualifying words: quinary, quinate, quincentenary, quincentennial, quindecade, quindecennial, quinquagenarian, quinquangular, quinquefoliate, quinquenniad, quinquennially, quinquennial, quinquennium,

quint-, quinti-, quintu- (L., fifth) Also see **quinqu-** for other "five" words and the NUMBERS section in **Appendix G** for other numerical elements.

Qualifying words: quintad, quintessence, quintessential, quintet, quintette, quintile, quintillion, quintipara, quintuple, quintuplet, quintuplicate

quir-, quisit-, quis-, que-, quest-, -quirement, -quirable, -quisition, -quisitive (L., ask, seek) Also see **peti-** and **rog-** for other "ask, seek" words.

Qualifying words: acquire, acquisition, acquisitive, conquer, conquest, conquistador, exquisite, inquest, inquirable, inquire, inquiringly, inquiry, inquisition, inquisitional, inquisitive, inquisitiveness, inquisitor, prerequisite, queried, query, quest, question, questionable, questioningly, questionnaire, request, require, requirement, requisite, requisition

quis- (L., ask; seek) See **quir-** for examples.

R r

rabbit, hare See **lepor-** for examples.

race (of people) See **ethno-** and **genus**.

rachio-, rachi-, rach-, rachis-, rhach-, rhachi-, rhachio- (Gk., spine) For additional "spine" words, see **spondylo-**.

> Qualifying words: rachial, rachialgia, rachianalgesia, rachianesthesia, rachicentesis, rachidial, rachidian, rachigraph, rachilysis, rachiocampsis, rachiocentesis, rachiodynia, rachiometer, rachiomyelitis, rachiopathy, rachiotome rachiotomy rachisagra, rachischisis, rachisensibilities, rachitis, rhachitis, rhachialgia, rhachiomyelitis

radi- (L., root) See **radic-** for examples.

radiance See **actino-** and **radio-** for examples.

radio-, rad- (L., ray, radiating [the Latin word for the spokes of a wheel is *radius*]) Also see **actino-** and **roentgeno-**.

> Qualifying words: irradiance, irradiant, irradiate, radial, radian, radiance, radiant, radiate, radiation, radiator, radiesthesia, radio (short for *radiotelegraphy*), radioactivity, radioautograph, radiobiologist, radiobiology, radiocardiography, radiodermatitis, radioodontist, radiograph, radiologist, radiology, radiolucent, radiometer, radiomicrometer, radionecrosis, radiophobia, radiophone, radioplastic, radioscope, radiosensibility, radiosensitive, radiosurgery, radiothanatology, radiotherapeutics, radiotherapist, radiothermy, radiotropism, radii(pl.), radium, radius(s.), ray, Rayon (French for *ray*)

radiance, radiating See **actino-, radio-,** and **roentgeno-** for other examples.

radic-, radi- (L., root) Also see **rhizo-**.

> Qualifying words: eradicable, eradicate, eradication, radical, radicalism, radicant, radicate, radicicole, radicicolous, radiciflorous, radiciform, radicivorous, radicivory, radicle, radicular, radicule, radiculose, radiectomy, radish, radix

radiculo-, radicul- (L., little root; pertaining to nerve roots)

> Qualifying words: radicula, radiculalgia, radicular, radiculectomy, radiculitis, radiculoganglionitis, radiculomedullary, radiculomyelopathy, radiculopathy

rain See **hyeto-, ombro-, pluv-, udo-, urino-,** and **uro-** for examples.

-rama (Gk., view) See **-orama** for examples.

rani-, ran- (L., frog) Also see **batracho-**

> Qualifying words: rana, Rana casadae, ranarium, Ranidae, raniform, ranine, ranivorous

rank, series See **ord-** for examples.

rap- (L., tearing away, seizing, swift, rapid; snatch away, seize, carry off)

> Qualifying words: eurapture, rapacious, rape, rapid, rapids, rapine, rapt, rapture, ravage, ravenous, ravine, ravish, surreptitious, usurp

rapid, swift Examine **agito-, celer-, tacho-,** and **veloci-** for examples.

raw, unripe, immature See **omo-** (Gk.).

ray See **actilno-, radio-,** and **roentgeno-**.

razor See **xyro-** for examples.

re-, red- (L., back, backward, again) Also see **ana-(#2), pali-,** and **retro-** for additional "back, again" words.

> Qualifying words: react, recalcitrance, recalcitrant, recant, recapitulate, recapitulation, recede, receipt, receive, recitation, recite, reclaim, recline, recluse, recognition, recommend, recommit, reconvert, recount, recur, recurrence, recycle, rededicate, reduce, reduction, redundancy, redundant, reduplicate, re-echo, refer, reference, reflect, reflection, reflex, reflexive, refrigerator, refuge, refugee, refuse, refute, regenerate, regress, regression, reject, rejection, rejoin, rejuvenate, rejuvenation, rejuvenator, relax, reluctant, remedial, remedy, remember, reminisce, remit, remittance, remunerate, remuneration, renovate, renovation, repatriate, repel, repellent, replicate, reply, report, repose, repository, repugnant, repulse, rescind, reside, residence, resident, residue, resilience, resilient, resist, resistance, resonance, resonant, resonator, respect, respiration, respirator, respire, resume, retain, retard, retort, retract, reverse, review, revise, revision, revival, revive, revoke, revolt, revolution, revolve, revue

reach, hold, clasp See **prehend-** for examples.

read, readable, See **legi-** for examples.

real, true See **etym-** and **veri-** for examples.

rear end, back side See **pygo-** for examples.

recent, new See **ceno-, neo-,** and **nov-**.

receptacle, container See **theco-** for examples.

recite, read See **legi-** for examples.

recognition See **gno-** for examples.

reckon, consider See **put-** for examples.

record, write See **glyph-, gram-, grapho-,** and **scrib-** for examples.

recti-, rect- (L., right, straight; to lead, to rule) Also see **dexter-, ortho-,** and **regi-**.

> Qualifying words: correct, correctional, corrective, direct, direction, director, directory, erect, erectile, erection, erector, insurrection, insurrectionist, rectangle, rectangular, rectifiable, rectification, rectifier, rectify, rectilineal, rectitude, rector, resurrect, resurrection

recto-, rect- (L., straight [intestine], direct, right; that is, "the part of the large intestine which ends at the anus") Also see **procto-** for other "rectum" words.

> Qualifying words: anorectal, rectalgia, rectitis, rectoabdominal, rectoanal, rectocolitis, rectocolonic, rectocystotomy, rectopexy, rectophobia, rectoplasty, rectorrhagia, rectorrhagy, rectoscope, rectoscopy, rectotomy, rectum, rectus

rectum See **procto-** and **recto-** for examples.

recurrence, repetition See **pali-, re-,** and **retro-** for examples.

red (the color) See **erythro-, rube,** and **rhodo-** (rose) for examples.

regi-, reg-, rex (L., rule, govern) For words with similar meanings, see **-arch, -crat,** and **recti-**.

> Qualifying words: corrigibility, corrigible, dirigible, incorrigibility, incorrigible, insurgence, insurgency, insurgent, interregnum, Tyrannosaurus Rex, regal, regent, regicide, regime, regimen, regiment, regina, regnant, regulate, regular, regulation, reign,

related to See **-ac** (Gk. > L.) for examples.

remember See **memor-** and **mne-**.

remove from, deprive of See **ex-** (L.).

rend, tear See **rupt-** for examples.

reno-, ren-, reni- (L., kidney or kidneys) Also see **nephro-** and **pyelo-**.

> Qualifying words: renal, renarium, renicapsule, renicardiac, reniculi, reniculus, reniform, renin, renipelvic, reniportal, renipuncture, renocutaneous, renogastric, renogram, renography, renointestinal, renopathy, renotrophic, renotropic

reproach, mark See **stigma** for examples.

reproductive organs (female) Examine **colpo-, episio-, hystero-, utero-, vagino-** and **vulvo-** for appropriate words.

reptil-, rept- (L., creeping) Also see **angui-, herpeto-, ophio-,** and **sauro-** for other "creeping" creatures.

> Qualifying words: reptant, reptatory, reptile, Reptilia, reptilian, reptiliferous, reptiliform, reptilism, reptilivorous, reptiloid, subreption

reptile, snake See **angui-, herpeto-, ophio-, reptil-,** and **sauro-** for examples.

request, ask See **peti-, rog-,** and **quir-**.

rest, quiet See **quies-** for examples.

reservoir, well, ground water See **phreato-**.

reticulo-, reticul-, reti- (L., net, small net; a netlike structure or a network)

> Qualifying words: reticle, reticula, reticular, reticulate, reticulation, reticulocyte, reticulocytopenia, reticulocytosis, reticuloid, reticulose, reticulum, retiform

retino-, retin- (L., innermost tunic of the eye; from L., *ret[e]*, "net")

> Qualifying words: retina, retinal, retinitis, retinoblastoma, retinodialysis, retinograph, retinoid, retinomalacia, retinopapillitis, retinopathy, retinopexy, retinoschisis, retinoscopy, retinosis, retinotoxic, retispersion

retro- (L., back, backward, behind) Also see **ana-** (#2), **pali-** and **re-** for other "back, behind" words.

> Qualifying words: retroaction, retroactive, retroauricular, retrocede, retrocession, retrocolic, retrocursive, retroflection, retroflex, retroflexion retrograde, retrography, retrogress, retrogression, retrogressive, retrolingual, retromammary, retromorphosis, retrorocket, retrorse, retrospect, retrospection, retrosternal, retroversion, retrovirus

return home See **nosto-** for examples.

resembling See **-oid** and **simal-** for examples.

result, completion See **teleo-** for examples.

reverse See **de-** (#4) for examples.

-rexia (appetite or hunger) See **orexi-** for examples.

rhach- See **rachio-** for examples.

-rhaph, -rhaphy, -orrhaphy, -rrhaphy (Gk., suture, stitching, joining in a seam)

> Qualifying words: blepharorrhaphy, celiorrhaphy, cystorrhaphy, gastrorrhaphy, glossorrhaphy, hepatorrhaphy, laryngorraphy, nephrorrhaphy, neurorrhaphy, orchidorrhaphy, perineorrhaphy, ureterorrhaphy

rhe- (flow, wave) See **rheo-** for examples.

rheo-, rhe-, rhy-, rheum- (Gk., a flow, wave; current of a stream, current) For other "wave" words, see **cymo-, fluct-, kymo-, liqu-, rheum-, -rrhea, undu-,** and **vacilla-**.

> Qualifying words: rheocrene, rheological, rheologist, rheology, rheometer, rheometry, rheophile, rheophilous, rheophily, rheophobe, rheophobous, rheophoby, rheophyte, rheoplankton, rheoscope, rheostat, rheostosis, rheotachygraphy, rheotactic, rheotaxis, rheotome, rheotrophic, rheotropic, rheotropism, rheotropism, rheoxene, rheoxenous, rhyme, rhyolite, rhysimeter, rhythmic, rime, terza rima

rheum-, rheuma- (Gk., flux, that which flows; a stream; discharge) Also see **cymo-, fluct-, rheo-, undu-,** and **vacilla-**.

> Qualifying words: rheumapyra, rheumarthritis, rheumatalgia, rheumatic, rheumatism, rheumatogenic, rheumatogenenis, rheumatoid, rheumatologist, rheumatology, rheumatopyra, rheumatosis, rheumy

-rhexis (Gk., rupture) See **-orrhexis** for examples.

rhino-, rhin-, -rhinia, -rhine (Gk., nose, nostrils) Also see **naso-** and **rhyncho-** for other "nose" words.

Qualifying words: Acorhinotermes, arhinia, dirhinous, holorhinal, macrorhinia, oxyrhine, Platyrrhina, platyrrhine, Prorhinotermes, rhinal, rhinalgia, rhinaria, rhinarium, rhinectomy, rhinesthesia, rhiniatry, rhinism, rhinitis, rhinoanemometer, rhinoantritis, rhinocanthectomy, rhinocerous, rhinocheiloplasty, rhinodymia, rhinodynia, rhinogenous, rhinohyperplasia, rhinolalia, rhinolaryngitis, rhinolith, rhinologist, rhinology, rhinonecrosis, rhinopathy, rhinophonia, rhinoplasty, rhinorrhea, rhinoscope, rhinoscopy, Rhinotermes, rhinotheca, rhinotomy, rhinovirous, Schedorhinotermes, schizorhinal

rhitid- (Gk., wrinkle, wrinkling) See **rhytid-** for other "wrinkle" words.

rhizo-, rhiz- (Gk., root) Also see **radic-**.

Qualifying words: heterorhizal, mycorrhiza, rhizanthous, rhizobenthic, rhizobenthos, rhizobia, Rhizobium, rhizocarp, rhizocarpous, Rhizocephalia, rhizocephalous, rhizodermis, rhizogenesis, rhizogenic, rhizogenous, rhizoid, rhizome, rhizomeningomyhelitis, rhizomorph, rhizomorphoic, rhizomorphous, rhizophagous, rhizophagy, rhizophile, rhizophilous, rhizophily, rhizophorous, rhizopod, rhizophorous, Rhizopoda, rhizosphere, rhizotaxis, rhizotomist, rhizotomy

rhodo-, rhod- (Gk., rose [red]) Also see **erythro-, roseo-,** and **rube** for additional "red" words and see COLORS for other elements.

Qualifying words: cynorrhoden, oorhodein, rhodamine, rhodium, rhodizite, Rhododendron, rhodogenesis, rhodolite, rhodonite, rhodophyll, rhodora

rhy- (flow, wave) See **rheo-** for examples.

rhyncho-, rhynch-, -rhyncha, -rhynchous (Gk., snout, beak) Also see **naso-** and **rhino-** for other "nose" words.

Qualifying words: Menorhyncha, ornithorhynchus, Oxyrrhyncha, Rhynchosia

rhypo-, rhyp- (Gk., filth) Also see **myso-** for other "filth" examples. Compare with **sapro-** and **sepsi-** for similarities.

Qualifying words: rhyparia, rhyparography, rhypophagy, rhypophobia, rhyptic

rhytid-, rhitid- (Gk., wrinkle, wringling; folding) Also see **rugo-** for more "wrinkle" words.

Qualifying words: rhyssoid, rhytidectomy, rhytidome, rhytidoplasty, rhytidosis, Rhytina, rhytiphobia, rhytiscopia

rib See **costo-** for examples.

rice See **Oryza** for examples.

rich See **pluto-, lucr-,** and **opulen-** for examples.

ridge; crest See **lopho-** for examples.

right (to the right side) See **dexter-** for examples.

right (correct) See **ortho-** and **recti-** for examples.

right, justice See **jus-** for examples.

rigi-, rig- (L., stiff, hard, numb) Also see **dur-** and **sclero-** for other "stiff, hard" words.

Qualifying words: calcium rigor, corrigible, de rigueur, dirigible, frigid, frigidity, heat rigor, regiment, regescent, rigid, rigidify, rigidity, rigidness, rigor, rigor mortis, rigorism, rigorist, rigorous, rigorously, rigour, water rigor, incorrigible

ring, circle See **orb-** for examples.

rising, becoming visible See **oriri-** for examples.

river See **fluvio-** and **potamo-** for examples.

road, way See **hodo-, odo-,** and **via-** for examples.

rock, stone See **lapid-, litho-, petro-,** and **saxi-** for examples.

rod, rod shaped See **bacilli-** and **rhabdo-** for examples.

rod-, ros- (L., gnaw, eat away)

Qualifying words: corrode, corrodible, corrosion, corrosive, erode, eroded, erosion, erosive, rodent, Rodentia, rodenticide

roentgeno-, roentgen- (German, radiation, x-ray) Also see **actino-** and **radio-** for similar examples. So called after its discoverer, a German physicist Wilhelm Konrad Roentgen (1845-1923), who discovered roentgen rays in 1895; winner of the Nobel prize in physics in 1901.

Qualifying words: roentgenism, roentgenize, roentgenocardiogram, roentgenogram, roentgenography, roentgenologist, roentgenology, roentgenolucent, roentgenometer, roentgenometry, roentgenopaque, roentgenoparent, roentgenoscope, roentgenoscopy, roentgenotherapy, roentgentherapy

rog-, roga-, -rogate, -rogation, -rogatory (L., ask, inquiry, request, beg) Also see **peti-** and **quir-** for other "ask, request" words.

Qualifying words: abrogate, abrogation, arrogant, arrogate, derogate, derogatory, interrogate, interrogation, interrogative, interrogatory, prerogative, prorogation, prorogue, rogation, subrogate, supererogation, supererogatory, surrogate

R roof ➥ rupture of an organ or vessel

roof, house See **calypo-** and **stego-** for other "roof" words.
rooster, cock See **alectryo-** for examples.
root See **radio-** and **rhizo-** for examples.
ros- (gnaw, eat away) See **rod-** for examples.
rose See **rhodo-** for examples.
roseo-, ros- (L., rose-colored) For other "red" words, see **rhodo-** and **rub-**.
> **Qualifying words:** rosarian, rosary, rose, roseate, roseola, Rosicrucian, rosiness, *sub rosa*

rot- (L., wheel) See **roti-** for examples.
roti-, rot- (L., wheel [turn])
> **Qualifying words:** rotate, rotation, rotator, rotatory, rotiform, rotor

rotten, putrid See **sapro-** and **sepsi-**.
rotundi-, rotundo-, rotund- (L, round) Also see **circ-, -cycle, cyclo-, orb-, peri-,** and **sphere** for words with similar meanings.
> **Qualifying words:** orotund, orotundity, rotund, rotunda, rotundate

rough See **rudi-** and **trachy-** for examples.
roughness, rudeness, bristling, shaking See **hor-** for examples.
round, around See **ambi-, amphi-, circum-, cyclo-, orb-, peri-,** and **sphero-** for examples.
round, ball See **glob-** and **sphere** for examples.
rove, wander See **err-, migr-, nomad,** and **vaga-** for examples.
row, rank See **ord-** for examples.
-rrhaphy (Gk., suture, stitching) See **-rhaph** for examples.
-rrhea, -rrhoea, -orrhea (Gk. > L., flow, flowing) Also see **fluct-, liqu-, rheo-, rheum-, undu-,** and **vacilla-** for additional "flow" words.
> **Qualifying words:** arrhythmia, diarrhea, gonorrhea, hemorrhage, hemorrhoid, hepatorrhea, hidrorrhea, logorrhea, otorrhea, pyorrhea, rhinorrhea, seborrhea, verborrhea

-rrhexis (rupture) See **-orrhexis** for examples.
rub, friction See **bruxo-, tribo-,** and **-tripsy** for examples.
rub-, rubi- (L., red [color]) For other "red" words, see **erythro-, rhodo-** (rose), and **roseo-**. Also examine COLORS for related words
> **Qualifying words:** erubescence, erubescent, rubefacient, rubefaction, rubella, rubeola, ruberal, rubescence, rubicund, rubicundity, rubify, rubiginous, rubigo, rubric, rubricate, rubrication, ruby

rudi-, rud- (L., rough, unformed, unwrought; ignorant, untutored) Also see **trachy-** for other "rough" words.
> **Qualifying words:** erudite, eruditely eruditeness, erudition, rude, rudely, rudeness, rudiment, rudimental, rudimentary, rudish

rugo-, rug- (Gk. > L., wrinkle, ridge, fold) Also see **rhytid-** for other "wrinkle" words.
> **Qualifying words:** arroyo (Spanish, from Latin), corrugate, corrugated, corrugation, corrugator, ruga, rugae, rugate, rugoscopy, rugose, rugosity, rugous, rugulose

rule, govern See **-arch, -crat,** and **regi-** for examples.
rump, buttocks See **pygo-** for examples.
run, go See **cur(r)-** and **dromo-** for examples.
rut or track See **orb-** for examples.
running (course) See **cur(r)-** and **dromo-** for examples.
rupt-, -rupting, -ruption (L., break, tear, rend) Also see **clast-** and **frag-** for other "break" words.
> **Qualifying words:** abrupt, bankrupt, corrupt, corruption, disrupt, disruption, erupt, eruption, incorruptible, interrupt, interruption, irruption, rupture, rut

rupture of an organ or vessel See **-orrhexis** for examples.

S s

sacchar-, sacchari-, saccharo- (Gk. > L., sugar; originally from Sanskrit, "gravel, grit") Also see **dulci-, gluco-** and **glyco-** for additional "sugar" or "sweet" words.

> **Qualifying words:** saccharide, sacchariferous, saccharify, saccharimeter, saccharometer, saccharin, saccharine, Saccharomyces, saccharose

sacer- (L., sacred, holy) See **sacro-**.

sack, pouch For examples, see **marsupium, scroto-** and **thyla-**.

sacred, holy See **hagio-, hiero-, sacro-,** and **sanct-** for examples.

sacro-, sacr-, sacer- (L., ¹sacred, holy; ²*os sacrum,* "sacred bone" [so called because it was thought never to disintegrate]; the triangular bone just below the lumbar vertebrae, usually formed by five fused vertebrae (sacral vertebrae) that are wedged dorsally between the two hip bones) Also see **hagio-, hiero-,** and **sanct-** for other "sacred" words.

> **Qualifying words:** ¹[sacred, holy] consecrate, consecration, desecrate, desecration, sacerdotal, sacrament, sacramental, sacred, sacrifice, sacrilege, sacrilegious, sacrosanct, sacrosanctity
>
> ²[bone] sacrad, sacral, sacralgia, sacrarthrogenic, sacrectomy, sacroanterior, sacrocygeal, sacrococcyx, sacrocoxalgia, sacrocoxitis, sacrodynia, sacroiliac, sacroilitis, sacroposterior, sacrolumbar, sacrotomy, sacrovertebral, sacrum

sag-, sagaci- (L., wise, shrewd, keen perception) Also see **sap-** and **soph-**.

> **Qualifying words:** presage, sagacious, sagacity, sage

sagging, drooping See **-ptosia** for examples.

sagitto-, sagitt- (L., arrow) Also see **toxo-** for other "arrow" words.

> **Qualifying words:** sagittal, Sagittarius, sagittoform, sagittoid

sail, float See **pleusto-** for examples.

sailor, ship See **naus-, naut-,** and **nav-**.

sal-, sali- (L., salt) Also see **halo-** for additional "salt" words.

> **Qualifying words:** *cum grano salis,* salad, salami, salary, salicylate, salicylemia, saliferous, salify, salimeter, saline, salinity, salinometer, *sal petrae,* salt, saltpeter, Salzburg, sauce, saucer, sausage, silt, soused

sale, selling See **-poly** and **onio-** for examples.

saliva (L., spittle, the fluid secreted in the mouth) Also see **sialo-** for other "spittle" words.

> **Qualifying words:** saliva, salivary, salivate, salivation

salt See **halo-** and **sal-** for examples.

same, similar See **equ-, homo-, iso-, -oid, pari-, peer-, simal-,** and **tauto-**.

sana-, sani-, san- (L., healthy, whole; *by extension:* cure, heal, take care of) Also see **cura-, iatro-, medi-,** and **therap-** for "cure, heal" words and **hygieio-** for "healthy" words.

> **Qualifying words:** insane, insaneness, insanitary, insanity, sanatorium, sanatory, sane, saneness, sanitarian, sanitarium, sanitary, sanitation, sanitization, sanitize, sanity

sanct- (L., sacred, holy) For other "sacred" words, see **hagio-, hiero-,** and **sacro-**.

> **Qualifying words:** sanctum sanctorum, sacrosanct, sanctification, sanctify, sanctimonious, sanctimoniously, sanction, sanctity, sanctorium, sanctuary, sanctum

sand See **amatho-, ammo-, arena, psammo-,** and **silico-** for examples.

sandbank, shore Examine **aigialo-** and **thino-** for related words.

sangui-, sanguin-, sanguino- (L., blood) For other "blood" words, examine **-emia** and **hemo-**.

> **Qualifying words:** consanguineous, consanguinity, ensanguine, exsanguine, exsanguinous, exsanguious, *sang royal,* sangaree, *sang-de-boeuf, sang-froid,* sanguicole, sanguicolous, sanguiferous, sanguification, sanguimotor, sanguinmotory, sanguinary, sanguine, sanguineous, sanguinivorous, sanguinolent, sanguinopoietic, sanguinous, sanguirenal, sanguis, sanguisuction, Sanguisuga, sanguisuga, sanguisugent, sanguisugous, sanguivore, sanguivorous

sani- (L., healthy; cure) See **sana-** for examples.

sap-, sapi- (L. [*sapere*], wise, wisdom, to be wise, to have wisdom; to know, knowledge; to taste [of], to perceive) Also see **sag-** and **soph-** for other "wise" words. Don't confuse this **sap-** with another **sap-** (sapo-) meaning "soap."

> **Qualifying words:** homo sapiens, insipid, insipidity, sage, sapid, sapidity, sapience, sapient, sapiential, sapiently, sapor, saporific, saporous, savant, savoir-faire (L. > Fr.), savoir-vivre (L. > Fr.), savor, savvy (slang, L. > Sp.)

sapo-, sap-, saponi- (L., soap)

> **Qualifying words:** saponaceous, saponatus, saponification, saponify

sapro-, sapr-, sap- (Gk., rotten, putrid, decaying) Also see **sepsi-** for other "rotten" words. Compare with **myso-** and **rhypo-** for words with similar meanings.

> **Qualifying words:** holosaprophyte, mesosaprobe, mesosaprobic, sapine, saprine, saprobe, saprobic, saprobiont, saprodontia, saprogen, saprogenic, saprogenous, saprolite, sapromyiophile, sapromyiophilous, sapromyiophily, sapronosis, sapropel, saprophage, saprophagic, saprophagous, saprophagy, saprophilous, saprophyte, saprophytic, saprophytism, saprophytophage, saprophytophagous, saprophytophagy, saproplankton, sapropyra, saprostomous, saprotroph, saprotrophic, saprotyphus, saprovore, saprovorous, saproxylobios, saprozoic, saprozoite, saprozoonosis, zoosaprophage, zoosaprophagous, zoosaprophagy

sarco-, sarc-, -sarcous, -sarc, -sarcoma, -sarcomatous, -sarcomatoid (Gk., flesh, meat) Also examine **carno-** and **creo-** for other "flesh, meat" words.

> **Qualifying words:** caulosarc, ectosarc, endosarc, fibrosarcoma, leukosarcoma, lymphosarcoma, perisarc, perisarcous, sarcasm, sarcobiot, sarcoblast, sarcocarp, sarcoderm, sarcogenic, sarcoid, sarcoleukemia, sarcology, sarcolysis, sarcolyte, sarcoma, sarcophago, sarcophagous, sarcophagus, sarcophagy, sarcoplasm, sarcoplast, sarcosis, sarcosoma, sarcosomes, sarcotheca, sarcotherapeutics, sarcotherapy, sarcotic, sarcous

Satan (Hebrew and Greek, the devil, the adversary) Also see **demono-, diablo-,** and **Lucifer** for words with similar meanings.

> **Qualifying words:** Satan, satanic, satanically, Satanology, Satanophobia

satis-, sati-, sat- (L., enough)

> **Qualifying words:** assets dissatisfaction, dissatisfy, insatiability, insatiable, insatiate, sad, sate, sated, satiate, satiated, satisfaction, satisfactory, satisfy, saturate, unsatisfactorily, unsatisfactory

sauro-, saur-, -saurus, -saurid, -saur, -sauria, -saurian (Gk., lizard) Also see **angui-** (snake), **herpeto-** ("serpent"), **ophio-** ("snake"), and **reptil-** ("creeping") for words with related meanings.

> **Qualifying words:** aachenosaurus, abrictosaurus, acrocanthosaurus, adasaurus, aegyptosaurus, aepisaurus, aetosaurs, aetosaurus, agrosaurus, alamosaurus, albertosaurus, alectrosaurus, algoasaurus, allosaurid, allosaurus, ammosaurus, amphisaurus, amtosaurus, anatosaurus, anchisaurid, anchi-

saurus, ankylosaur, ankylosaurid, ankylosaurus, anodontosaurus, anoplasaurus, antarctosaurus, apatosaurus, aralosaurus, archosaur, archosauria, arctosaurus, argyrosaurus, aristosaurus, asiatosaurus, atlantosaurus, austrosaurus, azendohsaurus, bactrosaurus, bahariasaurus, barapasaurid, barapaasaurus, barosaurus, blikanasauridae, blikanasaurus, brachiosaurids, brachiosaurus, brachylophosaurus, brachypodosaurus, brontosaurus, calamosaurus, camarasaurid, camarasaurus, camptosaurid, camptosaurus, carcharodontosaurus, carnosaurs, carnotaurus, carnotaur, carnotosaurus, centrosaurus, ceratosaurid, ceratosaurus, cetiosaurid, cetiosauriscus, cetiosaurus, champsosaurus, champsosaurs, chaoyoungosaurid, chaoyoungosaurus, chasmosaurus, cheneosaurus, chialingosaurus, chiayuesaurus, chinkosaurus, chilantaisaurus, chingkankousaurus, chinshakiangosaurus, chondrosteosaurus, chubutisauridae, chubutisaurus, claosaurus, clasmodosaurus, coelosaurus, coelurosaurs, colonosaurus, coloradisaurus, corythosaurus, cotylosaurs, cotylosaurus, cotylosauria, craterosaurus, cryptosaurus, danubiosaurus, daspletosaurus, deinocheirosauria, deinonychosaur, dilophosaurus, dimodosaurus, dinosaur, dinosauria, dinosaurid, dinosaurian, dinosauroid, dinosaurologist, dinosaurology, dinosaurus, doryphorosaurus, dravidosaurus, dromaeosaur, dromaeosaurus, dromeosaurids, dromicosaurus, dryosaurus, dryptosaurid, dryptosauroides, dryptosaurus, dynamosaurus, dyoplosaurus, dysalotosaurus, edaphosaurus, edmontosaurus, elaphrosaurus, elasmosaurid, elasmosaurus, elmisaurid, elmisaurus, embasaurus, erlikosaurus, eucerosaurus, eucnemesaurus, euoplocephalus, euskelosaurus, fabrosaurids, fabrosaurus, fenestrosaurus, gadolosaurus, geosaurus, geranosaurus, gigantosaurus, gilmoreosaurus, gongubusaurus, gorgosaurus, gresslyosaurus, griphosaurus, gryposaurus, gyposaurus, hadrosaurid, hadrosaurine, hadrosaurus, haplocanthosaurus, halticosaurus, hecatasaurus, heishansaurus, herrerasaurid, herrarasaurus, hierosaurus, heterodontosaurids, heterodontosaurus, hoplitosaurus, hoplosaurus, huayangosaurus, hylaeosaurus, hypacrosaurus, hypselosaurus, ichthyosaur, ichthyosauria, ichthyosaurous, ichthyosaurus, inosaurus, ischisaurus, ischyrosaurus, jaxartosaurus, kangnasaurus, kelmayisaurus, kentrosaurus, kentrosaurus, kentrurosaurus, kritosaur, kritosaurus, kronosaurus, kuehneosaurus, labrosaurus, lambeosaurine, lambeosaurus, lametasaurus, lanasaurus, laosaurus, laplatasaurus, leipsanosaurus, lepidosaur, lesothosaurus, lexovisaurus, likhoelesaurus, limnosaurus, loncosaurus, loricosaurus, lotosaurus, lufengosaurus, lukosaurus, lusitanosaurus, lystrosaurus, macrurosaurus, maiasaura, maiasaurus, magnosaurus, magyarosaurus, majungasaurus, mamenchisaurus, mandschurosaurus, marshosaurus, megalosaurid, megalosaurus, melanorosaurids, melanorosaurus, mesosauria, metriacanthosaurus, hadrosaurus, micropachycephalosaurus, microsaur, microsaurus, millerosaurus, mixosaurus, mongolosaurus, morinosaurus, mosasaurs, mosasaurus, mussaurid, mussaurus, muttaburrasaurus, nanosaur, nanosaurus, nanshiungosaurus, nemegtosaurus, neosaurus, nipponosaurus, noasaurids, noasaurus, nodosaurids, nodosaurs, nodosaurus, nothosaur, nyasasaurus, ohmdenosaurus oligosaurus, omeisaurus, omosaurus, onychosaurus, oplosaurus, orinosaurus, ornithominosauria, ornithominosaurus, orosaurus, orthogoniosaurus, ouranosaurus, pachycephalosaurid, pachycephalosaurus, pachyrhinosaurids, pachyrhinosaurus, pachysaurus, palaeosauriscus, palaeosaurus, panoplosaur, panoplosaurus, parasaurolophus, pareiasaurids, parksosaurus, parrosaurus, patagosaurus, peishansaurus, pelorosaurus, pelycosaur, pelycosauria, peoycosaur, petrolacosaurus, phaedrolosaurus, phytosaur, piatnitzkysaurus, pinacosaurus, pisanosaurus, piveteausaurus, plateosaur, plateosaurus, plateosaurid, plateosaurus, plesiosaur, plesiosaurus, pliosaur, pododesaurus, podokesaurus, polyodontosaurus, priveteausaurus, probactrosaurus, proceratosaurus, procerosaurus, procheneosaurus, prosaurolophus, prosauropods, protosauria, protosaurus, psittacosaurs, psittacosaurus, psittacousaurid, psittacousaurus, pterosaur, pterosauria, pterospondylus, rebbachisaurus, regnosaurus, rhodanosaurus, rhoetosaurus, rhynchosaur, riojasaurus, roccosaurus, saltasaurus, sanpasaurus, sarcosaurus, sauria, saurian, saurischia, saurischians, saurodont, saurognathous, sauroid, saurolophine, saurolophus, saurophagous, sauroplites, sauropod, sauropoda, sauropodomorphs, sauropsida, sauronithoidid, saurornithoidids, sauronitholestes, saury, scelidosaur, scelidosaurus, scolosaurus, scutellosaurus, secernosaurus, segisaurid, segisaurus, segnosaur, segnosauria, segnosaurid, segnosaurus, seismosaurus, sellosaurus, shamosaurus, shanshanosaurid, shanshanosaurus, shantungosaurus, shonisaurus, shuosaurus, silvisaurus, sinosaurus, spinosaurid, spinosaurus, staurikosaurid, staurikosaurus, stegosauria, stegosaurids, stegosaurs, stegosaurus, stenonychosaurus, stephanosaurus, stokesosaurus, strenusaurus, stretosaurus, struthiosaurus, styracosaurus, supersaurus, syrmosaurus, symphyrosaurus, syngonosaurus, syrmosaurus, szechuanosaurus, tarbosaurus, tatisaurus, teinurosaurus, teleosaurus, telmatosaurus, temnodontosaurus, tenchisaurus, tenontosaurus, teratosaurid, teratosauridae, teratosaurus, tetragonosaurus, thecodontosaurus, therizinosauria, therizinosaurids, therizinosaurus, thescelosaurid, thescelosaurus, thotobolosauurus, tianchungosaurus, tienshanosaurus, titanosaurid, titano-

saurus, torosaurus, torvosaurus, tovosaurus, tsintaosaurus, tugulusaurus, tuojiangosaurus, tylasaurus, tyrannosaurus, tyrannosauridae, tyrannosaurids, tyrannosaurus, Tyrannosaurus Rex, ultrasaurus, unquillosaurus, valdosaurus, vectisaurus, wannanosaurus, wuerhosaurus, yaleosaurus, yunnanosaurus, yangchuanosaurus, zephyrosaurus, zigongosaurus

save, protect See **alexo-, -fend-,** and **phylacto-**.

saxi-, sax- (L., rock, rocky, stone) Also see **lapid-, litho-,** and **petro-**.

Qualifying words: saxatile, saxicavous, saxicole, saxicoline, saxicolous, saxifrage, saxifragous

say, talk For examples, examine **cit-, clam-, dic-, fa-, lalo-, legi-, locu-, logo-, loqu-, mythico-, ora-, -phasia, -phemia,** and **voc-**.

scale, flake See **lepido-** for examples.

scan-, sca- (L., climb, mount) Also see **scend-** for additional "climb" words.

Qualifying words: escalate, escalation, escalator, scandal, scandalize, scandalmonger, scandalous, scandel, scandent, scansion, scansorial, slander

scapho-, scaph- (Gk., boat-shaped; shaped like the hull of a boat)

Qualifying words: bathyscaphe, scapha, scaphium, scaphocephalic, scaphognathite, scaphoid

scapulo-, scpul-, -scapula, -scapular (L., the flat, triangular bone in the back of the shoulder; the shoulder blade) Also see **omo-** (L.) for other "shoulder" words.

Qualifying words: scapula, scapulalgia, scapular, scapulary, scapulectomy, scapuloanterior, scapuloclavicular, scapulodynia, scapulohumeral, scapulopexy, scapuloposterior

scar See **cicatri-** for examples.

scarce See **spano-** for examples.

scato-, scat-, skato-, skat- (Gk., dung, feces, excrement) Also see **copro-, feco-,** and **fimbri-** for other "dung" words.

Qualifying words: scat, scatemia, scatologia, scatologic, scatology, scatoma, scatomancy, scatophagous, scatophagy, scatophilia, scatophobia, scatoscopy, skatologic, skatophagy

scatter, sprinkle See **-sperse** for examples.

scel- (Gk., leg) See **skel-** for examples.

scend-, scen- (L., climb, mount) Also see **scan-** for other "climb" words.

Qualifying words: ascend, ascendance, ascendancy, ascendant, ascension, ascent, condescend, condescending, condescension,

S save ➥ scend-

descend, descendant, descent, echelon, escalate, escalator, scale, scansion, transcend, transcendence, transcendency, transcendent, transcendental, transcendentalism

schisto-, schist- (Gk., split, cleft) Also see **schizo-** for other "split" words.

Qualifying words: schistasis, schistocyte, schistoglossia, schistometer, schistosomiasis, schistothorax, schistotrachelus, trichoschisis

schizo-, schiz-, schis- (Gk., split, cleft) Also see **schisto-** for other "split" words.

Qualifying words: mitoschisis, onychoscizia, retinoschisis, schism, schismatic, schisogenesis, schisophrenic, schisopod, schizocarp, schizocarpic, schizogenesis, schizogenetic, schizognathous, schizoid, schizoidism, schizokinesis, schizolysis, schizonychia, schizophasia, schizophrenia, schizophrenic, schizophyte, schizorhinal, schizothecal, schizotrichia

sci-, -science, -sciently, -scientific, -scientifically, -scient, -sciently (L., know, learn, knowledge) Also see **cogni-, epistemo-, gno-, intellect-, mne-,** and **not-.**

Qualifying words: conscience, conscientious, conscious, consciousness, nescience, nescient, omniscience, omniscient, parviscient, prescience, prescient, science, scientific, scientifically, scientist, subconscious, subsconsciously, unconscionable, unconscious

scia- (Gk., shade, shadow) See **scio-** for examples.

scintill- (L., light, shine, spark, sparkle, twinkle) Also see **luco-, lumen, luna-, lustr-, phospho-,** and **photo-.**

Qualifying words: scintigram, scintigraphy, scintilla, scintillascope, scintillate, scintillation, scintillescent, scintiphotograph, scintiscan, scintiscanner

scio-, sci-, scia- (Gk., shade, shadow; ghost) Also see **skio-** and **umbra-.**

Qualifying words: amphiscian, amphiscii, antiscians, antiscii, ascian, heliosciophyte, sciagram, sciagraph, sciagraphy, scialytic, sciamachy, sciametry, sciascope, sciascopy, sciatheric, sciomancy, sciomantic, sciophile, sciophilous, sciophyllous, sciophyte, sciotheism, scioptic

sclero-, scler- (Gk., hard, hardening) For other "hard" words, see **dur-** and **rigi-.**

Qualifying words: acrosclerosis, arteriosclerosis, otosclerosis, phlebosclerosis, sclera, scleradenitis, sclerectomy, sclerencephaly, scleriasis, scleritis, scleroadipose, sclerocarp, sclerodactylia, sclerodactyly, scleroderm, scleroderma, sclerodermatous, sclerodermic, sclerogen, sclerogenic, sclerogenous, scleroid, scleroma, scleromalacia, sclerometer, sclero-

nychia, sclerophyll, sclerophyllous, sclerophylly, sclerose, sclerosing, sclerosis, scleroskeleton, sclerotherapy, sclerotic, sclerotitis, sclerotome, sclerotomy, sclerous, sclerozone, sklerectasia, sklerema

scoleco-, scolec-, scoleci- (Gk., worm) Also see **helmintho-** and **vermo-.**

Qualifying words: scoleces(pl.), scoleciform, scolecite, scolecoid, scolecology, scolex(s.), scolite

scolio- (Gk., curvature, curved, twisted, crooked)

Qualifying words: rachioscoliosis, scoliokyphosis, scoliometer, scoliosciometry, scoliosis, scoliosometer, scoliotic, scoliotone

scop-, scopo-, scept-, skept-, -scope-, -scopy, -scopia, -scopic, -scopist (Gk., see, view, sight, look at, examine) For other "see" words, examine **-orama, spec-,** and **vid-.**

Qualifying words: abdominoscope, amblyoscope, arcoscopic, basiscopic, bishop, bronchoscope, bronchoscopic, bronchoscopy, chromatoscope, chromoscope, cinemascopia, cinemascope, cryoscope, cryoscopy, cystoscope, endoscope, endoscopy, gastroscope, horoscope, hydroscope, kaleidoscope, kaleidoscopic, macroscopic, microscope, microscopic, mixoscopia, ophthalmoscope, orthoscope, orthoscopic, oscilloscope, periscope, pharyngoscope, phonendoscope, photoscope, polariscope, pseudoscope, radarscope, radioscope, radiotelescope, retinoscope, sceptic, sceptical, scepticism, scope, scopograph, scopophilia, scopophobia, scopophobiac, skeptic, skeptical, skepticism, skopometer, sniperscope, snooperscope, spectroscope, stereoscope, stethoscope, stethoscopic, stroboscope, telescope, telescopic, videolaseroscopy

scoto-, scot- (Gk., darkness; blindness) Also see **cecum-, nocti-, nycti-** and **skoto-.**

Qualifying words: scotia, scotochromogen, scotochromogenic, scotodinia, scotogram, scotograph, scotography, scotoma, scotomagraphy, scotomata, scotometer, scotometry, scotomization, scotomy, scotophilia, scotophiliac, scotophobia, scotophobic, scotopia, scotopic, scotoplankton, scotoscopy, scototaxis, scototherapy

scratch See **acaro-** and **amycho-** for examples.

scrib-, script-, -scribe, -scription, -scriptive (L., write, record) Also see **glypto-, gram-,** and **grapho-.**

Qualifying words: adscript, ascribe, ascription, circumscribe, circumscription, conscript, conscripted, conscription, describe, describing, description, descriptive, indescribable, inscribe, inscription, interscribe, manuscript, nondescript, nondescription, postscript, post-script, prescribe, prescript, prescription, prescriptive, proscribe, pro-scripted, proscription, rescribing, rescript, rescriptive, scribble, scribbler, scribbling, scribe, scrip, script, scription, scriptorium, scriptory, scriptural, scripture, scrivener, subscribe, subscriber, subscript, subscription, superscribe, superscript, superscription, transcribe, transcribing, transcript, transcription, typescript

script- (L., write, record) See **scrib-**.

scroto-, scrot- (L., the pouch that holds the testes; a purse; probably a variant of *scortum*, a skin, hide, prostitute, or of *scrautum*; a leather bag for holding arrows; akin to *scrupus*, a sharp stone)

> **Qualifying words:** scrotal, scrotectomy, scrotitis, scrotocele, scrotopexy, scrotoplasty, scrotum

scrut- (L., search, investigation)

> **Qualifying words:** inscrutable, scrutable, scrutate, scrutator, scrutinize, scrutinizing, scrutiny

se- (L., aside, apart from, without, by itself)

> **Qualifying words:** desegregate, secede, secession, seclude, seclusion, secret, secrecy, secretary, secure, security, sedition, sedulous, seditionist, seduce, seduction, segregate, segregation, select, selection, separate, separation, severance

sea See **mare, pelago-,** and **thalasso-**.

sea bottom See **bentho-** for examples.

sea shells See **concho-** for examples.

search, investigate See **scrut-** for examples.

seashore, beach See **aigialo-** for examples.

sebo-, seb-, sebi- (L., tallow, suet; grease)

> **Qualifying words:** sebaceous, sebaceus, sebagogic, sebiferous, sebiparous, sebolith, seborrhea, seborrheic, sebum, seborrheal, seborrheid, sebotropic

sec-, seg-, -sect, -section, -sectional (L., to cut) Also see **-cise, -ectomy, -tom,** and **tomo-** for other "cut" words.

> **Qualifying words:** antivivisectionism, antivivisectionist, bisect, bisection, bisector, dissect, dissection, insect, intersect, intersection, multisect, multisection, resect, resection, secant, sect, sectarian, sectary, section, sectional, sectionalism, sector, segment, trisect, trisection, vivisect, vivisection, vivisectionist

second, two See **deutero-** for examples.

secret, hidden For examples, examine **adelo-, calypto-, clandestine, crypto-, myster-,** and **occult.**

secut- (follow) See **sequ-** for examples.

sed-, sedat-, -sid, -sess (L., sit)

> **Qualifying words:** assess, assiduity, assiduous, dissidence, dissident, insidious, insidiously, obsess, obsessed, obsession, ob-

sessive, possess, prepossess, preside, president, reside, residence, resident, residual, residuary, residue, seance, sedan, sedate, sedative, sedentary, sediment, sedimentary, sedimentation, sedimentological, sedimentology, sedulous, session, siege, subside, subsidiary, subsidize, subsidy, supersede, superseding

see, look at See **-orama, -scope, spec-,** and **vid-** for examples.

seed See **semen, spermo-** and **sporo-** for examples.

seek, ask See **quir-, peti-,** and **rog-** for examples.

seg- (L., cut) See **sec-** for examples.

seismo-, seism-, -seism, -seisma, -seismically, -seismical, -seismal, -seismic (Gk., shake, earthquake [move to and fro'; to shake, move violently]) Also see **pall-** for additional "shaking" words.

> **Qualifying words:** aseismic, atmoseisma, baryseisma, baryseismic, bathyseism, bioseisma, bradyseism, bradyseismic, coseism, coseismic, geoseism, helioseismology, isoseismal, isoseismic, lithoseisma, macroseism, macroseismic, megaseism, megaseismic, meizoseismal, microseism, microseismic, pyroseismic, seismaeshesia, seismesthesia, seismic, seismically, seismicity, seismism, seismocardiogram seismocardiography, seismogram, seismograph, seismographic, seismography, seismological, seismologist, seismology, seismometer, seismometry, seismoscope, seismotactic, seismotaxis, seismotherapy, seismotropic, seismotropism, teleseism, teleseismic, thalassoseisma

seize, clasp, reach See **prehend-** for examples.

seize See **cap-** for examples.

seize and carry off See **rap-** for examples.

seizing, violent attack See **-lepsy** for examples.

seizure See **hapto-** for examples.

seleno-, selen- (Gk., moon) Also see **luna-**.

> **Qualifying words:** geoselenic, Selene, selenite, selenium, Selene, selenocentric, selenodesy, selenodont, selenogamia, selenogault, selenograph, selenographer, selenographic, selenography, selenol, selenological, selenologist, selenology, selenomorphology, selenophobia, selenoplegia, selenoplexia, selenotrope, selenotropic, selenotropism, tetraselenodont

self See **auto-, ipse,** and **sui-** for examples.

self love See **narciss-** for examples.

sell, for sale See **poly-** and **vend-** for samples. Don't confuse this **-poly** with another **poly-** which means "many." Also compare this element with **onio-**.

sema- (signal) See **semeio-** for examples.

-semble See **simil-** for examples.

semeio-, sema-, semio- (Gk., signal, sign) Also see **sig-** for other "sign" words.

> **Qualifying words:** asemantic, asemasia, asemia, semantic, semantics, semaphore, semasiology, sematic, semeiography, semeiology, semeiopathic, semeiosis, semeiotic, semeiotics, semiography, semiologic, semiology, semiopathic, semiosis, semiotic, semiotics, zoosemiotics

semen, semin- (L., seed) Also see **spermo-** and **sporo-** for other "seed" words.

> **Qualifying words:** disseminate, dissemination, inseminate, insemination, semen, seminal, seminar, seminarian, seminarist, seminarium, seminary, semination, seminiferous, seminist, seminivorous

semi- (L., half, partly, twice) Also see **demi-** and **hemi-** for additional "half" words.

> **Qualifying words:** semiannual, semiaquatic, semiarid, semiautomatic, semiautonomous, semicentennial, semicircle, semicircular, semicolon, semicomplete, semiconscious, semicylindrical, semiformal, semiherbaceous, semilethal, semiliterate, semilunar, semimetamorphosis, semimicro, semiopaque, semiviparous, semipermeable, semiplume, semirigid, semiskilled, semitone, semiterrestrial, semitransparent, semitropical, semiyearly

semper (L., always, ever, at all times, on each occasion)

> **Qualifying words:** *semper fidelis*, *semper paratus*, sempervirent, sempervivum, Sempervivum, sempiternal, sempre

sen-, sene-, seni- (*senex*) (L., old age, old, elder) Also see **gero-** and **presbyo-**.

> **Qualifying words:** monseigneur, monsieur, seigneur, seigneury, seignior, seigniorage, seignorage, seignioral, seigniorial, seignorial, seignoral, seigniory, signory, senate, senator, senectitude, senescence, senescent, senex, senicide, senile, senilism, senility, senior, seniority, senium, senopia, senor, signore, sir, sire, surly (originally, *sirly*, *sirlike*, i.e., assuming "lordly airs")

send, throw See **ballo-, jet-,** and **miss-**.

seni- (old age, old) See **sen-** for examples.

sens-, senso-, sensori-, sent- (L., feeling, sensation, perception through the senses, be aware, discern by the senses) Also see **aesth-, pass-,** and **patho-**.

> **Qualifying words:** assent, clairsentience, consensus, consent, desensitize, dissension, dissent, dissenter, extrasensory, insensate, insensibility, insensible, insensitive, nonsense, nonsensical, photosensitive, presentiment, resent, resentful, resentment, scent, sensation, sensational, sensationalism, sensationalist, sense, sensibilities, sensibility, sensible, sensiferous, sensimeter, sensitive, sensitivity, sensitize, sensitometer, sensomotor, sensor, sensorial, sensorimetabolism, sensorimotor, sensorium, sensorivascular, sensory, sensual, sensuous, sentence, sententious, sentience, sentient, sentiment, sentimental, sentimentalism, sentimentalist, sentimentality, sentimentalize, sentinel, supersensible

sensation, feeling See **aesth-, pass-, patho-,** and **sens-** for examples.

sent- (L., feeling) See **sens-** for examples.

sepsi-, septi-, septico-, -sepsis, -septic, -septicemia, -septicemic (Gk., decay, putrefactive) Also see **sapro-** for additional "decay, putrid" words. Don't confuse this **sepsi-** with another **septi-** which means "seven." Compare with **myso-** and **rhypo-** for similarities.

> **Qualifying words:** antiseptic, asepsis, aseptic, autosepticemia, pneumosepticemia, pneumosepticemic, pyrosepticemia, sepsis, septal, septic, septicemia, septicine, septicophlebitis, septicopyemia, septineuritis, septopyemia

septi-, sept-, septem- (L., seven, seventh) See the NUMBERS section in **Appendix G** for other numerical elements. Don't confuse this **septi-** with the **septi-** which means "decay."

> **Qualifying words:** septangle, September, septemvirate, septennial, septennium, septet, septicentennial, septilateral, septillion, septivalent, septuagenarian, septuple, septuplet, septuplicate

sequ-, sequi-, secut-, suit-, -sue (L., follow)

> **Qualifying words:** consecutive, consequence, consequently, ensue, execute, execution, executive, executor, executrix, obsequies, obsequious, obsequiously, obsequiousness, persecute, persecution, prosecute, prosecutor, prosecution, pursuance, pursue, pursuit, second, secondary, sect, sectarian, sequacious, sequel, sequence, sequencial, sequent, sequential, sequester, subsequent, subsequently, sue, suit, suitable, suite, suitor

serico-, seric-, seri- (L., silk) Don't confuse this **seri-** with another **seri-** in "serial" or "series" and **serio-** in "serious," etc.

> **Qualifying words:** sericate, sericeous, sericin, sericite, sericocarpous, sericultural, sericulturalist, sericulture, serigraph, serigrapher, serigraphic, serigraphy

series, order See **ord-** for examples.

serpent, snake See **angui-, herpeto-** (reptile, serpent), **ophio-, reptil-,** and **sauro-** (lizard) for examples.

serendipity (Arabic, the gift of finding interesting things by chance; the faculty of finding valuable or agreeable things *not sought for*; an apparent aptitude for making fortunate discoveries accidently) Coined by English novelist Horace Walpole (fourth Earl of Oxford [1717-1797]) in a letter written on January 28, 1754 to his friend Sir Horace Mann, a British diplomat.

Qualifying words: pseudoserendipitous, pseudoserendipity, serendipitous, serendipity

sesqui- (L., one and a half) Also examine the NUMBERS section in **Appendix G** for other numerical elements. In chemistry, three atoms or equivalents of the (specified) element or radical are combined with two of another, as in iron sesquioxide, $Fe_2 O_3$.

Qualifying words: hippopotomonstrosesquipedalian, sesquialter, sesquialtera, sesquibasic, sesquicarbonate, sesquicentennial, sesquiduplicate, sesquinona, sesquioxide, sesquipedal, sesquipedalia, sesquipedalian, sesquipedalianism, sesquipedalianist, sesquipedality, sesquiquadrate, sesquibasic, sesquichloride, sesquihydrate, sesquihydrated, sesquioxide, sesquiplicate, sesquisalt, sesquisulfide, sesquisulphate, sesquitertian

-sess (sit) See **sed-** for examples.

set free See **solv-** for examples.

set in motion See **ag-** for examples.

seven See **hepta-** and **septem-** for examples. Also see NUMBERS in **Appendix G** for other numerical elements.

sex-, sexi-, sext- (L., six) Also see **hex-** for additional "six" words and the NUMBERS section in **Appendix G**. Don't confuse this **sex-** with another **sex** which refers to "mating" or "gender."

Qualifying words: sexagenarian, sexagonal, sexangular, sexadecimal, sexcentenary, sexdigitate, sexennial, sexennium, sexidigitate, sexivalent, sexradiate, sextet, sextillion, sextuple, sextuplet, sextuplicate

sext- (L., sixth) See **sex-** (above) for examples.

sexual procreation See **gono-** for examples.

shade See **scio-, skio-,** and **umbra-** for examples.

shadow See **scio-, skio-,** and **umbra-** for examples.

shake See **pall-** and **seismo-** for examples.

shaking, trembling See **hor-** for examples.

shape, figure See **form-, morpho-,** and **-oid** for examples and also see **eido-, icono-,** and **idol** for words with similar meanings.

shaping, forming See **ag-, fac-, -ize, plasmo-,** and **stru-** for examples.

sharp, sour See **acerb-, acid-, acri-, acut-, oxy-,** and **picro-** for examples.

sheath, scabbard See **vagino-** for examples.

sheep See **ovi-,** but don't confuse this **ovi-** with the one which means "egg."

shell See **concho-** for examples.

shell, snail See **cochle-** for examples.

shield See **aspido-** for examples.

shine, light See **ethero-, luco-, lumen-, lun-, lustr-, phospho-, photo-,** and **scintill-** for examples.

ship, sailor See **naus-, naut-,** and **nav-**.

shore, sandband See **thino-** for examples.

short See **brachy-** and **brevi-** for examples.

shoulder See **omo-** (L.) for examples.

shoulder blade See **scapulo-** for examples.

shout See **clam-** for examples.

show, make visible See **phanero-** and **phant-** for examples.

shut, close See **clud-** for examples.

sialo-, sial- (Gk., saliva; spittle, foam from the mouth; the salivary glands) Also examine **saliva** for other "spittle" words.

Qualifying words: sialaden, sialadenectomy, sialadenitis, sialadenography, sialadenotomy, sialadenotropic, sialagogic, sialagogue, sialine, sialoaerophagia, sialoaerophagy, sialodochoplasty, sialogenous, sialogogic, sialogogue, sialogram, sialograph, sialography, sialoid, sialolith, sialolithotomy, sialology, sialometer, sialometry, sialophagia, sialorrhea, sialosis, sialotic

sicca-, sicc- (L., drying, dry, withered) Also see **xero-** for other "dry" words.

Qualifying words: desiccant, desiccate, desiccation, exsiccate, exsiccation, exsiccative, siccation, siccative, siccific

sid- (L., sit) See **sed-** for examples.

side See **costo-** (rib) and **latero-** for examples.

side of head See **temporo-** for examples.

sidero-, sider- (Gk., iron) Also see **ferro-**. Don't confuse this element with the next **sidero-** which means "star."

Qualifying words: siderite, siderochrome, siderocyte, sideroderma, siderodromophobia, siderofibrosis, siderogenous, siderolite, siderophage, siderophagia, siderophil(e), siderophilous, siderophily, siderphone, sideroscope, siderosilicosis, siderosis, siderotic, siderotrophic, silicosiderosis

sidero-, sider- (L., star) In addition, see **aster-,
astra-, astro-,** and **stell-.** Don't confuse
this **sidero-** (L.) with the previous **sidero-**
(Gk.) which means "iron."

> **Qualifying words:** consider, considerable,
consideration, considered, considering, desideratum, desirability, desirable, desire, de-
sirous, sidereal, siderograph, siderography,
sideromancer, sideromancy, sideromantic, siderophobia, siderostat

sideways, side See **latero-** for examples.
sight, view See **-orama, -scope, spec-,** and
vid- for examples.
sign, signal See **semeio-** and **sign-.**
sign- (L., mark, token, sign) Also see **semeio-.**

> **Qualifying words:** assign, consign, con-
signment, countersign, design, designate, de-
signation, ensign, insignia, insignificant, re-
sign, resignation, signal, signature, signet,
significance, significant, signify

signal See **semeio-** and **sig-** for examples.
silico-, silic- (L., flint, quartz, sand; a crystalline compound [SiO_2]) For other "sand"
words, examine **amatho-, arena,** and
psammo-.

> **Qualifying words:** pneumonoultramicro-
scopicsilicovolcanoconiosis, silex, silica, silicate, silicatosis, siliceous, silicic, silicious, si-
licity, silicole, silicolous, siliciferous, silicify,
silicoflagellate, silicoflouric, silicon, silicone,
siliconoma, silicosiderosis, silicosis, silicotu-
berculosis, siliculose, siliculous, tuberculo-
silicosis

silk See **serico-** for examples.
silv- (L., forest, woods) See **sylv-.**
silver See **argent-** and **argyro-** for examples.
simal-, simil-, simul-, -semble (L., same, like,
alike; same time) Also see **equ-, homeo-,
homo-** (Gk.), **iso-, -oid, pari-, peer,** and
tauto- for words with similar meanings.

> **Qualifying words:** assemble, assembly,
assimilate, assimilation, dissemble, dissimi-
lar, dissimilate, ensemble, facsimile, resemblance, resemble, semblance, similar, simi-
larity, simile, similitude, simple, simplicity,
simplify, simulacrum, simulate, simulation,
simulator, simultaneity, simultaneous, si-
multaneously, verisimilar, verisimilitude

simil- (same) See **simal-** for examples.
similar See **equ-, homo-** (Gk.), **iso-, -oid,
pari-, simal-,** and **tauto-.**
simia-, simi- (L., ape, monkey) Also examine
pitheco- for other "ape" words.

> **Qualifying words:** simiad, simial, simian,
simianity, simious

simple, single See **haplo-** for examples.

simul- (same) See **simal-** for examples.
sinew, tendon See **achilles, tendo-,** and **teno-.**
single, alone See **haplo-, hyphen, mono-,
soli-,** and **uni-** for examples.
sinistro-, sinistr- (L., left, on the left side; at,
toward, or using the left; left-handed)
Also see **levo-** for similarities and compare with **dexter-** for words with opposite
meanings.

> **Qualifying words:** sinister, sinistra, sinis-
trad, sinistral, sinistrality, sinistraural, sinistraurality, sinistrocardia, sinistrocerebral,
sinistrocular, sinistrocularity, sinistrodextral,
sinistrogyration, sinistromanual, sinistro-oc-
ular, sinistropedal, sinistrophobia, sinistroro-
tation, sinistrorse, sinistrosis, sinistrotorsion,
sinistrous

siphono-, siphon- (Gk., tube, siphon) Also see
syringo- for other "tube" words.

> **Qualifying words:** siphon, Siphonaptera,
siphonaceous, siphoneous, siphonet, Sipho-
niulida, siphonogamous, siphonogamy, Siph-
onophora, siphonophore, Siphonophorida,
siphonostele, Siphonostomatoida

-sis (Gk. > L., state or condition) A suffix
formed from **-osis,** which you should see
for examples. Also see the SUFFIXES
section in **Appendix K** for other word
endings.
sist- (L., cause to stand, put, place; to stand
still) Also see **loco-, pon-, stato-, the-,**
and **topo-** for additional "place, stand"
words.

> **Qualifying words:** assist, assistance, as-
sistant, assisting, consist, consistency, consistent, consistory, desist, exist, existence,
existent, *in situ,* insist, insistence, insistent,
interstice, interstitial, irresistibility, irresist-
ible, persist, persistence, persistency, persistent, resist, resistance, resistant, resistible,
subsist, subsistence, subsistent

sister See **soror-** for examples.
sit See **sed-** for examples.
sitio-, siti-, sito-, sit- (Gk., food) Also examine
alimento-, bromato-, cibo-, and **tropho-.**

> **Qualifying words:** apositia, autosite, au-
tositic, coenosite, ectoparasite, eusitia, om-
phalosito, parasite, parasitic, parasiticide,
parasitism, parasitize, parasitology, parasito-
sis, sitiergeia, sitiology, sitiomania, sitiophobia, sitology, sitomania, sitophobia, sitotaxis,
sitotherapy, sitotoxin, sitotoxism, sitotropic,
sitotropism

sito- (food) See **sitio-** for examples.
six See **hex-** and **sex-** for examples.
skia- (Gk., shadow) See **skio-** for examples.
skler- (Gk., hard) See **sclero-** for examples.

skato- (Gk., dung, excretion) See **scato-** for examples.

skel-, scel- (Gk., leg)

> Qualifying words: isosceles, microskeles, scelalgia, sceloncus, skelalgia, skelasthenia, skelatony

skeleto-, skelet- (Gk. > Mod. L., dried up, withered, mummy; the bony and some of the cartilaginous framework of the body of animals)

> Qualifying words: endoskeleton, exo-skeleton, skeletal, skeletogenous, skeletoge-ny, skeletography, skeletology, skeletomotor, skeletomuscular, skeleton, skeletopia, skele-topy,

skill, art, craft See **art-** and **-techn-** for examples.

skillful See **dexter-** for examples.

skin See **cuti-**, **dermo-**, and **hymeno-** for examples.

skio-, ski-, skia- (Gk., shade, shadow) Also see **scio-** and **umbra-**.

> Qualifying words: skiagram, skiagraph, skiagraphy, skiametry, skiaphyte, skiascope, skiascopy, skiophil, skiophilous, skiophyll, skiophyte, skioscope, skioscopy

skoto- (Gk., dark, darkness; blindness) Also see **nocti-**, **nycti-**, and **scoto-**.

> Qualifying words: skotophilia, skotophi-lic, skotophile, skotophily, skotophobia, sko-toplankton, skototaxis, skototropic, skototro-pism

sky, heaven See **celest-** and **urano-**.

slack, loose See **lax-**, **-lysis,** and **solv-**.

slant, slope; bed See **clino-** and **loxo-** for examples.

slave See **dulo-** for examples.

sleep, sleeping See **coma**[1], **dorm-**, **hypno-**, **narco-**, **somni-**, and **sopor-** for examples.

slip, fall See **laps-** for examples.

slope, slant; bed See **clino-** for examples.

slow, delayed See **brachy-** and **brady-** for examples.

sluggish, stupor See **narco-** and **torp-** for examples.

small For related words, examine **-cle, -cule, -et** (Fr.), **-lepto-, micro-, mini-, nano-, oligo-, pauci-, pico-,** and **-ule.**

smell See **bromo-** (stench), **odori-** (smell), **osphresco-** (smell), **osmo-** (odor), and **ol-fact-** (to smell) for examples.

smoke, vapor See **capno-**, **fumi-**, and **typho-** for examples.

smooth See **leio-** for examples.

snake, serpent See **angui-, herpeto-** (reptile), **ophio-,** and **sauro-** (lizard) for examples.

snout, beak See **rhyncho-** for examples.

snow See **chiono-** and **nivi-** for examples.

soap See **sapo-** for examples.

soft See **malaco-** for examples.

soft part of the body See **laparo-** for examples.

soil, earth See **agra-, chthon-, geo-, humus,** and **terr-** for examples.

sol-, soli-, solo- (L., sun) Also see **helio-**. Don't confuse this **sol-, soli-** with the **soli-, sol-** meaning "one" or "alone."

> Qualifying words: girasol, insol, insolate, insolation, hippolarium (hippo-solarium), parasol, Sol, solair, solaire, solano, solar, so-laria, solarimeter, solarism, solarium, solar-ization, solarize, soliform, sol-lunar, soloform, solograph, solstice, solstitial, turnsole

soldier See **milit-** for examples.

soli-, sol- (L., one, alone, only) For more "one-type" words, see **eremo-** (solitary), **mono-,** and **uni-** and also examine the NUMBERS section in **Appendix G** for ad-ditional numerical elements. Don't con-fuse the **sol-** in this element with another **sol-** which means "sun."

> Qualifying words: desolate, desolated, desolation, isolate, isolation, isolationism, isolationist, sole, solely, soliloquize, soliloquy, soliped, solipsism, solitaire, solitary, solitude, solo, sullen

solid, firm See **stereo-** for examples.

solitary, lonely See **eremo-** and **soli-** for examples.

solu- (L., loosen) See **solv-** for examples.

solv-, -solu-, solut-, -sol, -soluble, -solubility (L., loosen, untie, set free) Also see **lax-** and **-lysis** for other "loosen" words.

> Qualifying words: absolute, absolution, absolutism, absolve, aerosol, dissolute, disso-lution, dissolve, dissolved, dissolving, hydro-sol, indisoluble, insoluble, insolvable, insol-vency, insolvent, irresolute, irresolution, res-olute, resolution, resolve, solubility, soluble, solute, solution, solvability, solvable, solve, solvency, solvent

soma-, som-, somat-, somato-, -soma, -some, -somus, -somia, -somic, -somal, -somite, -somatous, -somatia, -somatic (Gk., body) Also see **corp-** for related words.

> Qualifying words: acrosome, actinosoma, autosome, chromosome, heterosomatous, mesosoma, metasomatic, microsome, micro-somia, prosoma, psychosomatic, soma, so-mactids, somacule, somaesthesis, somaes-

thetic, somal, somaplasm, somasthenia, somatalgia, somatesthesia, somatesthetic, somatic, somatism, somatization, somatoderm, somatogenic, somatogram, somatology, somatome, somatometry, somatopathic, somatopathy, somathophrenia, somatophyte, somatoplasm, somatopsychic, somatopsychosis, somatoschisis, somatoscopy, somatosensory, somatosexual, somatotherapist, somatotherapy, somatotomy, somatotonia, somatotrophic, somatotropic, somatotype, somatropic, somatropin (HGH), somesthesia, somesthetic, somosphere

-some (Gk., body) See **soma-** for examples.

somni-, somno-, somn-, -somnia, -somniac (L., sleep; dream) Also see **coma**[1], **dorm-, hypno-, narco-,** and **sopor-** for other "sleep" words.

  Qualifying words: cacosomnia, dyssomnia, dyssomniac, hypersomnia, hyposomnia, hyposomny, insomnia, insomniac, insomnolence, levisomnous, parasomnia, somnambulant, somnambulate, somnambulates, somnambulating, somnambulation, somnambulator, somnambulism, somnambulist, somnifacient, somniferous, somnific, somniloquence, somniloquism, somniloquist, somniloquy, somnipathist, somnipathy, somnocinematograph, somnokinematograph, somnolence, somnolency, somnolent, somnolentia, somnolently, somnolescent, somnolism, somnovigil, Somnus

son, daughter See **fili-** for examples.

son-, sona-, -sonous, -sonic, -sonically (L., sound) Also see **echo** and **phono-** for other "sound" words.

  Qualifying words: assonance, assonant, consonance, consonant, dissonance, dissonant, electrosonic, hypersonic, infrasonic, radiosonic, resonance, resonant, resonate, resonator, sonar, sonata, sone, sonic, sonically, sonication, sonifer, soniferous, sonitus, sonnet, sonobuoy, sonochemical, sonoencephalograph, sonogram, sonograph, sonoluminescence, sonoluminescent, sonometer, sonora, sonority, sonorous, sonorously, sonorousness, stereosonic, subsonic, supersonic, transonic, ultrasonography, unison

song, poem See **ode** for examples.

-sonic (L., sound) See **son-** for examples.

-sonous (L., sound) See **son-** for examples.

sooty See **capno-** for examples.

sopho-, soph-, -sophic, -soph, -sopher, -sophy, -sophical, -sophically, -sophist (Gk., wise, wisdom; knowledge) Also see **sag-** and **sap-** for more "wise" words.

  Qualifying words: anthroposophy, pansophic, pansophism, pansophy, philosopher, philosophic, philosophical, philosophize, philosophy, physiosophic, sophia, sophism,

sophist, sophistic, sophisticate, sophisticated, sophistication, sophistry, sophomania, sophomore, sophomoric, theosophic, theosophy

sopor-, sop- (L., sleep, deep sleep) Also see **coma**[1], **dorm-, hypno-, narco-,** and **somni-** for more "sleep" words.

  Qualifying words: sopite, sopor, soporiferous, soporiferously, soporific, soporifical, soporifically, soporous

soro-, sorori- (L., sister) Also see FAMILY GROUPS.

  Qualifying words: soroptimist, sororate, sororial, sororicidal, sororicide, sororities, sorority

soul, spirit See **anima-** and **spir-** for examples.

sound (in body), healthful See **hygieio-**.

sound, voice See **echo, phono-, son-,** and **ton-**.

sour See **acerb-, acid-,** and **acri-**.

south See **austro-** for examples.

sorrow, grief See **doloro-** for examples.

sowing, seed See **spermo-** and **sporo-**.

spano-, span- (Gk., scarce, scarcity)

  Qualifying words: spanaemia, spanandry, spanemia, spanemic, spanemy, spanogamy, spanogyny, spanomenorrhea, spanopnea, spanopnoea

sparkle, twinkle See **scintill-** for examples.

speak, talk For examples, see **cit-, clam-, dic-, fa-, lalo-, legi-, locu-, logo-, loqu-, mythico-, ora-, -phasia, -phemia,** and **voc-**.

spec-, spic-, spect-, spectat-, spectro-, spect-, -spectr, -spectful, -spection, -spective (L., see, sight, look, appear, behold, and examine) Also see **-orama, scop-,** and **vid-** for more "see, look" words.

  Qualifying words: aspect, auspices, auspicious, circumspect, circumspection, conspicuous, conspicuousness, despicable, despise, despite, episcopal, especial, espionage, expect, expectant, expectation, haruspex, haruspicate, haruspication, haruspicy, inauspicious, inspect, inspection, inspector, introspection, introspective, kaleidoscope, microscope, periscope, perspective, perspicacious, perspicacity, perspicuity, perspicuous, prospect, prospective, prospectus, respect, respectable, respectful, respective, respite, retrospect, retrospection, sceptic, special, specie, species, specific, specification, specify, specimen, specious, spectacle, spectacles, spectacular, spectator, specter, spectral, spectrocolorimeter, spectrograph, spectroheliogram, spectroheliograph, spectrology, spectrophobia, spectrophone, spectroscope, spectrum, speculate, speculation, speculative, speculator, spite, spy, suspect, suspicion

speech   Examine **cit-, clam-, dic-, fa-, lalo-, legi-, locu-, logo-, loqu-, mythico-, ora-, -phasia, -phemia,** and **voc-** for samples.

speed, rapid   See **celer-, tacho-,** and **veloci-** for examples.

speleo-, spele-, spelaeo-, spelae-, spel-, -spelean, -spelaean (Gk. > L., cave, cavern) Also see **antro-** for other "cave" words.

> **Qualifying words:** biospeleologist, biospeleology, spelaeological, spelaeologist, spelaeology, speleobiologist, speleobiology, spelaeology, spelean, speleograph, speleography, speleohydrology, speleologist, speleology, speleometeorology, speleothemes, spelunk, spelunker, *Ursus spelaeus*

spermo-, sperm-, spermato-, spermat- (L., seed, germ) Also see **semen** and **sporo-**.

> **Qualifying words:** angiosperm, gymnosperm, monospermous, polyspermy, spermal, spermateleosis, spermatheca, spermatid, spermatiferous, spermatogenesis, spermatogenous, spermatoid, spermatophyte, spermatorrhea, spermatorrhoea, spermatosome, spermatoxin, spermatozoid, spermatozoon, spermiocalyptrotheca, spermocarp, spermoderm, spermology, spermophile, spermophyte, spermotoid, trispermous

-sperse, -spersed, -spersing, -spersion (L., from *spagere*, to scatter, strew, sprinkle)

> **Qualifying words:** asperse, disperse, intersperse

sphero-, spher-, -sphere (Gk., ball, round) Also see **glob-** for more "ball" words.

> **Qualifying words:** allobiosphere, athenosphere, athenospheric, atmosphere, autobiosphere, barysphere, bathysphere, biogeosphere, biosphere, biospherian, biospherarium, blastosphere, centrosphere, chemosphere, chromosphere, chromospheric, cosmosphere, ecosphere, eubiosphere, exosphere, geosphere, hemisphere, hemispherical, hydrosphere, ionosphere, lithosphere, magnetosphere, mesosphere, microsphere, noosphere, ozonosphere, petrosphere, photosphere, pyrosphere, spheroid, sphere, spherical, sphericity, spherocylinder, spherocyte, spheroid, spheroidal, spherometer, spherule, stratosphere, technosphere, tectosphere, thermosphere, troposphere, vivosphere, zoosphere

sphygmo-, sphygm-, -sphyxia (Gk., pulse)

> **Qualifying words:** asphyxia, asphyxiant, asphyxiate, sphygmic, sphygmocardiograph, sphygmocardioscope, sphygmochronograph, sphygmodynamometer, sphygmogram, sphygmograph, sphygmography, sphygmoid, sphygmology, sphygmomanometer, sphygmometer, sphygmopalpation, sphygmophone, sphygmoscope, sphygmoscopy, sphymosignal, sphygmotonograph, sphygmotonometer, sphygmoviscosimetry, sphygmus, sphymic,

-sphyxia (pulse) See **sphygmo-** for examples.

spic- (see) See **spec-** for examples.

spider   See **arachno-** and **arano-** for examples.

spine   See **coccygo-** (end of spine), **rachio-,** and **spondylo-** for examples.

spinning   See **gyro-** for examples.

spiny, thorny   Examine **acantho-, chaeto-,** and **echino-** for examples.

spir-, spira-, spirat-, -spire, -spiring, -spiration, -spirational (L., breath of life, breath, "soul") Also see **bio-, pneo-, pneumato-, pneumo-, vita-,** and **viv-** for related words.

> **Qualifying words:** aspirate, aspiration, aspire, conspiracy, conspirator, conspire, esprit, *esprit de corps*, expiration, expire, expiration, inspiration, inspirational, inspire, perspiration, perspire, photorespiration, respiration, respirator, respiratory, spiracle, spirant, spirit, spiritual, spiritualistic, spirogram, spirograph, spirography, spirometer, spirometrics, suspire, transpiration, transpire

spiral, coil   See **cochle-** and **helico-** for examples.

spirit   See **pneumato-** and **spir-** for examples.

spittle, saliva   See **saliva** and **sialo-** for examples.

spleen   See **lieno-** and **spleno-** for examples.

spleno-, splen-, splenico-, spleni-, -splenism, -splenia, -splenic (Gk., spleen, "the inward parts;" the elongated accessory lymphatic organ of the vascular [blood] system. The spleen is a large glandlike, but ductless, organ situated in the upper part of the abdominal cavity on the left side and lateral to the cardiac end of the stomach. It is also called the *lien*. The largest structure in the lymphoid system, it is a flattened oblong shaped structure of about 125 mm. in length. It disintegrates the red blood cells and sets the hemoglobin free, which the liver converts into bilirubin; it gives rise to new red blood cells during fetal life and in the newborn; serves as a reservoir of blood; produces lymphocytes and plasma cells; and has other important functions, the full scope of which has not been entirely determined. Also see **lieno-** for related words.

> **Qualifying words:** asplenia, hepatosplenitis, hypersplenia, megalospelenia, hepatosplenomegaly, phrenosplenic, splenalgia, splenectomize, splenectomy, splenectopy, splenicogastric, splenicopancreatic, spleniform, splenitis, splenodynia, splenogenous, spleno-

gram, splenography, splenohepatomegalia, splenohepatomegaly, splenoid, splenology, splenolysis, splenoma, splenomalacia, splenomegaly, splenometry, splenonephric, splenopathy, splenaphrenic, splenorrhagia, splenorrhaphy, splenotomy, splenotoxin

split See **schisto-** and **schizo-** for examples.

spodo-, spod- (Gk., ashes; waste materials) Also see **ciner-** and **tephro-** for examples.

> **Qualifying words:** spodium, spodogenous, spodogram, spodography, spodomancy, spodophagous, spodophorous

spond-, spon-, spons-, spondency, -spondence, -spondent, -spondencies, (L., bind oneself; promise, pledge)

> **Qualifying words:** correspond, correspondent, despond, despondent, espouse, irresponsible, reposte, respond, response, responsible, responsive, sponsor, sponsorship, spontaneous, spontaneously, spouse

spondylo-, spondyl- (Gk., spine, vertebra) Also see **rachio-** for other "spine" words.

> **Qualifying words:** platyspondulia, spondylalgia, spondylarthritis, spondyloarthropathy, spondylitic, spondylitis, spondylodynia, spondylolysis, spondylomalacia, spondylopathy, spondylosis, spondylotherapy, spondylotomy

spores, pollen See **palyn-** and **pollen** for examples.

sporo-, spor- (Gk., seed, a sowing) Also see **semen** and **spermo-** for additional "seed" words.

> **Qualifying words:** homosporous, spore, sporiferous, sporiparous, sporoduct, sporogenous, sporoid, sporokinete, sporophyll, sporophyte, sporotheca, sporozoan, sporozoid, synsporous, tachysporous, zoospore

spouse (wife) See **uxor-** for examples.

spread See **pand-** for examples.

spread, disperse See **-chore** for examples.

spring, mineral spring See **creno-** and **pego-** for examples.

sprinkle, scatter See **-sperse** for examples.

sta- (standing, fixed) See **stato-** for examples.

stalac-, stalag- (Gk., dropping, dripping)

> **Qualifying words:** stalactic, stalactical, stalactiform, stalactite, stalactitic, stalagmite, stalagmitic, stalagmometer

stalag- (Gk., dropping) See **stalac-** for examples.

stalk, stem See **cauli-** for examples.

stand, put, place See **sist-** and **stato-** for examples.

standard, flag See **vexill-** for examples.

standing, not moving See **stato-** for examples.

star See **aster-, astro-, sidero-,** and **stell-**.

startch See **amylo-** for examples.

stasi- (Gk., standing) See **stato-** for examples.

-stasis (standing, fixed) Examine **stato-** for examples.

stato-, -stat-, sta-, -static, -stasi, -stasis, -stasia, -stacy, -stitute, -sist, -stasic, -stit- (Gk., standing, stay, make firm, fixed) Also see **sist-** for other "stand" words.

> **Qualifying words:** aerostat, aerostatic, aerostatics, amyostasia, ananastasia, apostasy, armistice, arrest, arteriostasis, astasia, bacteriostat, barostat, circumstance, circumstantial, coelostat, constable, constancy, constant, constituency, constituent, constitute, constitution, contrast, cryostat, cytostasis, desisted, destination, destine, destitute, distance, distant, ecstatic, enterostasis, equidistant, establish, estate, existentialism, extant, fungistasis, fungistat, gyrostat, heliostat, hemostasis, hemostat, humidistat, hydrostat, hypostasis, iconostasis, inconsistency, inconsistent, instance, instant, instantaneous, instate, institute, institution, institutional, isostasy, lymphostasis, metastasis, microstat, mycostasis, mycostat, obstacle, obstetrics, obstinancy, obstinate, orbitostat, phlebostasis, prostitute, prostitution, pyrostat, reinstate, reinstatement, rest, restate, restitute, restitution, restive, rheostat, siderostat, solstice, stability, stable, stage, stagnant, staid, stamen, stamina, stance, stanchion, stanza, state, stately, statement, static, station, stationary, stationery, statistics, statoblast, statoscope, statuary, statue, stature, status, status quo, statute, statutory, staunch, substance, substantial, substantiate, substantive, substitute, substitution, substitutive, superstition, thermostat, transubstantiation, venostasis

steal, thief See **klepto-** and **plagiar-** for examples.

steam, vapor See **atmo-** for examples.

stearo- (Gk., fat) See **steato-** for examples.

steato-, steat-, stearo- (Gk., fat) Also examine **adipo-, eleo- (oil), lipo-,** and **oleo-** (oil) for other "fat" words.

> **Qualifying words:** stearate, stearic, stearin, steatite, steatitis, steatocystoma, steatogenesis, steatogenous, steatolysis, steatolytic, steatoma, steatonecrosis, steatopyga, steatopygia, steatopyga, steatopygia, steatopygic, steatopygous, steatorrhea, steatosis, steatozoon

stego-, steg-, stegano- (Gk., covered, to cover, roof, or house) Also see **calypo-**.

> **Qualifying words:** steganography, steganopod, stegnosis, stegodon, stegosaur, Stegosaurus

stell- (L., star) Also see **aster-, astra-, astro-,** and **sidero-** (L.) for more "star" words.

> **Qualifying words:** circumstellar, constellation, Estella, Estelle, interstellar, Stella, stellar, stellarator, stellate, stelliferous, stelliform, stellify, stellula, stellular, stellulate

stem, stalk See **cauli-** for examples.

stench, bad odor See **bromo-** and **osmo-**.

steno-, sten- (Gk., narrow, contracted) See **eury-** for *antonymous* words.

> **Qualifying words:** sclerostenosis, stenobaric, stenobary, stenobathic, stenobathy, stenobenthic, stenobionic, stenocephalic, stenochoric, stenochorous, stenoecious, stenographer, stenography, stenohaline, stenohydric, stenohygric, stenoionic, stenolumic, stenomorph, stenomorphic, stenophagous, stenophagy, stenophotic, stenophyllous, stenosis, stenostomatous, stenotele, stenotherm, stenothermal, stenothermia, stenothermic, stenothermophile, stenothermophilic, stenothermy, stenotopic, stenotropic, stenoxenous

stentor (Gk., Greek herald in the Trojan war [Greek mythology]; powerful voice [literally, "groaner, roarer"]) Also examine **cerauno-** for "thunder" words which are similar in meanings.

> **Qualifying words:** Stentor, stentorian

step, step around See **ambul-** and **grad-** for examples.

stereo-, stere- (Gk., solid, firm; three-dimensional)

> **Qualifying words:** cholesterol stereobate, stereochemistry, stereochromy, stereognosis, stereognostic, stereogram, stereograph, stereography, stereoisomerism, stereological, stereology, stereometry, stereomicroscope, stereo-music, stereophonic, stereopticon, stereoscope, stereoscopic, stereoscopy, stereotactic, stereotaxis, stereotropic, stereotropism, stereotype, stereotyped, stereotypical

sterno-, stern- (Gk., chest, breast, breast bone) Also see **pectoro-, stetho-,** and **thoraco-** for other "chest, breast" words.

> **Qualifying words:** sternalgia, sternoclavicular, sternodymia, sternodynia, sternoid, sternomastoid, sternopericardial, sternoschisis, sternotomy, sternoxiphopagus, sternum

stetho-, steth- (Gk., chest) Also see **pectoro-, sterno-,** and **thoraco-** for other "chest" words.

> **Qualifying words:** stethacoustic, stethalgia, stethemia, stethendoscope, stethogoniometer, stethograph, stethography, stethometer, stethomyositis, stethoparalysis, stethophone, stethophonometer, stethopolyscope, stethoscope

stheno-, sthen-, -sthenia, -sthenic, -asthenic (Gk., strength) For other words with similar meanings, see **dyna-, firm-, fort-, poten-,** and **valid-.**

> **Qualifying words:** adenohypersthenia, amyosthenia, amyosthenic, angiasthenia, angioasthenia, angiosthenia, asthenia, asthenic, asthenobiosis, asthenometer, asthenophobia, asthenopia, calisthenics, cardiasthenia, hypersthenia, myasthenia, myasthenic, neuroasthenia, sthenia, sthenic, sthenophotic

stick, rod See **rhabdo-** for examples.

stick to See **her-** for examples.

stiff, har See **ankylo-, dur-, rigi-,** and **sclero-.**

stigma (Gk. > L., mark, reproach [from Greek, "puncture, brand"])

> **Qualifying words:** astigmatic, astigmatism, instigate, stigma, stigmata, stigmatic, stigmatiferous, stigmatism, stigmatist, stigmatize, stigmatization, stigmatose

sting, pierce See **pung-** for examples.

sting, sharp See **acerb-, acid, acri-, acut-,** and **oxy-** for examples.

stink, bad odor See **bromo-** and **osmo-** for examples.

stitching, suture See **-rhaph** for examples.

stomach (belly) For examples, see **abdomino-, coelio-, gastro-,** and **ventri-.**

stomato-, stomat-, stom-, stoma, -stomatous, -stomous, -stome, -stomy (Gk., mouth) Also see **ora-, os-,** and **oscula-** for other "mouth" words.

> **Qualifying words:** anastomosis, colostomy, cyclostome, hypostoma, protostoma, pseudostoma, stenostomatous, stomach, stomal, stomatalgia, stomatitis, stomatodynia, stomatodysodia, stomatognathic, stomatolalia, stomatologist, stomatology, stomatomalacia, stomatomenia, stomatomology, stomatomy, stomatomycosis, stomatonecrosis, stomatonoma, stomatopathy, stomatoplastic, stomatoplasty, stomatopod, stomatorrhagia, stomatoscopy, stomatoscopy, stomatotomy, stomatous

stone, pebble See **calci-** for examples

stone, rock See **lapid-, litho-, petro-** and **saxi-** for examples.

stork See **ciconi-** for examples.

story See **mythico-** for examples.

straight, correct See **ortho-** and **recti-** for examples.

strain (draw tight) See **string-** for examples.

strange, foreign See **barber-, Gallo-,** and **xeno-** ("zeno") for examples.

strati-, strato-, strat- (L., horizontal layer; "stretched, spread out;" layer, cloud layer) Don't confuse this **strati-, strato-** with the next **strato-** which means "army."

Qualifying words: prostrate, stratal, straticulate, stratification, stratiform, stratify, stratigram, stratigraphy, stratocirrus, stratocumulus, stratopause, stratosphere, stratospheric, stratovolcano, stratum, stratus, substratum

strato- (Gk., army) Also see **arm-** for other "army" words. Don't confuse this **strato-** with the previous **strati-.**

Qualifying words: strategem, strategy, stratocratic, stratocracy, stratography

stray, wander See **err-, migr-, nomad-,** and **vaga-** for examples.

street See **agyio-** for examples.

strength For examples, see **dyna-, firm-, fort-, poten-, stheno-, valid-,** and **vir-.**

stretch, move in a certain direction See **tend-, tendo-, teno-,** and **ton-** for examples.

stretch, spread See **-pand-** for examples.

strict- (draw tight) See **string-** for examples.

strike See **flic-, flig-** for examples.

string, cord See **lin-** and **mito-** for examples.

string-, strict-, strain-, -stringence, -stringency, -stringe, -stringent (L., draw tight, compress)

Qualifying words: astringe, astringent, constrain, constraint, constrict, constriction, constrictor, constringent, distress, distressing, district, obstriction, perstringent, prestige, restrain, restraint, restrict, restriction, restrictivre, strain, strainer, strait, straiten, strand, strangle, strangulate, stress, strict, strictness, striction, stricture, string, stringent

strive after See **peti-, quir-,** and **rog-.**

strong For examples, see **dyna-, firm-, fort-, poten-, stheno-, valid-,** and **vir-.**

strong tendency toward See **philo-.**

stroph-, -strophy, -strophe, -strophical, -strophism, -strophic, -strophes (Gk., turn, twist) Also see **flect-, gyro-, -plex, tors-, trop-, verg-, vers-,** and **volv-.**

Qualifying words: anastrophe, angiostrophe, angiostrophy, antistrophe, apostrophe, catastrophe, catastrophic, diastrophe, diastrophism, epistrophe, exstrophy, geostrophic, geostrophy, monostrophe, phallanastrophe, strophic, strophical, syringosystrophy

stru-, struct-, -structure, -struction, -structive (L., build, place together, arrange) Also see **ag-, fac-,** and **-ize.**

Qualifying words: construct, construction, constructive, construe, destroy, destroyer, destruct, destructible, destruction, destructive, destructor, industrial, industry, instruct, instruction, instructor, instrument, instrumental, obstruct, obstruction, reconstruct, reconstruction, structural, structure, structured, substructure, supersturcture

struggle, contest See **agon-** and **ath-.**

study of See **-ology** for examples.

stupor, numb See **ambly-, narco-,** and **torp-.**

sub- (L., under, below [**suc-, suf-, sug-, sum-, sup-, sur-, sus-**]) Also see **hypo-, infra-,** and **subter-** for other "under" words. Don't confuse the **sur-** in this element with the **sur-** in **super-.** Note: **sub-** regularly means "under," but it often changes its form as it retains its meaning: **suc-** before **c** (succumb), **suf-** before **f** (suffocate), **sug-** before **g** (suggest), **sup-** before **p** (support), **sum-** before **m** (summon), and **sur-** before **r** (surrogate). **Sub-** is simplified to **su-** before **sp.** Before **c, p,** and **t,** it is sometimes formed into **sus-.**

Qualifying words: subaqueous, subaquatic, subarctic, subatomic, subaudition, subboreal, subcelestial, subcellar, subclavian, subcompact, subconscious, subcontinent, subcontract, subcutaneous, subcutical, subcuticula, subcuticular, subcutis, subdermal, subdivide, subdivision, subdorsal, subduction, subdue, subepiglottic, subglossal, subject, subjection, subjective, subjectivity, subjugate, subjunctive, sublet, sublimate, submation, sublime, subliminal, sublingua, sublingual, sublunar, submarine, submariner, submerge, submergence, submergible, submerse, submersible, submersion, submicroscopic, submission, submissive, submit, suboral, suborbital, subnormal, subordinate, subordination, subphylum, subscribe, subscriber, subscript, subscription, subsequence, subsequent, subservience, subservient, subside, subsidence, subsidiary, subsidize, subsidy, subsist, subsistence, subsistent, subsoil, subsonic, substance, substandard, substantial, substantiality, substantiate, substellar, substitute, substitution, substitutional, substrata, substratosphere, substratum, substructure, subsurface, subtenant, subterfuge, subterraneal, subterranean, subterraneous, subtle, subtlety, subtonic, subtotal, subtract, subtraction, subtractive, subtrahend, subtropic, subtropical, suburb, suburban, suburbanite, suburbia, subversion subversive, subvert, succeed, success, succession, succinct, succor, succumb, suffer, sufficient, suffocate, suffrage, suffuse suggest, summon, sumptuous, supplement, supplicate, supply, suppose, support, suppress, suppression, surrender, surreptitious, surrogate, suspend, suspicion, suspension, sustain, souvenir (Fr.)

subsequent, later See **post-** and **postero-**.

substance, matter See **hylo-** for examples.

subter- (L., under, beneath, secretly, less than; formed from **sub-**) Also see **hypo-** and **infra-** for other "below, under" words.

> **Qualifying words:** subterfluent, subterfluous, subterfuge, subternatural

suc- (L., under) See **sub-** for examples.

sudor-, sudo-, suda- sud-, sudori- (Gk. > L., sweat, sweating) Also see **hidero-** for other "sweat" words.

> **Qualifying words:** exudation, exude, sudarium, sudation, sudatoria, sudatorium, sudatory, sudogram, sudokeratosis, sudomotor, sudor, sudoral, sudoresis, sudoriceratosis, sudoriferous, sudorific, sudoriparous, sudorometer, sudorrhea, transude

suet, tallow; grease See **sebo-** for examples.

suf (L., under) See **sub-** for examples.

suffer, suffering See **pass-** and **patho-**.

SUFFIXES See **Appendix K**.

sug- (L., under) See **sub-** for examples.

sugar, sweet See **gluco-**, **glyco-**, and **sacchar-**.

sui- (L., self, of oneself) Also see **auto-**, **ego** (I), and **ipse** for other "self" words.

> **Qualifying words:** suicidal, suicide, suicidology, suigenderism, *sui generis*, *sui juris*, suimate

sum- (L., highest, topmost, chief point) Also see **acro-**, **alti-**, and **hypso-** for other "high" words.

> **Qualifying words:** consummate, consummation, sum, summary, summation, summit

sum- (L., under) See **sub-** for examples. Don't confuse this **sum-** with the preceding one which means "highest."

sun See **helio-** and **sol-** for examples.

sup- (L., under) See **sub-** for examples.

super-, supra-, sur- (L., above, over, more than; excessive) Also see **epi-**, **hyper-**, and **ultra-** for other "above" words. **Sur-** is a form of **super-** formed through the French and should not be confused with another assimilated **sur-** form which comes from **sub-** which means: "under, below, beneath." In some words, **super-** is amplified to mean: "on top of; higher in rank or position than; superior to; greater in quality, amount, or degree than others of its kind; to a degree greater than others of its kind; to a degree greater than normal; extra, additional."

> **Qualifying words:** superabundant, superannuate, superannuated, superb, supercar-

go, supercarpal, supercilia, supercilious, supercilium, superego, supererogate, supererogatory, superficial, superfluity, superfluous, supergalaxy, superglottal, superhuman, superimpose, superimposition, superincumbent, superintendent, superior, superiority, superjet, superlactation, superlative, superlunary, superman, supernatural, supernaturalism, supernormal, supernova, supernumerary, superovulation, superparasite, superphysical, superpower, supersatuate, superscribe, superscript, supersede, superseding, supersensible, supersensitive, supersonic, supersonics, superstition, superstitious, superstructure, supervention, supervise, supervision, supervisor, supraglottal, supraglottic, suprahepatic, supralabial, supraliminal, supranasal, supraorbital, suprascapular, supremacist, supremacy, supreme, surbase, surcharge, surface, surmise, surmount, surname, surpass, surplus, surprint, surprise, surrealism, surround, surtax, surveillance, survey, survive

supra- (L., above, over) See **super-** for examples.

sur- (L., above, over, more) See **super-** for examples.

sur- (L., under, below) See **sub-** for examples.

surface, face See **-hedral** for examples.

surgical removal Examine **-cise**, **-ectomy**, **sec-**, **seg-**, and **-tom** for examples.

surrounding For examples, see **ambi-**, **amphi-**, **circ-**, **circum-**, **cyclo-**, and **peri-**.

suture, stitching See **-rhaph** for examples.

swamp, marsh See **tipho-** for examples.

swan See **anseri-** and **cyg-** for examples.

sweat, sweat gland See **hidero-** and **sudor-**.

sweet, sweetness See **dulci-**, **gluco-**, **glyco-**, and **sacchar-**.

swelling, tumor See **carcino-**, **-oma**, and **onco-** for examples.

swift, rapid For examples, see **agito-**, **celer-**, **tacho-**, and **veloci-**.

swimming See **nata-**, **necto-**, **neusto**, and **pleusto-** for examples.

sword See **gladi-** and **xipho-** for examples.

syl- (together, with) See **syn-** for examples.

sylv-, silv- (L., wood, forest) Also see **also-**, **arbor-**, **dendro-**, **hylo-**, **ligni-**, **nemo-**, and **xylo-**.

> **Qualifying words:** Pennsylvania, savage, silva, silvan, silvate, Silvester, silvicole, silvicolous, silvics, silvicultural, silviculture, silviculturist, sylvan, Sylvania, Sylvester, sylvestral, Sylvia, sylvian, sylvics, sylvicole, sylvicolous, sylviculture, sylviculturist, transylvania, Transylvania

sym- (together, with) See **syn-** for examples.

syn- (**sy-, sym-, syl-, sys-**) (Gk., together, with, along with) Also see **com-** for additional "together" words.

> **Qualifying words:** asystole, asystolic, ectosymbiont, ectosymbiosis, endosymbiont, endosymbiosis, endosymbiotic, holosystole, holosystolic presystole, presystolic, syllable, syllogism, symbiology, symbiont, symbiosis, symbiote, symbiotic, symbol, symbolic, symbolism, symbolist, symbolize, symmetrical, symmetry, sympathetic, sympathize, sympathy, sympetalous, symphile, symphilous, symphonic, symphonious, symphony, symphytic, symphytism, symplastic, symposiarch, symposium, symptom, symptomatic, synaesthesia, synaesthetic, synagogue, synalgia, synanthous, synanthropy, syncarp, syncarpous, syncarpy, synchrocyclotron, synchronic, synchronistic, synchronology, syncryptic, synchronism, syndactly, syndactylism, syndrome, syndromesystem, synecology, synergagogy, synergogy, synergetic, synergic, synergism, synesthesia, synesthesialgia, synesthesis, syngenesis, syngenetic, syngnathia, syngnaths, synkinesia, synkinesis, synkinetic, synnecrosis, synod, synonymic, synonymous, synonyms, synopsis, syntactic, syntax, syntaxis, synthermal, synthesis, syntonic, syntrophism, syntropic, syntropy, synxemic, syssarcotic, syssarcosis, system, systematic, systematization, systematology, systole, systolic, systolometer, systremma, syzygiology, syzygy, telesystole, telesystolic

syphilo-, syphil-, syphili-, syphi- (From L., *Syphil[us]*, the eponymous main character of Girolamo Fracastoro's poem *Syphilus sive Morbus Gallicus* ["Syphilus, or the French Disease"], published at Verona. *Syphilus*, a venereal disease [of which Fracastoro's hero *Syphilis*, was a victim] which is caused by the microorganism *Treponema pallidum*) Syphilis was a shepard whose name literally means a "friend of swine."

> **Qualifying words:** antisyphilitic, dermosyphilopathy, neurosyphilis, syphilide, syphilis, syphilize, syphiloderm, syphilogenesis, syphilologist, syphilology, syphilopathy, syphilophobia, syphilotherapy, syphitoxin, syphilionthus, syphiliphobia

syringo-, syring- (Gk., pipe, tube, fistula; spine) Also see **siphono-** for other "tube" words.

> **Qualifying words:** syringe, syringeal, syringectomy, syringitis, syringobulbia, syringocarcinoma, syringocele, syringoencephalomyelia, syringoid, syringoma, syringosystrophy, syringotomy, syrinx

sys- (together, with) See **syn-** [shown above] for examples.

systol-, systole, -systolic, -stole (Gk. > L., contraction; to draw together)

> **Qualifying words:** bradydiastole, diastole, diastolic, extrasystole, hypodiastole, hyposystole, peridiastole, sphygmosystole

T t

tacho, tach-, tachy- (Gk., fast, speed, swift, rapid) Also see **agito-, celer-,** and **veloci-** for other "fast" words. Compare with **brady-** ("slow") for words with opposite meanings.

> **Qualifying words:** tachistesthesia, tachistoscope, tachogram, tachograph, tachography, tachometer, tachymetry, tachyarrhythmia, tachycardia, tachycardiac, tachygen tachygenesis, tachyglossus, tachygraph, tachygrapher, tachygraphist, tachygraphy, tachylalia, tachylogia, tachymeter, tachymetry, tachyon, tachyphagia, tachyphagy, tachyphasia, tachyphemia, tachyphrasia, tachyphrenia, tachyphylaxis, tachypnea, tachypnoea, tachypneic, tachypsychia, tachyrhythmia, tachyscope, tachysporous, tachytelic, tachytrophism, tachyzoite

tachy- (Gk., fast, speed) See **tacho-** for examples.

tact- (Gk., arrangement) See **taxi-** for examples.

tact- (L., touch) See **tang-** for examples.

-tag (L., touch) See **tang-** for examples.

tail See **caudo-, peni-,** and **uro-** for examples.

-tain (L., hold) See **ten-** for examples.

take, carry See **-phore** and **port-** for examples.

take, lead See **-agogue** and **duc-** for examples.

take, seize See **cap-** for examples.

take steps See **ambul-, grad-,** and **gress-** for examples.

talk, say See **cit-, clam-, dic-, fa-, lalo-, legi-, logo-, locu-, loqu-, mythico-, ora-, -phasia, -phemia,** and **voc-** for examples.

tall, high See **acro-, alti-,** and **hypso-.**

talo-, tal- (L., the ankle, anklebone) Also examine **astragalo-** for additional "ankle" words.

> **Qualifying words:** talalgia, talocrural, talofibular, talomalleolar, talon, talonavicular, talonid, taloscaphoid, talotibial, talus

tallow, suet; grease See **sebo-** for examples.

tang-, tact-, ting-, -tig -tag, -teg- (L., touch, reach, handle) For other "touch" words, see **hapto-** and **thigmo-.**

> **Qualifying words:** attainment, contact, contactual, contagious, contain, contaminate, contiguous, contingent, entire, intact, intangible, integer, integral, integrate, integration, integrity, tact, tactful, tactile, tactility, tactilogy, taction, tactometer, tactor, tactual, tangent, tangential, tangibility, tangible, tango, tangoreceptor, taste, tasteless, tax

tapho-, -taph (Gk., burial, grave; funeral)

> **Qualifying words:** bibliotaph, bibliotaphic, cenotaph, cenotaphic, coenotaph, epitaph, epitapher, taphephobia, taphiphobia, taphonomy, taphophilia, taphophiliac, taphophobia, taphophobiac, tritaph

tardy, delayed See **brady-** for examples.

tarso-, tars- (Gk. > L., ankle, tarsal plate of the eyelid [from Gk. *tarsos*, frame of wickerwork; broad, flat surface, as also in *tarsos podos*, the flat of the foot; the edge of the eyelid]) Also see **eury-** and **platy-** for other "broad, flat" words.

> **Qualifying words:** tarsal, tarsalgia, tarsalia, tarsalis, tarsectomy, tarsectopia, tarsen, tarsitis, tarsocheiloplasty, tarsoclasis, tarsomalacia, tarsomegaly, tarsometatarsal, tarsometatarsus, tarso-orbital, tarsophalangeal, tarsoplasia, tarsoplasty, tarsorrhaphy, tarsotarsal, tarsotibial, tarsotomy, tarsus

taste, tasting See **geus-, gust-,** and **sap-** for examples.

tauro-, taur-, tauri- (Gk., >L., bull) Also see **bou-** (ox) for related words.

> **Qualifying words:** Minotaur, taurian, tauricide, Taurids, tauriform, taurine, taurobolium, tauroboly, taurocephalous, tauroesque, taurokathapsia, taurolatry, tauromachian, tauromachy, tauromorphic, tauromorphous, taurophobia, Taurus, Thoreau

tauto- (Gk., same) Also see **equ-, homeo-, homo-** (Gk.), **iso-, -oid, pari-,** and **simal-** for more "same" examples.

> **Qualifying words:** tautochrome, tautochromism, tautochrone, tautochronous, tautological, tautologist, tauromorphy, tautologize, tautology, tautonym, tautophony, tautotype

taxi-, tax-, taxo-, taxio-, -taxia, -taxis, -taxy, tact-, -tactic, -tactical, -tactics (Gk., arrangement, order, put in order) Also see **cosmo-** for related words. Compare this element with **nomo-,** "law" for similarities. Don't confuse this **tax** with the one which is paid to the government, nor the **taxi** in **taxi**cab; neither of which is related to this element. Nor is there any relationship to the Latin **tact-,** which means "touch."

> **Qualifying words:** aerotaxis, anemotaxis, atactic, atactiform, ataxaphasia, ataxia, ataxiadynamia, ataxiagram, ataxiagraph, ataxiameter, ataxiamnestic, ataxiaphasia, ataxiophemia, ataxiophobia, ataxoadynamia, ataxophobia, ataxy, barotactic, barotaxis, biotaxis, chaetotactic, electrotaxis, electrotactic, chemotaxis, chemotactic, chemotaxonomic, diaphototactic, diaphototaxis, chemotaxonomy, eutaxy, geotactic, geotaxis, homotaxis, hydrotaxis, hypotaxis,

isotactic, leukotoctic, leucotaxis, omphalotaxis, orthotactic, paratactic, phobotactic, phobotaxis, phototactic, phototaxis, phyllotaxy, rheotaxis, syndiotactic, syntactic, syntactical, syntax, tactician, tactics, taxidermist, taxidermy, taxon, taxonomy, thermotactic, thermotaxis

teach See **doc-** for examples.

tear, break See **clast-, frag-, -orrhexis,** and **rupt-** for examples.

tear, pull See **tillo-** for examples.

tear, tears (in the eyes) See **dacryo-** and **lacri-** for examples.

tearing away See **rap-** for examples.

techno-, techn-, tect-, -technic(s), -technique, -technology, -technical, -technically (Gk., art, skill, craft; *techne,* "art, skill, craft;" *tekton,* "builder") Also see **art-** for other "skill" words.

> **Qualifying words:** architect, biotechnics, eutechnics, hydrotechny, iatrotechnic, iatrotechnique, machinotechnic, microtechnic, pantechnic, philotechnic, polytechnic, pyrotechnic, pyrotechny, polytechnic, pyrotechnics, technic, technical, technician, technicolored, technique, technocracy, technology, tectonic, zootechnic, zootechny

tect- (Gk., art, skill) See **techno-** for examples.

teeth, tooth Examine **dent-** and **odonto-** for examples.

teeth gnashing See **bruxo-** for examples.

-teg- (L., touch) See **tang-** for examples.

tele-, tel-, telo-, -telic, -telical (Gk., far away, far off, at a distance) Don't confuse this **tele-** with the **teleo-** which means "end, last."

> **Qualifying words:** autotelic, hypertelic, telalgia, Tel Autograph, teleaesthesia, telebinocular, telecardiogram, telecardiography, telecardiophone, telecast, teleceptive, teleceptor, telecinesis, telecommunication, telecord, telecourse, telecurietherapy, teledactyl, teledendrite, teledendron, telefluoroscopy, telegamid, telegenesis, telegenic, telegnosis, telegony, telegram, telegraph, telegrapher, telegraphic, telegraphically, telegraphist, telegraphy, telekinesis, telekinetic, telelectrocardiogra, telelectrocardiograph, telemeter, telemetrically, telemetry, telemnemonike, telencephal, telencephalic, telencephalization, teleneuron, teleost, teleostean, teleotherapeutics, telepathic, telepathically, telepathy, telepatist, telephone, telephoned, telephonic, telephonically, telephoning, telephony, telephoto, telephotograph, telephotography, telephotographic, teleplay, teleport, teleportation, teleprinter, telepromter, teleradiography, teleradium, teleran, telergic, telergy, telescope, telescopic, telescopically, telescopist, telescopy, telespectroscope, telesthesia, telesthetic, teletactor, teletherapy, telethermometer, telethermoscope, telethon, teletranscription, teletype, teletyped, teletyper, teletypewriter, teletyping, teletypist, teleview, televiewer, televise, televised, televising, television, televisional, televisionally, televisor, Telex, teleodynamic, teloreceptor, telpher, telphreage, telstar

teleo-, tel-, telo- (Gk., end, last; result, completion, perfection, fulfillment) Also see **fin-, omega, term-,** and **ultim** for other "end" related words. Don't confuse this element with **tele-,** which means "far away, at a distance," etc.

> **Qualifying words:** atelectasis, ateleosis, ateliotic, atelocardia, ateloencephalia, atelencephalis, atelocheilia, atelocheiria, ateloencephalia, ateloglossia, atelognathia, atelomyelia, atelophobia, atelopodia, ateloprosopia, atelostomia, autotelic, bradytelic, dysteleology, horotelic, spermateleosis, tachytelic, telangiitis, teledendron, teleological, teleologist, teleology, teleonomic, teleonomy, teleoptile, teleorganic, teleosis, telesis, telestich, telobiosis, teloblast, telokinesis, telopause, telophase, telotaxis

telmato-, telmat-, telmi-, telm- (Gk., marsh, pool, standing water, mud of a pool) Also examine **helo-, tipho-,** and **limno-** for other "marsh" words.

> **Qualifying words:** telmatology, telmatophile, telmatophilous, telmatophily, telmatophyte, telmatoplankton, telmicole, telmicolous

telmi- (Gk., marsh) See **telmato-** for examples.

telo- (far away *or* end) See **tele-** and **teleo-,** both of which may have different meanings.

tempo-, tempor- (L., time, occasion) Also see **chrono-** and **horo-** for other "time" words. Don't confuse this **tempo-** element with other words that refer to the *temples,* such as the flattened sides of the forehead or the building used for religious worship or services.

> **Qualifying words:** contemporaneous, contemporary, contretemps, extemporaneous, extemporaneously, extemporary, extempore, extemporization, extemporize, *pro tempore,* tempest, tempo, temporal, temporarily, temporary, temporize, *tempus fugit*

temporo-, tempor- (L., side of the head near the eye; temple) Also see **mastoid-** for related words.

> **Qualifying words:** auriculotemporal, frontotemporal, temporal, temporoauricular, temporofacial, temporomastoid, temporopontile, temporosphenoid

temporal bone See **mastoid-** for examples.

ten See **deca-** and **decim-** for examples. Also see the NUMBERS section in **Appendix G** for other examples of numerical elements.

ten-, tent-, tin-, -tain, -tainment, -tenance, -tinence (L., hold, grasp, have) Also see **cap-** and **prehend-**.

Qualifying words: abstain, abstention, abstinence, abstinent, appertain, appurtenance, attain, attainment, attentive, contain, container, containment, content, contention, continance, continent, continue, continuity, continuum, detain, detained, detention, entertain, entertainment, impertinent, incontinent, lieutenant, maintain, maintenance, malcontent, obtain, pertain, pertinent, retain, retainer, retention, retentive, retentivity, retinue, sustain, sustaining, sustenance, tenable, tenacious, tenacity, tenant, tenement, tenet, tennis, tenon, tenor, tenure, untenable

tend-, ten-, tens-, tent-, ton-, -tend, -tension, -tend, -tent, -tense, -tensive, -tentious (L., to move in a certain direction; to stretch, hold out) Also see **achillo-, tendo-, teno-,** and **ton-**.

Qualifying words: antenna, appertain, atonic, attend, attendant, attention, attenuate, barytone, catatonic, contend, contention, contentious, countenance, detente, detonate, distend, distention, entente, extend, extension, extensive, extensor, extent, extention, extenuate, hypertension, hypotension, intend, intendant, intense, intensity, intensive, intent, intention, intone, monotonous, ostensible, ostentation, ostentatious, oxytone, peritoneum, portent, portentious, pretend, pretense, pretentious, pretone, standard, subtend, superintend, superintendent, tenable, tenacious, tenacity, tenancy, tend, tendency, tendentious, tender, tendon, tendons, tendril, tennis, tense, tensile, tensimeter, tensiometer, tension, tensor, tent

tend toward, incline See **flect-, gyro-, -plex, stroph-, tors-, trop-, verg-, vers-,** and **volv-** for examples.

tenden See **achillo-, tend-, tendo-,** and **teno-**.

tendency toward See **philo-** for examples.

tendo-, tend- (Gk. > L., tendon, sinew [related to "stretch, move in a certain direction"]) Also see **achillo-, nervo-, neuro-, tend-,** and **teno-** for other related words.

Qualifying words: tendolysis, tendon, tendonitis, tendophony, tendoplasty, tendotome, tendotomy, tenectomy

teno-, tenon-, tenonto-, tenont-, ten- (Gk., tendon, sinew [related to "move in a certain direction, stretch"]) Also see **achillo-,** and **tend-**.

Qualifying words: tenalgia, tenodynia, tenofibril, tenolysis, tenomyoplasty, tenomyotomy, tenonectomy, tenonitis, tenonometer, tenontinitis, tenontodynia, tenontography, tenontology, tenontomyoplasty, tenosynovectomy, tenosynovitis, tenontoplastic, tenontoplasty, tenophony,

tenophyte, tenoplastic, tenoplasty, tenositis, tenotome, tenotomy

tens- (L., to move in a certain direction; to stretch) See **tend-** for examples.

tension, pressure See **tono-** for examples.

tephro- (Gk., ash-gray; volcanic material such as ash, dust, cinders, etc.) Also see **ciner-** and **conio-,** and **spodo-** for other words with similar meanings.

Qualifying words: tephra, tephrite, tephritic, tephrochronological, tephrochronology

tera- (Gk., one trillion ["monster"]; 10^{12} [1 000 000 000 000] or a milion milion) Also see **terato-** (from which this **tera-** is supposed to have come) and also take a look at the METRIC GROUPS section in **Appendix F** for other numerical units.

Qualifying words: terabit, terabyte, teracycle, terahertz, teraohm, teraohmmeter, terapascal, terasecond, teravolt, terawatt

tera- (Gk. > L., monster, marvel) See **terato-** for examples.

terato-, terata-, terat-, tera- (Gk. > L., marvel, omen, monster; malformation)

Qualifying words: teracurie, teras, teratism, terata, teratic, teratical, teratocarcinoma, teratogen, teratogenic, teratism, teratogenesis, teratogenetic, teratoid, teratological, teratologist, teratology, teratoma, teratophobia, teratoscopy, teratosis

terce-, ter- (*tierce*) (L., third, thrice) Also see **tri-** for other "three" words.

Qualifying words: tercel, tercentenary, tercentennial, tercet, tierce

term-, termin- (L., end, last, final, boundary) Also see **fin-, omega, teleo-,** and **ultim-** for other words with similar meanings.

Qualifying words: conterminous, determinable, determinant, determinate, determination, determine, determined, exterminate, extermination, exterminator, indeterminable, indeterminate, indetermination, interminable, predetermine, term, terminable, terminal, *Terminalia* (Roman festival), terminate, termination, terminator, terminology, terminous, terminus, Terminus (Roman god of boundaries), undetermined

Henry Thoreau in *Walden* wrote about an old fence: "I sacrificed it to Vulcan, for it was past serving the god Terminus."

termin- (end, last) See **term-** for examples.

terr-, -ter (L., earth, dry land, land) Also see **agra-, chtho-, geo-, humus,** and **pelo-** [mud]) for other "earth" words. Don't confuse this element with words which are spelled in a similar way, such as "terrify" or "terrible." Such words are not from the same combining element.

Qualifying words: circumterrestrial, disinter, disinterment, extraterrestrial, extraterritorial, extraterritoriality, inter, interment, Mediterranean, mediterranean, semiterrestrial, subterranean, *terra cotta*, *terra incognita*, terrace, *terra firma*, terraform (verb), terraformer, terraforming, terraformist, terrain, terramycin, terrane, terraneous, terraqueous, terrarium, terrazzo, Terre Haute (Indiana), terreous, terrestrial, terrevert, terricole, terricolous, terrier, terrigenous, territorial, territoriality, territory, tureen

terror (extreme fear) of something For examples, see the PHOBIA WORDS section in **Appendix I**.

testi-, test- (L., a witness, testicle; one of the two oval male gonads supported in the scrotum by its tissues and suspended by the spermatic cord) It is thought that under Roman law no man was admissible as a witness unless his testicles were present as evidence of virility. Also see **orchio-** for other "testicle" words.

Qualifying words: attest, contest, intestate, protest, protestant, protestantism, protestation, testalgia, testament, testate, testator, testatrix, testectomy, testes(pl.), testicle, testicond, testicular, testiculoma, testiculus, testify, testimonial, testis(s.), testitis, testitoxicosis, testoid, testiopathy, testopathy

tetarto-, tetart- (Gk., one fourth)

Qualifying words: tetartohedral

tetra-, tetr- (Gk., four) Also see **qauadri-** for other "four" words and see the Numbers section in **Appendix G** for other numerical elements.

Qualifying words: tetrabasic, tetracerous, tetrachloride, tetracyclic, tetracyclis, tetrad, tetradactyl, tetradactylous, tetradymite, tetradynamous, tetraglot, tetragon, tetragonal, tetragram, tetragymous, tetrahedral, tetrahedrite, tetrahedron, tetralogy, tetrameter, tetramorphic, tetramorphy, tetrandrous, tetraphony, tetraphyllous, tetraploid, tetrapneumonous, tetrapod, tetrapolis, tetrapterous, tetraradiate, tetrarch, tetrarchic, tetrarchy, tetraselenodont, tetrasome, tetrasomic, tetrathecal, tetratheism, tetratomic, tetravalent, tetrode, tetroxide

thalasso-, thalass-, thalassi-, thalassio-, thalatto-, thalatt- (Gk., sea) Also see **mare** and **pelago-**.

Qualifying words: thallassic, Panthallassa, thalassemia, thalassian, thalassic, thalassigenous, thalassin, thalassocracy, thalassocrat, thalassographer, thalassographic, thalassographical, thalassography, thalassoid, thalassomania, thalassometer, thalassophile, thalassophilous, thalassophily, thalassophobia, thalassophyte, thalassoplankton, thalassoposia, thalassoseisma, thalassotherapy

thalatto- (Gk., sea) See **thalasso-**.

thanas- (Gk., death) See **thanato-**.

thanato-, thanat-, thanas-, -thanasia, -thanasic (Gk., death, dead) Also see -cide, letha-, mort-, neci-, and necro- for other "death" words.

Qualifying words: apothanasia, athanasia, cacothanasia, dysthanasia, electrothanasia, euthanasia, orthothanasia, thanatism, thanatobiologic, thanatobiology, thanatocenosis, thanatocoenosis, thanatogeography, thanatognomic, thanatognomonic, thanatography, thanatoid, thanatological, thanatologist, thanatology, thanatomania, thanatometer, thanatomusia, thanatophidia, thanatophidial, thanatophobia, thanatophoric, thanatopsis, thanatopsy, Thanatos, thanatos, thanatosia, thanatosis, thanatotic

thaumato-, thaumat- (Gk., wonder, miracle)

Qualifying words: thaumatologist, thaumatology, thaumatolatry, thaumatrope, thaumatropy, thaumaturge, thaumaturgic, thaumaturgist, thaumaturgy

the-, theo- (God, god) See **theo-**.

the- (Gk. > L., placing, setting; place, put) Also see **loco-, pon-, sist-,** and **topo-**.

Qualifying words: anathema, antithesis, apothecary, diathesis, epithet, hypothesis, metathesis, parenthesis, prosthesis, prothesis, synthesis, synthetic, theme, thesis, thetic

theco-, thec-, theca-, theci-, -thecial, -thecae, -thecas, -thecium, -theca, -thec, -thecal, -thecial, -thecae, -thecas, -thecs Gk., case, capsule, container, receptacle [also: a placing, a setting, a putting]; "a place where" something is kept)

Qualifying words: apothecary, bibliotheca, bibliothecary, cleistothecium, dactylotheca, ectoathecal, ectotheca, endothecium, epithet, exothecium, gnathotheca, hydrotheca, hypothec, ootheca, oothecae, oothecal, perithecium, pinacotheca, podotheca, pseudothecium, pterotheca, rheotheca, sarcotheca, schizothecal, spermatheca, spermiocalyptrotheca, sporotheca, tetrathecal, theca, thecae, thecaphore, thecasporous, thecate, thecium, theocodont, thecosome

theft, thief, steal See **klepto-** and **plagiar-**.

theo-, the-, -theism, -theist, -theistic (Gk. (*theos*), God, god, deity, divine) Also see **dei-** for additional "God *or* god" words.

Qualifying words: allotheism, anthropotheism, apotheosis, atheism, atheist, atheistic, autotheism, dithesim, entheomania, enthuse, enthusiasm, henotheism, herotheism, hylotheism, hylotheist, misotheism, monotheism, monotheist, monotheistic, myriotheism, panentheism, panentheist, pantheism, pantheist, pantheon, philotheism, philotheist, philotheistic, physitheism, polytheism, polytheist, polytheistic, psychotheism, theanthropic, theanthropism, theanthropist, theanthroposophy, theism, thearchy, theistic, theist, theocentric, theocentricity, theocentrism, theocracy, theocrasia, theocrasy, theocrat, theocratic, theodicy, Theodora, Theodore, theogonist, theogony, theolatry, theolepsy, theoleptic, theologian, theological, theologism, theologue, theology, theomachist, theomachy, theomancy, theomania, theomaniac, theomorphic, theomorphism, theonomy, theopathetic, theopathic, theopathy, theophagite, theophagous, theophagy, theophanic, theophany, Theophilus, theophilous, theophily, theophobia, theopneustic, theosophic, theosophical, theosophy, theurgy, tritheism, tritheist, zootheism, zootheist, zootheology

ther- (Gk., wild animal) See **therio-** for examples.

therap-, -therapeutics(s), -therapeutically, -therapy, -therapies, -therapist (Gk., heal, cure) Also see **cura-, iatro-, medi-,** and **sana-** for other "healing" or "curing" words.

    Qualifying words: alimentotherapy, alkalitherapy, alkalotherapy, ammotherapy, apiotherapy, balneotherapy, bibliotherapeutics, bibliotherapist, bibliotherapy, chemotherapeutic, chemotherapist, chemotherapeutic, chemotherapy, crymotherapy, chronotherapy, cryotherapy, dermatotherapy, dipsotherapy, electrotherapeutic, ergotherapy, helioaerotherapy, heliotherapy, hemeotherapy, hemotherapeutic, hemotherapy, hidrotherapy, hierotherapy, hippotherapy, homeotherapeutics, homeotherapy, hydrotherapy, hydrotherapeutics, hyperthermotherapy, hypnotherapy, immunotherapy, kinesitherapy, lactotherapy, limotherapy, mechanotherapeutics, melissotherapy, nosotherapy, oncotherapy, pelotherapy, pharmacotherapeutics, phototherapy, physiotherapist, physiotherapy, pneumotherapy, pseudotherapy, psychotherapy, psychrotherapy, pyretotherapy, seismotherapy, thalassotherapy, theotherapy, therapeusis, therapeutic, therapeutical, therapeutics, therapeutist, therapist, therapy, thermotherapeutics, thermotherapy, vapotherapy, vulcanotherapy

-theria (Gk., wild animal) See **therio-** for examples.

therio-, theri-, thero-, ther-, -there, -therium, -theria, -theridae, -therian, -therioid, -theroid (Gk., animal, wild beast, wild animal) Also see **anima-, fauna,** and **zoo-** for other "animal" words.

    Qualifying words: Allotheria, allotheria, amphitherium, brontotherium, dinothere, Dino-

therum, Dintherium, eutheria, eutherian, megathere, megatherium, Megatherium, Metatheria, paleothere, pantotheria, Prototheria, prototheria, theria, theriac, therian, therianthropia, therianthropic, therianthropism, theriatrics, Theridiidae, theriogenology, theriolatry, theriomancy, theriomimicry, theriomorphic, theriomorphism, theriomorphous, theriophobia, theriopod, therium, therioid, theriotherapy, therodont, theroid, therolatry, therology, theromorph, theromorphia, theromorphism, Theropoda, theropodous, Titanothere

thermo-, therm-, thermi-, -thermia, -therm, -thermal, -thermic, -thermous -thermy (Gk., heat) Also see **calor-** and **ferv-** for other "heat" words.

    Qualifying words: acrohypothermy, adiathermancy, allotherm, anathermal, athermal, athermancy, athermanous, athermic, athermobiosis, athermy, autotherm, catathermal, diathermia, diathermic, diathermy, dysthermosia, ectotherm, ectothermic, endotherm, endothermia, endothermic, endothermy, eurythermic, eurythermal, exothermia, exothermic, geothermal, geothermics, geothermometry, haematothermal, heterotherm, homeotherm, homeothermal, homeothermic, hydrothermal, hydrothermia, hyperthermia, hyperthermy, hypothermal, hypothermia, hypothermy, isobathytherm, isotherm, isothermal, microthermophile, microthermophilous, microthermophily, pantothermal, philotherm, philothermic, philothermy, photothermal, photothermy, poikilotherm, poikilothermal, poikilothermia, poikilothermic, poikilothermy, radiothermy, stenothermal, thermaesthesia, thermal, thermalgesia, thermantidote, thermatology, thermesthesia, thermic, thermionic, thermium, thermoacoustic, thermoalgesia, thermobiology, thermochemical, thermochemist, thermochemistry, thermocleistogamy, thermocline, thermoduric, thermodynamic, thermodynamical, thermodynamicist, thermodynamics, thermoesthesia, thermogenesis, thermogenic, thermogenous, thermogeny, thermogeography, thermographer, thermographic, thermography, thermohaline, thermoimaging, thermokinematic, thermokinematics, thermology, thermoluminescence, thermoluminescent, thermolysis, thermolytic, thermometer, thermometric, thermometry, thermonasty, thermoneurosis, thermonuclear, thermopegic, thermoperiodic, thermoperiodicity, thermoperiodism, thermophagy, thermophase, thermophil, thermophile, thermophilic, thermophillic, thermophilous, thermophily, thermophobia, thermophobic, thermophylactic, thermophyte, thermoplegia, thermoplume, Thermopolis (Wyoming), thermopolypnea, thermoreceptor, thermoregulation, thermos, thermoscope, thermoscopic, thermosphere, thermostat, thermotactic, thermotaxic, thermotaxis, thermotherapeutics, thermotherapy, thermotics, thermotoxic, thermotoxin, thermotoxy, thermotropic, thermotropism, thermovision thermovisual

T

thero- (Gk., animal) See **therio-**.

thesaur- (Gk. > L., treasure, treasury, storehouse, chest; a treasury of words)

> Qualifying words: thesaural, thesauri(pl.) *or* thesauruses, thesaurus(s.)

thick See **densi-**, **pachy-**, and **pykno-**.

thicket, bush See **lochmo-** for examples.

thief, steal See **klepto-** and **plagiar-** for examples.

thigh See **femoro-** and **mero-** for examples.

thigmo-, thig-, thixo- (Gk., touch) Also see **hapto-** and **tang-** for other "touch" words.

> Qualifying words: thigmaesthesia, thigmocyte, thigmokinesis, thigmomorphic, thigmomorphic, thigmomorphosis, thigmotaxis, thigmotactic, thigmotaxis, thigmotherm, thigmothermic, thigmotropic, thigmotropism, thixotropic, thixotropy

thin, delicate See **lepto-** and **nemato-** for examples.

think over See **put-** for examples.

thino-, thini-, thin- (Gk. > L., sandbank, shore) Also see **aigialo-** for similarities.

> Qualifying words: thinicole, thinicolous, thinophile, thinophilous, thinophily, thinophyte

third See **terce** and **tri-** for examples.

thirst See **dipso-** for examples.

thixo- (Gk., touch) See **thigmo-** for examples.

thoraco-, thorac-, -thoracic (Gk., thorax, chest [part of the body between the neck and the abdomen; "breastplate, breast, chest"]) Also see **cervico-**, **esophago-**, **gutturo-**, **laryngo-**, **pectoro-**, **pharyngo-**, **sterno-**, **stetho-**, and **trachelo-** for other words with similar meanings.

> Qualifying words: hydropneumothorax, infrathoracic, pneumohydrothorax, scapulothoracic, subthoracic, thoracal, thoracectomy, thoracentesis, thoracic, thoracicoabdominal, thoracobronchotomy, thoracocautery, thoracodelphus, thoracodynia, thoracograph, thoracolysis, thoracometer, thoracometry, thoracomyodynia, thoracopathy, thoracoplasty, thoracopneumograph, thoracoscopy, thoracostenosis, thoracostomy, thoracotomy, thorax

thorny, spiny For examples, see **acantho-**, **chaeto-**, and **echino-**.

thousand See **kilo-** and **milli-** for examples.

thousand (ten thousand) See **myria-**.

thread, string See **fibro-**, **lin-**, and **mito-** for examples.

three See **tri-** and **terce-** for examples.

three-dimiensional See **stereo-** for examples.

threshold of consciousness See **limen** for examples.

-thrix (Gk., hair) See **tricho-** for examples.

throat, neck Examine **cervico-**, **esophago-**, **gutturo-**, **laryngo-**, **pharyngo-**, **thoraco-**, and **trachelo-** for examples.

thrombo-, thromb- (Gk., clot, lump; aggregation of blood factors.)

> Qualifying words: thrombectomy, thrombi, thromboangiitis, thromboarteritis, thrombocyte, thrombocythemia, thrombocytolysis, thrombocytopathia, thrombocytopathic, thrombocytopoiesis, thrombocytopoietic, thromboembolism, thromboendocarditis, thrombogenesis, thrombogenic, thromboid, thrombokinesis, thrombokinetics, thrombolysis, thrombolytic, thrombopathia, thrombopathy, thrombopenia, thrombophilia, thromboplastic, thromboplastin, thrombopoiesis, thrombopoietic, thrombosis, thrombotic, thrombus

through, across See **dia-**, **per-**, and **trans-** for examples.

throw, send See **ballo-**, **jet-**, and **miss-** for examples.

thrust, push See ^{2}**osmo-** and **trud-** for examples.

thunder See **bronto-**, **cerauno-**, **kerauno-**, and **tonitro-** for examples.

thunderbolt See **bronto-**, **cerauno-**, **kerauno-**, and **tonitro-** for examples.

thyla- (Gk., pouch, sack) For other "pouch" words, see **marsupium**.

> Qualifying words: thylacine, thylakoid

thyro-, thyr-, thyre-, thyreo-, thyroid-, thyroido-, -thyrea, -thyreosis, -thyroidism, -thyroid (Gk., pertaining to the thyroid gland; literally, "shield-shaped [cartilage];" from *thyre[os]*. A "shield," originally, "a large stone placed against a door [*thyra*] to keep it closed.")

> Qualifying words: athyrea, hypothyrea, hyperthyrea, thyreoitis, thyrofissure, thyroglossal, thyroidectomy, thyroid, thyroidotoxin, thyrotoxia, thyrotoxin, thyrotherapy, thyrotoxicosis, thyrotropin

till (the ground), care See **cult-** for examples.

tillo-, till- (Gk., to pluck, tear, pull)

> Qualifying words: onychotillomania, trichotillomania

timi-, tim- (L., to fear; faint-hearted, cowardly) Also see **-phobia**, for other "fear" words.

> Qualifying words: intimidate, intimidation, timid, timidity, timidly, timorouis

time See **chrono-**, **horo-**, and **tempo-** for examples.

-tin (hold) See **ten-** for examples.

ting- (L., touch) See **tang-** for examples.

tiny, small For examples, see **-cle, -cule, -icle, -le, lepto-, -let, -ling, micro-, mini-, nano-, oligo-, pauci-, pico-,** and **-ule.**

tip, top See **acro-, alti-,** and **hypso-** for examples.

tipho-, tiph, tiphi- (Gk., pool, pond, marsh, swamp) See **helo-, limno-,** and **telmato-** for words with similar meanings.

    Qualifying words: tiphicole, tiphicolous, tiphophile, tiphophilous, tiphophily, tiphophyte

tiro (L., beginner) See **tyro** (L.) for examples.

tissue See **arachno-** and **histo-** for examples.

titano-, titan- (Gk. > L., any person or thing of enormous size or power; from Greek mythology, one of the primitive gigantic deities, the children of Uranus and Gaea; the sun god, Helios, was the son of the Titan Hyperion)

    Qualifying words: Titan, titan, Titanesque, Titaness, Titanic, titanic, titaniferous, titanism, titanium, Titanomachy, Titanosaurus, titanothere

to, at See **ad-** for examples.

toad See **bufo-** and **phryno-** for examples.

toco-, -toky, -tocia, toko-, -tokia (Gk., childbirth) Also see **genus, nasc-,** and **para-** for words with similar meanings.

    Qualifying words: atocia, bradytocia, ditocous, dystocia, embryotocia, eutocia, eutokia, mogitocia, monotocous, oxytocia, oxytocic, polytocous, thelytocia, tocodynagraph, tocodynamometer, tocogeny, tocograph, tocography, tocological, tocologist, tocology, tocomania, tocometer, tocopherol, tocophobia, tocus, tokodynagraph, tokodynamometer, tokological, tokologist, tokology, tokophobia

toe, finger See **dactylo-** and **digit.**

toe nail See **onycho-** for examples.

together, in one, as a single word See **hyphen.**

together, between See **inter-** for examples.

together, with See **com-** and **syn-.**

toil, labor See **pono-** for examples.

token, mark See **sign-** for examples.

toko- (Gk., childbirth) See **toco-** for examples.

-tom, -toma, -tomic, -tomize, -tome, -tomical, -tomically, -tomist, -tomous, -tomy (Gk., cut, incision) Also see **-cise, -ectomy, sec-,** and **tomo-** for other "cut" examples.

    Qualifying words: anatomy, atom, cephalotomy, cirsotomy, colostomy, costotomy, craniotomy, crystolithotomy, cystotomy, dermatome, dermatotomy, diatom, dichotomous, dichotomy, encephalotomy, entomology, entomotomy, episiotomy, epitome, gonotome, herniotomy, labiotome, leucotomy, leukotomy, lobotomy, mastotomy, mastotomy, microtome, micro-

tomy, myotome, necrotomy, Neotoma, nephrotomy, osteotome, osteotomy, ototomy, ovariotomy, phlebotomy, rachiotome, tome, tracheotomy, varicotomy

tomo- (Gk., cut, section) Also examine **-cise, -ectomy, sec-,** and **-tom** for other "cut" examples.

    Qualifying words: tomogram, tomograph, tomography, tomolevel, tomomania

ton-, tono-, -tonia, -tonic, -tonous, -tony (L., sound, tone; [from Greek *tonos*, "that which is stretched, a stretching, a straining, pitch of the voice, musical note"]) Don't confuse this **ton-** with another **tono-,** meaning "tension." Also examine **echo-, phono-,** and **son-** for additional "sound" words.

    Qualifying words: atonal, atonic, baritone, barytone, betone, detonate, diatonic, ditone, entone, hypertonic, intonate, intonation, intone, isotonic, monotone, monotonous, monotony, myotonia, overtone, oxytone, pretone, semitone, subtone, syntonize, syntony, tonal, tonality, tonaphasia, tone, tonetic, tonic, tonicity, tonological, tonology, tonometer, tonometric, tonometrist, tonometry, tonophant, tonoplast, tonoscope, tonotopic, tonotopicity, tritone

tongue, or language See **glosso-** and **linguo-** for examples.

tonitro-, tonitru- (L., thunder) For other "thunder" words, see **bronto-** and **cerauno-.**

    Qualifying words: tonitrophobia, tonitruphobia

tono- (Gk., tension, pressure) Don't confuse this **tono-** with another **ton-** which means "sound."

    Qualifying words: angiohypertonia, angiohypotonia, ecotone, tonicity, tonoplast, tonoclonic, tonofibril, tonofilament, tonogram, tonograph, tonography, tonometer, tonometry, tonoscillograph, tonoscope

tonsil See **amygdal-** and **tonsillo-.**

tonsillo-, tonsillo-, tonsill- (L., small rounded mass of tissue, especially of lymphoid tissue) Also see **amygdal-** for other "tonsil" words.

    Qualifying words: peritonsillar, tonsil, tonsilla, tonsillar, tonsillectome, tonsillectomy, tonsillith, tonsillitic, tonsillitis, tonsilloadenoidectomy, tonsillohemisporosis, tonsillolith, tonsillomycosis, tonsillopathy, tonsilloscopy, tonsillotome, tonsillotomy, tonsillotyphoid, tonsolith

too little, less than See **hypo-** for examples.

tooth, teeth See **dent-** and **odonto-** for examples.

top, tip See **acro-, alti-,** and **hypso-.**

topmost, highest See **sum-** for examples.

topo-, top-, -topia, -topy, -topism, -topic, (Gk., place, a position, region, local, localized) Also see **loco-, pon-, the-,** and **sist-** for other "place" words.

    Qualifying words: biotope, biotopic, dystopia, dystopian, ectopia, heterotopia, isotope, isotopic, normotopia, skeletopia, topagnosia, topagnosis, topalgia, toparchy, topesthesia, topiary, topic, topical, topoanesthesia, topognosis, topographer, topographic, topographical, topography, topolatry, topological, topology, toponarcosis, toponeurosis, toponym, toponymics, toponymy, topophobe, topophobia, topophone, toposcopy, topothermesthesiometer, topotype, torpescent, topovaccinotherapy, utopia, utopianism, utopianist

torp- (L., stupor, numb, sluggish) Also see **ambly-** and **narco-**.

    Qualifying words: torpedo, torpid, torpify, torpor, torporific

tors-, tort-, tortu-, torqu- (L., bend, curve, turn, twist) Also see **flect-, gyro-, -plex, stroph-, trop-, verg-, vers-,** and **volv-**.

    Qualifying words: contort, contortion, contortionist, distort, distortion, extort, extortion, extortioner, extortionist, retort, torch, torment, tormentum, toroid, torque, torquemeter, torsiometer, torsion, tort, tortilla, tortion, tortoise, tortuose, tortuosity, tortuous, torture, torturous

torqu- (bend, curve) See **tors-** for examples.

tort- (bend, curve) See **tors-** for examples.

tortoise See **chelono-** for examples.

tortu- (bend, curve) See **tors-** for examples.

touch See **hapto-, tang-,** and **thigmo-**.

toward, to See **ad-** for examples.

tox- (poison) See **toxico-** for examples.

toxic- (poison) See **toxico-** for examples.

toxico-, toxic-, toxi-, tox-, toxin-, -toxically, -toxaemia, -toxemia, -toxaemic, -toxemic, -toxical, -toxy, -toxis, -toxicosis, -toxism, -toxia, -toxin, -toxicity, (Gk., poison) Examine **veno-** and **viru-** for other "poison" words.

    This Greek element originally meant "bow," then it became "arrow," than a "poisoned arrow" and finally "poison." In most cases, **toxico-** means poison, but in a few situations it refers to the original meaning of "arrow," as in **toxophilite, toxophily** ("love" of or *fondness* for archery) and should not be confused with **toxophil, toxophile** (having an affinity for a *toxin* or "poison").

    Qualifying words: aflatoxicosis, aflatoxin, anagotoxic, antitoxic, antitoxin, autotoxin, bac-teriotoxemia, biotoxic, biotoxication, biotoxicology, biotoxin, bufotoxin, crinotoxin, cytotoxicity, detoxicate, detoxication, detoxification, detoxify, ecotoxicology, endotoxic, endotoxin, exotoxin, ecotoxicologist, fungitoxic, genotoxicity, hemotoxin, hypertoxicity, intoxicate, intoxicated, intoxication, lymphoidtoxemia, lymphotoxin, mycotoxincosis, mycotoxic, mycotoxin, neurotoxia, neurotoxic, ophiotoxemia, peptinotoxin, phototoxins, phototoxicity, pyrotoxic, thyrotoxia, toxaemia, toxemia, toxenzyme, toxic, toxicant, toxicide, toxicity, toxicoderma, toxicodermia, toxicodermic, toxicodynamics, toxicogenic, toxicokinetics, toxicologist, toxicology, toxicomania, toxicomaniac, toxicopathic, toxicopexis, toxicophidia, toxicosis, toxiferous, toxigenic, toxiglossate, toxignomic, toxin, toxinantitoxin, toxinemia, toxinicide, toxinology, toxinosis, toxinotherapy, toxiphobia, toxiphrenia, toxogen, toxognaths, toxoid, toxoinfection, toxolysin, toxophile, toxophilic, toxophilous, toxophorous, urotoxia

toxo- (Gk., bow, arrow) Also see **sagitto-** for other "arrow" words.

    Qualifying words: toxophilite, toxophily

tra-, tract-, trac-, -tractive, -traction, -tracting, treat-, trai- (L., drag, draw together) Don't confuse the **tra-** in this element with the **tra-** in **trans-**.

    Qualifying words: abstract, abstracted, abstraction, abstractionism, attract, attraction, attractive, contract, contractile, contractility, contraction, contractor, contractual, detract, detraction, detrain, distract, distraction, distraught, entrain, entreat, extract, intractable, maltreat, mistreat, portrait, portray, protract, protractile, protraction, protractor, retract, retraction, retreat, subtract, subtraction, subtrahend, trace, tract, tractability, tractable, tractableness, tractile, traction, tractor, trail, trailer, train, trainee, trainer, trait, trawler, treat, treatise, treaty, trial

trace, tract, fooprint See **ichno-** for examples.

trachelo-, trachel- (Gk., neck, throat) See **cervico-, esophago-, gutturo-, laryngo-, pharyngo-,** and **thoraco-** for other "neck, throat" words.

    Qualifying words: trachelitis, trachelodynia, trachelogist, trachelologist, trachelology, trachelomyitis, tracheloplasty, trachelotomy

tracheo-, trache- (Gk., windpipe) Also see **aorta, broncho-, cervico-, esophago-, gutturo-, laryngo-, phrango-,** and **thoraco-** for other "throat" words.

    Qualifying words: laryngotracheal, trachea, tracheal, trachealgia, tracheitis, trachelectomy, trachelitis, tracheogenic, tracheopathia, tracheopathy, tracheophonesis, tracheophony, tracheoplasty, tracheoscopy, tracheostoma, tracheotomy

trachy-, trach- (Gk., rough) Also see **rudi-** for other "rough" words.

> **Qualifying words:** trachoma, trachomatous, trachychromatic, trachyphonia, trachyte

track, trace, footprint See **ichno-** for examples.

track, rut See **orb-** for examples.

tract- (L., drag, draw together) See **tra-**.

trader, traveler See **empori-** for examples.

tragico-, tragi-, trago-, trag- (Gk., goat; pertaining to "tragedy;" which refers to a play or other serious literary work having an unhappy ending. Literally, *goat song*, supposedly because the actors or singers in Greek tragedies were originally dressed in goatskins to represent satyrs, and thereby became actors in satyric drama from which "tragedy" was later developed. Another theory is that a goat may have been the prize to an actor for the best performance in a Greek play.) Also see **aego-, capri-,** and **hirco-** for other "goat" words.

> **Qualifying words:** tragacanth, tragal, tragedy, tragic, tragical, tragomaschalia, tragicomedy, tragicomic, tragion, tragopan, tragophonia, tragophony, tragopodia, Tragopogon, tragus

trago- (Gk., goat) See **tragico-** for examples.

tranquil (L., peaceful, quiet, calm) Formed from **trans-** (through, across) and **quiet** (*quies*, rest, quiet). See **trans-**.

trans-, tran-, tra- (L., across, through, over, beyond, on the far side of) Also see **dia-** and **per-** for other "across" or "through" words. Don't confuse the **tra-** in this element with another **tra-** in "drag" or "draw." **Trans-** becomes **tra-** before the consonants **-d, -j, -l, -m, -n,** and **-v**.

> **Qualifying words:** traduce, traject, trajection, trajectory, tranquil, tranquility, tranquillity, tranquilize, tranquillize, tranquilly, tranquilness, transact, transaction, transactional, transalpine, transatlantic, transcend, transcendence, transcendentalism, transcontinental, transcribe, transcript, transcription, transcutaneous, transdermal, transdermic, transducer, transduction, transect, transfer, transferable, transference, transfigure, transform, transformation, transformer, transfuse, transgenic, transfusion, transgress, transgression, transience, transient, transit, transition, transitional, transitive, transitory, translation, translator, transliterate, transliteration, translocate, translucence, translucency, translucent, transmigrate, transmigration, transmission, transmit, transmitter, transmutation, transmute, transoceanic, transonic, transpacific, transparence, transparency, transparent, transpiration, tran-

spire, transplant, transpolar, transport, transportation, transpose, transposition, transsexual, transsonic, transubstantiation, transversal, transverse, Transylvania, Transylvanian, transverse, travesty

transparent, glassy See **hyalo-** and **vitreo-** for examples.

traumato-, traumat-, trauma-, traum-, traumatic, -traumatically, -trauma (Gk., > L., wound, bodily injury)

> **Qualifying words:** barotrauma, microtrauma, neurotrauma, trauma, traumasthenia, traumataxis, traumatic, traumatin, traumatism, traumatology, traumatonasty, traumatopathy, traumatophilia, traumatophobia, traumatopnea, traumatopyra, traumatotactic, traumatotaxis, traumatotherapy, traumatropic, traumatropism

travel, journey See **empori-** and **itiner-**.

traveling, way See **empori-, odo-,** and **via-**.

treasure, treasury See **thesaur-** for examples.

treat, cure See **cura-, -iatry, medi-, sana-,** and **therap-** for examples.

trembling, shaking See **hor-** for examples.

tree See **arbor-, dendro-, nemo-,** and **sylvan**.

tri- (Gk. > L., three, thrice, threefold) Also see **terce-** for other "three" words and examine the NUMBERS section in **Appendix G**.

> **Qualifying words:** triactinal, triad, triadelphous, triandrous, triangle, triannual, trianthous, triarch, triarchy, triaster, triathlon, triaxial, tricentric, triceps, trichromatic, tricolor, tricycle, tridactyl, tridecaphobia, trident, tridimensional, triennial, triennium, trifocal, trifoliate, trigamy, trigon, trigonometry, trilateral, trilingula, trilogy, trillion, trimester, trinity, trinomial, trio, trionym, trioxide, triphyllous, triple, triplex, triplicate, tripod, trisect, trisection, triskaidekaphobia, trisyllable, tritheism, triumvirate, trivia, trivial, trivium

tribe See **phylo-** for examples.

tribo-, trib- (Gk., friction, rub, grind, wear away) Also see **bruxo-** and **-tripsy**.

> **Qualifying words:** nanotribologist, nanotribology, triboelectric, triboelectricty tribological, tribology, triboluminescence, triboluminescent, tribometer, tribulation

tricho-, trich-, -tricha, -trichia, -trichan, -trichic, -trichosis, -trichous, -thrix, -trichum, -trichy (Gk., hair) Also see **coma**[2], **crino-, dasy-, hirsute, pilo-, barba-** (beard), and **pogo-** (beard).

> **Qualifying words:** achromatrichia, atrichia, atrichic, atrichosis, chromotrichial, clastothrix, cymotrichy, endoectothrix, eutrichosis, glossotrichia, gynetrichosis, hypertrichosis, hypotrichia, hypotrichiasis, hypotrichosis, hypotrichous, leiotrichous, leiotrichy, leipotrichia,

leptotrichia, liparotrichia, lipsotrichia, oligotrich, oligotrichia, oligotrichosis, melanotrichous, paratrichosis, polytrichia, rhinothrix, schizotrichia, sclerotrichia, sclerothrix, trichaesthesia, trichalgia, trichiasis, trichina, trichinosis, trichites, trichoaesthesia, trichoanesthesia, trichobacteria, trichobezoar, trichocardia, trichocarpous, trichochromogenic, trichoclasis, trichoclasty, trichocutis, trichoderm Trichoderma, trichoesthesia, trichoesthesiometer, trichogen, trichogenous, trichoglossia, trichogyria, trichoid, trichologia, trichology, trichoma, trichomania, trichoma, trichome, trichomycosis, trichomoniasis, trichonosis, trichopter, trichopathic, trichopathophobia, trichopathy, trichophagy, trichophilous, trichophobia, trichopteron, trichornation, trichorrhea, trichorrhexis, trichoschisis, trichosiderin, trichosis, trichotaxis, trichotillomania, tricological, tricologist, tricology, trimachia, trimachy, ulotrichous, ulotrichy

trickle, dropping See **stalac-** for examples.

trim, prune See **put-** for examples.

-tripsy, -tripsis, -tripic (Gk., crush; from Greek, "massage, rubbing, friction, grind") Also examine **bruxo-** and **tribo-** for other "grinding" words.

> **Qualifying words:** anatripsis, angiotripsy, biotripis, cephalotripsy, cleidotripsy, hepaticolithotripsy, histotripsy, lithotripsy, neurtripsy, xerotripsis

-trix (L., woman who...) Also see **fem-** and **gyno-** for other "woman" words and see the SUFFIXES section in **Appendix K** for other word endings.

> **Qualifying words:** aviatrix, coadministratrix, curatrix, directrix, executrix, fornicatrix, impersonatrix, janitrix, mediatrix, negotiatrix, obstetrix

-tron, -tronic (Gk., device, instrument; more generally, used in the names of any kind of chamber or apparatus used in experiments [possible allusion to the Greek instrumental suffix, as in *árotron*, "plow," U.S.; "plough," British; from the Greek stem *aroun* "to plow"]. Examine the SUFFIXES section in **Appendix K** for other word endings.

> **Qualifying words:** betatron, biotron, cosmotron, cryotron, cyclotron, dynatron, electron, electronic, ignitron, isotron, klystron, magnetron, megatron, phanatron, phanotron, synchrotron

trop-, tropo-, -tropal, -trope(s), **-tropic, -tropism, -tropia, -tropous, -tropy** (Gk., bend, curve, turn, a turning) For additional "bend, curve," or "turn" words, see **flect-, gyro-, -plex, stroph-, tors-, verg-, vers-,**

and **volv-**. Don't confuse this **trop-, -tropy** element with **tropho-, troph-**, which means "food, nourishment, nutrition."

> **Qualifying words:** ageotropic, allotropism, allotropy, anisotropic, atropos, Atropos, autotropic, autotropism, barotropic, barotropism, chemotropism, dextrotropic, diageotropic, diageotropism, entropy, eutropism, eutropous, geonyctitropic, geonyctitropism, geotropic, geotropism, heliotrope, heliotropic, heliotropism, hydrotropism, isotropic, phototropic, phototropism, rheotrope, thermotropism, trope, trophotropic, trophy, tropic, Tropic of Cancer, Tropic of Capricorn, tropical, tropism, tropology, tropometer, tropoparasite, tropopause, tropophil, tropophilous, tropophyte, troposphere, tropospheric, tropotaxis

tropho-, troph-, -trophy, -trophs, -trophically, -trophic, -trophous (Gk., food, nutrition, nourishment) Also see **alimento-, bromato-, cibo-,** and **sitio-** for other "food" words.

> **Qualifying words:** abiotrophia, abiotrophy, acardiotrophia, allotrophia, allotrophic, atrophy, autotroph, autotrophic, autotrophically, autotrophy, chemoautotrophic, chemolithotrophic, chemotrophic, chemotrophy, diaheliotropic, diaheliotropism, diaphototropic, diaphototropism, diatropic, diatropism, dromotropic, dromotropism, dystrophy, ectotrophic, embryotroph, endotrophic, entrophicate, exendotrophic, eutrophic, eutrophication, eutrophy, glycotrophic, hemiatrophy, hemotroph, hemotrophy, heterotroph, heterotrophic, histotroph, hypertrophic, hypertrophy, hypotrophic, hypotrophy, metatroph, microheterotrophs, oligotrophic, osmotroph, osmotrophic, pedotrophy, phagotroph, polytrophic, trophallactic, trophallaxis, trophic, trophobiont, trophobiosis, trophobiotic, trophoblast, trophoblastic, trophocytes, trophoderm, trophodynamics, trophogenesis, trophology, trophoneurotic, trophonosis, trophopathia, trophopathy, trophophyll, trophospongium, trophotaxis, trophotherapy, trophotropic, trophotropism, trophozooid

trud-, -trude, trus-, -trusion (L., thrust, push)

> **Qualifying words:** abstruse, abstrusely, abstruseness, extrude, extrusion, extrusive, inobtrusive, intrude, intrusion, intrusive, obtrude, obtrusion, obtrusive, protrude, protrusion, protrusive

true, truth See **etym-, ortho-,** and **veri-** for examples.

trus- (L., push, thrust) See **trud-** for examples.

-trusion (L., push, thrust) See **trud-** for examples.

trust, faith See **cred-, dox-,** and **fid-** for examples.

truth, real See **etym-** and **veri-** for examples.

tube, pipe See **siphono-** and **syringo-**.

-tude (L., state, quality, condition of) A suffix which forms nouns from adjectives and past participles. Also see the SUFFIXES section in **Appendix K** for other word endings.

>   **Qualifying words:** altitude, aptitude, fortitude, gratitude, ineptitude, ingratitude, lassitude, latitude, longitude, multitude, plenitude, senectitude, servitude, similitude, solitude

tumor See **cancero-, carcino-, omo-,** and **onco-** for examples.

turb-, turbin- (L., turmoil, commotion, disorderly, agitated, confusion)

>   **Qualifying words:** disturb, disturbance, imperturbable, perturb, perturbation, trouble, turbellarian, turbid, turbidimetry, turbine, turbofan, turbojet, turboprop, turbulence, turbulency, turbulent

turmoil, commotion See **turb-** for examples.

turn, bend Check **flect-, gyro-, helico-, -plex, stroph-, tors-, trop-, verg-, vers-,** and **volv-** for examples.

turtle, tortoise See **chelono-** for examples.

twenty See **icosa-** for examples.

twice, half See **semi-** for examples.

twinkle, sparkle See **scintill-** for examples.

twist, turn See **flect-, gyro-, -plex, stroph-, tors-, trop-, verg-, vers-,** and **volv-** for examples.

two See **bi-, deutero-, di-, dicho-,** and **duo-** for examples.

tycho-, tych- (Gk., accident, chance, fortune, fate, providence)

>   **Qualifying words:** tychastics, Tyche (Greek goddess of fortune), tychite, tychoparthenogenesis, tychopelagic, tychoplankton, tychoplanktonic, tychoplanktont, tychopotamic

tympano-, tympan-, tympani- (Gk., *tympanon*, drum, kettledrum; from "blow, impression, to beat") Also see **myringo-** for other "membrane" words.

>   **Qualifying words:** tympanal, tympanectomy, tympania, tympanic, tympanichord, tympanicity, tympanion, tympanism, tympanist, tympanites, tympanitic, tympanitis, tympanocentesis, tympanogenic, tympanogram, tympanolabyrinthopexy, tympanomastoid, tympanomastoiditis, tympanometry, tympanophonia, tympanoplasty, tympanoplastic, tympanosclerosis, tympanosympathectomy, tympanotomy, tympanous, tympanum

typhlo-, typhl- (Gk., blind, blindness [*typhlos*, blind]; denotes relationship to the *cecum* or the first part of the large intestine, forming a dilated pouch; also called the "blindgut" or "blind intestine" [*caecum*, "blind, blind gut"; *typhlon, cecum*])

>   **Qualifying words:** 1. [blind]: typhlolexia, typhlology, Typhlolops, typhlophile, typhlophobia, Typhlophthalmi, typhlosis, typhlotic, typhlophile, typhlosis, typhloti
>   2. [blindgut]: typhlectasis, typhlectomy, typhlenteritis, typhlitis, typhlocolitis, typhlohepatitis, typhlolithiasis, typhlomegaly, typhlotomy

typho-, typh-, -typhoidal, -typhus, -typhic (Gk., [from *typhein, to smoke*], smoke, mist, vapor, cloud; in medicine, fever accompanied by stupor or a clouding of the mind resulting from a fever) Also examine **capno-** and **fumi-** for other "smoke" words.

>   **Qualifying words:** meningotyphoid, nephrotyphoid, paratyphoid, pleurotyphoid, pretyphoid, post-typhoid, typhemia, typhobacillosis, typhoid, typhomalarial, typhomania, typhorubeloid, typhous, typhus

tyro-, tyr- (Gk., cheese) Also see **case-** for other "cheese" words. Don't confuse this element with the next Latin **tyro** which means "beginner."

>   **Qualifying words:** tyrein, tyrogenous, tyroid, tyroma, Tyrophagus, tyrosin, tyrosine, tyrotoxicon, tyrotoxicosis, tyrotoxism

tyro, tiro (L., beginner, novice [also, originally, a "young soldier" or "recruit."]) Don't confuse this **tyro** with the previous **tyro-** meaning "cheese."

>   **Qualifying words:** tiros, tiro, tyro, tyros

U u

udo- (L., rain) Also see **hyeto-, ombro-,** and **pluv-** for other "rain" words.

> **Qualifying words:** udograph, udometer, udometric, udometry

-ula (L., little, small) See **-ule** for examples.

-ule, -ula (L., little, small) For other "little" words, see **-cle, -cule, lepto-, micro-,** and **mini-.**

> **Qualifying words:** capsule, globule, molecule

ulno-, uln- (L., elbow; larger bone of the forearm) Also see **ancon-** for other "elbow" words.

> **Qualifying words:** ulna, ulnad, ulnar, ulanaris, ulnen, ulnocarpal, ulnometacarpal, ulnoradial

ult- (L., beyond, excessive) See **ultra-** for examples.

ultim- (L., end, last, final) Also see **fin-, omega, teleo-,** and **term-** for other "end" words.

> **Qualifying words:** antepenultimate, antepenult, penultimate, penult, penultima, ultima, ultimate, ultimately, ultimatum, ultimo, ultimogeniture, *ultimum moriens*

ultra-, ult- (L., beyond, on the other side; excessive, to an extreme degree) Also see **epi-, hyper-,** and **super-** for other "beyond" words.

> **Qualifying words:** ulterior, ultimate, ultraconservative, ultrafiche, ultrafiltration, ultrahigh, ultraism, ultraliberal, ultramarine, ultramicrometer, ultramicroscope, ultramicroscopic, ultramicrotome, ultramilitant, ultraminiature, ultramodern, ultramundane, ultranationalism, ultrapure, ultrasonic, ultrasonics, ultrasonography, ultrasophisticated, ultrasound, ultratechnical, ultrathin, ultraviolet

-um (Gk. > L., a suffix which forms singular nouns) See **Appendix L** for a list of **-um** suffixes and also see **Appendix K** for a list of other SUFFIXES.

umbel (L., shade) See **umbra-** for examples.

umbili-, umbil- (L., pertaining to the navel, umbilical cord; a protuberance or swelling; related to *umbo,* the boss [a convex elevation or knob] of a shield) See **omphalo-** for other "navel" or "umbilical" references.

> **Qualifying words:** umbilectomy, umbilical, umbilicate, umbilication, umbilici(pl.), umbilicus(s.)

umbra-, umbro-, umbr-, umbel- (L., shade, shadow) Also see **scio-** and **skio-** for other "shadow" examples.

> **Qualifying words:** adumbral, adumbrate, adumbration, penumbra, penumbral, umbraticole, umbraticolous, penumbrous, somber, sombrero, umbel, umbellate, umbella, umbelliform, umber, umbra, umbraculate, umbrage, umbrageous, umbrageously, umbral, umbratile, umbrella, umbriferous, umbrophile, umbrophilic, umbrophily

un- (one, single) See **uni-** for examples.

uncia- (L., inch; ounce; a twelfth) Also see NUMBERS in **Appendix G** for other numerical elements.

> **Qualifying words:** inch, ounce, uncial

unclean, filthy See **myso-** and **rhypo-** for examples.

uncovered, naked See **gymno-** and **nudo-** for examples.

under, below See **hypo-, infra-, sub-,** and **subter-** for examples.

undu-, und- [*-ound,* through French] (L., flow, wave, billow) Also see **cymo-, fluct-, liqu-, rheo-, rheum-, -rrhea,** and **vacilla-.**

> **Qualifying words:** abound, abundance, abundant, abundantly, inundate, inundation, ondograph, redound, redundance, redundancy, redundant, sound, superabound, superabundance, superabundant, surround, surrounded, surrounding, undine, undulant, undulate, undulation, undulous

unequal, unsymmetrical See **aniso-** .

unguo-, ungu- (L., nail, claw, hoof) For other "nail" words, see **chela-** and **onycho-.**

> **Qualifying words:** subungual, ungual, unguicorn, unguiculate, unguiferous, unguiform, Ungulata, ungula, ungular, ungulate, unguligrade

uni-, un- (L., one, single) Also see **mono-** and **soli-** for other "one" words. In addition, see the NUMBERS section in **Appendix G** for other numerical elements.

> **Qualifying words:** disunite, *E pluribus unum,* reunite, triune, unanimous, unicameral, unicellular, unicentric, unicolor, unicorn, unicycle, unidactyl, undecennary, undecennial, unification, uniflorous, unifoliate, uniform, unify, unilateral, unilinear, unilingual, unimanual, union, uniparous, uniped, uniplicate, unipod, unipolar, unique, uniradiate, unisexual, unison, unisphere, unit, unitary, unite, united, univalent, universal, universe, university, univocal, univore, univorous, univory

union, marriage See **gamo-** for examples.

unite, join See **junct-** for examples.

universe See **cosmo-** for examples.

unmovable See **ankylo-** for examples.

unripe, raw See **omo-** (Gk.) for examples.

unseen, invisible See **adelo-** for examples.

untie, loosen See **lax-, -lysis,** and **solv-**.

untimely birth, miscarriage See **abort-** and **ectro-** for examples.

untrue, deception See **fals-** and **pseudo-** for examples.

unwrap, raw See **omo-** (Gk.) for examples.

up, upward See **ana-** for examples.

upon, over, above See **epi-, hyper-, super-,** and **ultra-** for examples.

urano-, uran- (Gk., heaven[s], sky; from Uranus, the god of the sky; in medicine, the palate, roof, or top of the mouth) Also see **celest-** for other "heaven" words.

   Qualifying words: transuranic, Urania, uranic, uranium, uranographer, uranographic, uranographist, uranography, uranographical, uranolite, uranology, uranometria, uranometrical, uranometry, uranophobia, uranoplasty, uranoplegia, uranorrhaphy, uranoschism, uranoscopy, Uranus

urban, urb-, -urban, -urbia (L., city) Also see **civi-** and **polis-** for other "city" words. The reference to a city which connotes cultivation, refinement, and elegance.

   Qualifying words: amburbial, conurbation, exurb, exurbanite, exurbia, interurban, interurbanite, penturban, penturbia, suburb, suburbia, suburban, suburbanite, urban, urbane, urbanism, urbanity, urbanize, urbanology, urbicole, urbicolous, urbiculture

-ure (L., denoting an act or result) Also see **Appendix K** for other SUFFIXES.

   Qualifying words: composure, legislature, literature, nature, primogeniture, rupture, scripture, structure, torture

urg-, (erg-), -urgy, -urgia, -urgical, -urgically, -urgist, -urge (Gk., work) This **urg-** is a transformation of *erg-*) Also see **ergo-, labor, oper-,** and **pono-** for other "work" words.

   Qualifying words: chemurgic, chirurgeon, chirurgery, -chirurgia (suffix), chirurgic, chirurgical, demiurge, dramaturge, dramaturgic, dramaturgy, George, liturgy, maneuver, manure, metallurgic, metallurgy, neururgic, panurgy, surgeon, surgery, symurgy, thaumaturgic, thaumaturgy, theurgic

-urnal (*-urnus*) (Gk., > L., a suffix which forms adjectives of time) Also see the SUFFIXES section in **Appendix K** for other word endings.

   Qualifying words: diurnal, nocturnal, terdiurnal

uretero-, ureter- (Gk., urinary canal; either of two tubes that carry urine from the kidneys to the bladder; the walls of each ureter have three layers—a fibrous outer layer, a muscular middle layer, and an inner memberane and are supplied by blood vessels and nerves) Also see **colpo-, episco-, hystero-, vagino-,** and **vulvo-** for additional "female-reproductive-organ" words.

   Qualifying words: ureter, ureteralgia, ureterectomy, ureteric, ureteritis, ureterocele, ureterocelectomy, ureterocolic, ureterocolostomy, ureterocutaneostomy, ureteroduodenal, ureterogram, ureterography, ureterolith, ureterolithotomy, ureterolysis, ureteromegtaly, ureteropathy, ureteroplasty, ureteroproctostomy, ureteropyelitis, ureteropyelography, ureteropyeloneostomy, ureteropyelonephritis, ureteropyelonephrostomy, ureteropyeloplasty, ureteropyelostomy, ureteropyosis, ureterorectal, ureterorrhatgia, ureterorrhaphy, ureterostenosis, ureterostomy, ureterotomy, ureteroureteral, ureteroureterostomy, ureterouterine, ureterovaginal,

urethro-, urethr- (Gk., *urethra,* a slitlike tube conveying urine from the internal urethral orifice of the bladder)

   Qualifying words: urethra, urethral, urethralgia, urethrectomy, urethrism, urethritis, urethrocutaneous, urethrocystitis, urethrocystography, urethrocystometry, urethrodynia, urethrogram, urethrograph, urethrography, urethrometer, urethrometry, urethropenile, urethropexy, urethroplasty, urethrorectal, urethrorrhagia, urethrorrhaphy, urethrorrhea, urethroscope, urethroscopy, urethroscrotal, urethrospasm, urethrostenosis, urethrostomy, urethrotome, urethrotomy, urethrovaginal

-uria (L., a characteristic or constituent of urine) See **urino-** for examples.

urinary canal See **uretero-** for examples.

urino-, urin-, uri-, -uria, -ure(a) (L., water, rain, wet; urine) Also see **aqua-, hydro-, hyeto-, ombro-, pluv-, udo-,** and **uro-** for other "water, rain" words.

   Qualifying words: albuminuria, hemoglobinuria, lithuria, oliguria, paruria, pneumaturia, polyuria, polyuric, pollakiuria, proteinuria, pyuria, urea, urease, urethra, uricolysis, uricolytic, uridrosis, uriesthesis, urina, urinable, urinacidometer, urinal, urinalysis, urinary, urinate, urination, urinative, urine, urinemia, urinidrosis, urinific, uriniferous, uriniparous, urinocryoscopy, urinogenous, urinologist, urinology, urinoma, urinometer, urinometry, urinous, urinophilous, uriposia, urinosanguineous

uro-, ur- (Gk., urine [water, rain, wet]) Also see **aqua-, hydro-, hyeto-, ombro-, pluv-,** and **udo-** for other "water" words. Don't confuse this **uro-** with the next one which means "tail."

> **Qualifying words:** uroacidimeter, urodynamic, urodynamics, uroerythrin, urodynia, urogenous, urogram, urography, urokinetic, urolith, urolithology, urologic, urologist, urology, uromancy, uromantia, uronology, uronophile, uronoscopy, uropathogen, uropathy, uropenia, urophobia, uropoiesis, uropoietic, uropsammus, urotoxic, urotoxin, uroxanthin

uro-, ur-, -urous, -ura, -uroid, -urus, -uridae (Gk., tail, tail-like) Also see **caudo-** and **peni-** for other "tail" examples. Don't confuse this **uro-** with the previous one which means "urine."

> **Qualifying words:** anthurium, anurous, brachyurous, cynosure, urochord, urodele, uropod, Uropygi, uropygi, uropygial, uropygium

ursus (L., bear) Also see **arcto-**.

> **Qualifying words:** Orson, ursa, Ursa major, Ursa minor, Ursidae, ursiform, ursine, urson, Ursula, Ursus, *Ursus spelaeus*

utero-, uter- (L., womb) Also examine **calpo-, episio-, hystero-, vagino-,** and **vulvo-**.

> **Qualifying words:** uteralgia, utercystostomy, uteri, uterine, uterismus, uteroabdominal, uterocervical, uterocolic, uterocystostomy, uterodynia, uteroenteric, utergenic, uterogestation, uterography, uterolith, uterometer, uterometry, utero-ovarian, uteroparietal, uteropelvic, uteropexy, uteroplasty, uteroscope, uterothermometry, uterotomy, uterotonic, uterotropic, uterotubal, uterovaginal, uteroventral, uterus

uterus, womb Examine **hystero-, metro-,** and **utero-** for related words.

Utopia (Gk., literally, "no where") Coined by Sir Thomas More [1779-1852] from Greek "not," and "place."

> **Qualifying words:** dystopia, Utopia, Utopian, utopianism, utopianist, utopianize, utopistic

uvulo-, uvul- (L., a pendent, fleshy mass; the small, fleshy mass hanging from the soft palate above the root of the tongue, composed of the levator and tensor palati muscle of the uvula, connective tissue, and mucous membrane; literally, *little grape*)

> **Qualifying words:** uvula, uvular, uvularis, uvulatome, uvulatomy, uvulectomy, uvulitis, uvulopalatopharyngoplasty, uvuloptosis, uvulotome, uvulotomy

uxor- (L., wife, spouse [female]) Also see FAMILY GROUPS for other family words.

> **Qualifying words:** uxorial, uxoricidal, uxoricide, uxoricidic, uxoricidomania, uxorilocal, uxorious, uxoriously, uxoravalence, uxorovalence

V v

vacc- (L., cow) Also see **bou-** and **bovi-** for other "cow" words.

> **Qualifying words:** vaccinate, vaccination, vaccine, vaccinotherapy

vacilla-, vacillat- (L., flow, wave, back) Also see **cymo-, fluct-, liqu-, rheo-, -rrhea,** and **undu-** for other "flow" words.

> **Qualifying words:** vacillant, vacillate, vacillating, vacillation, vacillator

vacu-, vaca- (L., empty)

> **Qualifying words:** evacuate, evacuation, vacancy, vacant, vacate, vacation, vacuist, vacuity, vacuole, vacuometer, vacuous, vacuum

vaga-, vag- (L., wander, move around) Also see **migr-** and **nomad-.**

> **Qualifying words:** extravagance, extravagant, *Nervus vagus,* vagabond, vagabondage, vagary, vagrancy, vagrant, vague, vagus

vagina See **vagino-** for examples.

vagino-, vagin- (L., originally, sheath, scabbard, the husk of grain; in medical science, the vagina or lowest part of the female genital tract, the canal which leads from the vulva to the uterus) Also see **colpo-, episio-, hystero-, vulvo-,** and **utero-** for related "female-reproductive-organ" words.

> **Qualifying words:** evaginate, vagina(s.), vaginae(pl.), vaginal, vaginalectomy, vaginatitis, vaginapexy, vaginate, vaginectomy, vaginiferous, vaginiform, vaginiperineotomy, vaginismus, vaginitis, vaginoabdominal, vaginocele, vaginocutaneous, vaginodynia, vaginofixation, vaginogram, vaginography, vaginolabial, vaginometer, vaginomycosis, vaginopathy, vaginoperineal, vaginoperineotomy, vaginopexy, vaginoplasty, vaginoscope, vaginoscopy, vaginotomy, vaginovesical, vaginovulvar, vaginula

-vail (L., power) See **valid-** for examples.

val- (L., power) See **valid-** for examples.

-valence (L., power) See **valid-** for examples.

-valent (L., power) See **valid-** for examples.

valid-, val-, vale-, -vail, -valent, -valence (L., power, strength, be strong; or "fare well") Also see **dyna-, firm-, fort-, poten-,** and **stheno-** for other "power" words.

> **Qualifying words:** ambivalence, ambivalent, avail, availability, available, bivalence, carnival, convalesce, convalescent, countervail, devaluate, devaluation, devalue, equivalence, equivalency, equivalent, evaluate, evaluation, hexavalent, invalid (IN vuh lid), invalid (in VAL id), invalidate, invalidity, invaluable, multivalence, multivalent, octavalent, pentavalent, prevail, prevalence, prevalent, quadrivalence, quinquivalent, tetravalence, trivalence, univalence, univalent, valediction, valeditorian, valedictory, valence, valency, valetudinarian, valetudinary, valiance, valiancy, valiant, valid, validate, valor, valorization, valorous, valuable, value

vapor, gas See **atmo-** for examples.

vapor, smoke See **capno-, fumi-,** and **typho-** for examples.

vari- (L., different, diversity, change) Also see **ali-, alio-, alter-, hetero-,** and **poikilo-** for other "different" words.

> **Qualifying words:** divaricate, invariable, prevaricate, prevarication, prevaricator, unvarying, variable, variance, variant, variation, varicolor, varicolored, varied, variegate, variety, variform, variometer, various, vary

varied, irregular See **poikilo-** for examples.

vaso-, vas-, vasi- (L., vessel, duct) Also see **angio-, arterio-, phlebo-,** and **veno-** for other "vessel" words.

> **Qualifying words:** circumvascular, vasalgia, vascular, vascularity, vasculitis, vasculogenesis, vasculotoxic, vase, vasectomy, vasiform, vasodilation, vasodilator, vasography, vasohypertonic, vasohypotonic, vosomotion, vasomotor, vasopuncture, vasoreflex, vasorelaxation, vasosensory, vasotomy, vasotrophic, vasotropic

vein (blood) See **angio-, arterio-, phlebo-, vaso-,** and **veno-** for examples.

veloci-, velo- (L., fast, speed, swift, and rapid) Also see **celer-** and **tacho-.**

> **Qualifying words:** velocimeter, velocipede, velocity, velodrome, velogenic

ven- (poison) See **veno-** for examples.

ven-, vent-, veni-, ventu- (L., come) Don't confuse the **vent-** here with the **vent-** for "wind."

> **Qualifying words:** advent, adventitious, adventive, adventure, adventuresome, avenue, circumvene, circumvent, circumvention, contravene, convene, convenient, conveniently, convent, conventicle, convention, conventional, covenant, event, eventual, eventually, eventuate, inconvenience, inconvenient, intervene, intervention, invent, invention, inventive, inventory, parvenu, peradventure, prevent, preventative, prevention, provenance, revenue, souvenir, subvene, subvention, supervene, uneventful, venire, venture, venturesome, venue

venari- (love, reverence) See **vener-** for examples.

vend- (L., to sell, to give [*i.e.* offer] for sale) Also see **-poly** for other "sale, selling" words.

> **Qualifying words:** vend, vendable, vendee, vender, vendible, vending, vendition, vendor, vendue

vener-, venari- (L., love, sexual desire, loveliness, beauty, attractiveness, charm; by extension "to reverence, worship, venerate") Also examine **amat-, aphrodi-, eroto-,** and **philo-** for other "love" words. Venery, "hunting" (archaic), "to hunt" from Latin *venari,* "to hunt, pursue;" the act, art, or sport of hunting; "the love for the pursuit [hunt]."

    Qualifying words: venerable, venerate, veneration, venereal, venerealize, venerealization, venereologist, venereology, venereophobia, venery, venial, venison, Venus

Venereal Terms or Terms of Venery See the GROUP NAMES section in **Appendix M** for an extensive list of venery terms.

veni- (L., come) See **ven-** for examples.

veno-, ven- (L., poison) Also see **toxico-** and **viru-** for other "poison" words. Don't confuse this **veno-** with the next one meaning "blood veins."

    Qualifying words: antivenen, antivenom, envenom, venenation, veneniferous, venenosity, venenous, venom, venomication, venomosalivary, venomous

veno-, veni-, -venous, -venously (L., blood veins) Also see **angio-, arterio-, phlebo-,** and **vaso-** for other "vein" words. Don't confuse this **veno-** with the previous **veno-** which means "poison."

    Qualifying words: intravenous, intravenously, paravenous, paravenously, venofibrosis, venogram, venography, venomotor, venopressor, venose, venosity, venostasis, venostat, venotomy, venous

vent- (L., come) See **ven-** for examples.

vent- (L., air, wind) Also see **aero-, anemo-, pneo-, pneumato-,** and **pneumo-** for other "air" words. Don't confuse this **vent-** with the one which means "to come."

    Qualifying words: hyperventilate, hyperventilating, hyperventilation, vent, ventiduct, ventifact, ventilate, ventilation, ventilator, ventile, ventometer, ventose

ventri-, ventro-, ventr- (L., stomach, belly [or a relationship to the front or anterior aspect of the body]) Also see **abdomino-, coelio-,** and **gastro-** for other "stomach" examples.

    Qualifying words: ventral, ventricle, ventricose, ventriduct, ventriduction, ventriloquism, ventriloquist, ventriloquy, ventripotent, ventrodorsal, ventroposterior, ventroscopy, ventrotomy

ventu- (L., come) See **ven-** for words which mean "come."

Venus (goddess of love; love, sexual desire, loveliness, attractiveness, beauty, charm) See **vener-** for derivations.

ver- (truth) See **veri-** for examples.

verb (L., word) Also see **legi-, lexico-,** and **logo-** for other "word" examples.

    Qualifying words: adverb, adverbial, cruciverbalist, cruciverbalophile, proverb, proverbial, verb, verbal, verbalism, verbalist, verbalization, verbalize, verbalizer, verbally, verbatim, verbiage, verbicide, verbify, verbigerate, verbigeration, verbomania, verbomaniac, verbophobia, verborrhea, verbose, verbosity

verd- (L., green) See **verdant** for examples.

verdant, verd- (L., green, yellow-green) Also see **chloro-** and **virid-.**

    Qualifying words: verdancy, verdant, verdantique, verdigris, verdohemochrome, verdohemoglobin, verdure, Vermont, viridescent

verg-, -vergent, -vergence (L., bend, curve, turn, tend toward, incline) Also see **flect-, gyro-, -plex, stroph-, tors-, trop-, vers-,** and **volv-** for other "bend, turn" words.

    Qualifying words: converge, convergence, convergent, diverge, divergence, divergent, verge

veri-, ver- (L., true, truth, real, truthfulness) Also see **etym-** for other "truth" words.

    Qualifying words: aver, veracious, veracity, veridicial, verdict, verifiable, verification, verify, veriloquence, veriloquent, verily, verisimilar, verisimilitude, veritable, verity, Veronica, very

vermo-, verm-, vermi- (L., worm) For other "worm" words, see **ascari-, helmintho-,** and **scoleco-.**

    Qualifying words: Vermes, vermian, vermicidal, vermicide, vermicelli, vermicular, vermiculate, vermiculation, vermicule, vermidice, vermiform, vermifugal, vermifuge, vermin, verminate, vermination, verminosis, verminous, vermiophobia, vermiphagia, vermiphile, vermivorous, vermography

vers-, vert-, -verse, -version, -version, -versation, -versary, -vert, vort-, vors- (L., bend, turn) Also see **flect-, gyro-, -plex, stroph-, tors-, trop-, verg-,** and **volv-.**

    Qualifying words: adversary, adversative, adverse, adversity, advert, advertise, advertisement, animadversion, animadvert, anniversary, averse, avert, aversion, controverse, controversy, controvert, conversant, conversation, converse, conversely, conversion, convert, convertible, dextrorse, divers, diverse, diversion, diversity, divert, diverticulum, divorce, divorcee, eversion, evert, extrorse, extroversion, extrovert, inadvertent, incontrovertible, introrse, introversion, introvert, inverse, inversion, invert, invertibrate, malversation, obverse, obversion, obvert, perverse, perversion, pervert, quaquaversal, retrorser, retroversion, reversal, reverse, reversible, reversion, revert, sinistrorse, subversion, subversive, subvert, tergiversate, tergiverse, tetrovert, transverse, traverse, universal, universe, university, versatile, verse, versed, versicle, versicolor, versify, version, verso, versus, vertebra, vertebrate, vertex, vertical, verticil, verticillation, vertiginous, vertigo, vervel, vice versa, vortex, vortical, vorticism, vortiginous

vert- (L., bend, turn) See **vers-** for examples.

vertebra, spinal chord See **coccygo-** (end of the spine)**, rachio-** and **spondylo-** for examples.

vesper (L., evening; pertaining to the evening) Also see **hesperian.**

> **Qualifying words:** vesperal, vespers, Vespertilio, vespertilionid, Vespertilionidae, vespertine

vespertilio (L., bat[s])

> **Qualifying words:** Vespertilio, vespertilian, vespertilionid, vespertilionine, Vespertilionidal, pipestrel, pipistrelle

vespi-, vesp- (L., wasp)

> **Qualifying words:** vespiary, Vespidae, vespiform, vespine, vespoid

vessel (blood) See **angio-, arterio-, phlebo-, vaso-,** and **veno-** for examples.

vexill- (L., flag, standard)

> **Qualifying words:** vexillary, vexillium, vexillologist, vexillology, vexillomania, vexillomaniac, vexillophillia, vexillophilliac, vexillum

via- (**-vey, -voy-**) (L., way, road, path) Also see **odo-** for other "way" words.

> **Qualifying words:** convey, convoy, deviant, deviate, deviation, deviationism, deviationist, devious, envoy, evitable, impervious, invoice, obviate, obvious, pervious, previous, previously, quadrivium, Traviata, trivia, trivial, triviality, trivialization, trivialize, trivialness, trivium, vehicle, via, viaduct, viatic, viaticum, voyage

vibration, shake See **pall-** and **seismo-.**

vict- (L., conquer, overcome) See **vinc-.**

vid-, video-, vis-, -vision, -visional, -visionally, visuo-, -vey (L., see, sight, view, look, perceive) Also see **-orama, -scope,** and **spec-** for other "see" words.

> **Qualifying words:** advice, advisable, advise, advised, advisement, advisory, belvedere, belvue, clairvoyant, *deja vu*, envisage, envision, envy, evidence, evident, evidently, improvidence, improvident, improvisator, improvise, interview, invidious, invisible, jurisprudence, preview, previse, prevision, provide, provider, providence, provident, providential, providing, provision(s), provisional, proviso, provisory, prudence, prudent, purvey, purview, review, revis-

al, revise, revision, revisit, revisory, revue, supervise, supervision, supervisor, surveillance, survey, surveying televise, television, videlicet, video, videodisc, videogenic, videognosis, videolaseroscopy, videophone, videopoly, videotape, videotext, *vide supra*, vidette (vedette), view, viewpoint, visa, visage, *vis-a-vis*, vise, visible, vision, visionary, visit, visitant, visor, vista, visual, visualphone, visuognosis, visuosensory, vizard

view, sight See **-orama, -scope, spec-,** and **vid-** for examples.

vigi-, vig- (L., watchful, wakeful, alert)

> **Qualifying words:** vigil, vigilance, vigilant, vigilante

vinc-, vict-, -vince, -vincible, -vincibility (L., conquer, overcome)

> **Qualifying words:** convict, conviction, convince, convincible, convincing, convincingly, evict, eviction, evince, evincible, *Invictus*, invincibility, invincible, vanquish, victor, Victor, Victoria, victorious, victory, victrix, Vincent, vincible

vini- (L., wine) See **vino-** for examples.

vino-, vin-, vini- (L., wine) Also see **oeno-** for other "wine" words. A related element is *viticulture* (cultivation of grapes)

> **Qualifying words:** vignette, vignettist, vinaceous, vine, vinegar, vinery, vineyard, vinic, vinicultural, viniculture, viniculturist, viniferous, vinification, vinology, vinometer, vinosity, vinous, vinously, vintage, vintner, vintry, vinyl

viper See **echidno-** for examples.

vir-, viri- (L., man, manliness; manhood; husband) Also see **andro-, anthropo-** (humans *or* mankind), and **homo-** (L.) (humans) for other "man" words. Don't confuse this **vir-** with others which mean either "poison" or "green" [as shown below].

> **Qualifying words:** centumvir, decemvir, septemvir, triumvir, triumvirate, virile, virilescence, virilescent, virility, viripotent, virtual, virtue, virtuoso, virtuous

vir- (L., poison) Examine **viru-** and **virid-.**

virgin See **virgo-** for examples.

virgo-, virg-, virgi- (L., a marriageable girl, maiden; related to "a young shoot, twig") Also see **partheno-** for additional related words.

> **Qualifying words:** virgin, virginal, Virginia, virginity, Virgo, *virgo intacta*

virid-, vir- (L., green) Also see **chloro-** and **verdant** for other "green" examples.

> **Qualifying words:** virescent, virid, viridescence, viridescent, virididity, viridigenous

viru-, vir- (L., poison) Also see **toxico-** and **veno-** for other "poison" words. Don't confuse this **vir-** with another **vir-** which means "man."

> Qualifying words: viral, viricide, viroid, virologic, virological, virologist, virology, virophobia, virosis, virucidal, virucide, virulence, virulent, viruliferous, virus, viruses

vis- (L., see, sight, view) See **vid-**.

viscero- (L., internal organs; any large interior organ in any of the three great cavities of the body, especially in the abdomen)

> Qualifying words: viscera, viscerad, visceral, visceralgia, visceralism, viscerimotor, viscerogenic, viscerography, visceromotor, viscerosensory, viscerosomatic, viscerotomy

visible display See **phanero-** and **phant-** for examples.

-vision (L., see, sight) See **vid-** for examples.

vist- (L., sight) See **vid-** for examples.

visu- (L., see, sight) See **vid-** for examples.

vita-, vito-, vit- (L., life, living, pertaining to life, essential to life) Also see **bio-** and **viva-** for other "life" words.

> Qualifying words: aquavit, aquavitae, *curriculum vitae*, devitalize, revitalization, revitalize, vitae, vitaglass, vitagonist, vitagraph, vital, vitality, vitalism, vitalize, vitameter, vitamin, vitaminogenic, vitaminoid, vitaminology, vitaminoscope, vitaphone, vitascope, vitadynamic

vitreo-, vitr- (L., glass) Also see **hyalo-** for other "glass" words.

> Qualifying words: in vitro, vitrain, vitrege, vitreous, vitrescence, vitrescent, vitrescible, vitric, vitrics, vitrifiable, vitrification, vitriform, vitrify, vitrine, vitriol, vitriolic, vitrite

viv- (L., life) See **viva-** for examples.

viva-, vivi-, vivo- (L., life) Also see **bio-** and **vita-** for other "life" words.

> Qualifying words: antivivisection, antivivisectionism, antivivisectionist, *bon vivant*, convivial, conviviality, *in vivo*, nonviable, ovoviviparous, revival, revive, revivescence, reviviscent, *sempervivum*, survival, survive, survivor, viability, viable, viand, victual, viva, *viva voce*, vivacious, vivacity, vivaria(pl.), vivarium(s.), vivary, vive, vivication, vivid, vividialysis, vividiffusion, vivification, vivifier, vivify, vivipara, viviparity, viviparous, vivipary, viviperception, vivisect, vivisection, vivisectionist, vivisector, vivisectorium, vivisepulture

voc-, voca-, vocat-, -voke, -vocation, -vocative, -vocable, vok- (L., call, talk, speak, say, voice, word) See **cit-, clam-, dic-, fa-, locu-, logo-, mythico-, -ology, ora-, -phasia,** and **-phemia** for other "talk, speak" words.

> Qualifying words: advocacy, advocate, advocation, avocation, avouch, convocation, con-

voke, equivocal, equivocate, equivocation, evocative, evoke, intervocalic, invocation, invoke, irrevocable, provocation, provocative, provoke, revoke, revocation, univocal, *viva voce*, vocable, vocabulary, vocal, vicalic, vocalize, vocation, vocational, vocative, vociferate, vociferous, voice, voiced, vouch, voucher, vouchsafe, vowel, vox, *vox populi*

voice, sound See **phono-** for examples.

voke-, vok- (call, talk) See **voc-** for examples.

volcan-, vulcan- (L., fire, burn) For other "fire" words, see **caust-, crema-, flagr-, flam-, ign-, incend-,** and **pyro-**.

> Qualifying words: cryptovolcanic, volcanic, volcaniclastic, volcanism, volcanologist, volcano, volcanogenic, volcanological, volcanology, Vulcan, vulcanize, vulcanology

volen, voli-, vol- (L., will, free choice, wish)

> Qualifying words: benevolence, benevolent, malevolence, malevolent, volition, volitive, voluntarily, voluntary, volunteer

voli- (L., wish) See **volen-** for examples.

volu- (L., bend, curve) See **volv-** for examples.

volut- (L., bend, curve) See **volv-** for examples.

volv-, volu-, -volve, volut-, -volute, -volution (L., bend, curve, turn, twist, roll) For more "bend, turn" words, see **flect-, gyro-, -plex, stroph-, tors-, trop-, verg-,** and **vers-**.

> Qualifying words: circumvolve, circumvolution, convolute, convoluted, convolution, devolve, evolution, evolutionary, evolutionism, evolutionist, evolvable, evolve, evolvement, evolver, involute, involuted, involution, involutional, involve, involved, involvement, obvolute, obvolution, revolt, revolution, revolve, revolver, vault, volt, voluble, volume, volute

vomit See **emeto-** for examples.

vor-, vora-, -vore, -vorous, -vores, -vora, -vory (L., eat, consume, devour) Also see **phago-** for other "eating" words.

> Qualifying words: algivorous, amphivorous, aphidivore, aphidivorous, aphidivory, apivorous, arachnivorous, baccivorous, bacterivore, bacterivorous, batrachivorous, calcivore, calcivorous, calcivory, cancrivorous, Carnivora, carnivore, carnivorous, cepivorous, detritivore, detritivorous, devour, equivorous, erucivorous, exudativore, exudativorous, exudativory, fructivore, folivore, folivory, fructivorous, frugivore, frugivorous, frugivory, fungivorous, gallivore, gallivorous, gallivory, graminivore, graminivorous, granivorous, Herbivora, herbivore, herbivorous, hominivorous, Insectivora, insectivore, insectivorous, larvivorous, lignivorous, limivorous, merdivorous, mulluscivorous, nectarivorous, nucivorous, omnivore, omnivorous, omnivorousness, ornithivorous, oryzivorous, pani-

vorous, phytivorous, piscivorous, pupivorous, pomivorous, radicivorous, sanguivore, sanguivorous, seminivorous, univore, univorous, univory, vermivorous, voracious, voraciously, voraciousness, voracity, xylivore, xylivorous, xylivory

-vore (L., eat) See **vor-** for examples.

-vorous (L., eat) See **vor-** for examples.

vors- (L., turn) See **vers-** for examples.

vort- (L., turn) See **vers-** for examples.

vot- (L., vow, affirm) See **vov-** for examples.

vov-, vot- (L., vow, affirm, wish, commit)

> **Qualifying words:** avow, avowal, devote, devoted, devotion, devout, votary, vote, voting, votive, votive candle, vow

vow, affirm See **vov-** for examples.

vulcan- (L., fire) See **volcan-** for examples.

vulg- (L., common people, multitude, common) Also see **ceno-**[1], **commu-, demo-, ethno-, pleb-, popu-,** and **publi-** for references to "common" and "people."

> **Qualifying words:** divulge, divulged, divulgence, divulger, divulging, vulgar, Vulgar Latin, vulgarian, vulgarism, vulgarity, vulgarization, vulgarize, Vulgate

vulpi-, vulp- (L., fox) *Vixen* is a female fox from Middle English while *vix* is the male fox. See the ANIMAL CATEGORIES section in **Appendix A** for additional information about the family names of animals.

> **Qualifying words:** Vulpecula, vulpecular, Vulpes, vulpicidal, vulpicide, vulpicidism, Vulpinae, vulpine, vulpinism

vulvo-, vulv- (L., womb, matrix; literally, "a covering, wrapper") See **colpo-, episio-, hystero-,vagino-,** and **utero-** for additional "female-reproductive-organ" words.

> **Qualifying words:** vulva, vulvar, vulvectomy, vulvitis, vulvopathy, vulvorectal, vulvouterine, vulvovaginal, vulvovaginitis

W w

walk See **ambul-** and **grad-** for examples.

wander, moving See **err-, migr-, nomad-,** and **vaga-** for examples.

wandering, drifting See **plankton** for examples.

war, fight See **belli-, -machy, milit-,** and **pugn-** for examples.

ward off, keep away See **alexo-** and **-fend-** for examples.

wash See **balneo-, lav-, luto-,** and **purg-** for examples.

wasp See **vespi-** for examples.

watchful, alert See **vigi-** for examples.

water See **aqua-, hydro-, hyeto-, ombro-, phreato-** (ground water), **pluvial, udo-,** and **uro-** for related words.

wave, flow See **fluct-, liqu-, rheo-, rheum-, undu-,** and **vacilla-** for examples.

wave, sprout See **cymo-** and **kymo-** for examples.

waver See **vacilla-** for examples.

wax See **cero-** and **cerum-** for examples.

way, road See **hodo-, odo-** and **via-** for examples.

wealth, wealthy See **lucr-, opulen-,** and **pluto-** for examples.

weapon See **arm-** and **strato-** (army) for examples.

wear away, rub See **bruxo-, tribo-,** and **-tripsy** for examples.

weave See **-plex** for examples.

web (tissue) See **arachno-** and **histo-.**

weigh, hang See **pend-** for examples.

weight, weighty See **baro-** and **grav-** for examples.

wellhead, spring See **creno-** and **pego-** for examples.

well, good See **bene-, bon-,** and **eu-** for examples.

well, reservoir, ground water See **phreato-** for examples.

west, evening See **hesperian** and **vesper** for examples.

wet, moist See **hygro-, humid-,** and other elements which mean "water" for examples.

wide, broad See **eury-** and **platy-.**

whale See **ceto-** for examples.

wheel See **roti-** for examples.

whip, beat See **flagello-** for examples.

whirling object See **turb-** for examples.

whirling, turning See **gyro-** and **volv-** for examples.

white For examples, see **albo-, albumino-, cand-** (glow), and **leuco-.**

whole, complete See **holo-** for examples.

wholesome, healthy See **hygieio-** for examples.

wholly, completely See **de-** for examples.

whore, whoring See **fornicate** and **porno-** for examples.

wide, flat See **eury-** and **platy-** for examples.

wife See **uxor-** for examples.

wild animal, wild beast See **theiro-** for examples.

will, free choice See **volen-** for examples.

wind See **aero-, anemo-, pneo-, pneumato-, spir-,** and **vent-** for examples.

wind pipe See **aorta-, broncho-,** and **tracheo-** for examples.

wine See **oeno-** (*eno-*) and **vino-** for examples.

wing, feather See **plum-, ptero-, pterygo-,** and **ptilo-** for examples.

wise, wisdom See **sag-, sap-,** and **sopho** for examples.

winter See **chimno-** for examples.

with, together See **com-** and **syn-** for examples.

withered, dry See **sicca-** and **xero-** for examples.

within, inside Examine **en-, endo-, ento-, eso-, intra-,** and **intro-** for examples.

without See **a-, an-** (Gk.) and **se-** (L.) for examples.

wolf See **lupus** and **lyco-** for examples.

wood See **hylo-, ligni-,** and **xylo-.**

woodland (open) See **orgado-** for examples.

woodpecker See **pici-** for examples.

woods, forest See **also-** and **sylv-** for examples.

woman See **fem-** and **gyno-** for examples.

womb, uterus See **colpo-, episco-, hystero-, metro-, vagino-, vulvo-,** and **utero-** for examples.

wonder, miracle See **thaumato-** for examples.

wonderful, marvelous See **prodigy** for examples.

word See **legi-, lexico-, logo-,** and **verb-** for examples.

work See **ergo-, labor-, oper-, pono-,** and **urg-** for examples.

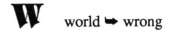

world See **cosmo-, geo-,** and **mundan-** for examples.

worm See **ascari-, helmintho-, scoleco-,** and **vermo-** for examples.

worse See **pejor-** for examples.

worship excessively See **-latry** for examples.

wound, bodily injury See **traumato-** for examples.

wrinkle See **rhytid-** and **rugo-** for examples.

wrist See **carpo-** for examples.

write, record See **glypto-, -gram, grapho-,** and **scrib-** for examples.

wrong, poor, bad See **caco, dys-, mal-, mis-,** and **para-** (see **para-** for other meanings).

X x

xantho-, xan-, xanth-, zantho, zanth (Gk., yellow) Also see **auri-, chryso-,** and **ochro-** for other "yellow" words. See COLORS for other color words

    Qualifying words: axanthopsia, ooxanthine, xanchromatic, xanthemia, xanthia, xanthic, xanthocarpous, xanthochroia, xanthochroic, xanthochroid, xanthochromia, xanthochromatic, xanthocyanopsia, xanthocyanopsy, xanthocyte, xanthoderm, xanthoderma, xanthodermic, xanthodont, xanthodontia, xanthodontous, xanthoerythroderma, xanthofibroma, xanthoma, xanthomelanous, xanthophyl, xanthophyll, xanthophylls, xanthophyte, xanthopia, xanthopsia, xanthopterin, xanthopsia, xanthosomes, xanthospermous, xanthous, xanthrochromatic, xanthrochromic, zanthine, zanthoxylum

xen- (Gk., foreign, strange) See **xeno-.**

xeno-, xen- (Gk., foreign, foreigner, strange, stranger) Also see **barbar-** for other "foreign, stranger" words. The *x* in **xeno-** is pronounced as *z* (*zeno*).

    Qualifying words: autoxenous, axenous, axeny, dixenous, dixeny, euxenite, heteroxenous, lipoxeny, monaxenic, monoxenous, monoxeny, oligoxenous, oligoxeny, rheoxene, rheoxenous, perixenitis, pleioxenous, pyroxene, trixenous, trixeny, xenembole, xenagogue, xenia, xeniobiosis, xenobiology, xenobiosis, xenobiotic, xenocurrency, xenocytophilic, xenodiagnosis, xenodochial, Xenodusa, xenoecic, xenoecy, xenogamous, xenogamy, xenogenesis, xenogenetic, xenogenic, xenogenous, xenogeny, xenoglossy, xenograft, xenolith, xenology, xenmancy, xenomancy, xenomania, xenomaniac, xenomorphic, xenomorphosis, xenon, xenoparasite, xenoparasitism, xenophilia, xenophilic, xenophily, xenophobia, xenophobic, xenophthalmia, xenoplastic, xenopus, Xenopus

xero-, xer-, xir- (Gk., dry) Also see **sicca-** for other "dry" words.

    Qualifying words: antixerotic, elixer, helioxerophile, helioxerophilous, helioxerophily, larynoxerosis, pharyngoxerosis, xerantic, xerarch, xeric, xeriscape, xerocheilia, xerochore, xerocleistogamic, xerocleistogamy, xerocole, xerocolous, xeroderma, xerodermatic, xerodermia, xerodermosis, xerogel, xerogeophyte, xerography, xerohylophile, xerohylophilous, xerohylophily, xerohylophyte, xerolith, xeromorph, xeromorphic, xeromorphy, xerophagia, xerophagy, xerophile, xerophilous, xerophily, xerophobia, xerophobious, xerophonia, xerophthalmia, xerophthalmus, xerophyte, xerophyton, xerosere, xerosis, xerostomia, xerotes, xerotherm, xerothermic, xerotherous, xerotripsis, xerotropic, xerotropism, Xerox ™

xipho-, xiphi- (Gk., sword) Also see **gladi-** for other "sword" words.

    Qualifying words: xiphias, Xiphias gladius, xiphidion, xiphisternum, xiphocostal, xiphodont, xiphodynia, xiphoid, xiphoiditis, xiphopagus, xiphophyllous

xir- (dry) See **xero-** for examples.

x-ray See **roentgeno-** for examples.

xylo-, xyl- (Gk., wood) Also see **also-, arbor-, dendro-, hylo-, ligni-,** and **sylv-** for other "wood, woods" words.

    Qualifying words: protoxylen, pyroxylophile, pyroxylophilous, pyroxylophily, saproxylobios, saproxylobios, saproxylobiotic, xylan, xylanthrax, xylem, xylivorous, xylobalsamum, xylocarp, xylocarpous, xylochrome, xylogen, xyloglyphy, xylograph, xylographer, xylographic, xylographical, xylographically, xylo- graphy, xyloic, xyloid, xylology, xyloma, xylomancy, xylonite, xylophage, xylophagous, xylophagy, xylophile, xylophilous, xylophily, xylophone, xylophonist, xylopolist, xylopoly, xystus, xylophyte, xylotherapy, xylotomist, xylotomous, xylotomy

xyro- (Gk., razor)

    Qualifying word: Xyrichthys, xyrid, Xyris, xyrophobia, xyrospasm

Y y

year See **ann-** and **-enni-** for examples.

yellow, gold See **auri-, chryso-, ochro-,** and **xantho-** for examples.

yellow-green, green See **chloro-, verd-,** and **virid-** for examples.

yield, go See **-cede** for examples.

yoke, pairs See **zygo-** for examples.

young, youthful See **fili-, juveni-, pedo-** (Gk.), and **puer-** for examples.

young girl See **partheno-** and **virgo-** for examples.

Z z

zantho- (Gk., yellow) See xantho-.

zoo-, zo-, -zoic, -zoid, -zoite, -zoal, -zonal, -zooid, -zoon, -zoa, -zoan (Gk., animal) Also see anima-, fauna-, and therio-.

Qualifying words: agrizoiatrist, agrizoiatry, agrizoic, agrizoology agrizoon, Anthozoa, anthozoa, anthozoan, anthozoic, anthozoon, bryozoa, bryozoans, celozoic, azoic, cenozoic, cytozoic, dactylozooid, dermatozoon, ecozoiatry, enterozoic, enterozoon, entozoa, entozoal, entozoic, entozoon, enzootic, Eozoic, eozoic, epizoic, epizoicide, epizoon, epizootic, epizootology, gastrozooid, holozoic, hydrozoa, hylozoism, gonozooid, malacozoology, Mesozoic, mesozoic, mesozoon, metazoa, metazoans, microzoon, microzoophilous, microzoophily, neozoic, oozoa, oozooid, Paleozoic, paleozoic, paleozoon, panzoic, parazoon, proterozoic, protozoa(pl.), protozoon(s), spermatozoon, trophozooid, zoa, zoanthropy, zodiac, zoiatria, zoidal, zoo, zooanthus, zoobenthos, zoobenthic, zoobiology, zoochorous, zoochory, zoocoenosis, zoodomatia, zoodynamics, zooecology, zooerythrin, zooneuston, zooneustonic, zoogamous, zoogamy, zoogenesis, zoogenic, zoogenous, zoogeny, zoogeographer, zoogeography, zoogony, zoography, zooid, zoomimic, zoolater, zoolatrous, zoolatry, zoolith, zoological, zoological gardens, zoologist, zoology, zoomantist, zoomancy, zoomania, zoometry, zoomorphic, zoomorphism, zoomorphosis, zooplankton, zoon, zoonerythrin, zoonomia, zoonomist, zoonomy, zoonoses, zoonosis, zooparasite, zoopathology, zoopathy, zooperal, zoopery, zoophagous, zoophagy, zoophile, zoophilia, zoophilism, zoophilist, zoophilous, zoophobia, zoophobic, zoophysical, zoophysics, zoophysiology, zoophyte, zoophytic, zoophytoic, zoophytological, zoophytology, zooplankton, zooplanktonic, zooplastic, zooplasty, zoopsia, zoopsychology, zoosaprophage, zoosaprophagous, zoosaprophagy, zooscopy, zoosemiotics, zoosis, zoosperm, zoosphere, zoospore, zoosuccivorous, zoosuccivory, zootaxy, zootechnics, zootechny, zootheism, zootheist, zootomy, zootoxin

zygo-, zyg- (Gk., yoke, forming pairs)

Qualifying words: azygous, dizygotic, heterozygosis, heterozygosity, heterozygous, homozygosity, homozygous, monozygosis, monozygotic, syzygy, zygal, zygodactyl, zygodont, zygolysis, zygoma, zygomorphic, zygomorphism, zygomorphous, zygophyte, zygose, zygosis, zygospore, zygotactic, zygotaxis, zygote, zygotic

zymo-, zym-, -zymic (Gk., ferment, fermentation [leavening agent, leavening catalyst])

Qualifying words: azyme, cytozyme, enzyme, histozyme, lysozyme, microzyme, preenzyme, proenzyme, vitazyme, zymase, zymochemistry, zymogen, zymogenesis, zymogenic, zymogenous, zymogic, zymogram, zymohydrolosis, zymoid, zymologic, zymologist, zymology, zymolysis, zymolytic, zymophore, zymorphorous, zymophosphate, zymoscope, zymosis, zymosthenic, zymotic, zymurgy, zythepsary (brewery), zythum (beer)

APPENDIX A, ANIMAL and BIRD CATEGORIES

antelopes (alcelaphine, antelopine)

female	doe
intact male	buck
immature	
newborn	kid
group	herd

asses (asinine), donkeys

female	jenny
intact male	jack, jackass
immature	
newborn	colt, foal, filly
group	herd, drove, pace

badger (meline)

female	sow
intact male	boar
immature	
newborn	cub
group	cete, colony

bear (ursine)

female	
intact male	
immature	yearling
newborn	cub, cub of the year
group	sloth

beaver

female	
intact male	
immature	kit
newborn	kit, kitten
group	

boar

female	
intact male	
immature	calf
newborn	squeaker
group	singular

buffaloes or buffalos

female	cow
intact male	bull
immature	
newborn	calf
group	herd

camels (cameline)

female	cow
intact male	bull
immature	colt
newborn	foal, calf
group	herd, flock

cat (feline)

female	queen, tabby, puss, she-cat
intact male	tom
castrated	gib
immature	
newborn	kitten
group	clowder, cluster, glaring dout, destruction (wild cats), litter (kittens), kindle (kittens)

cattle (bovine), bulls (taurine)

female	cow, dam
intact male	bull, sire
castrated male	steer, ox
immature	heifer (female) bullock (male) yearling
newborn	calf, stick
group	herd, drove, team; yoke (oxen)

chickens (galline)

female	hen
intact male	rooster, cock
castrated male	capon
immature	pullet (female), pullard (when fattened) cockerel (male)
newborn	chick
group	brood, flock

chinchillas

female	dam
intact male	sire
castrated	neutered
immature	grower
newborn	kit
group	

deer (cervine)

female	doe, hind
intact male	buck, hart, stag
immature	yearling
newborn	fawn, calf, kid, pricket
group	herd, leash, parcel (hinds)

dogs (canine)

female	bitch, slut
intact male	hound, dog
castrated dog	neutered
immature	
newborn	puppy, whelp
group	pack, kennel, litter

donkeys (see asses)

ducks (anatine)

female	duck
intact male	drake
immature	
newborn	duckling
group	team (in flight), paddling (in water)

eagles (aquiline)

female	
intact male	
immature	
newborn	eaglet
group	convocation

elephants (elephantine)

female	cow
intact male	bull
immature	
newborn	calf
group	herd

elks (cervine)

female	cow
intact male	bull
immature	
newborn	calf
group	gang

ferrets

female	bitch, doe, jill
intact male	dog, buck, jack, hob
immature	
newborn	kit
group	business, fesnying, cast, fusiness

foxes (vulpine)

female	vixen, bitch-fox, she-fox
intact male	vix, dog, dog-fox
immature	vulpecular
newborn	pup, cub
group	earth, skulk, lead

frog (ranine)

female	
intact male	
immature	
newborn	tadpole, polliwog
group	army, colony

geese (anserine)

female	goose
intact male	gander
immature	
newborn	gosling
group	flock, skein (when flying), gaggle (on water)

goats (hircine, caprine)

female	doe, nanny, dam
intact male	buck, billy
castrated male	weather
immature	yearling
newborn	yeanling, kid
group	flock, herd, tribe

hares (leporine)

female	doe, puss
intact male	jack, buck
immature	leveret (female)
newborn	
group	trace, drove, down, husk, leash, trip

hawks (accipitrine)

female	
intact male	
immature	eyas
newborn	
group	flight

hippopotamus (s.), **hippopotami** (pl.) (hippopotamine)

female	
intact male	
immature	
newborn	calf
group	bloat

horses (equine)

female	mare, dam
intact male	stallion, sire, stud
castrated male	gelding
immature	filly (female)
	colt (male)
	yearling
newborn	foal
group	herd, stable, team, harras, troop, race, rake (of colts)

kangaroos (macropine, macropodine)

female	blue doe, blue flier
male	boomer, buck
immature	
newborn	joey
group	troop, mob, herd

leopards (leopardine, pardine)

female	leopardess
male	leopard
immature	
newborn	cub
group	leap, lepe

lions (leonine)

female	lioness
male	lion
immature	
newborn	cub
group	pride, flock, troop, sault

moles (talpine)

female	
intact male	
immature	
newborn	
group	company, labor, movement

monkeys

female	
intact male	
immature	
newborn	
group	tribe, troop, cartload

moose [singular and plural] (cervine)

female	cow, dam
intact male	bull
immature	yearling
newborn	calf
group	

otters (lutrine)

female	bitch
intact male	dog
immature	cub
newborn	cub
group	bevy, family

peafowls (pavonine)

female	peahen
intact male	peacock
immature	
newborn	peachick
group	muster

pigeons (columbine)

female	hen
intact male	cock
immature	weanling squab
newborn	squab, squealer, squeaker
group	flight, flock

pigs (see **swine** for examples)

polecats (musteline)

female	jill
intact male	hob
immature	
newborn	kit
group	chine

rabbits (oryctolagine, leporine)

female	doe
intact male	buck
immature	junior
newborn	kit, nestling
group	nest, warren, herd

rats (murine)

female	doe
intact male	buck
immature	pup
newborn	nestling
group	colony

rhinoceros (ceratorhine)

female	cow
intact male	bull
immature	
newborn	calf
group	crash

seals (phocine)

female	cow
intact male	bull
immature male	bachelor
newborn	pup, cub
group	crash, colony, harem, bob, herd, pod, team

sheep [singular and plural] (ovine)

female	ewe, dam
intact male	ram, tup
castrated male	wether
immature	lamb (male/female) kid (male/female) yearling (male/female)
newborn	yeanling
group	flock, drove, trip, hurtle, down, fold

snakes (anguine)

female	
intact male	
immature	
newborn	
group	den, pit, nest

squirrels (sciurine)

female	
intact male	
immature	
newborn	nestling
group	dray, scurry

swans (cygnine)

female	pen
intact male	cob
immature	
newborn	cygnet
group	herd, wedge

swine (porcine)

"pigs" (under 120 pounds)
"hogs" (over 120 pounds)   [U.S. terms]

female	sow, dam
intact male	boar, sire
castrated male	barrow (young boar)
	tag (old boar)
immature	shoat (male)
	gilt (female)
newborn	piglet, pigline
litter of piglets	farrow
group	sounder, herd

tigers (tigrine)

female	tigress
intact male	tiger
immature	
newborn	cub
group	ambush, streak

turkeys (meleagrine)

female	hen
intact male	tom
immature	poult
newborn	poult
group	flock, rafter

walruses (odobenine)

female	cow
intact male	bull
immature	
newborn	calf
group	pod, herd

whales (cetacine)

female	cow
male	bull
immature	calf
newborn	calf, cub
group	gam, pod, herd, school

wolves (lupine)

female	bitch, she-wolf
male	dog wolf, dog, he-wolf
immature	whelp, cub
newborn	whelp, cub
group	pack, herd, rout

zebras (zebrine, hippotigrine)

female	mare
male	stallion
immature	colt (male), filly (female)
newborn	foal
group	herd

APPENDIX B

DAYS OF THE WEEK

Although many of the following languages use different scripts with a variety of accent marks, all of the days have been written in Latin or Roman-style letters, except the Greek, without accents for purposes of linguistic comparisons.

Anglo-Saxon days of the week:
sunnandaeg (Sun's day), monandaeg (Moon's day), Tiwesdaeg (Tiw's-day), Wodensdaeg (Woden's day), Thuresdaeg (Thor's day), Frigedaeg (Frigg's day), Saeternesdaeg (Saturn's day)

Arabic days of the week:
al-ahad, youm al-itsnain, youm al-tsoulatsa, youm al-arabaa, youm al-chamis, al goumaa, al-sabt

Catalonian days of the week:
diumenge, dilluns, dimars, dimecres, dijous, divendres, dissabte

Czechoslovakian days of the week:
nedele, pondeli, utery, streda, ctvrtek, patek, sobota

Danish days of the week:
sondag, mandag, tirsdag, onsdag, torsdag, fredag, lordag

Dutch days of the week:
Zondag, Maandag, Dinsdag, Woensdag, Donderdag, Vrijdag, Zaterdag

English days of the week:
Sunday, Monday, Tuesday, Wednesday, Thursday, Friday, Saturday

Esperanto days of the week:
dimanco, lundo, mardo, merkredo, jaudo, vendredo, sabato

Finnish days of the week:
sunnuntai, maanantai, tiistai, keskiviikko, torstai, perjantai, lauantai

French days of the week:
dimanche, lundi, mardi, mercredi, jeudi, vendredi, samedi

German days of the week:
Sonntag, Montag, Dienstag, Mittwoch, Donnerstag, Freitag, Samstag (sometimes, Sonnabend is used instead of Samstag)

Greek days of the week:
Κυριακη (Kyriake, *Kyriaki'*), Δευ–τερα (Deutera, *Defte'ra*), Τριτη (Trite, *Tri'ti*), Τεταρτη (Tetarte, *Teta'rti*), Πεμπτη (Pempte, *Pem'p-ti*), Παρασκευη (Paraskeue, *Paraskevi'*), Σαββατο (Sabbato, *Sa'v-vaton*)

Hebrew days of the week:
yom rischon, yom scheni, yom schelischi, yom reviie, yom chamischi, yom schischi, schabat

Hungarian days of the week:
vasarnap, hetfo, kedd, szerda, csutortok, pentek, szombat

Italian days of the week:
domenica, lunedi, martedi, mercoledi, giovedi, venerdi, sabato

Japanese days of the week:
nichiyoobi, getsuyoobi, kwayoobi, suiyoobi, mokuyoobi, kin'yoobi, doyoobi

Korean days of the week:
il yo il, whal yo il, wha yo il, soo yo il, mok yo il, khum yo il, toh yo il

Latin days of the week
See **Roman days of the week.**

Norwegian days of the week:
sondag, mandag, tirsdag, onsdag, torsdag, fredag, lordag

Polish days of the week:
niedziela, poniedzialek, wtorek, sroda, czwartek, piatek, sobota

Portuguese days of the week:
domingo, segunda feira, terca feira, quarta feira, quinta feira, sexta feira, sabado

Roman days of the week:
dies solis, dies lunae, dies Martis, dies Mercurii, dies Jovis, dies Veneris, dies Saturni

Rumanian days of the week:
duminica, luni, marti, miercuri, joi, vineri, simbata

Russian days of the week:
voskresyenye, panidyelnik, ftornik, sreda, chetverk, pyatnitsa, subota

Serbo-Croat days of the week:
nedelja, ponjedeljak, utorak, srijeda, cetortak, petak, subota

Spanish days of the week:
domingo, lunes, martes, miercoles, jueves, viernes, sabado

Swahili days of the week:
Jumatatu, Jumapili, Jumanne, Jumatano, Alhamisi, Ijumaa, Jumamosi

Swedish days of the week:
sondag, mandag, tisdag, onsdag, torsdag, fredag, lordag

Turkish days of the week:
pazar, pazartesi, sali, carsamba, per sembe, cuma, cumartesi

Yiddish days of the week:
suntog, montog, diensttog, mitvoch, donnerschtog, freitog, schabbes

Appendix C

Decibels

A decibel [dB] (DES uh buhl) is a unit for measuring the relative intensity of sounds, equal to one-tenth of a *bel*. A bel is used in physics to measure the difference in the intensity level of sounds to normal human ears, equal to ten decibels. It is estimated that 0 dB corresponds roughly to the quietest sound which can be heard by a healthy young adult. Normal conversation has a level of 60-70 dB, while sounds above about 100 dB tend to be uncomfortably loud and can damage our ears if heard for a long time. Sounds with a level above 120 dB can damage peoples's ears within quite a short time, perhaps only a few minutes. When the level of a sound is increased by 10 dB, the subjective loudness roughly doubles, whereas the sound power actually increases by a factor of 10. The smallest detectable change in level is about 1 dB. The system was named after Alexander Graham Bell (1847-1922), who is given credit for being the inventor of the telephone.

"Numerous studies have shown prolonged exposure to 85 decibels or more can cause permanent hearing loss. Other physiological damage can occur at lower levels."

"A single, explosive noise is capable of damaging hair cells, but hearing loss is usually the result of continual exposure to volumes over 80-85 decibels" (Arline Bronzaft, *Harvard Medical School Health Letter*, Vol. II, No. 8, 1986, pp. 1-4).

Decibel Levels

180   rocket launching pad (hearing loss inevitable)

140   gunshot blast, jet plane take-off at close range (approximately 200 feet), air raid siren (any length of exposure time is dangerous and is at the threshold of pain)

130   sound vibrations felt, as with thunder or near a four-engine jet at thirty meters

125   diesel engine room

120   amplified rock concert in front of speakers, sand-blasting, thunderclap (immediate danger), a nearby airplane engine, some rock or hard-metal cacophony groups, pneumatic hammer at one meter, thunderclap overhead **(at around 120 dB, the sensation of hearing is replaced by that of pain)**

110   deafening factory noises and some "musical boxes" turned up too loudly, discotheque, thunder, rock-n-roll band

108   the *coqui* frog croak of Puerto Rico (*up* to 108 decibels)

100   chain saw, boiler shop, pneumatic drill, printing plant, jackhammer, speeding express train, some car horns at five meters, farm tractor, riveting machine, some noisy subways (about 20 feet)

90   police whistle, heavy traffic, truck traffic, noisy home appliances, subway-rail train, pneumatic drill (or hammer) at one meter, "walk-man" ear phones (*average* volume), rock drill at 100 feet, some motorcycles at 25 feet, shouted conversation

80   heavy city traffic (25-50 ft.), alarm clock at two feet, factory noise, vacuum cleaner, heavy truck, loud radio music, garbage disposal; **75** telephone bell at three meters, shouting, quiet vacuum cleaner, side street in New York city with no traffic

70   typewriter, average factory noise, busy traffic (at one meter), office tabulator, noisy restaurant (constant exposure), quiet vacuum cleaner, TV

60   air conditioner at 20 feet, conversation (at one meter), sewing machine, large transformer, ordinary or average street traffic

50   quiet radio, average home, light traffic at a distance of 100 ft., refrigerator, gentle breeze, average office, typewriter, ordinary spoken voice

40   quiet office, living room, bedroom away from traffic, residential area (no traffic); many computer hard drives range an average of 40-50 dB, soft whisper (five feet)

30   quiet conversation, soft whisper, quiet suburb, speech in a broadcasting studio, "quiet" home sounds

20   whispering, ticking of a watch (by the ear), rural area (without loud farm machinery or other excessive noises)

10   rustling of leaves

0-1   the faintest sounds which can be heard, threshold of audibility

Appendix D

Hippocratic oath

Hippocrates of Cos (late 5th century B.C. [about 460 - 377 B.C.]), the famous Greek physician who is generally considered as the "Father of Medicine." An oath which is included in the body of written materials, attributed to Hippocrates and his school, known as the *Hippocratic oath*, has been the ethical guide to the medical profession since Hippocrates' time. There are some who believe that it may have been an ancient oath of the Aesclepiads (Greek., *Asklepios* > Latin, *Aesculapius*, the mythical Greek god of healing, son of Apollo and the nymph Coronis). It appears in a book of the hippocratic collections, however, it wasn't written by Hippocrates himself. The "oath" contains the Greek medical thought and practices of his day and embodies his ideals. He is credited with separating medicine from superstition and his observations have been used in medical teaching for centuries. One version of the oath follows:

"I swear by Appollo the physician, by Aesculapius, Hygeia, and Panacea, and I take to witness all the gods, all the goddesses, to keep according to my ability and my judgment the following Oath:

"To consider dear to me as my parents him who taught me this art: to live in common with him and, if necessary, to share my goods with him; to look upon his children as my own brothers, to teach them this art if they so desire without fee or written promise; to impart to my sons and the sons of the master who taught me and the disciples who have enrolled themselves and have agreed to the rules of the profession, but to these alone, the precepts and the instruction. I will prescribe regimen for the good of my patients according to my ability and my judgment and never do harm to anyone. To please no one will I prescribe a deadly drug, nor give advice which may cause his death. Nor will I give a woman a pessary to procure abortion. But I will preserve the purity of my life and my art. I will not cut for stone, even for patients in whom the disease is manifest; I will leave this operation to be performed by practitioners (specialists in this art). In every house where I come I will enter only for the good of my patients, keeping myself far from all intentional ill-doing and all seduction, and especially from the pleasures of love with women or with men, be they free or slaves. All that may come to my knowledge in the exercise of my profession or outside of my profession or in daily commerce with men, which ought not to be spread abroad, I will keep secret and will never reveal. If I keep this oath faithfully, may I enjoy my life and practice my art, respected by all men and in all times; but if I swerve from it or violate it, may the reverse be my lot."

A few Hippocratic quotes—

Everything in excess is opposed to nature.

The art has three factors, the disease, the patient, and physician. The physician is the servant of the art. The patient must co-operate with the physician in combating the disease.

Who could have foretold, from the structure of the brain, that wine could derange its functions?

Healing is a matter of time, but it is sometimes also a matter of opportunity.

A wise man ought to realize that health is his most valuable possession.

Natural forces are the healers of disease.

We must turn to nature itself, to the observations of the body in health and disease to learn the truth.

As to diseases, make a habit of two things—to help, or at least to do no harm.

Appendix E

Mancy Words (Words of Divination)

-mancy, -mancer, -mantic, -mantical, (Gk., divination, prophecy; to interpret signs so "practical" decisions can be made [related to *mania*]) Divination is considered the willful exploration of the future or the discovery of hidden things by various practices. The most common divinations are *astrology, dowsing, interpretation of dreams, cards, numerology, crystal-gazing, omens,* and *palmistry.*

acuto-mancia (also spelled *manzia*), a form of divination which uses pins. Thirteen tacking pins are used, ten of them are straight and the remainder bent. The pins are shaken and when they fall on a table covered with a light film of talcum-powder, their formations are studied for possible revelations about the future.

aeromancy, divination by observing substances in the air or wind, such as cloud shapes; weather forecasting; atmospheric phenomena (comets, etc.).

aichomancy, divination or fortune-telling by interpreting sharp points.

ailuromancy, divination as determined by the way a cat jumps; a black cat crossing one's path is a bad omen in the U.S. and Germany, although it is considered as lucky in Britain. Owning a black cat is also considered to be lucky. It is a widespread belief that killing or mistreating a cat will bring ill fortune. This may arise from ancient religious beliefs as a sacred animal.

air (wind), **aeromancy**

air (activities [rain, thunder, lightning, etc.]), **ceraunomancy**

alectoromancy, divination by the observation of a rooster eating corn scattered on letters; crowing, etc. In Africa, a black hen or a gamecock is used. An African diviner sprinkles grain on the ground and when the bird has finished eating, the seer interprets the designs or patterns left on the ground.

alectromancy, see **alectoromancy.**

alectryomancy or **alectroyomancy,** divination by the observation of a rooster eating corn scattered on letters and writing down the letters as the rooster touches them; crowing, etc.

aleuromancy, divination of meal or flour; predictions written on paper and baked in cakes or cookies, such as Chinese "fortune cookies" which are a form of this type of *mancy.* The ancient Greeks wrote sentences on pieces of paper rolled up in balls of flour. The balls were mixed up nine times and distributed to those who wanted to know their future.

all objects (any available object), **apantomancy**

alomancy, divination by means of salt; today, some people still respond to spilt salt on the table by throwing some over the left shoulder so bad luck will go away (a variant of halomancy); the diviner interprets future events from the patterns made from the sprinkled salt.

alphitomancy, divination with barley meal and honey loaves; once it was used as a method to determine if one were guilty of some crime by having the accused try to eat a barley cake and if he couldn't swallow it or if he got sick, he was considered guilty (this same method is said to have been used by the Chinese with rice cakes).

amathomancy, divination by observing the arrangement of dust or dirt.

ambulomancy, divination by observing how someone walks.

amniomancy, divination by the examination of the caul, or membrane, which sometimes envelopes the head of a child at birth; embryonic sac. From an examination of the caul, there was a prediction about the baby's future; if red, happy days; if lead-colored, he will have misfortunes.

animal (skins, bones, and droppings): **spatalomancy, spatilomancy**

animal feces: **spatalamancy, spatalomancy**

animals, **zoomancy**

animals (wild): **thieromancy, theriomancy**

anthomancy, divination with flowers (could "She loves me, she loves me not" have anything to do with this ancient method?).

anthracomancy, fortune-telling by analyzing burning coals.

anthropomancy, divination by examining the entrails of a person during a sacrifice or slaughter, usually those of virgins or young children. This form of *mancy* was practiced in ancient Egypt (Roman Emperor Heliogabalus is said to have done this).

antinopomancy, divination by analyzing the sacrifices of children.

apantomancy, divination by the examination of any objects which happen to present themselves; omens drawn from chance meetings with a rabbit, an eagle, etc.

arithmancy, divination with numbers, numerology; practiced by Greeks and Chaldeans. The Greeks would analyze the names of warring enemies and determine their numerical values and from this they would predict the result of the battle. The Chaldeans divided their alphabet into three sections of seven letters and made a symbolic link to the seven planets.

appearance of a person, **schematomancy**

armomancy, divination by inspection of the shoulders to determine whether a victim was suitable for sacrifice to the gods.

arrows: **belomancy, bolomancy**

ashes: **ceneromancy, spondomancy, tephramancy, tephromancy**

aspidomancy, divination with a shield by sitting on it within a magic circle and going into a trance; predictions from the devil.

astragalomancy, divination with dice, knuckle bones, stones, small pieces of wood, or ankle bones which have been marked with letters, symbols, or dots. Using dice for divination is a form of astragalomancy.

astromancy, divination by interpreting the stars, astrology; one of the ancient systems of prophecy.

austromancy, divination by observing winds, especially the south winds, with special significance attached to their direction and intensity.

axhead, **axinomancy**

axinomancy, divination with an axhead and a "jet-stone" placed on a bed of hot embers; or with a marble. Practiced by the ancient Greeks to discover a crime. An agate or piece of jet (stone) was placed on a red-hot axe which indicated the guilty person by its motion.

babies (nursing), **mazomancy**

barley meal, **alphitomancy**

beans/bones, **cleromancy**

belomancy, divination with arrows; one method was to throw a certain number of arrows into the air and note the directions in which the arrows inclined as they fell; said to be used by the Chaldeans and Scythians and passed on to some Germanic tribes. "Another method was to have three arrows upon one of which was written, 'God forbids it me;' upon another, 'God orders it me;' and upon the third nothing at all. These were put into a quiver, out of which one of the three was drawn at random. If the arrow without the inscription was drawn, they drew again." *-Demonologia,* John Bumpus, London: 1827

A different procedure was to place labels to a given number of arrows which archers would shoot and the advice on the arrow which went the farthest would be followed. Babylonians were said to use this method.

bibliomancy, divination by picking Bible or other book passages at random; several church councils were formed in the fifth century A.D. to study and forbid this "common" practice. One of the methods used was for a person to point to a line or passage with his eyes closed. In the Middle Ages, it was trendy to use Virgil's *Aeneid* and Homer's *Illiad.* Also known as **rhapsodomancy** and **stichomancy.**

Bible verses, **bibliomancy**

birds: **ornithomancy, ornomancy, orthinomancy**

blood: **dririmancy, haematomancy, hematomancy**

body, **somatomancy**

bolomancy, divination with arrows thrown at random from a container.

bones: **ossomancy, osteomancy**

bones (knuckle), **astragalomancy**

book passages, **bibliomancy**

botanomancy, divination with plants, herbs; a method of divination by burning the branches of vervein [now, *vervain*; "*verbena,* sacred boughs or certain medicinal plants"] and brier, upon which were carved the questions of the diviner. Variations included scattering the leaves of vervein [*vervain*] or heather in a high wind. Another method was by writing sentences on leaves which were exposed to the wind, the divination would be gathered from those leaves which were left. Interpretations were also made from the crackling sounds made when certain plants were thrown on the fire or crushed in the hands.

brazen vessels, cattabomancy

brizomancy, divination with the inspiration of Brizo, goddess of sleep; therefore, divination by the interpretation of dreams.

breastbone, **sternomancy**

brontomancy, divination by interpreting thunder or thunderstorms.

capnomancy, divination by observing smoke from victims who were sacrificed by fire
"The general rule was that when the smoke was thin and light and ascended straight up, it was a good omen; if it were heavy, it was an ill omen. There was another species of capnomancy which consisted of observing the smoke arising from poppy and jessamin seeds cast upon burning coals." -*Demonologia*, John Bumpus, London: 1827

cards: **cartomancy, catopromancy**

cartomancy, see **catoptromancy**.

catopromancy, prophecy with playing cards; similar to tarot cards.

catoptromancy or **catotromancy,** divination with a crystal ball, a lens, or mirrors. The Greeks put metal "mirrors" under the water or held them in a fountain and interpreted the reflections.

catoxtromancy, divination with a mirror or some other reflective surface.

cats: **ailuromancy, felidomancy**

cattabomancy, prophecy with the use of brazen vessels.

caul or after birth membrane, **amniomancy**

causimomancy, divination with fire; "it is a happy presage when combustible objects don't burn when thrown into the fire;" it was a good omen if something failed to burn or took a long time to catch on fire.

ceneromancy, divination by interpreting the ashes from a sacrifice.

cephalomancy, divination by boiling a donkey's head on burning coals.

ceraunomancy, divination from activities in the air (rain, thunder, lightning, etc.).

ceramancy, divination by dropping melted wax into water and observing (interpreting) the figures made there. During the Middle Ages, wax would be melted in a brass container and poured into another vessel containing cold water.

ceromancy, see **ceramancy**.

chalcomancy, divination by striking copper or brass bowls.

chaomancy, divination by observing and interpreting confusion or disorder; observed in clouds, airborne apparitions, aerial visions, or comets.

chartomancy, divination with maps; interpreting inscriptions.

cheese: **tiromancy, tyromancy**

cheiromancy, divination with palmistry or the analysis of the various shapes and forms of the hands reading lines, moisture, scars, dirt, etc. in/on a person's hand to deduce character, temperament, fortune, the future, etc. This was practiced by ancient Greeks, Chaldean astrologers, gypsies, and others..

chilomancy, divination performed with keys.

chiromancy, see **cheiromancy**.

chresmomancy, divination by interpreting the utterences of a person who is in a frenzy; dating back to the Greek Oracle of Delphi.

christallomancy, divination with a crystal ball.

chronomancy, divination by the determination of the precise time for some action.

chyromancy, divination with the hands. Also **chiromancy** (*q.v.*).

circle (walking until dizzy), **gyromancy**

cledonomancy, divination with omens or lucky charms, by listening to utterances of mantic significance, or by interpreting unplanned events.

cleidomancy, divination with a key; a pendulum; sometimes with a key hanging from a young girl's third-finger nail; sometimes with a moving key hanging from a Bible.

cleromancy, divination by throwing black and white beans, little bones, dice, and perhaps, stones; anything suitable for casting lots. Studying shapes formed as pebbles are thrown into still water; in Rome these objects were sacred to Mercury. The Masai of East Africa shake stones in a buffalo horn. In at least one Bantu tribe, a diviner used twenty-seven objects, mostly pairs and most of them knuckle bones. Some of the bones client's family, and others were from sows, gazelles, and wild boars. The future is predicted by interpreting the patterns formed by the bones.

clothes (brushed), **petchimancy**

clidomancy, see **cleidomancy.**
clouds, **chaomancy**
coals (burning), **anthracomancy**
conchomancy, divination with sea shells.
copper bowls, **chalcomancy**
coscinomancy, divination by turning a sieve held on a pair of shears or tongs (as in voodoo). "The art of divination by means of a sieve. A very ancient practice mentioned by Theocritus, and still used in some parts of England, to find out persons unknown." -Chambers from *A Dictionary of the English Language,* 3rd Ed., 1765, compiled by Samuel Johnson. Pebbles or other fine substances have also been known to be sifted through a sieve and then interpretations were made of the patterns formed.
cosinomancy, see **coscinomancy.**
counting, **mathemancy**
crithomancy, divination by spreading grain or cake dough over sacrificed victims.
cromniomancy, divination with names, significant happenings, or missing persons which were written on onions, planted, and observed to see which one would sprout first. The onion which sprouted most rapidly indicated that the person whose name had been inscribed on it was enjoying vigorous health. Another application was that wishes would come true if one burnt onion skins on a fire. Sometimes the onions had to be placed on the altar at Christmas before they had any divine significance.
cromnyomancy, divination by using onions.
cryptomancy, divination with secret signs, words, etc.; some unrevealed method used by mantics.
crystal ball: **catoptromancy, catotromancy, christallomancy, crystallomancy, spheromancy**
crystallomancy, divination with crystal gazing as in a crystal ball, with a precious stone, or with a bright-metal surface. Sometimes a mirror-like pool of water was used. By gazing steadily and deeply into a polished crystal ball, it was believed that those possessing the gift could see what was about to happen or what was actually happening at some other place.
cubomancy, divination with thrown dice or with cubed bones.
cup: **scyhomancy, seyomancy**

cyclomancy, divination with some revolving device.
dactyliomancy, divination with finger rings ". . . by holding a ring suspended by a fine thread over a round table on the edge of which were a number of marks with the 24 [Greek] letters of the alphabet. The ring was consecrated with a great deal of mystery." -*Demonologia*, John Bumpus, p. 146, London: 1827. A ring was suspended on a string as it swang unassisted against the side of a glass indicating "yes" or "no" to questions. A ring might also be used as a pendulum to point out letters. One technique is to let a ring swing from one's hand by a string or human hair over a circle, often the rim of a wide vase, on which letters are written. The swinging of the ring spells out the answers to questions. Some groups use other objects; for example, the Malaysians use lemons; the Cherokees used stones or ancient arrowheads, and a modern version of the method is the *Ouija* board.
dactylomancy, see **dactyliomancy.**
daphnomancy, divination by throwing laurel leaves on a sacred fire from a grove sacred to Appollo. If the leaves crackled in the flames, the forecast would be favorable; if they burned quietly, the prophecy was negative.
dead, **necromancy, nycromancy**
demonomancy, divination by calling on demons for prophecies as in black magic.
dice: **astragalomancy, cleromancy, cubomancy**
dirt (earth), **geomancy**
divination, **manticism**
dogs (howling), **ololygmancy**
donkey's head, **cephalomancy**
dophonomancy, divination by interpreting the crackle of a laurel branch on a fire (the same as *daphnomancy*).
dreams, **brizomancy, oneiromancer, oneiromancy, oniromancy**
drug (induced sleep), **narcomancy**
dung (or seeds in dung), **stercomancy**
dust (dirt), **amathomancy**
dressing, **stolisomancy**
dririmancy, divination by observing dripping blood.
eggs, **oomancy, ovomancy**

elaeomancy, divination with olive oil or another kind of oil; by the observation of a liquid surface.

empyromancy, divination by observing fire and smoke or the objects on a sacrificial fire. Eggs, flour, and incense were used for this purpose as well as shoulder blades of the sacrificed victim.

enoptromancy, divination by the use of a mirror and its reflections.

entrails (includes human inner parts, such as the intestines, etc.), **anthropomancy, spleanchomancy**

eromancy, Oriental (Persian) divination in which a person covered his head with a cloth and muttered questions above a vase of water. Stirrings on the surface would be regarded as a good omen.

excrement, **scatomancy**

eychnomancy, divination with lamps.

eyes, **oculomancy, ophthalmomancy**

face (especially, the forehead), **metopomancy, physiognomancy**

false divination, **pseudomancy**

fig leaves, **sychomancy**

feet: **pedomancy, podomancy**

felidomancy, divination by observing the behavior or actions of a cat, ranging from changes in weather to unexpected visitors.

finger nails: **onimancy, onychomancy, onycomancy, onymancy, onyomancy**

finger rings: **dactyliomancy, dactylomancy**

fire (burning): **causimomancy, empyromancy, pyromancy**

fire, earth, air, water: **stareomancy**

flames: **lampadomancy, lychnomancy**

floromancy, divination with flowers or plants, including their colors, petals, and time and place of planting. A belief that flowers radiate vibrations and have curative properties in healing disease.

flowers: **anthomancy, floromancy**

foliomancy, divination with tea leaves.

footprints, **ichnomancy**

fortune teller, **mantologist**

frenzy, **chresmomancy**

gastromancy, divination by listening to stomach sounds or the use of ventriloquism, and/or with the marks on the stomach; also, divination by crystal-gazing.

gelomancy, divination by translating hysterical laughter into coherent terms.

geomancy, divination by the analysis of figures or lines drawn in dirt (or on paper); a system of divination by scattering pebbles, dust, sand grains, or seed on the ground and interpreting their shapes and positions; making marks on the ground with a stick (now with a pencil or pen on paper); still used by modern-day Chinese in Hong Kong and other places before construction of a building takes place; in modern Germany, a geobiologist checks water and magnetic veins in the earth so living-quarters (bed room, etc.) can be "properly" arranged.

grain, **crithomancy**

graphomancy, divination with handwriting analysis.

graphtomancy, see **graphomancy**.

gyromancy, divination by walking in a circle until dizziness causes one to fall and this is interpreted in various ways.

haematomancy, divination with blood.

halomancy, divination with the use of salt (one method was by interpreting the shape of salt which was thrown on a flat surface). Interpretation of the shapes which are formed after salt is thrown on a surface or by throwing salt into flames and observing the nature of the flames, their color, speed, and direction.

hands: **cheiromancy, chiromancy, chyromancy**

handwriting: **graphomancy, graphtomancy**

haruspimancy, divination by the "reading" of livers.

head, **kephalonomancy**

heavens: **ouranomancy, uranomancy**

hematomancy, divination with blood.

hematomancy, see **hematomancy**.

hidromancy, divination with water, tides, and ebbs.

hieromancy, divination with sacrificial remains or sacred objects; by observing the things offered as sacrifices.

hippomancy, divination with horse(s); the Celts kept white horses in consecrated groves; ancient Germans kept similar steeds in their temples. If on leaving the temple at the out-break of hostilities, the horses crossed the temple threshold with the left forefoot first, the prophecy was regarded as an evil omen and the war was abandoned. A horse's pace was also interpreted.

horses, **hippomancy**

hydromancy, divination with water or other liquids; such as, tides and ebbs; by having a small boy tell what he has seen in the water. Interpreting the color and patterns of flowing water; sometimes ripples are studied as stones are dropped into quiet water.

hyomancy, divination with wild swine; or by the tongue or the "tongue bone."

ichnomancy, divination with the interpretations of personality and appearances of people by studying their footprints, posture and position.

ichthyomancy, divination by examining the heads and/or entrails of fish for prophetic signs or the next fish caught.

iconomancy, divination of pictures or icons or with special images.

idolomancy, divination with idols or images.

images: **iconomancy, idolomancy**

imbecility, **moromancy**

incense: **knissomancy, libanomancy, livanomancy**

iron, **sideromancy**

kephalonomancy, divination used by some of the Lombards in which lighted carbon was poured on the baked head of a goat as the names of those who were accused of crimes were called out. If crackling occurred as a name was called, it was assumed that the accused was guilty. The head of an ass was also used.

keraunomancy, divination by interpreting thunder and lightning.

keys: **chilomancy, cleidomancy, clidomancy, kleidomancy**

kidneys, **mephromancy**

kleidomancy, divination with a key or a pendulum (**cleidomancy**).

knissomancy, divination with burning incense.

knives, **macharomancy**

labiomancy, divination with lip reading.

lampadomancy, divination with the flame of a torch, candles, or substances which are burned in their flames. The actions and movements of the flames were interpreted and a flame with a single point was believed to indicate good fortune, but if it had two points, this signaled bad luck. Sparks were said to indicate news and sudden extinction of the flame meant disaster.

lamps, **eychnomancy**

land contours, **topomancy**

largest object at hand, **macromancy**

laughter, **gelomancy**

laurel branch, dophonomancy

laurel leaves, **daphnomancy**

lead, **molybdomancy**

leaves, **phyllomancy, phyllorhodomancy**

lecanomancy, divination with water in a basin into which plates of gold and silver were put with jewels. Sometimes a stone, or similar object, was thrown into a basin of water and the sounds it made as it dropped to the bottom were interpreted. Another method involved placing water in a silver vase on a clear moonlit night. The light from the candle was reflected on the water by the blade of a knife and the diviner concentrated on the image formed in the water. In addition, other objects were dropped into the water; such as, melted metals (lead or tin), silver and gold, oil, wax, or egg whites.

letters, **nomancy**

lungs and/or air, **pneumancy**

libanomancy, fortune telling by observing incense smoke.

licanomancy, divination by the study of reflections in still water.

lip reading, **labiomancy**

lithomancy, divination with rocks or stone charms; with meteorites.

livanomancy, divination with incense.

liver, **haruspimancy**

logarithmancy, divination with mathematical logarithms.

logomancy, divination by the observation of words and discourse; with the use of magic words.

Lucifer, **necyomancy**

lychnomancy, divination with flames of three identical candles arranged in a triangle. Success was indicated by one flame burning brighter than the other two, a wavering flame indicated travel, a spiral flame meant plots by enemies, an uneven flame presaged danger, sparks called for caution, and a sudden extinction indicated bad luck.

macharomancy, divination by using knives or swords.

macromancy, divination with the largest thing at hand (nearby).

maculmancy, divination with stains or anything made impure; with spots.

magastromancy, divination with magic or astrology.

magic, **magastromancy**

mantic, one who divines and/or makes a prophecy; one blessed with prophetic powers.

manticism, the art of divination and prophecy.

mantologist, one who tells fortunes.

mantology, the art of fortune-telling or divining past, present, and/or future events.

maps, **chartomancy**

margaritomancy, divination with pearls; covered with a vase and put near a fire, names of suspects were pronounced and when the guilty name was uttered the pearl was supposed to jump up and "pierce" the bottom of the vase.

mathemancy, divination by counting.

mazomancy, divination by observing nursing babies.

meal (flour), **aleuromancy**

meconomancy, divination with opium and its effects; drug-induced sleep.

meteormancy, divination by observing thunder, lightning, weather, meteors, etc.

meteoromancy, see **meteormancy**.

metopomancy, divination by examining the lines, etc. of the face or forehead.

mice (or rats), **myomancy**

micromancy, divination with the smallest thing available.

mineralmancy, divination with minerals.

minerals, **mineralmancy**

mirrors: **catoptromancy, catotromancy, catoxtromancy, enoptromancy**

molybdomancy, divination by observing the motion of molten lead on a flat surface or in water and the interpretations made of the hissing sounds.

moon, **selenomancy**

moromancy, divination by interpreting imbecility or through nonsense; foolish divination.

mountains, **oromancy**

myomancy, divination by the movements of mice and rats; used by ancient Assyrians, Romans, and Egyptians. The cries and activities of the mice and/or rats were often said to indicate the presence of evil. The peculiar cries, or some devastation they

were responsible for, was understood as a prognostication of evil. The Greek historian, Herodotus, wrote about a King Sennacherib when he invaded Egypt. The mice (or rats) gnawed on his soldiers' quivers and bows so that in the morning they were without arms. As they fled in confusiion, many of them were slain. Horapollo, in his curious work on the Hieroglyphics of Egypt, describes the rat as a symbol of destruction.

name: **onomancy, onomatomancy**

narcomancy, divination with opium and its effects or with drug-induced sleep.

navel (observing it), **omphalomancy**

necromancy, divination by communication with the dead by raising them back to "life" (not with a ghost); early Greeks were supposed to descend into Hades to consult the dead rather than summoning the dead into the mortal sphere again; more recently, it is claimed that ghosts or spirits are summoned to speak to the living.

necyomancy, divination by summoning Lucifer.

nephelomancy, divination with tobacco smoke or the formation and direction of clouds.

nephromancy, divination by looking at the kidneys.

nomancy, divination by graphological examination of letters, usually in a name.

numbers, **arithmancy**

nursing babies, **mazomancy**

nycromancy, divination by communication with the dead.

oculomancy, divination by interpretating the eyes of certain human subjects.

odontomancy, divination by interpreting aches and pains of the teeth or by other types of teeth examinations.

oenomancy, divination by observing the colors and other features of wine or the interpretation of the patterns made by wine that had been poured out as an offering to the gods.

oil, **elaeomancy**

oinomancy, see **oenomancy**.

ololygmancy, divination by interpreting the howling of dogs.

omens (lucky charms), **cledonomancy**

omphalomancy, divination by contemplation of one's own navel (as in yoga?) or by counting the knots in the umbilical cord of a mother's first child to predict the number of children she will have.

oneiromancy, see **oniromancy**.

oniromancy (oneiromancy), divination or the interpretation of dreams. More than 36 references to dreams are mentioned in the Bible, the most famous being the interpretations of dreams made by Joseph in Egypt in the book of Genesis, chapters 40 and 41.

onimancy, divination by observing fingernails or olive oil on the finger nails of an "unpolluted boy" or a young female virgin.

onions: **cromniomancy, cromnyomancy**

onomancy, see **onomatomancy**.

onomatomancy, divination by interpreting the names, or the number of vowels (even/odd) in a name, or the total number of letters, or the sum of the numerical values of the letters.

onychomancy (onimancy), divination of fingernails or the reflection of bright sunlight on a person's fingernails and noting any symbols that might appear there (as with crystal gazing or teacup reading).

onycomancy, see **onychomancy**.

onymancy, divination by interpreting the fingernails.

onyomancy, see **onychomancy**.

oomancy, divination with eggs (usually when they have been broken).

ophthalmomancy, divination by interpreting reflections, colors, etc. of the eyes.

ophiomancy, divination by watching snakes.

opium: **meconomancy, narcomancy**

ornithomancy, divination by the observation and interpretation of birds; a Greek term for Roman augury, which interpreted the flight or song of birds. The Romans had a distinct order of priests who were responsible for determining auspicious or inauspicious undertakings [*auspicious* means "viewing" or "watching the birds" in flight and making interpretations that show that their behavior and sounds were good omens while *inauspicious* would be the result of bad omens].

ornomancy, see **ornithomancy**.

oromancy, divination by observing mountain shapes, etc.

orthinomancy, divination with birds in flight; birds are also involved with **orniscopy, ornithoscopy,** and **ornomancy.**

oryctomancy, divination from things dug up.

ossomancy, divination with bones.

osteomancy, see **ossomancy**.

ouranomancy, divination by observing the heavens.

ovomancy, divination with eggs.

pearls, **margaritomancy**

pebbles: **pessomancy, psephomancy**

pedomancy, divination by observing the soles or bottoms of the feet.

pegomancy, divination by observing the way air bubbles are rising in springs or fountains; dropping stones in sacred pools or springs and observing their movements.

pendulum, **cleidomancy**

person who divines, **mantic, mantologist**

pessomancy, divination with pebbles or beans marked with symbols and colors relating to health, communications, success, travel, etc. The stones were either thrown out after shuffling (mixing) in a bag or drawn out at random.

petchimancy, divination by observing the results of brushed clothes.

phyllomancy, divination with leaves.

phyllorhodomancy, divination by clapping rose leaves against the side of the hand and noting the sounds that they make; used for divination by ancient Greeks

physiognomancy, divination by observing the facial expressions of a subject and interpreting forms, lines, etc. of the face

pictures, **iconomancy**

pins, **acutomancia**

plants, **botanomancy**

pneumancy, divination by interpreting air, wind, or the lungs; by blowing [especially by blowing out a candle] It exists today in the act of blowing out the candles on a [festival] birthday cake.

podomancy [also, **pedomancy**, L.], divination by interpreting someone's feet.

psephomancy, prophecy with pebbles (heaped in a pile).

pseudomancy, fraudulent or misleading fortune telling; pretended divination.

psychomancy, divination through men's souls and affections; conjuring or evoking the dead; with some object or piece of clothing connected with the person.

pyromancy, divination with fire or flames; a *good omen* resulted when the flames were vigorous and quickly consumed the sacrifice and when the smoke was transparent, neither red nor dark in color, when it didn't crackle, but burnt silently in a pyramidal form; but a *bad omen* when it was difficult to kindle, disturbed by wind or slow to consume the victim. Mantics also observed flames of torches by throwing powdered pitch into the flames. Another aspect is pyroscopy (based on the burn stains left on a light surface after burning a sheet of paper).

retromancy, divination by things seen over one's shoulder.

revolving device, **cyclomancy**

rhabdomancy, divining by rods, sticks, or wands; dowsing for water. Usually a forked branch of hazel or willow, which when manipulated by the diviner or *dowser,* inclined toward the place where a concealed spring or a metallic vein (lode) was to be found. Zulu divining sticks answered "yes" or "no," depending on whether they fell or rose.

rhapsodomancy, divination with verses; divination took place by opening and orally reading the first verses seen; sometimes as a needle is stuck into a closed book. Also **bibliomancy** and **stichomancy**.

roads (sticks, wands), **rhabdomancy**

rocks, **lithomancy**

rods, sticks, or wands: **rhapdomancy**

rings (finger): **dactyliomancy, dactylomancy**

rooster: **alectromancy, alectroyomancy**

rose leaves, **phyllorhodomancy**

sacred objects: **hieromancy, theomancy**

salt: **alomancy, halomancy**

sacrifices (children), **antinopomancy**

scapulimancy, divination by observing charred or cracked shoulder blades or markings on the shoulder bone of an animal (especially a sheep).

scapulomancy, divination from charred or cracked shoulder blades of an animal that had been burned in sacrifice.

scarpomancy, reading character by studying a person's old shoes.

scatomancy, divination by examining excrement or feces.

schematomancy, divination by the examination of a person's appearance or form so as to determine his personal history.

sciomancy, divination through communication with shadows (spirits) of the dead; also concerned with the evocation of astral reflections to ascertain future events.

scyphomancy, divination by using a cup of water and reading the signs indicated by certain articles floating on the water.

selenomancy, divination by moon gazing.

seyomancy, divination with a cup.

shadows, **sciomancy**

sharp points, **aichomancy**

shells (sea), **conchomancy**

shield, **aspidomancy**

shoes (old), **scarpomancy**

shoulders: **armomancy, retromancy, scapulimancy, scapulomancy, spatulomancy, spatulomantic, spealomancy**

sideromancy, divination by observation of the stars or the interpretation of burning straw smoke and the patterns made by the burnt straw on a hot iron. *Sidero* refers to "stars" (L., *q.v.*) or to "iron" (Gk., *q.v.*)

sieve: **coscinomancy, cosinomancy**

signs (secret), **cryptomancy**

smallest thing available, **micromancy**

smoke: **capnomancy, empyromancy, nephelomancy**

snakes, **ophiomancy**

somatomancy, divination by observing a body.

souls, **psychomancy**

spasmatomancy, divination by interpreting spasms or the twitching body of a potential sufferer.

spatalamancy, divination by the observation of animal droppings, feces, or their skins and bones..

spatalomancy, see **spatalamancy**.

spatilomancy, see **spatalamancy**.

spatulamancy, divination by observing or examining burned, chracked, or charred animal shoulder blades.

spatulomancy, see **spatulamancy**.

spealomancy, see **spatulamancy**.

spheromancy, divination with a crystal ball.

sphondulomancy, divination with spindles.

spindles, **sphondulomancy**

splanchomancy, divination in the form of **anthropomancy** practiced by ancient Etruscans from the study of the entrails of sacrificed victims.

spodomancy, divination by examining ashes, especially those of a sacrifice.

spots (stains), **maculmancy**
spring water, **pegomancy**
stareomancy, divination through the observations of the ancient elements of fire, earth, air, and water.
stars: **astromancy, sideromancy**
stercomancy, divination by observing dung or seeds found in dung.
sternomancy, divination by examining the breastbone.
stichomancy, divination by the lines or the passages in a book of poetry. Also known as **bibliomancy** and **rhapsodomancy**.
stignomancy, divination by examining the writings or carvings on tree bark.
stigomancy, divination by observing the writings or carvings on tree bark.
stigonomancy, divination by examining the writings or carvings on tree bark
stoicheomancy, divination by opening the works of Homer or Virgil and reading orally the first verses seen which are considered prophetic.
stolisomancy, divination by the manner in which a person dresses himself. In ancient Rome, Emperor Augustus believed a military revolt was predicted on a particular morning of the occurrence because his attendant (valet) had buckled the emperor's right sandal on his left foot.
stranger, **xenomancy**
stomach sounds, **gastromancy**,
sun, **heliomancy**
swine, **hyomancy**
swords, **macharomancy**
sycomancy, divination by writing names or messages on leaves from a fig tree and letting them dry out; modern version involves the use of ivy leaves; if leaves dried quickly, it was an evil omen, but a good augury if the leaf dried slowly.
tasseomancy, divination by interpreting the sediment of the tea leaves or coffee grounds which were left after the liquid was been poured off or consumed.
tea leaves: **foliomancy, tasseomancy**
teeth, **odontomancy**
tephramancy, see **tephromancy.**
tephromancy, divination by examining the ashes from an altar which have been blown or thrown up into the air after consumation of the victims of a sacrifice.

theiromancy, divination by observing wild animals and interpreting their behavior and movements.
theomancy, mysteries of a divine majesty sought the sacred names; the possessor of such a "science" knew the future, commanded nature, had full power over angels and demons, and could perform miracles; by the answers of divinely inspired oracles.
theriomancy, see **theiromancy.**
thunder: **brontomancy, keraunomancy, meteormancy**
time, **chronomancy**
tiromancy, divination by watching cheese coagulate.
tobacco smoke, **nephelomancy**
tongue, **hyomancy**
topomancy, divination by observing the contour of the land.
transataumancy, divination by interpreting something seen or heard accidentally or unexpectedly.
tree bark; **stignomancy, stigomancy, stigonomancy**
trochomancy, divination by looking at wheel tracks.
tyromancy, divination by watching cheese coagulate.
unexpected sights or sounds, **transataumancy**
uranomancy, divination by observing the sky or natural phenomena in the sky.
urimancy, see **urinomancy.**
urine: **urimancy, urinomancy, uromancy**
urinomancy, divination by interpretating the characteristics of urine *or* a medical prognosis based on the examination of urine to diagnose diseases.
uromancy, see **urinomancy.**
vase, **eromancy**
ventriloquism, **gastromancy**
verses: **rhapsodomancy, stichomancy, stoicheomancy**
walking, **ambulomancy**
water: **hydromancy, lecanomancy, licanomancy, ydromancy**
water (tides, ebbs), **hidromancy**
weather, **meteormancy, meteoromancy**
wheels, **trochomancy**
wind, **austromancy**
wine: **oenomancy, oinomancy**
wood, **xylomancy**
words, **logomancy**

xenomancy, divination by observing the first stranger who appears.

xylomancy, divination with small pieces of wood; interpreting the forms or appearance of fallen tree branches or other wood seen on the ground; also the positions of logs and the manner of burning in a fire.

ydromancy, divination with water (obsolete form of **hydromancy**).

zoomancy, divination with observations of animals or their movements under particular circumstances; imaginary animals that people claim to have seen such as a salamander playing around in a fire or a sea serpent riding ocean waves.

zygomancy, divination with weights.

Bibliography for **-mancy** words

Bumpus, John. *Demonologia.* London: 1827

Dickson, Paul; *Words.* New York: Delacorte Press, 1982

Drury, Nevill. *Dictionary of Mysticism and the Occult.* San Francisco: Harper & Row Publishers, 1985

Gibson, Walter B. and Litzka R. *The Complete Illustrated Book of Divination and Prophecy.* Garden City, New York: Doubleday & Co., Inc., 1973

Roget's International Thesaurus. 4th ed. Revised by Robert L. Chapman, New York: Harper & Row, Publishers, 1977

Shepard, Leslie, Ed. *Encyclopedia of Occultism & Parapsychology,* Volumes I & II. Detroit: Gale Research Co., 1979

Appendix F

Metric Groups

SI units (*Systeme International d'Unites*) or the **International System of Units** of the modern metric system, are recommended for all scientific purposes. Since the system has been adapted by international agreement [according to the 1960 *Eleventh General Congress on Weights and Measures*], it is supposed to be the basis of all national measurements throughout the world and it integrates such measurements for science, industry, and commerce. Thus there is only one unit for a particular quantity, whether thermal, electrical, or mechanical.

The SI system is formed on a foundation of seven base units:

1. Length = meter (*metre*, British)
2. Mass = kilogram (*kilogramme*, British)
3. Time = second
4. Temperature = Kelvin (in 1967, the *General Conference on Weights and Measures* gave the name Kelvin to the SI of temperature and assigned to this temperature unit the symbol **K** without the associated symbol for the degree)
5. Electrical current = ampere
6. Luminous intensity = candela
7. Amount of substance = mole (decided at the 1971 conference)

Decimal multiples of the units are indicated by a set of prefixes as shown on this and the following page.

The prefixes which follow have been verified by a hand-out sheet entitled: "Les Prefixes SI.", dated 16.9.1974, CCU/74-23 obtained from Mr. R. P. Hudson, editor of METROLOGIA (an international journal of scientific metrology) at the Bureau International des Poids et Mesures, Pavillon de Breteuil, F-92310 Sevres, FRANCE with a letter dated July 22, 1987.

METRIC MULTIPLES and SUBMULTIPLES

WHOLE NUMBERS

exa- [EKS uh] (Gk.), from **hexa**, "six," [Symbol = E]: 10^{18} (1 000 000 000 000 000 000); U.S., quintillion; U.K. trillionfold

    Qualifying word: exameter

peta- [PE tuh] (Gk.), from **penta**, "five," [Symbol = P]: 10^{15} (1 000 000 000 000 000); U.S., quadrillion; U.K. thousand billionfold

    Qualifying words: petacurie, petacycle, petameter

tera- [TE ruh] Gk.), "monster, omen, marvel," [Symbol = T]: 10^{12} (1 000 000 000 000); U.S., trillion; U.K. billionfold

    Qualifying words: terabit, teracurie, teracycle, terahertz, terameter, teraohm, teraohmmeter, terawatt

giga- [JIG uh *or* GIG uh] (Gk.), "giant," [Symbol = G]: 10^{9} (1 000 000 000); U.S. billion; U.K., thousand millionfold

    Qualifying words: gigabit, gigacycle, gigaelectronvolt, gigaelectrovolt, gigahertz, gigameter, giganewton, gigasecond gigawatt, gigohm

mega- [MEG uh] (Gk.), "big, great, large," [Symbol = M]: 10^{6} (1 000 000); U.S., million; U.K. millionfold

    Qualifying words: megabit, megacycle, megahertz, megameter, megaton, megavolt, megawatt, megohm

kilo- [KIL oh *or* KEEL oh] (Gk.),"thousand," [Symbol = k]: 10^{3} (1 000); U.S., thousand; U.K. thousandfold

    Qualifying words: kiloampere, kilobar, kilobit, kilocalorie, kilocycle, kilogram, kilohertz, kilohm, kilojoule, kiloliter, kilometer, kilovolt, kilowatt

hecto- [HEK toh] (Gk.), "hundred," [Symbol = h]: 10^{2} (100); U.S., hundred; U.K., hundredfold

    Qualifying words: hectare, hectogram, hectoliter, hectometer

deka-, deca- [DEK uh] (Gk.), "ten" [Symbol = da]: 10^{1} (10); U.S., ten; U.K., tenfold

    Qualifying words: decagram, dekaliter, dekameter

FRACTIONS

deci- [DE si] (L.), "ten," [Symbol = d]: 10^{-1} (0.1); or one-tenth U.S., tenth; U.K., tenth part

    Qualifying words: decibel, decigram, deciliter, decimeter

centi- [SEN ti] (L.), "one-hundred," [Symbol = c]: 10^{-2} (0.01) or one-hundredth; U.S., hundredth; U.K., hundredth part

    Qualifying words: centibar, centigram, centiliter, centimeter

milli- [MIL i] (L.), [Symbol = m]: "a thousand," 10^{-3} (0.001) or one-thousandth; U.S., thousandth; U.K., thousandth part

    Qualifying words: milliampere, millicycle, millifarad, millihertz, milliliter, millirad, milliroentgen, millivolt, milliwatt

micro- [MIGHK roh] (Gk.) [Symbol = μ]: "small," 10^{-6} (0.000 001); U.S., millionth; U.K., millionth part

    Qualifying words: microampere, microfarad, microhenry, microlambert, microsecond, microvolt, microwatt

nano- [NA noh] (Gk.) [Symbol = n]: "dwarf," 10^{-9} (0.000 000 001); U.S., billionth; U.K., thousand-millionth part

    Qualifying words: nanoampere, nanocurie, nanofarad, nanogram, nanoliter, nanometer, (nanometre, British), nanomole, nanosecond

pico- [PEE koh] (It.) [Symbol = p]: "small quantity," 10^{-12} (0.000 000 000 001); U.S., trillionth; U.K., billionth part

    Qualifying words: picoampere, picocurie, picofarad, picogram, picoliter, picometer, picomole, picopicogram, picosecond, picowatt

femto- [FEM toh] (Danish) [Symbol = f]: "fifteen," 10^{-15} (0.000 000 000 000 001); U.S., quadrillionth; U.K., thousand-billionth part

    Qualifying words: femtoampere, femtogram, femtojoule, femtoliter, femtometer, femtomole, femtosecond, femtovolt, femtowatt

atto- [A toh] (Danish), [Symbol = a]: "eighteen," 10^{-18} (0.000 000 000 000 000 001); U.S., quintillionth; U.K., trillionth part

    Qualifying words: attoampere, attosecond, attotesla

Appendix G

mono-, nom- (Gk., one) See **mono-** for examples.

soli-, sol- (L., one) See **soli-** for examples. Don't confuse this element with another **sol-**, which means "sun."

uni- (L., one) See **uni-** for examples.

sesqui- (L., one and one half [$1^{1/2}$]) See **sesqui-** for examples.

bi-, bin- (L., two) See **bi-** for examples. Don't confuse this element with another **bio-, bi-** which means "life."

deutero-, deuter- (Gk., second) See **deutero-** for examples.

di-, dicho-, dich- (Gk., two) See **di-** for examples.

duo-, du- (L., two) See **duo-** for examples.

terce-, ter- (L., thrice, three) See **terce-** for examples.

tri- (Gk., > L., three) See **tri-** for examples.

quadri-, quad-, quadru-, quatr- (L., four) See **quadri-** for examples.

tetarto-, tetart- (Gk., one fourth) See **tetarto-** for examples.

tetra-, tetr- (Gk., four) See **tetra-** for examples.

penta-, pent- (Gk., five) See **penta-** for examples.

quinqu-, quinque-, quin- (L., five) See **quinqu-** for examples.

hex-, hexa- (Gk., six) See **hex-** for examples.

sex- (L., six) See **sex-** for examples.

hepta-, hept- (Gk., seven) See **hepta-** for examples.

septem-, septi-, sept- (L., seven) See **septem-** for examples.

octo-, oct- (Gk. > L., eight) See **octo-** for examples.

ennea- (Gk., nine) See **ennea-** for examples.

nona- (L., nine) See **nona-** for examples.

novem- (L., nine) See **novem-** for examples.

deca-, dec-, deka- (Gk., ten) See **deca-** for examples.

decem-, decim-, deci- (L., ten) See **decem-** for examples. In the metric system, **deci-** is used to show 1/10 of a unit.

hendeca- (Gk., [*hen-*, "one"] eleven) See **hendeca-** for examples.

dodeca-, dodec- (Gk., twelve) See **dodeca-**for examples.

duodeci- (L., twelve) See **duodeci-** for examples.

uncia (L., inch, ounce, a twelfth) See **uncia** for examples.

icosa-, icos-, icosi- (Gk., twenty) See **icosa-** for examples.

centi-, cent- (L., hundred) See **centi-** for examples. In the metric system, **centi-** denotes 1/100 of a unit.

hecto-, hect- (Gk., hundred) See **hecto-** for examples.

kilo- (Gk., thousand) See **kilo-** for examples.

mille-, milli- (L., thousand) See **mille-** for examples. In the metric system, **milli-** denotes 1/1000 of a unit.

myria-, myri- (Gk., ten thousand or "very numerous") See **myria-** for examples.

40 - 49	quadragenarian
50 - 59	quinquagenarian
60 - 69	sexagenarian
70 - 79	septuagenarian
80 - 89	octogenarian
90 - 99	nonagenarian

The following are **U.S.** and **Canadian** numerical systems with **British, French,** and **German** variations in brackets. The U.S. practice "was modeled on the French system but more recently the French system has been changed to correspond to the German and British systems." *Webster's Ninth New Collegiate Dictionary*, Merriam-Webster, Inc., 1983.

ten (10^1) 10 [British use the same, 10^1]

hundred (10^2) 100 [British use the same, 10^2]

thousand (10^3) 1 000 [British use the same, 10^3]

million (10^6) 1 000 000 [British use the same, 10^6]

billion (10^9) 1 000 000 000 [British use milliard, 10^{12}]

trillion (10^{12}) 1 000 000 000 000 [British, 10^{18}]

quadrillion (10^{15}) 1 000 000 000 000 000 [British, 10^{24}]

quintillion (10^{18}) 1 000 000 000 000 000 000 [British, 10^{30}]

sextillion (10^{21}) 1 000 000 000 000 000 000 000 [British, 10^{36}]

septillion (10^{24}) 1 000 000 000 000 000 000 000 000 [British, 10^{42}]

octillion (10^{27}) 1 000 000 000 000 000 000 000 000 000 [British, 10^{48}]

nonillion (10^{30}) 1 000 000 000 000 000 000 000 000 000 000 [British, 10^{54}]

decillion (10^{33}) 1 000 000 000 000 000 000 000 000 000 000 000 [British, 10^{60}]

undecillion (10^{36}) 1 000 000 000 000 000 000 000 000 000 000 000 000 [British, 10^{66}]

duodecillion (10^{39}) 1 000 000 000 000 000 000 000 000 000 000 000 000 000 [British, 10^{72}]

tredecillion (10^{42}) 1 000 000 000 000 000 000 000 000 000 000 000 000 000 000 [British, 10^{78}]

quattuordecillion (10^{45}) 1 000 000 000 000 000 000 000 000 000 000 000 000 000 000 000 [British, 10^{84}]

quindecillion (10^{48}) 1 000 000 000 000 000 000 000 000 000 000 000 000 000 000 000 000 [British, 10^{90}]

sexdecillion (10^{51}) 1 000 000 000 000 000 000 000 000 000 000 000 000 000 000 000 000 000 [British, 10^{96}]

septendecillion (10^{54}) 1 000 000 000 000 000 000 000 000 000 000 000 000 000 000 000 000 000 000 [British, 10^{102}]

octodecillion (10^{57}) 1 000 000 000 000 000 000 000 000 000 000 000 000 000 000 000 000 000 000 000 [British, 10^{108}]

novemdecillion (10^{60}) 1 000 000 000 000 000 000 000 000 000 000 000 000 000 000 000 000 000 000 000 000 [British, 10^{114}]

vigintillion (10^{63}) 1 000 000 000 000 000 000 000 000 000 000 000 000 000 000 000 000 000 000 000 000 000 [British, 10^{120}]

googol (10^{100}) 1 000 000 000 000 000 000 000 000 000 000 000 000 000 000 000 000 000 000 000 000 000 000 000 000 000 000 000 000 000 000 000 000 000 000 000 000 000 000 000 000 000 000 000

Although not from a Greek or Latin source, this nomenclature is frequently used in mathematics for such a numerical group. Credit for coining this term is given to Milton Sirotta, the nine-year-old nephew of Dr. Edward Kasner, an American mathematician, when the boy was asked, c. 1940, to give a name to such a large unit of numbers. A *googol* is also called *ten duotrigintillion*. In addition to googol, Dr. Kasner (1878-1955) also credits his nephew with contributing *googolplex* which is ten raised to the power of a googol or $10^{10^{100}}$ or the number 1 followed by 10^{100} zeros.

centillion (10^{303}) 1 000 [British, 10^{600}]

See **Cardinal numbers** on the next page.

Cardinal numbers from Latin

unus (masculine), **una** (feminine),
   unum (neuter), one
duo, duae, duo, two
tres, tria, three
quattuor, four
quinque, five
sex, six
septem, seven
octo, eight
novem, nine
decem, ten
undecim, eleven
duodecim, twelve
tredecim, thirteen
quattuordecim, fourteen
quindecim, fifteen
sedecim, sixteen
septendecim, seventeen
duodeviginti, eighteen
undeviginti, nineteen
viginti, twenty
viginti unus, etc., twenty-one, etc.
duodetriginta, twenty-eight
undetriginta, twenty-nine
triginta, thirty
quadraginta, forty
quinquaginta, fifty
sexaginta, sixty
septuaginta, seventy
octoginta, eighty
nonaginta, ninety
centum, hundred
centum et unus, etc., hundred and
   one, etc.
ducenti (masculine, plural),
   ducentae (feminine, plural),
   ducenta (neuter, plural), two
   hundred
trecenti, three hundred
quadringenti, four hundred
quingenti, five hundred
sescenti, six hundred
septingenti, seven hundred
octingenti, eight hundred
nongenti, nine hundred
mille, thousand

Appendix H

OXYMORA

Oxymoron, pronounced ahk" si MOR ahn, is singular, **oxymora**, pronounced ahk" si MOR uh, is plural, [pointedly foolish, Greek, *oxy-*, "point, sharp" and *moron*, "foolish, dull"]. *Oxymora* are the combinations of contradictory or incongruous words, often for literary effect; a figure of speech in which opposite or contradictory ideas or terms are combined; a wittily paradoxical turn of phrase which appeals to "unconscious responses instead of rational examinations."

The use of the oxymoron is considered an effective figure of speech which works especially well in poetry, political rhetoric, and humorous writing. As mentioned above, like all poetic devices, it appeals to the reader's unconscious responses, not so much to his/her reason.

According to Evan Esar in *Esar's Comic Dictionary*, an oxymoron is "a figure of speech that stands for a self-contradictory expression, like a chaste whore or an honest politician." Malcolm Muggeridge, who predated Esar, said, "Good taste and humor are a contradiction in terms, like a chaste whore." Could this be a case of *honest plagiarism*?

Oxymora List

A Fine Mess
"Alone Together"
abundant poverty
accidentally on purpose
accurate rumors
acrophobic mountain-climbers
act naturally
acute apathy
acute dullness
airline food
airline schedules
a little pregnant
almost always
almost candid
almost exactly
almost impossible
almost perfect
almost persuaded

almost pregnant
almost safe
almost suddenly
almost surprised
almost totally
Amtrak schedule
anonymous colleague
anticipated serendipity
anxious patient
apathetically urged
apathetic interest
approximate solution
arrogant humility
athletic scholarship
awfully good
baby grand
Back to the Future
bad health
bad luck
balanced insanity
barely dressed
benevolent despot
benign neglect
beyond infinity
biomortia (living dead)
bipartison cooperation
bittersweet
black light
blameless culprit
blue rose
brilliantly dull
build down
business ethics
calculated spontaneity
cardinal sin
casual formality
casually concerned
casual sex
cavalier concern
certainly unsure
chaotic organization
cheerfully mournful
cheerful pessimist
cheerful undertaker
chilling fever
CIA cooperation
civil engineer
civilized warfare
civil war
Classic New Homes
clean dirt
clean kill

clearly confused
clearly obscure
cold toast
combative apology
commercial art
comparatively unique
compassionate editor
completed research
completely educated
completely succinct in depth
congressional accountability
congressional action
congressional cooperation
congressional responsibility
conscripted volunteer
conservative liberal
considerate boss
consistent discrepancies
conspicuously absent
constant variable
constructive criticism
contra aid
contra assistance
controlled enthusiasm
controlled skeptic
conventional wisdom
corporate family
criminal justice
cruel kindness
cryocaustic
current history
deafening silence
deaf piano tuner
death benefits
definite maybe
deliberately thoughtless
deliberate mistake
deliberate speed
demanding patient
designer jeans
devout atheist
diligent sloth
diminished confidence
diminutive giants
direct circumvention
disciplined gluttony
distant relatives
Dodge Ram
divorce court
domestic cooperation
down escalator
dry ice

dull acupuncturists
dull roar
dull shine
dynamic monotone
easy task
economic forecast
educated guess
educational administration
educational television
elected king
elevated subway
eloquent silence
enough time
entertaining sermon
enthusiastic indifference
eschew obfuscation
eternal life
even odd
exact estimate
expected serendipity
expected surprise
explicit innuendo
explicitly ambiguous
expressive silence
extensive briefing
extremely average
extremely bland
extremely neutral
faculty cooperation
faculty understanding
fairly explicit
fairly obvious
false fact
famous anonymous
fast-mail service
fast food
fast waiter
faultily faultless
fearful bravery -William Shakespeare
fiery ice
filing system
final conclusion
finally again
financially strong savings and loan
      associations and banks
fire water
firm maybe
first annual
first conclusions
first deadline
fish farm
flat busted

flexible freeze
foreign policy continuity
free love
free prisoner
free society
freezer burn
fresh-frozen jumbo shrimp
fresh prunes
fresh raisins
fresh yogurt
fried roast
friendly enemies
friendly fire (from one's own military)
friendly rocket death
friendly takeover
friendly war
frozen food
full-time hobby
functional illiterate
future history
genuine fake
genuine imitation
genuine imitation leather
glacier-like rapidity
global village
good garbage
good grief
good lawyer
good stuff
gourmet hamburger
graphic language
gregarious recluse
grotesque beauty
growing small
gummily brittle
half-true
half dead
half naked
happy apathy
happy demise
happy fault
happy pessimist
harmonious discord
hasten slowly
highly visible covert operation
hilarious funeral
holy wars
home office
honest convict
honest insurance companies
honest plagiarism
hopeful pessimist

hospital food
horribly decent
hot ice
humane robotics
human robot
idiot savant
idly laborious
ill fortune
ill health
important trivia
incomplete cure
incredibly real
indifferently attentive
indirect communication
industrial park
initial conclusion
initial results
initial retirement
inside out
insincere thanks
insincere vow
instant classic
instant folk hero
intelligent fight
intelligent news coverage
intense apathy
intense disinterest
interested students
internal exile
intimate strangers
junk bonds
justifiably paranoid
known-covert operation
lady mud wrestler
laid-back compulsive
larger half
lasting aid
least favorite
legal brief
legitimate conspiracy
legitimate politics
lesser evil
less is more
liberal conservative
liberal fundamentalists
light heavyweight
limited immunity
linear curve
liquid gas
liquid smoke
literary illiterates
little big

little bit big
little deceptive
little giant
live television
living end
local network
long recess
loose tights
loquacious librarian
loss prevention specialist
love-hate relationship
low-fat icecream
lower inflation
loyal opposition
mail delivery
major minority
man child
meaningful nonsense
meaningful overnight relationship
meatless meat
micro-mainframe
mild interest
mildly psychotic
military accountablility
military intelligence
military justice
military system
minor miracle
mobile home
mobile house
modern history
modern maturity
modestly arrogant
moral majority
morbid humor
more unique
most unique
motorcycle safety
mournful optimist
nameless celebrity
nasty politeness
natural artifact
natural synthetic
near miss
neat office
negative growth
negative momentum
new classic
new cliché
noiseless sound
nonalcoholic beer
nondairy creamer

non-fat icecream
nonstick velcro
nonworking mother
normal deviation
normal espionage
normal human
obedient defiance
objective rating
oddly natural
old news
100%+
open secret
orderly confusion
original copies
parents without partners
partial conclusion
partially organized
partial silence
partial success
passive challenge
passive confrontation
passively aggressive
passively tried
peace offensive
perfect misfit
permanent guest host
persistent ambivalence
personalized form letter
pianoforte
pious atheist
planned exodus
planned serendipity
planned spontaneity
plastic glass
plastic silverware
player coach
pleasant hell
pleasing pain
politely insulting
political ethics
political promise
poor intelligence
positive resistance
postal service
practical joke
preliminary conclusion
pretty bad
pretty ugly
pro-contra
pronounced silence
proud humility
                    -Edmund Spencer

public service
pure .999
pure speculation
qualified success
randomly organized
random order
rational ravings
re-create
real fantasy
real magic
real polyester
real potential
Rebel Without a Cause
recent history
recreational burning
regional pantheists
regular special
relative truth
remotely obvious
required elective
resolute ambivalence
restless sleep
rising deficits
rock music
rock opera
rolling stop
routine emergency
sadly amused
sad optimist
safe sex
same difference
scalding coolness -Ernest Hemingway
school system
science fiction
scientific creationism
sea farming
secretarial science
secret rumor
semiboneless
semiprecious
semiprivate
semiprofessional
semiretired
Senate Intelligence Committee
serious humor
shared monopoly
shyly pompous
sight unseen
silent applause
silent barber
silent scream
silent testimony

simple technology
simply superb
sincere lie
single thought
slight hernia
slightly pregnant
slightly used dental floss
slight surprise
small crowd
smaller half
small fortune
smokeless cigarette
social security
solid rumor
somewhat awesome
somewhat destroyed
somewhat functional
somewhat legal
sophisticated New Yorker
sophomore
spendthrift
splendidly dull
standard deviation
stand down
straight forward subterfuge
strangely familiar
student athlete
student teacher
studious students
subjective data
sugarless candy
superette
sweet pain
sweet pickle
sweet sorrow -William Shakespeare
sweet sour
systematic chaos
systematic disorder
systematic variance
talk show
taped live
tax-free
tax return
tax simplification
teacher union
tentative conclusion
terribly enjoyable
terribly good
Texas chic
three originals
thunderous silence
tight slacks

totalitarian democracy
traditionally radical
tragic comedy
train schedule
tremendously small
true illusion
truth in advertising
turkey ham
unbiased opinion
uncommonly common
uncrowned king
understanding editors
United Nations
unrepeatable pleonasm
unspoken suggestion
unsung hero
unusual routine
unwelcome recess
vaguely aware
virgin wool
war games
waste management
wealthy professor
weather forecaster
wedded bliss
well-preserved ruins
white chocolate
white gold
white rose
whole half
whole hemisphere
whole part
wise fool (sophomore)
withheld contribution
working breakfast
working hobby
working lunch
working vacation
young Republican
young sixty
zero defects
zero deficit

Oxymoron Quotations

A little pain never hurt anyone.

A unified, neutral Germany? Given that nation's heritage, such a phrase may prove to be the oxymoron of the decade.
-Kevin M. Matarese,
Fulda, West Germany;
as seen in "Letters,"
Time magazine, p. 5, March 5, 1990.

A verbal contract isn't worth the paper it's written on. Include me out.
-Samuel Goldwyn

Christ was born in 4 B.C.

Clichés are a dime a dozen—avoid them like the plague.

Cum tacent, clamant. When they are silent, they shout. -Cicero

Cure suggestibility with hypnosis.

Gentlemen, I want you to know that I am not always right, but I am never wrong.
-Samuel Goldwyn

Goes (Went) over like a lead balloon.

Honk if you are against noise pollution!

I'll give you a definite maybe
-Samuel Goldwyn

I'm not going to say, "I told you so."

I've told you a million times, "Don't exaggerate!"

I am a deeply superficial person.
-Andy Warhol

I am proud of my humility.

I can resist everything but temptation.
-Mark Twain

If Roosevelt were alive, he'd turn over in his grave.   -Samuel Goldwyn

If I could drop dead right now, I'd be the happiest man alive! -Samuel Goldwyn

If you fall and break your legs, don't come running to me.

I never put on a pair of shoes until I've worn them five years. -Samuel Goldwyn

Is that a mirage or am I seeing things?

It's bad luck to be superstitious.

It isn't an optical illusion. It just looks like one.

It's more than magnificent–it's mediocre.   -Samuel Goldwyn

I used to be an agnostic, but now I'm not so sure.

May I ask a question?

No one goes to that restaurant anymore—it's always too crowded.
                -Yogi Berra

Our comedies are not to be laughed at.
                -Samuel Goldwyn

Our similarities are different.
                -Dale Berra, Yogi's son

Parting is such sweet sorrow.
                -William Shakespeare

Procrastination means never having to say you're sorry.

Professional certification for car people may sound like an oxymoron
                -*The Wall Street Journal*,
        p. B1, Tuesday, July 17, 1990.

Referring to a book: "I read part of it all the way through."
                -Samuel Goldwyn

Smoking is the leading cause of statistics.

Some bachelors want a meaningful overnight relationship.

Talking about a piece of movie dialogue:
        "Let's have some new clichés.
                -Samuel Goldwyn

The scene is dull. Tell him to put more life into his dying.   -Samuel Goldwyn

Thank God I'm an atheist.

This report is filled with omissions.

We are not anticipating any emergencies.

We're overpaying him, but he's worth it.   -Samuel Goldwyn

Appendix I

PHOBIA WORDS

-phobia, -phobias, -phobe, -phobiac, -phobist, -phobic, -phobism, -phobous; phobo-, phob- (Gk., fear: *extreme, morbid, excessive, illogical, exaggerated, irrational* fear or terror of something or someone; however, sometimes this Greek element also means a strong *dislike* or *hatred* for something) Noun endings are formed with **-phobia** and **-phobe**; while adjectives end with **-phobic.**

ablutophobia, excessive fear of bathing

acarophobia, excessive fear of skin infestation by mites or ticks; fear of itching

accidents: **diplychiphobia, dystychiphobia**

acerbophobia, excessive fear of sourness

achluophobia, an abnormal fear of darkness

acidophobia, in plants, an inability to tolerate acid soils

acid soils (intolerance by plants): **acidophobia, acidophobic**

acousticophobia, an abnormal fear of hearing noises in general or specific noises

acrophobia, excessive fear of heights, elevators, climbing ladders, pinnacles, etc; fear of sharp points

adipophobia, an abnormal fear of being fat

aelurophobia, an abnormal fear of cats

aerohygrophobia, intolerant of high atmospheric humidity

aeronausiphobia, intensive fear of airplanes

aerophobia, an excessive fear of wind, air, or an intensive hatred of drafts; as in cases of **hydrophobia,** hysteria, and other nervous ailments

aging, **gerascophobia**

agoraphobia, agorophobia: excessive fear of crowded, public places (like markets), or of the necessity of leaving the sheltering protection of home, parents, friends, etc; considered the most common phobia known in the U.S.

agraphobia, a fear of sexual abuse

agrizoophobia, an abnormal or excessive fear of wild animals

agyiophobia, an abnormal fear of busy streets; fear of crossing a busy street; excessive fear of public places where help might not be available or from which escape might be difficult to achieve

agyrophobia, an abnormal fear of crossing a street

aichmophobia, an abnormal or morbid fear of being touched by pointed objects, such as knives

AIDS, a terrible fear of getting AIDS [*Acquired Immune Deficiency Syndrome*], **AIDSaphobia, AIDSophobia**

AIDsaphobia, AIDSophobia: intensive fear of getting AIDS

ailourophobia, ailurophobia: an excessive fear of cats

air: **aerophobia, airphobia, pneumatophobia**

airplanes, **aeronausiphobia**

akousticophobia, an abnormal fear of sounds

albumin in one's urine (as a sign of kidney disease), **albuminurophobia**

albuminurophobia, excessive fear of albumin in one's urine as a sign of kidney disease

alektorophobia, a fear of chickens

aleurophobia, excessive fear of cats

algophobia, excessive fear of pain

alkaline soils (plants): **basiphobia, basophobia**

alliumphobia, an excessive fear of garlic

allodoxaphobia, an intensive fear or hatred of the opinions of others

alone: **autophobia, eremiophobia, eremitophobia, eremophobia, monophobia**

altophobia (preferred usage is **acrophobia**), an abnormal or excessive fear of heights

alychiphobia, excessive fear of failure

amathophobia, excessive fear of dust

amaxophobia, excessive fear of being in, meeting in, driving in, or riding in certain kinds of vehicles; or of vehicles in general

ambulophobia, excessive fear of walking

amnesia, **amnesiophobia**

amnesiophobia, a fear of having amnesia

amychophobia, an excessive fear of scratches or of being scratched

anablepophobia, an excessive fear of looking up at high places

ancraophobia, excessive fear of wind

androphobia, excessive fear or hatred of men

anemophobia, abnormal fear of drafts, winds, cyclones, hurricanes, etc.

anginaphobia, excessive fear of a sore throat or severe heart pain

Appendix I, PHOBIAS: anginophobia ➡ beautiful women

anginophobia, angionophobia: an extreme fear of choking or painful constriction about the heart; heart attack; narrowness

Anglophobia, fear or hatred of England and all things which are English

animals in general or specific animals, zoophobia; animals (wild), agrizoophobia

anopheliphobia, fear or hatred of mosquitoes (especially malarial mosquitoes)

ankylophobia, excessive fear of immobility (of a joint)

anthophobia, excessive fear of flowers

anthropophobia, an abnormal fear of people or human society or a particular individual

antlophobia, excessive fear of floods

ants: formiphobia, myrmecophobia

anuptaphobia, an excessive fear of remaining unmarried or single

anxiety (general), panophobia

apeirophobia, excessive fear of infinity

aphephobia, excessive fear of touching or of being touched by other persons

aphidiophobia, an illogical, or irrational fear of reptiles

apiophobia, apiphobiaa: morbid fear of bees or of being stung by bees

aquaphobia, an irrational fear of water

arachibutyrophobia, a fear of peanut butter sticking to the roof of one's mouth

arachnephobia, arachnophobia: excessive fear of spiders

arachnoophobia, excessive fear of spider eggs

arrangement: phobotactic, phobotaxis

arrhenophobia, an excessive fear of men

arsonophobia, excessive fear of fire or of setting something on fire

asleep, hypnophobia

asthenophobia, unexplained fear of weakness

astraphobia, an excessive fear of being struck by lightning or of thunderstorms

astrapophobia, intensive fear of being struck by lightning

astrophobia, excessive fear of stars

ataxiophobia, ataxophobia: an excessive fear of disorder

atelophobia, excessive fear of imperfection or incompleteness

atephobia, an excessive fear of ruins

atmospheric, humidity or moisture (intolerance of): aerohygrophobe, aerohygrophoby

atomic energy or nuclear weapons, nucleomitophobia

atychiphobia, excessive fear of failure

aulophobia, excessive fear of flutes

aurophobia, strong dislike of gold

auroraphobia, a fear of the northern lights

automobiles (vehicles), ochophobia

automysophobia, an excessive fear of being dirty or of personal filth

autophobia, excessive fear of being by oneself or of being in solitude

aversion to phobia words, phobologophobia

avoidance reaction of a motile organism: phobotactic, phobotaxis

bacilli, bacillophobia

bacillophobia, a fear of germs or bacilli

bacteria: bacteriaphobia, bacteriophobia, microbiophobia

bacteriaphobia, bacteriophobia: an abnormal fear of being in contact with germs or bacteria

bad men, scelerophobia

bad water, cacohydrophobia

baldness: peladophobia, phalacraphobia

ballistophobia, ballistrophobia: an exaggerated fear of missles or of being shot

barophobia, a fear of gravity or heaviness

barren spaces: cenophobia, kenophobia

basiphobia, basophobia: in plants, an inability to adapt to alkaline soils; in humans, the inability to stand or walk for fear of falling

basistasiphobia, basostasophobia: an exaggerated fear of standing or walking

bathing: ablutophobia, bathophobia

bathmophobia, bathomophobia: an overly intensive fear or hatred of walking

bathophobia, excessive fear of depths or of descending into depths, such as when looking down into a well; an intense dislike of bathing

bathysiderodromomophobia, a morbid fear of subways or any similar situation which exists underground (the North Sea Chunnel?)

batophobia, an abnormal fear of passing or walking close to high objects, such as buildings; dread of heights

batrachophobia, excessive fear of frogs (and of toads)

bats, vespertiliophobia

beards, pogonophobia

beaten (flogged), mastigophobia

beatings, rhabdophobia

beautiful women, venustaphobia

208   Words for a Modern Age

becoming ill, **nosophobia**

bed (going to), **clinophobia**

bees: **apiophobia, apiphobia, melissophobia**

belonephobia, belonophobia: an exaggerated fear of pins and needles or of anything sharp

bibliophobia, excessive fear of books

big words: **sesquipedalophobia, sesquipedalophobe**

birds, **ornithophobia**

birth of a monster, **teratophobia**

blennophobia, excessive fear of slime

blenophobia, an abnormal fear of pins and needles

blood: **haematophobia, hemaphobia, hematophobia, hemophobia**

blushing: **ereuthrophobia, erythrophobia**

body odors: **bromhidrosiphobia, bromidrosophobia, osphresiophobia**

bogyphobia, fear of demons and goblins

books, **bibliophobia**

boredom, **thaasophobia**

botanophobia, an abnormal or excessive fear of plants in general or of specific plants (such as poison ivy and poison oak?)

botophobia, excessive fear of cellars

bound (tied with ropes), **merinthophobia**

bradycardiaphobia, a fear that one's heart is beating too slowly

brain disease, **meningitophobia**

bridges: **gephydrophobia, gephyrophobia**

bromhidrosiphobia, bromidrosophobia: an abnormal fear of personal body odors

brontephobia, brontophobia: an exaggerated fear of thunder and thunderstorms

bulls, **taurophobia**

burglars, **scelerophobia**

buried alive: **taphephobia, taphophobia**

busy streets, **agyiophobia**

cacohydrophobia, a fear of bad water.

cainophobia, cainotophobia: an exaggerated fear of novelty or newness in general

calciphobia, the inability of some plants to grow in lime-rich soil

cancer: **cancerophobia, cancerphobia, carcinomatophobia, carcinophobia**

cancerphobia, cancerophobia, carcinomatophobia, carcinophobia: an excessive fear of cancer

cardiophobia, excessive fear of heart disease

carnophobia, excessive fear of a meat diet

catagelophobia, excessive fear of ridicule

catapedaphobia, an abnormal fear of jumping (from both high and low places)

categelophobia, excessive fear of ridicule

cathisophobia, excessive fear of sitting down

catopthrophobia, catoptrophobia: excessive fear of mirrors

cats: **aelurophobia, ailourophobia, ailurophobia, aleurophobia, elurophobia, felinophobia, galeophobia, gatophobia**

cellars, **botophobia**

cemeteries: **coimetrophobia, taphephobia**

cenophobia, cenotophobia: an abnormal fear of empty rooms, barren spaces, or of large spaces

ceraunophobia, fear of thunder and lightning as those which exist in storms

chaetophobia, excessive fear of hair

changes (new things, new approaches): **kainophobia, kainotophobia, neophobia**

changes by moving, **tropophobia**

charminphobia, a fear of being squeezed

cheerfulness, **cherophobia**

cheimaphobia, cheimatophobia: an abnormal fear of cold or frost, especially of winter

cherophobia, excessive fear of gaiety, happiness, or cheerfulness

chickens, **alektorophobia**

childbirth: **maieusiophobia, tocophobia, tokophobia**

children (young): **paediophobia, pediophobia**

Chinese (customs or influences), **Sinophobia**

chins, **geniophobia**

chionophobia, an excessive fear of snow or of snow storms

choking: **angionophobia, pnigeraphobia, pnigerophobia, pnigophobia**

cholera, **cholerophobia**

cholerophobia, excessive fear of cholera

choreophobia, chorophobia: excessive fear of dancing

chrematophobia, chrometophobia: a fear of having money or wealth

chromatophobia, chromophobia: an abnormal fear of certain colors

chronophobia: discomfort concerning time (a common psycho-neurosis of prison inmates)

churches: **ecclesiaphobia, ecclesiophobia**

cibophobia, an irrational fear of food

claustrophobia, an intense fear of being shut up in a small or confined space

cleistophobia, cleithrophobia: intensive fear of closed spaces or of being locked in

cleptophobia, excessive fear of having one's property stolen or of becoming a thief

clergymen, **hierophobia**

cliffs, **cremnophobia**

climacophobia, excessive fear of stairs or of falling down the stairs

climbing ladders, **acrophobia**

clinophobia, excessive fear or strong dislike of going to bed

clithrophobia, excessive fear of being enclosed

closed spaces: **claustrophobia, cleistophobia, cleithrophobia, clithrophobia**

clothing, **vestiophobia**

clouds: **nebulaphobia, nephophobia**

clubs (rods), **rhabdophobia**

cnidophobia, excessive fear of nettles, plant stings, or insect stings

coimetrophobia, excessive fear of cemeteries

coitophobia, fear of sexual intercourse

cold: **cheimaphobia, cheimatophobia, cryophobia, frigophobia, psychrophobia**

cold weather, **psychrophobia**

colors: **chromatophobia, chromophobia**

cometophobia, excessive fear of comets

comets, **cometophobia**

computerphobia, an intense dislike or exaggerated fear of computers or any association with them

computers: **computerphobia, cyberphobia**

confined space, **claustrophobia**

constipation, **coprostasophobia**

contact with other people, **aphephobia**

contamination: **misophobia, molysmophobia, molysomophobia, mysophobia**

contamination by dirt, **misophobia**

contracting (catching) a disease, **nosophobia**

contrectophobia, fear of sexual abuse

coprophobia, fear of feces or excrement

coprostasophobia, fear of constipation

corpses, **necrophobia**

counterphobia, searching for what is feared; preferring that which one is afraid of

cremnophobia, an abnormal fear of steep cliffs (precipices)

cremophobia, an excessive fear of being alone or of solitude

criticism, **enissophobia**

cross (crucifix), **staurophobia**

crossing a bridge, **gephydrophobia**

crossing a busy street, **agyiophobia**

crossing streets: **agyrophobia, dromophobia**

crossing over a bridge, **gephyrophobia**

crowds: **agaraphobia, agorophobia, demophobia, enochlophobia, ochlophobia, demophobia**

crucifix, **staurophobia**

cryophobia, excessive fear of cold, ice, or frost

crystal: **crystallophobia, hyalophobia**

crystallophobia, fear of glass or crystal

cyberphobia, an abnormal fear of computers

cyclones, **anemophobia**

cymophobia, an abnormal fear of sea swells, or waves

cynophobia, excessive fear of intense dread of dogs or of rabies

cypridophobia, excessive fear of sexual intercourse or of catching a venereal disease

cyprinophobia, fear of lewd, immoral women; fear of prostitutes

cypriphobia, an abnormal or intensive fear of getting a venereal disease

daemonophobia, an intensive fear of demons (spirits, goblins, etc.)

dampness, **hygrophobia**

dancing, **chorophobia**

darkness: **achluophobia, lygophobia, nyctophobia, sciaphobia, sciophobia, scotophobia**

dawn, **eosophobia**

daylight, **phengophobia**

dead bodies, **necrophobia**

death: **necrophobia, thanatophobia**

decaying matter, **septophobia**

decidophobia, fear of making decisions

decisions (making), **decidophobia**

defeat: **kakorraphiaphobia, kakorraphiophobia**

defecalgesiophobia, an abnormal fear of having painful defecation

defecation (painful), **defecalgesiophobia**

defecation, **rhypophobia**

definite disease, **monopathophobia**

deformed child, **teratophobia**

deformities: **dysmorphobia, dysmorphophobia**

deipnophobia, an abnormal fear of dining and dinner conversation

dementophobia, fear of being insane

demons, evil sprits: **bogyphobia, daemonophobia, demonophobia**

demophobia, a fear or intense dislike of crowds of people

dendrophobia, excessive fear of trees

dentists, **dentophobia**
dentophobia, fear of being around a dentist
depths, **bathophobia**
dermatophobia, dermatopathophobia, dermatosiophobia: an excessive fear of skin disease, lesions, or cracks of the skin
descending into depths (such as looking down into a well), **bathophobia**
deserted places: **eremiophobia, eremitophobia, eremophobia**
devil/demons: **demonophobia, satanophobia**
dextrophobia, excessive fear of things on the right side of the body
diabetes, **diabetophobia**
diabetophobia, fear of having diabetes
didaskaleinophobia, an abnormal or intense fear of going to school
dikephobia, excessive fear of justice
dining, **deipnophobia**
dinner conversation, **deipnophobia**
dinophobia, fear of whirlpools and of dizziness
diplopiaphobia, an exaggerated fear of having double vision
diplychiphobia, an excessive fear of accidents
dipsomanophobia, dipsophobia: intense fear or hatred of drinking
dirt: **misophobia, musophobia, mysophobia, rupophobia**
dirty (personal), **automysophobia**
disease (getting one), **pathophobia**
disease (some *definite* kind), **monopathophobia**
disease contraction, **nosophobia**
diseases (strange), **xenophobia**
dishabillophobia, an exaggerated or abnormal fear of undressing in front of someone
disorder: **ataxiophobia, ataxophobia**
dizziness, **dinophobia**
doctors (medical), **iatrophobia**
dogs: **cynophobia, kynophobia**
dolls: **paedophobia, pediophobia, pediphobia, pedophobia**
domatophobia, excessive fear of one's home or of being confined in a house
doraphobia, an exaggerated fear of fur or the skin of animals
dormatophobia, an irrational fear of being confined in a house or in one's home
double vision, **diplopiaphobia**
drafts: **aerophobia, anemophobia**
dreams (wet), **oneirogmophobia**
dreams, **oneirophobia**

drinking: **alcoholophobia, dipsomanophobia, dipsophobia, phobodipsia, potophobia**
dromophobia, an abnormal fear of crossing streets or of wandering (roaming)
drug addict, **pharmacophobia**
drugs in general, **pharmacophobia**
drugs (new), **neopharmaphobia**
dryness, **xerophobia**
dry places (deserts, etc), **xerophobia**
dust: **amathophobiat, koniophobia, koniphobia**
dying, **thanatophobia**
dysmorphophobia, excessive fear of deformity, usually in others
dystychiphobia, excessive fear of accidents
eating: **phagophobia, sitiophobia, sitophobia**
ecclesiaphobia, ecclesiophobia: an irrational fear of a church or of churches in general
ecophobia, fear of home surroundings or home life
eisoptrophobia, fear of mirrors *or* termites
electricity: **electrophobia, elektrophobia**
electrophobia, elektrophobia, an abnormal fear of electricity
eleutherophobia, excessive fear of freedom
elevators, **acrophobia**
elurophobia, excessive fear of cats
emetophobia, excessive fear of vomiting
emptiness, **kenophobia**
empty rooms, **cenophobia**
enclosed, **clithrophobia**
enetephobia, enetophobia: an abnormal fear of pins or needles
England or things English, **Anglophobia**
enissophobia, fear of criticism or sin
enochlophobia, an abnormal fear of crowds
enophobia, excessive hatred of wine
enosiophobia, excessive fear of sin
entomophobia, excessive fear of insects
entonophobia, excessive fear of ticks
eosophobia, an abnormal fear of the dawn
eremiophobia, eremitophobia, eremophobia: an abnormal fear of stillness, being alone, or of deserted places
ereuthrophobia, excessive fear of blushing
ergasiophobia, ergasophobia: an excessive fear or hatred of work
ergophobia, see **ergasiophobia** (an antonym would be **ergomania** [an excessive desire to work]

ermitophobia, excessive fear of solitude of being alone

erotophobia, excessive fear of sexual feelings and their physical expressions

errors, **hamartophobia**

erythrophobia, excessive fear of the color red or of blushing

esodophobia, fear of losing one's virginity

euphobia, abnormal fear of good news

everything: **panphobia, panophobia, pantophobia**

evil spirits, **demonophobia**

examinations, **kopophobia**

excrement: **coprophobia, scatophobia**

exerting one's self, **ponophobia**

exhaustion, **kopophobia**

eyes (opening them), **optophobia**

eyes: **ommatophobia, ommetaphobia**

fabrics (specific kinds), **textophobia**

failure: **alychiphobia, atychiphobia, kakorraphiaphobia, kakorraphiophobia, kakorrhaphiophobia**

falling down stairs, **climacophobia**

false rabies, **pseudohydrophobia**

false statements (a fear of making false statements), **mythophobia**

family relations, **symmetrophobia**

fat (of being fat): **adipophobia, lipophobia**

fatigue: **kopophobia, ponophobia**

fear (absence of), **hypophobia**

fear (affected with morbid terror of something), **phobic**

fear (caused by fear): **phobogenic, phobogenous**

fear (excessive), **phobism**

fear (mild), **paraphobia**

fear (morbid), **phobia**

fear (a nonspecific fear of everything): **panophobia, panphobia, pantaphobia, pantophobia**

fear (seeking out), **counterphobia**

fear (which can be controlled with reasoning), **paraphobia**

fear of fear itself, **phobophobia**

fear of just one thing, **monophobia**

fear of one's own fears: **autophobia, phobophobia**

fear of phobia words, **phobologophobia**

feathers, **pteronophobia**

febriphobia, excessive fear of having a fever

feces, **coprophobia**

felinophobia, excessive fear of cats

feminophobia, an abnormal or intense fear of women

fever: **febriphobia, fibriphobia, pyrexeophobia, pyrexiophobia**

fibriphobia, excessive fear of having a fever

filth (personal), **automysophobia**

filth: **mysophobia, rhypophobia, rupophobia, rypophobia**

filth contamination, **musophobia**

filthy language, **scatophobia**

fire (setting on fire): **arsonophobia, pyrophobia**

fish, **ichthyophobia**

flashes of light, **selaphobia**

flavors (strange): **geumaphobia, geumophobia, geumatophobia**

flogged (beaten), **mastigophobia**

floods, **antlophobia**

flowers, **anthophobia**

flutes, **aulophobia**

fog: **homichlophobia, nebulaphobia**

food: **cibophobia, sitiophobia, sitophobia**

foreign things, **xenophobia**

foreigners: **xenophobia, zenophobia**

forests: **hylephobia, hylophobia, xylophobia**

forgetting a password, **friendorphobia**

formiphobia, excessive fear of ants

France: **Francophobia, Gallophobia**

Francophobia, dislike or hatred of the French or French customs, influences, etc.

freedom, **eleutherophobia**

freezing: **frigophobia, psychrophobia**

French customs or influences, **Francophobia**

friendorphobia, fear of forgetting a password

friendships, **sociophobia**

frigophobia, fear of being cold or freezing

frogs, **batrachophobia**

frost: **cheimaphobia, cheimatophobia, cryophobia**

fur, **doraphobia**

gaiety, **cherophobia**

gaining weight: **obesophobia, pocrescophobia**

galeophobia, intense fear of cats *or* of sharks

Gallophobia, excessive fear of France or anything having to do with France

gametophobia, gamophobia: an exaggerated fear of marriage

garlic, **alliumphobia**

gatophobia, excessive fear of cats

gelophobia, excessive fear of laughter

general anxiety, **panophobia**

geniophobia, excessive fear of chins

genophobia, excessive fear of sex

genuphobia, fear of servility or submissiveness (a reference to the knees)

gephydrophobia, gephyrophobia: a fear of crossing a bridge or passing under a bridge

gerascophobia, excessive fear of growing old

Germans and their culture: **Teutonophobia, Germanophobia**

Germanophobia, fear of Germany, its people, its culture, or of German ideas

germs: **bacillophobia, bacteriophobia, spermatophobia, spermophobia**

gerontophobia, fear of growing old

geumaphobia, geumatophobia, geumophobia: a fear of unfamiliar tastes or flavors

ghosts: **phasmophobia, spectrophobia**

girls (their company), **parthenophobia**

glares, **photangiaphobia**

glass: **crystallophobia, hyalophobia, hyelophobia, nelophobia**

glass bottoms, **hyalinopygophobia**

glossophobia, an abnormal fear of speaking in public or of trying to speak (often associated with stuttering)

goblins: **bogyphobia, daemonophobia**

God's punishment for sin, **theophobia**

gold, **aurophobia**

good news, **euphobia**

graphophobia, a dislike of writing or a morbid fear of having to write

graves, **taphophobia**

gravity, **barophobia**

Greek (and Latin) terms, **Hellenophobia**

gringophobia, in Spain or Latin America, an intense dislike of North Americans or white strangers

growing old: **gerascophobia, gerontophobia**

gymnophobia, excessive fear of nudity or the sight of nakedness

gynephobia, gynophobia: an abnormal fear or hatred of women or any association with them

hadephobia, excessive fear of hell

haematophobia, morbid fear of seeing blood

hagiophobia, excessive fear or intense dislike of saints or of holy objects or concepts

hair (certain colors), **trichophobia**

hair: **chaetophobia, trichophobia**

hair disease: **trichopathophobia, trichophobia**

hair growth (certain kinds), **trichophobia**

hair on the body, **hypertrichophobia**

halophobia, the inability of some plants to grow in salt-rich soil

hamartophobia, a fear of errors or sins

hamaxophobia, fear of being in or riding in a vehicle

haphephobia, haphophobia, hapnophobia, haptephobia, haptophobia: an exaggerated fear or hatred of touching or of being touched

happiness, **cherophobia**

harmartophobia, fear of making errors or of sinning

harpaxophobia, a fear of robbers or thieves or of being attacked by a robber or a thief

hatred of a stepmother, **novercaphobia**

hearing noises, **acousticophobia**

heart attack: **anginophobia, angionophobia**

heart beating too slowly, **bradycardiaphobia**

heart constriction (painful): **anginaphobia, angionophobia**

heart disease, **cardiophobia**

heat, **thermophobia**

heaven: **ouranophobia, uranophobia**

heaviness, **barophobia**

hedenophobia, hedonophobia: an illogical or exaggerated fear of having pleasure

heights: **acrophobia, altophobia, batophobia**

heliophobia, abnormal sensitivity to the effects of sunlight; abnormal fear of sunlight

hell: **hadephobia, stygiophobia**

Hellenophobia, an irrational fear or hatred of Greek (and Latin) words

helminthophobia, fear of worm infestations

hemaphobia, an abnormal fear of the sight of blood or of transfusions

hematophobia, an abnormal fear of the sight of blood or of transfusions

hemophobia, an abnormal fear of the sight of blood or of transfusions

hereditary disease, **patroiophobia**

herpes disease through sexual activity, **herpetophobia**

herpetophobia, an abnormal fear of reptiles or snakes; intense fear of catching the herpes disease through sexual activity

herptophobia, excessive fear of snakes

hierophobia, fear of sacred or religious objects or clergymen

high objects, **batophobia**

high places: **hypsiphobia, hypsophobia**

high places (looking up at), **anablepophobia**

high temperatures, **thermophobia**
hippophobia, excessive fear of horses
hodophobia, fear or hatred of traveling
holy object: **hagiophobia, hierophobia**
home (fear of returning to one's home): **nostophobia, vokephobia**
home, **domatophobia**
home life, **ecophobia**
home surroundings: **ecophobia, oecophobia, oikophobia**
homichlophobia, an abnormal fear of fog or humidity
homilophobia, hatred for sermons or a fear of being preached to
homophobia, fear of or intense apprehension about homosexuality; a strong dislike of monotony
homosexuals, **homophobia**
hormephobia, excessive fear of shock
horses, **hippophobia**
hospitals, **nosocomephobia**
house confinement: **domatophobia, dormatophobia**
human beings, **phobanthropy**
human society, **anthropophobia**
humidity, **homichlophobia**
hurricanes: **anemophobia, lilapsophobia**
hyalinopygophobia, an excessive fear of glass bottoms
hyalophobia, a fear of crystal or glass
hydrargyrophobia, a fear of mercurial medicines
hydrophobia, what is thought to be a fear of water, especially by those who have rabies; the inability to drink (swallow liquids) because of throat constrictions, not a fear of water itself, gives the impression that the rabies victim is afraid of water
hydrophobobphobia, an intense fear of having rabies or with symptoms simular to the disease, sometimes resulting in hysterical conditions resembling hydrophobia
hyelophobia, excessive fear of glass
hygrophobia, a fear or strong dislike of liquids in any form, especially wine and water; an aversion to dampness
hylephobia, hylophobia: excessive fear or hatred of forests, woods, or of materialism
hypegiaphobia, morbid fear of responsibility
hypengyophobia, fear of responsibility
hypertrichophobia, excessive fear of hair on the body

hypnophobia, excessive fear of being asleep
hypophobia, lack of normal fear; not being afraid enough
hypsiphobia, hypsophobia: an abnormal fear of high places
iatrophobia, an abnormal fear of going to a doctor (physician)
ice, **cryophobia**
ichthyophobia, excessive fear of fish or of anything related to fish
ideas, **ideophobia**
ideophobia, excessive fear of ideas
idleness: **thaasophobia, thassophobia**
illness (becoming), **nosophobia**
illness: **nosemaphobia, pathophobia**
illyngophobia, excessive fear of vertigo
immobility (of a joint), **ankylophobia**
immoral women, **cyprinophobia**
imperfection, **atelophobia**
incompleteness, **atelophobia**
incorrectness, **mythophobia**
infants: **paedophobia, pediophobia, pediphobia, pedophobia**
infected with worms, **vermiphobia**
infection: **molysmophobia, molysomophobia**
infinity, **apeirophobia**
injections, **trypanophobia**
injury, **traumatophobia**
innovation, **neophobia**
inoculations, **trypanophobia**
insanity: **dementophobia, lyssiophobia, lyssophobia, maniaphobia**
insects: **acarophobia, entomophobia**
insect stings, **cnidophobia**
intimacy with a different life form, **symbiophobia**
iophobia, excessive fear of poisons or of rust
isolophobia, excessive fear of solitude
isopterophobia, an abnormal fear of termites
itching, **acarophobia**
Japan (or the Japanese), **Japanophobia**
jealousy, **zelophobia**
joint immobility, **ankylophobia**
jumping (from both high and low places), **catapedaphobia**
justice, **dikephobia**
kainophobia, kainotophobia: excessive fear of anything new or of change
kakorraphiaphobia, kakorraphiophobia, kakorrhaphiophobia: an irrational fear of failure or defeat
katagelophobia, excessive fear of ridicule

kathisophobia, excessive fear of sitting down

kenophobia, excessive fear of open spaces, of emptiness, or of barren spaces

keraunophobia, excessive fear of thunder and lightning (lightning in general)

keraunothnetophobia, an excessive fear of being hit by man-made satellites

kidney disease, **albuminurophobia**

kinesophobia, kinetoptophobia: an excessive fear of movement

kissing: **philemaphobia, philematophobia**

kleptophobia, excessive fear of thieves or of loss through thievery; of becoming a **kleptomaniac**

knives (or other sharp objects), **aichmophobia**

knowledge, **sophophobia**

koinoniphobia, excessive fear of being in a room full of people

koniophobia, koniphobia: an excessive fear of dust

kopophobia, an abnormal fear of fatigue or exhaustion or fear of mental or physical examinations

kynophobia, an abnormal fear of someone who is assumed to have rabies; a fear of dogs

kyphophobia, excessive fear of stooping

lachanophobia, intense dislike of vegetables

lakes in general, **limnophobia**

laliophobia, lalophobia: an intense fear of talking (or stuttering)

language (obscene or filthy), **scatophobia**

large objects, **megalophobia**

large spaces, **cenophobia**

latrophobia, an intense fear of being robbed either at home or in public

laughter, **gelophobia**

learning, **sophophobia**

leaves of plants, **phyllophobia**

left (objects on the left side of the body): **levophobia, sinistrophobia**

lepraphobia, leprophobia: an excessive fear of leprosy

leprosy: **lepraphobia, leprophobia**

levophobia, excessive fear of objects on the left side of the body

lewd women, **cyprinophobia**

lice: **pediculophobia, phthiriophobia**

light (flashes of), **selaphobia**

light (plants which thrive or survive in reduced light), **photophobia**

light, (painful sensitivity to light), **photophobia**

light directed upon the eyes which may cause photalgia, **photaugiaphobia**

lightning and thunder: **ceraunophobia, keraunophobia**

lightning strike: **astrapophobia, astraphobia**

ligyrophobia, excessive fear of noise

lilapsophobia, excessive fear of tornadoes or hurricanes

lime-rich soil (plants), **calciphobia**

limnophobia, an abnormal fear of marshes, of marshy lakes, or lakes in general

linonophobia, excessive fear of string

lipophobia, excessive fear of being fat

liquids in any form, **hygrophobia**

locked in (closed in): **claustrophobia, cleistophobia, cleithrophobia**

logophobia, excessive fear of words

loneliness: **autophobia, cremophobia**

looked at, **scopophobia**

looking up at high places, **anablepophobia**

loved (being loved), **philophobia**

love-play: **sarmassophobia**

lygophobia, excessive fear of darkness

lyophobia (lyophobic), having little attraction between particles and the medium of dispersion

lyssiophobia, lyssophobia: an intense fear of becoming mad, insane, or of having a nervous break-down; a fear of catching rabies

machinery, **mechanophobia**

machines (technical), **technophobia**

macrophobia, an abnormal fear of having to wait for long periods of time

madness: **lyssophobia, lyssiophobia**

magic, **rhabdophobia**

maieusiophobia, an intense fear of pregnancy or childbirth

man, **androphobia**

maniaphobia, excessive fear of insanity

many things, **polyphobia**

marriage: **gametophobia, gamophobia**

marshes, **limnophobia**

mastigophobia, fear of being flogged (beaten)

materialism, **hylephobia**

matter (decaying), **septophobia**

meat diet, **carnophobia**

mechanophobia, morbid fear of machines

medicine (new), **neopharmaphobia**

medicine, **pharmacophobia**

megalophobia, excessive fear of large objects

melissophobia, excessive fear of bees

men: **androphobia, arrhenophobia**

meningitis (brain disease), **meningitophobia**

meningitophobia, excessive fear of meningitis or brain disease

menophobia, abnormal fear of menstruation

menstruation, **menophobia**

mercurial medicines, **hydrargyrophobia**

merinthophobia, an abnormal fear of being bound or tied up with ropes

metallophobia, excessive fear of metals or objects made of metal

metals (objects made of metal), **metallophobia**

meteorites, **meteorophobia**

meteorophobia, excessive fear of meteors or meteorites; or an extreme fear of certain weather phenomena

meteors, **meteorophobia**

metrophobia, excessive fear of poetry

mice: **muriphobia, murophobia, musophobia, mysophobia**

microbes, **microbiophobia**

microbiophobia, excessive fear of microbes or bacteria

microphobia, a fear of microbes or very small objects

mind (contents of one's own mind), **psychophobia**

mirrors: **eisoptrophobia, catopthrophobia, catoptrophobia, spectrophobia**

misophobia, excessive fear of dirt, especially of being contaminated by dirt

missles: **ballistophobia, ballistrophobia**

mites (or itching), **acarophobia**

moisture, **hygrophobia**

molysomophobia, an abnormal fear of infection or contamination

money: **chrematophobia, chrometophobia**

monopathophobia, an abnormal fear of sickness in a specified part of the body or some definite disease

monophobia, an excessive fear of being left alone or of just one thing

monotony, **homophobia**

monsters (or giving birth to), **teratophobia**

moon, **selenophobia**

morbid fear, **phobia**

mosquitoes, **anopheliphobia**

mother-in-law (irritation by being around her), **pentheraphobia**

motion: **dromophobia, kinesophobia, kinetophobia**

motorphobia, a fear of motor vehicles

motor vehicles, **motorphobia**

movement: **kinesophobia, kinetoptophobia**

moving around, **tropophobia**

muriphobia, murophobia: an excessive fear of mice

music, **musicophobia**

musicophobia, an intense hatred of or fear of music

musophobia, excessive fear of dirt, especially of being contaminated with filth; an abnormal fear of mice

myrmecophobia, excessive fear of ants

mysophobia, excessive fear of filth, contamination, or dirt; an excessive fear of mice

mythophobia, excessive fear of making false statements or of untrue stories; extreme fear of incorrectness

myxophobia, excessive fear of slime

nakedness: **gymnophobia, nudiphobia, nudophobia**

names (certain ones): **nomatophobia, onomatophobia**

narrow spaces, **stenophobia**

nebulaphobia, excessive fear of fog or clouds

necrophobia, excessive fear of death and/or dead bodies

needles: **belonephobia, belonophobia, blenophobia**

neglect of some duty, **paralipophobia**

nelophobia, excessive fear of glass

neopharmaphobia, an exaggerated or excessive fear of a new medicine

neophobia, intense fear of novelty, new things, or unfamiliar things

nephophobia, an abnormal fear of clouds

nervous breakdown: **lyssiophobia, lyssophobia**

nettles, **cnidophobia**

new: **kainophobia, neophobia**

new medicine, **neopharmaphobia**

newness, **kainotophobia**

news (good), **euphobia**

new things: **cainophobia, cainotophobia**

night: **noctiphobia, nyctophobia**

noctiphobia, excessive fear of night or of what might happen at night

noise: **acousticophobia, ligyrophobia, phonophobia**

nomatophobia, excessive fear of names

nonspecific fear: **panophobia, panphobia**

North Americans (intense dislike of), **gringophobia**

northern lights, **auroraphobia**

nosemaphobia, an exaggerated or excessive fear of illness

nosocomephobia, excessive fear of hospitals

nosophobia, an intense fear of contracting a disease or of becoming ill

nostophobia, an irrational fear of returning to one's home

novelty: **cainophobia, cainotophobia, kainotophobia, kainophobia, neophobia**

novercaphobia, an exaggerated, irrational, or excessive fear or hatred of a stepmother

nuclear weapons, **nucleomitaphobia**

nucleomitaphobia, fear of death by nuclear weapons

nudiphobia, nudophobia: an abnormal fear of nakedness

nudity: **gymnophobia, nudiphobia, nudophobia**

number thirteen: **terdekaphobia, tredecaphobia, triakaidekaphobia, tridecaphobia, triskadekaphobia, triskaidekaphobia**

nyctophobia, fear of darkness or night

obesophobia, fear of gaining weight

obscene language, **scatophobia**

oceans, **thalassophobia**

ochlophobia, an abnormal fear of crowds

ochophobia, excessive fear of vehicles

odontophobia, fear of teeth, especially those of animals

odor (personal): **bromidrosiphobia, ophresiophobia**

odors (certain kinds), **osmophobia**

odors (smells), **olfactophobia**

odynephobia, odynophobia: an abnormal fear of pain

oecophobia, fear of home surroundings

oenophobia, oinophobia: fear of wine; hatred or extreme dislike of wine

oikophobia, fear of home surroundings

old (growing): **gerascophobia, gerontophobia**

old age, **gerontophobia**

olfactophobia, an extreme hatred or fear of having certain odors

ombrophobia, excessive fear of rain

omission of some duty, **paralipophobia**

ommatophobia, ommetaphobia: an exaggerated fear of eyes

oneirogmophobia, fear of having wet dreams

oneirophobia, an intense fear of dreaming or of what they might mean

one thing, **monophobia**

one who is terrified of something or someone, **phobiac**

onomatophobia, an irrational fear of a certain name or hearing a certain word or words

opening one's eyes, **optophobia**

open space: **agoraphobia, cenophobia, kenophobia**

ophiciophobia, ophidiophobia: an excessive fear of snakes

ophresiophobia, excessive fear of odors

ophthalmophobia, an abnormal fear of being stared at

opinions of others, **allodoxaphobia**

optophobia, fear of opening one's eyes

order: **phobotactic, phobotaxis**

ornithophobia, excessive fear of birds

osmophobia, excessive fear of certain odors

osphresiophobia, fear of bodily odors

ostraconophobia, abnormal fear of shellfish

ouranophobia, abnormal fear of heaven or the sky

overworking (fatigue), **ponophobia**

paedophobia, excessive fear of dolls or infants

pain (from over exertion), **ponophobia**

pain (rectum), **proctophobia**

pain: **algophobia, odynephobia, odynophobia**

pain caused by light in the eyes: **photaugiaphobia, photangiophobia**

panophobia, panphobia, pantophobia: an irrational fear of a nonspecific fear; a fear of everything; a state of general unexplained anxiety

pantaphobia, lacking fear, having no fear; an abnormal fearlessness

papacy, **papaphobia**

papaphobia, fear of the pope or the papacy

paper, **papyrophobia**

papyrophobia, an abnormal fear of paper

paralipophobia, fear of the neglect or omission of some duty; or fear of having a responsibility

paraphobia, a moderate fear, especially one which a person can control with reasoning

paraphobia, morbid fear of sexual perversion

parasites (borers), **trypanophobia**

parasites: **parasitophobia, phthiriophobia**

parasitophobia, excessive fear of parasites

parents-in-law, **soceraphobia**

parthenophobia, an abnormal fear of young girls (virgins) or of their company

passing near high objects, **batophobia**

password (forgetting), **friendorphobia**

pathophobia, fear of becoming ill or of getting a disease

patroiophobia, excessive fear of heredity

peanut butter sticking to the roof of someone's mouth, **arachibutyrophobia**

peccatiphobia, peccatophobia: an excessive fear of sinning

pediculophobia, an abnormal fear of lice

pediophobia, pediphobia, pedophobia: an abnormal terror or fear of infants, dolls, or young children

peladophobia, morbid fear of becoming bald

pelagra (catching it): **pellagraphobia, pellagrophobia**

pellagraphobia, pellagrophobia: an intense fear of catching pellagra (a deficiency of niacin which results in dermatitis, inflammation of mucous membranes, diarrhea, and psychic disturbances which include depression, irritability, anxiety, delusions, and hallucinations)

peniaphobia, an exaggerated fear of being in a state of poverty

pentheraphobia, fear of having a mother-in-law or irritation by being around her

people: **anthropophobia, demophobia**

performing in public, **topophobia**

personal body odors: **bromhidrosiphobia, bromidrosophobia**

person who has a morbid terror of something, **phobiac**

phagophobia, an abnormal fear of eating or swallowing certain kinds of food

phalacraphobia, a fear of becoming bald

phantoms, **spectrophobia**

pharmacophobia, fear of drugs or medicine or of becoming a drug addict

phasmophobia, excessive fear of ghosts

phengophobia, excessive fear of daylight or of sunlight

philemaphobia, philematophobia: an intense fear of kissing

philophobia, excessive fear of falling in love or being loved

phobanthropy, excessive fear of humans

phobia, a morbid, unexplained terror of something

phobiac, one who has a morbid or unexplained terror of something

phobic, relating to, or affected by, a morbid, unexplained terror of something or someone

phobism, constituting an excessive fear of or a morbid, unexplained terror of something

phobodipsia, excessive fear of drinking or of excessive drinking (alcohol, for example)

phobogenic, phobogenous: something which is induced or caused by fear

phobologophobia, an aversion to or dislike of **phobia** words

phobophobia, excessive fear of fear itself or of one's own fears

phobotactic, a fear of arrangement or order; avoidance reaction of a motile organism

phobotaxis, a fear of arrangement or order; avoidance reaction of a motile organism

phonophobia, an excessive or abnormal fear of noise, sounds, or of speaking out loud

photalgia: **photalgiophobia, photaugiaphobia, photaugiophobia**

photalgiaphobia, photalgiophobia: a fear of photalgia (pain in the eyes caused by light)

photaugiaphobia, photaugiophobia: an abnormal, pathological fear of light directed upon one's eyes which may cause photalgia (pain caused by light in the eyes)

photophobia, excessive fear of light; painful sensitivity to light, especially visually; tendency to thrive in *reduced* light, as with certain plants

phronemophobia, excessive fear of thinking

phthiriophobia, phthisiophobia, phthisophobia: an intense fear of tuberculosis

phyllophobia, excessive fear of leaves

physical-sexual expressions, **erotophobia**

physical injury, **traumatophobia**

physicians, **iatrophobia**

pins: **belonephobia, belonophobia, blenophobia, enetephobia, enetophobia**

places (certain ones), **topophobia**

placophobia, excessive fear of tombstones

plants, **botanophobia**

pleasure: **hedenophobia, hedonophobia**

pluviophobia, excessive fear of rain

pneumatophobia, intense fear of incorporeal (disembodied) beings (ghosts, sprits); drafts

pnigeraphobia, pnigerophobia, pnigophobia: an excessive fear of smothering or choking

pocrescophobia, an abnormal fear of gaining weight

poetry, **metrophobia**

pogonophobia, a fear or hatred of beards

poinephobia, excessive fear of punishment

points, **aichmophobia**
poisoning: **iophobia, toxicophobia, toxophobia, iophobia, toxicophobia, toxiphobia**
politicians, **politicophobia**
politicophobia, excessive fear of politicians
polyphobia, excessive fear of many things
ponophobia, fear of fatigue, especially through overworking; a hatred for exerting one's self; dread of pain
pope, **papaphobia**
porphyrophobia, an excessive fear of purple
potamophobia, potomophobia: a morbid fear of rivers or of running water
potophobia, excessive fear of drinking
poverty, **peniaphobia**
preaching, **homilophobia**
precipices, **cremnophobia**
preferring that which one is afraid of, **counterphobia**
pregnancy, **maieusiophobia**
primeisodophobia, an abnormal fear of losing one's virginity
proctophobia, an intense fear of pain experienced by those who suffer with a rectum disease or mental apprehension about such a disease
progress, **prosophobia**
prosophobia, fear of or aversion to progress
prostitutes: **cyprianophobia, cypridophobia, cyprinophobia, cypriphobia**
protein foods, **proteinphobia**
proteinphobia, intense dislike of or aversion to protein foods
psellismophobia, excessive fear of stuttering
pseudohydrophobia, an excessive fear of what is assumed to be **hydrophobia**, but which may only seem to be **hydrophobia**; any animal disease that has symptoms similar to rabies
pseudorabies, **kynophobia**
psychophobia, a pathologic fear of the mind or psyche and, in particular, of the contents of one's own mind
psychrophobia, an abnormal fear of coldness or cold weather
pteronophobia, excessive fear of feathers
public places: **agarophobia, agoraphobia, agyiophobia**
punishment, **poinephobia**
punishment by whipping, **rhabdophobia**
purple, **porphyrophobia**

pyrexeophobia, pyrexiophobia: an excessive fear of having a fever
pyrophobia, an intense fear of fire
rabies: **cynophobia, hydrophobia, lyssophobia**
radiophobia, excessive fear of x-rays
railroads, **siderodromophobia**
rain: **ombrophobia, pluviophobia**
rape, **virgivitiphobia**
razors, **xyrophobia**
rectal pain: **proctophobia, rectophobia**
rectal excreta, **coprophobia**
rectophobia, excessive fear of pain experienced by those who suffer with rectum disease or mental apprehension about such a disease
red, **erythrophobia**
relatives: **syngenescophobia, syngenesophobia**
religious ceremonies, **teleophobia**
religious concepts, **hagiophobia**
religious objects, **hierophobia**
reptiles: **aphidiophobia, herpetophobia**
responsibility (fear of having it): **hypegiaphobia, hypengyophobia, paralipophobia**
responsibility: **hypegiaphobia, hypengyophobia**
returning home, **vokephobia**
returning to one's home, **nostophobia**
rhabdophobia, excessive fear of being beaten or a general fear of sticks or clubs (rods); criticism or punishment; or a fear of magic
rhypophobia, fear of filth or defecation
rhytiphobia, excessive fear of getting wrinkles
ridicule (of being ridiculed): **catagelophobia, categelophobia, katagelophobia**
right side of the body (things there), **dextrophobia**
rivers: **potamophobia, potomophobia**
robbers, **harpaxophobia**
robbery (being robbed), **latrophobia**
rods, **rhabdophobia**
room (full of people), **koinoniphobia**
ruins, **atephobia**
running water, **potomophobia**
rupophobia, excessive fear of dirt or filth
Russian culture, **Russophobia**
Russophobia, an excessive fear of Russians or Russian motives, culture, etc.
rust, **iophobia**
rypophobia, excessive fear of soiling or of filth
sacred objects, **hierophobia**
saints, **hagiophobia**

salt-rich soil (plants), **halophobia**
sarmassophobia, an abnormal fear of love-play
Satan, **Satanophobia**
Satanophobia, excessive fear of Satan
satellites (being hit by man-made satellites), **keraunothnetophobia**
scabies (itch), **scabiophobia**
scabiophobia, excessive fear of scabies (itch)
scatophobia, intense fear or extreme hatred of obscene or filthy language; fear of being around excrement
scelerophobia, excessive fear of bad men
scholionophobia, fear of going to school
school: **didaskaleinophobia, scholionophobia**
sciaphobia, sciophobia: an abnormal fear of shadows
scoleciphobia, excessive fear of worms
scopophobia, scoptophobia: an excessive fear of being stared at
scotophobia, an abnormal fear of darkness or of having blind areas in the visual field
scratched by someone or by something, **amychophobia**
scratches, **amychophobia**
scriptophobia, excessive fear of writing
seas, **thalassophobia**
sea swells, **cymophobia**
selaphobia, fear or strong dislike of flashes of light
selenophobia, an abnormal fear of the moon
self, **autophobia**
semen (losing it): **spermatophobia, spermophobia**
septophobia, excessive fear of decaying matter
sermons, **homilophobia**
servility, **genuphobia**
sesquipedalophobia, a hatred or a fear of big words
sex, **genophobia**
sexual abuse: **agraphobia, contrectophobia**
sexual feelings, **erotophobia**
sexual intercourse: **coitophobia, genophobia**
sexual perversion, **paraphobia**
shadows: **sciaphobia, sciophobia, skiaphobia**
sharks, **galeophobia**
sharp objects, **belonephobia**
sharp points, **acrophobia**
shellfish, **ostraconophobia**
shock, **hormephobia**
shot: **ballistophobia, ballistrophobia**

shut up in a small space, **claustrophobia**
sickness (wasting sickness), **tabophobia**
sickness in a particular part of the body, **monopathophobia**
siderodromophobia, an excessive fear of railroads or of traveling on trains
siderophobia, excessive fear of stars
sin: **enissophobia, enosiophobia, hamartophobia**
single (remaining unmarried), **anuptaphobia**
single fear, **monophobia**
sinistrophobia, excessive fear of things on the left side
sinning: **enissophobia, enosiophobia, harmatophobia, hamartophobia, peccatiphobia, peccatophobia**
Sinophobia, an excessive fear of China or of things related to the Chinese
sitiophobia, sitophobia, an abnormal fear of food or of eating; or an intense hatred of food or of eating
sitting, **thaasophobia**
sitting down: **cathisophobia, kathisophobia**
skiaphobia, excessive fear of shadows
skin disease: **dermatopathophobia, dermatophobia, dermatosiophobia**
skin infestation by mites or ticks, **acarophobia**
skin of animals, **doraphobia**
sky: **ouranophobia, uranophobia**
sleep, **hypnophobia**
slime: **blennophobia, myxophobia**
small things: **microbiophobia, microphobia, tapinophobia**
smells (odors), **olfactophobia**
smothering: **pnigeraphobia, pnigerophobia, pnigophobia**
snakes: **herpetophobia, herptophobia, ophiciophobia, ophidiophobia, ophiophobia**
snow: **chinophobia, chionophobia**
soceraphobia, a fear or strong dislike of one's parents-in-law
society in general, **sociophobia**
sociophobia, an abnormal fear or hatred of any social friendships or situations
soiling, **rypophobia**
soleciphobia, excessive fear of worms
solitude: **autophobia, ermitophobia, eremiophobia, eremophobia, isolophobia, monophobia**
sophophobia, intense fear of knowledge or of learning

sore throat, **anginaphobia**

sounds: **acousticophobia, akousticophobia, phonophobia**

sourness: **acerbophobia, acerophobia**

speaking in public: **glossophobia, lalophobia, phonophobia**

specters, **spectrophobia**

spectrophobia, excessive fear of specters, or of phantoms, or of looking in a mirror at one's own image or seeing the images of others

speed, **tachophobia**

spermatophobia, an intensive fear of losing semen or a morbid fear of germs

spermophobia, an excessive fear of germs

spheksophobia, excessive fear of wasps

spider eggs, **arachnoophobia**

spiders: **arachnephobia, arachnophobia**

spirits (evil), **daemonophobia**

squeezed, **charminphobia**

stage fright, **topophobia**

stairs, **climacophobia**

standing (fear of attempting to stand or walk): **stasibasiphobia, stasophobia**

standing (for fear of falling), **basophobia**

standing: **basistasiphobia, basostasophobia**

standing and walking: **stasobasiphobia, stasophobia**

stared at: **ophthalmophobia, scopophobia, scoptophobia**

stars: **astrophobia, siderophobia**

stasibasiphobia, stasobasiphobia: an abnormal conviction that one cannot stand or walk

stasiphobia, stasophobia: an abnormal conviction that one cannot stand or walk; an intense fear of attempting to stand or to walk

staurophobia, an excessive fear of a crucifix

staying single, **anuptaphobia**

stealing, **cleptophobia**

stenophobia, a fear of narrow spaces

stepfather, **vitricophobia**

stepmother (fear of or an abnormal hatred of), **novercaphobia**

sticks, **rhabdophobia**

stillness: **eremiophobia, eremitophobia, eremophobia**

stings, **cnidophobia**

stolen from, **kleptophobia**

stooping, **kyphophobia**

strangers: **xenophobia, zenophobia**

strange things, **xenophobia**

streets: **agyiophobia, agyrophobia**

string: **linonophobia, linophobia**

stuttering: **glossophobia, laliophobia, psellismophobia**

stygiophobia, an excessive fear of going to hell [*stygio-* is based on *crossing the river Styx*]

submissiveness, **genuphobia**

subways, **bathysiderodromophobia**

sunlight: **heliophobia, phengophobia**

surgical operations, **tomophobia**

swallowing, **phagophobia**

symbiophobia, a fear of any intimate association with another life form

symbolophobia, fear of symbols

symmetrophobia, a fear or dislike of symmetry

syngenescophobia, sygenesophobia: an intense or strong dislike or fear of one's relatives

syphiliphobia, syphilophobia: a dread of being infected with syphilis

syphilis: **syphilidophobia, syphiliphobia, syphilophobia**

tabophobia, a fear of any wasting sickness

tachophobia, an excessive fear of speed

taeniophobia, morbid fear of tapeworms

talking: **glossophobia, laliophobia, lalophobia, phonophobia**

tapeworms: **taeniophobia, teniophobia**

taphephobia, taphiphobia, taphophobia: an intense fear of being buried alive or an extreme fear of cemeteries and graves

tapinophobia, an excessive fear of small things

tastes (strange): **geumatophobia, geumaphobia, geumophobia**

taurophobia, an excessive fear of bulls

technical machines, **technophobia**

technophobia, a fear of technical machines

teeth, **odontophobia**

teleology (dislike and rejection of): **teleophobia, telophobia**

teleophobia, a fear of religious ceremonies or an intense dislike and rejection of teleology

telephone, **telephonophobia**

telephonophobia, a fear of using the telephone

telophobia, a strong dislike for teleology

temperatures which are high, **thermophobia**

teratophobia, an intense fear of monsters or of giving birth to a monster or a deformed child

terdekaphobia, an excessive fear of the number thirteen

termites: **eisopterophobia, isopterophobia**

terror (morbid or abnormal): **phobia, phobism, phobogenic**

Teutonophobia, an excessive fear of Germans and German culture

textophobia, an excessive fear of specific kinds of fabrics

thaasophobia, thassophobia: excessive dislike of sitting or of being idle, intense hatred of boredom

thalassophobia, an excessive fear of seas or oceans

thanatophobia, an unwarranted apprehension of imminent death or a morbid dread of death or of dying

theaters, **theatrophobia**

theatrophobia, an excessive fear of theaters

theologicophobia, abnormal fear of theology

theology, **theologicophobia**

theophobia, an excessive fear of God, the wrath of God, or of God's punishment for sin

thermophobia, an excessive fear of or aversion to heat or high temperatures

thief (of becoming one), **cleptophobia**

thieves: **cleptophobia, harpaxophobia, kleptophobia**

thinking, **phronemophobia**

thirteen: **terdekaphobia, tredecaphobia, triakaidekaphobia, tridecaphobia, triskadekaphobia, triskaidekaphobia**

thixophobia, an excessive fear of touching or of being touched

thunder: **brontephobia, brontophobia, ceraunophobia, tonitrophobia, tonitruphobia**

thunder and lightning, **keraunophobia**

thunderstorms: **astraphobia, brontephobia, brontophobia**

ticks, **entonophobia**

tied with ropes (bound), **merinthophobia**

time (discomfort), **chronophobia**

toads, **batrachophobia**

tocophobia, tokophobia: an excessive fear of childbirth

tombstones, **placophobia**

tomophobia, a fear of surgical operations

tonitrophobia, tonitruphobia: an excessive fear of thunder

topophobia, fear of certain places or of performing (stage fright); also **agoraphobia**

tornadoes, **lilapsophobia**

touched: **haphephobia, haptephobia, haptophobia, thixophobia**

touched by pointed objects (such as knives), **aichmophobia**

touching: **aphephobia, thixophobia**

toxicophobia, a fear of poisoning, of poisons, or of being poisoned

toxiphobia, toxophobia: an abnormal fear of poisoning, of poisons, or of being poisoned

trains (traveling on), **siderodromophobia**

transfusion of blood, **hemaphobia**

traumatophobia, an intense disabling fear of war or physical injury, wounds, etc.

traveling, **hodophobia**

tredecaphobia, a fear of the number thirteen

trees, **dendrophobia**

trembling, **tremophobia**

tremophobia, an excessive fear of trembling

triakaidekaphobia, a fear of the number thirteen

trichinophobia, an abnormal or excessive fear of trichinosis (a disease caused by intestinal worms)

trichinosis (intestinal worms): **trichinophobia, trichopathophobia, trichophobia**

trichopathophobia, a fear of trichinosis (a disease caused by worms which come from raw or insufficiently cooked meat, especially pork); fear of a certain hair color, hair growth, hair disease, etc

trichophobia, a fear of trichinosis or of certain kinds of hair growth, hair color, hair disease, etc

tridecaphobia, a fear of the number thirteen

triskadekaphobia, triskaidekaphobia: an excessive fear of the number thirteen

tropophobia, a fear of making changes or of moving

trypanophobia, a fear of parasites (borers) or of inoculations or injections

tuberculophobia, an excessive fear of tuberculosis

tuberculosis: **phthisiophobia, phthisophobia, tuberculophobia**

tyrannophobia, a fear or hatred of tyrants

tyrants, **tyrannophobia**

undressing in front of others, **dishabillophobia**

unfamiliar tastes, **geumaphobia**

unmarried, **anuptaphobia**

untrue stories, **mythophobia**

uranophobia, a fear of heaven or of the sky

urinating, **urophobia**

urophobia, a fear of urinating; an intense fear of *not being able* to urinate

vaccinations, **vaccinophobia**

vaccines, **vaccinophobia**

vaccinophobia, an intense fear of vaccines and vaccinations

vegetables, **lachanophobia**

vehicles: **amaxophobia, ochophobia**

venereal disease: **cypridophobia, cypriphobia, venereophobia**

venereophobia, fear of venereal disease

venustaphobia, a fear of beautiful women

verbaphobia, verbophobia: an excessive fear or hatred of words

vermiphobia, an abnormal fear of being infected with worms

vertigo, **illyngophobia**

vespertiliophobia, an abnormal fear of bats

vestiophobia, an excessive fear of clothing

virginity (losing): **esodophobia, primeisodophobia**

virgins, **parthenophobia**

virgivitiphobia, excessive fear of being raped

vitricophobia, an excessive fear of step-fathers

void, **kenophobia**

vokephobia, a fear of returning home

vomiting, **emetophobia**

walking: **ambulophobia, basiphobia, basistasiphobia, basophobia, basostasophobia, bathmophobia, bathomophobia, stasibasiphobia**

walking or standing: **stasobasiphobia, stasophobia**

wandering (roaming), **dromophobia**

war (being wounded in war), **traumatophobia**

wasps, **spheksophobia**

water: **aquaphobia, hydrophobia, potamophobia, potomophobia**

waves, **cymophobia**

weakness, **asthenophobia**

wealth: **chrematophobia, chrometophobia**

weather phenomena, **meteorophobia**

weight (gaining): **obesophobia, pocrescophobia**

wet dreams, **oneirogmophobia**

whirlpools, **dinophobia**

white strangers, **gringophobia**

wild animals, **agrizoophobia**

wind: **aerophobia, ancraophobia, anemophobia**

wine (hatred or strong dislike of): **enophobia, oenophobia, oinophobia**

women (beautiful), **venustaphobia**

women): **feminophobia, gynephobia, gynophobia**

women (lewd), **cyprinophobia**

wooden objects, **xylophobia**

woods: **hylephobia, hylophobia, xylophobia**

words, big: **sesquipedalophobia**

words (hearing a certain word or words), **onomatophobia**

words: **logophobia, verbaphobia, verbophobia**

work (hatred of): **ergasiophobia, ergasophobia, ergophobia, ponophobia**

worm infestations: **helminthophobia, vermiphobia**

worms: **scoleciphobia, soleciphobia**

wounds, **traumatophobia**

wrinkles, **rhytiphobia**

writing: **graphophobia, scriptophobia**

x-rays, **radiophobia**

xenophobia, a fear or hatred of foreigners and of strange or foreign things

xenophoby, a fear of strange diseases

xerophobia, an abnormal fear of dryness or of dryplaces, such as deserts; an aversion to dry places or an inability to survive in dry places

xylophobia, an excessive fear of wooden objects or forests

xyrophobia, an abnormal fear of razors

young children: **pediophobia, pediphobia**

young girls, **parthenophobia**

zelophobia, an excessive fear of jealousy

zenophobia (a misspelling of **xenophobia**), an excessive fear of strangers or foreigners

zoophobia, a morbid fear of animals in general or of a specific animal

Appendix J

PLEONASMS

Pleonasms are the opposite (antonyms) of oxymora. A pleonasm consists of two concepts (usually two words) that are *redundant* or pleonastic.

academic scholar
anonymous stranger
bad evil
cash money
classic tradition
cold frost
cold ice
continuing on
dark night
exact same
federal deficit
free gift
frozen ice
good luck
growing greater
hear with one' own ears
hot fire
hot water heater
indulgent patience
intentional planning
killed dead
last will and testament
literate English teachers
literate readers
marital spouse
microdot
negative misfortune
nocturnal-night vampires
nonreading illiterates
old customs
old senior citizens
personal individual
play actor
positive praise
rags and tatters
real actual
redundancies, tautologies, and pleonasms
redundant redundancies
redundant repetitions
repeated redundancies
retreating back

see with one's own eyes
sharp point
shape and form
small speck
staged scenario
tiny speck
unhealthy sickness
university college students
unmarried bachelor
unmarried old maid
wet water
widow woman
widower man
youthful teenagers

"It's déjàvu all over again." -Yogi Berra

"Smoking can kill you, and if you've been killed, you've lost a very important part of your life."

-attributed to Brooke Shields

Appendix K, SUFFIXES

The following suffixes don't include all of the possible meanings attributed to them by various authorities. An attempt has been made to give some of the most important "definitions" for a general understanding of the most commonly used suffixes which have come from Latin and Greek sources.

Also see **-um** for other suffixes (singular and plural forms). *Some* of the following suffixes and a few others, which may not be shown here, are listed throughout other parts of this book.

-able (L., capable of, fit for, tending to, given to)
>   **Qualifying words:** amicable, culpable, laudable, portable, reasonable, teachable

-ac (Gk. > L., like, pertaining to)
>   **Qualifying words:** aphorodisiac, cardiac, hypochondriac, insomniac, maniac, phobiac, pyromaniac

-aceous (L., pertaining to, like, having the quality of, resembling, made of)
>   **Qualifying words:** carbonaceous, cretaceous, herbaceous, subaceous

-acious (L., inclined to, abounding in)
>   **Qualifying words:** audacious, fallacious, loquacious, pugnacious, tenacious, vivacious

-acity (L., a quality or state of being, denoting quality of)
>   **Qualifying words:** audacity, pugnacity, tenacity, veracity

-acy (L., condition of, quality of, state of, office of)
>   **Qualifying words:** celibacy, delicacy, democracy, fallacy, legacy, lunacy, magistracy, papacy, piracy

-ade (L, forms nouns and, sometimes, verbs)
>   **Qualifying words:** cannonade, cavalcade, tirade

-age (L., quality of, act of, process, function, condition, or place)
>   **Qualifying words:** acreage, breakage, brokerage, courage, coverage, herbage, marriage, parsonage, passage, spoilage, usage, voyage

-al (L., act or process of)
>   **Qualifying words:** acquittal, ceremonial, denial, dismissal, final, original, refusal, principal

-al (L., of, belonging to, suitable to, pertaining to, relating to, resembling)
>   **Qualifying words:** accidental, educational, global, maternal, natural, neanderthal, oral, scriptural, seasonal, suicidal, tribal

-an (L., connected with, belonging to)
>   **Qualifying words:** American, Chicagoan, Cuban, European, human, Roman, Russian, Tibetan, urban

-an (-ane), (L., pertaining to, belonging to, or resembling)
>   **Qualifying words:** American, amphibian, crustacean, European, human, urban

-an (L., a person who specializes in something)
>   **Qualifying words:** comedian, Episcopalian, logician, pedestrian, Puritan, Republican, veterinarian

-ance (L, process, degree, action, state of)
>   **Qualifying words:** abundance, ambulance, appearance, brilliance, continuance, dissonance, forbearance, importance, vigilance

-ancy (L, process, degree, action of)
>   **Qualifying words:** abundancy, buoyancy, brilliancy, continuancy, hesitancy, obstinancy, vacancy

-ane (L., connected with, belonging to)
>   **Qualifying words:** humane, mundane, urbane

-ant (L., a person who, the thing which)
>   **Qualifying words:** claimant, contestant, defendant, defiant, deodorant, emigrant, immigrant, radiant, servant, tenant, vacant, vigilant

-ant (L., denoting impersonal physical agents in technical and commercial coinages)
>   **Qualifying words:** lubricant, propellant, immigrant

-ar (L., like, pertaining to, of the nature of, or belonging to)
>   **Qualifying words:** circular, insular, lunar, polar, solar, titular, singular

-arian (L., a believer, advocate, or one who practices a set of principles)
>   **Qualifying words:** authoritarian, equalitarian, establishmentarian, millenarian, totalitarian, vegetarian

-arian (L., a person who is or is part of something; pertaining to his/her state or condition)
>   **Qualifying words:** libertarian, librarian, nonagenarian, octogenarian, proletarian, seminarian, sexagenarian

-arium (s.), **-aria** (pl.), **-ariums** (pl.) (Gk. > L., a place for; abounding in or connected with something; "a place containing or related to" that which is specified by the root) Also see **-ary, -orium,** and **-ory.**

> **Qualifying words:** aquarium, caldarium, calidarium, cinerarium, frigidarium, herbarium, hippolarium (hippo-solarium), insectarium, leprosarium, ossuarium, panarium (bread), planetarium, pollenarium, ranarium, sanitarium, solarium, septarium, sudarium, tepidaria, termitarium, terrarium, vaporarium, vivaria, vivarium

-ary (L., a place for, or abounding in something)

> **Qualifying words:** aviary, dictionary, glos- sary, granary, library, sanctuary, sedentary, stationary

-ary (L., of or pertaining to, connected with)

> **Qualifying words:** bacillary, boundary, dignitary, lapidary, sanctuary

-ary (L., pertaining to, connected with, like, belonging to)

> **Qualifying words:** arbitrary, complimentary, customary, inflationary, luminary, revolu- tionary, secondary, sedentary, solitary, visionary, voluntary

-ary (L., having [some number of] parts)

> **Qualifying words:** binary, quaternary, quinary, ternary, trinary, unitary

-ate (L., being, like, or possessing)

> **Qualifying words:** affectionate, alternate, collegiate, delicate, desolate, dispassionate, fortunate, indiscriminate, irate, obstinate, passionate, sedate

-ate (L., derivative of a specified chemical compound or element, used to indicate a salt of an acid ending in **-ic**)

> **Qualifying words:** aluminate, nitrate, opiate, silicate, sulfate

-ate (L., indicates rank, office, insitutions, or collective bodies)

> **Qualifying words:** consulate, delegate, electorate, graduate, magistrate, potentate, primate, senate, triumvirate

-ate (L., to do, make, cause, act upon)

> **Qualifying words:** annihilate, captivate, concentrate, detoxicate, evaporate, liberate, medicate, placate, salivate, vaccinate, venerate

-atic (Gk. > L., pertaining to: of the nature of)

> **Qualifying words:** aquatic, dramatic, erratic, grammatic, pneumatic

-ation (L., state, result, act, effect, or product of)

> **Qualifying words:** civilization, personification, visitation

-ation (L., action or process of)

> **Qualifying words:** negotiation, perspiration, separation, starvation

-cle (L., diminutive, small, little)

> **Qualifying words:** article, corpuscle, denticle, particle

-cule (L., diminutive, smallness)

> **Qualifying words:** animalcule, majuscule, miniscule, minuscule, molecule

-cy (L., state of, condition of, act of, or denoting rank or office)

> **Qualifying words:** accuracy, agency, bankruptcy, captaincy, celibacy, democracy, expediency, fallacy, infancy, literacy, lunacy, occupancy, stagnancy, vacancy

-ee (Fr., one who receives *or* the performer of an action)

> **Qualifying words:** addressee, divorcee, donee, draftee, employee, payee, referee

-eer (L., a person who is concerned with, produces, handles, or is otherwise significantly associated with the referent of the base)

> **Qualifying words:** auctioneer, buccaneer, charioteer, engineer, mountaineer, mutineer, pioneer, racketeer, volunteer

-ence (L., condition of, quality of, act of)

> **Qualifying words:** abstinence, continence, dependence, difference, evidence, existence, independence, opulence

-ency (L., condition of, quality of, act of)

> **Qualifying words:** consistency, dependency, emergency, exigency, fluency

-ent (L., a person or thing that performs an action)

> **Qualifying words:** accident, client, correspondent, dependent, dissident, evident, incombent, insurgent, referent, resident, solvent, student, subsequent

-ent (L., relating to, like, belonging to)

> **Qualifying words:** dependent, evident, permanent

-eous (L, having, full of, abounding in)

> **Qualifying words:** beauteous, courteous, gaseous, hideous, igneous, ligneous, righteous, vitreous

-esce (L., this once had the basic meaning of "beginning to," but this meaning has been lost in most words)

> **Qualifying words:** acquiesce, effloresce

-escence (L., the process or state of becoming)

> **Qualifying words:** acquiescence, adolescence, convalescence, luminescence

-escent (L., increasing)

> **Qualifying words:** acquiescent, adolescent, crescent

-fy (L, to make, to cause)

> **Qualifying words:** mortify, petrify, rectify, justify

-ia (Gk. > L., names of areas and countries)

> **Qualifying words:** Australia, California, Italia, Manchuria, Mauritania, Rumania, suburbia, utopia

-ia (L., names of Roman feasts)

> **Qualifying word:** Lupercalia

-ia (Gk. > L., names of diseases and disorders)

> **Qualifying words:** alexia, amnesia, anemia, aphasia, diphtheria, dysphagia, malaria, mania, neuralgia, nostalgia, phobia, pneumonia

-ia (Gk. > L., names of plants or animals and their orders or classes)

> **Qualifying words:** Amphibia, begonia, poinsettia

-ia (Gk. > L., names of alkaloids)

> **Qualifying word:** morphia

-ia (Gk. > L., collective nouns)

> **Qualifying words:** juvenilia, media, memorabilia, paraphernalia, trivia

-ia (Gk. > L., names of things relating to or belonging to)

> **Qualifying words:** gynephobia, hydrophobia, kleptomania, megalogastria, monomania, pedodontia, pyromani

-ial (L., of, pertaining to)

> **Qualifying words:** celestial, imperial, senatorial, tutorial

-ian (L., belonging to, derived from)

> **Qualifying words:** mammalian, Tunisian, Washingtonian

-ibility (L., able to be or to do, a variation of **-ability**)

> **Qualifying words:** defensibility, flexibility, reducibility, sensibility

-ible (L., ability, capacity, fitness)

> **Qualifying words:** audible, credible, collapsible, edible, legible, visible

-ic (L., state of, act of, quality of)

> **Qualifying words:** alcoholic, anemic, critic, logic, lunatic, magic, moronic, music, titanic

-ic (Gk. > L., relating to, like, belonging to, pertaining to, of the nature of)

> **Qualifying words:** alcoholic, anemic, aromatic, chronic, dynamic, gymnastic, kinetic, moronic, rhythmic, sarcastic, Slavonic, titanic, volcanic

-ical (L., quality, degree)

> **Qualifying words:** anthological, economical, farcical, logical, poetical

-ice (L., state, art, quality of; dependence, attached to)

> **Qualifying words:** accomplice, justice, malice, notice, novice, prejudice

-ician (L., a specialist or practitioner in some field of work)

> **Qualifying words:** beautician, mortician, musician, physician, statistician

-id (L, state or condition; having, being, pertaining to)

> **Qualifying words:** avid, florid, fluid, frigid, horrid, incipid, intrepid, invalid, lucid, placid, rabid

-id (L., pertaining to, of the nature of, descendant of)

> **Qualifying words:** acid, arachnid, humid, lipid, rigid

-ier (L., denotes an occupation, a variation of **-er**; a noun suffix occurring mainly in loan words from French, often simply a spelling variant of **-eer**, with which it is etymologically identical)

> **Qualifying words:** bombardier, brigadier, cashier, cavalier, clothier, financier, furrier, gondalier

-il (L., capable of being, pertaining to [variation of **-ile**])

> **Qualifying word:** civil

-ile (L., ability or capacity, relating to, like, suitable, susceptibility, liability [often British])

> **Qualifying words:** agile, docile, fragile, hostile, missile, mobile, prehensile, puerile, senile, virile, volatile

-ine (L., of, pertaining to, of the nature of, like) This group is also listed in the main body of the book.

> **Qualifying words:** aquiline, asinine, canine, crystalline, divine, elephantine, equine, feline, feminine, marine, saline, suine, taurine, ursine, viperine

-ine (L., used in chemical compounds or elements)

> **Qualifying words:** arsine, bromine, caffeine, chlorine, cocaine, gasoline, quinine, quinoline

-ion (L., an act or process or the outcome of an act or process)

    Qualifying words: abortion, allusion, aversion, coercion, communion, creation, destruction, distortion, fusion, indention, legion, notion, opinion, rebellion, tortion

-ious (L. > Fr., of, pertaining, relating to, or resembling [variant of **-ous**])

    Qualifying words: ambitious, atrocious, furious, glorious, hilarious, religious, sagacious

-ise (Gk. > L., to act upon, treat, make, or affect)

    Qualifying words: chastise, compromise, despise, franchise

-ise (L., British spelling of American **-ize** words)

    Qualifying words: botanise (Brit.), botanize (U.S.); equalise (Brit.), equalize (U.S.)

-ish (L., belonging to or having a charateristic of)

    Qualifying words: British, devilish, fiftyish, freakish, knavish, Spanish

-ish (L., do, make, perform)

    Qualifying words: abolish, astonish, ravish

-ism (Gk., an action, practice, or process)

    Qualifying words: baptism, barbarism, communism, criticism, favoritism, plagiarism, terrorism

-ism (Gk., a state, condition of being, act of)

    Qualifying words: antagonism, despotism, parallelism, pauperism, phobism

-ism (Gk., a characteristic behavior or quality of)

    Qualifying words: heroism, individualism, intellectualism, realism

-ism (Gk., a distinctive usage or feature, especially of language)

    Qualifying words: Anglicism, Latinism, malepropism

-ism (Gk., a doctrine, theory, system, or principle)

    Qualifying words: agnosticism, atheism, capitalism, communism, expressionism, pacifism, Platonism

-ist (Gk. > L., a person who does, makes, uses, believes, or is an expert in)

    Qualifying words: antagonist, apologist, biologist, chemist, communist, dentist, dramatist, epidemologist, machinist, militarist, novelist, nudist, philanthropist, psychologist, radiologist, realist, romanticist

-ition (L., forms nouns indicating action)

    Qualifying words: acquisition, cognition, expedition, extradition, prohibition

-itious (L., of, pertaining to, relating to, or resembling)

    Qualifying words: adventitious, expeditious, fictitious, repetitious

-ity (L., an action, practice, or process; a quality, state, or degree)

    Qualifying words: agility, annuity, audacity, authenticity, civility, gravity, opacity, pugnacity, sagacity, sanity, tenacity, veracity

-ive (L., tending to, having the nature of)

    Qualifying words: abusive, active, creative, disruptive

-ize (L., to act in a certain way, to treat in a certain way, to make into)

    Qualifying words: advertize, Americanize, Anglicize, apologize, baptize, barbarize, catechize, chastize, civilize, computerize, democratize, dramatize, economize, epitomize, etymologize, eulogize, exorcize, fossilize, humanize, itemize, moralize, nasalize, oxidize, philosophize, sterilize, sympathize, terrorize, theorize, tyrannize, verbalize, vocalize

-ment (L., product, means, action of, result)

    Qualifying words: abridgment, environment, fragment, government, implement, judgment, measurement, ornament

-mony (L., a resulting thing, condition, status, role, or function)

    Qualifying words: acrimony, alimony, ceremony, matrimony, patrimony, sanctimony, testimony

-or (L., indicates persons or things performing some action)

    Qualifying words: harbor, sailor, sculptor, valor

-or (L., indicates a state, quality, or activity)

    Qualifying words: advisor, ardor, demeanor, elevator, honor, horror, pallor, squalor, orpor, tremor, vendor, vigor

-oria (L., a place used for something) For examples, see **-orium**.

-orium, -oria (L., a place or a thing used for something) Also see **-arium** and **-ary** for other examples.

    Qualifying words: auditorium, conservatorium, crematorium, ejaculatorium, emporium, incubatorium, lavatorium, lubritorium, natatorium, oratorium, sanitorium, scriptorium (s.), scriptoria (pl.), sensorium, sudoria, sudorium, vaporium

-ory (from Latin, **-orium**) (L., place where) Also see **-ary** (-arium) for additional elements.

    Qualifying words: conservatory, crematory, directory, dormitory, factory, laboratory, lavatory, observatory, oratory, purgatory

-ory (L., a suffix which forms nouns)

    Qualifying words: accessory, inventory, trjectory, victory

-ory (L., a suffix which forms adjectives; pertaining to; of the nature of)

    Qualifying words: ambulatory, auditory, compulsory, cursory, declamatory, hortatory, laudatory, mandatory, obligatory, predatory, preparatory, respiratory

-ose (L, in chemistry: a carbohydrate)

    Qualifying words: fructose, glucose, lactose

-ose (L., containing, full of, given to, possessing the qualities of)

    Qualifying words: bellicose, comatose, verbose

-ous (L., having, full of, abounding in)

    Qualifying words: contiguous, covetous, famous, hazardous, ludicrous, nervous, stupendous

-ous (L., in chemistry, this means "having a lower valence than is expressed by the suffix **-ic**")

    Qualifying words: ferrous, sulfurous

-ous (L., state of, act of, doctrine, or quality of)

    Qualifying words: gracious, ludicrous, vivacious

-sis (L., state or condition of)

    Qualifying words: biosis, cirrhosis, paralysis, psychosis

-tion (L., action or condition of)

    Qualifying words: absorption, benediction, commendation, contrition, malediction, revolution, starvation

-tious (L., of, pertaining to, relating to, or resembling)

    Qualifying words: cautious, infectious

-tor (L., a doer, an agent)

    Qualifying words: administrator, actor, aviator, benefactor, dictator, director, executor, janitor, legislator, narrator, orator, procurator, proprietor, victor

-trix (L., a doer, an agent; the feminine equivalent of **-tor**)

    Qualifying words: administratrix, aviatrix, benefactrix, executrix, inheritrix, oratrix, procuratrix, proprietrix

-tron (Gk., instrument [used especially in forming names of devices in electronics and nuclear physics])

    Qualifying words: biotron, cosmotron, cryotron, cyclotron, electron, ignitron, klystron, magnetron

-tude (L., condition or state of being)

    Qualifying words: altitude, certitude, fortitude, gratitude, latitude, longitude, magnitude, multitude, platitude

-ty (L., condition, quality, state of)

    Qualifying words: amity, audacity, beauty, diety, enmity, liberty, novelty, piety, poverty, sanity, unity, verity

-ule (L., diminutive, small, little)

    Qualifying words: capsule, globule, module, nodule, tubule

-um (Gk. > L., singular suffix) See **-um** in **Appendix L** for a list of examples.

-ure (L., act of; state of; result of)

    Qualifying words: legislature, pleasure, pressure, procedure, rupture, scripture, torture

-y (Gk. > L., a specified state, condition, or quality)

    Qualifying words: carpentry, democracy, infamy, monogamy

Appendix L

-um (Gk. > L., a suffix which forms singular nouns) The plural of **-um** is **-a.** Also see **Suffixes** in **Appendix K** for other word endings.

Singular	Plural	Singular	Plural
addendum	addenda	optimum	optima
agendum	agenda	ovum	ova
aquarium	aquaria	palladium	palladia
arboretum	arboreta	penicillium	penicillia
arcanum	arcana	planetarium	planetaria
atrium	atria	plectrum	plectra
bacterium	bacteria	phylum	phyla
brachium	brachia	podium	podia
candelabrum	candelabra	postulatum	postulata
cerebellum	cerebella	referendum	referenda
cerebrum	cerebra	risiduum	risidua
cilium	cilia	rostrum	rostra
cinerarium	cineraria	sanatorium	sanatoria
compendium	compendia	sanitarium	sanitaria
consortium	consortia	scriptorium	scriptoria
continuum	continua	septum	septa
corrigendum	corrigenda	serum	sera
cranium	crania	solarium	solaria
curriculum	curricula	spectrum	spectra
datum	data	speculum	specula
delirium	deliria	sputum	sputa
desideratum	desiderata	stadium	stadia
dictum	dicta	stratum	strata
duodenum	duodena	substratum	substrata
effluvium	effluvia	sudatorium	sudatoria
emporium	emporia	terrarium	terraria
encomium	encomia	trapezium	trapezia
erratum	errata	tympanum	tympana
exordium	exordia	ultimatum	ultimata
fulcrum	fulcra	vacuum	vacua
gymnasium	gymnasia	viaticum	viatica
herbarium	herbaria		
honorarium	honoraria		
interregnum	interregna		
marsupium	marsupia		
mausoleum	mausolea		
maximum	maxima		
medium	media		
memorandum	memoranda		
millenium	millenia		
minimum	minima		
momentum	momenta		
moratorium	moratoria		
natatorium	natatoria		

Words for a Modern Age

Appendix M

GROUP NAMES

There are many group names from traditional terms of the hunt and some current creations which attempt to describe group characteristics. Such historical nomenclature or terminology, called VENEREAL TERMS or TERMS OF VENERY, were said to refer to a gathering of *group names* or collective nouns from the hunt and social functions.

Venereal terms, or the language of the chase (hunt), were in general use as well-established hunting terms. The nomenclature in italics were considered the proper terms for groups of beasts, fish, fowls, insects, or whatever was designatged and "codified in the fifteenth century." According to James Lipton, in his *An Exaltation of Larks*, 1968, surviving lists include: *The Egerton Manuscript* (106 terms, 1450) and *The Book of St. Albans* (164 terms, 1486). The groups are referred to as: "nouns of multitude, group terms," and "terms of venery."

Lipton also says, "*venery* and *venereal* are most often thought of as signifying love, and more specifically physical love. From *Venus* we have the Latin root *ven* which appears in the word *venari*, meaning 'to hunt game'."

Eric Partridge, a specialist in lexicography, says in his etymological dictionary, *Origins*, that *ven* in *venari* has its original meaning of "to desire and pursue." *Venery* came to signify the hunt and it was used in all the early works on the chase, including the earliest known on the subject of English hunting.

Dr. Ernest Klein in his *A comprehensive Etymological Dictionary of the English Language* writes that *venery* means hunting (archaic), from Latin *venari*, "to hunt, pursue," which probably derives from I.E., "to strive after."

These terms were part of the education of the wealthy. "Willam Blades in his Introduction to the 1881 facsimile edition of *The Book of St. Albans*, refers to the book's subjects as 'those with which, at that period, every man claiming to be gentle was expected to be familiar; while ignorance of their laws and language was to confess himself a churl' " (Lipton, p. 10, 1968).

Many of the words in the following list have no authoritive basis and have been created to express possible names for the groups represented.

accountants, a column of accountants
actors, a cast of actors; a company of actors; a troupe of actors
acupuncturists, a sting of acupuncturists
air conditioners, a drone of air conditioners
airplanes, a flight of airplanes; a squadron of airplanes
allergists, a patch of allergists; a hive of allergists
amoebas, an ooze of amoebas
anatomists, a corps of anatomists; a body of anatomists
angels, *a host of angels* [angels were considered *warriors* of God, from Latin *hostis* (enemy) -Lipton]
antelopes, a herd of antelopes
anthropologists, a tribe of anthropologists
ants, *a colony of ants*; a union of carpenter ants; a picnic of ants
apes, *a shrewdness of apes*
arachnologists, a web of arachnologists
arrows, a sheaf of arrows; a quiver of arrows
assassins, a slew of assassins
asses, a herd of asses; a drove of asses
astronomers, a galaxy of astronomers
audiologists, a heard of audiologists
bachelors, a debauchery of bachelors; a score of bachelors
badgers, *a cete of badgers*
bakers, an aroma of bakers
bananas, a bunch of bananas
barbers, a babble of barbers
barflies, a buzz of barflies
barnacles, a fixture of barnacles
baseball players, a team of baseball players
bass, *a shoal of bass*
bats, a hanger of bats; a cloud of bats
bears, *a sloth of bears*; a sleuth of bears
beauties, *a bevy of beauties*
beepers, an embarrassment of beepers; an annoyance of beepers
bees, *a swarm of bees*; a grist of bees; an apiary of bees; *a colony of bees*; *a hive of bees*
bells, a peal of bells
biologists, a cell of biologists
birds; *a dissimulation of birds*; *a flight of birds*, a flock of birds

boa constrictors, a crush of boa constrictors
bowls, a set of bowls
bread, a batch of bread
brokers, a portfolio of brokers
buffaloes, a herd of buffaloes
bullets, a fusillade of bullets
buses, a lurch of busses
camels, a herd of camels; a flock of camels
candidates, *a slate of candidates* (perhaps a reference to a time when nominees were chalked on a slate -Lipton)
cards, a pack of cards; a deck of cards
cardinals, a synod of cardinals; a college of cardinals
cardiologists, a flutter of cardiologists; a click of cardiologists; a fibrillation of cardiologists
cars, a fleet of cars
caterpillars, *an army of caterpillars*
cats, *a clowder of cats; a clutter of cats* ("clouder" is the same word as "clutter" according toLipton), a kindle of young cats; a cluster of house cats
cattle, *a drove of cattle*; a herd of cattle
cellular phones, a babel of cellular phones
centerfolds, a spread of centerfolds
cheerleaders, a frenzy of cheerleaders
cheetahs, a dash of cheetahs
chickens, *a peep of chickens*; a brood of chickens; a flock of chickens; a clutch of chickens
chicks, *a brood of chicks; a clutch of chicks*
chinaware, a set of chinaware; a service of chinaware
chiropractors, a crack of chiropractors
cigarettes, a carnage of cigarettes; a coffin of cigarettes; a pack of cigarettes
city-dwellers, a strangle of city-dwellers
clams, *a bed of clams*; a squirt of clams
clans, a gathering of clans
cockroaches, an intrusion of cockroaches; a repugnance of cockroaches; an embarrassment of cockroaches; an eternity of cockroaches
commuters, a dash of commuters; a scurrying of commuters
cottontails, a nest of cottontails
creditors, a curse of creditors
crocodiles, a bask of crocodiles
crows, *a murder of crows;* a hover of crows
cryptologists, a secrecy of cryptologists
dancers, a troupe of dancers

debt, a mountain of debt
deer, a herd of deer; a flight of deer
democrats, an inflation of democrats
dentists, a wince of dentists
dermatologists, a rash of dermatologists
diagnosticians, a guess of diagnosticians
dietitians, a bland of dietitians
dodos, an extinction of dodos
dogs, a pack of dogs; a kennel of dogs
drinks, a round of drinks
drunks, a load of drunks
ducks, *a paddling of ducks* (on water); a brace of ducks; a team of ducks (in flight); a plump of ducks (in flight); a dopping of ducks (diving)
bureaucrats, a maze of bureaucrats
eagles, a convocation of eagles
eels, a swarm of eels; a congeries of eels
eggs, *a clutch of eggs*
electors, a college of electors
electric eels, a battery of electric eels
electricians, an ohm of electricians
elephants, *a herd of elephants*
elks, *a gang of elks*
engineers, a corps of engineers
epidemiologists, a plague of epidemiologists
equestrians, a prance of equestrians
falcons, a cast of falcons
fax machines, a discourse of fax machines
ferrets, *a business of ferrets*; a fusiness of ferrets; a fesnyng of ferrets
finches, *a charm of finches;* a trimming of finches; a trembling of finches; a flock of finches
fireflies, a sprinkle of fireflies
fish, *a school of fish* ("school" is a corruption of *shoal* [O.E. *sceald*, meaning "shallow"] -Lipton); *a shoal of fish*; a run of fish; a catch of fish
fishermen, *a drift of fishermen*; an exaggeration of fishermen; a fib of fishermen
flamingoes, a stand of flamingoes
flies, a swarm of flies
flowers, a bunch of flowers; a bouquet of flowers
football players, a team of football players
foxes, *a skulk of foxes*; *a leash of foxes,* an earth of foxes
frigatebirds, a fleet of frigatebirds
frogs, an army of frogs; a colony of frogs
game birds, a raft of game birds (afloat on water)

gardeners, a sprinkling of gardeners; a slug of gardeners

geese, *a gaggle of geese* (on water and the ground); *a flock of geese*; *a skein of geese* (when flying)

geologists, a conglomerate of geologists; a stratum of geologists

giraffes, a tower of giraffes; a gawk of giraffes; a herd of giraffes

girls, a bevy of girls

gnats, *a cloud of gnats*; *a horde of gnats*; a swarm of gnats

goats, *a trip of goats* (this might be a corruption of "tribe" -Lipton); *a tribe of goats*; a herd of goats; a flock of goats

goldfinches, a charm of goldfinches; a chattering of goldfinches; a troubling of goldfinches

goldfish, a lode of goldfish

golf-clubs, a set of golf-clubs

gorillas, *a band of gorillas*

graduates, an unemployment of graduates; a vale of graduates

grammarians, a conjunction of grammarians

grapes, *a cluster of grapes* (a 500-year old venery term -Lipton); a bunch of grapes

graphologists, a doodle of graphologists

grasshoppers, a cloud of grasshoppers

graffitti, an eyesore of graffitti

greyhounds, a leash of greyhounds; a brace of greyhounds

grouse, a covey (a single brood or family) of grouse; a pack (larger group or several broods) of grouse; a pageant of grouse

gulls, a colony of gulls; a scavenging of gulls

hares, *a husk of hares*; *a down of hares*, a drove of hares; a trace of hares

harts, a herd of harts

hawks, *a cast of hawks;* a flight of hawks; a leash of hawks

hedgehogs, a clip of hedgehogs

hematologists, a bank of hematologists; a vein of hematologist

hens, *a brood of hens*; a layer of hens

herons, *a siege of herons*; a sedge of herons

herring, an army of herring; a shoal of herring

highways, a parking lot of highways

hippopotami, a bloat of hippopotami

hogs, *a drift of hogs;* ("drift is defined as a driving of beasts -Lipton)

horseplayers, a parlay of horseplayers

horses, a harness of horses; *a harras of horses* (the Latin word *hara* meant a pigsty, hence any enclosure for animals; while in French, *haras* means "stud" -Lipton); a team of horses; a herd of horses; a stable of horses

hounds, a cry of hounds; a pack of hounds; a sleuth of hounds

hummingbirds, a charm of hummingbirds

hunters, *a blast of hunters*

Indians, a tribe of Indians

jack rabbits, a husk of jack rabbits

jays, a party of jays; a band of jays

jellyfish, *a smack of jellyfish*

jewelers, a ring of jewelers

judges, *a sentence of judges*; a bench of judges

junk mail, a swamp of junk mail

kangaroos, *a troop of kangaroos*; a mob of kangaroos

kine, a drove of kine

kittens, *a kindle* (or *kendle*) *of kittens* (*kindle* means "to give birth" -Lipton); *a litter of kittens*

knots, *a cluster of knots*

laborers (Brit., labourers), a gang of laborers

lady bugs, a harem of lady bugs; a swarm of lady bugs

larks, *an exaltation of larks*; an ascension of larks; a bevy of larks

lawyers, *an eloquence of lawyers*; a subtlety of lawyers

leopards, *a leap of leopards*; a spot of leopards

lexicographers, a logorrhea of lexicographers

librarians, a shush of librarians; a stack of librarians; a media center of librarians

lice, a flock of lice

lies, a pack of lies

lions, *a pride of lions;* a flock of lions; a troop of lions

locusts, *a plague of locusts*; a host of locusts; a swarm of locusts

machine guns, a nest of machine guns

mackerel, a shoal of mackerel

magpies, *a tidings of magpies*; a tittering of magpies

mallard ducks, a sord of mallards; a puddling of mallard ducks (on water)

malls, a sprawl of malls

manicurists, a file of manicurists; a clip of manicurists

maps, a latitude of maps

mares, a stud of mares

martens, *a richness of martens*

masseurs, a pummel of masseurs

mechanics, a torque of mechanics

men, *a band of men*; *a host of men*

messengers, *a diligence of messengers*

meteorologists, a shower of meteorologists

mice, a nest of mice

minstrels, a troupe of minstrels

misers, a horde of misers

mockingbirds, a plagiarism of mockingbirds

moles, *a labor of moles*

monkeys, a troop of monkeys; a tribe of monkeys; a barrel of monkeys

mosquitoes, a swat of mosquitoes; a swarm of mosquitoes

mules, *a barren of mules* (also spelled "baren", it is probably a corrruption of Middle English *berynge*, "bearing" -Lipton); *a span of mules*; a rake of mules

musicians, a band of musicians, an orchestra of muscians

nightingales, *a watch of nightingales*; a match of nightingales

oncologists, a lump of oncologists

onions, a rope of onions

ophthalmologists, a spectacle of ophthalmologists

ornithologists, a flock of ornighologists

orthodontists, a brace of orthodontists

orthopedists, a brace of orthopedists; a cast of orthopedists

osteopaths, a joint of osteopaths

otologists, a heard of otologists

otorhinolaryngologists, a snootful of otorhinolaryngologists

owls, *a parliament of owls*

oxen, *a yoke of oxen*; a herd of oxen; a drove of oxen; a team of oxen

oysters, *a bed of oysters*

palmists, a line of palmists

paranoids, a panic of paranoids

parasites, a host of parasites

parasitologists, a host of parasitologists

parrots, *a company of parrots*; a flock of parrots

partridges, *a covey of partridges* (covey refers to nesting habits -Lipton); a bevy of partridges

peacocks, *an ostentation of peacocks*; a muster of peacocks; a pride of peacocks

pearls, a rope of pearls; a string of pearls

pelicans, a gulp of pelicans

penguins, a colony of penguins; a rookery of penquins

people, a throng of people; a crowd of people; a congregation of people

pharmacists, a dose of pharmacists

pheasants, *a bouquet of pheasants*; *a nest of pheasants*; *an eye of pheasants*; a nide of pheasants (in a nest); a nye (young) of pheasants; a brood of pheasants

philologists, a gloss of philologists

photographers, a click of photographers

pianists, a pound of pianists

pigeons, a flight of pigeons; a flock of pigeons

pigs, *a litter of pigs*; a farrow of pigs; a herd of pigs

plumbers, a flush of plumbers

podiatrists, an arch of podiatrists

ponies, *a string of ponies*

pornographers, a pander of pornographers

porpoises, a school [*or* shoal] of porpoises

poultry, a run of poultry

princes, *a state of princes*

procrastinators, a delay of procrastinators; a stall of procrastinators; a put-off of procrastinators

psychiatrists, a shrinking of psychiatrists; a gab of psychiatrists

psychoanalysts, a complex of psychoanalysts

punsters, a groan of punsters

puppies, a piddle of puppies

pups, *a litter of pups*

quails, *a bevy of quail*; a covy (or *covey*) of quail

rabbits, *a nest of rabbits*; a colony of rabbits

racehorses, a field of racehorses

rams, a thump of rams

ravens, *an unkindness of ravens*

realtors, a lot of realtors

relatives, a descent of relatives

repairmen, an overcharge of repairmen

republicans, a deficit of republicans

rheumatologists, a crutch of rheumatologists; a pain of rheumatologists

rhinoceroses (rhinoceri), *a crash of rhinoceroses* (rhinoceri)

robbers, a band of robbers; a gang of robbers

roebucks, *a bevy of roebucks* (it seems that bevy comes from the French word *boire*, meaning to "drink" as roes are seen drinking together at streams, etc. -Lipton)

runners, a field of runners
sailors, a gob of sailors; a crew of sailors
salts, a dose of salts
savages, a horde of savages
schizoids, a split of schizoids
scrabblers, a logomania of scrabblers
seals, *a pod of seals* (like a "pod of peas," sailors made the same connection for groups of seals -Lipton); a trip of seals; a herd of seals; a crash of seals
servants, a staff of servants
sheep, *a flock of sheep*; a cumulus of sheep; *a drove of sheep*; a fold of sheep
ships, a fleet of ships; a squadron of ships; a flotilla of ships
smokers, a hack of smokers; a cancer of smokers; a cloud of smokers
snakes, a ripple of snakes
soldiers, *a boast of soldiers; a troop of soldiers*; a muster of soldiers (for inspection)
sparrows, *a host of sparrows*; a quarrel of sparrows; a tribe of sparrows
spiders, a network of spiders; a web of spiders
squirrels, *a dray of squirrels* (*dray* is a Middle English word for their "nest," according to Lipton)
stairs, a flight of stairs
starlings, *a murmuration of starlings*; a chattering of starlings
stars, a galaxy of stars; a cluster of stars; a constellation of stars
statesmen, a disagreement of statesmen
statisticians, a number of statisticians; a graph of statisticians
steps, a flight of steps
storks, *a mustering of storks*
stud horses, a haras of stud horses (French)
Sundays, a month of Sundays
swallows, *a flight of swallows*
swans, a band of trumpeter swans; *a wedge of swans*; *a bevy of swans*; a herd of swans; a game of swans; a squadron of swans; a whiteness of swans
swifts, a flock of swifts; a flight of swifts
swine, *a sounder of swine* (Originally an Old English word *sunor*, meaning "herd." The Norman French changed *sunor* to *sounder* -Lipton); a drift of swine; a dolt of swine
teetotalers, a wagon of teetotalers
television antennas, a forest of TV antennas

teratologists, a distortion of teratologists
thanatologists, a terminus of thanatologists
thieves, a gang of thieves; a den of theives
tigers, a prowl of tigers
toads, *a knot of toads*
toll booths, a bottleneck of toll booths
tomorrows, a promise of tomorrows
tree surgeons, a graft of tree surgeons
trees, a clump of trees
troubles, a sea of troubles
trout, *a hover of trout*
trustees, a board of trustees
turkeys, *a rafter of turkeys* (*raft* here refers to "a large and often motley collection of people and things, as a raft of books," according to Lipton); a flock of turkeys; a dole of turkeys; a dule of turkeys; a raft of turkeys; a raffle of turkeys
turtles, *a bale of turtles*
udertakers, an extreme unction of undertakers
urologists, a piddle of urologists; a void of urologists
vendors, a haggle of vendors
venereal terms, a plentitude of venereal terms
vigilantes, a posse of vigilantes
violinists, a string of violinists
vipers, a nest of vipers
voters, a constituency of voters
vulcanologists, an eruption of vulcanologists
waiters, an indifference of waiters; an order of waiters
wasps, a colony of wasps; a vespiary of social wasps in a nest; a nest of wasps
whales, *a gam of whales;* a *pod of whales*; a syndicate of killer whales; a bank of sperm whales; a herd of whales; a school of whales
wheat, a sheaf of wheat
wildcats, a clowder of wildcats
witches (males, *warlocks*), a congeries of withces
witches (females), a coven of witches
wives, *an impatience of wives*
wolves, *a rout of wolves* (in O.Fr., *route* meant "a troop" or "throng" -Lipton); *a pack of wolves*
woodpeckers, *a descent of woodpeckers*; a gatling of woodpeckers
worms, a can of worms
worshippers, a congregation of worshippers

wrestlers, a crunch of wrestlers
writers, a pen of writers
yesterdays, a flight of yesterdays
zebras, a herd of zebras

The previous list of Venery Terms (or *group names*) is based on information found in a variety of sources, but especially from the following:

Bernstein, Theodore M. *Bernstein's Reverse Dictionary*, 2nd. edition. New York: Times Books, 1988.

Illustrated Reverse Dictionary. Pleasantville, New York: The Reader's Digest Association, Inc., 1990.

Informatin Please Almanac Atlas & Yearbook. Boston: Houghton Mifflin Co., 1990.

Inpress Print. Philadelphia: Lea & Febeger Publishers, April, 1969.

Lipton, James. *An Exaltation of Larks or the Veneal Game*. New York: Grossman Publishers, Inc., 1968.

Lipton, James. *An Exaltation of Larks, The Ultimate Edition*. New York: Viking Penguin, 1991.

Wallechinsky, David and Wallace, Irving. *The People's Almanac* Presents the Book of Lists. Garden City, New York: Doubleday & Co., Inc., 1975.

The following pages consist of Latin abbreviations, phrases, words, and sentences (unless another language is indicated). Such references are used in law, medicine, music, philosophy, business, history, and many literary works.

@ (**ad**, at, or to) "I purchased two books @ $15.00 each."

A.B. or **B.A.** (**Artium Baccalaureus**, Bachelor of Arts) A university or college degree which is usually given after four years of successful course work.

Abeunt studia in mores. (studies change into habits) "Pursuits done with constant and careful attention become habits." -Ovid

ab ex. (**ab extra**, from without)

ab extra (**ab ex**, from without)

Abiit ad majores. "He has gone to his forefathers." He's dead.

ab imo pectore (from the bottom of [one's] heart)

ab incunabulis (from the cradle) Used in connection with early printed books, especially those published before the end of the 15th century. Such books are called *incunabula* (swaddling clothes).

ab intestato (from or by a person dying intestate, *i.e.*, without a valid will) A reference to someone who has died and left no will and testament.

A bove majori discit arare minor. "From the older ox, the younger learns to plow."

ab ovo (from the egg; from the beginning)

ab ovo usque ad mala (from eggs to apples) Roman banquets began with eggs and ended with apples. Now we say, "from soup to nuts."

abs. feb. (**absente febre**, while fever is absent) A medical direction.

absente febre (**abs. feb.**, while fever is absent) A medical direction.

absit invidia "Let there be no ill will."

absit omen "Let there be no evil omen [because of the word just used]."

abs. re. (**absente reo**, the defendant being absent) Used in legal matters.

ab uno ad omnes (from one to all)

Ab uno disce omnes. (from one learn all) "From one sample, judge the rest or know all the rest." -Vergil

ab urbe condita (A.U.C., from the founding of the city [Rome], *c.* 753 B.C.)

a.c. (**ante cibum**; before food) A direction on prescriptions indicating that medicine should be taken before meals.

Accusare nemo se debet. "No one is obliged to incriminate himself." A legal maxim.

Acta est fabula. "The play is over." Words used at the close of a dramatic performance in the ancient Roman theater. They are said to be the dying words of Emperor Augustus.

Actus non facit reum nisi mens est rea. "The act does not make a criminal unless the intention is criminal." A legal maxim.

ad (@, at, or to) Used to express cost of individual items.

A.D. (**anno Domini**, in the year of the Lord [Jesus Christ]) Some people translate *anno Domini* as "in the year of *our* Lord," but there is no Latin *noster*, "our," in the phrase. **A.D.** is written before the year, usually with small capital letters, with no separating comma, as: A.D. 1995; or informally, after the year, as: about 1450 A.D. *Anno Domini* is supposed to indicate the number of years from the birth of Chirst. In the sixth century, Dionysius Exiguus initiated the system of expressing dates by referring events to the birth of Christ. According to his calculations, Christ was born in 754 A.U.C. (*q.v.*). However, it is generally agreed that Christ was born at least four years before the date which was set by Dionysius.

a.d. (**ante diem**, before the day)

ad absurdum (to what is absurd) A reference to an argument demonstrating the absurdity of an opponent's proposition.

addenda ([plural], things to be added or already added)

addendum ([singular], something to be added or already added)

Ad astra per aspera. (to the stars through difficulties or in spite of difficulties) The motto of the state of Kansas.

Adeo in teneris consuescere multum est. "So imperative it is to form habits in early years." -Vergil

adeptus (adept) "One who has attained." The alchemists applied the term **vere adeptus** to anyone who claimed to have found the Elixir of Life or the Philosopher's Stone.

ad die (from that day)

a die datus (dated from a certain day)

ad fin. (ad finem, to the end)

ad finem (ad fin., to the end)

ad gustum (to one's taste)

ad hoc (toward this) Referring to this, for this thing, for a particular purpose or occasion; as a committe might be, said of an argument or reason which applies only to a specific case. An *ad hoc* committee is one whose existence is limited to the time it takes to dispose of the matter at hand; when the problem is solved, the committee goes out of existence.

ad inf. (ad infinitum, to infinity, endlessly)

ad infinitum (ad inf., without limit; indefinitely into the future)

ad init. (ad initium, at the beginning)

ad initium (ad init., at the beginning)

ad int., a.i., (ad interim, in the meantime or mean while)

ad interim (ad int., a.i.; for the interval, temporarily, in the meantime)

ad Kalendas Graecas "[It shall be done] on the Greek Calends," *i.e.* never. In the Roman calendar, the Calends meant the first day of the month. Since the Greeks did not have this term, the expression was used by the Romans to designate an event that would never occur. Suetonius wrote that Caesar Augustus made this statement as he was asked when he was going to pay his creditors.

ad lib. (ad libitum, at pleasure, freely, unscripted, improvised)

ad libitum (ad lib., at pleasure; according to one's pleasure; freely, unscripted, improvised) This is usually shortened to *ad lib.* [with *or* without a period] *Ad lib* is used both as a verb and as a noun. When used in the entertainment world, to *ad lib* means to improvise, to add an impromptu word or statement to a script. As a noun, an *ad lib* is an "off-the-cuff" or unprepared remark.

ad loc. (ad locum, at the place)

ad locum (ad loc., at the place)

ad multos annos (for many years)

ad nauseam (to the point of disgust, to sickness)

adst. feb. (adstante febre, while fever is present) A medical direction.

adstante febre (adst. feb., while fever is present) A medical direction.

ad val., ad v., a/v (ad valorem [*q.v.*], according to the value)

ad valorem (according to value) Referring to taxes: "In proportion to invoiced value of goods." A term used when imposing customs and stamp duty, the duty increasing according to the value of the transaction of goods involved.

ae., aet. (aetatis, aged; of age)

affidavit "He has pledged." A sworn statement.

a fortiori (all the more so; with even greater or stronger reason) Literally, "from the stronger [point];" it is used to initroduce a statement that, assuming a previous statement is accepted as true, must be all the more true. When arguing a point, *a fortiori* means "all the more so." If statement "A" is true, then *a fortiori*, *i.e.*, all the more so, statement "B" must be true. If students can't (or won't) do twenty minutes of homework each night, *a fortiori*, they can't (or won't) do sixty minutes each night.

agape (Gk., love) A love-feast. The early Christians held a love feast in conjunction with the Lord's Supper when the rich provided food for the poor. Eventually they became a scandal and were condemned by the Council of Carthage in A.D. 397. Today it may be considered a feast or gathering characterized by friendliness and good feeling. For some people, it also represents *God's* love and is not considered to be the same *love* as between human beings.

age hoc (attend to this) During a sacrifice, the Roman crier repeated these words to keep the attention of those in attendance.

agenda, [plural]; **agendum,** [singular] (things to be done, memoranda of items to be considered at a meeting) *Agenda* was plural in form in the original Latin, but now has been generally accepted as singular in English, in the sense of "list," and followed by a singular verb. So well established is *agenda* as a singular that *agendas* is now commonly heard and seen as the plural form. However, the correct Latin singular is *agendum*; as,

"The *agendum is* whether we want an extended school year or not." "The *agenda have been* established for the meeting." You have the choice to follow *hoi polloi* or to write it "correctly."

Alea jacta est! "The die is cast!" Also **Jacta alea est!** Supposedly spoken by Julius Caesar, 49 B.C., when he crossed the Rubicon to challenge the Senate and Pompey's forces for supremacy of Rome. Crossing the Rubicon resulted in the civil war and Pompey's defeat by Julius Caesar's forces. Suetonius wrote that Caesar said, "Let us go forward whither the signs of the gods and the injustice of our enemies call us. *The die is cast!*"

alma mater (nourishing or foster mother) The Romans used this term to refer to various goddesses, such as Ceres; now it refers to a person's old school, college, or university.

almanac A medieval Latin word of obscure origin which referred to a calendar of days and months with astronomical data, etc. Now it is an annual publication which includes calendars with weather forecasts, astronomical information, tide tables, lists, charts, and tables "of useful information."

alt. dieb. (alternis diebus) Every other day, on alternate days. Medical directions in a prescription.

alter ego (other "I") An inseparable friend [your *other self*].

Alter ipse amicus. "A friend is a second self."

alumna ([feminine, singular], foster child; former student, as of an **alma mater**)

alumnae ([feminine, plural], foster children; former students, as of an **alma mater**)

alumni ([masculine, plural], foster children; former students, as of an **alma mater**) Graduates and former students of a coeducational institution are generally referred to by this masculine plural form, *i.e. alumni.*

alumnus ([masculine, singular], foster child; former student, as of an **alma mater**)

a.m., A.M. (ante meridiem, before noon [meridiem], before the middle of the day)

A.M. or M.A. (Artium Magister) Master of Arts. A university or college degree which is received after an additional year of successful graduate work after the **A.B.** degree.

a maximis ad minima (from the greatest to the least)

amicus curiae (a friend of the court) A person appointed by a judge to assist by giving advice in the handling of a legal case.

amor patriae (love for one's native country)

Amor vincit omnia. "Love conquers all." Normally, the order in Latin is **Omnia vincit amor.**

Anathema sit. "Let him be accursed."

anguis in herba (a snake in the grass) A traitor or disloyal friend; an unsuspected danger.

animal bipes implume "A two-footed animal without feathers." A Latinized form of Plato's definition of mankind.

anno Domini (in the year of the Lord [Jesus Christ]) See **A.D.** for more information.

anno urbis conditae (A.U.C., Ab urbe condita; from the founding of the city [Rome]) The traditional date for the founding of Rome is 753 B.C.

annuit coeptis "He [God] has favored our undertakings." This motto, adapted from Vergil's *Aeneid, IX, 625,* in which Ascanius prays to Jupiter for help in slaying an enemy, appears on the Great Seal of the United States. The words at the bottom of the seal, *Novus ordo seclorum (q.v.),* mean "The new order of the ages."

annus mirabilis (year of wonders) Great achievements or disasters, or the like; the London fire of 1666 and the plague in the same year are examples of such a year.

ante bellum (before the war) Specifically, in the United States, before the "Civil War" or "The War between the States."

ante cibum (a.c.; before food) A direction on prescriptions indicating that a medicine should be taken before meals.

ante diem (a.d., before the day)

ante meridiem (a.m., A.M.; before the middle of the day, before noon [*meridiem*])

a posteriori (from effect to cause, from facts to generalizations, inductively [applied to reasoning]) *A posteriori* is a conclusion which is reached by examination and analysis of the specific facts, as happens in a science laboratory, where a person reasons from actual observation of data and comes to a conclusion from the observed facts. Contrasted with *a priori* .

a primo ad ultimum (from first to last)

a priori (from what comes before, from cause to effect, deductively [applied to reasoning]; from the general to the particular; self-evident, known independently of experience) In *a priori* reasoning, one works from a known premise (or premises) to a reasonably assumed effect. By extension the phrase is also used to mean, "to the best of one's knowledge."

aqua (an aqueduct which was used to supply water to the city of Rome) During the Republic, aqueducts, and the water supplied, were cared for by water companies hired under contract by the censors.

A.U.C. (Ab urbe condita, from the founding of the city [Rome]) See **anno urbis conditae** for more details. A reference to the founding of the city of Rome.

augur A priest who was a member of the College of Augurs which numbered twelve, six patrician and six plebeian. Before the *lex Domitia de sacerdotiis* was passed by Gnaeus Domitius Ahenobarbus in 104 B.C., new augurs were chosen by those who were already in the college. After the law came into effect, augurs were to be publicly elected. Augurs did not predict the future, nor did they make personal interpretations of the objects or signs to determine whether or not the proposed undertaking had the approval of the gods. There was a guide book which was to be followed exactly to find out if a meeting, a proposed new law, a war, or any other State or government business should take place.

aurora australis (dawn of the southern wind, the southern lights)

aurora borealis (dawn of the northern wind, the northern lights)

Ave, Imperator, morituri te salutant. "Hail, Caesar, they who are about to die salute you!" Spoken to Claudius by gladiators prior to entering the arena to fight. This may have been a sarcastic salutation.

Bene vale. "Farewell."

Beware of the dog. (**Cave canem.**)

Bis pueri senes. "Old men are twice children."

bona fide (in good faith) "Genuine *or* sincere."

B.S., B.Sc. (Baccalureus Scientiae) Bachelor of Science

buyer beware, Let the: **Caveat emptor.**

C (centum, 100)

c., ca. (circa; about, around) Used in giving approximate dates, *e.g.* "It happened *ca.* 1500 A.D."

cacoethes loquendi (an uncontrollable desire or mania for talking or making speeches)

cacoethes scribendi (the writer's itch, an uncontrollable desire to write, a mania for authorship) *Tenet insanabile multos scribendi cacoethes*. -Juvenal "The incurable itch for scribbling [*or* writing] affects many."

Caesarean section There are claims that Gaius Julius Caesar was delivered by such an operation, but evidence disputes such a claim. Fact: the first known successful Caesarean section was recorded in Pavia, Italy, April, 1876 from a Julie Covallini. Fact: although the operation was occasionally used in ancient times, the Caesarean section usually resulted in death for both the child and the mother. There were some occasions when the child survived, but the mother inevitably perished. Caesar's mother, Aurelia, lived to be at least seventy years old and was apparently in good health up until the time of her death. This would suggest that she never had the deadly operation.

calends (**calare,** "to call") The first day of the Roman month. Varro said the term was first used to call the people together on the first day of the month when the *pontifex* told them of the time of the new moon, the day of the nones, and the festivals and sacred days to be observed. The custom continued until A.U.C. 450 when the *fasti* or calendar was posted in public places.

Came, saw, conquered (**Veni, vidi, vici.**) See **Veni,** etc. for information.

Carpe diem, quam minimum credula postero. "Seize the day *or* take advantage of today and place no trust in tomorrow." "Enjoy the present moment and don't depend on there being a tomorrow."

-Horace

cave (beware) "Look out, be careful."

Cave ab homine unius libri. "Beware the man of one book." Be careful of the person who owns just one book.

Cave canem. "Beware of the dog." An inscription found in a vestibule at Pompeii.

caveat (let him beware) A warning or caution.

Caveat emptor. "Let the buyer beware." The principle that a purchaser cannot assume that his or her purchase will be exactly as hoped [or promised]. The full maxim is *Caveat emptor quia ignorare non debuit quod jus alienum emit.* "Let the buyer beware because he should not be ignorant of the property that he is buying."

c.e. (Caveat emptor, at buyer's risk) "Buyer beware."

centum (C., 100)

centum weight (**cwt.,** hundred weight)

cf. (confer, compare) "Refer to, *or* see."

circa (**c., ca.;** about, around) Approximate, such as a date.

citius, altius, fortius (faster, higher, stronger) Motto of the Olympic Games.

Civis Romanus sum! "I am a Roman citizen!" No Roman citizen could be condemned unheard; by Valerian Law, he could not be bound; by Sempronian Law, it was forbidden to beat him with rods (sticks). At different times both of his parents had to be Roman citizens, at other times only his father. The citizen was required to serve in the military, although prior to Gaius Marius, only if he owned sufficient property to buy his arms and support himself on campaigns beyond the little money he was paid by the State, which was usually at the end of a campaign.

Cogito, ergo sum. "I think; therefore I am." Credited to Descartes [French philosopher] as *a priori* proof of one's existence.

Compliments of the publisher [not the editor] (**Hommage d'éditeur.** [French])

compos mentis (of sound mind, sane)

confer (**cf.,** compare, refer to, or see) "A good motto to live by is **Vincit qui se vincit,** *cf.*"

corpus Christi (the body of Christ)

corpus delicti (the basic [*or* body] of facts [necessary to prove the existence of a specific crime]) This refers to evidence which can be used to convict a thief, such as catching him with stolen goods; or proof in a murder trial of the actual death of the victim. It doesn't mean the *body* of the victim.

corrigenda ([plural], a list of errors to be corrected, inserted in a book after it has been printed) Equivalent to **errata** (*q.v.*).

corrigendum ([singular], an error to be corrected, especially one in a completed publication) Also **erratum** (*q.v.*).

criteria (Gk., [plural]) Standards for judgment. There is no such thing as "one *criteria.*" "These are the *criteria* you must follow if you want to succeed."

criterion (Gk., [singular]) A standard, rule, or test by which something can be judged. There is no such thing as "one *criteria.*" "We have just one *criterion* for you to follow."

Cui bono? "Who benefits?" or "What good is it?" The real meaning is, "Who gains by it?" "To whom is it an advantage?" This phrase is often but erroneously translated "for what good?"

Cujus est solem ejus est usque ad coelum. "The person who owns the land owns it all the way up to the sky."

cum grano salis (with a grain of salt) -Pliny It means that one should not believe certain things fully or literally. "There is some truth in the statement, but we must be careful about accepting it as correct, take it *cum grano salis.*"

cum laude (with praise) A reference to a good examination grade or an earned degree from a school.

Cum tacent, clamant. "When they are silent, they shout." -Cicero. An example of an oxymoron (*q.v.*).

curriculum vitae (course of life) Outline or résumé, as for a job application which shows one's job qualifications and previous work experiences.

cwt. (centum weight, hundred weight)

data [plural] "Things known or assumed, information, facts or figures from which conclusions can be inferred." *Data,* as the plural of *datum,* requires a plural verb in Latin and in English. However, one often reads, especially in technical, scientific, and business writings, such usages as "The *data is* inconclusive." It should be: "The *data are* inconclusive."

datum [singular] "Something known or assumed, a fact or figure from which a conclusion, or conclusions, can be inferred." Although rarely used properly (if at all), *datum* should be expressed in the singular sense. "There is one *datum* on this page which is not correct." Using the word *fact* instead of *datum* probably would make one's writing easier to understand and decrease anxiety about accuracy.

D.D. (Divinitatis Doctor) Doctor of Divinity A degree granted after a required curriculum of theological studies have been accomplished.

decessit sine prole (d.s.p., died without issue or offspring [children])

de facto (in reality, actually) Functioning or existing in fact, regardless of legal status.

De gustibus non est disputandum. "There must be no disputing about taste." There is no accounting for tastes.

desideratum ([singular], what is desired but not yet on hand)

desiderata ([plural], things that are desired but not yet on hand or in one's possession, *e.g.* provisions for travel)

deus ex machina (god [or *dea*, goddess] out of a machine) A person or thing that suddenly resolves a problem or a device providing a contrived resolution in a play. In Greek or Roman dramas, this was a device by which a god appeared on the stage at a crucial moment to help solve the dilemma. Now it refers to a person or thing that solves a problem in a drama by some artificial or abrupt means.

die is cast, The (**Alea jacta est.** *or* **Jacta alea est.**) See **Alea jacta est.**

dies nefastus (contrary to divine law) An unlucky or inauspicious day. For the Romans, **dies nefasti** were days on whilch no judgments could be pronounced nor any public business transacted.

Divide et impera. "Divide and conquer." A reference to the policy of stirring up dissension and rivalries within the ranks of one's enemies, as Caesar did in Gaul and elsewhere.

D. Litt. or Litt. D. (Doctor Litterarum) Doctor of Literature or Letters

D.M.D. (Dentariae Medicinae Doctor) Doctor of Dental Medicine

Dulce et decorum est pro patria mori. "It is sweet and proper *or* fitting [honorable] to die for one's country." *–Horace, Odes,* III, *ii,* 13 A carving in stone over the entrance to the Amphitheater at Arlington National Cemetery in Virginia.

editio princeps (first edition)

e.g. (exempli gratia, for example) Use *e.g.* only when giving an example to illustrate a point. Always precede this Latin term with a comma or a semicolon.

emporium In Roman times, this word had two meanings. It refered to a seaport whose commercial life primarily consisted of maritime trade *or* it could denote a large building on the waterfront of a port where importers and exporters (businessmen) had their "offices."

e pluribus unum (from many, one *or* one out of many) A reference to the many states in the United States as being one nation. Adapted from Vergil's poem, *Moretum.* The Continental Congress ordered the President of Congress to have a seal in 1776 and *E Pluribus Unum* appeared on the first seal, as well as on many early coins. Congress adopted the motto in 1781 and it still appears on U.S. coins as well as on the Great Seal.

ergo (therefore, hence) "He was caught with the smoking gun, *ergo* he is the killer."

errata ([plural], mistakes or errors) Placed in a published book to point out errors which were discovered after it was printed. Also **corrigenda** (*q.v.*).

erratum ([singular], an error or mistake) Also **corrigendum** (*q.v.*).

error(s): **corrigenda, corrigendum, errata, erratum**

et al. (et alii, and others [people, not things])

et alii (et al., and others [people, not things])

etc., &c (et cetera, and so forth, and other [things]) It is redundant to say or write "and *et cetera*" since *et* means "and."

et cetera (etc., and so forth; and the other things [not people]) It is redundant to say or write "and *et cetera*" since *et* means "and."

et seq., seq., sq. (et sequens, and the following)

et sequens (et seq., seq., sq.; and the following)

Et tu, Brute! (And you [too], Brutus!) Included in Shakespeare's play, *Julius Caesar*, in which Caesar's last words expressed his shock as Brutus stabbed him after the other assasins had mortally wounded him.

et ux. (**et uxor**, and wife)

et uxor (**et ux.**, and wife)

et vir (and man; and husband)

Eureka! (Gk., I have found it!) The exclamation of Archimedes who, while bathing, discovered how to determine the gold content of a crown made for King Hiero II of Syracuse. This experiment led to the discovery of the law of specific gravity. Motto of California. Based on the fact that gold was discoverd there.

ex animo (from the heart) "Sincerely."

ex capite (out of the head) "From the head."

ex cathedra (from the chair or throne, with authority) Dogmatic utterances of the Pope on matters of faith and morals when he is seated on his "holy" throne: spoken with an infallible voice as the successor and representative of St. Peter. The term is sometimes applied to the arrogant, possitive expressions of the uninformed when they speak as if they were representing some high authority.

excelsior (higher) "Aim for higher things." This is the motto of the state of New York.

ex curia (out of court)

exempli gratia (**e.g.**, for example, for [the sake of] example) Use *e.g.* only when giving an example to illustrate a point. This Latin term should be preceded by a comma or a semicolon.

Exempta juvat spiris e pluribus unus. "Better one thorn plucked than all remain."

Exeunt. (they go out) This is a common stage direction that characters leave the stage.

Exeunt omnes. (all go out) All leave the stage.

ex gratia (out of goodness) Referring to a payment made as a favor, not an obligation.

ex libris (from the books) Phrase used before the owner's name on bookplates.

ex post facto (arising or enacted after the fact, retroactive) An *ex post facto law* is one which sets a penalty for an act that was not illegal at the time it was performed. Such laws are forbidden by the United States Constitution.

Fauna The animals of a country or region at any given period. The term was first coined by Linnaeus in his *Fauna Suecica* (1746).

Faunus A good spirit of forests and fields, and a god of prophecy. He had the form of a Satyr and is identified with the Greek god Pan. At his festivals, called *Faunalia*, peasants brought rustic offerings and had a "merry" time.

fasces A bundle of birch rods tied around in a crisscross pattern with red leather thongs. In ancient Rome, **fasces** were assigned to the higher magistrates as symbols of authority, an might represent power over life. Carried by men called *lictors*, they preceded the *curule magistrate* as well as the *proconsul* and *propraetor*, as a symbol of his imperium. Within the *pomerium*, only the rods went into the bundles, to signify that the *curule magistrate* had only the power to chastise; outside the *pomerium*, axes were inserted into the bundles, to signify that the *curule magistrate* also had the power to execute. The number of **fasces** indicated the degree of imperium. A dictator had twenty-four, a *consul* or **proconsul** twelve, a *praetor* or *propraetor* six, and a *curule aedile* two.

fasti In ancient Rome, working days when the law courts were open for business. Holy days, when the law courts, etc., were not open were called **dies nefasti**. The **dies fasti** were listed in calendars and the list of events occurring during the year of office of a pair of consuls was called **fasti consulares**; therefore, any chronological list of events of office-holders were known as **fasti**.

Festina lents. "Hasten slowly; more speed, less haste; make haste slowly." -Horace

fiduciary (trust) A trustee of a trust or the executive administrator of a will.

flagrante delicto (with the crime blazing) Caught in the act of committing a crime.

Flora, the Roman goddess of flowers especially associated with Spring. Her festivals, the *Floralia*, were from April 28-May 3. The term **Flora** also refers to native plants of a region or country.

Founding of the city [Rome] (**ab urbe condita.**)

gladiators (from **gladius,** sword) Soldiers of the sand (*arena*), who performed for an audience as entertainment. Inherited from the Etruscans, the gladiator performed throughout Italy, including Rome. Whether military deserters, condemned criminals; slaves, or freemen; in all cases, they were thought to be volunteers because, otherwise, they probably wouldn't be worth the expense of training in the special schools (*ludi*). The gladiator could be a very profitable investment and many of them became very wealthy and were as popular as professioinal athletes are today.

Graecum est; non potest legi. "It is Greek; it cannot be read." Probably from medieval times. "It's Greek to me." "...for mine own part, it was Greek to me."-Casca, *Julius Caesar*, William Shakespeare

gtt. (guttal, drops) A medical/pharmaseutical term.

habeas corpus ([that] you may have the body) A writ requiring a person to be brought before a court or judge to determine his legal rights.

hic jacet "Here lies... [on tombstones]."

h.l. (hoc loco, in this place)

hoc loco (h.l., in this place)

hoc titulo (h.t., in, or under, this title)

hoi polloi (Gk., the many) A term applied to the masses, the common, ordinary people. *The* is not needed in front of *hoi polloi*, because *hoi* means *the*. Purists who maintain the redundancy of *the* probably are fighting a losing battle because many professional writers continue to use "*the* hoi polloi*." The phrase also has derogatory implications, often being equated with *the rabble* and the *rag tag masses*.

Hommage d'éditeur. (French; With the compliments of the publisher [not the editor].)

homo sapiens "Man as a rational being." The genus of mankind as distinct from other animals.

honoraria [plural] or **honorarium** [singular], Honorary payments; fees for professional services on which no fixed prices were set.

H. (hora, hour) Used in medical prescriptions.

h.s. (horo somni) "At the hour of sleep; bedtime." Used with medical prescriptions.

h.t. (hoc titulo; in, *or* under, this title)

ib., ibid. (ibidem; in the same place)

ibid. (ibidem, in the same place [or book])

ibidem (ibid., in the same place [or book]) In books and articles with many references, a writer may mention several sources on the same page. To avoid the constant repetition of the name of the author and the title of the work quoted or cited, the writer saves space by using *ibid.*, a shortcut for saying "in the same book listed above."

I came, I saw, I conquered. **(Veni, vidi, vici.)** See **Veni,** etc. for information.

id. (idem, the same)

idem (id., the same) The same word, the same author, or the same publication.

Ides "Originally the day of the full moon of the lunar month. In months of 31 days (March, May, July, October), the *Nones* were the seventh day and the *Ides* the fifteenth, while in the shorter months (all of the months except March, May, July, and October), the *Nones* fell on the fifth and the *Ides* on the thirteenth day.

id est (i.e., that is [to say]) Introduces a definition. Use *i.e.* only when rephrasing a statement to make it more understandable.

i.e. (id est, that is[to say]) See **id est** above.

ign. (ignotus; unknown)

ignis fatuus (foolish fire) A light that misleads; a name given to a light that sometimes appears at night, usually over marshes, probably because of the combusion of marsh gas. This expression refers to a false hope, an illusion, a vain hope.

Ignorantia legis neminem excusat. "Ignorance of the law excuses no one."

ignotus (ign., unknown)

imprimatur (let it be printed) An official license from the Roman Catholic Church to print or publish a book.

inf. (infra, inferior; below)

in flagrante delicto (red handed) Caught in the very act of committing a crime.

in folio "Once-folded sheet of printed matter."

infra (inf., inferior, below)

infra dig. (infra dignitatem, beneath [one's] dignity)

infra dignitatem (infra dig., beneath [one's] dignity)

in lim. (in limine, at the outset)

in limine (in lim., at the outset) "On the threshold."

in loco parentis (in the place of a parent) Having the responsibilities or role of a parent, *e.g.* teachers during the time students are under their charge *or* the legal position of a guardian.

in medias res (into the midst of things) The way a story or play might begin, as when a story begins in the middle and then flashes back to the cause of a character's trouble or perdicament.

in perpetuum (forever, in perpetuity)

I.N.R.I. (Jesus Nazarenus, Rex Judaeorum) "Jesus of Nazareth, King of the Jews."

inter vivos (among the living) A kind of trust created during the lifetime of the trustor.

in toto (completely, as a whole, totally)

intra muros (within the walls)

in utero (in the womb) Prenatal; not yet born.

in vacuo (in emptiness) In a vacuum or void; without reference to one's surroundings; without regard for reality.

in vino veritas (in wine is truth) When a person is intoxicated, he/she utters many things which at other times would be concealed or disguised.

in vitro (within glass) Observable as in a test tube; *e.g.,* "an *in vitro* birth."

in vivo (in or upon a living organism) As opposed to **in vitro** (*q.v.*).

Ipse dixit. "He himself has said it." An assertion made without proof.

ipso facto (by that fact) As an immediate consequence of that fact or act.

i.q. (idem quod, the same as)

Jacta alea est! "The die is cast!" Said to be the words uttered by Julius Caesar when he crossed the Rubicon River. Also see **Alea jacta est!** for additional information.

J.D. (Jurum Doctor) Doctor of Laws

lapsus linguae (a slip of the tongue) A word spoken by mistake.

lb. (libra, pound)

l.c. (loco citato, in the place cited)

libra (lb. pound)

lingua franca (the Frankish tongue) A jargon used for elementary communication by medieval traders and sailors in the Mediterranean, derived for the most part from the Romance languages [Italian mixed with French, Greek, Arabic, etc.]. Generally, it describes a mixture of languages used as a means of communication in business.

litterati (men of letters) A reference to scholarly people.

Litt.D. (Litterarum Doctor) Doctor of Literature

loco citato (loc. cit., in the place already cited)

loc. cit. (loco citato, in the place already cited)

locus delicti "The place where a crime was committed."

locus in quo (the place in which) The place in question or the spot mentioned.

locus sigilli (L.S., place of *or* for the seal)

LL.B. (Legum Baccalaureus) Bachelor of Laws

LL.D. (Legum Doctor) Doctor of Laws

L.S. (locus sigilli, place of *or* for the seal)

Lupercalia An ancient Roman festival with fertility rites, held on February 15 in honor of Lupercus, a pastoral god sometimes identified with Faunus. The festival started at the Lupercal where Romulus and Remus were said to have been suckled by the *lupa* or she-wolf. Dogs and goats were sacrificced to Faunus and *Luperci* or *Creppi,* young men dressed in goat-skins (or in the nude), ran around the base of the Palatine hill striking women with goat-hide strips, or thongs, called *amicula Iunonis* or "mantles of Juno." The touch of the lash, or whip, was supposed to make the women fertile. It was at the Lupercalia in 44 B.C. that Antony, himself a Lupercus, offered Caesar a crown and Shakespeare has Julius Caesar instruct Antony to "touch Calpurnia" so she might become fertile and be rid of her barren condition.

m. (meridies, noon; *or* **mille,** thousand)

Macte! "Well done!" Bravo! Good luck!

magnum cum laude "With great praise or distinction." Used especially on a diploma to designate a grade of work higher than *cum laude,* but lower than *summa cum laude.*

Magna est vis consuetudinis. "Great is the force of habit." -Cicero

magnum opus (great work) Major work of a writer, composer, or the like.

mali exempli (of bad example)

malis avibus (bad birds) "With unlucky birds." Under bad auspices.

many, [The masses] (**hoi polloi**)

mare clausum (a closed sea) A sea that is under the jurisdiction of one nation only.

mare liberum (a free sea) A sea that is open to the navigation of all nations.

margaritas ante porcos (pearls before swine) "[Don't throw] pearls before swine."

Maximum remedium est irae mora. The best remedy for anger is delay." -Seneca

M.D. (Medicinae Doctor) Doctor of Medicine

mea culpa (my fault) Personal acknowledgment of one's fault or guilt.

media [plural] (middle) Forms of communication. "The *media* are presenting different viewpoints."

medium [singular] (middle) A form of communication. "The favorite *medium* of entertainment and information for most people **is** television."

Memento mori. (remember death) "Remember that you must die." An object (such as a skull) is usually displayed as a reminder of death.

memorabilia (remembrances) "Things worthy to be remembered."

memoria in aeterna (in eternal remembrance)

memoria technica (system of memory) A mnemonical system or use of mnemonics.

mens sana in corpore sano (a sound mind in a sound body) -Juvenal

meo periculo (at my own risk)

meridies (**m.**, noon, middle of the day)

miliaria [plural], **miliarium** [singular] (thousand; milestone) The *miliaria* were erected every 1,000 paces, or **Roman mile**, on all Roman roads after 123 B.C. It was a massive cylindrical stone, over six feet in height and weighing two or more tons. The *miliarium* generally gave the distance from the town where the road originated, the name and titles of the emperor under whose auspices the road was built, sometimes the names of those who built it, and sometimes the date when it was finished. In addition the *miliarium* generally specified whether the road was repaired (*ristituit*) or built at the emperor's own expense (*pecunia sua*) and whether it was a gravel road (*via glarea*) or a paved road (*via stata*). Thousands of *mil-

iaria have been removed from the roads; many are found to have been used in building houses, churches, and foundations, while others have been moved to museums.

In addition to milestones, there were the *itineraria* to guide tourists, military commanders and commercial travelers over the Roman roads. The *itineraria* were schematic maps with symbols to indicate such geographical features as mountains, rivers, and lakes, as well as way-stops, official night quarters (*mansiones*), military bases (*castra praetoriana*), and post-houses, (*mutationes*) where horses were kept in readiness. The *itineraria* also gave the distances between points on the road. -Victor W. Von Hagen, *The Roads that Led to Rome*

mille (**m.**) "A thousand."

minutiae (trifling, unimportant details)

mirabile dictu (wonderful to relate) -Vergil

mist. (**mistura**, mixture) A medical term used in prescriptions.

mob (See **mobile vulgus**)

mobile vulgus (moving common [people]) "The mob, the fickle or excited crowd."

modus operandi (**M.O.**, way of working) Method of proceeding with a task. Characteristic manner of operation or procedure; as with a criminal who uses a unique *modus operandi* (**M.O.**)and can thus be identified because of his special way of committing his criminal activities.

modus vivendi (way of living) Compromise or living arrangement between people of differing interests. Temporary arrangement between two or more parties to enable them to get along together, pending a full settlement of a dispute.

Morituri te salutamus. "We who are about to die salute you." See **Ave, Imperator** for information.

n.b., N.B. (nota bene, note well, take careful note)

nefasti dies (unlucky days) No official business was allowed to be conducted on such dates.

ne quid nimis (nothing in excess)

n.l. (non liquet) "It isn't clear." A term used by lawyers when a case is not proven.

n.l. (non licet) "[It is] not permitted."

nil. *or* nil (short for nihil, nothing)

Nemo solus satis sapit. "No one is sufficiently wise by himself." Two heads are better than one. -Plautus

ne plus ultra (no more beyond) "The limit, perfection, or peak of achievement."

Ne puero gladium. "Don't give a sword to a boy."

Nescit vox missa reverti. "The word once spoken can never be recalled." -Horace

noct. (nocte) "At night." A medical term used in prescriptions.

Noli me tangere. "Don't touch me."

Nolo contendere. "I do not wish to contest the suit." A plea entered in law by the defendant which subjects him to a judgment of conviction; by so doing he does not necessarily admit his guilt, but he also declares that he will not offer any defence.

non compos mentis (not of sound mind) Said of a lunatic, idiot, drunkard, or one who has lost his memory and understanding by accident or disease.

nones In the ancient Roman calendar, the ninth day before the ides.

non licet (n.l., it is not permitted)

non placet "It is unpleasing." The term used for expressing a negative vote, especially by the governing body of a university.

Non scholae, sed vitae discimus. "We don't learn just for school, but we learn for life." -Seneca, Jr.

non seq. (non sequitur) "It does not follow."

non sequitur (non seq.) "It does not follow." An illogical remark or inapplicable statement; a conclusion or inference that does not follow from a previous statement from which it is supposed to be inferred.

Nosce te ipsum. "Know yourself." A motto on the temple of Apolllo at Delphi.

novus ordo seculorum "A new order of the ages [is born]" *or* "new world order." Adapted from Vergil, this motto appears on the Great Seal of the United States and it is Yale University's founding slogan. See annuit coeptis for additional information.

nulla poena sine lege (no punishment without a law) If a law didn't exist before a specific action was committed, one can't be sentenced to prison for that activity.

nulli secundus (second to none)

nunc aut nunqum (now or never)

ob. (obiit) "He [or She] died."

obiit (ob., obit.; obituary) "A death list."

obit. (obiit, obituary) "A death list."

obiter dictum [singular] (obiter dicta [plural], said by the way) An incidental remark or opinion by a judge that is not binding on the final decision; a digression; a casually interjected comment or reflection.

Omnia vincit amor. "Love conquers everything." -Vergil

Omnis cognitio fit a sensibus. "All knowledge comes through the senses." –Lucretius

op. (opus, work)

op. cit. (opere citato, in the work cited)

opere citato (op.cit., in the work cited)

os. (os, ora; mouth) A medical term used in prescriptions.

opus (op., work, opera)

ovem lupo committere "To set a fox to keep the geese." Don't get a fox to guard the geese [or chickens, ducks, etc.].

p.a., per an. (per annum, by the year)

p.ae. (partes aequales, equal parts)

pace (by the leave of) Used in expressing polite disagreement. When used in front of someone's name, it is used as an apology when contradicting him or her, as: "pace Dr. Smith."

pallida mors (pale Death) Part of the quotation: *pallida mors aequo pulsat pede pauperum tabernas regumque turres.* "Pale Death, with impartial step, knocks at the cottages of the poor and the palaces of kings." -Horace

panem et circenses (bread and circuses) The cry of the Roman mob for food and entertainment. -Juvenal. Food and amusements were said to be the sole interests of the common Romans and the rulers of Rome used this as a means of keeping the masses "satisfied" instead of coming up with real solutions to their economic problems.

parent, in place of: in loco parentis (*q.v.*).

passim (here and there) Applied to words used many times in a piece of writing.

paterfamilias (father of a family) Head of the household.

pater patriae (father of his country)

pax Romana. (Roman peace.) A peace dictated and enforced by Roman armies.

p.c. (post cibum, after food) Used in medical prescriptions as directions for proper consumption after meals.

pearls before swine: **(margaritas ante porcos)**

per (by) A person authorized to sign someone else's name to any document should add his/her own signature preceded by *per.*

per annum (p.a., per an., by the year)

per capita (measured *by head* of the population, for each person)

per cent (per centum, by the hundred)

per diem (p.d., by the day)

per mensem (by the month)

per os (through the mouth) Direction for administration of medicine.

per procurationem (by proxy) "Proxy vote, by authorization." In some situations, it is also expressed as **per procuratorem.**

per se (by itself) "In itself, as such, intrinsically."

persona grata (an acceptable person)

persona non grata (unacceptable person) Person, especially a diplomat, whose presence is not welcome in a country. Although normally of diplomatic usage, it may be used in any situation which expresses the undesirability of someone.

Ph.D. (Philosophiae Doctor) Doctor of Philosophy

phenomena [plural] (Gk. > LL., to appear) *Phenomenon* is the singular form in English while *phenomena* is the plural form. *Phenomena* should never be used with a singular verb.

phenomenon [singular] (Gk. > LL., to appear) *Phenomenon* is the singular form in English while *phenomena* is the plural form.

placebo (I shall please) In medicine, a prescription given to please a patient who, in the physician's opinion, needs no medication.

plebeians, blebs All of those Roman citizens who were not patricians were plebeians. By the time of Gaius Marius, *c.* 110 B.C., there were very few politically unimportant posts which remained as strictly the province of the patricians.

Pleno jure. With full right or authority.

p.m., P.M. (post meridiem, after noon) After the middle of the day.

P.O. (per os, by mouth) A medical term used in prescriptions.

pollice verso (with thumb turned [downward]) Traditionally, the signal by which spectators condemned a vanquished gladiator to death.

pons asinorum (bridge of donkeys; test for beginners; problem that the slow-witted cannot solve) It is anything except a "bridge"; it is really *pedica asinorum,* the "dolt's stumblingblock." (*Brewer's Dictionary of Phrase & Fable*)

Pontifex Maximus The chief (or senior) priest and head of the State religion of Rome. At first he was probably required to be a patrician, but by the middle Republic era he was more than likely to be a plebeian. He supervised all of the various members of the priestly colleges—augurs, *pontifices,* other minor priests, and the Vestal Virgins.

posse comitatus (the power of the county) The power of a sheriff to round up forces to preserve law and order.

Possunt quia posse videntur. "They can because they think they can." -Vergil

post cibum (after meals) Used in medical prescriptions, often with the abbreviation **p.c.**

Post cineres gloria sera venit. "After one is reduced to ashes, fame comes too late." Too often fame comes after one's death.

post diem (after the [appointed or proper] day) Used in law.

post meridiem (p.m., P.M.; after the middle of the day) Afternoon.

post mortem (after death) This expression is often used to indicate an examination or investigation after death, carried out for medical or legal purposes.

post obitum (after death)

post partum (after birth)

precocious (before cooking or before being cooked) Premature; development of mind and/or body before one's age.

prima facie (first face) "At first consideration before there has been time for inquiry or examination; at first glance; apparent; self-evident."

primus inter pares (first among equals)

p.r.n. (pro re nata) "As the occasion arises, as needed."

pro bono publico (for the public good)

procurator bibliothecarum Dir. of libraries

pro forma (for [the sake of]) "Form; as a matter of form." In commercial use it is an account drawn up to show market value of certain products. Used for importing pro- ducts, a *pro forma* invoice must sometimes be presented in advance to arrange for payment or permits. It is understood that this preliminary estimate may not be as exact as the actual invoice to be presented later as the final bill to be paid.

pro et con(tra) (for and against)

pro mundi beneficio "For the benefit of the world."

pro rata (in proportion)

pro re nata (**p.r.n.**) As the occasion arises, as needed."

Prosit. "May it profit you; to your health." A Latin toast frequently used by Germans.

pro tem. (**pro tempore**, for the time being)

pro tempore (**pro tem.**, for the time being, temporarily)

PS (**post scriptum, post script**) "Anything which is written [added] after the main message of a letter." An afterthought.

pulv. (**pulvis**, powder) A medical term used in prescriptions.

PPS (**post postscriptum**) "That which is written after the **post script** as an additional after thought."

Publisher's compliments [A free book sent by the publisher, not the editor]: (**Hommage d'éditeur.** [French])

q.e. (**quod est**, which is)

Q.E.D. (**quod erat demonstrandum**, the thing to be demonstrated) Examine *quod erat demonstrandum* for more information.

Q.h. *or* **q.h.** (**quaque hora**) "Every hour." Used in medical prescriptions.

q.i.d. (**quater in die**) "Four times a day."

q.i.n. (**quater in nocte**) "Four times a night." Used in medical prescriptions.

q.p. (**quantum placet**) Used in prescriptions to signify that the quantity may be as little or as much as you like.

q.s. (**quantum sufficit**; as much as suffices) See **quantum sufficit** for more information.

quantum placet (**q.p.**) Medical directions indicating that the quantity may be as much or as little as you like.

quantum sufficit (**q.s.**, as much as suffices) A term used on medical prescriptions to in- dicate that as much of a certain component should be used as is sufficient, a decision left to the pharmacist.

quater in die (**q.i.d.**) "Four times a day."

quater in nocte (**q.i.n.**) "Four times a night."

quaque hora (**Q.h.** *or* **q.h.**) "Every hour." Used in medical prescriptions.

Qui docet discit. "He who teaches, learns."

Quid nunc? "What now?" One who is curious to know everything that passes; a gossip.

quid pro quo (something for something) Something given in return for something else; a favor in return, a substitution or fair exchange.

quintessence (Gk., the fifth essence) The ancient Greeks said there are four elements or forms in which matter can exist: fire, air, water, and earth. The Pythagoreans added a fifth element known as the fifth essence—quintessence—ether, more subtle and pure than fire, and consisted of a spherical or circular motion which flew upwards at creation and formed the basis of the stars. It was considered the ultimate substance of which the heavenly bodies were thought to ge composed. Now the word stands for the essential principle or the most subtle extract [pure, undiluted essence] of a body which can be obtained.

Quo vadis? (Whither goest thou? *or* Where are you going?) These words were supposedly spoken by Christ when He met the discouraged Apostle Peter as he was leaving Rome.

Quod dixi dixi. What I have said, I have said.

quod erat demonstrandum (**Q.E.D.**, which was the thing to be demonstrated) A formula appended at the end of a proof in geometry.

Quod est? (**q.e.**, which is)

Quod nota. (which [you should] note)

Quod vide. (**q.v.**) (which [you should] see) Used when the writer wants the reader to see a specific cross-reference. See **q.v.** for additional information. Always use **q.v.** in parenthesis (*q.v.*) after the desired reference.

quorum (of whom) The lowest number of members of a committee or board, etc., the presence of whom is necessary before business may be transacted.

Quot homines, tot sententiae. (as many minds as men) "There are as many opinions as there are men to hold them." There are as many viewpoints as there are people.

Quot linguas calles, tot homines vales. "As many languages as you know, so many separate individuals you are worth." You are worth as many different people as the number of languages you know.

> Attributed to Charles V, Holy Roman Emperor.

quotid. (quotidie) "Every day." Used in medicine for prescriptions.

q.v. (quod vide; which see, consult) Often inserted in a text to indicate that the reader, unacquainted with some term or fact, may find an explanation under the word preceding the *q.v.* It should be used in parenthesis (*q.v.*) after the word or phrase involved.

Q.v., q.v. (quantum vis) "As much as you wish." Used in medical prescriptions.

R (recipe, take) An abbreviation used at the beginning of a medical prescription. See **Rx** for more information.

rara avis (rare bird) An unusual or exceptional person or thing; someone out of the ordinary. It was first used figuratively by the Roman satirist Juvenal. *Rara avis in terris nigroque simillima cygne.* "A bird rarely seen on earth, and very like a black swan." Juvenal chose a black swan for his comparison because the Romans had no idea that black swans existed.

rep. (repetatur) "Let it be repeated." Used in medical prescriptions.

requiem (rest) "A Mass for the dead." A Roman Catholic Church term.

Requiescat in pace (R.I.P.) "May he [*or* she] rest in peace." Often seen on tombstones or literature concerning death.

Res ipsa loquitur. "The matter speaks for itself." In a trial involving an accident, the damage is evident; the defendant must prove that the accident was not due to negligence on his part.

rigor mortis "Stiffness occurring after death."

R.I.P. (Requiescat in pace) "May he [*or* she] rest in peace." This symbol is used on tombstones, cards of mourning, etc.

Roman Republic, The: The Roman Republic was established in 509 B.C. after the overthrow of the last of the seven kings, Tarquinius Superbus. It was superseded by the Roman Empire in 27 B.C.

Rx (recipe; take) An abbreviation used at the beginning of a medical prescription. This has been a symbol used by pharmacists since ancient times. There is supposed to be a slant bar across the base of the R and it represents the sign of the Roman god Jupiter, under whose special protection all medicines were placed. The letter itself and its flourish may be paraphrased: "Under the good auspices of JOVE, the patron of medicines, take the following drugs in the proportions set down."

sanctum sanctorum (the holy of holies) A place of utmost privacy and sacredness.

salutatorian (salutator) "The person who gives the welcoming address at a graduation." Usually a speech given by the person with the second highest grade average in a particular graduating class.

Scribendi recte sapere est et principium et fons. "Knowledge is the prime source of good writing."

Scripta manent, verba volant. "When words are written, they remain; when they are spoken, they fly in the air."

semel in die (s.i.d., once a day) Used with medical prescriptions.

semper fidelis (always faithful) Motto of the U.S. Marine Corps.

semper idem (always the same)

semper paratus (always prepared) Motto of the U.S. Coast Guard.

senatus populusque Romanus (S.P.Q.R.) The Senate and the People of Rome. See **S.P.Q.R.** for more information.

seq. (sequens, the following)

sesquipedalia verba (one and a half foot long words)-Horace A reference to very "big" words.

s.d. (sine die, without a day)

sic (so, thus) Inserted to confirm a quotation even when the original is incorrect. It is inserted in brackets [*sic*] to indicate that the copy follows the original exactly as it was written. Inserted in a quotation when the writer who is quoting wishes to disclaim responsibility for some error in grammar, spelling, or fact, *e.g.* "There's [*sic*] several reasons why we shouldn't do this." "This is the song that they sung [*sic*]." Never use a period after *sic*, in or out of the brackets. It is not an abbreviation.

sic passim (so [it is] everywhere) Used to indicate that the same sentiment or expression is found in other passages of a book.

sic semper tyrannis "May it ever thus be to tyrants" or "Thus always to tyrants." Motto of the state of Virginia. There are some who say these words were shouted by John Wilkes Booth as he leaped to the stage after shooting President Abraham Lincoln. Other witnesses thought he said something else.

sic transit gloria mundi "So passes away the glory of the world."

s.i.d. (**semel in die**, once a day)

Si monumentum requiris, circumspice. "If you seek a monument, look about you." An inscription on Sir Christopher Wren's tomb in St. Paul's Cathedral, London, England. Wren was the architect of the cathedral.

sine anno (s.a.) "Without the [year] date of publication."

sinecure (without cares) An office [or position] which requires no work, yet provides compensation.

sine die (s.d.; without a day) In parliamentary procedure, without appointing a day to assemble again.

sine loco (s.l., without a place)

sine prole (s.p., without issue, *i.e.*, no children)

sine qua non (without which not *or* without which nothing) The phrase refers to a necessity, something indispensable; an indispensable condition or qualification for a particular purpose.

Sit tibi terra levis. "May the earth rest lightly upon thee." A line often found on Roman tombstones.

s.l. (sine loco) "Without a place."

slip of the tongue (**lapsus lingual,** *q.v.*)

s.p. (sine prole) "Without issue, *i.e.*, no children."

S.P.Q.R. (senatus populusque Romanus) "The Senate and the People of Rome." The initials *S.P.Q.R.* appeared on many ancient official standards [flags] and emblems and they still exist on manhole covers in modern Rome.

st., (stet) "Let it stand."

status quo (the present position) "The existing state of affairs as it has been and is." Indicates the idea of preserving something without change, just the way it is now; leave things the way they are.

status quo ante (the previous position) Commonly used in international dealings to indicate that nothing is to be changed, or that there is to be a return to an earlier state of affairs, such as the *status quo ante bellum.*

stat. (statim, immediately) A medical direction in a prescription.

stet (st.) "Let it stand." Used in proofreading to indicate that something queried or removed from the text should be retained.

stet processus "Let the process stand." A court order suspending further action.

Suave, mari magno turbantibus aequora ventis, e terra magnum alterius spectare laborem. "It is pleasant when safe on the land to watch the great struggle of another out on a swelling sea, amid winds churning the deep." -Lucretius

sub poena [also written as **sub pena**] (under punishment or penalty) A *sub poena* is a court order requiring a person to appear in court, usually unwillingly, on pain of punishment if he does not do so. Usually a *sub poena* is ordered so someone can give evidence or "bear witness" for a specified trial.

sub rosa (under the rose) "Secretly, confidentially, privately."

sub specie Under the appearance of.

sub verbo [**voce**] (under the word [title]) "A term used in cross references in dictionaries, etc."

sub vi (s.v., under compulsion) A person who is forced to sign a confession, might want to try to write *s.v.* after his name to indicate that he did so against his will.

sub voce (under the word) Referring to an entry in an index, vocabulary, etc.

sui generis (of its own kind) "Unique, in a class by itself." Having a distinct character of its own; unlike anything else.

sui generis sine dubio "In a class by itself, without doubt." Unique.

sui juris (of his or her own right) Of full legal capacity.

summa cum laude (with the highest praise) Normally a reference to graduates of schools or universities.

summum bonum (the highest good) The highest attainable good.

Summum jus, summa injuria. "Extreme justice is extreme injustice." -Cicero, *On Duties*, I, x, 33

Sum quod eris, fui quod sis. "I am what you will be; I was what you are." A message engraved on tombstones as a reminder to the living.

s.v. (sub vi; under compulsion) When a person is forced to sign something against his will, he might write *s.v.* after his name.

tabula rasa (an erased tablet, a clean slate) John Locke's image of the mind at birth. John Locke (1632-1704) was an English empirical philosopher.

Tempus fugit. "Time flies."

Tempus omnia revelat. "Time reveals everything."

terra firma (solid earth) "Ground, dry land [as opposed to the sea or water]."

terra incognita [singular] (unknown land *or* territory) An unexplored region. This phrase is often used in referring to matters about which one is uninformed, *e.g.* "I don't think I can do this because it is *terra incognita* to me."

terrae incognitae [plural] (unknown land) "Unexplored lands or regions."

that is (**id est**) (*q.v.*)

t.i.d. (ter in die) "Three times a day."

t.i.n. (ter in nocte) "Three times a night."

tongue, a slip of the: (**lapsus linguae**) (*q.v.*)

triumvir (three men) In ancient Rome, one of a group of three men acting as joint magistrates for some special purpose or function. In Roman history the most famous triumvirate was that of Octavian, Anthony (Antony), and Lepidus in 43 B.C., which was known as the *Second Triumvirate* to distinguish it from the combination of Caesar, Pompey, and Crassus in 60 B.C., which is known as the *First Triumvirate*.

Ubi libertas, ibi patria. "Where there is liberty, there is my country."

ubi supra (u.s., where cited above) In the place (in the book, etc.) mentioned above.

u.d., ut dict. (ut dictum, as directed)

u.i. (ut infra, as below) "As cited below."

ung. (unguentum, ointment) A medical term used in prescriptions.

unum post aliud (one after the other) One thing at a time.

urbi et orbi "To the city [Rome] and the world." A papal statement.

ursa major (the bigger bear) A constellation known as the Great Bear or the Big Dipper, two stars of which point toward the North Star.

ursa minor (little bear) A northern constellation, it includes the stars of the little dipper, with the North Star at the end of the handle.

ut infra (u.i., as below) "As cited below."

u.s. (ubi supra) "Where cited above."

ut sup. (ut supra, as above) "As cited above."

ut supra (ut sup., as above) "As cited above."

v. *or* vid. (vide, see)

Vade mecum. (go with me) A guide and constant companion. Today it designates a special kind of reference work, a handbook, or manual, something ready and close at hand, like a guidebook.

Vale. ([singular]; farewell, goodbye) Used when addressing one person. Also see **Valete** [plural].

valedictorian (valedictor, farewell words or speech) The person who gives the closing address at a graduation ceremony, usually the one with the highest grade average in the graduating class.

Valete. ([plural]; farewell, goodbye) Used when addressing more than one person. Also see **Vale** [singular].

Veni, vidi, vici. "I came, I saw, I conquered." Attributed to Julius Caesar's summary of his swift victory at Zela in 47 B.C. over King Pharnaces of Pontus in the Pontic campaign; according to Plutarch; but Gaius **Suetonius** Tranquillus, 69?–140? A.D., a Roman biographer and historian, doesn't ascribe the words to Caesar, saying only that they were displayed before his title after his victories at Pontus. [*Encyclopedia of Word and Phrase Origins* by Robert Hendrickson]

venue (to come) The locality where a crime is committed or a cause of action occurs; the county or locality where a jury is drawn and a case tried. A "**change of**

venue" is a substitution of another place for a trial as when the jury or court may be prejudiced for or against a defendant.

Verba volant, scripta manent. "Spoken words fly through the air, but written words endure."

verbatim (word for word) "Exactly as said or written."

verbatim et litteratim (word for word and letter for letter)

verbi gratia (v.g., as for example)

Verbum sapienti sat est. (a word to the wise is enough) A simple hint is sufficient (enough) for any intelligent person.

Veritas omnia vincet. "Truth conquers all things."

versus (vs., against)

v.g. (**verbi gratia**, as for example)

via (by way of) Used to describe routes or Roman roads.

v.i. (**vide infra**, see below)

vice versa (the other way round) The order or relation being reversed; in reverse order.

vid. (**vide**, see)

vide (vid., see)

vide infra (v.i., see below) An instruction in a document to look for a citation which follows.

videlicet (viz., one may *or* can see, to wit, that is to say, namely)

Vide post. "See the following."

Vide supra. (v.s.) "See above." See the previous reference or citation.

Vincit omnia veritas. "Truth conquers everything."

Vincit qui se vincit. "He wins control who controls himself." –Seneca

Vino vendibili hedera non opus est. "A popular wine needs no ivy." A good product needs no special advertising. The ivy was sacred to Bacchus, and its bush was displayed as a sign outside of Roman taverns. Bacchus was an ancient Greek and Roman god of wine and revelry. Earlier Greeks called him *Dionysus.*

Vir sapit qui pauca loquitur. "He is a wise man who speaks but little."

Vita brevis, longa ars. "Life is short and art is long." It is often quoted as **Ars longa, vita brevis.** (q.v.). -Seneca

Vita sine litteris mors est. "Life without learning [education] is death."

viva voce (by word of mouth) "Orally, with the living voice." A *viva voce* examination is one in which the respondent gives spoken answers instead of written responses.

viz. (**videlicet,** namely) "That is to say."

Vox audita perit, littera scripta manet. "The word that is spoken dies in the air, the written word remains."

vox et praeterea nihil (a voice and nothing more) Empty words; a threat but nothing more.

vox populi (the voice of the people) "Public opinion."

vox pop. (**vox populi,** the voice of the people) "Public opinion."

vox populi, vox Dei "The voice of the people is the voice of God."

v.s. (L, **vide supra,** see above)

vs. (**versus,** against)

Important Sources of Information
Used for This Book

I remember seeing somewhere that *research is just the re-arrangement of the bones in a cemetery.* I don't want anyone to think that I am implying that the books listed below are equivalent to cemeteries, but I do feel that I have arranged the "bones" in such a way that people can find the important Latin and Greek elements easier. The listed sources have given me many *bones* and, after twenty-four years of sorting and re-arranging (many times and in many ways), I want to acknowledge the contributions the following sources have made toward the completion of this monumental task.

Ayers, Donald M. *English Words from Latin and Greek Elements.* Tucson: The University of Arizona Press, 1965.

American Heritage Dictionary of the English Language, The. Boston: Houghton Mifflin Co., 1981.

British Museum Library (London, England), c. 1964-1967. This is the first major source for the research I did for the book. It was also where I met Eric Partridge, renowned philologist and independent compiler of word books, including: *Origins, A Short Etymological Dictionary of Modern English; A Dictioinary of Slang & Unconventional English; A Dictionary of the Underworld,* and others. Although very busy doing his own research, he gave me words of encouragement, a list of possible publishers, and words of advice: "Don't tell any of the publishers that I told you to write to them. You won't impress them by using my name. In fact it probably would have the opposite result." He also told me how he regretted the absence of Latin in the curricula of almost every school, pointing out that Cambridge and Oxford had dropped Latin as a prerequisite for entrance to their universities.

Brown, Roland Wilbur. *Composition of Scientific Words.* Washington, D.C.: Smithsonian Institution Press, 1956.

Dorland's Illustrated Medical Dictionary, 26th ed. Philadelphia: W.B. Saunders Co., 1985.

Greene, Amsel. *Word Clues.* Evanston, Illinois: Harper & Row, Publishers, 1949.

International Dictionary of Medicine and Biology, three volumes. New York: John Wiley & Sons, Inc., 1986.

Klein, Dr. Ernest. *A Comprehensive Etymological Dictionary of the English Language,* two volumes. New York: Elsevier Publishing Co., 1966. One of the most useful sources of information for this book.

Library of Congress, Washington, D.C., so much information to gather in such a short time. A very valuable resource.

Lincoln, R.J. & Boxshall, G.A. *The Cambridge Illustrated Dictionary of Natural History.* Cambridge, England: Cambridge University Press, 1987.

McGraw-Hill Dictionary of Scientific and Technical Terms, 4th ed. New York: McGraw-Hill Book Co., 1989.

Monson, Samuel C. *Word Building*. New York: The MacMillan Co., 1958 and 1968.

Random House Dictionary of the English Language, The. 2nd ed., unabridged. New York: Random House, Inc., 1987.

Saint Deniol's Residential Library (Hawarden, Northern Wales), summer of 1987. As far as I know, this is the only residential or "live-in" (room and board) library in the world. Located near Chester, England, the library was established in 1896 by W.E. Gladstone as a foundation or trust where others could "share his love of books in a peaceful environment." Gladstone served as Queen Victoria's Prime Minister on four different occasions. Part of the trust he established included thirty thousand volumes of his own library which has since "grown to over 165,000 printed items."
I was like a child in a candy store with so many choices and so little time to fill my desires. Many early dictionaries, especially Samuel Johnson's *A Dictionary of the English Language*, 3rd ed., 1765; and *An English Dictionary*, 1677, by E. Cole, were of special interest. St. Deiniol's Library was one of those rare experiences which came about because of my research for this book.

Sloat, Clarence and Taylor, Sharon. *The Structure of English Words*, 3rd ed. Dubuque, Iowa: Kendall/Hunt Publishing Co., 1985.

Smith, Robert W.L. *Dictionary of English Word-Roots*. Totowa, New Jersey: Littlefield, Adams & Co., 1966.

Stedman's Medical Dictionary, Illustrated; 24th ed. Baltimore: Williams & Wilkins, 1982.

Taber's Cyclopedic Medical Dictionary, 14th ed. Philadelphia: F.A. Davis Co., 1981.

Urdang, Laurence. *-Ologies & -Isms*, 3rd ed. Detroit: Gale Research Co., 1984.
Prefixes and Other Word-Initial Elements of English. Detroit: Gale Research Co., 1984.
Suffixes and Other Word-Final Elements in English. Detroit: Gale Research Co., 1982.

Webster's New World Dictionary of the American Language, 2nd ed. Cleveland: William Collins + World Publishing Co., Inc., 1974 and 1976.

Webster's Ninth New Collegiate Dictionary. Springfield, Massachusetts: Merriam-Webster, Inc., 1983.

Webster's Third New International Dictionary of the English Language, 2nd ed., unabridged. Springfield, Massachusetts: G. & C. Merriam Co., 1934.

Webster's II New Riverside University Dictionary. Boston: The Riverside Publishing Co., A Houghton Mifflin Co., 1984.

John G. Robertson

Your Contributions

Although every effort has been made to find and correct all *errata* (*q.v.*) by checking and rechecking the text in this important reference, I expect someone will find a slip of the finger resulting in a typo error or what might even be an inaccuracy. You are welcome to write to me about anything that you feel should be rectified and all corrections will be included in future editions. If you have any contributions, please send them to me at the address shown below.

Copies of this book are available from the publisher at special discount prices when purchased in quantity for classroom or seminar use. Write or send a fax for quantity prices.

John Robertson

Send all inquiries to

Senior Scribe Publications
4105 Oak Street
Eugene, OR 97405

Phone numbers:

(503) 343 8384 (in the U.S.) *or*
011-49-6122-12273 *or*
06122-12273 (within Germany)

Fax numbers:

011-49-6122-76659 *or*
06122-76659 (within Germany)

Robertson's Words for a Modern Age was printed and bound by Edwards Brothers Incorporated, Ann Arbor, Michigan, on acid-free paper.

Notes

Notes